P9-DNF-512

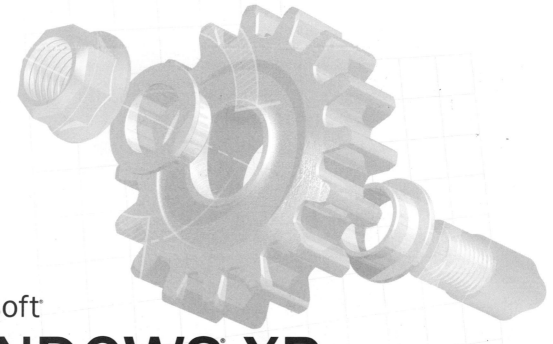

Microsoft®
WINDOWS® XP
REGISTRY GUIDE

Jerry Honeycutt

PUBLISHED BY
Microsoft Press
A Division of Microsoft Corporation
One Microsoft Way
Redmond, Washington 98052-6399

Library of Congress Cataloging-in-Publication Data
Honeycutt, Jerry.
    Microsoft Windows XP Registry Guide / Jerry Honeycutt.
        p. cm.
    Includes index.
    ISBN 0-7356-1788-0
    1. Microsoft Windows (Computer file)   2. Operating systems (Computers)   I. Title.

    QA76.76.O63 H6636 2002
    005.4'4769--dc21   2002075317

Printed and bound in the United States of America.

1 2 3 4 5 6 7 8 9   QWT   7 6 5 4 3 2

Distributed in Canada by H.B. Fenn and Company Ltd.

A CIP catalogue record for this book is available from the British Library.

Microsoft Press books are available through booksellers and distributors worldwide. For further informa-
tion about international editions, contact your local Microsoft Corporation office or contact Microsoft
Press International directly at fax (425) 936-7329. Visit our Web site at www.microsoft.com/mspress.
Send comments to *mspinput@microsoft.com*.

For Microsoft Press:
Acquisitions Editor: Alex Blanton
Project Editors: Jenny Moss Benson and
    Kristen Weatherby

Body Part No. X08-81847

For Online Training Solutions, Inc.:
Project Managers: Joyce Cox, Nancy Depper, and
    Joan Preppernau
Technical Editor: Keith Bednarczuk
Copy Editor: Nancy Depper
Compositors: RJ Cadranell and Liz Clark
Proofreader: Lisa Van Every

For Carlo and Kay

Contents at a Glance

Contents

Acknowledgments

Never let authors tell you that they wrote their books all by themselves. Creating a book out of an author's gibberish takes a lot of work from a lot of people with a lot of different skills. Some crack the whip and others are artisans. They all deserve credit.

First I'd like to thank my acquisitions editor, Alex Blanton. Alex holds up well under pressure, pushing me to get things done without breaking my will to do things right. The result is the right mix of quality and timeliness. The folks who I had the most contact with were Jenny Benson and Kristen Weatherby, though. They were this book's project editors with the responsibility of managing the overall process. Kristen worked on the early stages of this book, getting the whole project moving forward, and Jenny had the unenviable job of getting it finished. I bow to both of them and chant, "I'm not worthy."

A number of other people have my admiration as well. Nancy Depper was this book's copy editor, correcting my brutal use of the language. Lisa Van Every proofed the book's contents, and Keith Bednarczuk was the book's technical editor. I think this book's layout looks great, and the credit goes to RJ Cadranell and Liz Clark. Finally, Joyce Cox and Joan Preppernau provide their project management skills. Thank you one and all.

Introduction

The registry is the heart and soul of Microsoft Windows XP. In my other registry books, I said the same thing about the registry in every version of Windows since Microsoft Windows 95, and by the time you're finished reading this book, I hope you'll agree. The registry contains the configuration data that makes the operating system work. The registry enables developers to organize configuration data in ways that are impossible with other mechanisms, such as INI files. It's behind just about every feature in Windows XP that you think is cool. More importantly, it enables you to customize Windows XP in ways you can't through the user interface.

Windows XP and every application that runs on Microsoft's latest desktop operating system do absolutely nothing without consulting the registry first. When you double-click a file, Windows XP consults the registry to figure out what to do with it. When you install a device, Windows XP assigns resources to the device based on information in the registry and then stores the device's configuration in the registry. When you run an application such as Microsoft Word 2002, the application looks up your preferences in the registry. If you were to monitor the registry during a normal session, you'd see the registry serves up thousands of values within minutes.

In this book, you will learn how to customize the registry, but you must also learn how to take care of the registry. You must learn how to back up the registry so you can restore it if things go awry. You must also learn the best practices for editing the registry safely.

The registry isn't just a hacker's dream, though. The registry is an invaluable tool for the IT professional deploying, managing, and supporting Windows XP. Did you know that most policies in Group Policy and system policies are really settings in the registry? Does that give you any ideas? Did you know that scripting registry edits is one of the best ways to deploy settings to users? This book teaches you about policies, scripting, and much more. For example, you will learn how to deploy registry settings during Windows XP and Microsoft Office XP installations. Some deployment problems can be solved only by using the registry, so I describe the most common IT workarounds, too. For example, I'll show you how to prevent Windows XP from creating the Microsoft Outlook Express icon on the desktop when a user logs on to the computer for the first time.

This Book Is Different—Really

This book contains information that you're not going to find in any other book about the Windows XP registry. You'll learn how to track down where Windows XP and other programs store settings in the registry. You'll learn how to write scripts to edit the registry. You'll discover registry hacks that are both unique and useful. And you'll read about my personal experiences with the registry and what I consider my best practices. For example, in Chapter 2, "Using the Registry Editor," you'll learn how I quickly document my changes to the registry—right in the registry itself.

That's all stuff for power users, but more than half of this book is for IT professionals. Whether you're a desktop engineer, deployment engineer, or a support technician, you'll learn techniques that will make your job easier. A lot of the book focuses on how the registry affects Windows XP and Office XP deployment. You'll learn about creating and deploying effective default user profiles. You'll learn how to deploy settings with Windows XP and Office XP. You'll even learn how to build your own Windows Installer package files expressly for managing settings in the registry. The best part is that just about every tool I suggest in this book is either free or very inexpensive.

Power Users First; Then IT Professionals

Even the most focused IT professional is a power user at heart, so this book presents information for power users first. Thus, here are the first five chapters in Part I, "Registry Overview":

- **Chapter 1, "Learning the Basics"**   This chapter is an overview of the registry in Windows XP. It includes common terminology and an explanation of how Windows XP organizes the registry. You'll learn important concepts, such as the different types of data that you can store in the registry and the difference between little-endian and big-endian storage of double-word values. What exactly *is* a GUID, anyway? You'll find out here.

- **Chapter 2, "Using the Registry Editor"**   Registry Editor is your window into the registry, so this chapter teaches you how to use it effectively.

- **Chapter 3, "Backing Up the Registry"**   Backing up the registry protects your settings. This chapter shows quick-and-dirty ways to back up settings as well as methods for backing up the entire registry.

- **Chapter 4, "Hacking the Registry"**   This chapter is a power user's dream because it describes some of the coolest hacks for Windows XP. For example, it shows you how to customize the dickens out of Windows Explorer.

- **Chapter 5, "Mapping Tweak UI"**   Microsoft now has an updated version of Tweak UI, and this chapter describes it in detail. You don't just learn how to use Tweak UI; there's no sport in that. You'll learn exactly where in the registry Tweak UI stores each setting so you can apply them using your own scripts.

Part II, "Registry in Management," contains information useful to both power users and IT professionals. In this section, you'll learn how to manage Windows XP's registry. You'll also learn how to use the registry as a management tool:

- **Chapter 6, "Using Registry-Based Policy"**   This chapter focuses on Group Policy and system policies. You'll learn the differences between them and how each policy can be used to manage computers and users. Importantly, you'll learn how to build your own policy templates for Group Policy.

- **Chapter 7, "Managing Registry Security"**   Windows XP secures settings in the registry. This chapter shows you how to manage the registry's security. It also shows you how to poke selective holes in the registry's security so that you can deploy and run legacy applications on Windows XP.

- **Chapter 8, "Finding Registry Settings"**   Finding the location where Windows XP stores a setting in the registry is easy, as long as you know which tools to use. I'll give you a hint: Microsoft Word 2002 is the second best registry tool. You'll also learn about tools that you can use to remotely monitor the registry.

Part III, "Registry in Deployment," is primarily for IT professionals. This part of the book helps you use the registry to deploy Windows XP and Office XP more effectively. It includes the following chapters:

- **Chapter 9, "Scripting Registry Changes"**   A plethora of methods are available to you for customizing registry edits. This chapter teaches the best of them, including REG files, INF files, and Windows Installer package files. It also describes tools such as Console Registry Tool for Windows, which comes free with Windows XP. This is useful for editing the registry from batch files.

- **Chapter 10, "Deploying User Profiles"**   Default user profiles are an effective way to deploy default settings to users. This chapter describes not only default user profiles, but mandatory and roaming user profiles as well. What's unique about this chapter is that it describes a useful process for building profiles that ensures they'll work for all users in your organization.

- **Chapter 11, "Mapping Windows Installer"**   Windows Installer is a relatively new service that's a better way to install applications. This chapter describes how Windows Installer interacts with the registry. It will also help you clean up the registry when things go wrong with some Windows Installer–based applications.

- **Chapter 12, "Deploying with Answer Files"**   This chapter shows you how to script Windows XP's installation and how to add registry settings to the mix.

- **Chapter 13, "Cloning Disks with Sysprep"**   Many companies that maintained up to 50 Microsoft Windows 2000 disk images now can use just a single Windows XP disk image. They do that by generalizing their disk images so that they work on the widest possible variety of hardware. That's the topic of this chapter. This chapter also shows how Sysprep interacts with the registry.

- **Chapter 14, "Microsoft Office XP User Settings"**   A big part of an Office XP deployment project is deploying user settings. This chapter describes a variety of ways to do just that. You'll learn about tools that come with the Office XP Resource Kit, for example, as well as techniques for using them.

- **Chapter 15, "Working Around IT Problems"**   This is a special chapter that addresses the comments and questions I frequently hear from IT professions. How should you handle coexistence issues between Microsoft Access 97 and Microsoft Access 2002? That's just one of many IT issues you can address by using Windows XP's registry.

Part IV, "Appendices," is a reference that describes the contents of the registry. In the few pages available in this book, I can't possibly describe every registry value. But Part IV describes the most interesting settings. These appendices describe the relationships between different portions of the registry, including how a variety of registry keys and values interact.

Some Terminology

Most of the terminology I use in this book is fairly standard by now, but to avoid confusion, I'll take a moment to describe how I use some of it.

Rather than give you hardcode paths, I use the standard environment variables that represent those paths instead. That way, when you read the instructions, you'll be able to apply them to your scenario regardless of whether you're using a dual-boot configuration or where on your computer user profiles exist (C:\Documents and Settings or C:\Winnt \Profiles). Additionally, on your computer, the folder that contains Windows XP's system files might be in a different location depending on whether you upgraded to Windows XP, installed a clean copy of the operating system, or customized the installation path in an answer file. Thus, I use the following environment variables throughout this book. (You can see these environment variables by typing **set** at an MS-DOS command prompt.)

- %USERPROFILE% represents the current user profile folder. Thus, if you log on to the computer as Jerry and your profile folders are in C:\Documents and Settings, you'd translate %USERPROFILE% to C:\Documents and Settings\Jerry.

- %SYSTEMDRIVE% is the drive that contains Windows XP's system files. That's usually drive C, but if you installed Windows XP on a different drive, perhaps in a dual-boot configuration, it could be drive D, E, and so on.

- %SYSTEMROOT% is the folder containing Windows XP. In a clean installation, this is usually C:\Windows, but if you upgraded from Windows NT or Windows 2000, it's probably C:\Winnt.

Aside from the environment variables, I also use abbreviations for the various root keys in the registry. HKEY_CLASSES_ROOT and HKEY_LOCAL_MACHINE are unwieldy, for example, and cause lines to wrap in funny places. To make the book more readable, I use the following instead:

HKCR	HKEY_CLASSES_ROOT
HKCU	HKEY_CURRENT_USER
HKLM	HKEY_LOCAL_MACHINE
HKU	HKEY_USERS
HKCC	HKEY_CURRENT_CONFIG

Gotta Love Windows XP

Before we move on to the rest of the book, I thought I'd share with you why I love Windows XP so much. It makes all my various jobs much easier; it even made writing this book easier than any book I've ever written.

For example, one of my favorite features is Remote Desktop. Before I got Windows XP, either I had to have several computers sitting on my desk to test instructions, dig around in the registry, take screen shots, and so on, or I had to walk back and forth between my lab and my office, which was a major productivity bust. For this book, I configured Remote Desktop on each Windows XP–based computer in my lab so I could connect to them from my production computer. That way, I could have two or three Remote Desktop connections open, each with a different experiment running. Remote Desktop reduced writing time by a huge amount. It also reduced the number of times that I was tempted to experiment on my production computer (which can result in a day of lost work because I trashed the computer's configuration). Remote Desktop was worth the cost of Windows XP alone.

And did I mention wireless networking? Windows XP enables me to get out of my office—in which I have 10 or so computers running, with the fan and hard drive noise that entails. Thanks to wireless networking, which Windows XP makes a no-brainer to configure, I could find a quiet place in my house to hide while I was writing this book. No fans. No noise. And even when I was hiding in the bedroom, I could still connect to the computers in my lab.

Regarding the registry itself, there are a few changes that struck me right away. First Microsoft got rid of the dueling registry editors. Windows 2000 had two editors: Regedit and Regedt32. Both had strengths and weakness, and you had no choice but to flip back and forth between each. Windows XP combines both editors into a single registry editor. Another new feature is Console Registry Tool for Windows (Reg). Windows XP includes this tool by default, whereas in Windows 2000 you had to install it from the support tools. This makes it a more viable tool for scripting registry edits using batch files. And it's free!

Final Note

This is the registry book that I've been waiting two years to write. I hope that it makes your Windows XP experience even better. I also hope it will make you more productive and more effective.

If you have any comments or questions, please feel free to send them my way at *jerry@honeycutt.com*. I answer my e-mail. You can also visit my Web site, *http://www.honeycutt.com*, to download the samples that you see in this book. You'll also find mailing lists you can join and additional articles that I've written about Windows XP, the registry, and various deployment topics.

Registry Overview

Working with the registry is daunting if you know little about it. Thus, in this part, you master the basic information you need to successfully leverage the registry. For example, you learn about the contents of the registry and the types of data you find in it. You learn how to back up and restore the registry, and how to edit the registry using Registry Editor.

This part is for IT professionals and power users. Aside from learning the basics and backing up the registry, for example, it describes how to hack settings in the registry to customize Windows XP. Many of the settings you learn about in this part aren't available through the user interface. This part also describes one of the most popular downloads on the Internet: Tweak UI. Instead of showing you how to use this simple program, however, it describes where the program stores each and every one of its settings in the registry.

Read this part from beginning to end. Don't skip it. With the basics under your belt, and a sense of what you can do with the registry, you'll be better prepared to tackle the content elsewhere in this book.

Learning the Basics

The registry has a subtle but important role in Microsoft Windows XP. On one hand, the registry is passive—it's just a big collection of settings sitting on your hard disk, and you probably don't think much about it while you're editing a document, browsing the Internet, or searching for a file. On the other hand, it plays a key role in all those activities. The settings in the registry determine how Windows XP appears and how it behaves. They even control applications running on your computer. This gives the registry great potential as a tool for power users or IT professionals, enabling them to customize settings that aren't available in the user interface.

This chapter introduces the registry to you. First you learn about the registry's role and how it fits into your world. Then I explain some important terminology to ensure that we're speaking the same language, and you see how Windows XP organizes the registry. Next you learn about the tools I use to edit the registry. And last, you see how Windows XP stores the registry on the hard disk. Throughout this chapter, you'll find several tidbits that are useful beyond the registry. For example, you learn about the two different architectures for storing numbers in memory, which IT professionals run into as much outside the registry as inside.

This is all basic information, but don't skip this chapter. Read it once, and you'll be set for the rest of this book.

Heart and Soul of Windows XP

Windows XP stores configuration data in the registry. The registry is a hierarchical database, which you can describe as a central repository for configuration data (Microsoft's terminology) or a configuration database (my terminology). A hierarchical database has characteristics that make it ideally suited to storing configuration data. Lay out the database in a diagram, like the one shown in Figure 1-1, and it looks like an outline or organization chart. This allows settings to be referenced using paths, similar to file paths in Windows XP. For example, in Figure 1-1, the path A\G\M references the shaded box. Also, each setting is an ordered pair that associates a value's name with its data, similar to the way the IRS associates your social security number with your tax records. The registry's hierarchical organization makes all settings easy to reference.

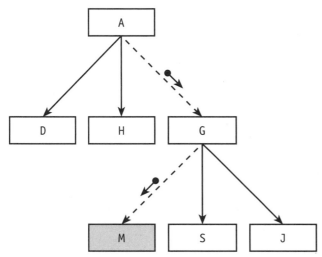

Figure 1-1   *The registry is a hierarchical database that contains most of Windows XP's settings.*

You can do nothing in Windows XP that doesn't access the registry. I use a tool to monitor registry access and often leave it running while clicking around the operating system's user interface. I almost never see this monitor idle. With every click, Windows XP consults the registry. Every time I launch a program, the operating system consults the registry. Every application I use looks for its settings in the registry. The registry is certainly the center of attention.

I've written other books about the registry, and in them I call the registry *the operating system's heart and soul*. Aside from being a central place to store settings, the registry by its very nature allows complex relationships between different parts of Windows XP, applications, and the user interface. For example, right-click different types of files and you see different shortcut menus. Settings in the registry make this type of context-sensitive user interface possible. The settings for each user who logs on to Windows XP are separate from those of other users—again because of the registry. Windows XP's ability to use different configurations for laptop computers depending on whether they're docked or undocked is due in large part to the registry. Even Plug and Play depends on the registry.

For Power Users

So the registry is important, but what good is learning about it for power users? Well, first, being a technology enthusiast (the high-brow way to say *geek*) implies that you like to dabble with technology to learn more about it. What better way to learn more about Windows XP than to figure out how and where it stores settings? The process is analogous to tearing apart your VCR so that you can learn how it works. If you've ever wondered why the operating system behaves a certain way, the answer is often found by consulting the registry.

Mastering the registry has concrete advantages for power users, though. Because it is the operating system's configuration database, backing up your settings is a bit easier than it would be without the registry. And unlike in the old days when settings were stored in INI files, you always know where to begin looking when you need to find a value. But the biggest advantage of mastering the registry is more exciting and very real: You can customize Windows XP and the applications that run on it in ways that aren't otherwise possible. Windows XP has thousands of settings that you'll never see in any dialog box but that you might want to customize. For example, you can redirect your Favorites folder to a different place, improve your Internet connection's performance, and add commands to any type of file's shortcut menu. Chapter 4, "Hacking the Registry," details many different customization possibilities.

For IT Professionals

IT professionals rely on the registry because it enables most of the management features they use. Large portions of this book focus on those features and how they use the registry.

Policy management is the biggest feature. IT professionals use policies to configure computer and user settings to a standard, and users can't change those settings. For example, I recently used policies to configure users' screen savers so that they lock the desktop after 15 minutes of idle time, which secures users' computers if they walk away from their desks without logging off from Windows XP. Policy management is a great boon to every IT organization because it can lower costs and boost user productivity.

IT professionals can manage the registry's security, which lets users run legacy applications in their restricted accounts instead of logging on to their computers as Administrator (a bad idea in any enterprise environment). You can manage the registry's security directly or using a tool such as Security Configuration And Analysis to automate the process. (For more information, see Chapter 7, "Managing Registry Security.")

Also, IT professionals can use a combination of scripts and the registry to automate customizations. One IT professional with whom I worked recently wrote scripts to clean up and configure users' computers after installing Windows XP on them. You can address most needs with a good script.

An indirect but important benefit of the registry to IT professionals is application compatibility. Microsoft defines standards for where different types of settings belong in the registry. The company has standards for file associations, Plug and Play configuration data, printer settings, application settings, and much more. Applications that follow these standards are more likely to work well with the operating system, not to mention other applications, because they're all looking for the same settings in the same places. For that matter, most applications that work well in Microsoft Windows 2000 will work just fine in Windows XP, given that the overall structure of the registry doesn't change much between the operating systems.

The registry enables too many other management features for IT professionals to neglect mastering it. Some of those features include the following (see Figure 1-2):

- Deployment customization
- Folder redirection
- Hardware profiles
- Offline files
- Performance monitoring
- Roaming user profiles
- Windows Management Instrumentation

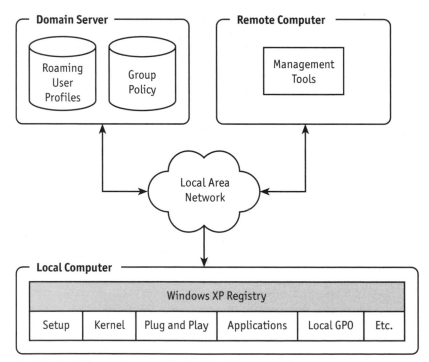

Figure 1-2   *The registry enables local and remote administration.*

Brief History of the Registry

MS-DOS got its configuration data from Config.sys and Autoexec.bat. The primary purpose of Config.sys was to load device drivers, and the primary purpose of Autoexec.bat was to prepare MS-DOS for use by running programs, setting environment variables, and so on. Every application that ran on MS-DOS was responsible for managing its own settings. Neither of these configuration files is useful in Windows XP.

Microsoft Windows 3.0 alleviated the limitations of Autoexec.bat and Config.sys a bit by providing INI files for storing settings. INI files are text files that contain one or more sections with one or more settings in each section. You've undoubtedly seen plenty of them. The problem with INI files is that they provide no hierarchy, storing binary values in them is cumbersome (although not impossible), and they provide no standard for storing similar types of settings. INI files have other subtle problems, all related to the configuration file's inability to build complex relationships between applications and the operating system. A bigger problem with INI files and early versions of Windows was the sheer number of them that floated around the average computer. Every application had its own INI files.

Windows 3.1 introduced the registry as a tool for storing OLE (object linking and embedding) settings, and Windows 95 and Windows NT 3.5 expanded the registry to the configuration database that Windows XP uses now. Even though INI files are no longer necessary because applications now have a far better way to store settings, you'll always find a handful on any computer, including Win.ini.

A few years ago, people were more interested in the history of the registry than they are now. The registry has been around since before 1995, and everyone pretty much takes it for granted these days, so I won't waste any more book pages on its lineage. The history lesson is over; now you're living in the present.

Registry Warnings and Myths

For all of its benefits, the registry is a great paradox. On the one hand, it's the central place for all of Windows XP's configuration data. It's the keystone. On the other hand, the fact that the registry is so critical also makes it one of the operating system's weaknesses. Take out the keystone, and the arch crumbles. If the registry fails, Windows XP fails. Fortunately, total failure is less likely than my winning the lottery before you finish this book, and partial failure that doesn't prevent you from starting the computer is often easily overcome.

The registry's keystone role is one of the reasons for its mythical stature. Microsoft doesn't say much about it. You don't find the registry's editor on the Start menu. You find very little information about the registry in Help. Microsoft doesn't provide white papers that help users unlock its secrets. And why should they? Do you really want the average user mucking around in the registry? The dearth of information coming from Microsoft led to home-grown registry Web sites and FAQs, which are still somewhat popular. All these factors contribute to the myth of the registry as a magical configuration play land. Woo hoo!

I want to debunk that myth. Don't get me wrong: There is a lot of power packed into the registry. But there is no magic and there's nothing to fear. Simply put, the registry is nothing more than your computer's settings. After you're used to working in the registry, doing so no longer gives you chills of excitement; it barely gets a yawn.

The warnings you see in most documents that contain instructions for editing the registry are definitely overblown, particularly for readers of this book, who are either power users or IT professionals. (I wouldn't say that if the book were for novice or intermediate users.) You can do very little damage to the registry that you can't undo, assuming you take the straightforward precautions of backing up settings before you change them and backing up your computer on a regular basis. Failing that, use one of the many troubleshooting tools you learn about in this book to fix problems. Chapter 3, "Backing up the Registry," contains a lot of troubleshooting help. Use a bit of common sense and you'll do just fine.

Must-Know Concepts

Learning the concepts in the following sections is important to your satisfaction with this book. These are the things you must know to work efficiently with the registry. For example, the registry is filled with hexadecimal numbers, and if you don't understand hexadecimal, they're not going to make sense to you. If you're a programmer, you can probably skip these sections; otherwise, *don't*.

The following sections walk you through the most important of these concepts, beginning with security and globally unique identifiers. You learn how to read hexadecimal numbers and convert them to binary and decimal notation and use them as bit masks. You learn the difference between Unicode and ANSI character encoding. You even learn how Intel-based computers store numbers in memory. All of these topics are significant to your ability to use the registry as a tool.

Security Identifiers

Computer accounts, user accounts, groups, and other security-related objects are *security principles*. *Security Identifiers* (SIDs) uniquely identify security principles. Each time Windows XP or Active Directory creates a security principle, they generate a SID for it. Windows XP's Local Security Authority (LSA) generates SIDs for local security principles and then stores them in the local security database. The Domain Security Authority generates SIDs for domain security principles and then stores them in Active Directory. SIDs are unique within their scope. Every local security principle's SID is unique on the computer. And every domain security principle's SID is unique within any domain in the enterprise. What's more, Windows XP and Active Directory never reuse a SID, even if they delete the security principle to which that SID belonged. Thus, if you delete an account and then add it back, the account gets a new SID.

The important thing to remember is that every account has a SID. It's kind of like having a passport number that uniquely identifies you to immigration. You can refer to an account by its name or by its SID, but in practice you seldom use the SID because its format is cumbersome. You frequently see accounts' SIDs in the registry, though, and that's why you're learning about them here.

An example of a SID is S-1-5-21-2857422465-1465058494-1690550294-500. A SID always begins with S-. The next number identifies the SID's version—in this case, version 1. The next number indicates the identifier authority and is usually 5, which is NT Authority. The string of numbers up to 500 is the domain identifier, and the rest of the SID is a relative identifier, which is the account or group. This is a real rough overview of the format of a SID, which is much more complex than this brief example. If you want to learn more about SIDs, see *http://www.microsoft.com/windows2000/techinfo/reskit/en/distrib/dsce_ctl_xgqv.htm*, which is a section in the Windows 2000 Resource Kit about SIDs.

Some SIDs are shorter than the previous example, such as S-1-5-18. These are *well-known SIDs*, and they are the same on every computer and in every domain. They are interesting because they pop up over and over again in the registry and in other places. Table 1-1 describes Windows XP's well-known SIDs. I've italicized the names of SIDs that are of particular interest to you while you're reading this book. The placeholder *domain* is the SID's domain identifier.

Table 1-1   Well-Known SIDs

SID	User or Group name
S-1-0	Null Authority
S-1-0-0	Nobody
S-1-1	World Authority
S-1-1-0	*Everyone*
S-1-2	Local Authority
S-1-2-0	Local
S-1-3	Creator
S-1-3-0	Creator Owner
S-1-3-1	Creator Group
S-1-3-2	Not used in Windows XP
S-1-3-3	Not used in Windows XP
S-1-4	Nonunique Authority
S-1-5	NT Authority
S-1-5-1	Dialup
S-1-5-2	Network
S-1-5-3	Batch
S-1-5-4	Interactive

Table 1-1   Well-Known SIDs *(continued)*

SID	User or Group name
S-1-5-5-*X-Y*	Logon Session
S-1-5-6	Service
S-1-5-7	Anonymous
S-1-5-8	Not used in Windows XP
S-1-5-9	Enterprise Domain Controllers
S-1-5-10	Self
S-1-5-11	Authenticated Users
S-1-5-12	Restricted
S-1-5-13	Terminal Service User
S-1-5-14	Remote Interactive Logon
S-1-5-18	*LocalSystem* or *System*
S-1-5-19	*LocalService*
S-1-5-29	*NetworkService*
S-1-5-*domain*-500	*Administrator*
S-1-5-*domain*-501	*Guest*
S-1-5-*domain*-502	krbtgt
S-1-5-*domain*-512	Domain Admins
S-1-5-*domain*-513	Domain Users
S-1-5-*domain*-514	Domain Guests
S-1-5-*domain*-515	Domain Computers
S-1-5-*domain*-516	Domain Controllers
S-1-5-*domain*-517	Cert Publishers
S-1-5-*root domain*-518	Schema Admins
S-1-5-*root domain*-519	Enterprise Admins
S-1-5-*root domain*-520	Group Policy Creator Owners
S-1-5-*domain*-553	RAS and IAS Servers
S-1-5-32-544	*Administrators*
S-1-5-32-545	*Users*
S-1-5-32-546	*Guests*
S-1-5-32-547	*Power Users*

SID	User or Group name
S-1-5-32-548	Account Operators
S-1-5-32-549	Server Operators
S-1-5-32-550	Print Operators
S-1-5-32-551	Backup Operators
S-1-5-32-552	Replicator
S-1-5-32-554	Pre-Windows 2000 Compatible Access
S-1-5-32-555	*Remote Desktop Users*
S-1-5-32-556	Network Configuration Operators
S-1-6	Site Server Authority
S-1-7	Internet Site Authority
S-1-8	Exchange Authority
S-1-9	Resource Manager Authority

Globally Unique Identifiers

Globally unique identifiers are better known as *GUIDs* (pronounced *goo id*). They are numbers that uniquely identify objects, including computers, program components, devices, and so on. These objects often have names, but their GUIDs remain unique even if two objects have the same name or their names change. In other words, an object's GUID is similar to a security principle's SID. You see GUIDs scattered all over the registry, so you should get used to them.

All GUIDs have the same interesting format. They're 16-byte hexadecimal numbers in groups of 8, 4, 4, 4, and 12 digits (0 through 9 and A through F). A dash divides each group of digits, and curly brackets enclose the whole number. An example of a real GUID is {645FF040-5081-101B-9F08-00AA002F954E}, which represents the Recycle Bin object that you see on the desktop. The GUID {127A89AD-C4E3-D411-BDC8-001083FDCE08} belongs to one of the computers in my lab.

Programmers often use the tool Guidgen.exe to create GUIDs, but Windows XP generates them, too. Regardless of the source, Microsoft guarantees that GUIDs are globally unique (hence the name). No matter how many times Guidgen.exe or Windows XP generates a GUID, the result is always unique. That's what makes GUIDs perfect for identifying objects like computers, devices, and what have you.

Hexadecimal Notation

Ninety-nine percent of the data you see in the registry is hexadecimal. Computers use hexadecimal notation instead of decimal for a good reason, which you'll learn in a bit. You must learn how to read and convert hexadecimal numbers to use the registry as an effective tool. And that's the point of this section.

Binary and decimal notations don't get along well. You learned decimal notation as a child. In this notation, 734 is $7 \times 10^2 + 3 \times 10^1 + 4 \times 10^0$, which is $7 \times 100 + 3 \times 10 + 4 \times 1$. Easy enough, right? The digits are 0 through 9, and because you multiply each digit right to left by increasing powers of 10 (10^0, 10^1, 10^2, and so on), this notation is called *base 10*. The problem is that decimal notation doesn't translate well into the computer's system of ones and zeros. Binary notation does. In this notation, 1011 is $1 \times 2^3 + 0 \times 2^2 + 1 \times 2^1 + 1 \times 2^0$ or $1 \times 8 + 0 \times 4 + 1 \times 2 + 1 \times 1$ or 11. The digits are 0 and 1, and because you multiply each digit right to left by increasing powers of 2 (2^0, 2^1, 2^2, and so on), this notation is called *base 2*. Converting a binary number to a decimal number is a lot of work, and binary numbers are too cumbersome for people to read and write.

That brings us to hexadecimal notation. Hexadecimal notation is *base 16*, and because you can evenly divide 16 by 2, converting between binary and hexadecimal is straightforward. The digits are 0 through 9 and A through F. Table 1-2 shows the decimal equivalent of each digit. In hexadecimal, A09C is $10 \times 16^3 + 0 \times 16^2 + 9 \times 16^1 + 12 \times 16^0$ or $10 \times 4096 + 0 \times 256 + 9 \times 16 + 12 \times 1$, or 41,116 in decimal notation. As with the other examples, you multiply each hexadecimal digit right to left by increasing powers of 16 (16^0, 16^1, 16^2, and so on).

Table 1-2   Hexadecimal Digits

Binary	Hexadecimal	Decimal
0000	0	0
0001	1	1
0010	2	2
0011	3	3
0100	4	4
0101	5	5
0110	6	6
0111	7	7
1000	8	8
1001	9	9
1010	A	10
1011	B	11
1100	C	12
1101	D	13
1110	E	14
1111	F	15

Converting between binary and hexadecimal notations might be straightforward but it is time consuming, so I'm offering you a trick. When converting from binary to hexadecimal, use Table 1-2 to look up each group of four digits from left to right, and jot down its hexadecimal equivalent. For example, to convert 01101010 to hexadecimal, look up 0110 to get 6, and then look up 1010 to get A, so that you end up with the hexadecimal number 6A. If the number of digits in the binary number isn't evenly divisible by 4, just pad the left side with zeros. To convert hexadecimal numbers to binary, use Table 1-2 to look up each hexadecimal digit from left to right, and jot down its binary equivalent. For example, to convert 1F from hexadecimal to binary, look up 1 to get 0001, look up F to get 1111, and string them together to get 00011111.

One last problem: Is 12 a decimal number or a hexadecimal number? You don't have enough information to know for sure. The solution is to always use the prefix 0x at the beginning of hexadecimal numbers. 0x12 is then a hexadecimal number, whereas 12 is a decimal number. This is the standard format for hexadecimal numbers, and it's the format that Microsoft uses in its documentation and in all the tools you'll use in this book.

Tip   If converting binary, hexadecimal, and decimal numbers is too much work for you, as it certainly is for me, use Windows XP's Calculator. Click Start, All Programs, Accessories, and Calculator. Make sure you change to scientific view by clicking Scientific on the View menu. In the top left part of Calculator's window, you see four buttons: Hex, Dec, Oct, and Bin. Click the button corresponding to the notation in which you want to input a number, type the number, and then click the button corresponding to the notation to which you want to convert the number.

Bits and Bit Masks

You have binary and hexadecimal notations under your belt, and now you need bit masks. In the registry, Windows XP sometimes groups settings together in one number. Each bit within that number is a different setting. Thus, you can store eight settings in a byte, 16 settings in a word, and so on. In this book and elsewhere, you'll see instructions that tell you that a setting's bit mask is 0x20, which simply means that you turn on that setting by enabling the bits that 0x20 represents. This will make more sense soon.

You count a binary number's bits from right to left, starting with 0. The number in Figure 1-3 on the next page is 0x26. The top part shows the binary equivalent, and the second part shows each bit's number. The bit on the far right is bit 0. In this example, bits 1, 2, and 5 are 1, whereas the remaining bits are 0. If you saw instructions that tell you to turn on bit 7, you'd change the number to 10100110.

Many times, instructions you read aren't always so nice as to give you an exact bit number, so you have to do a bit of math. Often, all you'll see is a bit mask, and you have to figure out which bits the mask actually represents. For example, to turn on bit 0x40 in the number 0x43, convert both numbers to binary, figure out which bits the mask represents, change those bits to ones in the number, and then convert the number back to hexadecimal. Calculator in Scientific Mode is the easiest way to do these steps. You'd do the same to turn off the setting, except that you'd change the target bits to 0. After a while, you get pretty good at figuring out which bits a mask represents, though. Moving from right to left, each bit's mask is 0x01, 0x02, 0x04, 0x08, 0x10, 0x20, 0x40, and 0x80. The bottom part of Figure 1-3 illustrates this.

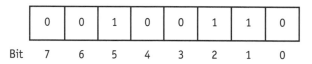

Figure 1-3   *When fooling around with bits, a binary 1 is the same thing as yes or true, and a binary 0 is the same thing as no or false. In other words, they are Boolean values.*

Note   Turning on and off bit masks is even easier if you use bitwise math. To turn a bit mask on in a number, OR the two numbers together. To turn a bit mask off in a number, reverse the bits in the mask, and then AND it together with the number: *number* AND NOT *mask*. Calculator in Scientific Mode supports all these operations.

Little-Endian and Big-Endian

In a hexadecimal number such as 0x0102, the 0x01 is the most significant byte and the 0x02 is the least significant. The left-most bytes are more significant because you multiple these digits by a higher power of 16. The right-most digits are less significant, and the digits become more significant as you move from right to left.

Programs store numbers in memory in two ways: big-endian or little-endian. When a program stores a number using big-endian (*big end first*) storage, it stores the most significant bytes in memory first, followed by the less significant bytes. When stored in memory using big-endian storage, the number 0x01020304 is 0x01 0x02 0x03 0x04. Makes sense, doesn't it? The problem is that Intel-based processors don't store numbers in memory this way. Intel-based processors use the little-endian (*little end first*) architecture, which means they store the least significant bytes first, followed by the more significant bytes. Thus, the number 0x01020304 is 0x04 0x03 0x02 0x01 in memory.

Although most of the tools you'll use display all numbers—little-endian or big-endian—correctly, you'll have to pay careful attention when you're looking at numbers in binary values because the tools won't automatically reverse the order of the bytes for you. Thus, if you see the number 0x34 0x77 in a binary value, you'll have to remember to reverse the order of bytes to get the result 0x7734.

ANSI and Unicode Encoding

The first prominent character encoding scheme was ASCII, and it's still in use today. In ASCII character encoding, each character is 8 bits, or a single byte. Because ASCII was for western languages, its use was limited in European countries and regions whose languages contained characters that weren't included in the 256 characters that ASCII supported. To get around this limitation, the International Standards Organization (ISO) created a new character encoding standard called Latin-1 that included European characters left out of the ASCII set. Microsoft enhanced Latin-1 and called the standard ANSI. But ANSI is still an 8-bit character encoding that can represent only 256 unique characters. Many languages have thousands of symbols, particularly Asian languages such as Chinese, Korean, and Japanese.

To overcome the limitations of an 8-bit character encoding standard, Microsoft, in cahoots with companies such as Apple Computer, Inc., and IBM, created the non-profit consortium Unicode, Inc., to define a new character encoding standard for international character sets. The work done at Unicode merged with work already in progress at ISO, and the result is the Unicode standard for character encoding. Unicode is a 16-bit encoding standard, which provides for 65,536 unique characters—more than enough to represent all of the world's languages. It even supports arcane languages, such as Sanskrit and Egyptian hieroglyphs, and includes punctuation marks, mathematical symbols, and graphical symbols.

Unicode is Windows XP's native character encoding, but it also supports ANSI. Internally, the operating system represents object names, paths, and file names as 16-bit Unicode characters. Also, it usually stores data in the registry using Unicode. If a program stores the text *Jerry* using ANSI, it looks like 0x4A 0x65 0x72 0x72 0x79 in memory. However, if the program stores the same string using Unicode, it looks like 0x4A 0x00 0x65 0x00 0x72 0x00 0x72 0x00 0x79 0x00 in memory. Why? Because Unicode text is 16-bits, and Windows XP stores 16-bit numbers in little-endian format (see "Little-Endian and Big-Endian Storage," earlier in this chapter). Thus, it writes the *J* into memory as 0x004A (with the bytes reversed), followed by the *e* as 0x0065, and then the remaining characters as 0x0072, 0x0072, and 0x0079.

Null and Empty Strings

If you've written programs using a language such as C, the concept of *null* isn't foreign to you. Null is the null character, or 0x00. Windows XP terminates strings with the null character so that programs know where strings end.

In the registry, a similar concept is that a value can have null data, meaning that it contains no data at all. It's empty. Usually, when you're looking at the null value in the registry, you see the text *(value not set)*. This is different from a value that contains an empty string—text that's zero characters in length, or "". The following values are not the same:

- null
- ""

Structure of the Registry

The structure of Windows XP's registry is so similar to the structure of its file system that I can't help but make the analogy. Figure 1-4 compares Registry Editor, the tool you use to edit the registry, and Windows Explorer. (You learn how to use Registry Editor in Chapter 2, "Using the Registry Editor.") In the editor's left pane, which is called the *key pane*, you see the registry's hierarchy, just as you see the file system's hierarchy in Windows Explorer's left pane. Each folder in the key pane is a registry *key*. In the editor's right pane, which is called the *value pane*, you see a key's *values*, just as you see a folder's contents in Windows Explorer's right pane.

Take another look at Figure 1-4. In Windows Explorer, you see each of the computer's disks under My Computer. Likewise, in Registry Editor, you see each of the registry's *root keys* under My Computer. Although you see the full name of each root key in Registry Editor, I tend to use the standard abbreviations you see in Table 1-3. The abbreviations are easier to type and read, and in a book like this one, they usually keep long names from splitting in unfriendly places when they wrap across two lines.

Table 1-3   Root Keys

Name	Abbreviation
HKEY_CLASSES_ROOT	HKCR
HKEY_CURRENT_USER	HKCU
HKEY_LOCAL_MACHINE	HKLM
HKEY_USERS	HKU
HKEY_CURRENT_CONFIG	HKCC

Keys

Keys are so similar to folders (Registry Editor even uses the same icon for keys as Windows Explorer uses for folders) that they have the same naming rules. You can nest one or more keys within another key as long as the names are unique within each key. A key's name is limited to 512 ANSI or 256 Unicode characters, and you can use any ASCII character in the name other than a backslash (\), asterisk (*), and question mark (?). In addition, Windows XP reserves all names that begin with a period for its own use.

The similarities between the registry and file system continue with paths. C:\Windows \System32\Sol.exe refers to a file called Sol.exe on drive C in a subfolder of \Windows called System32. HKCU\Control Panel\Desktop\Wallpaper refers to a value called Wallpaper in the root key HKCU in a subkey of Control Panel called Desktop. This notation is a *fully qualified path*. I often refer to a key and all its subkeys as a *branch*.

Keys and folders

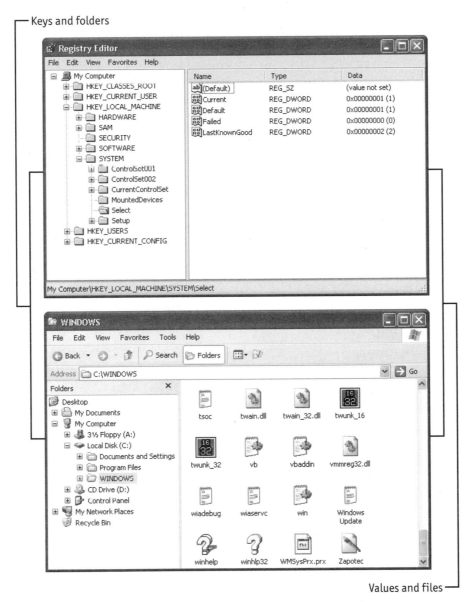

Values and files

Figure 1-4 *If you're familiar with Windows Explorer, and I'll bet you are, you won't have any trouble understanding the registry's structure, which is similar to that of the file system.*

Note I usually use the term *key*, but occasionally I use *subkey* to indicate a parent-child relationship between one key and another. Thus, when you see something that describes the key Software and its subkey Microsoft, it indicates that Microsoft is a child key under Software.

The last thing to tackle in this section is the concept of *linked keys*. Windows XP stores hardware profiles in `HKLM\SYSTEM\CurrentControlSet\Hardware Profiles\`. Each hardware profile is a subkey *nnnn*, where *nnnn* is an incremental number beginning with `0000`. The subkey `Current` is a link to whichever key is the current hardware profile, and root key `HKCC` is a link to `Current`. It all sounds terribly convoluted until you see the relationship in Figure 1-5. Think of links as aliases or shortcuts, if you care to continue the file system analogy.

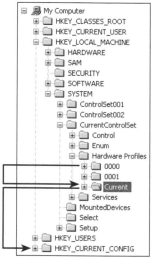

Figure 1-5   *When one key is linked to another, as in this example, the same subkeys and values appear in both places.*

Values

Each key contains one or more values. In my analogy with Windows Explorer, values are similar to files. A value's *name* is similar to a file's name. A value's *type* is similar to a file's extension, which indicates its type. A value's *data* is similar to the file's actual contents. Click a key in Registry Editor's key pane, and the program shows the key's values in the value pane. In the value pane, you see three columns, which correspond to the three parts of a value:

- **Name.** Every value has a name. The same rules for naming keys apply to values: up to 512 ANSI or 256 Unicode characters except for the backslash (\), asterisk (*), and question mark (?), with Windows XP reserving all names that begin with a period. Within each key, value names must be unique, but different keys can have values with the same name.

- **Type.** Each value's type determines the type of data that it contains. For example, a `REG_DWORD` value contains a double-word number, and a `REG_SZ` value contains a string. The section "Types," later in this chapter, describes the different types of data that Windows XP supports in the registry.

- **Data.** Each value can be empty, or null, or can contain data. A value's data can be a maximum of 32,767 bytes, but the practical limit is 2 KB. The data usually corresponds to the type, except that binary values can contain strings, double-words, or anything else for that matter.

Every key contains at least one value, and that's the default value. When you look at the registry through Registry Editor, you see the default value as (Default). The default value is almost always a string, but ill-behaved programs can change it to other types. In most cases, the default value is null, and Registry Editor displays its data as (value not set). When instructions require that you change a key's default value, they usually say so explicitly: "Set the key's default value."

Note When looking at a key's fully qualified path, you have to figure out whether the path includes a value or not. Usually, the text is clear about whether the path is to a key or includes a value, but sometimes it isn't. For example, does HKCR\txtfile\EditFlags refer to a key or a value? In this case, it refers to a value, and I prefer to use explicit language, such as "the value HKCR\txtfile\EditFlags," to make the reference clear. Sometimes, paths that don't include a value name end with a backslash (\). If there is no backslash, pay particular attention to the context to make sure you know whether the path is just a key or includes a value. Sometimes a bit of common sense is all you need.

Types

Windows XP supports the following types of data in the registry. As you look through this list, realize that REG_BINARY, REG_DWORD, and REG_SZ account for the vast majority of all the settings in the registry:

- **REG_BINARY.** Binary data. Registry Editor displays binary data in hexadecimal notation, and you enter binary data using hexadecimal notation. An example of a REG_BINARY value is 0x02 0xFF 0xA9 0x38 0x92 0x38 0xAB 0xD9.

- **REG_DWORD.** Double-word values (32-bits). Many values are REG_DWORD values used as Boolean flags (0 or 1, true or false, yes or no). You also see time stored in REG_DWORD values in milliseconds (1000 is 1 second). 32-bit unsigned numbers range from 0 to 4,294,967,295 and 32-bit signed numbers range from -2,147,483,648 to 2,147,483,647. You can view and edit these values in decimal or hexadecimal notation. Examples of REG_DWORD values are 0xFE020001 and 0x10010001.

- **REG_DWORD_BIG_ENDIAN.** Double-word values with the most significant bytes stored first in memory. The order of the bytes is the opposite of the order in which REG_DWORD stores them. For example, the number 0x01020304 is stored in memory as 0x01 0x02 0x03 0x04. You don't see this data type much on Intel-based architectures.

- **REG_DWORD_LITTLE_ENDIAN.** Double-word values with the least significant bytes stored first in memory (reverse-byte order). This type is the same as REG_DWORD, and because Intel-based architectures store numbers in memory in this format, it is the most common number format in Windows XP. For example, the number 0x01020304 is stored in memory as 0x04 0x03 0x02 0x01. Registry Editor doesn't offer the ability to create REG_DWORD_LITTLE_ENDIAN values, because this value type is identical to REG_DWORD in the registry.

- **REG_EXPAND_SZ.** Variable-length text. A value of this type can include environment variables, and the program using the value expands those variables before using it. For example, a REG_EXPAND_SZ value that contains %USERPROFILE%\Favorites might be expanded to C:\Documents and Settings\Jerry\Favorites before the program uses it. The registry API (Application Programming Interface) relies on the calling program to expand the environment variables in REG_EXPAND_SZ strings, so it's useless if the program doesn't expand them. See Chapter 10, "Deploying User Profiles" to learn how to use this type of value to fix some interesting problems.

- **REG_FULL_RESOURCE_DESCRIPTOR.** Resource lists for a device or device driver. This data type is important to Plug and Play, but it doesn't figure much in your work with the registry. Registry Editor doesn't provide a way to create this type of value, but it does allow you to display it. See HKLM\HARDWARE\DESCRIPTION\Description for examples of this data type.

- **REG_LINK.** A link. You can't create REG_LINK values.

- **REG_MULTI_SZ.** Binary values that contain lists of strings. Registry Editor displays one string on each line and allows you to edit these lists. In the registry, a null character (0x00) separates each string, and two null characters end the list.

- **REG_NONE.** Values with no defined type.

- **REG_QWORD.** Quadruple-word values (64-bits). This type is similar to REG_DWORD but contains 64 bits instead of 32 bits. The only version of Windows XP that supports this type of value is Windows XP 64-Bit Edition. You can view and edit these values in decimal or hexadecimal notation. An example of a REG_QWORD value is 0xFE02000110010001.

- **REG_QWORD_BIG_ENDIAN.** Quadruple-word values with the most significant bytes stored first in memory. The order of the bytes is the opposite of the order in which REG_QWORD stores them. See REG_DWORD_BIG_ENDIAN for more information about this value type.

- **REG_QWORD_LITTLE_ENDIAN.** Quadruple-word values with the least significant bytes stored first in memory (reverse-byte order). This type is the same as REG_QWORD. See REG_DWORD_LITTLE_ENDIAN for more information. Registry Editor doesn't offer the ability to create REG_QWORD_LITTLE_ENDIAN values, because this value type is identical to REG_QWORD in the registry.

- **REG_RESOURCE_LIST.** List of REG_FULL_RESOURCE_DESCRIPTION values. Registry Editor allows you to view but not edit this type of value.

- **REG_RESOURCE_REQUIREMENTS_LIST.**   List of resources that a device requires. Registry Editor allows you to view but not edit this type of value.

- **REG_SZ.**   Fixed-length text. Other than REG_DWORD values, REG_SZ values are the most common types of data in the registry. An example of a REG_SZ value is Microsoft Windows XP or Jerry Honeycutt. Each string ends with a null character. Programs don't expand environment variables in REG_SZ values.

Data in Binary Values

Of all the values in the registry, binary values are the least straightforward. When an application reads a binary value from the registry, deciphering its meaning is up to the program. This means that applications can store data in binary values using their own data structures, and those data structures mean nothing to you or any other program. Also, applications often store REG_DWORD and REG_SZ data in REG_BINARY values, which makes finding and deciphering them difficult, as you learn in Chapter 8, "Finding Registry Settings." In fact, some programs use REG_DWORD and four-byte REG_BINARY values interchangeably; thus, keeping in mind that Intel-based computers use little-endian architecture, the binary value 0x01 0x02 0x03 0x04 and the REG_DWORD value 0x04030201 are exactly the same thing.

Now I'm going to make things more difficult. The registry actually stores all values as binary values. The registry API identifies each type of value by a number, which programmers refer to as a *constant*, and which I tend to think of as the *type number*. You'll notice this type number mostly when you export keys to REG files—something you learn how to do in Chapter 2. For example, when you export a REG_MULTI_SZ value to a REG file, Registry Editor writes a binary value with the type number 7. Normally, the type number associated with each value type doesn't matter because you refer to them by their names, but there are times when the information in the Table 1-4 will come in handy:

Table 1-4   Value Types

Type	Number
REG_NONE	0
REG_SZ	1
REG_EXPAND_SZ	2
REG_BINARY	3
REG_DWORD	4
REG_DWORD_LITTLE_ENDIAN	4
REG_DWORD_BIG_ENDIAN	5
REG_LINK	6
REG_MULTI_SZ	7
REG_RESOURCE_LIST	8

Organization of the Registry

Part IV, "Appendices," describes the contents of the registry in detail. The overview in this section makes getting around in the registry easier until you get there.

Of the five root keys you learned about earlier, HKLM and HKU are more important than the others. These are the only root keys that Windows XP actually stores on disk. The other root keys are links to subkeys in HKLM or HKU. HKCU is a link to a subkey in HKU. HKCR and HKCC are links to subkeys in HKLM. Figure 1-6 illustrates this relationship between root keys and their links to keys.

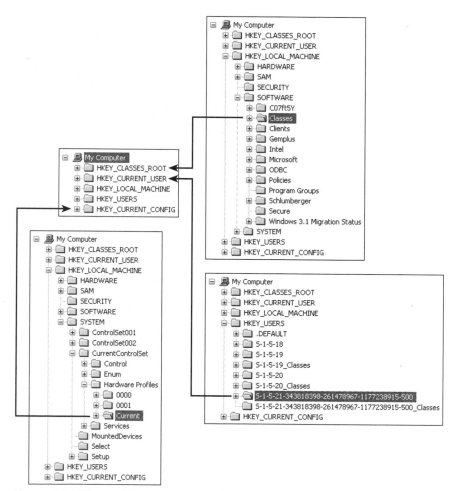

Figure 1-6   *Three of the registry's root keys are links to subkeys in* HKU *and* HKLM.

Throughout this book, you'll see the terms *per-user* and *per-computer*, which indicate whether a setting applies to the user or the computer. Per-user settings are user specific—for example, whether or not a user prefers to display Windows Explorer's status bar. Per-computer settings apply to the computer and every user who logs on to the computer—for example, network configuration. Per-user settings are in HKCU, and per-computer settings are in HKLM. In Chapter 10, "Deploying User Profiles," you learn how Windows XP keeps one user's settings separate from every other user's settings.

HKEY_USERS

HKU contains at least three subkeys:

- .DEFAULT contains the per-user settings that Windows XP uses to display the desktop before any user logs on to the computer. This isn't the same thing as a default user profile, which Windows XP uses to create settings for users the first time they log on to the computer.

- *SID*, where *SID* is the security identifier of the *console user* (the console user is the user sitting at the keyboard), contains per-user settings. HKCU is linked to this key. This key contains settings such as the user's desktop preferences and Control Panel settings.

- *SID*_Classes, where *SID* is the security identifier of the console user, contains per-user class registrations and file associations. Windows XP merges the contents of keys HKLM\SOFTWARE\Classes and HKU*SID*_Classes into HKCR.

You'll usually see other SIDs in HKU, including the following (see Table 1-1 for a refresher):

- S-1-5-18 is the well-known SID for the LocalSystem account. Windows XP loads this account's profile when a program or service runs in the LocalSystem account.

- S-1-5-19 is the well-known SID for the LocalService account. Service Control Manager uses this account to run local services that don't need to run as the LocalSystem account.

- S-1-5-20 is the well-known SID for the NetworkService account. Service Control Manager uses this account to run network services that don't need to run as the LocalSystem account.

You can ignore these SIDs when working in HKU.

Any other subkeys in HKU belong to secondary users. For example, if you use Windows XP's Run As command to run a program as a different user, the operating system loads that user account's settings into HKU. This feature, called *secondary logon*, enables users to run programs with elevated privileges without requiring them to actually log on to a different account. For example, if I'm logged on to the computer using the account Jerry, which is in the Power Users group, but I need to do something in a program as an administrator, I hold down the Shift key, right-click the program's shortcut, click Run As, and then type the Administrator account's name and password. The program runs under the Administrator account and, in this case, HKU contains settings for both the Jerry and Administrator accounts. This technique helps prevent human error as well as opportunistic viruses.

Figure 1-7 shows a typical HKU and describes each of its subkeys. You'll see the same default and service account settings on your computer that you see in the figure. The remaining subkeys and their SIDs will be different, depending on the SID of the console user account and whether other accounts have logged on to Windows XP.

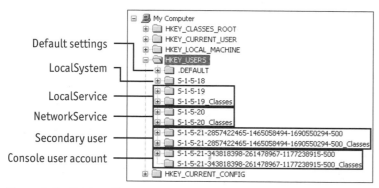

Figure 1-7 *Each subkey in* HKU *contains an account's settings.*

HKEY_CURRENT_USER

HKCU contains the console user's per-user settings. This root key is a link to HKU*SID*, where *SID* is the console user's security identifier. This branch includes environment variables, desktop settings, network connections, printers, and application preferences. Here's a snapshot of some of this root key's subkeys:

- **AppEvents.**   Associates sounds with events. For example, it associates sounds with opening menus, minimizing windows, and logging off Windows XP.

- **Console.**   Stores data for the console subsystem, which hosts all character-mode applications, including the MS-DOS command prompt. In addition, the Console key can contain subkeys for custom command windows.

- **Control Panel.**   Contains accessibility, regional, and desktop appearance settings. You configure most of these settings in Control Panel. However, this key contains a handful of useful settings that have no user interface; you can configure them only through the registry.

- **Environment.**   Stores environment variables users have set. Each value associates an environment variable with the string that Windows XP substitutes for the variable. The default values for these entries are in the user's profile.

- **Identities.**   Contains one subkey for each identity in Microsoft Outlook Express. Outlook Express uses identities to allow multiple users to share a single mail client. With Windows XP's support for user profiles, one user's settings are separate from other users' settings, so this key is seldom necessary.

- **Keyboard Layout.** Contains information about the installed keyboard layouts.

- **Network.** Stores information about mapped network drives. Each subkey in Network is a mapped drive to which Windows XP connects each time the user logs on to the computer. The subkeys' names are the drive letters to which the drives are mapped. Each drive's key contains settings used to reconnect the drive.

- **Printers.** Stores user preferences for printers.

- **Software.** Contains per-user application settings. Windows XP stores much of its own configuration in this key, too. Microsoft has standardized its organization so that programs store settings in HKCU\Software*Vendor**Program**Version*\. *Vendor* is the name of the program's publisher, *Program* is the name of the program, and *Version* is the program's version number. Often, as is the case with Windows XP, *Version* is simply CurrentVersion.

- **Volatile Environment.** Contains environment variables defined when the user logged on to Windows XP.

Other subkeys you see in HKCU are usually legacy leftovers or uninteresting. They include UNICODE Program Groups, SessionInformation, and Windows 3.1 Migration Status.

HKEY_LOCAL_MACHINE

HKLM contains per-computer settings, which means the settings in this branch apply to the computer's configuration and affect every user who logs on to it. Settings run the gamut from device driver configurations to Windows XP settings. HKLM contains the following subkeys (notice that these subkeys are capitalized; I'll explain why later):

- **HARDWARE.** Stores data describing the hardware that Windows XP detects as it starts. The operating system creates this key each time it starts, and it includes information about devices and the device drivers and resources associated with them. This key contains information that IT professionals find useful during a network inventory, as you learn in Chapter 15, "Working Around IT Problems."

- **SAM.** Contains Windows XP's local security database, the Security Accounts Manager (SAM). Windows XP stores local users and groups in SAM. This key's access control list (ACL) prevents even administrators from viewing it. SAM is a link to the key HKLM\SECURITY\SAM.

- **SECURITY.** Contains Windows XP's local security database in the subkey SAM, as well as other security settings. This key's ACL prevents even administrators from viewing it, unless they take ownership of it.

- **SOFTWARE.** Contains per-computer application settings. Windows XP stores settings in this key, too. Microsoft standardized this key's organization so that programs store settings in HKLM\SOFTWARE*Vendor**Program**Version*\. *Vendor* is the name of the program's publisher, *Program* is the name of the program, and *Version* is the program's version number. Often, as is the case with Windows XP, *Version* is CurrentVersion. HKCR is a link to the key HKLM\SOFTWARE\Classes.

- **SYSTEM.**   Contains control sets, one of which is current. The remaining sets are available for use by Windows XP. Each subkey is a control set named ControlSet*nnn*, where *nnn* is an incremental number beginning with 001. The operating system maintains at least two control sets to ensure that it can always start properly. These sets contain device driver and service configurations. HKLM\SYSTEM\CurrentControlSet is a link to ControlSet*nnn*, and the key HKLM\SYSTEM\Select indicates which ControlSet*nnn* is in use.

HKEY_CLASSES_ROOT

HKCR contains two types of settings. The first is file associations that associate different types of files with the programs that can open, print, and edit them. The second is class registrations for Component Object Model (COM) objects. This root key is one of the most interesting in the registry to customize, because it enables you to change a lot of the operating system's behavior. This root key is also the largest in the registry, accounting for the vast majority of the space that the registry consumes.

Before Windows 2000, HKCR was a link to the key HKLM\SOFTWARE\Classes, but this root key is more complicated now. To derive HKCR, the operating system merges two keys: HKLM\SOFTWARE\Classes, which contains default file associations and class registrations; and HKCU\Software\Classes, which contains per-user file associations and class registrations. HKCU\Software\Classes is really a link to HKU*SID*_Classes, which you learned about in the "HKEY_USERS" section. If the same value appears in both branches, the value in HKCU\Software\Classes has higher precedence and wins over the value in HKLM\SOFTWARE\Classes. This new merge algorithm has several benefits:

- Programs can register per-computer *and* per-user program file associations and program classes. (One user can have file associations that other users who share the computer don't have.) This is probably the biggest benefit of the merge.

- Users who share a single computer can use two different programs to edit the same type of file without affecting each other.

- Because per-user file associations and class registrations are in the users' profiles, they follow users from computer to computer when using roaming user profiles.

- IT professionals can limit access to HKLM\SOFTWARE\Classes without preventing users from changing HKCU\Software\Classes, allowing for greater security in the registry without crippling users' ability to change associations.

Create a new key in the root of HKCR, and Windows XP actually creates it in HKLM\SOFTWARE\Classes. Windows XP doesn't provide a user interface other than Registry Editor to add class registrations to HKCU\Software\Classes, because the intention is to allow programs to register per-user program classes. When you edit an existing program class, the change is reflected in HKLM or HKCU, depending on where the program class already exists. If the program class exists in both places, Windows XP updates only the version in HKCU.

Note HKCR is significant enough that it gets its own appendix. Appendix A, "File Associations," describes this root key in detail. You learn how it associates file extensions with file types, how Windows XP registers COM objects, and which subkeys are the most interesting to customize.

HKEY_CURRENT_CONFIG

HKCC is a link to configuration data for the current hardware profile, the key HKLM\SYSTEM \CurrentcontrolSet\Hardware Profiles\Current. In turn, Current is a link to the key HKLM \SYSTEM\CurrentcontrolSet\Hardware Profiles*nnnn*, where *nnnn* is a incremental number beginning with 0000. For more information, see Appendix C, "Per-Computer Settings."

Registry Management Tools

Hundreds of third-party and shareware registry tools are available. You learn about many of them throughout this book. Some tools I use more often than others, though, and here's an introduction to them:

- **Registry Editor.**   You learn about Registry Editor in Chaper 2, "Using Registry Editor." This is the primary tool you use to edit settings in the registry.

- **Console Registry Tool for Windows (Reg.exe).**   This command-line registry tool supports most of the capabilities of Registry Editor. The significance of this tool is that it allows you to script edits in batch files. For more information about Reg.exe, see Chapter 9, "Scripting Registry Changes."

- **WinDiff.**   This tool comes with the Windows XP Support Tools, which you install from \Support\Tools on the Windows XP CD. It's the best program I've found for comparing files, a useful technique for tracking down settings in the registry. For more information about using this tool, see Chapter 8, "Finding Registry Changes."

- **Microsoft Word 2002.**   This application might not seem like a registry management tool, but I use Word when WinDiff isn't available to compare files so I can figure out where a program stores a setting in the registry. I also use Word to edit scripts so that I can take advantage of its built-in version control and revision tracking features.

If you used the Windows 2000 Resource Kit tools, you'll notice the absence of tools from the Windows XP Resource Kit. The CD contains a copy of the kit's documentation and that's all. This is partially because Windows XP includes many of these tools, as does the Windows XP Support Tools (these are on your Windows XP CD in \Support\Tools). Most of the Windows 2000 Resource Kit tools still work well in Windows XP, and you can download many of them from Microsoft's Web site at *http://www.microsoft.com /windows2000/techinfo/reskit/tools/default.asp*.

Note   If you're looking for a particular type of tool that I don't discuss in this book, finding it is easy: Open the ZDNet Downloads site at *http://downloads-zdnet.com.com* in Internet Explorer, and then search for *registry* in the Windows category. The result is a list of hundreds of registry tools with a wide variety of special features, such as search and replace. Make sure that you download a program that works with Windows XP, though.

Registry Hive Files

In Registry Editor, you see the registry's logical structure. This is how Windows XP presents the registry to you and the programs that use it, regardless of how the operating system actually organizes it on disk, which is much more complicated.

Physically, Windows XP organizes the registry in *hives*, each of which is in a binary file called a *hive file*. For each hive file, Windows XP creates additional supporting files that contain backup copies of each hive's data. These backups allow the operating system to repair the hive during the installation and boot processes if something goes terribly wrong. You find hives in only two root keys: HKLM and HKU. (All other root keys are links to keys within those two.) The hive and supporting files for all hives other than those in HKU are in %SYSTEMROOT%\System32\config. Hive files for HKU are in users' profile folders. Hive files don't have a file name extension but their supporting files do, as described in Table 1-5.

Table 1-5   Hive File Name Extensions

Extension	Description
None	Hive file
.alt	Not used in Windows XP. In Windows 2000, System.alt is a backup copy of the System hive file
.log	Transaction log of changes to a hive
.sav	Copy of a hive file made at the end of the text-mode phase of the Windows XP setup program

Note   The Windows XP setup program has two phases: text-mode and graphics-mode. The setup program copies each hive file to a SAV file at the end of the text-mode phase so that it can recover if the graphics-mode phase fails. If graphics-mode phase does fail, the setup program repeats that phase after restoring the hive file from the SAV file.

Hives in HKLM

Table 1-6 shows the relationship between each registry hive and its hive file. Notice that the name of each hive is capitalized in the registry, which is sometimes a useful reminder while you're editing. What you should get out of this table is that each hive in the first column comes from the files in the second column. Thus, Windows XP loads the hive HKLM \SOFTWARE from the hive file Software, which is in %SYSTEMROOT%\System32\config. It loads the hive HKLM\SYSTEM from the hive file System, which is in the same location. To see the hive files that Windows XP has loaded, see HKLM\SYSTEM\CurrentControlSet \Control\hivelist\.

Table 1-6 Hive Files

Hive	Hive, Supporting Files
HKLM\SAM	SAM, SAM.LOG
HKLM\SECURITY	SECURITY, SECURITY.LOG
HKLM\SOFTWARE	Software, Software.log, Software.sav
HKLM\SYSTEM	System, System.log, System.sav

Did you notice that you don't find a hive file for HKLM\HARDWARE in Table 1-6? That's because this hive is dynamic. Windows XP builds it each time the operating system boots, and it doesn't save the hive as a hive file when it shuts down.

Note Other files in %SYSTEMROOT%\System32\config seem conspicuously out of place. AppEvent.Evt, SecEvent.Evt, and SysEvent.Evt are Windows XP's event logs—Application, Security, and System, respectively. You can see in the registry where Windows XP stores each event log by looking at the subkeys of HKLM\SYSTEM\ControlSet001\Services \Eventlog. Userdiff is a file that Windows XP uses to convert user profiles from earlier versions of Windows (notably versions of Microsoft Windows NT) so that Windows XP can use them. The last out-of-place file is Netlogon.ftl, which remains a mystery to me.

Hives in HKU

Each subkey in HKU is also a hive. For example, HKU\.DEFAULT is a hive, and its hive file is %SYSTEMROOT%\System32\config\default. The remaining subkeys come from two different sources, though. The hive HKU*SID* is in the hive file %USERPROFILE%\Ntuser.dat, while the hive HKU*SID*_Classes is in the hive file %USERPROFILE%\Local Settings \Application Data\Microsoft\Windows\UsrClass.dat.

Each time a new user logs on to Windows XP, the operating system creates a new profile for that user using the default user profile. The profile contains a new Ntuser.dat hive file, which is the user profile hive. You learn much more about user profiles and how to deploy them in Chapter 10, "Deploying User Profiles."

To see which profiles Windows XP has loaded, and the hive file that corresponds to each hive, see the key HKLM\SOFTWARE\Microsoft\Windows NT\CurrentVersion\ProfileList. This key contains one subkey for each profile that the operating system has ever loaded, past or present. The subkey's name is the name of the hive in HKU, and the value ProfileImagePath contains the path to the hive file, which is always Ntuser.dat. ProfileList does not mention the *SID*_Classes hives, however; it contains only user profile hives.

Note   Windows 2000 limited the size of the registry, but Windows XP does not. This means that the operating system no longer limits the amount of space that the registry hives consume in memory or on the hard disk. Microsoft made an architectural change to the way Windows XP maps the registry into memory, eliminating the need for the size limit you might have struggled with in Windows 2000.

Using the Registry Editor

Registry Editor is the tool you use to edit the registry directly. You change the registry every time you log on to the computer, but you do it indirectly through Control Panel or the Run dialog box, which updates the registry's list of programs that you've run recently. With Registry Editor, you affect settings without the help of a user interface. That makes Registry Editor one of the operating system's most powerful and dangerous tools. On one hand, you can customize Microsoft Windows XP in ways that aren't possible through the user interface. On the other hand, nothing is checking the settings you change for sanity.

Every version of Windows since 3.1 has had a registry editor. The editor in Microsoft Windows 95 can search the registry and has a simple to use interface. Microsoft Windows NT 4.0 has an archaic editor that can't search and is more difficult to use than the editor in Windows 95, but it has capabilities unique to a secure operating system, such as the ability to set permissions on keys and edit more advanced data types like REG_MULTI_SZ. Microsoft Windows 2000 provides both editors, requiring you to switch back and forth to use each editor's unique abilities. Now, with Windows XP, you get the best of both editors in a single program (insert applause for the developers here).

Registry Editor in Windows XP is the tool you learn about in this chapter. It's the basis for just about every set of instructions you see in this book. It is also the basis for many solutions you find in Microsoft's Knowledge Base, the solutions that people post to UseNet, and so on. This chapter contains more than just instructions for how to use the editor, though. You'll find useful tidbits of information that come from my own experience using this program, such as how to search better and how to quickly back up settings before changing them, which will hopefully make your experience with the single most powerful tool in Windows XP a great one.

Running Regedit

You won't find a shortcut to Registry Editor (Regedit) on the Start menu. You don't *want* to find a shortcut to Regedit on the Start menu. Imagine what life as an IT professional or power user who supports friends and relatives would be like if Microsoft advertised this program to every Windows XP user on the planet. That's one reason why you find so little documentation about Regedit in Help or elsewhere. That's also why Windows XP provides policies that you can use to limit access to Regedit. IT professionals and power users have great need for Regedit, however—it's often the only way to fix a problem or customize certain settings. For example, I recently used a program that changed critical settings while it was running, and then restored them when the program shut down. Unfortunately, the program crashed without restoring the settings and the only way I could get them back to their original values was to edit the registry. Sometimes, it's the only tool for the job.

Note   Regedit and Registry Editor are one and the same. Regedit.exe is the name of Registry Editor's program file and it is easier to type, say, and read, so I will use the term *Regedit* for Registry Editor throughout the remainder of this book.

Regedit is in %SYSTEMROOT%, C:\Windows on most computers. Click Start, Run, and type **regedit** to run Regedit. You don't have to type the path. If you want to start Regedit even quicker, drag Regedit.exe to your Quick Launch toolbar or to the Start button to add it to the top of your Start menu.

IT professionals can prevent users from running Regedit. They can set the Disable registry editing tools policy in Group Policy, local or otherwise. When users try to run Regedit, they see an error message that says, "Registry Editing has been disabled by your administrator." Although it's probably not a good idea to prevent the setup program from installing Regedit.exe, you can set the Regedit.exe file's permissions to prevent users from running it or better yet, use Software Restriction Policies to prevent users from running Regedit.exe, regardless of the file's permissions or users' rights. I cover these topics in detail elsewhere in this book.

Note   For more information about Group Policy and Software Restriction Policies, see Chapter 6, "Using Registry-Based Policies." To learn the best way to deploy file and registry permissions, see Chapter 7, "Managing Registry Security."

Note   Administrators shouldn't rely on any of these methods to secure the registry completely. These simple barriers don't stop determined users from gaining access to the registry. For instance, dogged users can download shareware registry editors, most of which don't honor the Disable registry editing tools policy. Shareware registry editors also circumvent Software Restriction Policies and permissions that you apply to Regedit.exe. In reality, determined users will always find a way to hack away at the registry, so part of the solution must be a corporate IT policy that you clearly communicate to users.

Exploring Regedit

With all its power, Regedit is still a simple program with a straightforward user interface. Its few menus are simple. It has a status bar that displays the name of the current key. Its window contains two panes, split by a divider that you can drag left or right to change the size of both panes. On the left is the *key pane*; on the right is the *value pane*. The key pane displays the registry's keys and subkeys, analogous to folders and subfolders. This is the registry's hierarchy. The value pane displays the settings that each key contains. Click a key in the key pane, and you see that key's values in the value pane. This is so similar to Windows Explorer that I'll stretch to say that if you know how to use one, you know how to use the other. Figure 2-1 is a snapshot of Regedit.

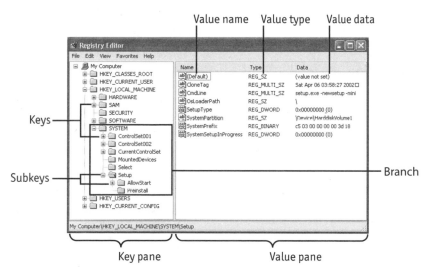

Figure 2-1   *Regedit is much easier to use when you maximize its window, which helps you to see the full names of subkeys and each value's data in its entirety.*

Regedit saves its settings every time you close it. The next time you start Regedit, the window will open to its last position and the window and panes will be the same size. The columns will also be the same size. Last, Regedit reselects the last key that you selected. At times, you'll want Regedit to forget these settings, though, particularly if you're writing a book about the registry and are doing screen captures. Chapter 9, "Scripting Registry Changes," shows you how to do just that. You create a script that automatically removes the key `HKCU\Software\Microsoft\Windows\CurrentVersion\Applets\Registry`. You can't just remove this key using Regedit, though, because Regedit creates this key each time you close it and will use the current settings to do so.

The following sections describe each pane in more detail, including special tips for working on each side of Regedit's window.

Regedit Got Better

Regedit in Windows XP makes several improvements over the version in Windows 2000:

- Access the features of both Regedit and Regedt32 (the second registry editor in Windows 2000) in a single editor. You no longer have to flip back and forth between both registry editors to complete most tasks.

- Search for keys, values, and data faster.

- Add the keys you use most frequently to the Favorites menu and then pop back to them just by clicking their friendly names on the menu.

- Return to the last key that you selected the next time you run Regedit.

- Export any portion of the registry to a text file that's much easier to read than anything earlier versions of either registry editor provided.

Additionally, Windows XP makes substantial improvements to the registry itself. Windows XP supports much larger registries than earlier versions of Windows; it's now limited only by the amount of disk space available. Second, the registry is faster in Windows XP than in earlier versions of Windows. Windows XP keeps related keys and values closer together in the database, preventing page faults that degenerate into disk swapping. Last, Windows XP reduces fragmentation by allocating space for large values in 16-KB chunks. All in all, the registry in Windows XP is significantly faster to query than it was in Windows 2000.

Key Pane

The key pane displays the registry's hierarchy. It is organized much like an outline, with each key's child keys, or subkeys, indented immediately below it. At the top, you see My Computer, which represents the local computer. When you connect to another computer's registry over the network, you see that computer's name at the top level of the key pane, too. Immediately under My Computer, you see each of the local registry's root keys. Following each root key are its subkeys. The term *branch* refers to a key and all its subkeys.

Click the plus sign (+) next to a key to expand that branch. Click the minus sign (–) next to a key to collapse that branch. Click any key to see its values in the value pane. You can use the mouse pointer to explore the registry, but using the keyboard is much more efficient when you know the keyboard shortcuts that are available. Table 2-1 describes the keyboard shortcuts that you can use. Of all the shortcuts available, the keys I use the most are Right Arrow and Left Arrow. These are quick ways to move around the registry while expanding and collapsing entire branches at the same time. The other shortcut I find most helpful is Ctrl+F, which quickly opens the Find dialog box.

Table 2-1 Keyboard Shortcuts

Key	Description
Searching	
Ctrl+F	Opens the Find dialog box
F3	Repeats the last search
Browsing	
Keypad +	Expands the selected branch
Keypad -	Collapses the selected branch
Keypad *	Expands all the selected branch's subkeys
Up Arrow	Selects the previous key
Down Arrow	Selects the next key
Left Arrow	Collapses the selected branch if it's not collapsed; otherwise, selects the parent key
Right Arrow	Expands the selected branch if it's not already expanded; otherwise, selects the key's first subkey
Home	Selects My Computer
End	Selects the last key that's visible in the key pane
Page Up	Moves up one page in the key pane
Page Down	Moves down one page in the key pane
Tab	Moves between the key and value panes
F6	Moves between the key and value panes
Other	
Delete	Deletes the select branch or value
F1	Opens Regedit's Help
F2	Renames the selected key or value
F5	Refreshes the key and value panes
F10	Opens Regedit's menu bar
Shift+F10	Opens the shortcut menu for the selected key or value
Alt+F4	Closes Regedit

As you learned in Chapter 1, "Learning the Basics," Windows XP stores different parts of the registry in different hive files. Regedit displays all the hive files together to show a single, unified registry, though. In Regedit, you can see when a branch is its own hive because its name is capitalized. For example, all the subkeys under HKLM are hives, so their names are capitalized. You find each subkey's hive file in %SYSTEMROOT%\System32\config. Notice in Figure 2-1 that all the subkeys under HKU are capitalized, because they are also hives. You find most of those hive files in %USERPROFILE%\Ntuser.dat. When you change a value in Regedit, Windows XP updates the appropriate hive file. While you're editing, you don't really care to which hive file a particular setting belongs, though. Refer back to Chapter 1 if you need a refresher on how Windows XP stores the registry on disk.

Value Pane

The value pane displays the selected key's values. In this pane, you see three columns: Name, Type, and Data. You can change the size of each column by dragging the dividers left or right. I typically use about half the pane to display the Name and Type columns and the remainder of the pane to display the Data column. Each row contains a single value. The first value in the value pane is always (Default), which is the key's default REG_SZ value. For more information about default values, see Chapter 1, "Learning the Basics."

The Name column contains the value's name. Next to the name, you see one of the icons in Table 2-2 that indicates the value's type: string or binary. The Type column indicates the type of data in that value. Unlike earlier versions of Regedit, Windows XP's Regedit properly displays all the different data types that Windows XP supports in the registry, and you can edit them. That includes not only REG_SZ, REG_DWORD, and REG_BINARY, but also REG_EXPAND_SZ, REG_MULTI_SZ, and so on. The Data column displays the value's contents. You'll easily recognize REG_DWORD and REG_SZ values in this column, but REG_BINARY and other types of values are much more difficult to view in their entirety. To get a better glimpse of binary values, click View, Display Binary Data.

Table 2-2   Binary and String Icons

Icon	Description
	Binary values, including REG_DWORD and REG_BINARY
	String values, including REG_SZ and REG_MULTI_SZ

Searching for Data

You're going to spend a lot of time searching the registry. I promise. This is particularly true if you're an IT professional responsible for helping users, deploying Windows XP, and so on. This is even true if you're a power user trying to figure out why a program is doing something that you don't particularly like. For instance, you might want to figure out why a program runs every time you start Windows XP. If you don't already know about the Run key, you'd have to search the registry for the program's file name. I spend a lot of time locating programs' settings in the registry and I do that by searching for their names and file names.

You can search key names, value names, and string data. You can also search for partial matches (searching for *Windows* matches both *C:\Windows* and *Windows XP*) or require full matches. The first hit can take a long while to show up, so be patient. It takes even longer if you're searching a remote computer's registry. After Regedit finds a hit, it selects the key or value it found. If Regedit searches to the end of the registry without a match, it displays a message that says, "Finished searching through the registry." Here's how to search using Registry Editor:

1. On the Edit menu, click Find.

2. In the Find dialog box, shown in Figure 2-2, type the text you want to find in the Find What box.

3. To find keys whose name contains the text, select the Keys check box. To find values whose name contains the text, select the Values check box. To find REG_SZ values whose data contains the text, select the Data check box.

4. Click Find Next.

5. Press F3 to repeat your search if necessary.

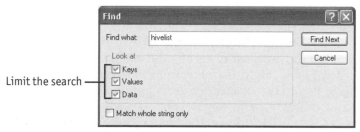

Figure 2-2   *Use fewer characters and partial matches to get more hits. Use more characters or require full matches to get fewer hits.*

You can significantly cut down the time it takes to search the registry by narrowing the focus to keys, values, or data. For example, if you know that you want to search only for values that contain certain characters in their names, limit your search to value names. If you know that you're searching for data, limit your search to value data. In the Find dialog box, shown in Figure 2-2, clear the Keys, Values, or Data check boxes to prevent Regedit from searching those areas. Selecting the Match Whole String Only check box won't improve turnaround time, but it will reduce the number of hits you receive and, because you don't have to look at as many hits, make searching quicker. Select this check box only if you're 100 percent certain about the name or data for which you're searching; otherwise, you won't find it.

Searching Incrementally

Incremental searching makes finding subkeys and values in long lists much faster. It's a life saver when you're trying to find a subkey in HKCR, because searching takes too long and paging down the long list is mind numbing. Here's how it works: Select the first item in a long list, and then start typing the item you want to find. Regedit selects the first item that matches what you've typed so far. So if you click the first subkey under HKCR and then type **wm**, Regedit selects wmafile. Type **d** (without delaying too long so as not to restart the incremental search) and Regedit selects WMDFile. You get the idea. Keep in mind that it won't find keys or values that are collapsed. That is, incremental searching only finds keys that you can see by scrolling the key pane up or down.

Searching in Binary Values

Regedit can't search for REG_DWORD or binary values. It searches only for key names, value names, or string values. This means that you can't use Regedit to find numeric values in REG_DWORD or REG_BINARY values, and you certainly can't find text that Windows XP stores as REG_BINARY values, which is very common.

The solution is straightforward, though. Export the branch that you want to search to a REG file. (See "Exporting Settings," later in this chapter, to learn how to create a REG file.) Then open the REG file in Notepad, and search for the number or binary string you want to find. You have to know how Regedit formats values in REG files to find them, however. Chapter 9, "Scripting Registry Changes," describes the format of REG files in detail. For now, you need to know what the different types of values look like in a REG file, which is what Table 2-3 describes. For example, if you want to find the word *Jerry* in a REG_BINARY value, you'd convert its letters to their Unicode values, a task that's easy if you know that a capital A has a hex value of 0x0041, a lowercase a has a hex value of 0x0061, and the number 0 has a hex value of 0x0030. Thus, *Jerry* as a binary string is 0x4A 0x00 0x65 0x00 0x72 0x00 0x72 0x00 0x79 0x00. (If you're not familiar with reverse byte notation and Unicode, see Chapter 1.) To find binary strings in a REG file that contain the word *Jerry*, search for 4a,00,65,00,72,00,72,00,79.

Table 2-3   REG File Data Formats

Type	In Regedit	In REG files
REG_SZ	Microsoft Windows XP	"Microsoft Windows XP"
REG_DWORD	0x00000009	dword:00000009
REG_BINARY	0XC2 0X00 0X02 0X9E 0X00 0X00 0X3D	hex:c2,00,02,9e,00,00,3d

Table 2-3 contains only REG_SZ, REG_DWORD, and REG_BINARY examples. That's because Regedit uses a variation of REG_BINARY to represent all other value types. In a REG file, for instance, a REG_MULTI_SZ looks like hex(7):4a,00,65,00,72,00,72,00,79,00,00,00. Chapter 9 describes the format of every value type and what they look like in REG files.

Bookmarking Favorite Keys

Regedit, including the versions that come with Windows 2000 and Windows XP, adopts one of Microsoft Internet Explorer's most useful features: Favorites. This enables you to bookmark the subkeys that you edit most frequently and return to them quickly. Clicking a subkey on the Favorites menu is certainly a better alternative to clicking your way through the key pane or, worse yet, trying to remember where Windows XP stores the Run key in the registry. Adding a key to Favorites is easy, and after you add it, you can click its name on the Favorites menu (Figure 2-3) and go straight to that key.

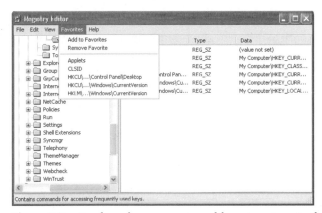

Figure 2-3   *Bookmark your most-used keys to return to them quickly.*

To add a key to Favorites, click it, and then click Favorites, Add To Favorites. In the Add To Favorites dialog box, type a descriptive name for your shortcut. I typically name shortcuts with the root key and last couple of subkeys, such as HKCU\...\Windows\CurrentVersion, so I can quickly tell whether the shortcut is in HKCU or HKLM (they have similar structures). Using the full name, like HKCU\Software\Microsoft\Windows\CurrentVersion, isn't practical, because it makes the menu too wide.

You might like to have some help getting your Favorites menu going. Thus, the following list shows you what I typically put on mine:

- HKCR\CLSID
- HKCU\Control Panel\Desktop
- HKCU\Software\Microsoft\Active Setup\Installed Components
- HKCU\Software\Microsoft\Internet Explorer
- HKCU\Software\Microsoft\Windows\CurrentVersion
- HKCU\Software\Microsoft\Windows\CurrentVersion\Explorer
- HKCU\Software\Policies
- HKLM\SOFTWARE\Microsoft\Active Setup\Installed Components
- HKLM\SOFTWARE\Microsoft\Windows\CurrentVersion
- HKLM\SOFTWARE\Microsoft\Windows\CurrentVersion\Explorer

- `HKLM\SOFTWARE\Policies`
- `HKLM\SYSTEM\CurrentControlSet\Control`

Removing a key from Favorites is also easy. On the Favorites menu, click Remove Favorite, and then click the keys you want to remove. If you want to rename keys in Favorites, you can edit the key `HKCU\Software\Microsoft\Windows\CurrentVersion\Applets\Regedit\Favorites` and rename shortcuts or change their targets.

Tip   Regedit displays keys in the order that you added them; it doesn't sort them alphabetically. If you really want this list to be in alphabetical order, export `HKCU\Software\Microsoft\Windows\CurrentVersion\Applets\Regedit\Favorites` to a REG file. Edit the REG file to sort the keys in alphabetical order, or any other order that you prefer, and then import the REG file back in to the registry after removing the `Favorites` key. The Favorites menu is resorted. Save this REG file, by the way, so you can use your favorites elsewhere.

Using Better Techniques

After a while, you'll know enough about the registry in Windows XP to make searching much faster. You'll know where to begin and end your searches so that you don't waste your time searching parts of the registry where you're not going to find what you want. Click a subkey near where you want to begin, and then search. As you repeat your search by pressing F3, keep an eye on the status bar and note the key that contains the current hit. After you've gone past the branch that you think should contain the value, quit searching.

Here's an example of focusing a search. When you build a default user profile, which you learn about in Chapter 10, "Deploying User Profiles," you'll load the hive file you're building and check it for references to the current user profile folder, which you don't want to deploy to desktops throughout the organization. To narrow your search on that hive, you'll select the hive's first key in the registry and then search for the path, deciding along the way about what to do with any references to it that you find. After you're out of that hive, though, quit searching so that you don't waste your time and accidentally change values you don't intend to change.

Other examples of focusing searches to find data faster are:

- Limiting your search to `HKCR` when you want to find values related to file associations. For that matter, do an incremental search to speed things up.

- Looking only in the branches `HKCU\Software` and `HKLM\SOFTWARE` to find programs' settings. And if you know the names of the vendor and program, you can go straight to the key that contains its settings because you know that programs store their settings in `HKCU` and `HKLM` in the branch `Software\Company\Program\Version`.

- Searching HKCU if you know you're searching for per-user settings, and search HKLM if you know you're searching for per-machine settings.

- Searching the branch HKLM\System if you're after device driver and service settings.

Shareware Search Tools

A variety of shareware tools are available for searching the registry. They are far more advanced than Regedit and designed specifically to make digging around the registry easier and quicker. You can download evaluation versions of these tools at any shareware site. Try *http://www.zdnet.com/downloads* or *http://www.tucows.com*. Here are some of the most popular:

- Registry Crawler 4.0 from 4Developers at *http://www.4developers.com*

- Registry Toolkit from Funduc Software at *http://www.funduc.com*

- Resplendent Registrar from Resplendence Sp at *http://www.resplendence.com*

- Registry Detective from PC Magazine at *http://www.pcmagazine.com*

Registry Crawler is my personal favorite but the other tools also get good results. Registry Crawler not only searches the registry faster than Regedit, but it has features that make the task easier. You can access it quickly from the system tray. It presents a list of matches that you see all at once, rather than bouncing around from hit to hit, and you can export the results to a REG file. It also enables you to search the registries of multiple computers at one time if you have access to them over a network. Its most powerful feature is its search-and-replace capability, however, which enables you to replace all instances of a value with another.

Editing the Registry

In Regedit, assuming that a key or value's permissions don't prevent it, you can add, delete, and rename keys and values. You can also change most values.

As you'd suspect, there's more than one way to do just about anything in Regedit. You'll find three different ways to change a value: through the main menu, through the shortcut menu, or with a keyboard shortcut. Use whichever method is right for you, but I prefer keyboard shortcuts because I deplore touching the desktop rodent without a reason. You can edit any value by selecting it and pressing Enter.

The following sections describe the features that Regedit provides for editing the registry. These are the basic steps that you'll rely on throughout this book.

Changing Values

I promise that 99.999 percent of the time (had to get the five 9s in there), when working with Regedit, you're going to double-click a value to change it. That's not going to stop me from telling you about other ways you can change a value, however. One way to change a value is to click Edit, Modify. Another way is to right-click the value and then click Modify on the shortcut menu.

Regedit displays a different editor depending on the value's type. For example, Regedit opens the Edit String dialog box when you edit a REG_SZ value. It displays the Edit DWORD Value dialog box when you edit a REG_DWORD value. Unlike the version of Regedit that comes with Windows 2000, the version in Windows XP doesn't toss you into the Edit Binary Value dialog box for values such as REG_MULTI_SZ. This version has dialog boxes for almost all the value types that Windows XP supports. The following graphics show what the different editors look like, with a description of each.

Use the Edit String dialog box to edit REG_SZ and REG_EXPAND_SZ values. Enclosing the value in quotes isn't necessary unless you intend to include the quotes in your value. You can copy values from this dialog box to the clipboard, which is a nifty way to get values into scripts and documents.

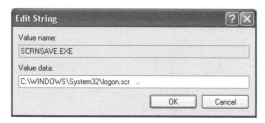

Use the Edit DWORD Value dialog box to edit REG_DWORD values. By default, you're editing a hexadecimal value, but you won't include any prefixes such as 0x in the value; you just type the hexadecimal digits. You can edit the value as a decimal number by selecting the Decimal option. Note that Regedit displays REG_DWORD values in the Value Data box using both notations.

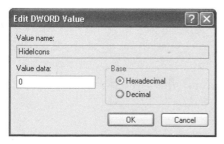

Use the Edit Binary Value dialog box to edit REG_BINARY values. The first column of numbers in this dialog box is the offset, starting from zero. The second column of numbers contains the binary string in hexadecimal notation. The last column shows the text representation of the binary string. You can edit either the second or third columns. You can type hexadecimal digits or plain text.

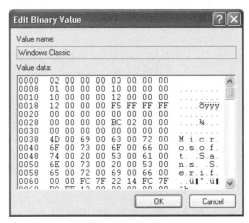

Use the Edit Multi-String dialog box to edit REG_MULTI_SZ values. Each string is on its own line with no blank lines.

To change a value, click Edit, Modify, and then type the value's new data in the Value Data box. When you change a value using Regedit, the editor immediately applies that change to the registry, but that doesn't mean Windows XP or other programs have noticed the change. In fact, all changes go unnoticed until the program or operating system has a reason to load or reload that value from the registry. For example, if you change the

Windows Explorer settings in the registry, open windows won't reflect those changes—you must close and reopen those windows. If you customize Microsoft Office XP, you must shut down and restart it before it'll recognize your changes. Settings that Windows XP loads only when you log on to the operating system and per-user settings, such as the location of shell folders like Favorites, require you to log off and back on to Windows XP for your changes to be reflected. Likewise, settings in HKLM and per-machine settings often require you to restart the computer in order for Windows XP to recognize them because the operating system loads those settings only as it starts.

Chances are pretty good that you're going to mess up something. Unless you have access to a test lab, you're likely to experiment on your production computer (read production as *essential*). If things get out of hand, don't panic, and by all means, don't make things worse by restarting your computer over and over again or whacking away at the registry until there's nothing left. Instead, see Chapter 3, "Backing up the Registry" to learn how to easily recover your recent working configuration.

Stupid Clipboard Tricks

If you're writing scripts, documentation, deployment plans, and so on, you'll be typing a lot of key names and values. This is an error-prone and painful process, and it's one that you can do much easier using the clipboard.

For instance, instead of trying to type a fully qualified key name, flipping back and forth between Regedit and your text editor, and trying to remember each subkey in the branch, just copy the key name to the clipboard and then paste it in to your document: In the key pane, right-click a key, and then click Copy Key Name.

You can copy value names and data to the clipboard, too. Value names don't tend to be long, but using the clipboard is the only way to ensure you have the value's data correct. In the value pane, right-click the value whose name you want to copy to the clipboard, and click Rename. Press Ctrl+C to copy the name to the clipboard, and then press Esc so that you don't accidentally change the name. If you prefer a less risky way to copy a value's name, edit the value, select the value's name, and then press Ctrl+C to copy it to the clipboard.

Copying a value's data to the clipboard is useful and easy: Edit the value, select the value's data, and then press Ctrl+C to copy it to the clipboard. This is a great way to back up data before changing it. Before changing a value, copy its data to the clipboard, create a new value of the same type, and paste the data on the clipboard into it. For example, if I wanted to change a REG_SZ value called Stubpath, I'd copy its data to the clipboard and then paste that data into a new REG_SZ value called StubpathBackup. Then, if the change doesn't work out, I could restore the original value and repair the problem that I created with my willy-nilly edits.

Adding Keys or Values

The only reason you would create keys and values is if you were instructed to do so; that is, you know adding the value will have some effect. For example, Microsoft's Knowledge Base often instructs you to add a value that fixes a certain problem. Throughout this book, you learn about values you can add to the registry that customize Windows XP. Otherwise, adding a value that no program reads doesn't accomplish anything. If you're itching to add something to the registry, take a look at some of the tips in Chapter 4, "Hacking the Registry," or Chapter 15, "Working Around IT Problems."

To create a new key, first click the key under which you want to create a subkey; click Edit, New, and Key; and then type a name for the new key. When you create a new key, Regedit names it New Key #N, where N is an incremental number beginning with 1, and then selects the name so you can change it.

Creating a new value is similar:

1. In the Key pane, click the key in which you want to add a value.

2. On the Edit menu, click New, and then click the type of value you want to create: String Value, Binary Value, DWORD Value, Multi-String Value, or Expandable String Value.

3. Type a name for the new value.

Regedit names the new value New Value #N and then selects it so you can type a new name. Windows XP requires all names contained in a key to be unique. No two subkeys can have the same name and no two values can have the same name. That's why Regedit names new values New Value #1, New Value #2, and so on. The default data for binary values is *null*, or no value whatsoever. The default value for strings is the empty string. The default value for REG_DWORD values is 0. After you create a new value, you edit it to change its value from the default.

Deleting Keys or Values

Click the key or value that you want to delete, and then click Edit, Delete. I don't delete settings often, but there are a few circumstances that recur. The first is when I want to reset a program's settings. For example, to reset Regedit's view settings, you must remove the value that contains them. You can wipe out most programs' settings by wiping them out of the registry. You just have to know where to look: the branch Software*Company**Program**Version*, under HKCU and HKLM. Although this works well for programs that re-create missing settings, it doesn't work for programs that fall over dead when their settings are missing.

Another circumstance is when I want to tidy up the registry a bit. Often, the registry contains references to files that don't exist (*orphans*) or settings that just shouldn't be in the registry anymore, particularly after removing a program. With a little thought and a little luck, you can clean these settings out of the registry. Chapter 3, "Backing up the Registry," is a helpful resource for either scenario.

Tip   There's a better, safer way to remove keys and values than just paving over them. You can rename settings you want to remove, which hides them from any code that's looking for them. Just add your initials to the beginning of the key or value's name. For example, I can hide a value called Session by renaming it JH-Session. Then if something goes terribly wrong, (and it happens from time to time when digging around in the registry), I can remove the current version of Session and give the old version its original name.

Renaming Keys or Values

In Regedit, you can't click a selected file to rename it like you can in Windows Explorer. Instead, you click the key or value that you want to rename, and then click Rename on the Edit menu. You can also click the key or value you want to rename, and then press F2.

In the previous section, "Deleting Keys and Values," you learned that one of the main reasons I rename keys and values is to hide them from Windows XP and other programs instead of permanently deleting them. Then, only after I'm happy with the result, I permanently remove the item. Sometimes I don't even bother to do that, as renamed keys serve as good documentation for the changes I make in the registry. To rename a key or value, select the key, click Edit, Rename, and type a new name.

Printing the Registry

Regedit has a feature that prints all or part of the registry. I confess that I've never printed anything in the registry; I just haven't found a good reason to do it. You can certainly print subkeys as a backup before making changes, but I tend to use hive files for that purpose, which doesn't require me to retype keys, values, and data to restore the old settings. You might not get much use out of this feature, but this chapter wouldn't be complete without describing how to use it. To print all or part of the registry, follow these steps:

1. Click the key you want to print, keeping in mind that you're going to print every subkey and value under it.

2. On the File menu, click Print to display the Print dialog box, shown in Figure 2-4.

3. Do one of the following:
   - To print the entire registry, click All.
   - To print the selected branch, click Selected Branch.
4. Click Print.

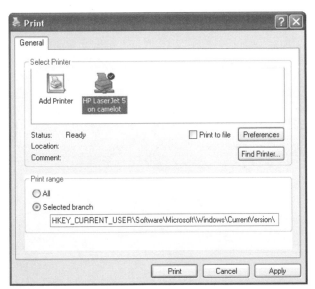

Figure 2-4 *The format of Regedit's printer output is the same as the format that Regedit uses when exporting portions of the registry to a text file.*

The following listing shows you what Regedit's printer output looks like. As you see, it's not very useful except maybe as a temporary way to remember values. Still, Microsoft greatly improved Regedit's printer output for Windows XP. Regedit now prints REG_DWORD values so they look like REG_DWORD values, rather than printing them as binary values in little-endian format (see Chapter 1, "Learning the Basics"). It also prints binary values along with their ASCII-equivalent text. Last, this version of Regedit actually prints each value's type rather than relying on you to figure it out while you're flipping through pages.

Listing 2-1   Sample Printer Output

```
Key Name:          HKEY_LOCAL_MACHINE\SYSTEM\Setup
Class Name:        <NO CLASS>
Last Write Time:   1/2/2002 - 1:16 AM
Value 0
  Name:            SetupType
  Type:            REG_DWORD
  Data:            0x0
```

```
Value 1
   Name:              SystemSetupInProgress
   Type:              REG_DWORD
   Data:              0x0
Value 2
   Name:              CmdLine
   Type:              REG_SZ
   Data:
Value 3
   Name:              SystemPrefix
   Type:              REG_BINARY
   Data:
00000000   cd 03 00 00 00 80 3c d2 - Í.....<Ò
Value 4
   Name:              SystemPartition
   Type:              REG_SZ
   Data:              \Device\HarddiskVolume1
Value 5
   Name:              OsLoaderPath
   Type:              REG_SZ
   Data:              \
```

Exporting Settings to Files

Exporting all or part of the registry is one of those things IT professionals and power users do often. By exporting, I mean copying portions of the registry to another file, typically a REG file but hive files are more useful. This is a great way to back up settings so you can easily restore them later, if necessary. It's also a good way to share settings with other users or computers. I often create REG files for settings I prefer so that I can change those settings simply by importing a REG file rather than clicking my way through the Windows XP user interface—one double-click replaces a hundred clicks.

In the IT world, exporting settings to REG files has practical purposes, too. First is deployment. REG files are the simplest and often the only way to deploy some settings with Windows XP. You can deploy REG files through your Windows XP answer file, for example, as you will learn in Chapter 12, "Deploying with Answer Files." It's also a convenient way to deploy settings from an intranet or helpdesk. Last, REG files are an easy way to add settings to your Office XP deployment. You can do this through the Office XP Resource Kit's Custom Installation Wizard. Chapter 14, "Deploying Office XP Settings," describes how to add REG files to Office XP's installation.

Regedit exports settings to four different types of files: registration, Win9x/NT4 registration, hive files, and text files. The differences between the four are significant, and you learn about them later in this chapter. Follow these steps to export branches of the registry to files:

1. Click the key at the top of the branch you want to export.

2. On the File menu, click Export to display the Export Registry File dialog box, shown in Figure 2-5.

3. In the File Name box, enter a name for the file you're creating.

4. Select the option for the export range you want:

    - To back up the entire registry, select the All option.

    - To back up the selected branch, select the Selected Branch option.

5. In the Save As Type list, click the type of file you want to create: Registration Files (*.reg), Registry Hive Files (*.*), Text Files (*.txt), or Win9x/NT4 Registration Files (*.reg).

6. Click Save.

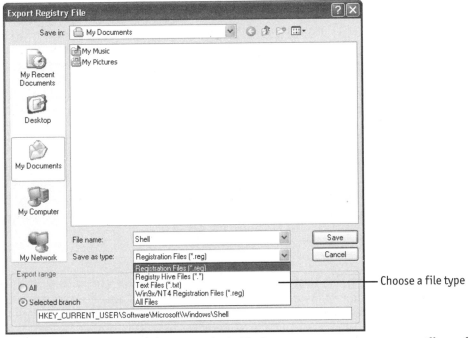

Figure 2-5 *Make sure you choose which file format you want to use, regardless of the file extension you type in the File Name box.*

Importing a file into the registry is similar to opening a file. Click File, Import; in the Files Of Type list, click the type of file that you're importing; then, in the File Name box, type the path and name of the file you're importing. The following sections describe each of the file types that you see in the Save As Type and Files Of Type lists. Each type is a different file format and thus suited to different purposes than the other types.

Registration Files

Registration files are version 5 REG files—plain text files that look similar to INI flies. Each section name represents a key, and each item in a section represents a value. The following listing is a sample of a version 5 REG file:

Listing 2-2   Sample Version 5 REG File

```
Windows Registry Editor Version 5.00

[HKEY_CURRENT_USER\Sample]
"String"="Jerry Honeycutt"
"Binary"=hex:01,02,03,04,05,06,07,08
"DWORD"=dword:00004377
"Expandable String"=hex(2):25,00,55,00,53,00,45,00,52,00,00,00
"MultiString"=hex(7):48,00,65,00,6c,00,6c,00,6f,00,00,00,00,00

[HKEY_CURRENT_USER\Sample\Subkey]
```

The most important thing to know about version 5 REG files is that they are Unicode, and some programs can't handle Unicode REG files properly. And because these files are Unicode, each character in REG_EXPAND_SZ and REG_MULTI_SZ values is two bytes wide. In the listing just shown, you'll notice this in the values called Expandable String and MultiString. For example, the letter A is 0x0041, not 0x41. For more information about Unicode-encoded text, see Chapter 1, "Learning the Basics." Windows 2000 and Windows XP are the only Microsoft operating systems that support version 5 REG files.

In the previous section, you learned how to import REG files using Regedit. You can also double-click a REG file to merge it into the registry. Regedit will prompt to merge the settings that the file contains into the registry and, after you click Yes, it will tell you when it's finished. If you're deploying a REG file to users, however, you don't want them to see the message or answer the prompt, so you'll use Regedit's /s command-line option to run it quietly. For example:

```
regedit settings.reg /s
```

Use this command line from batch files, scripts, answer files, or even from the Office XP Resource Kit's Custom Installation Wizard. For more information about creating and deploying REG files, see the following chapters:

- Chapter 9, "Scripting Registry Changes," describes the format of each value type in REG files and shows you how to build them manually.

- Chapter 12, "Deploying with Answer Files," describes how to deploy REG files as part of your Windows XP answer file—a great way to deploy user settings.

- Chapter 14, "Deploying Office XP Settings," describes how to deploy REG files as part of your Office XP customizations.

> **Caution**   Don't import a REG file that you create in one version of Windows into another version—at least not without thinking about it carefully. For example, exporting hard-ware settings from the Windows NT 4.0 registry and importing them into the Windows XP registry will likely wreak havoc with Windows XP. Some settings are fine to share across Windows versions, however, such as file associations in HKCR and some programs' settings. Use common sense.

Win9x/NT4 Registration Files

Win9x/NT4 registration files are version 4 REG files, which Windows 95, Windows 98, Windows Me, and Windows NT 4.0 support. The following sample is a version 4 ANSI REG file. The settings are the same as the version 5 Unicode REG file you saw in the previous section:

Listing 2-3   Sample Version 4 REG File

```
REGEDIT4

[HKEY_CURRENT_USER\Sample]
"String"="Jerry Honeycutt"
"Binary"=hex:01,02,03,04,05,06,07,08
"DWORD"=dword:00004377
"Expandable String"=hex(2):25,55,53,45,52,00
"MultiString"=hex(7):48,65,6c,6c,6f,00,00

[HKEY_CURRENT_USER\Sample\Subkey]
```

Instead of Unicode text, version 4 files are ANSI text files. That means that each character is a single byte wide. The letter A is 0x41. You notice the difference between this and the earlier Unicode REG file in the Expandable String and MultiString values. Characters in REG_EXPAND_SZ and REG_MULTI_SZ values are single bytes, which is more natural for most folks. This is the file format that's compatible with programs expecting ANSI REG files, and it has the added benefit of being compatible with earlier versions of Regedit.

Choosing Between REG and Hive Files

Registry Editor exports branches to four different file formats. Each format has strengths and weaknesses that make it appropriate for some tasks and useless for others. This section should help you choose the right format each time.

Exporting to hive files is my choice most of the time. The reason I like hive files so much is because they're much more accurate than either type of REG file. They are the same format as the Windows XP working hive files, so they represent settings exactly the same way. Also, when you import a hive file, Registry Editor deletes the branch it's replacing before importing the settings. In other words, the editor removes any settings that exist in the working registry but not in the hive file you're importing. When restoring keys from a backup after an unsuccessful registry edit, this is exactly the behavior you want. Hive files have one more strength that make them my choice most of the time: You can load them as new hives and view their contents without affecting other parts of the registry. Their only drawback is you can't view them in Notepad.

Although hive files are my choice most of the time, there are a few scenarios that require me to use REG files. First is when I'm working with programs that don't understand hive files. For example, the Office XP Resource Kit's Custom Installation Wizard can read REG files but not hive files. Second is when I'm exporting settings to different versions of Windows. Windows 98 doesn't provide a way to load hive files. Last, and important in my view, is when I'm trying to track down a setting in the registry by comparing snapshots. Comparing two hive files isn't feasible, but comparing two REG files is easy using Microsoft Word 2002.

Hive Files

Hive files are binary files that contain portions of the registry. As you recall from Chapter 1, "Learning the Basics," Windows XP stores different parts of the registry in different hive files. Regedit displays all these hives together in one logical unit. Hive files are useful tools, though. You can export branches to hive files that can then be imported to another computer or by another user. They're great backups.

Exported hive files have purposes similar to REG files. Hive files have most of the advantages of REG files, except that you can't view and edit them in a text editor. The advantage that hive files have over REG files is that you can load and edit them in Regedit without actually replacing your own settings. The section "Working with Hive Files," on the facing page, describes how to load hive files.

Text Files

You can export keys to text files, but you can't import them back into the registry. If you're curious what an exported text file looks like, take a look at the sample printer output in the

"Printing the Registry" section. They are one and the same. Regedit makes exported text files more readable than REG files, which can help you interpret settings better, but that's about the only use of text files.

Working with Hive Files

There are two scenarios in which working with hive files is an important part of an IT professional's job. The first is when creating a default user profile, which you learn how to do in Chapter 10, "Deploying User Profiles." The other is troubleshooting. You can take a hive file from a computer or user profile that's not working properly, repair it on another computer, and then replace it on the original computer.

Loading a hive file is different from *importing* a hive file. When you import a hive file, which you learned how to do in the previous section, you actually replace settings in the registry. In other words, you load the hive file over existing settings. When you load a hive file, you create a whole new branch in the registry that doesn't overlap or replace any other branch. This enables you to edit the settings in a hive file without changing your own settings. Here's how to load a hive file in to the registry:

1. In the key pane, click either HKU or HKLM.

2. On the File menu, click Load Hive.

3. In the File Name box, type the path and file name of the hive file you're loading, and then click Open.

4. In the Key Name box, shown in Figure 2-6, type the name you want to assign to the hive.

The name you give to the key is arbitrary. Use any name that helps you identify the hive file that you're loading. All you're doing in this step is creating a root key in which to load the hive file.

Figure 2-6 *Type a name that describes what the hive file contains.*

When you're finished editing settings in the hive file, you must unload it before doing anything else with it, such as copying it to a removable disk. That's because Windows XP locks the file until you unload it. Unloading a hive file is easy: Click the key into which you loaded the hive, which you specified in step 4, and then click Unload Hive on the File menu. If you get an error message when you try to copy the hive file or profile folder that contains a hive file, it's usually because you forgot to unload it from the registry.

Command-Line Alternative

Windows XP comes with a killer command-line alternative to Regedit. Anything you can do with Regedit you can do with Console Registry Tool for Windows. And this tool installs *with* Windows XP, unlike earlier versions of Windows, which required you to get the tool from the resource kits.

What's so great about a command-line registry editor? You can use it to script registry changes. For example, you can write a batch file that automatically backs up a portion of the registry. Imagine a batch file that extracts hardware information from a computer and dumps it on to a network share. That's a quick inventory system. Recently, I used Reg.exe to extract the GUID (see Chapter 1, "Learning the Basics") from every computer on a network so that I could configure them as managed computers in Active Directory. This was a huge timesaver.

Chapter 9, "Scripting Registry Changes," describes Console Registry Tool for Windows, otherwise known as Reg.exe, in great detail. If you want to learn more about it now, just type **Reg.exe** at the MS-DOS command prompt.

Getting Beyond Basics

This chapter described Regedit's essential features. These are the basics that you must know to perform routine tasks such as changing registry values. What you didn't learn in this chapter are some of the more advanced tasks that an IT professional or power user needs to truly master Windows XP. From this point forward, it's time to get past the basics and branch out in to other parts of this book. Learn more about Regedit in the following chapters:

- Chapter 3, "Backing Up the Registry," describes how to use Regedit as a trouble-shooting tool. You also learn how to protect the registry.

- Chapter 7, "Managing Registry Security," describes how to set subkeys' permissions using Regedit. You also learn how to secure remote registry editing to prevent users from gaining access to other users' registries.

- Chapter 10, "Deploying User Profiles," shows you how to use Regedit to edit the settings in a user profile so you can deploy those settings to hundreds or even thousands of desktops throughout the organization.

Backing Up the Registry

Mistakes happen—whether due to your own silly errors or users' meddling with the registry when they shouldn't. Nothing can happen that warrants large doses of anti-anxiety drugs, however. Ninety-nine times out of 100, the tools you learn about in this chapter can prevent or overcome any registry error. Because I know how to use these tools, there's only been one time when I busted a computer so badly that I gave up and reinstalled Microsoft Windows XP. The sad part is that after spending hours reinstalling the operating system and incumbent applications, I discovered an easy fix for the problem.

Most of these tools have a higher calling than just backing up and protecting the registry. They're features that push the reliability of Windows XP far beyond the levels of earlier versions of Windows. System Restore ensures that you can roll back the configuration of Windows XP to an earlier snapshot, which the operating system makes automatically. Other features that make Windows XP more stable include Device Driver Rollback, Error Reporting, and Windows Driver Protection. See *http://www.microsoft.com/windowsxp/pro/techinfo/planning /reliability* for the "Reliability Improvements in Windows XP Professional" white paper.

In this chapter, I show you many ways to restore a configuration, and you won't need all of them. Pick the one or two techniques that work for you and stick with them. In particular, decide which of the methods you're going to use to protect the registry while editing it. I prefer to save keys to hive files before making changes to the registry, but you might prefer to make backup copies of individual values. Also, you definitely want to know about System Restore and how to fix troublesome settings. The last part of this chapter describes the advanced troubleshooting tools, which you turn to only when things are so fouled up that you have no other choice.

Many of these tools require advance preparation. For example, to restore a backup copy of the registry, you must have made a backup. Likewise, to use Automated System Recovery, you must have created the disk. Thus, don't come to this chapter just when you have a problem. Read it first in preparation for problems that hopefully won't come.

Editing the Registry Safely

I must admit that I'm pretty bad about taking my own advice. It's easy to forget about backing up values before making what seem to be simple changes. But how do you know that some simple change isn't going to be the one that sinks the ship? You don't—so you should *do as I say and not as I do*: Back up values before changing or deleting them. There are easy and difficult ways to do this; I'm going to show you the easy ways.

You'll learn three techniques in this section. The first is making backup copies of values, which you can quickly restore in the registry. Backups also document the changes you make. The second is exporting the part of the registry in which you're working to a REG file. I don't like this method for reasons that I'll explain later, but it has the advantage of being readable. The third method (and my first choice when making significant changes) is to export branches to hive files. I prefer this method because it's the most accurate way to back up and restore parts of the registry. With any of these three methods, you'll cover most of the pitfalls in editing the registry.

If these techniques fail, or if you're planning on major registry surgery, move on to the techniques described later in this chapter. System Restore can get you out of trouble most of the time; it fails only when Windows XP is so far gone that it no longer starts properly. In that case, you're left with Automated System Recovery and Recovery Console, which are the last tools you learn about in this chapter. But first try starting Windows XP in Safe Mode and then running System Restore.

Tip   Do you find yourself making the same changes over and over again? I tend to customize the same settings every time I install Windows XP or every time I log on to a computer and get a new user profile. You don't have to worry about backing up the values you're changing if you write a script to change them automatically. Test the script carefully so you can apply it with assurance that it works properly. Chapter 9, "Scripting Registry Changes," shows you how to write these scripts. Test them *again* every time you change them.

Copying Single Values

The easiest way to leave a way out if things go wrong is to make backup copies of values before changing them.

Here's how to do it: Rename the original value to something like *Initials_ Name*, where *Initials* is your initials, and *Name* is the value's original name. Add a date if you think you're going to change the value often. Then add a new value using the original name and type, but with new data. Alternatively, create a new value of the same type as the value you're changing, but with a new name. Copy the original value's data to the clipboard, and then paste it in to the new value. You're all set to change the value, and if you don't like the result, you can restore the original value with little effort. Figure 3-1 shows backup settings in the key HKCU\Control Panel\Desktop.

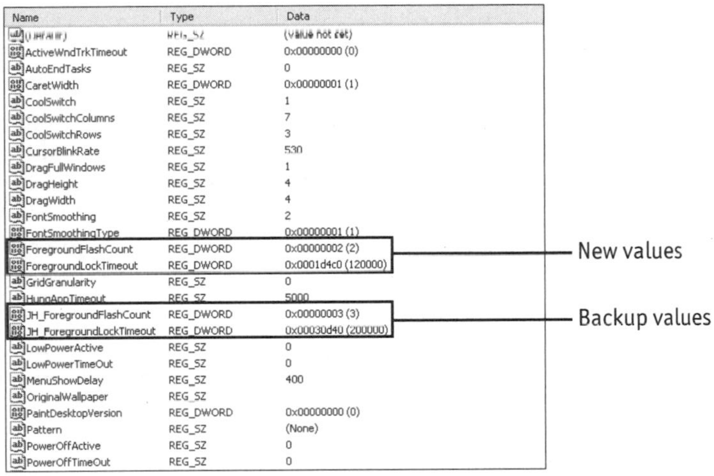

Name	Type	Data
(Default)	REG_SZ	(value not set)
ActiveWndTrkTimeout	REG_DWORD	0x00000000 (0)
AutoEndTasks	REG_SZ	0
CaretWidth	REG_DWORD	0x00000001 (1)
CoolSwitch	REG_SZ	1
CoolSwitchColumns	REG_SZ	7
CoolSwitchRows	REG_SZ	3
CursorBlinkRate	REG_SZ	530
DragFullWindows	REG_SZ	1
DragHeight	REG_SZ	4
DragWidth	REG_SZ	4
FontSmoothing	REG_SZ	2
FontSmoothingType	REG_DWORD	0x00000001 (1)
ForegroundFlashCount	REG_DWORD	0x00000002 (2)
ForegroundLockTimeout	REG_DWORD	0x0001d4c0 (120000)
GridGranularity	REG_SZ	0
HungAppTimeout	REG_SZ	5000
JH_ForegroundFlashCount	REG_DWORD	0x00000003 (3)
JH_ForegroundLockTimeout	REG_DWORD	0x00030d40 (200000)
LowPowerActive	REG_SZ	0
LowPowerTimeOut	REG_SZ	0
MenuShowDelay	REG_SZ	400
OriginalWallpaper	REG_SZ	
PaintDesktopVersion	REG_DWORD	0x00000000 (0)
Pattern	REG_SZ	(None)
PowerOffActive	REG_SZ	0
PowerOffTimeOut	REG_SZ	0

New values — ForegroundFlashCount, ForegroundLockTimeout

Backup values — JH_ForegroundFlashCount, JH_ForegroundLockTimeout

Figure 3-1   *Backing up values in the registry is like having a built-in revision tracking feature.*

Likewise, instead of deleting a value, which you can recover only by memory because Registry Editor (Regedit) does not have an Undo feature, rename the value to hide it from any program that's looking for it. The effect is the same, and you can always restore the value by restoring its name. Although you can't easily back up entire branches before changing settings in them, you can hide entire branches to make it seem like they no longer exist. This is a safe way to remove a program's settings from the registry in the hopes that the program re-creates them, for example. This *is* your Undo feature.

Printing portions of the registry isn't an alternative to creating a backup for them. You would have to manually restore each and every value from the information on the printout, and the format isn't easily readable. If you want just a quick snapshot of a value before you change it, take a screenshot instead: Press Alt+PrtSc, and then paste the screenshot into Paint. Print or save your screenshot for future reference.

Backing Up to REG Files

If you'd rather have a more tangible backup, one with which you can restore an entire branch, export that branch to a REG file. In Regedit, click the top-level key in the branch you're editing. Then on the File menu, click Export, type the name of the REG file to which you want to export the branch's settings, and then click Save. Your settings are tucked away safely, and you can edit that branch knowing that restoring the original values will be easy. Don't export the entire registry; back up only on the branch in which you're working. Exporting the entire registry takes so long that you likely won't make it a regular habit.

Restoring your backup REG file is easy, too. On Regedit's File menu, click Import. Type the name of the REG file that contains your settings, and then click Open. You can also double-click the file to import it. I mentioned earlier that I don't like using REG files to back up settings, and here's why: When you import a REG file, Regedit merges its settings into the registry rather than replacing them. That means Regedit replaces or creates any value that the REG file contains, but values that the REG file doesn't contain aren't removed from the registry. This creates a problem if you add values to the registry while editing it because importing the REG file doesn't get rid of them. See Table 3-1 for a summary of the merge process.

Table 3-1   Merging REG Files

Value Exists in REG File?	Value Exists in Registry?	Action
No	No	None
No	Yes	None—Regedit doesn't remove or change the value in the registry
Yes	No	Regedit adds the value
Yes	Yes	Regedit changes the value

Note   Most of the techniques you'll learn about in this chapter work remotely, too. You can back up and restore keys for other users. If you have a computer that fails while logging on to Windows XP, you can access the computer over the network and restore that computer's settings using Regedit. On the File menu, click Connect Network Registry, and type the name of the computer containing the registry you want to open. Not only can you edit the remote computer's registry, but you can also export hive files from and import hive files into it.

Backing Up to Hive Files

Hive files are a better than REG files for backing up the registry. When you import a hive file containing a key, Regedit completely replaces the current key and all of its subkeys with the contents of the hive file. That means that Regedit removes any value you added since backing up the registry to a hive file. This is a far more accurate way to back up branches before editing them.

Exporting branches to hive files is similar to exporting them to REG files; you just pick a different file type. On Regedit's File menu, click Export. In the Save As Type list, click Registry Hive Files, type the name of the new hive file, and then click Save. Reverse the process to restore your settings: Click File, Import; then click Registry Hive Files in the Save As Type list, type the name of the hive file to which you backed up your settings, and then click Open. You can use any file extension you like, but I prefer to give hive files the *.dat* extension. The *.hiv* extension is also common for hive files.

Don't confuse what you just learned about exporting and importing hive files with loading and unloading them. When you import a hive file, you're making changes to working parts of the registry. When you load a hive file, you're creating a whole new branch that Windows XP doesn't use. It doesn't read or change those settings, but they're visible in Regedit, so you can examine them. Unloading the hive file just unlinks the file from the registry. You can unload only hive files you manually loaded and not hive files Windows XP loaded.

Whereas importing a hive file is a great way to restore an entire branch, loading a hive file is a good method to restore settings surgically or just to check an original value. First load the file in to the registry: Click either HKLM or HKU in Regedit; on the File menu, click Load, type the name of the hive file that contains your settings, and then click Open. Regedit prompts you for a key name, and you can type any arbitrary name that'll help you identify the hive. You'll then see that hive file under the root key into which you loaded it. Figure 3-2 on the next page is an example of loading a hive file that contains a backup copy of the key HKU \Control Panel\Desktop. Examine the setting in the hive file you loaded, or even copy the backup setting and then paste it over the current value. Don't forget to unload the hive, or else you won't be able to remove the file later.

Now that I hopefully have you sold on using hive files to back up settings before changing them, I'm going to introduce you to the ultimate way to back up registry settings: Console Registry Tool for Windows (Reg.exe). This command-line tool comes with Windows XP and provides most of Regedit's features plus some. You learn its full use in Chapter 9, "Scripting Registry Changes." You can use it to save keys to hive files. You can also use it to restore, load, and unload hive files. With Reg.exe, saving a hive file is the same as exporting, and restoring a hive file is the same as importing. The best part is one of the tool's unique features: the ability to copy one key to another key, creating a quick backup copy of a key right there in the registry. So for example, I can copy HKCU\Control Panel \Desktop\ to HKCU\Control Panel\JH_Backup\ with a single command. Table 3-2 on the next page describes the Reg.exe command lines for each of these features. See Chapter 9 for a full explanation of all the different options.

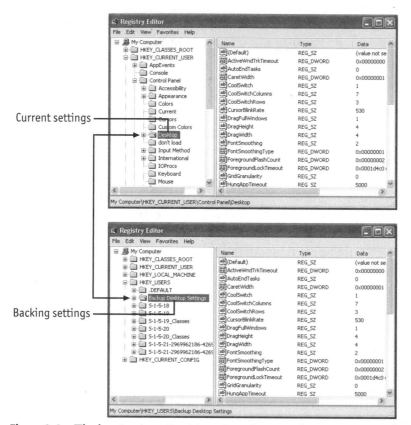

Current settings —

Backing settings —

Figure 3-2 *The key* Backup Desktop Settings *is a hive containing a backup copy of* HKCU\Control Panel\Desktop\ *that I've loaded into the registry.*

Table 3-2   Backing Up the Registry with Reg.exe

Command Line	Description
REG SAVE *keyname filename*	Save the branch starting with the key *keyname* to the hive file called *filename*. *Keyname* begins with one of the root key abbreviations, HKCR, HKLM, HKCU, HKU, or HKCC.
REG RESTORE *keyname filename*	Restore the hive file *filename* to the key *keyname*, replacing all of its contents. *Keyname* begins with one of the root key abbreviations, HKCR, HKLM, HKCU, HKU, or HKCC.
REG LOAD *keyname filename*	Load the hive file *filename* to a new temporary branch beginning with the key *keyname*. *Keyname* begins with one of the root key abbreviations, HKCR, HKLM, HKCU, HKU, or HKCC.
REG UNLOAD *keyname*	Unload the hive file in the temporary branch beginning with the key *keyname*. *Keyname* begins with one of the root key abbreviations, HKCR, HKLM, HKCU, HKU, or HKCC.
REG COPY *keyname1 keyname2* [/s]	Copy the values in the key *keyname1* to the key *keyname2*, creating it if it doesn't already exist. *Keyname1* and *keyname2* begin with one of the root key abbreviations, HKCR, HKLM, HKCU, HKU, or HKCC. The option /s copies the entire branch, not just the values in *keyname1*.

Fixing Corrupt Settings

Even if you've followed my advice to this point, you're going to run into problems. Sometimes a simple change to the registry has ripple effects that restoring a backup copy of a value won't fix. Windows XP and most applications are incredibly resilient, though, so fixing a problem is a simple matter of telling it to *heal thyself.*

The quickest route is to remove the offending value and allow the program to re-create it using a default. Windows XP and most programs re-create missing settings, which is what makes this work in most cases. This is tantamount to uninstalling and reinstalling an application. The difficult part is figuring out which value contains the troublesome setting. Chapter 8, "Finding Registry Values," helps you track down settings. For example, if your mouse pointer bounces around the screen in convulsive fits, remove the key HKCU\Control Panel\Mouse. When you log off and back on to Windows XP, the mouse settings are re-created. The operating system won't re-create everything you delete, though, particularly file associations in HKCR. So back up any setting you delete before you try this troubleshooting technique.

Managing Settings to Avoid Problems

IT professionals dodge most problems with settings by managing them properly. The first and most important practice is not to dump users into the local Administrators group. I understand the reasons you might do this, such as legacy applications that won't otherwise run properly, or users who can't change settings because their accounts are in the local Power Users or local Users groups. You can successfully deal with all these issues using tools such as Security Templates, which you learn about in Chapter 7, "Managing Registry Security." It's not difficult, and moving users from the local Administrators group to the Power Users or Users group can save professionals a lot of frustration, and save their companies serious loot.

Policies are another good way to manage settings. Policies accomplish two goals: first they configure settings for the user, if for example, he or she doesn't know the appropriate values. Policies also configure settings according to IT policy, and users can't change them. Moving users out of the local Administrators group saves your company money by reducing lost downtime and deviations from corporate standards, but policies actually help you recover money from your IT investment. Chapter 6, "Using Registry-Based Policy," describes exactly how policies benefit IT and how to use them.

In the Windows XP registry, you can also set keys' permissions to prevent users from changing those settings. This might sound like a great idea, but micro-managing settings is so cumbersome that it is almost impossible to maintain. If you need to manage a key's Access Control List (ACL), use Security Templates instead. Security Templates are much easier to deploy and maintain across the board, and you learn how to use them in Chapter 7.

For those settings that Windows XP or other programs don't re-create, you have other options. If you used Files And Settings Wizard to transfer your settings from an earlier version of Windows to Windows XP, you can reapply your old settings to your current configuration. IT professionals use the User State Migration Tool for the same purpose. Of course, there must be copies of the original user state data for this to be possible. Chapter 10, "Deploying User Profiles," describes this tool. Other options for repairing settings are described later in this chapter.

Allowing Windows XP to Fix Errors

Perhaps you can't find a setting in the registry, or removing that setting from the registry doesn't fix the problem. In that case, head for Control Panel. You can fix many per-user settings and a few per-computer settings in it. That includes the configuration of all your input and output devices, particularly the pointing device, keyboard, display, and printer. It also includes accessibility and regional options.

When a device just doesn't work, your best bet is often to remove and redetect the device. In my experience, this fixes a vast number of problems. You remove a device using Device Manager, restart the computer, and then have Windows XP redetect it. If the operating system doesn't redetect the device, use Add Hardware Wizard to detect it. You start Add Hardware Wizard on the Hardware tab of the System Properties dialog box. Removing a device directly from the registry isn't a good idea because Windows XP scatters devices' settings, and the linkages are difficult to remove accurately. Follow these instructions to reinstall a device:

1. Open Device Manager.

   To open Device Manager, click Start, and then click Control Panel. Click Performance And Maintenance, and then click System. On the Hardware tab, click Device Manager.

2. Click the device you want to remove, and then click Uninstall on the Action menu.

Tip   Sysprep is used to prepare a disk containing Windows XP for duplication and deployment; it can also used to set things straight when your configuration is seriously out of whack. When you restart a computer after running Sysprep, Mini-Setup Wizard configures the computer for use. It detects the computer's hardware, configures the network connections, and optionally joins the computer to a business network. Chapter 13, "Cloning Disks with Sysprep," describes Sysprep in more detail. To use Sysprep to repair a broken configuration and redetect your computer's hardware, run `sysprep -activated -pnp -quiet -reseal`. If you want to fully automate Mini-Setup Wizard, create the file Sysprep.inf you learn about in Chapter 13. This is a radical step—you'll lose the local Administrator user profile and a good number of per-computer settings—but it might give your configuration the refresh that it needs.

Repairing an Application's Settings

Predictability is a good thing when it comes to program settings. And most programs store their settings in the registry using the same organization. Per-user settings are in `HKCU\Software\`*`Company`*`\`*`Program`*`\`*`Version`*`\`, and per-computer settings are in the same branch of `HKLM`. *Company* is the name of application's publisher, *Program* is the name of the application, and *Version* is an optional version number. Some omit the version number, which isn't strictly by the rules but common nonetheless. Figure 3-3 shows where the TechSmith product SnagIt version 5 stores its settings. (This happens to be the killer program I use to capture screenshots.)

TechSmith SnagIt 5 settings

Figure 3-3 *TechSmith SnagIt is the best screen capture tool, and it works well with Windows XP.*

Well-designed applications re-create settings that they're missing. To reset the program's per-user settings, remove `HKCU\Software\`*`Company`*`\`*`Program`*`\`. You typically don't want to remove the program's per-computer settings because doing so is likely to adversely affect most applications. You can hide the program's per-computer settings to test the scenario first, just to be on the safe side.

Windows Installer–based applications are easier to reset because Windows Installer has repair functionality built right into it. Microsoft Office XP is an example of a Windows Installer–based application. To learn more about Windows Installer-based applications, see Chapter 11, "Mapping Windows Installer." For now, I will describe the three different ways you can have Windows Installer restore an application's original settings:

- On the application's Help menu, click Detect And Repair.

- Click Start, Control Panel, and then click Add Or Remove Programs. Click the application you want to repair, and then click Change. Follow the instructions you see on the screen to repair the application.

- In the Run dialog box, type **msiexec /f[u][m]** *package*, where *package* is the path and file name of the application's package file, which has the *.msi* file extension. Use /fu to repair per-user settings and /fm to repair per-computer settings. IT professionals like this command because it's the best way to repair settings without visiting the user's desk.

The last repair method for Windows Installer–based applications, particularly for Office XP, is Profile Wizard. Chapter 14, "Deploying Office XP Settings," describes how to use this tool to deploy settings with Office XP. Basically, you install and configure Office XP on a sample computer, capture Office XP settings to an OPS file using Profile Wizard, and then deploy the OPS file with your Office XP customizations. IT professionals should save that OPS file for use later. Think of it as a help desk tool. After users' 15 minutes of phone time is up (we both know there's a limit to how long you want calls to last), and before you throw new disk images at their computers, reapply the OPS file to restore their settings. The command that you're running on their computers is proflwiz /r *filename* /q, where *filename* is the name of the OPS file that contains Office XP per-user settings.

Removing Programs from the Registry

As I said earlier, predictability makes troubleshooting settings in the Windows XP registry possible. It also makes removing programs' settings possible but not a breeze. Some programs don't uninstall correctly, and you're left with no choice but to manually remove their settings from the registry. For example, if an uninstall program doesn't finish properly, it might fail to remove the entry from the list of programs in Add Or Remove Programs or orphan a file association, causing you to see an error message about Windows XP not finding a program when you double-click a file.

You can invest in a third-party tool to look for and remove the program's settings, or you can do it manually. Even though it's somewhat difficult, you can remove most programs' settings successfully. Doing so is more art than science, but here are the general steps involved in the process:

1. List the EXE and DLL files in the application's folder.

   You install most programs in %SYSTEMDRIVE%\Program Files*Program*, where *Program* is the name of the program. List the EXE and DLL files in that folder and all of its subfolders.

2. Remove keys and values that contain the application's installation folder.

   Search the registry for each of the application's folders and subfolders. For example, if an application installed in *C:\Program Files\Example* has two subfolders, *\Binary* and *\Templates*, search the registry for *C:\Program Files\Example*, *C:\Program Files \Example\Binary*, and *C:\Program Files\Example\Templates*. Choose the keys and values you remove carefully to avoid interfering with other programs that might require those settings.

3. Remove keys and values that contain the program's name.

   Search the registry for different versions of the program's name. For example, if the application is *Jerry's House of Horrors*, search for *Jerry's*, *Jerry's House*, and *House of Horrors*. Use any combinations you think you'll find in the registry. Choose the keys and values you remove carefully so that you don't break other applications that might also use those settings.

4. Remove keys and values that contain the EXE and DLL files you recorded.

   You recorded a list of EXE and DLL files in step 1. Search the registry for each of these program files. Search for the complete file name, including the extension, and remove the key or value only if the path matches the program's installation folder. Use caution here as with the other steps.

Removing Windows Installer-based applications manually is much more difficult because they knit themselves into the registry much tighter than programs packaged using other technologies. Chapter 11, "Mapping Windows Installer," is your best shot at figuring out these settings, but you still shouldn't remove them manually. Instead, Chapter 11 describes a tool called Msizap.exe that removes almost all traces of a program's Windows Installer data from the registry. This tool comes with the Windows XP Support Tools, and the command line is msizap T! *package*, where *package* is the path and file name of the package file from which you installed the application. Msicuu.exe is similar; you also learn about it in Chapter 11. After using either tool, remove any remaining settings using the instructions you read earlier in this section.

Msizap.exe Saves the Day

Msizap.exe has saved my hind end on more than one occasion. In one case, I was upgrading a customer's deployment servers with the latest version of Symantec Ghost Corporate Edition. The plan was to upgrade to the latest version in place.

Nothing ever goes as planned, eh? Ghost's Windows Installer data was corrupt on one particular server, and I was certain the customer wasn't going to believe me when I said, "I didn't do it." Because of the corrupt data, I couldn't upgrade to the newer version of Ghost. And my heart sank when I found out that I couldn't remove the earlier version, either.

I was close to swapping the server, but I remembered Msizap.exe and thought to give it a try. Sure enough, Msizap.exe yanked enough of Ghost's Windows Installer data out of the registry that I was able to install the new version. I credit this handy utility with saving me a lot of work and a lot of explaining. You learn more about Msizap.exe in Chapter 11, "Mapping Windows Installer." Keep it nearby.

Using Another Computer's Settings

If all else fails and you're desperate to set things straight, you can borrow settings from another computer. The only time I recommend doing this is when the settings are simple and contained within a small key. For example, restoring a file association or a small program's settings from another computer is straightforward enough, but borrowing a device's settings from another computer just isn't a good idea. There's no reason to believe that Windows XP will store the exact same settings for the exact same device on two different computers.

You can use either REG files or hive files for this technique. I prefer hive files because importing them completely replaces the key that they contain. First connect to the remote computer's registry and export the settings to a hive file. Regedit stores the hive file in a folder on your local computer so you don't have to copy it from the remote computer. Import the hive file to replace your old settings with the settings in the hive file. This is useful for IT professionals in a supporting role, too. You can borrow the key from one remote computer and then connect to another remote computer to restore the settings to the second computer's registry. For example, you can copy a file association from one remote computer to another remote computer—all without stepping down out of the ivory tower.

Using System Restore

System Restore returns your computer to a previous snapshot without losing recent personal information, such as documents, history lists, favorites, or e-mail. It monitors the computer and many applications for changes and creates restore points. I call these restore points *snapshots*, but they're really instructions for undoing recent changes.

You restore these snapshots when your configuration isn't working. By default, Windows XP creates restore points daily and when significant events such as installing an application or device driver occur. System Restore is ideal for serious work in the registry because you can create your own restore points any time you like. You can also change the snapshot schedule or even script System Restore. Yes, I'm going to show you how.

System Restore creates different types of restore points:

- **Initial system checkpoints.**   System Restore creates initial system checkpoints when Windows XP starts the first time. Restoring to this point returns Windows XP and programs to their state immediately after installing Windows XP.

- **System checkpoints.**   System Restore creates restore points regularly, whether or not the system changes. By default, it creates system checkpoints every 24 hours. If you turn the computer off for more than 24 hours, System Restore will create a system checkpoint the next time you start Windows XP.

- **Installation checkpoints.**   System Restore creates installation checkpoints when you install programs that use recent installer technologies, so you can restore the computer to its state before installing the programs. To reverse the changes made by other programs, restore the most recent checkpoint.

- **Automatic update checkpoints.**   System Restore creates a restore point before updating Windows XP using Automatic Update or Windows Update.

- **Manual checkpoints.**   System Restore or a script can be used to create your own restore points; I'll show you how later in this chapter. Create manual checkpoints before making significant changes to the registry.

- **Restore operation checkpoints.**   System Restore creates restore operation checkpoints each time you restore a checkpoint. You use restore operation checkpoints to undo a restoration if you don't like the results.

- **Unsigned device driver checkpoints.**   System Restore creates a restore point when you install an unsigned device driver. If installing the device driver interferes with your computer's stability, you can restore the computer to its state before installing the device driver.

- **Backup utility recovery checkpoints.**   System Restore creates a restore point before you use Backup to perform a recovery. You can restore the computer if the recovery leaves your computer in a questionable state.

Note   You must still uninstall programs using Add Or Remove Programs, even if you restore to a point prior to program installation. Removing the program and then restoring the checkpoint is the best sequence.

System Restore requires at least 200 MB of available disk space. If 200 MB of space isn't available, Windows XP disables System Restore. By default, Windows XP allocates 12 percent of the hard disk's size (or 400 MB on hard disks that are smaller than 4 GB), and this happens to be the most that Windows XP can give it. You can otherwise configure the amount of disk space System Restore consumes, though. On the System Restore tab of the System Properties dialog box, drag the slider left or right to adjust the amount of disk space it uses. To open System Properties, click Start, Control Panel, Performance And Maintenance, and then click System. However, don't reduce the amount much because doing so limits the number of restore points that System Restore can maintain at one time.

Taking Configuration Snapshots

Here's how to create a restore point using System Restore:

1. Start System Restore one of the following ways:

   - Click System Restore in Help and Support Center.

   - Click Start, All Programs, Accessories, System Tools, System Restore.

   - Run %SYSTEMROOT%\System32\Restore\rstrui.exe.

2. Select the Create A Restore Point option, and then click Next.

3. In the Restore Point Description box, type a descriptive name for the restore point, and then click Create. (System Restore adds the date and time to the name of the restore point.)

To restore a checkpoint, follow these steps:

1. Start System Restore using one of the three methods in the previous procedure.

2. Select the Restore My Computer To an Earlier Time option, and then click Next.

3. Select the restore point that you want to restore, and then click Next.

   System Restore maintains up to 90 days of restore points, given enough disk space, so you can move backward and forward in the calendar to see the restore points created on each day. In the calendar, shown in Figure 3-4, bold dates are those that contain restore points.

4. Click a date, and then click the restore point in the list.

5. Click Next again, and Windows XP restarts so it can restore your configuration to the restore point you selected.

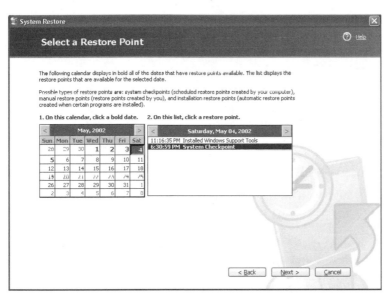

Figure 3-4   *Before continuing, make sure you save your documents and close any programs that are running. System Restore restarts your computer.*

Sometimes, if your configuration is unstable enough, you won't be able to start Windows XP normally. That leaves you with Safe Mode, which you'll learn about in "Advanced Options Menu," later in this chapter. In Safe Mode, you can't create restore points, but you can restore ones that have already been created. Thus, if Windows XP doesn't start normally, start it in Safe Mode, restore to an earlier configuration, and then restart the computer.

Peeking Under the Covers

Many of the files and folders System Restore uses are super hidden, so you won't see them unless you display system and hidden files. In Windows Explorer, click Tools, Options. On the Folder Options dialog box's View tab, select the Show Hidden Files And Folders option, and then clear the Hide Protected Operating System Files check box. System Restore's program files are in %SYSTEMROOT%\System32\Restore. Aside from the program file rstrui.exe, you'll find the super-hidden file filelist.xml, which lists the files and settings that System Restore monitors. Double-click this file to view the XML in Internet Explorer. It excludes a few legacy configuration files, for example Win.ini, System.ini, Autoexec.bat, and Config.sys. It excludes a handful of folders, too, most of which aren't important to the operating system's stability. What's interesting is the list of file extensions that it includes.

System Restore protects everything from EXE and DLL files to VBS and VXD files. If a file matches one of the included file extensions and it's not in a folder that filelist.xml excludes, System Restore monitors it. It also monitors the per-user hive files listed in the key `HKLM\SOFTWARE\Microsoft\Windows NT\CurrentVersion\ProfileList`.

The actual restore points are in each volume's System Volume Information folder. This folder is also super hidden, so you'll need to select the Show Hidden Files And Folders option and then clear the Hide Protected Operating System Files check box to see it. You'll have to add your name to the folder's ACL to open it. I don't recommend you do that on a production computer, however, because you risk blowing the file system. If you have a lab computer, go for it; otherwise, I'll describe this folder for you.

System Volume Information contains a subfolder called _restore*GUID*, where *GUID* is the computer's GUID (see Chapter 1, "Learning the Basics"). For example, my computer has _restore{4545302B-EA51-4100-A7E2-C7A37551AA83}. Beneath that folder is one folder for each restore point called RP*N*, where *N* is an incremental number beginning with 1. RP*N* contains backup copies of changed and deleted files. In fact, I opened my latest restore point folder, deleted a program file, and watched as System Restore added it to the restore point. It also backs up files that change so it can restore those. System Restore changes the file names, so you won't find missing files or documents in there. This folder also contains a list of the changes that System Restore must apply to the computer to restore the checkpoint. That includes instructions for restoring backup files.

The subfolder called \snapshot is in RP*N*. It contains backup copies of the registry's hive files. If you have access to System Volume Information, you can load these hive files in Regedit, examine them, or even recover settings from them. If you really need settings from these hive files, you're better off restoring them using System Restore. You can see System Volume Information in Figure 3-5; hopefully that will satisfy your curiosity enough to keep you out of it. The following is a list of the registry hive files you find in \snapshot:

- _REGISTRY_MACHINE_SAM
- _REGISTRY_MACHINE_SECURITY
- _REGISTRY_MACHINE_SOFTWARE
- _REGISTRY_MACHINE_SYSTEM
- _REGISTRY_USER_.DEFAULT
- _REGISTRY_USER_NTUSER_*SID*
- _REGISTRY_USER_USRCLASS_*SID*

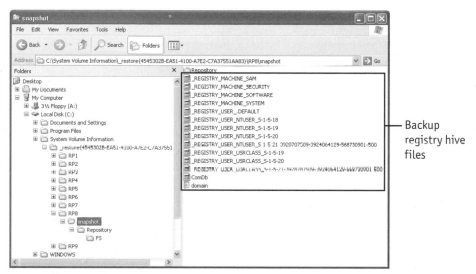

Figure 3-5   *System Restore backs up all the hive files so it can restore them if necessary.*

Managing System Restore

System Restore has sparse management options. You can change how much disk space it uses, which I've already covered, and you can even disable it altogether. There's only one good time to disable System Restore, and that's when you install Windows XP on sluggish computers. System Restore consumes a small slice of your computer's resources as it monitors the file system for changes, and disabling it can recover those resources. To disable System Restore, click Start, Control Panel, Performance And Maintenance, and then click System to open the System Properties dialog box. On the System Restore tab, select the Turn Off System Restore check box. But unless the computer is painfully slow, leave System Restore alone.

Two policies are available to IT professionals for managing System Restore. The first is Turn off System Restore, which disables System Restore altogether. I know some administrators who haven't embraced System Restore yet, and they're disabling it in their organizations. Their concern is the amount of disk space it uses and the small performance penalty for using it; both are negligible in my opinion. If you don't want users to be able to configure System Restore, enable the Turn off Configuration policy, which locks the user interface so users can't change System Restore's configuration. Users can still create their own restore points, however. Both of these policies are per-computer administrative settings (Computer Configuration\Administrative Templates) in \System\System Restore.

System Restore has a few other settings for which it doesn't provide a user interface or policy. These are mostly settings in the registry that control System Restore's schedule. You can build your own administrative template for these, however, which you learn about in Chapter 6, "Using Registry-Based Policy." Chapter 6 also shows you how to enable policies.

Hacking System Restore

`HKLM\Software\Microsoft\WindowsNT\CurrentVersion\SystemRestore` is the key where you find all of System Restore's settings. Unless otherwise noted, all the settings in the following list are `REG_DWORD` values:

- **CompressionBurst.** This value specifies the idle time compression in seconds. That is the amount of time to compress data after the computer becomes idle. System Restore can compress data for the amount of time specified, and then it must stop until after the next time the computer becomes idle.

- **DiskPercent and DSMax.** These values together specify how much disk space System Restore uses. System restore uses the greater of the two values. Thus, for hard disks smaller than 4 GB, System Restore uses 400 MB, which is the default value of `DSMax`. For hard disks larger than 4 GB, System Restore uses 12 percent, which is the default value of `DiskPercent`.

- **DSMin.** This value specifies the minimum amount of free disk space that System Restore requires during the installation process. This value also specifies the minimum amount of disk space that System Restore needs to reactivate and resume the creation of restore points after Windows XP disabled it due to low disk space.

- **RestoreStatus.** This value indicates whether the last restore operation failed (`0x00`), succeeded (`0x01`), or was interrupted (`0x02`).

- **RPGlobalInterval.** This value specifies the amount of time in seconds that System Restore waits between creating system checkpoints. The default value is 24 hours, or `0x15180`.

- **RPLifeInterval.** This value specifies the time in seconds that System Restore keeps restore points before removing them from the computer. The default value is `0x76A700`, or 90 days.

- **RPSessionInterval.** This value specifies the amount of time in seconds that System Restore waits before it creates the system checkpoints while the computer is turned on. The default value is zero, disabling this feature. You can change this value to `0xE10` to create a restore point every hour that the computer is in use. On a computer that you customize often, such as a lab computer, you might create a restore point every hour.

- **ThawInterval.** This value specifies the amount of time in seconds that System Restore waits before it reactivates itself after adequate disk space becomes available. Start the System Restore user interface, and it reactivates immediately.

The remaining settings you find in SystemRestore aren't useful to customize and Microsoft warns in no uncertain terms that you shouldn't change them. However, you can disable System Restore by setting DisableSR to 0x01, and doing so doesn't remove existing restore points like it does when you disable System Restore in the user interface. Editing the remaining settings can do bad things to your computer's performance, so limit yourself to the settings I described in this section.

Scripting System Restore

You can script System Restore using Windows Scripting Host (WSH) and Windows Management Instrumentation (WMI). Chapter 9, "Scripting Registry Changes," describes in detail how to script registry edits. But perhaps you want write scripts specifically to automate System Restore. These scripts are a handy way to get more control over the creation of restore points than the registry settings in the previous section give you.

Scripting System Restore relies on WMI and Srclient.dll, which is the System Restore client DLL. The account in which you run these scripts must have administrative privileges, which prevents them from being used by members of the Users or Power Users group. In Scheduled Tasks, you can schedule these scripts to run with elevated privileges, though. The following listing shows a script that automatically creates a restore point. It creates a System Restore object using WMI, and then creates a restore point by calling the method CreateRestorePoint(). The first parameter is the name of the restore point; you should use a descriptive name that begins with a verb, such as *Installed* or *Changed*.

```
Set SRP = GetObject( "winmgmts:\\.\root\default:Systemrestore" )
CSRP = SRP.CreateRestorePoint( "Hacked the registry", 0, 100 )
```

In addition to creating restore points, you can restore checkpoints using scripts. You can also configure System Restore; enable and disable it; or iterate through the list of restore points on the computer. For more information about System Restore's WMI classes, see *http://msdn.microsoft.com/library/en-us/sr/srstart_2dd1.asp*, which is the MSDN documentation for System Restore.

Backing Up the Registry Regularly

Backup Utility has come a long way since the original version that shipped with the earliest versions of Windows. Microsoft licenses Backup Utility from VERITAS Software Corporation (*http://www.veritas.com*), and it's a light edition of the company's Backup Exec. Users of the Microsoft Windows 2000 backup program are already familiar with this version. The user interfaces of the two versions are almost identical, and the steps to back up a computer are almost the same. Like the earlier version of this utility, you can back up to a file, tape, or other removable media. Enterprise users will likely have tape changers to automate a full backup schedule, including tape swapping.

Windows XP makes a few significant enhancements. The first is shadow copy. A volume shadow copy is an exact point-in-time copy of the contents of a hard disk, including open files. Users can continue to access files on the hard disk while Backup Utility backs them up during a volume shadow copy. In this way, it correctly copies files that change during the backup process. Shadow copy ensures that programs can continue to write to files on the volume, open files aren't omitted from the backup, and backing up the system doesn't lock users out.

Backing Up Using Symantec Ghost

I'm a big fan of Symantec Ghost Corporate Edition, which you can learn more about at *www.symantec.com*. It's the tool I prefer for deploying Windows XP in big environments. It's also useful as a backup utility, and you can use the Personal Edition of Ghost to back up a single computer.

The backup strategy for my home-office network uses both Ghost and Backup Utility. Backup Utility is better at protecting documents than it is at protecting entire configurations. To restore a computer from a backup tape, you first have to install Windows XP on the computer and honestly, it takes as much time to reinstall everything from scratch as it does to restore a good backup. That's why I prefer to protect my configurations using Ghost. After installing Windows XP and all of my applications on a computer, I create an image of the computer's disk on the server. I update that image any time I make a significant change to the computer, such as after installing new applications. If the computer fails, I can start the computer using a Ghost boot disk, restore the disk image, and I'm back up and running. The process takes less than 15 minutes whereas restoring the computer using Backup Utility can take a few hours.

I protect important documents and other important files using Backup Utility. Documents, images, and so on change often enough to make using Ghost to protect those impractical. Thus, I schedule Backup Utility to run each day so that I can restore any of my documents if something goes wrong.

I take this approach one step further by completely separating my configuration from my data. I use Folder Redirection to move users' My Documents folders from their local user profiles to a central location on the network. I back up all users' documents each time I back up their redirected folders on the server. For the most part, then, each computer's configuration is completely replaceable. I can restore its current disk image, log on to Windows XP, and I'm back where I was before the computer failed.

To open Backup Utility, click Start, All Programs, Accessories, System Tools, and then Backup. I have a preference for clicking the mouse as little as possible, so I just click Start, Run, and type **ntbackup** in the Run dialog box. Backup Utility has a robust set of command-line options you can use to script the backup process; you can learn more about those options in Backup Utility's Help. That's the hard way. The easy way is to schedule a job using Backup Utility, configure options in its user interface, and then copy the command line from Scheduled Tasks. Why spend an hour getting the command line just right when Backup Utility can do that for you?

Note   To back up a computer's file and folders, users must be in the Administrators or Backup Operators groups. If they aren't in either of those groups, they must have at least read permission on each file and folder they want to back up using Backup Utility. Alternately, you can give users the *Back up files and directories* and the *Restore files and directories* rights.

Planning a Backup Strategy

If you're an IT professional in a large enterprise, you already have a backup plan. Many small and home-based businesses go without backup plans or backing up their computers at all, and that's a shame. Unproductive downtime probably hurts small businesses more than it hurts huge enterprises, and they can easily avoid it. Whether you back up your computers using Backup Utility, Symantec Ghost, or any other method, just do it, and do it often.

The first part of a good strategy is rotation. That is, keeping backups around for a period of time so you can restore to any one of them later. For example, you might back up computers once a week and keep each backup set for a month. You'll always have the four most recent backups available. I use tapes and like to keep one set of tapes offsite in case of a disaster (I also store tapes in a fireproof safe, but you never know about those things until you try them). Use a rotation that works for you; on my server, I use the one shown in Figure 3-6 on the next page (backing up individual computers isn't necessary because I store anything I care to save on the server). I don't change my daily backup tapes because one tape holds a full week's worth of changes. That's why I can get away with having only nine sets of tapes. With more users, you might change tapes daily. Here's a summary of what you see in Figure 3-6:

- **Monthly.**   Move the most recent full-backup tape offsite (tape 5).
- **Weekly.**   Back up the entire server to tape (tapes 1 through 4).
- **Daily.**   Back up changed files to tape and mark those files as archived (tapes 6 through 9). The backup set includes system information, users' home folders, documents, mail folders, roaming user profiles, and so on.

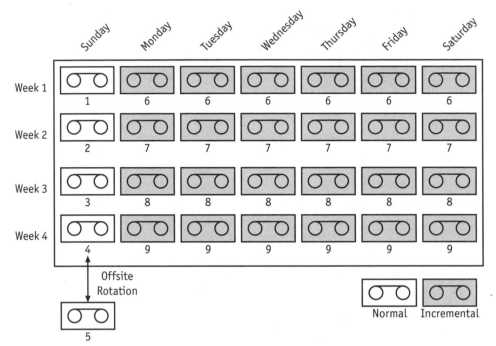

Figure 3-6   *Normal backup tapes contain all the server's files; incremental backup tapes contain only files that changed since the last normal or incremental backup.*

The second part of a good strategy is automation. You'll never stick to your backup plan if you don't automate it. Backup Utility integrates with Scheduled Tasks to schedule backup jobs through its own user interface, so this is easy. You can schedule your own backup jobs in Scheduled Tasks, but the command-line options are a bit intense, so I'd stick to the user interface. If your backup jobs require multiple tapes, as mine usually do, you'll have to be around to swap tapes. Large organizations will want to consider investing in a robotic tape changer or library, if they haven't already invested in large-scale backup technology.

Backing Up System State Data

In Backup Utility, you don't see an option to back up the registry. Furthermore, if you try to back up the hive files in %SYSTEMROOT%\System32\config, you'll fail. Instead, you back up the Windows XP *system state data*. System state data is the combination of the following system components (a server's system state data includes additional components, including Active Directory data, SYSVOL, and more):

- Registry
- COM+ Class Registration database
- Boot files, including the system files
- System files that are under Windows File Protection

To back up the registry, you have to copy all the system state data. Likewise, in order to restore the registry, you have to restore all the system state data. This makes Backup Utility a less-than-ideal way to back up the registry if that's all you're really trying to accomplish. To back up Windows XP system state data, select the System State check box in Backup Or Restore Wizard, shown in Figure 3-7; or click Only Backup The System State Data in Backup Wizard (yes, they are two different wizards). You can also select the System State check box on Backup Utility's Backup tab.

Backup Utility doesn't back up and restore everything on the computer, by the way. The key HKLM\SYSTEM\CurrentControlSet\Control\BackupRestore contains two interesting subkeys. The first subkey, FilesNotToBackup, contains a list of files and folders that Backup Utility skips. Each value contains a path to skip, and those values often contain wildcards. The second subkey, KeysNotToRestore, contains a list of keys not to restore to the computer. Likewise, each value contains a key to skip, and you see wildcards in many of the values. You'll find few surprises in either subkey. For example, Backup Utility doesn't back up System Restore's restore points because \System Volume Information _restore*GUID** is in FilesNotToBackup. It doesn't restore Plug and Play information, either, because CurrentControlSet\Enum\ is in KeysNotToRestore.

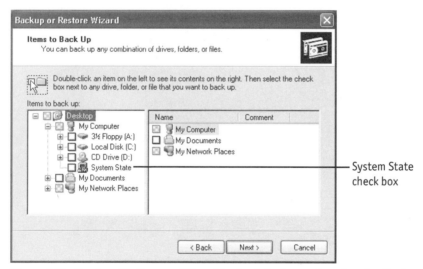

Figure 3-7 *Backup Or Restore Wizard is the default user interface for Backup Utility. If you'd rather use the classic user interface, click Advanced Mode on the first page.*

Restoring System State Data

Restoring system state data from a backup is similar to backing up the system state data in the first place. If all you backed up was system state data, just restore the entire backup. Otherwise, click System State in Backup Or Restore Wizard or on Backup Utility's Restore And Manage Media tab. If you restore the files to the original location, you'll restore your computer's settings, protected system files, boot files, and so on. This is the shotgun approach to restoring system state data from a backup.

Instead of the shotgun approach, the surgical approach is sometimes more appropriate. Restore the files to an alternate location. Backup Utility tells you that it won't restore all system state data to alternate locations, but don't worry; it does restore the registry hive files. Figure 3-8 shows you the contents of system state data as well as how Backup Utility restores the registry to an alternate location. When you restore system state data to a folder, the registry hive files are in the subfolder \Registry. You can load these hive files in Regedit and then copy settings from them to the working registry.

Figure 3-8   *Restoring system state data to an alternate location is the best choice if you want to restore a limited number of files or settings.*

You don't always have to restore a backup to get at the backup copy of the registry. If the most recent backup contains the settings you want to restore, you'll be happy to know that Backup Utility copies the hive files to %SYSTEMROOT%\repair. Don't try replacing the hive files in %SYSTEMROOT%\System32\config with the backup copies you find in %SYSTEMROOT%\repair—you can't because they're in use by Windows XP. You can load the backup hive files in Regedit to borrow settings from them, or you can start Recovery Console and then copy the backup hive files to %SYSTEMROOT%\System32\config. It's worth pointing out that System Restore does a far better job of restoring your settings than you can.

Backing Up User Settings

Backup Utility puts per-computer settings in system state data, but it doesn't back up per-user settings from users' profile folders. Those settings are in each profile folder's Ntuser.dat file. Don't forget the per-user class registrations that Windows XP stores in %USERPROFILE% \Local Settings\Application Data\Microsoft\Windows\UsrClass.dat. You have to pick these up manually either by selecting them in Backup or Restore Wizard or by using another means of backing up users' settings, such as backing up roaming user profiles. Windows XP does a great job of protecting per-computer settings and fixing them when they get out of whack, but it doesn't do as good of a job with per-user settings. My experience is that after users' settings are completely fouled, the support call lasts too long, and users don't always leave the experience as happy campers.

Backing up user profiles from each computer isn't practical on a large network. You can use System Restore to fix users' profiles because it backs up settings from the profiles in the key HKLM\SOFTWARE\Microsoft\Windows NT\CurrentVersion\ProfileList. You can take a more proactive stance, however. One solution is implementing roaming user profiles. Assuming they're compatible with your environment (roaming user profiles don't work well in mixed environments and when hardware configurations vary wildly from one computer to the next), the central storage of roaming user profiles makes it possible to back up users' settings as part of the server's normal backup routine. Even if users don't log on to multiple computers, roaming user profiles might be worth implementing just for this capability alone. Restoring a user's profile is a matter of logging the user off of Windows XP, restoring the user's profile folder to the server, and then logging the user back on to Windows XP.

Note   Chapter 10, "Deploying User Profiles," gives this subject more attention. You learn how to deploy different types of user profiles, back them up, and so on. You also learn about the many improvements that Windows XP makes to roaming user profiles, which just might make them more feasible in your organization.

Recovering from Disasters

Everything I've explained to this point assumes that you can start Windows XP. If you can't, your recovery options are a bit more limited and a lot more dramatic. If you have the money, I'd invest in Winternals Software Administrator's Pak. This is a set of advanced trouble-shooting tools that I use to recover configurations that are on the teetering edge of the trash bin. Learn more about it at *http://www.winternals.com*. I'll tell you more about these tools in Chapter 8, "Finding Registry Settings," because I use them to track down programs' settings in the registry (a hint of things to come).

It's fortunate that these types of problems don't occur as often as they once did. The reliability improvements in Windows XP mean that I don't have to recover nearly as many configurations as I did with Microsoft Windows 98 or Microsoft Windows NT 4.0. The tools available in Windows XP are similar to the ones that came with Windows 2000. The Advanced Options menu (the boot menu) offers a variety of modes in which to start Windows XP, including Safe Mode. Recovery Console is a limited command prompt with which you can fix certain classes of problems. And Automated System Recovery, which is the last resort, minimally reinstalls Windows XP on the computer. I'll present these in the order in which you should use each option.

Note   After a failure isn't the right time to master the advanced troubleshooting tools. Practice with them in a lab environment. Make them your own by scoping out their advantages and disadvantages well in advance of any problems. Master these tools now, and you'll enjoy that smug feeling you get by fixing a user's computer and walking away saying, "no worries," after just a few minutes of work.

Advanced Options Menu

Windows XP gives you a number of options for starting the computer. Safe Mode is the most common example. In Safe Mode, Windows XP uses default settings for the minimum set of device drivers required to start the operating system. When you can't start Windows XP normally, you can usually start it in Safe Mode and then repair the problem or use System Restore to restore a checkpoint. You can also remove programs using Add Or Remove Programs and uninstall cranky devices.

To start Safe Mode or one of the other modes, you have to display the Advanced Options menu. First restart the computer. When you see the message, "Please select the operating system to start," press F8 (you might start tapping F8 prior to seeing this message), and then select one of the options in the menu:

- **Safe Mode.**   Starts Windows XP using basic files and drivers (mouse, monitor, keyboard, mass storage, basic video, and default system services without network connections). If Windows XP doesn't start using safe mode, you might need to use Recovery Console to repair Windows XP.

- **Safe Mode With Networking.**   Starts Windows XP using basic files and drivers, as described in the last item, but includes network connections.

- **Safe Mode With Command Prompt.**   Starts Windows XP using basic files and drivers. After logging on to the operating system, you see a command prompt instead of the graphical user interface.

- **Enable Boot Logging.**   Starts Windows XP and logs all the device drivers and services that the operating system attempts to load. The log file is Ntbtlog.txt and is in the %SYSTEMROOT% folder. Safe Mode, Safe Mode with Networking, and Safe

Mode with Command Prompt add to the log a list of all the drivers and services that Windows XP loaded. The log is useful for determining which device driver or service is preventing Windows XP from starting properly.

- **Enable VGA Mode.**   Starts Windows XP using the basic VGA driver. This mode is useful after installing a new device driver for the video card when it's causing Windows XP not to start properly. Windows XP always uses the basic VGA driver when you start in Safe Mode, Safe Mode with Networking, or Safe Mode with Command Prompt.

- **Last Known Good Configuration.**   Starts Windows XP using the registry hive files and device drivers that Windows XP saved the last time it shut down. Any changes made since the last successful startup are lost. Use Last Known Good Configuration only when the problem is in the configuration because it doesn't solve problems that corrupt or missing files cause.

- **Directory Service Restore Mode.**   Restores the SYSVOL directory and the Active Directory directory service on a server. This option is irrelevant to Windows XP.

- **Debugging Mode.**   Starts Windows XP and sends debugging information to another computer through a serial cable.

Note   If you're unable to start Windows XP using the graphical user interface, you can usually start it using Safe Mode with Command Prompt. To run System Restore, which you're likely to do if you want to restore an earlier restore point, run the command %SYSTEMROOT% \System32\Restore\rstrui.exe.

Recovery Console

If Safe Mode doesn't do the trick, try Recovery Console. It offers commands that help fix varieties of system-related problems. You can enable or disable services; format disks; read and write files on a local NTFS volume; and perform a number of other administrative tasks. Notably, you can copy files from a floppy disk or CD to %SYSTEMROOT% in order to replace broken system files. Recovery Console is useful only if you're already familiar with the MS-DOS command prompt, and you must log on to the computer as an administrator to use it.

You start Recovery Console one of two ways:

- **From the Windows XP CD.**   Boot the computer using the Windows XP CD, and the setup program gives you the option of starting Recovery Console.

- **From the list of operating systems when the computer boots.**   First install Recovery Console on the computer by typing *D:\i386\winnt32.exe /cmdcons* in the Run dialog box, where *D* is the drive containing the Windows XP CD. Restart the computer, and choose Recovery Console in the list of operating systems.

Recovery Console has numerous commands, but it's missing a good chunk of the commands the MS-DOS command prompt provides. To see a list of commands and how to use them, type **help** at the Recovery Console command prompt. Here's a brief overview of each of them:

- `Attrib` Changes the attributes of a file or directory
- `Batch` Executes the commands specified in the text file
- `Bootcfg` Boot file (boot.ini) configuration and recovery
- `ChDir (Cd)` Displays the name of the current directory or changes the current directory
- `Chkdsk` Checks a disk and displays a status report
- `Cls` Clears the screen
- `Copy` Copies a single file to another location
- `Delete (Del)` Deletes one or more files
- `Dir` Displays a list of files and subdirectories in a directory
- `Disable` Disables a system service or a device driver
- `Diskpart` Manages partitions on your hard disks
- `Enable` Starts or enables a system service or a device driver
- `Exit` Exits the Recovery Console and restarts your computer
- `Expand` Extracts a file from a compressed file
- `Fixboot` Writes a new partition boot sector onto the specified partition
- `Fixmbr` Repairs the master boot record of the specified disk
- `Format` Formats a disk
- `Help` Displays a list of the commands you can use in Recovery Console
- `Listsvc` Lists the services and drivers available on the computer
- `Logon` Logs on to a Windows installation
- `Map` Displays the drive letter mappings
- `Mkdir (Md)` Creates a directory
- `More` Displays a text file
- `Net Use` Connects a network share to a drive letter
- `Rename (Ren)` Renames a single file
- `Rmdir (Rd)` Deletes a directory
- `Set` Displays and sets environment variables
- `Systemroot` Sets the current directory to the systemroot directory of the system you are currently logged on to
- `Type` Displays a text file

Policies that you can enable to add more *oomph* to Recovery Console are new for Windows XP. The policies `Recovery console: Allow automatic administrative logon` and `Recovery console: Allow floppy copy and access to all drives and folders` are per-computer administrative policies in `\Windows Settings\Security Settings \Local Policies\Security Options`. Enable `Recovery console: Allow automatic administrative logon` to automatically log on to Recovery Console as Administrator. Set `Recovery console: Allow floppy copy and access to all drives and folders` to allow access to all of the computer's drives and folders (Recovery Console limits access to %SYSTEMROOT% by default). After you enable this policy, you configure Recovery Console by setting environment variables: Type set *variable = true | false* at the command prompt (you must include a space on each side of the equal sign). Table 3-3 shows the default environment settings. To see the current settings, type **set**.

Table 3-3 Recovery Console Environment Settings

Setting	Default	Description
AllowWildCards	False	Enable wildcards for some commands
AllowAllPaths	False	Allow access to all files and folders
AllowRemovableMedia	False	Allow file copying to removable media
NoCopyPrompt	False	Don't prompt to overwrite existing files

Note You can't log on to Recovery Console if you installed Windows XP from a disk image prepared with Sysprep (see Chapter 13, "Cloning Disks with Sysprep"). This is due to changes that Sysprep makes in the way Windows XP stores password keys in the registry. These changes aren't compatible with Recovery Console. Microsoft publishes a fix for this problem in the Knowledge Base. Look for article Q308402, and download the files it lists. I expect that the first service pack for Windows XP will fix this problem.

Automated System Recovery

Create Automated System Recovery (ASR) backups frequently as part of your overall strategy. It's a last resort for system recovery, useful only if you've used up the other options that I've described in this chapter, including Safe Mode, Last Known Good Configuration, and Recovery Console.

Automated System Recovery is a two-part process. The first part is to back up the computer using Automated System Recovery Preparation Wizard, which is in Backup Utility. The wizard backs up system state data, services, and all operating system components. It also creates a file that contains information about the backup data, disk configurations, and how to restore the computer. Automated System Recovery does not back up or restore data files, programs, and so on. It only backs up the files necessary to start the computer in the event of failure. Here's how to prepare for Automated System Recovery:

1. Run Backup Utility.

   Click Start, All Programs, Accessories, System Tools, and then Backup.

2. If you see Backup or Restore Wizard, click Advanced Mode; otherwise, move on to the next step.

3. Click Automated System Recovery Wizard to start the wizard, and then follow the instructions you see on the screen to back up the computer and create an Automated System Recovery disk.

The second part of the process is to restore the computer. You use Automated System Recovery by pressing F2 when the setup program prompts you. Automated System Recovery reads the disk configurations from the file it created earlier, and restores all disk signatures, volumes, and disks containing operating system files. (It tries to restore all of the computer's disks but might not be able to do so successfully.) Automated System Recovery then installs Windows XP minimally, and then restores the backup created by Automated System Recovery Preparation Wizard. The whole process is similar to reinstalling Windows XP manually and then restoring your own backup. It's automated, however.

Administrator's Pak

Winternals Software Administrator's Pak contains tools that go far beyond Recovery Console and Automated System Recovery. You can also buy these tools individually if the price of the entire toolkit is a bit steep.

The first tool is ERD Commander. Using this tool, you can start computers directly from a CD into an environment similar to Windows XP. The environment gives you full access to all the computer's volumes. It's kind of like a graphical version of Recovery Console. You can even reset a forgotten Administrator password, edit the registry, and copy files from the computer to the network. If this tool is your last resort for fixing a downed computer, you're going to be in good hands.

Disk Commander is another tool in the kit that enables you to recover files from dead volumes. After scanning a volume, it presents the files it found in a user interface similar to Windows Explorer so you can copy them to a safe place.

Remote Recover is the last tool that I'm featuring here, but there are more in the Administrator's Pak. Use this tool to repair failed computers across a network. That is, it gives you access to a remote computer's disks as if you installed those disks on your computer. You have to boot the remote computer, though, and Remote Recover gives you two options. The first is to start the remote computer using a bootable floppy disk. The second, and the one I like best, is a PXE-based disk image that you can start remotely or add to a RIS (Remote Installation Service) server.

You can learn more about these notable tools by visiting Winternals Software's Web site at *www.winternals.com*. The wunderkind duo of Mark Russinovich and Bryce Cogswell, Winternals Software's founders, have developed these and other tools to such a high level of reliability that I often bet my job on them.

Hacking the Registry

This chapter covers hacking the registry to make Microsoft Windows XP look and feel the way you want. Rather than showing you how Windows XP organizes the registry, which is covered in the chapters in Part IV, "Appendices," I'll show you the brute force hacks that immediately change the way you use Windows XP. To make these customizations easier, I've included scripts for many of them. Download these and new scripts at *http://www.honeycutt.com*.

I use the term *hack* loosely. These aren't security hacks or hacks that give you more features than you're supposed to have. By no means am I helping you hack product activation. These are hacks that help you customize the operating system in ways that you can't through its user interface. For example, this chapter helps you customize the shortcut menus and the icons you see in the user interface and change how Windows XP behaves. It even describes how you can automatically log on to Windows XP, bypassing the Log On To Windows dialog box. You'll find some of these hacks on various Web sites and FAQs, but hopefully I'm giving you many new ones that you won't find anywhere else.

These hacks are for power users. If you're looking for customizations with an IT flavor, see Chapter 15, "Working Around IT Problems," which has customizations that help IT professionals deploy Windows XP and solve particular IT problems. But even though the chapter you're reading now is end user–oriented, IT professionals might find that its customizations are a good fit for their enterprise users, and professionals can deploy those customizations in a variety of ways, including default user profiles, policies, and scripts. For example, IT professionals frequently ask me how to simulate IntelliMirror features like Folder Redirection without using policies, and the first hack shows you how to do just that.

Redirecting Special Folders

Special folders include the My Documents, My Pictures, and Favorites folders, among many others. Table 4-1 shows the special folders that Windows XP creates after a fresh installation and their default paths. The first column contains each folder's internal name as Windows XP and other programs know it. The second column contains each folder's default path, which almost always starts with %USERPROFILE%, making these folders part of each user's profile folder. Chapter 10, "Deploying User Profiles," describes these user profile folders in depth.

Users might want to redirect special folders for a variety of reasons, but two come to mind. The first is to redirect the My Documents folder to a different volume. For example, users might redirect My Documents to drive D so they can reinstall Windows XP on drive C without losing their documents. The second scenario is when users have a network and want to access their documents from more than one computer. In that case, they can redirect both their My Documents and Favorites folders to a network location so they have access to them from anywhere. IT professionals frequently want to redirect My Documents to a network location, too, which makes backing up users' documents easier. This can be done with the IntelliMirror feature Redirected Folders. IT professionals can't use IntelliMirror features without Active Directory, but they can simulate Redirected Folders. Chapter 15, "Working Around IT Problems," shows how to use this hack in that scenario.

Table 4-1   Special Folders

Name	Default path
AppData	%USERPROFILE%\Application Data
Cache	%USERPROFILE%\Local Settings\Temporary Internet Files
Cookies	%USERPROFILE%\Cookies
Desktop	%USERPROFILE%\Desktop
Favorites	%USERPROFILE%\Favorites
History	%USERPROFILE%\Local Settings\History
Local AppData	%USERPROFILE%\Local Settings\Application Data
Local Settings	%USERPROFILE%\Local Settings
My Pictures	%USERPROFILE%\My Documents\My Pictures
NetHood	%USERPROFILE%\NetHood
Personal	%USERPROFILE%\My Documents
PrintHood	%USERPROFILE%\PrintHood
Programs	%USERPROFILE%\Start Menu\Programs
Recent	%USERPROFILE%\Recent
SendTo	%USERPROFILE%\SendTo
Start Menu	%USERPROFILE%\Start Menu
Startup	%USERPROFILE%\Start Menu\Programs\Startup
Templates	%USERPROFILE%\Templates

HKCU\Software\Microsoft\Windows\CurrentVersion\Explorer\User Shell Folders is the key where Windows XP stores the location of per-user special folders. Each value in this key is a special folder as shown in Table 4-1. These are REG_EXPAND_SZ values, so you can use environment variables in them. Use %USERPROFILE% in a path to direct the folder somewhere inside users' profile folders or %USERNAME% in a path to include users' names. To redirect users' Favorites folders to the network, set the value Favorites, which you looked up in Table 4-1, to *Server**Share*\%USERNAME%\Favorites, where *Server**Share* is the server and share containing the folders. The next time the user logs on, Windows XP updates a second key, HKCU\Software\Microsoft\Windows\CurrentVersion\Explorer\Shell Folders, with the paths from User Shell Folders, so you don't have to update it. In fact, Microsoft's documentation says Windows XP doesn't use Shell Folders.

The following listing shows you how to redirect special folders automatically. Save this listing to the text file Redirect.inf and replace the string PERSONAL with the location where you want to redirect the My Documents folder. (Use environment variables so the script works for all users.) Do the same for the strings FAVORITES, PICTURES, and APPDATA. To configure these settings, right-click Redirect.inf, and then click Install. Chapter 9, "Scripting Registry Changes," shows you other ways to deploy these settings. You can uninstall this script using Add Or Remove Programs.

Listing 4-1   Redirect.inf

```
[Version]
Signature=$CHICAGO$

[DefaultInstall]
AddReg=Reg.Settings
AddReg=Reg.Uninstall
CopyFiles=Inf.Copy

[DefaultUninstall]
DelReg=Reg.Settings
DelReg=Reg.Uninstall
DelFiles=Inf.Copy

[Reg.Settings]
HKCU,Software\Microsoft\Windows\CurrentVersion\Explorer\
\User Shell Folders,AppData,0x20000,"%APPDATA%"
HKCU,Software\Microsoft\Windows\CurrentVersion\Explorer\
\User Shell Folders,Personal,0x20000,"%PERSONAL%"
HKCU,Software\Microsoft\Windows\CurrentVersion\Explorer\
\User Shell Folders,My Pictures,0x20000,"%PICTURES%"
HKCU,Software\Microsoft\Windows\CurrentVersion\Explorer\User Shell \
Folders,favorites,0x20000,"%FAVORITES%"

[Reg.Uninstall]
HKCU,Software\Microsoft\Windows\CurrentVersion\Uninstall\%NAME%
HKCU,Software\Microsoft\Windows\CurrentVersion\Uninstall\
\%NAME%,DisplayName,,"%NAME%"
```

```
HKCU,Software\Microsoft\Windows\CurrentVersion\Uninstall\%NAME%,UninstallString\
,,"Rundll32.exe setupapi.dll,InstallHinfSection DefaultUninstall 132"\
" %53%\Application Data\Custom\Redirect.inf"

[Inf.Copy]
Redirect.inf

[DestinationDirs]
Inf.Copy=53,Application Data\Custom

[SourceDisksNames]
55=%DISKNAME%

[SourceDisksFiles]
Redirect.inf=55

[Strings]
NAME        = "Jerry's Redirect Folders"
APPDATA     = "\\Server\Folders\%USERNAME%\Application Data"
PERSONAL    = "\\Server\Folders\%USERNAME%\My Documents"
PICTURES    = "\\Server\Folders\%USERNAME%\My Documents\My Pictures"
FAVORITES   = "\\Server\Folders\%USERNAME%\Favorites"
DISKNAME    = "Setup Files"
```

Note   The special folders in this section are per-user and exist within users' profile folders. Windows XP also lists per-computer special folders in HKLM. Examples of per-computer folders include Common AppData, Common Desktop, and Common Documents. It's not as useful to customize per-computer folders, however. Regardless, the same rules apply. Change the location of the folder in User Shell folders; Windows XP automatically updates Shell Folders.

Customizing Shell Folders

Some folders you see in Windows Explorer, Control Panel, or on the desktop don't actually exist on the file system. They're objects based on classes registered in the key HKCR\CLSID. Some folders and files that do exist on the file system have special capabilities (the History and Briefcase folders for example), and those capabilities also come from objects based on classes registered in HKCR\CLSID. A class is essentially a template for creating something real, like an object in the user interface, and CLSID is where those classes register themselves so Windows XP knows about them.

Other programs might register additional classes, and you can easily spot interesting ones in HKCR\CLSID because they have the subkey ShellFolder and the value Attributes in that subkey. Appendix A, "File Associations," describes the value Attributes and what to make of each bit in it. Figure 4-1 shows what this subkey and value look like in the registry. Class registrations containing the value LocalizedString are also likely candidates for customization because they contain this value only if objects based on that class appear in the user interface. These classes have a variety of purposes, and you'll use them frequently to hack Windows XP.

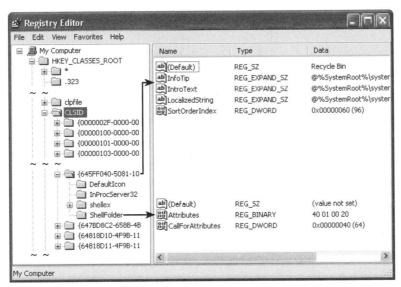

Figure 4-1 *You can find interesting object classes by searching for ShellFolder subkeys that contain the value Attributes. Look for LocalizedString, too.*

Table 4-2 on the next page lists the classes registered in HKCR\CLSID that I found the most interesting. I divided this table into four sections. The first is shell folders. These are special-purpose folders, such as My Computer, My Network Places, and so on. The second section is Control Panel folders, for example Administrative Tools and Scheduled Tasks. The third section is Control Panel icons. The fourth section is other interesting classes, such as the Run dialog box. Objects created from classes in the first two sections are folders. Objects created from classes in the last two sections are generally dialog boxes but sometimes add capabilities to files and folders, as is the case with Briefcase. The first column is the class's name and the second column is the class's GUID, or *class identifier*. I've italicized those that aren't useful for hacking but that you run into frequently while hacking the registry.

Table 4-2   Special Object Classes

Object	Class identifier
Shell folders	
ActiveX Cache	{88C6C381-2E85-11D0-94DE-444553540000}
Computer Search Results	{1F4DE370-D627-11D1-BA4F-00A0C91EEDBA}
History	{FF393560-C2A7-11CF-BFF4-444553540000}
Internet Explorer	{871C5380-42A0-1069-A2EA-08002B30309D}
My Computer	{20D04FE0-3AEA-1069-A2D8-08002B30309D}
My Documents	{450D8FBA-AD25-11D0-98A8-0800361B1103}
My Network Places	{208D2C60-3AEA-1069-A2D7-08002B30309D}
Offline Files	{AFDB1F70-2A4C-11D2-9039-00C04F8EEB3E}
Programs	{7BE9D83C-A729-4D97-B5A7-1B7313C39E0A}
Recycle Bin	{645FF040-5081-101B-9F08-00AA002F954E}
Search Results	{E17D4FC0-5564-11D1-83F2-00A0C90DC849}
Shared Documents	{59031A47-3F72-44A7-89C5-5595FE6B30EE}
Start Menu	{48E7CAAB-B918-4E58-A94D-505519C795DC}
Temporary Internet Files	{7BD29E00-76C1-11CF-9DD0-00A0C9034933}
Web	{BDEADF00-C265-11D0-BCED-00A0C90AB50F}
Control Panel folders	
Administrative Tools	{D20EA4E1-3957-11D2-A40B-0C5020524153}
Fonts	{D20EA4E1-3957-11D2-A40B-0C5020524152}
Network Connections	{7007ACC7-3202-11D1-AAD2-00805FC1270E}
Printers and Faxes	{2227A280-3AEA-1069-A2DE-08002B30309D}
Scanners and Cameras	{E211B736-43FD-11D1-9EFB-0000F8757FCD}
Scheduled Tasks	{D6277990-4C6A-11CF-8D87-00AA0060F5BF}
Control Panel icons	
Folder Options	{6DFD7C5C-2451-11D3-A299-00C04F8EF6AF}
Taskbar and Start Menu	{0DF44EAA-FF21-4412-828E-260A8728E7F1}
User Accounts	{7A9D77BD-5403-11D2-8785-2E0420524153}
Other	
Add Network Places	{D4480A50-BA28-11D1-8E75-00C04FA31A86}
Briefcase	{85BBD920-42A0-1069-A2E4-08002B30309D}
E-mail	{2559A1F5-21D7-11D4-BDAF-00C04F60B9F0}
Help and Support	{2559A1F1-21D7-11D4-BDAF-00C04F60B9F0}
Internet	{2559A1F4-21D7-11D4-BDAF-00C04F60B9F0}

Object	Class identifier
Network Setup Wizard	*{2728520D-1EC8-4C68-A551-316B684C4EA7}*
Run	{2559A1F3-21D7-11D4-BDAF-00C04F60B9F0}
Search	{2559A1F0-21D7-11D4-BDAF-00C04F60B9F0}
Windows Security	{2559A1F2-21D7-11D4-BDAF-00C04F60B9F0}

You can do a lot when armed with the information in Table 4-2. You can customize which folders you see in My Computer, for example. You can rename the icons you see on the desktop and, for that matter, configure which icons appear on the desktop at all. For example, administrators might put the Administrative Tools folder on their desktops to make it quicker to access. See the upcoming sections for information about the different ways I've found to use these classes.

Renaming Desktop Icons

On the desktop, you can rename the My Computer, My Network Places, My Documents, and Internet Explorer icons. Assuming you see these icons on your desktop, right-click them, and then click Rename. Other icons, like the Recycle Bin, aren't so easy. No Rename command is available for them.

You rename an icon without a Rename command by editing its class registration. Change the value of LocalizedString. Here's an example: In Table 4-1, you see the Recycle Bin's class ID is {645FF040-5081-101B-9F08-00AA002F954E}. To rename the Recycle Bin icon to *Trash Can*, set the value of LocalizedString in the key HKCR\CLSID\{645FF040-5081-101B-9F08-00AA002F954E} to Trash Can. Afterward, click the desktop, and press F5 to refresh its contents. The value LocalizedString usually contains something like @%SystemRoot%\system32\SHELL32.dll,-8964, which means that Windows XP uses the string with the ID 8964 from the file Shell32.dll. Just replace all that with the new name.

Tip LocalizedString is a REG_EXPAND_SZ value, so you can use environment variables. For example, set LocalizedString to %USERNAME%'s Garbage, and the user Jerry sees *Jerry's Garbage* below the icon. You can do this for other icons as well. My Computer's class ID is {20D04FE0-3AEA-1069-A2D8-08002B30309D}. Change LocalizedString in HKCR\CLSID\{20D04FE0-3AEA-1069-A2D8-08002B30309D} to %USERNAME%'s Computer, and the user Jerry sees *Jerry's Computer* instead of My Computer; the user Sally sees *Sally's Computer*.

You don't see the value LocalizedString in some class registrations. The absence of this value indicates that Microsoft didn't intend to display the names of those objects in the user interface. To rename a class that doesn't contain this value, change the default value of HKCR\CLSID*classID* or better yet, add LocalizedString to it. When Windows XP looks for an object's name, it looks first for LocalizedString and second for the class registration's default value.

Using Custom Icon Images

Each class registration you see in Table 4-2 contains the subkey DefaultIcon. This subkey's default value is the icon that Windows XP uses when it displays objects based on that class. For example, the default value of DefaultIcon in HKCR\CLSID\{20D04FE0-3AEA-1069-A2D8-08002B30309D} is the icon that Windows XP displays when it creates the My Computer object in the user interface, such as in Windows Explorer or on the desktop.

To use a different icon, change the default value of DefaultIcon. You can use the path and file name of an icon file, which has the *.ico* extension, or you can use a resource path. A resource path is either *Name,Index* or *Name,-resID*. *Name* is the path and name of the file containing the icon, which is usually a DLL or EXE file. Most of the icons that Windows XP uses come from %SystemRoot%\System32\Shell32.dll. *Index* is the index number of the icon, beginning with 0. *resID* is the resource identifier of the icon. Programmers assign resource IDs to resources they store in program files, including icons, strings, dialog boxes, and so on.

Tip   My favorite tool for finding icons in program files is PE Explorer from Heaven Tools. You can download an evaluation copy from the Web site at *http://www.heaventools.com*. This tool will even extract all the icons from DLL and EXE files so that you can use them individually.

Adding Desktop Icons

Windows XP has a much cleaner desktop than earlier versions of Windows. By default, you see only the Recycle Bin icon. You can add the typical icons, though: On the Display Properties dialog box's Desktop tab, click Customize Desktop. In the Desktop Items dialog box, choose the icons you want to display on the desktop. The icons you can add are My Documents, My Computer, My Network Places, and Internet Explorer. To open the Display Properties dialog box, click Start, Control Panel, Appearance And Themes, and then click Display.

If the icon you want to add isn't one of those four choices, if you want to script these changes, or if you want to add icons to other special folders, you must edit the registry. All the hacks you learn about in this section are in the branch SOFTWARE\Microsoft\Windows \CurrentVersion\Explorer. Change this branch in HKLM to affect all users; change it in HKCU to affect an individual user. Figure 4-2 shows the contents of this branch.

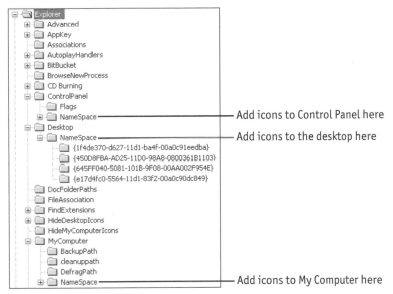

Figure 4-2 *The NameSpace subkeys of Explorer\ControlPanel, Explorer\Desktop, and Explorer\MyComputer determine the contents of each corresponding folder.*

You add icons to Control Panel, the desktop, and so on by editing the subkeys indicated in Table 4-3. Create a new subkey in NameSpace and name it the class ID of the object you want to add. For example, to add an icon to the desktop that opens the Run dialog box (see Table 4-2), add a new subkey called {2559A1F3-21D7-11D4-BDAF-00C04F60B9F0} to Desktop\Namespace. Then refresh the desktop by clicking it and pressing F5. As shown in Figure 4-3 on the next page, you can add folders to My Computer, too. In this case, I added the Administrative Tools and Network Connections folders to My Computer. Only folder objects are good candidates for My Computer, so pick class IDs from the first two sections of Table 4-1. Add class IDs from the last two sections of the table, and you'll see only those objects in the right pane of Windows Explorer. Objects based on classes in the second and third sections of Table 4-1 are good choices for Control Panel.

Table 4-3 NameSpace Subkeys

Folder	Subkey
Control Panel	ControPanel\NameSpace
Desktop	Desktop\NameSpace
My Computer	MyComputer\NameSpace
My Network Places	NetworkNeighborhood\NameSpace
Remote Computer	RemoteComputer\NameSpace

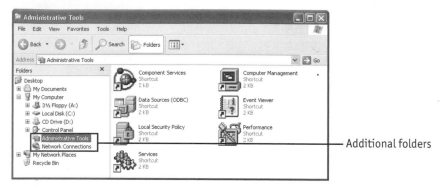

Additional folders

Figure 4-3   *By editing the registry, you can reorganize the contents of Windows Explorer.*

Hiding Desktop Icons

With earlier versions of Windows, you removed icons from the desktop by removing their subkeys from the key NameSpace. This often caused problems, especially when removing the Network Neighborhood icon from the desktop.

Windows XP makes a special provision for hiding desktop icons. You remove icons from the desktop or My Computer by editing in HKLM or HKCU the branch SOFTWARE \Microsoft\Windows\CurrentVersion\Explorer. To hide icons in My Computer, add a REG_DWORD value to HideMyComputerIcons—the name is the class ID of the icon you want to hide—and set it to 0x01. Refresh Windows Explorer to see your changes.

Hiding desktop icons is a hair more complicated. In HideDesktopIcons, you see two subkeys: ClassicStartMenu and NewStartPanel. The first subkey determines which icons to hide when Windows XP is using the classic Start menu. The second determines which icons to hide when Windows XP is using the new Start menu. Add a REG_DWORD value named for the icon's class ID to either subkey to hide it in that view. Set the value to 0x01. For example, to hide the Recycle Bin icon when the new Start menu is in use, create a REG_DWORD value called {645FF040-5081-101B-9F08-00AA002F954E} in the subkey HideDesktopIcons\NewStartPanel, and then set it to 0x01. Click the desktop and then press F5 to refresh.

Tip   When you add a class ID to HideMyComputerIcons or HideDesktopIcons, use the default value of that subkey to remind you which icon you're hiding. Windows XP doesn't use this subkey's default value, and putting the icon's name in it will help you figure out which subkey to remove in order to show that icon.

Customizing File Associations

File associations control the following aspects of how Windows XP treats files:

- Which icon Windows XP displays for a file
- Which application launches when users double-click files
- How Windows Explorer displays particular types of files
- Which commands appear on files' shortcut menus
- Other features, such as InfoTips

Appendix A, "File Associations," describes file associations in detail. In that chapter, you also learn how to customize file associations in ways that only programmers know—until now. Because Appendix A gives the full treatment to file associations and the root key that contains them, HKCR, I'm not going to duplicate that material here. I thought you'd have more fun with some specific file association customizations that I like, such as adding Tweak UI to the My Computer icon's shortcut menu or opening an MS-DOS command prompt at a particular folder.

File Associations in the Registry

I said that Appendix A, "File Associations," is the place to go to learn about file associations in HKCR, but a quick brain dump will help you use the hacks you see in this chapter. Take a look at Figure 4-4, which shows how Windows XP chooses what to display on a file's shortcut menu.

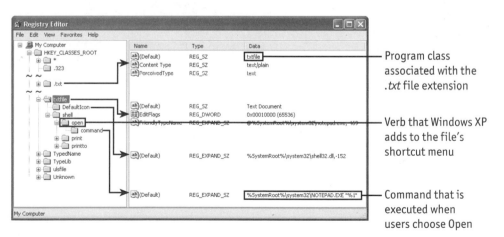

Figure 4-4   *A file extension key's default value indicates the program class with which it's associated. The program class's shell subkey contains commands you see on the shortcut menu.*

(continued)

In the figure on the previous page, you see the keys that Windows XP consults when you right-click a text file and then click Open. First the operating system looks up the file extension in HKCR. The default value, shown in Figure 4-4, indicates that the program class associated with the *.txt* file extension is txtfile. So the operating system looks in HKCR \txtfile for the subkey shell to find the commands it adds to the shortcut menu. For example, as shown in Figure 4-4, Windows XP adds Open to the shortcut menu, and when users choose Open, it runs the command in the command subkey.

The command in the command subkey is usually *"program" options "%1"*. *program* is the path and file name of the program you want to run. If you're using a script and change the default value of command to REG_EXPAND_SZ, you can use environment variables like %SYSTEMROOT% in it. Otherwise, use an explicit path. You use the %1 as a placeholder for the target file. Windows XP will add the path and name of the target file to the end of the command, but you don't want to leave this up to chance. Also, always enclose %1 in quotes in case the target path and file name include spaces.

You often see this same shell subkey in class registrations, too. For example, the class registration for My Computer contains a command for managing the computer. The class registration for Recycle Bin contains commands to empty and explore its contents.

Running Programs from My Computer

I'm all for any customization that makes things easier. There are some programs that I use over and over again, and I want a nice, easy place from which to run them. The Quick Launch toolbar is nice, as is the list of frequently used programs on the Start menu. I want a place where I can put system-oriented commands, though, so I like to put those commands on My Computer's shortcut menu. Then I can display the My Computer icon on the desktop and they're one mouse click away. You learned how to show the icon in the section "Hiding Desktop Icons."

To add commands to My Computer's shortcut menu, edit its class registration, which is in HKCR\CLSID\{20D04FE0-3AEA-1069-A2D8-08002B30309D}. Add the command to this key's shell subkey. For example, after installing Microsoft Tweak UI, which you learn about in Chapter 5, "Mapping Tweak UI," I like to add a command to My Computer's shortcut menu that opens Tweak UI. So I add the branch tweak\command to My Computer's class registration. I set the default value of tweak to Tweak UI, the menu item text, and the default value of command to C:\Windows\System32\Tweakui.exe, the path and file name of Tweak UI. After customizing the class registration for My Computer, starting Tweak UI is fast: Right-click My Computer, and then click Tweak UI.

The following INF file automates this setting. First install Tweak UI. Then save this script to the file Tweakui.inf, right-click the file, and then click Install. (Again, you can download these sample scripts from *http://www.honeycutt.com*.) See Chapter 9, "Scripting Registry Changes," for other ways to script this hack. You can uninstall these settings in Add Or Remove Programs.

Listing 4-2 Tweakui.inf

```
[Version]
Signature=$CHICAGO$

[DefaultInstall]
AddReg=Reg.Settings
AddReg=Reg.Uninstall
CopyFiles=Inf.Copy

[DefaultUninstall]
DelReg=Reg.Settings
DelReg=Reg.Uninstall
DelFiles=Inf.Copy

[Reg.Settings]
HKCR,CLSID\{20D04FE0-3AEA-1069-A2D8-08002B30309D}\shell\tweak
HKCR,CLSID\{20D04FE0-3AEA-1069-A2D8-08002B30309D}\shell\tweak,,,"%MENUITEM%"
HKCR,CLSID\{20D04FE0-3AEA-1069-A2D8-08002B30309D}\shell\tweak\command\
,,0x20000,"%SYSTEMROOT%\System32\Tweakui.exe"

[Reg.Uninstall]
HKLM,Software\Microsoft\Windows\CurrentVersion\Uninstall\%NAME%
HKLM,Software\Microsoft\Windows\CurrentVersion\Uninstall\%NAME%,DisplayName\
,,"%NAME%"
HKLM,Software\Microsoft\Windows\CurrentVersion\Uninstall\%NAME%,UninstallString\
,,"Rundll32.exe setupapi.dll,InstallHinfSection DefaultUninstall 132"\
" %17%\Tweakui.inf"
[Inf.Copy]
Tweakui.inf

[DestinationDirs]
Inf.Copy=17

[SourceDisksNames]
55=%DISKNAME%

[SourceDisksFiles]
Tweakui.inf=55

[Strings]
NAME     = "Jerry's Tweak UI Shortcut"
MENUITEM = "Tweak UI"
DISKNAME = "Setup Files"
```

You can add any command to any shortcut menu, and that command doesn't have to edit, print, or do anything at all with the menu's target. My Computer is a good place to park system-oriented commands like Tweak UI, but you could also put them on another object's shortcut menu, such as Recycle Bin, if you don't display the My Computer icon on the desktop.

Open Command Prompts at Folders

Another favorite customization, and the one I probably use the most, enables me to quickly open an MS-DOS command prompt with the targeted folder set as the current working directory. I add the command C:\WINDOWS\System32\cmd.exe /k cd "%1" to the Directory and Drive program classes. Then I right-click a folder and click CMD Prompt Here to open a command prompt with that folder set as the current working directory. This is a real time saver. Here are the settings to add to HKCR\Directory (repeat these settings in HKCR\Drive):

- In HKCR\Directory\shell, create the subkey cmdhere.

- In HKCR\Directory\shell\cmdhere, set the default value to CMD Prompt Here. This is the text you'll see on the shortcut menu.

- In HKCR\Directory\shell\cmdhere, create the subkey command.

- In HKCR\Directory\shell\cmdhere\command, set the default value to C:\Windows\System32\cmd.exe /k cd "%1".

The following script automatically adds this command to the Directory and Drive program classes. Save it to the text file Cmdhere.inf, right-click it, and then click Install. To understand how this script works, see Chapter 9, "Scripting Registry Changes." Remove these settings using Add Or Remove Programs.

Listing 4-3   Cmdhere.inf

```
[Version]
Signature=$CHICAGO$

[DefaultInstall]
AddReg=Reg.Settings
AddReg=Reg.Uninstall
CopyFiles=Inf.Copy

[DefaultUninstall]
DelReg=Reg.Settings
DelReg=Reg.Uninstall
DelFiles=Inf.Copy

[Reg.Settings]
HKCR,Directory\Shell\Cmdhere
HKCR,Directory\Shell\Cmdhere,,,"%MENUITEM%"
HKCR,Directory\Shell\Cmdhere\command,,,"%11%\cmd.exe /k cd ""%1"""
HKCR,Drive\Shell\Cmdhere
HKCR,Drive\Shell\Cmdhere,,,"%MENUITEM%"
HKCR,Drive\Shell\Cmdhere\command,,,"%11%\cmd.exe /k cd ""%1"""

[Reg.Uninstall]
HKLM,Software\Microsoft\Windows\CurrentVersion\Uninstall\%NAME%
HKLM,Software\Microsoft\Windows\CurrentVersion\Uninstall\%NAME%,DisplayName\
,,"%NAME%"
```

```
HKLM,Software\Microsoft\Windows\CurrentVersion\Uninstall\%NAME%,UninstallString\
,,"Rundll32.exe setupapi.dll,InstallHinfSection DefaultUninstall 132 "\
"%17%\Cmdhere.inf"

[Inf.Copy]
Cmdhere.inf

[DestinationDirs]
Inf.Copy=17

[SourceDisksNames]
55=%DISKNAME%

[SourceDisksFiles]
Cmdhere.inf=55

[Strings]
NAME     = "Jerry's CMD Prompt Here"
MENUITEM = "CMD &Prompt Here"
DISKNAME = "Setup Files"
```

Rooting Windows Explorer at a Folder

The idea behind this customization is to open Windows Explorer without all the usual clutter so you can focus on a single folder. Add the command `explorer.exe /e,/root,/idlist,%I` to the `Folder` program class's `shell` subkey. Then right-click any folder, choose the command you added, and another Windows Explorer window opens with that folder rooted at the top of the left pane.

Here are the settings you add to the `Folder` program class:

- In `HKCR\Folder\shell`, create the subkey `fromhere`.

- In `HKCR\Folder\shell\fromhere`, set the default value to `Explore from Here`. This is the text you'll see on the shortcut menu.

- In `HKCR\Folder\shell\fromhere`, create the subkey `command`.

- In `HKCR\Folder\shell\fromhere\command`, set the default value to `explorer.exe /e,/root,/idlist,%I`.

The following script automatically adds this command to the `Folder` program class. Save it to the text file Fromhere.inf, right-click it, and then click Install. To understand how this script works, see Chapter 9, "Scripting Registry Changes." Remove these settings using Add Or Remove Programs.

Listing 4-4   Fromhere.inf

```
[Version]
Signature=$CHICAGO$

[DefaultInstall]
AddReg=Reg.Settings
AddReg=Reg.Uninstall
CopyFiles=Inf.Copy

[DefaultUninstall]
DelReg=Reg.Settings
DelReg=Reg.Uninstall
DelFiles=Inf.Copy

[Reg.Settings]
HKCR,Folder\shell\fromhere
HKCR,Folder\shell\fromhere,,,"%MENUITEM%"
HKCR,Folder\shell\fromhere\command,,,"explorer.exe /e,/root,/idlist,%I"

[Reg.Uninstall]
HKLM,Software\Microsoft\Windows\CurrentVersion\Uninstall\%NAME%
HKLM,Software\Microsoft\Windows\CurrentVersion\Uninstall\%NAME%\
,DisplayName,,"%NAME%"
HKLM,Software\Microsoft\Windows\CurrentVersion\Uninstall\%NAME%\
,UninstallString,,"Rundll32.exe setupapi.dll,InstallHinfSection DefaultUninstall 132 "\
"%17%\Fromhere.inf"

[Inf.Copy]
Fromhere.inf

[DestinationDirs]
Inf.Copy=17

[SourceDisksNames]
55=%DISKNAME%

[SourceDisksFiles]
Fromhere.inf=55

[Strings]
NAME     = "Jerry's Explore from Here"
MENUITEM = "Explore from &Here"
DISKNAME = "Setup Files"
```

Adding InfoTips to Program Classes

I like InfoTips; you might not. Position the mouse pointer over an object in the user interface, and Windows XP displays the InfoTip associated with it in a small yellow box. For documents, the InfoTip typically includes the type of document, the date of its last modification, its size, and so on. You can further customize InfoTips, though.

Windows XP uses the REG_SZ value InfoTip to display InfoTips. The operating system uses this value it finds in the class registration or program class to which the object belongs. For example, if you position the mouse pointer over a file with the *.doc* file extension, Windows XP looks in the associated program class Wordpad.Document.1 for the value InfoTip. If it doesn't find the value there, it uses the value InfoTip that it finds in HKCR*. The default value of that is prop:Type;DocAuthor;DocTitle;DocSubject;DocComments; Write;Size.

Thus, you can customize individual classes or create an InfoTip that applies to all classes. If you're after a specific object or file type, add the REG_SZ value InfoTip to that specific class registration or program class. Otherwise, customize the value InfoTip in HKCR* to see that tip for all file classes.

So what does all that mean? The notation prop:*name* indicates to Windows XP that it should use the document property *name* in the InfoTip. Thus, the value you just saw means that Windows XP should display the document properties Type, DocAuthor, DocTitle, DocSubject, DocComments, Write, and Size in the InfoTip. You can also set InfoTip to an exact string that you want Windows XP to display when users position the mouse pointer over objects of that particular class. For example, you can set InfoTip for the txtfile program class to This is a text file, and that's what Windows XP displays when users position the mouse pointer over text files. Windows XP ignores any property in the InfoTip that the document doesn't define, and InfoTips can be up to six lines long. The following list shows just some of the document properties that you can add to an InfoTip (available properties depend on each individual program class):

- Access
- Album
- Artist
- Attributes
- Bit Rate
- CameraModel
- Company
- Copyright
- Create
- Dimensions
- DocAuthor

- DocCategory
- DocComments
- DocPages
- DocSubject
- DocTitle
- Duration
- FileDescription
- FileVersion
- Genre
- LinkTarget
- Name

- Owner
- ProductName
- ProductVersion
- Protected
- Size
- Status
- Track
- Type
- WhenTaken
- Write
- Year

Note   A related value is `TileInfo`. The contents of this value are the same as the contents of `InfoTip`. Windows XP displays `TileInfo` next to icons in Tile view. You're limited to two lines, however, so make good use of the space you have. I don't like the default value of `TileInfo` in most cases; I prefer to display more useful information such as a file's attributes. Thus, I like to set the value `HKCR\*\TileInfo` to `prop:Type;Attributes,` which is more useful to me. Although you don't have to log off and back on to Windows XP to see changes you make to `InfoTip`, you do have to log off of Windows XP to see changes you make to `TileInfo`.

Customizing Folders with Desktop.ini

This customization only marginally involves the registry, but it's too good to leave out. This chapter shows you how to customize files and other objects you see in the user interface, but customizing individual folders is good, too. For example, you might have a folder in My Documents that you want to stand out from others.

You do that by creating the file Desktop.ini in the folder. You can customize folders numerous ways using this file, but the two most interesting are setting unique icons for folders and displaying InfoTips when users position the mouse pointer over them. In this sample Desktop.ini file, the value `IconFile` points to the file containing the icon I want Windows Explorer to display for the folder. The value `IconIndex` is the index number of the icon, starting with 0, which is the first icon in the file. If you use an icon file instead of a DLL or EXE file, put the path of the file in `IconFile` and set `IconIndex` to 0. `InfoTip` is the text that I want Windows Explorer to display when I position the mouse pointer over the folder.

```
[.ShellClassInfo]
IconFile=C:\Windows\Regedit.exe
IconIndex=0
InfoTip="Manuscripts for my latest registry book."
```

Set the Desktop.ini file's Hidden And System attribute by typing the command **attrib +s +h** *filename* in the Run dialog box. You also set the folder's System attribute by typing the command **attrib +s** *foldername* in the Run dialog box. Figure 4-5 shows what the folder Registry Book looks like after creating this Desktop.ini file in it and setting the file and folder's attributes. Now whenever I position the mouse pointer over the folder, I am reminded of the important task at hand.

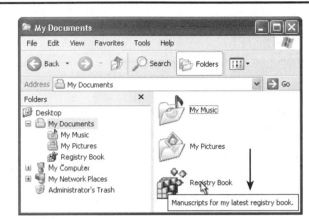

Figure 4-5   *When I hold the mouse pointer over the Registry Book folder, I see the text* Manuscripts for my latest registry book.

Adding File Templates

I'm sure you know about the New menu. Right-click within any folder, click New, and choose one of the templates available to create a new, empty file; then double-click the new file to edit it. By default, Windows XP provides the following templates: Briefcase, Bitmap Image, Wordpad Document, Rich Text Document, Text Document, Wave Sound, and Compressed (Zipped Folder). You can add templates, though, making the chore of starting new files quicker and easier.

Adding new templates is a two-step process:

1. In the file extension key HKCR\ *.ext*, create the ShellNew subkey.

2. Add one of the following four values to the ShellNew subkey to define how Windows XP creates new files of this type:

   - **NullFile.**   This is an empty REG_SZ value. Windows XP creates a zero-length file. Make sure that the associated program can handle empty files.

   - **FileName.**   This is a REG_SZ value that contains the name of a template file. By default, Windows XP looks in %USERPROFILE%\Templates for this file, but you can include an explicit path.

   - **Data.**   This is a REG_BINARY value containing a binary stream of data that Windows XP uses to create the new file.

   - **Command.**   This is a REG_SZ value. Windows XP executes the command in this value, passing it the path and name of the file it's to create.

For example, the template for the *.txt* file extension creates a null file. Then double-click the file to edit it in Notepad. If you'd rather create the file and open it in Notepad automatically, remove the value NullFile from the key HKCR\.txt\ShellNew. Then add the value Command, and set it to Notepad.exe "%1". When you create a new text file using the

New menu, Notepad starts and asks you if you want it create the new file. Ideally, any application you launch using the Command value would have a command-line option to suppress the prompt, though. Most don't, and you have no choice but to answer it.

Preventing Messenger from Running

Believe it or not, some people don't like Windows Messenger, and they tire of the program's constant nags to sign up for a Passport. Windows XP doesn't provide a user interface to remove Windows Messenger permanently (see Chapter 15, "Working Around IT Problems," for a simple way to uninstall it, though), but you can keep it from running. In Windows Messenger, click Tools, Options. On the Preferences tab of the Options dialog box, clear the Run This Program When Windows Starts check box. The problem with this setting is that the program still runs when other programs start. Clearing this check box removes the command that starts Windows Messenger from the key HKCU\Software\Microsoft\Windows\CurrentVersion\Run.

The most ironclad solution is to set the policy that prevents Windows Messenger from ever running. You can set this policy using Group Policy editor to edit the local Group Policy Object (see Chapter 6, "Using Registry-Based Policy"), or you can set the policy directly. To do that, create the REG_DWORD value PreventRun in HKLM\SOFTWARE\Policies \Microsoft\Messenger\Client and set it to 0x01. This setting affects all users who log on to the computer. When they try running Windows Messenger, they don't see an error message. It just doesn't run.

Personalizing the Start Menu

Windows XP has a nice new Start menu. And you can customize it more thoroughly than you could with any earlier version of Windows. Open the Taskbar And Start Menu Properties dialog box by clicking Start, Control Panel, Appearance And Themes, and then Taskbar And Start Menu. On the Start Menu tab, select either the Start Menu option or the Classic Start Menu option to choose which version of the Start menu to use, and then click Customize. The result is the Customize Start Menu dialog box, which you use to customize what Windows XP displays on the Start menu and in what form.

You can customize the Start menu other ways, too. For example, you can use Tweak UI to control which programs appear in the frequently used programs list. You learn how to use Tweak UI in Chapter 5, "Mapping Tweak UI." You can also use Tweak UI to customize which icons you see on the Start menu. In addition, Windows XP has dozens of policies that control the Start menu's behavior. Those policies aren't useful as hacks, however, because it's difficult to script and deploy policies to users in the Users and Power Users groups. Neither group can change settings in the Policies branch of the registry. This section focuses on deployable settings, and you can learn more about the policies in Appendix D, "Group Policies."

The following sections describe the most useful Start menu hacks. First you learn how to configure what appears and what doesn't appear on the Start menu. Then you learn how to prevent some programs from appearing on the frequently used programs list. You also learn how to restore the Start menu's sort order when it's not in alphabetical order.

Configuring the Menu's Contents

Even though you can completely customize the Start menu in the user interface, power users and IT professionals will likely want to script Start menu customizations. Power users don't want to reconfigure the Start menu every time they install Windows XP. IT Professionals can use scripts to deploy these settings or configure them automatically when creating default user profiles (see Chapter 10, "Deploying User Profiles").

If you want to script these settings, you need to know where to find them in the registry. As it happens, all these settings are in the same place: HKCU\Software\Microsoft\Windows \CurrentVersion\Explorer\Advanced. Table 4-4 describes the values you can add to this key if they aren't already present. You see two sections in this table. The first section, "Class Start Menu," contains values that affect the classic Start menu. The second section, "New Start Menu," contains values that affect the new Start menu, better known as the Start panel. Most of these settings are REG_DWORD values, but some are REG_SZ values. If the possible data for one of the settings in Table 4-4 includes 0x01, 0x02, and so on, it's a REG_DWORD value. If the possible data includes NO or YES, it's a REG_SZ value.

Table 4-4 Start Menu Settings

Name	Data
Classic Start Menu	
StartMenuAdminTools	NO—Hide Administrative Tools YES—Display Administrative Tools
CascadeControlPanel	NO—Display Control Panel as link YES—Display Control Panel as menu
CascadeMyDocuments	NO—Display My Documents as link YES—Display My Documents as menu
CascadeMyPictures	NO—Display My Pictures as link YES—Display My Pictures as menu
CascadePrinters	NO—Display Printers as link YES—Display Printers as menu
IntelliMenus	0x00—Don't use personalized menus 0x01—Use Personalized Menus
CascadeNetworkConnections	NO—Display Network Connections as link YES—Display Network Connections as menu
Start_LargeMFUIcons	0x00—Show small icons in Start menu 0x01—Show large icons in Start menu
StartMenuChange	0x00—Disable dragging and dropping 0x01—Enable dragging and dropping
StartMenuFavorites	0x00—Hide Favorites 0x01—Display Favorites
StartMenuLogoff	0x00—Hide Log Off 0x01—Display Log Off
StartMenuRun	0x00—Hide Run command 0x01—Display Run command

Table 4-4   Start Menu Settings *(continued)*

Name	Data
StartMenuScrollPrograms	NO—Don't scroll Programs menu YES—Scroll Programs menu
New Start Menu	
Start_ShowControlPanel	0x00—Hide Control Panel 0x01—Show Control Panel as link 0x02—Show Control Panel as menu
Start_EnableDragDrop	0x00—Disable dragging and dropping 0x01—Enable dragging and dropping
StartMenuFavorites	0x00—Hide Favorites menu 0x01—Show the Favorites menu
Start_ShowMyComputer	0x00—Hide My Computer 0x01—Show My Computer as link 0x02—Show My Computer as menu
Start_ShowMyDocs	0x00—Hide My Documents 0x01—Show My Documents as link 0x02—Show My Documents as menu
Start_ShowMyMusic	0x00—Hide My Music 0x01—Show My Music as link 0x02—Show My Music as menu
Start_ShowMyPics	0x00—Hide My Pictures 0x01—Show My Pictures as link 0x02—Show My Pictures as menu
Start_ShowNetConn	0x00—Hide Network Connections 0x01—Show Network Connections as link 0x02—Show Network Connections as menu
Start_AdminToolsTemp	0x00—Hide Administrative Tools 0x01—Show on All Programs menu 0x02—Show on All Programs menu and Start menu
Start_ShowHelp	0x00—Hide Help and Support 0x01—Show Help and Support
Start_ShowNetPlaces	0x00—Hide My Network Places 0x01—Show My Network Places
Start_ShowOEMLink	0x00—Hide Manufacturer Link 0x01—Show Manufacturer Link
Start_ShowPrinters	0x00—Hide Printers and Faxes 0x01—Show Printers and Faxes
Start_ShowRun	0x00—Hide Run command 0x01—Show Run command
Start_ShowSearch	0x00—Hide Search command 0x01—Show Search command
Start_ScrollPrograms	0x00—Don't scroll Programs menu 0x01—Scroll Programs menu

Trimming the Frequently Used Programs List

Each time you run a program, Windows XP adds it to the list of frequently used programs you see on the Start menu (see Figure 4-6). You might not want every program you open to appear in this list, however. For example, I don't want to see Notepad in this list, nor do I want to see Command Prompt. You can choose which programs do and don't pop up in this list by customizing `HKCR\Applications`.

`HKCR\Applications` contains subkeys for a variety of programs that Windows XP knows about. The name of each subkey is the name of the program file. Thus, you see the subkeys `notepad.exe` and `explorer.exe` in `HKCR\Applications`. If you want to customize another program, add its subkey to this key. For example, to customize whether Command Prompt appears in the list of frequently used programs, add the subkey `cmd.exe` to `HKCR\Applications`. Then, to keep the program off of the list, add the `REG_SZ` value `NoStartPage` to it.

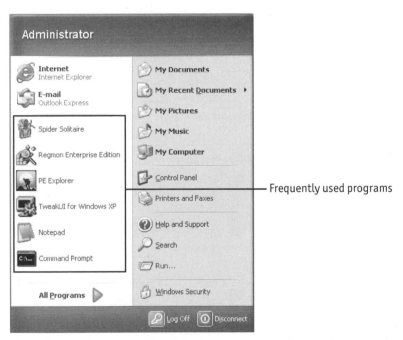

— Frequently used programs

Figure 4-6   *Windows XP displays the programs you frequently use on the Start menu.*

Restoring the Sort Order

Unless you disable dragging and dropping on the Start menu (see Table 4-4), users can sort the All Programs menu. Windows XP also sometimes adds new shortcuts to the bottom of the All Programs menu. In either case, finding the program you want to run is difficult when the sort order of the Start menu gets out of hand.

HKCU\Software\Microsoft\Windows\CurrentVersion\Explorer\MenuOrder contains the sort order of the Favorites menu and Start menu. The subkey Favorites contains the sort order of the Favorites menu. The subkey Start Menu contains the sort order of the classic Start menu, and the subkey Start Menu2 contains the sort order of the new Start menu. Deciphering the contents of these three keys is next to ridiculous, but you can remove any of them to re-sort the corresponding menu in alphabetical order. For example, to restore the All Programs menu to alphabetical order, remove the subkey Start Menu2. To restore the Favorites menu in both Windows Explorer and Internet Explorer, remove the subkey Favorites.

I like to keep a script handy that automatically removes MenuOrder. The following listing is an example. Save this listing to the text file Resort.inf, right-click it, and then click Install. This script is different from the others you've seen in this chapter because you can't uninstall it; its changes are permanent:

Listing 4-5   Resort.inf

```
[Version]
Signature=$CHICAGO$

[DefaultInstall]
DelReg=Reg.Settings

[Reg.Settings]
HKCU,Software\Microsoft\Windows\CurrentVersion\Explorer\MenuOrder
```

Tip   You sorted the Start menu just the way you wanted it—wouldn't it be dandy if you could transfer that sort order to another computer? You're in luck. Export the key MenuOrder to a REG file, and then import that REG file to the computer on which you want to use that sort order.

Customizing Internet Explorer

Windows XP comes with Internet Explorer 6. IT professionals can customize Internet Explorer in a number of ways using the Internet Explorer Administration Kit. This tool is available at *http://www.microsoft.com/downloads*, and it also comes with the Office XP Resource Kit. You can do the following with the kit:

- Tailor Internet Explorer and other Internet components to fit the needs of your enterprise or users. For example, you can customize the Links bar and Favorites menu to promote your intranet or provide helpful information.

- Configure and deploy settings without ever touching desktops.

- Customize the setup program so that it requires little or no user interaction.

- Control which settings users can change so that IT professionals can ensure that security, connection, and important settings stick to corporate standards.

For more information about the Internet Explorer Administration Kit, see *http://www.microsoft.com/windows/ieak/default.asp*. The following sections describe a few of my favorite customizations for Internet Explorer, including extending its shortcut menus, changing the toolbar's background, and adding search URLs to it.

Extending the Shortcut Menus

Right-click a Web page, and Internet Explorer displays a shortcut menu. You can customize this shortcut menu by adding commands to it that you link to scripts in an HTML file. For example, you can add a command to the shortcut menu that opens the current Web page in a new window or highlights the selected text on it.

`HKCU\Software\Microsoft\Internet Explorer\MenuExt` is where Internet Explorer looks for extensions. Add this key if it doesn't exist, and then add a subkey for each command that you want to add. Then set that subkey's default value to the path and name of the HTML file containing the script that carries out the command. For example, to add the command Magnify to the shortcut menu that runs the script in the HTML file C:\Windows \Web\Magnify.htm, add the subkey `Magnify` and set its default value to `C:\Windows\Web \Magnify.htm`. When you choose this command on Internet Explorer's shortcut menu, it executes the script that the file contains. Then you need to create Magnify.htm. The following listing is the contents of Magnify.htm. `external.menuArguments` is a property that contains the window object in which you executed the command. Because you have access to the window object, you can do almost anything you like in that window, such as reformatting its contents, and so on.

Listing 4-6   Magnify.htm

```
<HTML>
<SCRIPT LANGUAGE="JavaScript" defer>
var objWin = external.menuArguments;
var objDoc = objWin.document;
var objSel = objDoc.selection;
var objRange = objSel.createRange();
objRange.execCommand( "FontSize", 0, "+2" );
</SCRIPT>
</HTML>
```

You can configure the shortcut menus to which Internet Explorer adds your command. In the subkey you created for the extension, add the REG_DWORD value `Contexts`, and apply the bit masks shown in Table 4-5 (on the next page) to it. For example, to limit the previous example so that Internet Explorer displays it only for text selections, add the REG_DWORD value `Contexts` to `Magnify`, and set it to `0x10`.

Table 4-5   Internet Explorer Menu Extensions

Bit mask	Menu
0x01	Default
0x02	Image
0x04	Control
0x08	Table
0x10	Text Selection
0x11	Anchor
0x12	Unknown

Note   If you're interested in learning more about extending Internet Explorer, you should check out Microsoft's documentation for extending the browser. You find it at *http:// msdn.microsoft.com/workshop/browser/ext/overview/overview.asp*. This requires proficiency with writing scripts and HTML, though.

Changing the Toolbar Background

You can customize the background you see on Internet Explorer's toolbar. It's just a bitmap. To change the background, create a REG_SZ value called BackBitmap in HKCU\Software \Microsoft\Internet Explorer\Toolbar. Set this value to the path and name of the bitmap file you want to see in the toolbar's background. Internet Explorer tiles the bitmap horizontally and vertically to fill the toolbar.

Customizing Search URLs

Search URLs are a convenient way to use different Internet search engines. For example, you might have a search URL called *news* that searches Google Groups. Type **news Jerry Honeycutt** in the address bar to automatically search Google Groups for all UseNet articles that contain the words *Jerry* and *Honeycutt*.

HKCU\Software\Microsoft\Internet Explorer\SearchURL is where you create search URLs. If you don't see this subkey, create it. Then add a subkey for each search prefix you want to use. To use the example I just gave, create the subkey news. Set the default value of the prefix's subkey to the URL of the search engine. Use %s as a placeholder for the search string. Internet Explorer replaces the %s with any text you type to the right of the prefix. Continue the example, and set it to http://groups.google.com/groups?q=%s&hl=en.

Add the REG_SZ values shown in Table 4-6 to the prefix key you created. The purpose of these values is to describe what to substitute for special characters in your search string, including a space, percent sign (%), ampersand (&), and plus sign (+). These characters have special meaning when submitting forms to Web sites, so you must substitute a plus sign for a space, for example, or %26 for an ampersand. Thus, the browser translates the string *Ben & Jerry* to *Ben+%26+Jerry*.

Deriving the URL that you must use is easy. Open the search engine that you want to add to Internet Explorer's search URLs, and then search for something. When the browser displays the results, copy the URL from the address bar, replacing your search word with a %s. For example, after searching Google Groups for *sample*, the resulting URL is *http:// groups.google.com/groups?q=sample&hl=en*. Replace the word *sample* with %s to get `http://groups.google.com/groups?q=%s&hl=en`.

Table 4-6   Values in Search URLs

Name	Data
<space>	+
%	%25
&	%26
+	%2B

This hack is so useful that I have a script that automatically creates search URLs for the search engines I use most often. Copy the following listing to the file Search.inf, right-click it, and then click Install. You can remove this script and all its settings using Add Or Remove Programs. This script creates search URLs for the five search engines that I use most often. The search URL *news* searches Google Groups; *msn* searches MSN; *ms* searches Microsoft's Web site; *msdn* searches MSDN; and *technet* searches TechNet.

Listing 4-7   Search.inf

```
[Version]
Signature=$CHICAGO$

[DefaultInstall]
AddReg=Reg.Settings
AddReg=Reg.Uninstall
CopyFiles=Inf.Copy

[DefaultUninstall]
DelReg=Reg.Settings
DelReg=Reg.Uninstall
DelFiles=Inf.Copy

[Reg.Settings]
HKCU,Software\Microsoft\Internet Explorer\SearchURL

HKCU,Software\Microsoft\Internet Explorer\SearchURL\news,,0,"%GOOGLE%"
HKCU,Software\Microsoft\Internet Explorer\SearchURL\news," ",0,"+"
HKCU,Software\Microsoft\Internet Explorer\SearchURL\news,"%",0,"%25"
HKCU,Software\Microsoft\Internet Explorer\SearchURL\news,"&",0,"%26"
HKCU,Software\Microsoft\Internet Explorer\SearchURL\news,"+",0,"%2B"

HKCU,Software\Microsoft\Internet Explorer\SearchURL\msn,,0,"%MSN%"
HKCU,Software\Microsoft\Internet Explorer\SearchURL\msn," ",0,"+"
HKCU,Software\Microsoft\Internet Explorer\SearchURL\msn,"%",0,"%25"
```

```
HKCU,Software\Microsoft\Internet Explorer\SearchURL\msn,"&",0,"%26"
HKCU,Software\Microsoft\Internet Explorer\SearchURL\msn,"+",0,"%2B"

HKCU,Software\Microsoft\Internet Explorer\SearchURL\ms,,0,"%MICROSOFT%"
HKCU,Software\Microsoft\Internet Explorer\SearchURL\ms," ",0,"+"
HKCU,Software\Microsoft\Internet Explorer\SearchURL\ms,"%",0,"%25"
HKCU,Software\Microsoft\Internet Explorer\SearchURL\ms,"&",0,"%26"
HKCU,Software\Microsoft\Internet Explorer\SearchURL\ms,"+",0,"%2B"

HKCU,Software\Microsoft\Internet Explorer\SearchURL\msdn,,0,"%MSDN%"
HKCU,Software\Microsoft\Internet Explorer\SearchURL\msdn," ",0,"+"
HKCU,Software\Microsoft\Internet Explorer\SearchURL\msdn,"%",0,"%25"
HKCU,Software\Microsoft\Internet Explorer\SearchURL\msdn,"&",0,"%26"
HKCU,Software\Microsoft\Internet Explorer\SearchURL\msdn,"+",0,"%2B"

HKCU,Software\Microsoft\Internet Explorer\SearchURL\technet,,0,"%TECHNET%"
HKCU,Software\Microsoft\Internet Explorer\SearchURL\technet," ",0,"+"
HKCU,Software\Microsoft\Internet Explorer\SearchURL\technet,"%",0,"%25"
HKCU,Software\Microsoft\Internet Explorer\SearchURL\technet,"&",0,"%26"
HKCU,Software\Microsoft\Internet Explorer\SearchURL\technet,"+",0,"%2B"

[Reg.Uninstall]
HKCU,Software\Microsoft\Windows\CurrentVersion\Uninstall\%NAME%
HKCU,Software\Microsoft\Windows\CurrentVersion\Uninstall\%NAME%,DisplayName\
,,"%NAME%"
HKCU,Software\Microsoft\Windows\CurrentVersion\Uninstall\%NAME%,UninstallString\
,,"Rundll32.exe setupapi.dll,InstallHinfSection DefaultUninstall 132 "\
"%53%\Application Data\Custom\Search.inf"

[Inf.Copy]
Search.inf

[DestinationDirs]
Inf.Copy=53,Application Data\Custom

[SourceDisksNames]
55=%DISKNAME%

[SourceDisksFiles]
Search.inf=55

[Strings]
NAME     = "Jerry's IE Search URLs"
DISKNAME = "Setup Files"

; Search URLs

GOOGLE   = "http://groups.google.com/groups?q=%s&hl=en"
MSN      = "http://search.msn.com/results.asp?RS=CHECKED&FORM=MSNH&v=1&q=%s"
```

```
MICROSOFT = "http://search.microsoft.com/default.asp?so=RECCNT&siteid=us&p=1&"\
"nq=NEW&qu=%s&IntlSearch=&boolean=ALL&ig=1&ig=3&ig=5&ig=7&ig=9&ig=2&ig=4&ig=6&"\
"ig=8&ig=10&i=00&i=02&i=04&i=06&i=08&i=01&i=03&i=05&i=07&i=09"
MSDN      = "http://search.microsoft.com/default.asp?qu=%s&boolean=ALL&nq=NEW&"\
"so=RECCNT&p=1&ig=01&i=00&i=01&i=02&i=03&i=04&i=05&i=06&i=07&i=08&i=09&i=10&"\
"i=11&i=12&i=13&i=14&i=15&i=16&i=17&i=18&i=19&i=20&i=21&i=22&i=23&i=24&i=25&"\
"i=26&i=27&i=28&i=29&i=30&i=31&i=32&i=33&i=34&i=35&i=36&i=37&i=38&i=39&i=40&"\
"i=41&i=42&i=43&i=44&i=45&i=46&i=47&i=48&i=49&i=50&i=51&siteid=us/dev"
TECHNET   = "http://search.microsoft.com/default.asp?qu=%s&boolean=ALL&nq=NEW&"\
"so=RECCNT&p=1&ig=01&ig=02&ig=03&ig=04&i=00&i=01&i=02&i=03&i=04&i=05&i=06&i=07&"\
"i=08&i=09&i=10&i=11&i=12&i=13&i=14&i=15&i=16&i=17&i=18&i=19&i=20&i=21&i=22&"\
"i=23&i=24&i=25&i=26&i=27&i=28&i=29&i=30&i=31&i=32&i=33&i=34&i=35&i=36&i=37&"\
"i=38&i=39&siteid=us/itresources"
```

Clearing History Lists

So that you can quickly open documents and programs you use frequently, Windows XP keeps history lists. These are MRU or most recently used lists. Table 4-7 shows you where in the registry the operating system stores these lists. Clear these lists by removing the keys associated with them. After removing the `RecentDocs` key, make sure you delete the contents of %USERPROFILE%\Recent, too.

Search Assistant's history list deserves a bit more attention. The key `ACMru` contains a variety of subkeys, depending on the types of things for which you've searched. For example, if you search for files and folders, you'll see the subkey `5603`, which contains a list of the different search strings. If you search the Internet using Search Assistant, you'll see the subkey `5001`. You can remove each subkey individually to clear a specific type of query's history list, or you can remove the key `ACMru` to clear all of Search Assistant's history lists. The table contains a list of the subkeys that I've found in `ACMru`.

Table 4-7   History Lists

Location	Subkey
Internet Explorer's address bar	HKCU\Software\Microsoft\Internet Explorer\TypedURLs
Run dialog box	HKCU\Software\Microsoft\Windows\CurrentVersion\Explorer\RunMRU
Documents menu	HKCU\Software\Microsoft\Windows\CurrentVersion\Explorer\RecentDocs
Common dialog boxes	HKCU\Software\Microsoft\Windows\CurrentVersion\Explorer\ComDlg32\LastVisitedMRU
Search Assistant	HKCU\Software\Microsoft\Search Assistant\ACMru 5001. Internet 5603. Files and folders 5604. Pictures, music, and video 5647. Printers, computers, and people

Running Programs at Startup

The Run and RunOnce subkeys are useful for running programs automatically when the computer starts or when users log on to the computer. In fact, these keys are a handy way to deploy software that requires administrator privileges. You learn about this use for these keys in Chapter 15, "Working Around IT Problems."

The Run and RunOnce keys are in two different locations. First you see these subkeys in HKLM\SOFTWARE\Microsoft\Windows\CurrentVersion. Commands here run when any user logs on to the computer. You also see these subkeys in HKCU\Software\Microsoft \Windows\CurrentVersion. Commands in this branch run after the specific user logs on to Windows XP. As well, Windows XP treats commands in Run differently than commands in RunOnce:

- **Run.** Windows XP runs the commands in this subkey every time a user logs on to the computer.

- **RunOnce.** Windows XP runs the commands in this subkey once and then removes the key from RunOnce after the command completes successfully.

To add a command to Run or RunOnce in HKLM or HKCU, create a REG_SZ value that has an arbitrary but descriptive name. Put the command line you want to execute in the new value. For example, the Run key in HKCU has the value MSMSGS by default, and this value contains "C:\Program Files\Messenger\msmsgs.exe" /background, which runs Windows Messenger every time the user logs on to Windows XP. Although you might have occasion to add commands to the Run subkey, it's more common to remove commands from this subkey to prevent programs from running when you start or log on to Windows XP.

Controlling Registry Editor

Registry Editor (Regedit) has a few features that most users like but some prefer to disable. The following sections show you how to customize these features. First you customize the default action for REG files. In other words, you can control what Regedit does when you double-click a file with the *.reg* extension. Second you prevent Regedit from saving its settings when you close it. By doing so, Regedit opens the window to the same size and position every time.

Default Action for REG Files

When you double-click a file with the *.reg* extension, Regedit imports the file's settings into the registry after you click Yes when it prompts you to merge the file's settings. If you edit REG files frequently, this behavior might concern you because you might accidentally import a REG file when you meant to edit it. Conversely, if you frequently import REG files, you might want to prevent Regedit from prompting you to merge the file's settings into the registry. Here are how to accomplish both tasks:

- **Prevent Regedit from automatically importing REG files.**   To do this, you must make the default action for REG files something other than opening the file, such as editing the file. To do that, set the default value of `HKCR\regfile\shell` to `edit`. The next time you double-click a REG file, it'll open in Notepad.

- **Merge a REG file into the registry without prompting.**   To do this, change the command line that Windows XP executes when you open the file. Set the default value of `HKCR\regfile\shell\open\command` to `regedit.exe /s "%1"`.

Storing Window Position and Size

Each time you close Regedit, the program stores its view settings (window position and size, column sizes, last open key, and so on) in the registry. The next time you run Regedit, it restores the window using those settings. Many users like Regedit to forget these settings, but Regedit doesn't provide an option to do that.

`HKCU\Software\Microsoft\Windows\CurrentVersion\Applets\Regedit` is the key in which Regedit stores these settings. The trick is to set the key's ACL (Access Control List) so you can't write to it, and then Regedit can't store its last view settings there. You can either delete the values in this key so Regedit uses defaults every time it starts, or customize them so Regedit uses your custom settings every time it starts. In either case, set the key's ACL so you can read but not write values:

1. In Regedit, click the key `Applets\Regedit`.

2. On the Edit menu, click Permissions.

3. Click Advanced, clear the Inherit From Parent The Permission Entries That Apply To Child Objects check box, click Copy, and then click OK.

4. In the Group Or User Names list, select each account and group; then clear the Full Control check box.

Note   See Chapter 7, "Managing Registry Security," for more information about configuring keys' ACLs. In particular, if you decide that you don't like this customization, you'll have to take ownership of the key to gain full control of it again, assuming that you don't already own the key.

Logging On Automatically

Some users don't like having to log on to Windows XP. When they restart the computer, they want it to boot all the way to the desktop without stopping at the Log On To Windows dialog box along the way. Before I tell you that this is possible (oops), let me add that you should never skip the logon process if your computer is connected to a business network. Obvious security concerns are present when you allow anyone with access to your computer to have full access to all of its contents and the network.

`HKLM\SOFTWARE\Microsoft\Windows NT\CurrentVersion\Winlogon` is where you configure the ability to log on to Windows XP automatically. First you set the `REG_SZ` value `AutoAdminLogon` to 1, which turns on this feature. Just remember that this is a `REG_SZ` value and not a `REG_DWORD` value. Next set the values `DefaultUserName` and `DefaultPassword` to the user name and password that you want to use to log on to the operating system. Both are `REG_SZ` values. Last, set the `REG_SZ` value `DefaultDomainName` to the name of the domain that's authenticating your name and password. Table 4-8 summarizes these values, which you create if they don't already exist.

Table 4-8   Values in Winlogon

Name	Type	Data
HKLM\SOFTWARE\Microsoft\Windows NT\CurrentVersion\Winlogon		
AutoAdminLogon	REG_SZ	0 | 1
DefaultUserName	REG_SZ	*Name*
DefaultDomainName	REG_SZ	*Domain*
DefaultPassword	REG_SZ	*Password*

Changing User Information

On a regular basis, I get asked questions about changing user information. That's the information you provided when you installed Windows XP. You can change it. Both of the following values are in the key `HKLM\SOFTWARE\Microsoft\Windows NT\CurrentVersion`:

- `RegisteredOrganization`.   The name of the organization

- `RegisteredOwner`.   The name of the user

Both are `REG_SZ` values. Changing the registered organization and owner names doesn't affect installed applications. However, applications you install after changing these values are likely to pick up the new names.

Looking for More Hacks

This chapter just scratches the surface. If I had the space, I could fill another 50 pages with great Windows XP hacks. But you do find good hacks in other chapters:

- Chapter 5, "Mapping Tweak UI," shows you where all the settings in Tweak UI are in the registry. Tweak UI makes the most popular hacks available in one sleek user interface, and this chapter documents the corresponding hacks.

- Chapter 8, "Finding Registry Settings," helps you discover your own hacks.

- Chapter 15, "Working Around IT Problems," contains hacks that apply to IT scenarios, such as deploying software or fixing IT-unfriendly behavior.

- Appendix A, "File Associations," describes `HKCR` in detail, including hacking it.

And don't forget the chapters in Part IV, "Appendices." These chapters are the ultimate source for registry hacks because they document the most interesting settings found in the registry.

Note   Quite possibly the single largest and most usable source of registry hacks is published by WinGuides at *http://www.winguides.com/registry*. Download the Registry Guide, which is an HTML help file that's well organized and formatted. This guide contains hundreds if not thousands of useful settings that enable you to customize all versions of Windows. Another useful and popular Web site is Jerold Schulman's at *http://www.jsiinc.com*. He has put significant energy into the thousands of IT tips and tricks on his Web site.

Mapping Tweak UI

Microsoft Tweak UI is a must-have tool for anyone customizing Microsoft Windows XP. It prevents users from opening the registry and customizing settings that aren't available in the operating system's user interface. Tweak UI started as a grassroots utility built by a handful of rebellious programmers and ended up one of the most popular downloads on the Internet. Microsoft has released versions of this tool for every version of Windows since Microsoft Windows 95. The company even included it on the Microsoft Windows 98 CD. And now, it's available for Windows XP, and it includes even more customizations.

You can download Tweak UI from *http://www.microsoft.com /downloads* (Microsoft split the original Microsoft Power-Toys programs apart). You can also download it from *http://downloads-zdnet.com.com*, one of my favorite download Web sites. The file you download is called TweakUiPowertoy-Setup.exe. Run this program to install Tweak UI on your computer. To run Tweak UI, click Start, All Programs, Powertoys for Windows XP, and Tweak UI for Windows XP. In the left pane, click a category, and then in the right pane, edit the settings you want to change. The program is mostly self-explanatory; you see a description of each setting at the bottom of the window. Pay attention to the bottom part of the windows. It tells you whether the settings in that category are per-user or per-machine. Per-user settings sometimes require you to log off and back on to Windows XP in order for them to take affect. Per-machine settings affect every user who logs on to the computer.

This chapter isn't about *using* Tweak UI—that's too easy. Instead, I'll tell you where in the registry Tweak UI changes each setting. Information like this is powerful. You can script Tweak UI customizations. For example, power users can write a script to apply their favorite Tweak UI settings, and then apply all those settings to every computer they use simply by running the script. The process is streamlined—compare one double-click to dozens of clicks and edits—and the consistency doesn't hurt, either.

IT professionals can write a script to deploy useful settings to users or include those settings in default user profiles for new users (see Chapter 10, "Deploying User Profiles"). Scripting these settings is amazingly easy, and you learn how to do that in Chapter 9, "Scripting Registry Changes."

The sections in this chapter correspond to the major categories in Tweak UI. (I skipped the About and Repair categories because they have little to do with the registry. You should look at both, though. The About category contains useful tips for using Windows XP. The Repair category can fix a variety of small problems, including messed up icons, fonts, and folders.) Each section contains a brief description of the settings in that category and how to change them in the registry. In most cases, each section contains a table that describes each setting's value name, value type, and value data. Each table contains subheadings that show the key for the values following it.

General

The items in the Settings list in the General category are effects that you can enable or disable. In fact, the Settings list, shown in Figure 5-1, used to be called the Effects list in earlier versions of Tweak UI. Settings range from list box and window animations to menu fading. Disable these settings only on slower computers when you think you can improve the user interface's crispness; otherwise, these settings make Windows XP look great.

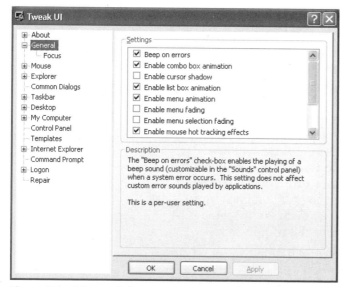

Figure 5-1 *Many of these settings are in the Performance Options dialog box. Right-click My Computer, click Properties, and in the Performance area of the Advanced tab of the Properties dialog box, click Settings.*

You see all the settings in the General category in Table 5-1. One value needs a bit of explaining, though: UserPreferencesMask. The bits in this REG_BINARY value are various settings, which Chapter 4, "Hacking the Registry," and Appendix B, "Per-User Settings," describe in detail. To turn on a setting, set the appropriate bit to 1 in UserPreferencesMask. To turn off a setting, clear the corresponding bit. The number in the Data column tells you which bit to toggle. The easiest way to toggle the bit is to use Calculator in scientific mode. Bitwise math is beyond most simple scripting techniques, including REG files. If you want to create a script to change the settings in UserPreferencesMask, use INF files or look to Windows Scripting Host (see Chapter 9, "Scripting Registry Changes").

Tip UserPreferencesMask is an example of a REG_DWORD value disguised as a REG_BINARY value. When you see a 32-bit binary value, chances are, it's really a double-word value. In that case, you can safely replace the value with a REG_DWORD. Don't forget that Windows XP uses the little-endian architecture, though, so it stores double-word values in reverse-byte order. In other words, you replace the REG_BINARY value 0x04 0x03 0x02 0x01 with the REG_DWORD 0x01020304. See Chapter 1, "Learning the Basics," for a refresher on little-endian architecture and bitwise math.

Table 5-1 Values in General

Setting	Name	Type	Data
HKCU\Control Panel\Sound			
Beep on errors	Beep	REG_SZ	Yes | No
HKCU\Control Panel\Desktop			
Enable combo box animation	UserPreferencesMask	REG_BINARY	Bit 0x0004
Enable cursor shadow	UserPreferencesMask	REG_BINARY	Bit 0x2000
Enable list box animation	UserPreferencesMask	REG_BINARY	Bit 0x0008
Enable menu animation	UserPreferencesMask	REG_BINARY	Bit 0x0002
Enable menu fading	UserPreferencesMask	REG_BINARY	Bit 0x0200
Enable menu selection fading	UserPreferencesMask	REG_BINARY	Bit 0x0400
Enable mouse hot tracking effects	UserPreferencesMask	REG_BINARY	Bit 0x0080
Enable tooltip animation	UserPreferencesMask	REG_BINARY	Bit 0x0800
Enable tooltip fade	UserPreferencesMask	REG_BINARY	Bit 0x1000
Show Windows version on desktop	PaintDesktopVersion	REG_DWORD	0X00 | 0X01
HKCU\Control Panel\Desktop\WindowMetrics			
Enable Window Animation	MinAnimate	REG_SZ	0 | 1

Tracking Down Tweak UI Settings

Are you curious about how I tracked down all the Tweak UI program's settings? I used the techniques you learn about in Chapter 8, "Finding Registry Settings." The first technique is a program from Winternals Software called Registry Monitor that monitors access to the registry. It reports every setting that Windows XP or other programs read or write.

The second technique, and the one that I used most, is to compare snapshots of the registry before and after making the change. Here's how that process worked for me while writing this chapter:

1. Export the branch of the registry that you suspect contains the setting to a REG file. If in doubt, export the entire registry. Name the file Before.reg.
2. Change the setting. In this case, change a setting in Tweak UI.
3. Export the same branch of the registry that you exported in step 1. Name the file After.reg.
4. Compare both files; the differences between them represent the changes in the registry.

The primary tool that I use to compare REG files is Windiff, which comes with the Windows XP Support Tools and the Windows 2000 Resource Kit. If you don't have Windiff, you can use Microsoft Word 2002 just as effectively: Open the first REG file in Word, and then click Tools, Compare And Merge Documents to compare it to the second file.

Focus

When an application needs your attention—or when it simply wants to annoy you—it steals the focus from the application in which you're currently working. This leads to frustration as you flip back and forth between windows. The settings in the Focus category prevent that scenario by causing applications to flash their taskbar buttons to get your attention rather than stealing focus from the application in the foreground.

Table 5-2 describes the settings in the Focus category. The default value for `ForegroundLockTimeout` is `0x00030D40`, or `200000`. This value is the time in milliseconds before Windows XP allows an application to steal the focus from the foreground application. To convert 200000 to seconds, divide it by 1000 (200 seconds). You see the value `ForegroundFlashCount` in the table twice, because setting it to `0` causes the taskbar button to flash until you click it; otherwise, the taskbar button flashes the number of times you set in `ForegroundFlashCount`.

Table 5-2   Values in Focus

Setting	Name	Type	Data
HKCU\Control Panel\Desktop			
Prevent applications from stealing focus	ForegroundLockTimeout	REG_DWORD	*N*
Flash taskbar button until I click on it	ForegroundFlashCount	REG_DWORD	0x00
Flash taskbar button *N* times	ForegroundFlashCount	REG_DWORD	*N*

Mouse

The settings in the Mouse category control the rodent's sensitivity. Before adjusting these values manually, use Tweak UI to figure out what the best settings are for you. You can use the test icon, shown in Figure 5-2, to try different values. After you've settled on a value, you're good to go.

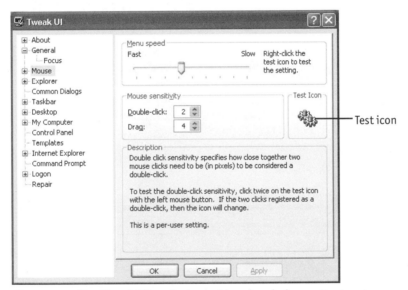

Figure 5-2   *Use Tweak UI to find suitable values before trying to set mouse sensitivity values manually.*

The first value in Table 5-3 (on the next page), MenuShowDelay, is the time in milliseconds that Windows XP waits before opening a menu to which you point. The default is 400, or .4 seconds, but you can cut that number in half if you want menus to open faster. The values DragHeight and DragWith are the settings that specify the distance (in number of pixels) that you must move the mouse with a button held down before Windows XP recognizes that you're dragging something. The default value is 4 pixels, and you should keep the height and width the same as each other. The last two values, DoubleClickHeight and DoubleClick-Width, are the settings that specify the maximum distance (in pixels) allowed between two mouse clicks before Windows XP recognizes that you're double-clicking something. The default value is 2. These are REG_SZ values; Windows XP expects decimal rather than hexadecimal numbers.

Table 5-3   Values in Mouse

Setting	Name	Type	Data
HKCU\Control Panel\Desktop			
Menu speed	MenuShowDelay	REG_SZ	0 to 65534
Drag	DragHeight DragWidth	REG_SZ	0 to N
HKCU\Control Panel\Mouse			
Double-click	DoubleClickHeight DoubleClickWidth	REG_SZ	0 to N

Hover

The settings in the Hover category are similar to the settings in the Mouse category. They control the size of the area in pixels and the time in milliseconds that the mouse pointer must remain in one spot before Windows XP recognizes that the mouse is hovering over something. Table 5-4 describes the values for this category. The default sensitivity is 2, and you should keep the height and width equal to each other. The default hover time is 400. Cut that number in half to select objects quicker when you point to them. If you don't see these values in the registry, create them.

Table 5-4   Values in Hover

Setting	Name	Type	Data
HKCU\Control Panel\Mouse			
Hover sensitivity	MouseHoverWidth MouseHoverHeight	REG_SZ	0 to N
Hover time (ms)	MouseHoverTime	REG_SZ	0 to N

Wheel

The setting in the Wheel category controls the mouse wheel. The value WheelScrollLines is the only value in Table 5-5. That's because the three different options in this category relate to the different data you can assign to this value. The default is 3, which enables the mouse wheel to scroll 3 lines at a time.

Table 5-5 Values in Wheel

Setting	Name	Type	Data
HKCU\Control Panel\Desktop			
Use mouse wheel for scrolling	WheelScrollLines	REG_SZ	0
Scroll a page at a time	WheelScrollLines	REG_SZ	-1
Scroll *N* lines at a time	WheelScrollLines	REG_SZ	0 to *N*

X-Mouse

The settings in the X-Mouse category, as described in Table 5-6, used to be one of my favorite customizations. I liked the idea of windows popping to the foreground when I pointed at them. It gets annoying after a while, but it's a novelty you should try because you might like it. Here's more on each of these settings:

- **Activation follows mouse (X-Mouse).** Gives focus to any window to which you point but doesn't raise the window to the foreground unless you check the next option in this list.
- **Autoraise when activating.** Brings the window that has focus to the foreground.
- **Activation delay (ms).** Specifies the delay (in milliseconds) before Windows XP brings the window to which you pointed to the foreground.

These settings in the value UserPreferencesMask are bits, which you learned about earlier in this chapter. The default value for ActiveWndTrkTimeout is 0, but 400 is a more reasonable delay. A higher timeout prevents windows from flipping between the foreground and background, making this feature much less annoying and more useful.

Table 5-6 Values in X-Mouse

Setting	Name	Type	Data
HKCU\Control Panel\Desktop			
Activation follows mouse (X-Mouse)	UserPreferencesMask	REG_BINARY	Bit 0x0001
Autoraise when activating	UserPreferencesMask	REG_BINARY	Bit 0x0040
Activation delay (ms)	ActiveWndTrkTimeout	REG_DWORD	0 to *N*

Explorer

The settings in the Explorer category are all over the map: You can customize the Start menu, enable smooth scrolling, and automatically clear the document history. Table 5-7 on the next page maps the settings in this category to their registry values. Create any keys and values that you don't see in the registry.

You'll notice that the setting Show Links On Favorites Menu is missing from Table 5-7. This is because that setting isn't in the registry. When you disable the Links menu, Tweak UI simply sets the Links folder's hidden attribute. Enable the folder, and Tweak UI clears the Links folder's hidden attribute. This is the only way to prevent Internet Explorer from displaying the Links folder on the Favorites menu.

Note Most of the settings in this category are policies, and you must pay attention to how the settings are phrased. For example, the Tweak UI setting Allow Help On Start Menu is positive. The corresponding value NoSMHelp is negative, which is true of most policies, as you will learn in Chapter 6, "Managing Registry Policies." Thus, to *enable* Help on Start Menu, you must disable NoSMHelp. To *disable* Help on Start Menu, you must enable NoSMHelp.

Table 5-7   Values in Explorer

Setting	Name	Type	Data
HKCU\Control Panel\Desktop			
Enable smooth scrolling	SmoothScroll	REG_DWORD	0x00 | 0x01
HKCU\Software\Microsoft\Internet Explorer\Main			
Use Classic Search in Internet Explorer	Use Search Asst	REG_SZ	Yes | No
HKCU\Software\Microsoft\Windows\CurrentVersion\Explorer			
Manipulate connected files as a unit	NoFileFolderConnection	REG_DWORD	0x00 | 0x01
Prefix "Shortcut to" on new shortcuts	Link	REG_DWORD	0x00 | 0x01
HKCU\Software\Microsoft\Windows\CurrentVersion\Explorer\Advanced			
Detect accidental double-clicks	UseDoubleClickTimer	REG_DWORD	0x00 | 0x01
HKCU\Software\Microsoft\Windows\CurrentVersion\Explorer\CabinetState			
Use Classic Search in Explorer	Use Search Asst	REG_SZ	Yes | No
HKCU\Software\Microsoft\Windows\CurrentVersion\Policies\Explorer			
Allow Help on Start Menu	NoSMHelp	REG_DWORD	0x00 | 0x01
Allow Logoff on Start Menu	NoLogoff	REG_DWORD	0x00 | 0x01
Allow Recent Documents on Start Menu	NoRecentDocsMenu	REG_DWORD	0x00 | 0x01
Allow Web content to be added to the desktop	NoActiveDesktop	REG_DWORD	0x00 | 0x01
Clear document history on exit	ClearRecentDocsOnExit	REG_DWORD	0x00 | 0x01
Enable Windows+X hotkeys	NoWinKeys	REG_DWORD	0x00 | 0x01
Lock Web content	NoActiveDesktopChanges	REG_DWORD	0x00 | 0x01
Maintain document history	NoRecentDocsHistory	REG_DWORD	0x00 | 0x01
Maintain network history	NoRecentDocsNetHood	REG_DWORD	0x00 | 0x01

Setting	Name	Type	Data
Show My Documents on classic Start Menu	NoSMMyDocs	REG_DWORD	0x00 | 0x01
Show My Pictures on classic Start Menu	NoSMMyPictures	REG_DWORD	0x00 | 0x01
Show Network Connections on classic Start Menu	NoNetworkConnections	REG_DWORD	0x00 | 0x01

Shortcut

When you create a shortcut, Windows XP adds an overlay to the original document's icon so you can easily identify it as a shortcut. The Shortcut category enables you to customize that overlay. You can choose not to add an overlay, to add a light arrow, to use the normal arrow, or to use a custom icon as the overlay. Table 5-8 shows the value and data that Tweak UI uses for shortcuts.

HKLM\SOFTWARE\Microsoft\Windows\CurrentVersion\Explorer\ShellIcons is the key where you customize the shortcut overlay. Create this key if you don't see it in the registry. You add the REG_SZ value 29, and set it to *filename,index*, where *filename* is the name of the file containing the icon, and *index* is the index of that icon. For more information about using icons, see Chapter 4, "Hacking the Registry." Tweak UI removes 29 from ShellIcons if you choose the default arrow. It sets 29 to C:\WINDOWS\system32\tweakui.exe,2 for a light arrow or C:\WINDOWS\system32\tweakui.exe,3 for no arrow.

Table 5-8 Values in Shortcut

Setting	Name	Type	Data
HKLM\SOFTWARE\Microsoft\Windows\CurrentVersion\Explorer\ShellIcons			
Arrow	29	REG_SZ	null
Light Arrow	29	REG_SZ	C:\WINDOWS\system32\tweakui.exe,2
None	29	REG_SZ	C:\WINDOWS\system32\tweakui.exe,3
Custom	29	REG_SZ	*filename,index*

Colors

Table 5-9, on the next page, describes the values in the Colors category. Create any values that you don't see in the registry. HotTrackingColor is a string value, and Windows XP expects an RGB value in decimal notation. For example, white is 255 255 255. The operating system expects binary RGB values in hexadecimal for the remaining values. Windows XP uses each color as follows:

- **Hot-tracking.** Windows XP displays file names in this color when you point to them and if you've enabled the single-click user interface.

- **Compressed files.**   Windows XP displays compressed files in this color.
- **Encrypted files.**   Windows XP displays encrypted files in this color.

Table 5-9   Values in Colors

Setting	Name	Type	Data
HKCU\Control Panel\Colors			
Hot-tracking	HotTrackingColor	REG_SZ	*RRR GGG BBB*
HKCU\Software\Microsoft\Windows\CurrentVersion\Explorer			
Compressed files	AltColor	REG_BINARY	*0xRR 0xGG 0xBB 0x00*
Encrypted files	AltEncryptionColor	REG_BINARY	*0xRR 0xGG 0xBB 0x00*

Thumbnails

The Thumbnails category controls the quality of thumbnails in Windows Explorer. Table 5-10 describes the values for Image Quality and Size. Create values that you don't see in the registry. The default value for ThumbnailQuality is 0x5A. The default value for ThumbnailSize is 0x60. Keep in mind that higher quality and larger thumbnails require more disk space, which is not usually a problem, but they also take longer to display. Changing the quality does not affect thumbnails that already exist on the file system.

Table 5-10   Values in Thumbnails

Setting	Name	Type	Data
HKCU\Software\Microsoft\Windows\CurrentVersion\Explorer			
Image Quality	ThumbnailQuality	REG_DWORD	0x32 - 0x64
Size (pixels)	ThumbnailSize	REG_DWORD	0x20 - 0xFF

Command Keys

If you have a keyboard with navigation keys, such as the Microsoft Internet Keyboard Pro (I use this keyboard; learn more about it at *http://www.microsoft.com/hardware*), you can customize them. For example, you can reassign the Calculator key to open your favorite calculator, instead of the program that comes with Windows XP.

HKCU\Software\Microsoft\Windows\CurrentVersion\Explorer\AppKey is the key where you customize the navigation keys. If you don't see this key, create it. Look up the keyboard key you want to customize in Table 5-11, and then add the corresponding subkey to AppKey. Within that subkey, create the REG_SZ value ShellExecute, and set it to the path and file name of the program you want to execute by pressing that key. If you want to disable the navigation key, set it to an empty string. You can restore the original behavior by removing the subkey you added to AppKey. For example, to run PowerToy Calculator by pressing the Calculator key, add 18 to AppKey. Then create the REG_SZ value ShellExecute in 18, and set it to PowerCalc.exe.

Table 5-11   Subkeys for Command Keys

Key	Subkey	Key	Subkey
Back (Internet browser)	1	New	29
Calculator	18	Open	30
Close	31	Paste	38
Copy	36	Print	33
Corrections	45	Raise microphone volume	26
Cut	37	Redo	35
Favorites	6	Refresh (Internet browser)	3
Find	28	Reply	39
Forward (Internet browser)	2	Save	32
Forward (mail)	40	Search	5
Help	27	Send	41
Lower microphone volume	25	Spelling checker	42
Mail	15	Stop (Internet browser)	4
Media	16	Toggle dictation and command/control	43
Mute microphone	24	Toggle microphone	44
Mute volume	8	Undo	34
My Computer	17	WebHome	7

Common Dialog Boxes

The common dialog boxes, such as the Save As dialog box, display the places bar on the left side. These are shortcuts to common folders, which make getting around much easier. By default, you see the History, Documents, Desktop, Favorites, and My Network Places folders there. You can customize the folders that appear in the places bar by using the Common Dialogs category in Tweak UI (see Figure 5-3 on the next page).

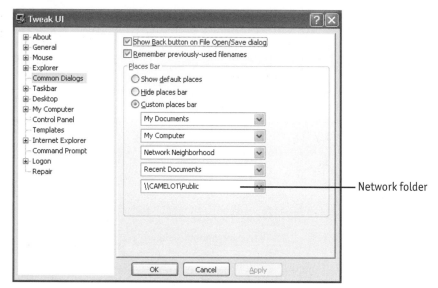

Figure 5-3 *Make network document folders easily accessible by adding them to the places bar.*

First things first: Table 5-12 describes the settings that enable you to remove the Back button and history from common dialog boxes. You can also hide the places bar altogether by setting the value `NoPlacesBar` to `0x01`. Create this value if it doesn't exist.

Table 5-12   Values in Common Dialog Boxes

Setting	Name	Type	Data
HKCU\Software\Microsoft\Windows\CurrentVersion\Policies\comdlg32			
Show Back button on File Open/Save dialog box	NoBackButton	REG_DWORD	0x00 | 0x01
Remember previously-used file names	NoFileMru	REG_DWORD	0x00 | 0x01
Hide places bar	NoPlacesBar	REG_DWORD	0x00 | 0x01

Customizing the places bar is a bit more complicated. First you add to `HKCU\Software\Microsoft\Windows\CurrentVersion\Policies\comdlg32\` the `PlacesBar` subkey. In `PlacesBar`, create the `REG_DWORD` values `Place0`, `Place1`, `Place2`, `Place3`, and `Place4`. These correspond to the five available buttons from top to bottom. The common dialog boxes will display only the buttons specified by these values; if there is a `PlacesBar` subkey with no values, an empty places bar will be displayed. Then set `Places`N to one of the settings in shown in Table 5-13. For example, to set the second button to My Music, create the `REG_DWORD` value `Places1` in `PlacesBar`, and set it to `0x0D`. You're not limited to the folders you see in Table 5-13, by the way. You can create the `Places`N value as a `REG_SZ` and then add the path of any folder. To restore the default places bar, remove the `PlacesBar` subkey and remove the `NoPlacesBar` value.

Table 5-13   Folders for the Places Bar

Folder	Value	Folder	Value
Desktop	0x00	Network Neighborhood	0x12
Favorites	0x06	History	0x22
My Documents	0x05	My Pictures	0x27
My Music	0x0D	Recent Documents	0x08
My Computer	0x11		

Taskbar

Table 5-14 describes the settings in the Taskbar category. Most notably, you can disable balloon tips by setting the REG_DWORD value EnableBallonTips to 0x00. Create this value if it doesn't already exist.

Table 5-14   Values in Taskbar

Setting	Name	Type	Data
HKCU\Software\Microsoft\Windows\CurrentVersion\Explorer\Advanced			
Enable balloon tips	EnableBalloonTips	REG_DWORD	0x00 | 0x01
HKCU\Software\Microsoft\Windows\CurrentVersion\Policies\Explorer			
Warn when low on disk space	NoLowDiskSpaceChecks	REG_DWORD	0x00 | 0x01

Grouping

The settings in the Grouping category, as described in Table 5-15, enable you to control how buttons group on the taskbar. Using the TaskbarGroupSize value, which you create if it doesn't already exist, you determine the applications that Windows XP collapses into groups first:

- **Group least used applications first.**   Windows XP groups least frequently used applications first, and groups more frequently used applications as necessary.

- **Group applications with the most windows first.**   Windows XP groups applications that have the most open windows first, and groups applications with fewer open windows only as necessary.

- **Group any application with at least *N* windows.**   Windows XP groups applications that have *N* windows open on the desktop.

Windows XP uses the same REG_DWORD value for all three cases. If you set TaskbarGroupSize to 0x00, Windows XP uses least-used grouping. If you set it to 0x01, Windows XP uses most-windows grouping. Finally, if you set it to any other value, Windows XP groups any application that has that number of open windows.

Table 5-15   Values in Grouping

Setting	Name	Type	Data
HKCU\Software\Microsoft\Windows\CurrentVersion\Explorer\Advanced			
Group least used applications first	TaskbarGroupSize	REG_DWORD	0x00
Group applications with the most windows first	TaskbarGroupSize	REG_DWORD	0x01
Group any application with at least N windows	TaskbarGroupSize	REG_DWORD	N

XP Start Menu

Windows XP displays the most frequently used programs on the bottom of the Start menu. This handy feature prevents you from having to hunt for applications you use often. Some applications don't belong on this list, however. I tire of seeing Notepad on the Start menu just because I happened to use it to view a text file. I also don't like seeing Command Prompt on the Start menu every time I type **cmd** in the Run dialog box. The solution is to tell Windows XP which applications you don't want it to add to the Start menu. Do that in the key HKCU\Software\Classes\Applications.

In Table 5-16, look up the application that you want to keep off the Start menu's list of frequently used programs. If you don't find the program in Table 5-16, find the program's file name by looking in the Program Files folder or at the program's shortcut on the Start menu. Then add a subkey to Applications, in which the name of the subkey is the program's file name (omit the path). Add the REG_SZ value NoStartPage to the program's subkey, and leave it blank. For example, to keep Notepad off the Start menu, create the subkey Notepad.exe in HKCU\Software\Classes\Applications, and add the value NoStartPage.

Table 5-16   Values in XP Start Menu

Application	File Name	Application	File Name
Accessibility Wizard	Accwiz.exe	Narrator	Narrator.exe
Address book	Wab.exe	Notepad	Notepad.exe
Backup	Ntbackup.exe	On-Screen Keyboard	Osk.exe
Calculator	Calc.exe	Outlook Express	Msimn.exe
Character map	Charmap.exe	Paint	Mspaint.exe
Command prompt	Cmd.exe	Pinball	Pinball.exe
Data sources (ODBC)	Odbcad32.exe	Remote Assistance	Rcimlby.exe

Application	File Name	Application	File Name
Disk cleanup	Cleanmgr.exe	Remote Desktop Connection	Mstsc.exe
FreeCell	Freecell.exe	Solitaire	Sol.exe
Files and Settings Transfer Wizard	Migwiz.exe	Sound Recorder	Sndrec32.exe
Hearts	Mshearts.exe	Spider Solitaire	Spider.exe
HyperTerminal	Hypertrm.exe	System Information	Msinfo32.exe
Internet Backgammon	Bckgzm.exe	System Restore	Rstrui.exe
Internet Checkers	Chkrzm.exe	Tour Windows XP	Tourstart.exe
Internet Explorer	Iexplore.exe	Utility Manager	Utilman.exe
Internet Hearts	Hrtzzm.exe	Windows Media Player	Wmplayer.exe
Internet Reversi	Rvsezm.exe	Windows Messenger	Msmsgs.exe
Internet Spades	Shvlzm.exe	Windows Movie Maker	Moviemk.exe
Magnifier	Magnify.exe	Windows Update	Wupdmgr.exe
Minesweeper	Winmine.exe	WordPad	Wordpad.exe
MSN Explorer	Msn6.exe		

Desktop

One of the most popular customizations for Windows 98 was to remove the icons from the desktop. That meant users did not display the My Documents icon and the Network Neighborhood icon. Windows XP caught up with users' tastes and displays only the Recycle Bin icon on the desktop by default.

If you miss the good old days, you can add the icons back to the desktop. Use the Tweak UI category Desktop. Table 5-17 describes the values corresponding to each icon. Add each value to the subkey NewStartPanel, creating it if it doesn't exist, and set it to 0x00 to hide the icon or 0x01 to display the icon.

Table 5-17 Values in Desktop

Setting	Name	Type	Data
HKCU\Software\Microsoft\Windows\CurrentVersion\Explorer\HideDesktopIcons \NewStartPanel			
Internet Explorer	{871C5380-42A0-1069-A2EA-08002B30309D}	REG_DWORD	0x00 | 0x01
My Computer	{20D04FE0-3AEA-1069-A2D8-08002B30309D}	REG_DWORD	0x00 | 0x01
My Documents	{450D8FBA-AD25-11D0-98A8-0800361B1103}	REG_DWORD	0x00 | 0x01
My Network Places	{208D2C60-3AEA-1069-A2D7-08002B30309D}	REG_DWORD	0x00 | 0x01
Recycle Bin	{645FF040-5081-101B-9F08-00AA002F954E}	REG_DWORD	0x00 | 0x01

First Icon

Using the First Icon category, choose the icon that you want to appear first on the desktop: My Documents or My Computer. Table 5-18 describes the settings you need to apply for either scenario.

Table 5-18   Values in First Icon

Setting	Name	Type	Data
HKCR\CLSID\{450D8FBA-AD25-11D0-98A8-0800361B1103}			
My Documents	SortOrderIndex	REG_DWORD	0x48
My Computer	SortOrderIndex	REG_DWORD	0x54

My Computer

Determine which icons you see in My Computer using the My Computer Category. Table 5-19 describes the settings you must apply to show the Control Panel and Files Stored On This Computer icons in My Computer.

Table 5-19   Values in My Computer

Setting	Name	Type	Data
HKCU\Software\Microsoft\Windows\CurrentVersion\Explorer\HideMyComputerIcons			
Control Panel	{21EC2020-3AEA-1069-A2DD-08002B30309D}	REG_DWORD	0x00 | 0x01
HKCU\Software\Microsoft\Windows\CurrentVersion\Policies\Explorer			
Files Stored on This Computer	NoSharedDocuments	REG_DWORD	0x00 | 0x01

Drives

Windows XP can hide drive letters. You hide them by setting NoDrives in the key HKCU \Software\Microsoft\Windows\CurrentVersion\Policies\Explorer, but it's easier using the Tweak UI category Drives. The trick is figuring out the value to put in the REG_BINARY value NoDrives.

Each bit in NoDrives, right to left, corresponds to the drive letters A through Z. To hide drive A, turn on the first bit. To hide drive B, turn on the second bit. Turn on the bit representing each drive that you want to hide. This math is easier if you use Calculator in Scientific mode. Also, see Chapter 1, "Learning the Basics," for some tips on doing bitwise math.

Note Hiding drive letters in Windows XP doesn't prevent users from accessing those drives through other means, including at the MS-DOS command prompt. This setting hides only those drives in Windows Explorer, the common dialog boxes, and so on. Thus, you can't rely on this as a security measure.

Special Folders

Windows XP users have special folders in their user profiles, such as the My Documents, My Pictures, and Favorites folders. The default location for these folders is in %USERPROFILE%, but you can redirect them to any location, including a location on the network. That's the purpose of the Tweak UI category Special Folders.

HKCU\Software\Microsoft\Windows\CurrentVersion\Explorer\User Shell Folders is the key where you find each of these special folders. You learn about them in detail in Chapter 4, "Hacking the Registry," and Chapter 17, "Per-User Settings." In Table 5-20 on the next page, look up the folder you want to redirect. Then in User Shell Folders, change the value shown in the Value Column to the folder's new location. I suggest that you use environment variables, particularly when referencing folders in %USERPROFILE% or %SYSTEMROOT%. The next time you log on to Windows XP, Windows XP updates HKCU\Software\Microsoft\Windows\CurrentVersion\Explorer\Shell Folders\ to reflect your changes. After relocating a shell folder, you must manually move your files and folders from the old location to the new location.

Tip I always relocate the My Documents, My Pictures, and Favorites folders to a network location. Doing so ensures that I always have access to my documents and Internet shortcuts from any computer on the network. I use Group Policy to automatically redirect the My Documents and My Pictures folders so I don't have to think about it. I use a script to relocate the Favorites folder on each computer that I use, however, because Group Policy doesn't support redirecting Favorites folders. Using a script makes redirecting Favorites easy but still not automatic.

Table 5-20   Values in Special Folders

Folder	Value	Default path
CD Burning	`CD Burning`	`%USERPROFILE%\Local Settings\Application Data` `\Microsoft\CD Burning`
Desktop	`Desktop`	`%USERPROFILE%\Desktop`
Document templates	`Templates`	`%USERPROFILE%\Templates`
Favorites	`Favorites`	`%USERPROFILE%\Favorites`
My Documents	`Personal`	`%USERPROFILE%\My Documents`
My Music	`My Music`	`%USERPROFILE%\My Documents\My Music`
My Pictures	`My Pictures`	`%USERPROFILE%\My Documents\My Pictures`
Programs	`Programs`	`%USERPROFILE%\Start Menu\Programs`
Send To	`SendTo`	`%USERPROFILE%\SendTo`
Start menu	`Start Menu`	`%USERPROFILE%\Start Menu`
Startup	`Startup`	`%USERPROFILE%\Start Menu\Programs\Startup`

AutoPlay

All the action in the AutoPlay category is in its subcategories: Drives, Types, and Handlers. In the Drives category, you can prevent specific drives from playing media automatically when you insert them. You use the value `NoDriveAutoRun`, which is a `REG_BINARY` value, just like the `NoDrives` value you learned about earlier. For each drive that you want to stop from playing disks automatically, set the bit, right to left, which corresponds to the drive letters A through Z. `NoDriveAutoRun` is in the key `HKCU\Software\Microsoft\Windows\CurrentVersion\Policies\Explorer`.

The next subcategory is Types. In this category, you can control whether CDs, DVDs, and removable drives automatically play when you insert disks. Table 5-21 describes the values that correlate to the settings you see in this category. Just like you did with the value `UserPreferencesMask`, you must toggle the bit shown in the Data column. To prevent CD drives from automatically playing, for example, set bit 0x20 in the `REG_DWORD` value `NoDriveTypeAutoRun`.

Table 5-21   Values in Autoplay Drive Types

Setting	Name	Type	Data
HKCU\Software\Microsoft\Windows\CurrentVersion\Policies\Explorer			
Enable Autoplay for CD and DVD drives	NoDriveTypeAutoRun	REG_DWORD	Bit 0x20
Enable Autoplay for removable drives	NoDriveTypeAutoRun	REG_DWORD	Bit 0x04

The last subcategory is Handlers. When Windows XP detects that you've inserted a CD, DVD, or removable disk, it automatically runs the program that it associates with the type of content on that disk. You control what programs are used with which types of content using the Handlers tab. This setting is much easier to configure in Tweak UI than manually, but we'll try it anyway.

HKLM\SOFTWARE\Microsoft\Windows\CurrentVersion\Explorer\AutoplayHandlers \EventHandlers is the key where you find these associations. In Table 5-22, look up the type of content you want to customize. Then open the subkey shown in the Subkey column for EventHandlers. In that subkey, add any of the following handlers as an empty REG_SZ value:

- MSCDBurningOnArrival
- MSOpenFolder
- MSPlayCDAudioOnArrival
- MSPlayDVDMovieOnArrival
- MSPlayMediaOnArrival
- MSPlayMusicFilesOnArrival
- MSPlayVideoFilesOnArrival
- MSPrintPicturesOnArrival
- MSPromptEachTime
- MSPromptEachTimeNoContent
- MSShowPicturesOnArrival
- MSTakeNoAction
- MSVideoCameraArrival
- MSWiaEventHandler

Table 5-22   Values in Autoplay Handlers

Media	Subkey	Media	Subkey
Generic	GenericVolumeArrival	Music files	PlayMusicFilesOnArrival
Blank CDR	HandleCDBurningOnArrival	Video files	PlayVideoFilesOnArrival
Mixed content	MixedContentOnArrival	Digital images	ShowPicturesOnArrival
CD audio	PlayCDAudioOnArrival	Video camera	VideoCameraArrival
DVD	PlayDVDMovieOnArrival		

Control Panel

The Control Panel category enables you to hide specific icons in Control Panel. Create a REG_SZ value in the key HKCU\Control Panel\don't load, and name it using the file name of the CPL file you want to hide. Set the value to Yes to display the icon or No to hide the icon. Table 5-23 shows the file names of the CPL files that come with Windows XP. For example, to hide the Internet Options icon, add the REG_SZ value Inetcpl.cpl to don't load, and set its value to No.

Table 5-23   Values in Control Panel

File name	Description	File name	Description
Access.cpl	Accessibility Options	Mmsys.cpl	Sounds and Audio Devices Properties
Appwiz.cpl	Add Or Remove Programs	Nusrmgr.cpl	User Accounts
Desk.cpl	Display Properties	Nwc.cpl	Client Service for NetWare
Hdwwiz.cpl	Add Hardware Wizard	Odbccp32.cpl	ODBC Data Source Administrator
Inetcpl.cpl	Internet Properties	Powercfg.cpl	Power Option Properties
Intl.cpl	Regional and Language Options	Sysdm.cpl	System Properties
Joy.cpl	Game Controllers	Telephon.cpl	Phone and Modem Options
Main.cpl	Mouse Properties and Keyboard Properties	Timedate.cpl	Date and Time Properties

Templates

Use the Templates category to customize the templates you see when you right-click the desktop or the unused space in a folder window, and then click New. Chapter 4, "Hacking the Registry," and Appendix A, "File Associations," describe how to build customized templates. Table 5-24 describes the values that Tweak UI uses for each of the default templates in Windows XP. Note that if you disable any of the templates shown in Table 5-24, Tweak UI hides the ShellNew key by renaming it to ShellNew- (adds a dash).

Table 5-24   Values in Templates

Setting	Name	Type	Data
HKCR			
Bitmap Image	HKCR\.bmp\ShellNew \NullFile	REG_SZ	""
Briefcase	HKCR\.bfc\ShellNew \Command	REG_EXPAND_SZ	%SYSTEMROOT%\system32 \rundll32.exe %SYSTEMROOT% \system32\syn- cui.dll,Briefcase_Create %2!d! %1

Setting	Name	Type	Data
Compressed (zipped) folder	HKCR\.zip \CompressedFolder \ShellNew\Data	REG_BINARY	0x50 0x4B 0x05 0x06 0x00 0x00 0x00 0x00 0x00 0x00 0x00 0x00 0x00 0x00 0x00 0x00 0x00 0x00 0x00 0x00 0x00 0x00
Rich Text Document	HKCR\.rtf\ShellNew \Data	REG_SZ	{\rtf1}
Text Document	HKCR\.txt\ShellNew \NullFile	REG_SZ	""
Wave Sound	HKCR\.wav\ShellNew \FileName	REG_SZ	sndrec.wav
WordPad Document	HKCR\.doc \WordPad.Document.1 \ShellNew\NullFile	REG_SZ	""

Internet Explorer

Table 5-25 describes the settings that Tweak UI establishes when you customize Internet Explorer and Windows Explorer toolbars with a bitmap image. These settings are in the Internet Explorer category.

Table 5-25 Values in Internet Explorer

Setting	Name	Type	Data
HKCU\Software\Microsoft\Internet Explorer\Toolbar			
Use custom background for Internet Explorer toolbar	BackBitmapIE5	REG_SZ	*Filename*
Use custom background for Windows Explorer toolbar	BackBitmapShell	REG_SZ	*Filename*

Search

This is my favorite customization. The Tweak UI's category Search enables you to add search URLs to Internet Explorer so that you can use search engines from the browser's address bar. For example, add the prefix news and set its URL to http://groups.google.com /groups?q=%s&hl=en; then you can quickly search Google Groups for *Windows XP* by typing **news Windows XP** in the address bar. Figure 5-4 shows a search URL.

Figure 5-4 *You don't need to download any search add-ins for Internet Explorer when using your favorite search engines is this easy.*

Add the subkey `SearchURL` to `HKCU\Software\Microsoft\Internet Explorer`. Then add a subkey for each search prefix you want to use. To use the example I just gave you, create the subkey `news`. Set the default value of the prefix's subkey, `news` in this example, to the URL of the search engine. Use the `%s` as a placeholder for the search string. Internet Explorer replaces the `%s` with any text you type to the right of the prefix. Continuing the Google Groups example, you'd set the default value to `http://groups.google.com/groups?q=%s&hl=en`.

Add the `REG_SZ` values shown in Table 5-26 to the prefix key you created. The purpose of these values is to describe what to substitute for special characters in your search string, including a space, percent sign (%), ampersand (&), and plus sign (+). These characters have special meaning when submitting forms to Web sites, so you must substitute a plus sign for a space, for example, or %26 for an ampersand. Thus, the browser translates the search string *Windows XP Bits & Pieces* to *Windows+XP+Bits+%26+Pieces*.

The only question left now is where to get the URL. That's easy. Open the search engine you want to add to Internet Explorer's search URLs, and then search for something—anything. When the browser displays the results, copy the URL from the Address bar, replacing your search word with a `%s`. For example, when searching Google Groups for *honeycutt*, the results are in a Web page with the URL *http://groups.google.com/groups?q=honeycutt&hl=en*. Replace the search word *honeycutt* with a `%s` to get `http://groups.google.com/groups?q=%s&hl=en`.

Note Searching from the address bar doesn't work properly with the original Windows XP RTM (Release to Manufacturing) bits. You must update the operating system using Windows Update or with the latest service pack from Microsoft.

Table 5-26   Values in Search

Name	Data
`<space>`	+
%	%25
&	%26
+	%2B

View Source

Use the View Source category in Tweak UI to change the program in which Internet Explorer displays a Web page's source. Set the default value of the key HKLM\SOFTWARE\Microsoft \Internet Explorer\View Source Editor\Editor Name to the path and file name of the program you want to use. Create this value if it doesn't already exist.

Command Prompt

If you're a command-line junkie like me, you'll appreciate file name and directory completion. The MS-DOS command prompt supports both of these features, but you have to enable them first. Table 5-27 describes the settings in the Command Prompt category in Tweak UI. Set the value CompletionChar to the keystroke you want to use for file name completion, and set the value PathCompletionChar to the keystroke you want to use for directory completion. You can use the same keystroke for both values. The value you use for *key* is the ASCII key code. Thus, Tab is 0x09. The value WordDelimiters is a string of characters that delimit words on the command line when you press Ctrl+Right Arrow or Ctrl+Left Arrow. Create these values if they don't exist.

Table 5-27   Values in Command Prompt

Setting	Name	Type	Data
HKCU\Software\Microsoft\Command Processor			
File name completion	CompletionChar	REG_DWORD	*key*
Directory completion	PathCompletionChar	REG_DWORD	*key*
HKCU\Console			
Word separators	WordDelimiters	REG_SZ	*separators*

Logon

In the Logon category, you toggle Autoexec.bat parsing by setting the REG_SZ value ParseAutoexec in the key HKCU\Software\Microsoft\Windows NT\CurrentVersion \Winlogon to 0 or 1. Set ParseAutoexec to 0 to prevent Windows XP from parsing Autoexec.bat for environment variables. Otherwise, set ParseAutoexec to 1, and Windows XP will parse it for environment variables.

Autologon

The last useful category in Tweak UI is Autologon, and it enables you to automatically log on to Windows XP without providing your name, domain, or password. Table 5-27 describes the values you must set to log on to the computer automatically. *Name* is the user name, and *Domain* is the domain name. To enable Autologon, you must set the REG_SZ value AutoAdminLogon to 1. Last, set the value REG_SZ value DefaultPassword in the subkey Winlogon to the password you want to use to automatically log on to the computer. You don't see this value in Tweak UI because it stores the password differently.

> **Note** This setting is useful for IT professionals deploying software. It's one way to install applications that require administrative access to the computer, which users in most enterprises don't have. Chapter 15, "Working Around IT Problems," discusses this setting in detail.

Table 5-27   Values in Autologon

Setting	Name	Type	Data
HKLM\SOFTWARE\Microsoft\Windows NT\CurrentVersion\Winlogon			
Log on automatically at system startup	AutoAdminLogon	REG_SZ	0 | 1
User name	DefaultUserName	REG_SZ	*Name*
Domain	DefaultDomainName	REG_SZ	*Domain*

Registry in Management

Managing the registry is easier when you are armed with the right tools. This part describes those tools. You learn about registry-based policies and how to use them to manage settings in the registry. You learn how to track down registry settings and write scripts to change them. You also learn about registry security.

Whereas the first part of this book was for both power users and IT professionals, this part tends more toward IT professionals. Power users can still benefit from giving this part a thorough read, though, because some of the better customizations are actually policies, and customizing Windows XP is better done through scripts. Still, I give this part an IT slant because these are valuable IT tools.

Using Registry-Based Policy

IT professionals use Group Policy to manage users' desktop environments. First introduced in Microsoft Windows 2000, Group Policy enables you to dramatically reduce the cost of deploying and managing desktops. Part of the trick to this is deploying standard desktop configurations rather than wasting money to support individual users. Using Group Policy in this way enforces corporate standards and configures users' computers, freeing them from this task and enabling them to do their jobs. For example, you enhance productivity by configuring users' applications, data, and settings so they follow users regardless of where users log on to the network. Microsoft Windows XP extends Group Policy with new settings, new features, and significant improvements.

In this chapter, I focus on local registry-based policies. Group Policy in the enterprise is a big subject, and one that requires familiarity with Active Directory. At the end of this chapter, however, you'll find a handful of resources that are useful for learning more about both Active Directory and Group Policy. Rather than teach you about sites, domains, and organization units, which are peripherally related to the Windows XP registry, I show you how to implement registry-based policies in a local Group Policy object. This information transfers intact to network Group Policy. Because of the focus of this book—more or less dirty tricks for the IT professional—I also show you how to define your own policies and even deploy Windows XP policies on networks that aren't based on Active Directory, including Microsoft Windows NT and Novell Netware.

This chapter is for you whether you're an IT professional or power user. If you're an IT professional, I assume you have the key Active Directory and Group Policy concepts under your belt. And if you're not an IT professional, I don't anticipate that you will try to use this information in an enterprise environment, so this information is fairly complete. For example, power users often define local policies to customize their computers, and this doesn't require a lot of information about Active Directory or policy inheritance. In fact, some of the most popular and interesting customizations are available in Group Policy already, so you don't need to hack the registry at all.

Editing Local Policies

Policies are different from preferences, and comparing the two helps you better understand how Windows XP uses policies. Users set preferences, such as their desktop wallpaper. They can change preferences any time. Administrators set policies, such as the location of the My Documents folder, and they have precedence over the equivalent user preference. Windows XP stores policies in the registry separately from user preferences. If the policy exists, the operating system uses the setting that policy specifies. If the policy doesn't exist, the operating system uses the user's preference. In the absence of the user's preference, the operating system uses a default setting. The important thing is that a policy does not change the equivalent user preference and, if they both exist at the same time, the policy has precedence. Also, if the administrator removes the policy, the user's preference is once again used. In other words, Group Policy does not *tattoo* the registry. (See the sidebar "Tattoos on the Registry," later in this chapter.) Table 6-1 summarizes this behavior.

Table 6-1 Policies Compared to Preferences

Policy defined?	Preference defined?	Behavior
No	No	Default
No	Yes	Preference configures
Yes	No	Policy configures
Yes	Yes	Policy configures, ignoring the preference

Windows XP combines policies together in a *Group Policy object* (GPO). In Active Directory, you have multiple GPOs, which apply to users and computers, depending on where they are in the directory. In Windows XP, you have only one GPO, and that's the *local GPO*. Settings in this GPO apply to the local computer and every user who logs on to it. Because the local GPO is the first GPO that Windows XP applies when it starts and when users log on to it, *network GPOs* can override settings in it. For example, if you define a local policy that enables you to install Windows Installer–based programs with elevated privileges but the network administrator sets a network policy that disallows that, the network policy wins, and you won't be able to install these programs unless you're a local administrator for that computer; otherwise, you can install Windows Installer–based programs no matter the group in which your account is a member.

GPOs include settings for both computer configurations and user configurations. Because Group Policy settings apply to either computers or users, GPOs contain branches for each:

- **Computer Configuration.**   These are per-computer policy settings that specify operating system behavior, desktop behavior, security settings, computer startup and shutdown scripts, computer-assigned applications, and application settings. Windows XP applies per-computer policies when the operating system starts and at regular intervals.

- **User Configuration.**   These are per-user policy settings that specify operating system behavior, desktop settings, security settings, assigned and published applications, folder redirection settings, user logon and logoff scripts, and application settings. Windows XP applies per-user policies when the user logs on to the computer and at regular intervals.

You edit the local GPO using the Group Policy editor, shown in Figure 6-1. To open the Group Policy editor, type **gpedit.msc** in the Run dialog box. The left and right panes you see in the editor are similar to those in Registry Editor (Regedit), so I won't explain how to use them here. Immediately under Local Computer Policy, you see Computer Configuration and User Configuration. Computer Configuration contains per-computer policies, and User Configuration contains per-user policies. Registry-based policies, this chapter's focus, are in Administrative Templates under either branch.

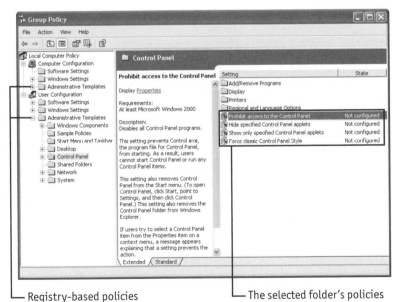

└─ Registry-based policies   └─ The selected folder's policies

Figure 6-1   *The Extended and Standard view tabs are new for Windows XP. Click the Extended tab to display help for the selected policy setting.*

Typing **gpedit.msc** in the Run dialog box is the quick way to edit the local computer's GPO, but you can create your own console in Microsoft Management Console (MMC) to edit a remote computer's GPO. Editing local policies on a remote computer is useful if your organization isn't using Active Directory, but it's too cumbersome to use as a general management tool, so I'd use it in one-off scenarios:

1. In the Run dialog box, type **mmc**, and press Enter.

2. On the File menu, click Add/Remove Snap-In.

3. In the Add Standalone Snap-In dialog box, on the Standalone tab, click Add.

4. Click Group Policy, and then click Add.

5. In the Select Group Policy Object dialog box, click Browse. In the Browse For A Group Policy Object dialog box, on the Computers tab, select the Another Computer option, type the remote computer's name in the space provided, and then click OK.

Note Windows XP doesn't allow you to specify security settings in a remote computer's local GPO. Thus, when you open Security Settings for a remote computer, you don't see these settings. Even though you can't apply these settings to remote computers, you can include them in a disk image for deployment, which you learn more about in the section "Deploying Registry-Based Policy," later in this chapter.

Tattoos on the Registry

Group Policy and System Policy, policies that versions of Windows earlier than Windows 2000 use, handle changes differently. Windows XP automatically removes a GPO's settings from the registry when the GPO no longer applies to the user or computer. Also, Group Policy doesn't overwrite users' preferences. So if you delete a GPO from Active Directory, Windows XP removes that GPO's settings from the registry and reverts back to users' preferences. Likewise, if you remove an individual policy from a GPO, Windows XP removes that setting from the registry and restores users' existing preferences. Group Policy doesn't make permanent, irreversible changes to the registry.

System Policy does make permanent, irreversible changes to the registry, though. In other words, it *tattoos* the registry. Removing System Policy leaves all the policies it contained in the registry. The only way to restore users' preferences, assuming these policies don't overwrite their preferences, is to manually remove the policy from the registry or explicitly change the setting in System Policy. This is one of the scenarios you learn to grapple with in Chapter 15, "Working Around IT Problems." One of the nastier incarnations of this behavior can occur when you upgrade from an earlier version of Windows to Windows XP. When you upgrade, policies in the registry are permanent, and you must manually remove them from the registry; Windows XP doesn't remove them automatically.

Group Policy Extensions

Group Policy has several extensions that you can use to configure GPOs. In fact, each of the different nodes that you see in the Group Policy editor is an extension. By default, the editor loads all the available extensions when you start it. There are different extensions in Computer Configuration and User Configuration, and you see more extensions when you're editing a network GPO in Active Directory than when you're editing a local GPO. The following list summarizes some of the extensions that Group Policy provides in a local GPO (network GPOs provide more):

- **Scripts.** You can assign scripts to users that run when they log on to or log off of Windows XP. You can assign scripts to computers that run when Windows XP starts and when it shuts down. You see this extension in the Windows Settings folder.

- **Security Settings.** You can manage security settings, including password, audit, and lockout policies. You can also manage user rights and restrict the applications that users can run. You see this extension in the Windows Settings folder.

- **Administrative Templates.** Group Policy creates a file containing registry settings that are written to HKCU or HKLM in the registry. Windows XP loads settings from this file as the operating system starts and when users log on to the computer. These are registry-based policies.

Registry-Based Policy

Registry-based policies and *administrative policies* are two names for the same thing. They're registry settings that override users' preferences, and users can't change them for good reasons that you'll learn about in this section. Other policies, including security settings, might or might not be registry settings. In the Group Policy editor, you find registry-based policies in the Administrative Templates folder under Computer Configuration or User Configuration.

Figure 6-2 on the next page shows the workflow using registry-based policies. Administrators define policies using the Group Policy editor, which you saw in Figure 6-1. *Administrative templates*, files with the *.adm* extension, define the policies they can set. Administrative templates and *policy templates* are the same thing, and you frequently see the short name *ADM files*. These templates describe the user interface for collecting settings from the administrator and their locations in the registry. When the administrator defines policies, the editor stores them in a file called Registry.pol. Windows XP loads the settings contained in the file Registry.pol when the operating system starts, when users log on to it, and at regular intervals. The next section describes where in the registry Windows XP stores policies and where you find the Registry.pol file.

The following components combine to implement registry-based policy:

- The Administrative Templates extension, which you use to edit policy settings. This extension is the Administrative Templates folder in the editor. It creates the Registry.pol file based on settings that the administrator defines.

- A built-in registry client-side extension, which processes policies and creates their corresponding values in the registry (available only in Windows 2000 or later). Although the client-side extension is responsible for reading settings from the Registry.pol file and writing them to the registry, Windows XP and other applications must look for and use these settings to give them meaning.

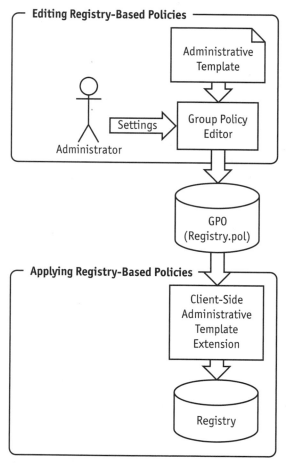

Figure 6-2 *Registry-based policies start with administrative templates, which define the settings that are available and the location where they are stored in the registry.*

Windows XP comes with administrative templates that define all the proper policies that the operating system supports. If you want to use policies for an application, such as one in Microsoft Office XP, you must load the administrative templates for it. In fact, the Office XP Resource Kit comes with a big handful of administrative templates that help IT professionals better manage the entire productivity suite. Windows XP provides the following administrative templates:

- **System.adm.**   Core settings and primary template file, defining most of the settings you see in Administrative Templates

- **Wmplayer.adm.** Windows Media settings
- **Conf.adm.** NetMeeting conferencing software
- **Inetres.adm.** Internet Explorer

All registry-based policies can be in one of three states: Enabled, Disabled, or Not Configured. Figure 6-3 shows these settings on a sample policy. *Enabled* explicitly turns on the setting by adding the setting to the registry with a value of 0x01. *Disabled* explicitly turns off the setting by adding the setting to the registry with a value of 0x00 or removing the value altogether. The *Not Configured option* removes the setting from the registry altogether, which yields to the user's preference. Many policies collect additional settings, as shown in the figure.

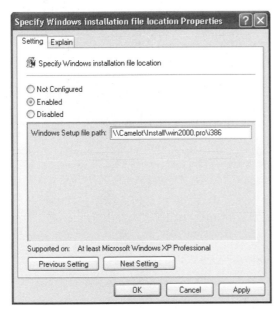

Figure 6-3 *Each policy has three states, Enabled, Disabled, or Not Configured, and some policies collect additional information.*

When setting a policy, pay particular attention to the language to ensure that you get the result you want. Some policies are positive, so enabling the policy turns on the feature. Other policies are negative, however, so turning on those policies actually disables those features. To make things more confusing, outside of Windows XP, you frequently see policies that you have to enable and then turn the setting on or off. In other words, to turn on a setting, you have to enable the policy and then select or clear a second check box to turn on or off the setting. The Office XP policy templates are notorious for this extra level of indirection. All this just illustrates that you have to pay close attention to the names of policies when setting them. Read their names out loud, prefixing the sentences with the words *enable* or *disable*—just to be sure.

Group Policy Storage

Where does Windows XP store policies in the registry and on the disk? The branch \Software \Policies is the preferred branch for registry-based policies. This branch in HKLM contains per-computer policies, and the branch in HKCU contains per-user policies. Another branch, inherited from earlier versions of Windows, is \Software\Microsoft\Windows\CurrentVersion \Policies. Policies in this branch tend to tattoo the registry, which means they make permanent changes to the registry that you must explicitly change. What prevents users from changing these keys, and thus the policies they enforce, is their ACLs (Access Control Lists). The Users and Power Users local groups do not have permission to change values in these keys. An administrator can overwrite these keys directly and change the policy, however.

That covers the location of policies in the registry; now for their location on the file system. The local GPO is in %SYSTEMROOT%\System32\GroupPolicy. This is a super-hidden folder. To show it in Windows Explorer, click Tools, Options; on the Folder Options dialog box's View tab, select the Show Hidden Files And Folders option, and then clear the Hide Protected Operating System Files check box. It contains the following subfolders and files (our focus is the file Registry.pol):

- **\Adm.**   Contains all the ADM files for the local GPO.

- **\User.**   Includes the file Registry.pol, which contains registry-based policies for users. When users log on to the computer, Windows XP applies these to HKCU.

- **\User\Scripts.**   Contains the local GPO's per-user scripts. The scripts in \Logon run when users log on to Windows XP, and the scripts in \Logoff run when they log off of the operating system.

- **\Machine.**   Includes the file Registry.pol, which contains registry-based policies for the computer. When Windows XP starts, it applies these settings to HKLM.

- **\Machine\Scripts.**   Contains the local GPO's per-computer scripts. The scripts in \Startup run when Windows XP starts, and the scripts in \Shutdown run when the operating systems shuts down.

If you're familiar with System Policy and the file Ntconfig.pol, you're probably wondering whether the files Registry.pol and Ntconfig.pol use similar formats. They don't. Both are binary files, but Registry.pol is much simpler. It contains a simple list of settings, including their value names, type, and data, in a binary format. Ntconfig.pol is actually a registry hive file that you can load and browse in Regedit. Unfortunately, you can't do the same with Registry.pol.

Note   Domain GPOs are more complicated than local GPOs. Active Directory stores policies in *Server*\SYSVOL*Domain*\Policies, where *Server* is the name of the domain controller, and *Domain* is the name of the domain. Each GPO is in a subfolder, and the name of the subfolder is the GPO's GUID (see Chapter 1, "Learning the Basics"). The structure of each GPO's subfolder is similar to the structure of the local GPO described in this chapter. The \User and \Machine folders have additional subfolders, though, and the various Group Policy extensions create these.

Extending Registry-Based Policy

You can extend registry-based policy by customizing existing administrative templates or by creating new ones. Windows XP provides administrative templates for its policies. Other applications, such as Office XP, also provide templates. When you install the Office XP Resource Kit, it adds the Office XP policy templates to %SYSTEMROOT%\Inf. You should never customize these templates. You might want to create your own templates that extend registry-based policy, though.

First the caveats: Extending registry-based policy is generally something that developers do to give administrators more control over users' applications. Remember that a registry-based policy requires developers to add code to their applications that read policies and enforce those settings. If developers added policies to their code, they almost certainly created policy templates for them, so you don't have to. On the other hand, if no code enforces a policy setting, creating an administrative template for it is useless. It almost sounds like extending registry-based policy is futile, eh? But there are still times when it's useful and some times that are extremely valuable:

- **Repairing broken policies.**   I don't run across broken policies often, but when I do, the only way to fix them is to create a custom template for them. For example, in the Windows XP beta, the screen saver policy stored the timeout period incorrectly in the registry. My simple fix was to create a custom template for it.

- **Creating custom administrative templates.**   Windows XP supports hundreds of policies, as does Office XP. Hunting for policies is sometimes frustrating. You can create a custom administrative template that assembles all the policies you're deploying in one place, making the job a bit easier. You can also rephrase the language of a policy with easier-to-understand descriptions.

- **Customizing Windows XP.**   Many of the registry settings you can use to customize Windows XP have no user interface. You can build a user interface for them by creating an administrative template and changing those settings with the Group Policy editor. For power users, this is a great reason to master this topic. This goes against one of the primary features of Group Policy, however, because settings you change outside the normal policy branches in the registry will tattoo the registry.

You can use any text editor to create an administrative template. Administrative templates have a language all their own, and you learn about that language in the remainder of this section. The Group Policy editor is very good about displaying useful errors when a template file contains an error. It gives you the line number, the keyword that's in error, and more information. In summary:

1. Create an administrative template using the language you learn about in this chapter. The template file is a text file with the *.adm* extension.

2. Load the template file in the Group Policy editor as you learn to do in the section "Deploying Registry-Based Policy."

3. Edit the settings that the administrative template defines.

The following listing is a sample administrative template that doesn't do much but illustrates what a template file looks like. Figure 6-4 shows what this template looks like in the Group Policy editor. The figure's annotations show some of the keywords that are responsible for different portions of a policy. For example, the keyword EXPLAIN is responsible for displaying the policy's description that you see in the figure. Throughout the remainder of this section, you'll see dozens more examples that give you the building blocks for creating your own administrative templates. Take these building blocks and copy them right into your file to get started straightaway.

Listing 6-1   example.adm

```
CLASS USER

CATEGORY "Sample Policies"
  #if version >= 4
    EXPLAIN "These are sample policies that don't do anything."
  #endif

  POLICY "Sample Policy"
    #if version >= 4
      SUPPORTED "At least Microsoft Windows XP Professional"
    #endif
    EXPLAIN "This is a sample policy that doesn't do much."
    KEYNAME "Software\Policies"
    VALUENAME Sample
    VALUEON NUMERIC 1
    VALUEOFF NUMERIC 0
  END POLICY

END CATEGORY
```

Note   The statements #if and #endif enclose statements that work with only certain versions of System Policy or Group Policy. Using these statements, the developer can write one administrative template that works with different versions of Windows, including Windows NT, Windows 2000, and Windows XP. System Policy in Windows NT is version 2. Windows 2000 is version 3. Windows XP is version 4. Thus, to make sure that the Group Policy editor in Windows 2000 ignores keywords that only Windows XP supports, the developer encloses those keywords between #if version >= 4 and #endif. To ensure that only System Policy Editor in Windows NT sees a block of keywords, enclose them between #if version = 2 and #endif. These conditional statements show that Microsoft was thinking far into the future, even back in the old days.

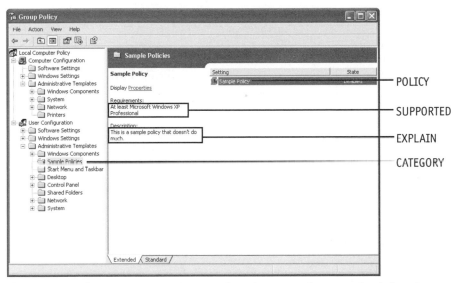

Figure 6-4   *Administrative templates, such as the one in this example, define the user interface for collecting settings that the editor stores in the file Registry.pol.*

Comments

Comments are useful and necessary to document the contents of your policy templates. You can add comments to template files two different ways. Precede the comment with a semicolon (;) or two forward slashes (//). You can also place comments at the end of any valid line. You see examples of comments throughout this chapter; I've documented each example using them. Each line in the following example is a valid comment. I prefer using // for comments.

Listing 6-2   example.adm

```
; This is a comment
// This is also a comment
CLASS USER // Per-user settings
CLASS MACHINE ; Per-computer settings
```

Strings

In a one-off, quick-and-dirty template file, don't feel bad about hard-coding strings. That means adding the string where you need it and repeating the same string as often as necessary. The listing you saw in the section "Extending Registry-Based Policy" uses hard-coded strings. If you're using enterprise-class template files, or if you're managing the files over time, use string variables. Using string variables makes it easier to maintain template files that use the same strings more than once. More importantly, it makes localization of template files far easier and much less error prone.

Define strings at the end of your template file in the [strings] section. The format of each string is name="string". You must enclose the string in double quotation marks. To use string variables in your template file, use the format !!*name*. Each time the Group Policy editor sees !!*name*, it substitutes the string for the name. Incidentally, the !! makes searching template files for strings easy—just search the file for the double exclamation marks. The following listing is an example of how strings and string variables are used in template file:

Listing 6-3   example.adm

```
POLICY !!Sample                           // Defined in [strings] section
  SUPPORTED "At least Microsoft Windows XP" // Hard-coded string
  EXPLAIN !!Sample_Explain                 // Defined in [strings] section

...

[strings]
Sample="Sample Policy"
Sample_Explain="This sample policy doesn't do much of anything."
```

Note   In this chapter, I tend not to use string variables for clarity. Avoiding string variables prevents you from having to look up each string as you're wading through the listings. Keep in mind that you'll want to use string variables if you plan on localizing your files.

CLASS

The first entry in a template file is the keyword CLASS. It defines whether the policies following it are per-user or per-computer, that is, it specifies where in the Group Policy editor you see the policy: User Configuration or Computer Configuration. You can use multiple CLASS keywords in a template file. When the Windows XP client-side extensions process the file, it merges the settings defined in the CLASS USER sections and does the same for the settings defined in all the CLASS MACHINE sections. Then it loads the settings defined in the CLASS USER sections in HKCU and the settings defined in the CLASS MACHINE sections in HKLM.

Syntax

CLASS *Name*

Name	This must be MACHINE or USER. MACHINE specifies that the policies following the CLASS keyword are per-computer policies, and USER specifies that the policies following the keyword are per-user policies. This keyword persists until you change it using additional CLASS keywords.

Example

Listing 6-4   example.adm

```
CLASS MACHINE

// Policies here are per-computer policies

CLASS USER

// Policies here are per-user policies

CLASS MACHINE

// Policies here are per-computer policies
```

CATEGORY

After you define whether your policy will appear under the Computer Settings or User Settings branch of the Group Policy editor using the CLASS keyword, use the CATEGORY keyword to create subfolders in that branch. The editor displays your settings in that folder. Just as you can create subkeys within keys in the registry, you can create subcategories within categories by nesting the CATEGORY keyword. Just keep in mind that all the CATEGORY keyword does is create folders.

   Categories can include zero or more policies. Categories that contain no policies usually contain one or more subcategories, at a minimum. You define a registry key in which the Group Policy editor creates settings for that category using the KEYNAME keyword, which you learn about in the next section. Using the KEYNAME keyword here is optional if you're defining the key elsewhere. Last, you end a category with END CATEGORY.

Syntax

```
CATEGORY Name
  KEYNAME Subkey

  Policies

END CATEGORY
```

Name	This is the folder name you want to see in the Group Policy editor. Use a string variable or a string enclosed in quotes.
Subkey	This is an optional subkey of HKLM or HKCU to use for the category. Do not include either root key in the path, though, because the preceding CLASS keyword specifies which of these root keys to use. If you specify a subkey, all subcategories, policies, and parts use it unless they specifically provide a subkey of their own. Enclose names that contain spaces in double quotes.

Example

Listing 6-5   example.adm

```
CLASS USER // Settings are per-user in HKCU

CATEGORY "Desktop Settings"
  KEYNAME "Software\Policies\System"

  // Add policies for the Desktop Settings category here

  CATEGORY "Custom Application Settings"
    KEYNAME "Software\Policies\CustomApps"

    // Add policies for the custom applications subcategory here

  END CATEGORY
END CATEGORY
```

Keywords

The valid keywords you can use within a CATEGORY section are the following:

- CATEGORY
- END
- KEYNAME
- POLICY

KEYNAME

Use the KEYNAME keyword within a category to define which subkey of HKCU or HKLM (depending on the CLASS keyword) contains the value you're changing. Do not include a root key in the path because the CLASS keyword defines it. If the name contains spaces, you must enclose the string in double quotation marks. The example in the previous section, "CATEGORY" shows how to use the KEYNAME keyword.

POLICY

Use the POLICY keyword to define a policy that the administrator can change. The policy editor displays the policy and its controls in a dialog box that the administrator uses to change the policies state and settings. You can include multiple POLICY keywords in a single category, but you don't need to include the KEYNAME keyword before each POLICY keyword. The most recent KEYNAME keyword applies for each policy. You end a policy with END POLICY.

Each policy contains a VALUENAME keyword to associate a registry value with it. By default, the policy editor assumes it's a REG_DWORD value and stores 0x01 in it when you enable the policy. The policy editor also removes the value when you disable the policy. You must use the VALUEON and VALUEOFF keywords if you don't want the policy editor to remove the value when you disable the policy. You don't have to use any keywords other than VALUENAME to get this behavior. You can include optional PART keywords that specify additional options, however, such as drop-down list boxes, check boxes, text boxes, and so on. You see these controls in the bottom part of the policy's dialog box (see Figure 6-3).

Syntax

```
POLICY Name
[KEYNAME Subkey]
EXPLAIN Help
VALUENAME Value

  [Parts]

END POLICY
```

Name	This is the name of the policy as you want to see it in the Group Policy editor. Use a descriptive but short name.
Subkey	This is an optional subkey of HKLM or HKCU to use for the category. Do not include either root key in the path, though, because the preceding CLASS keyword specifies which of these root keys to use. If you specify a subkey, all subcategories, policies, and parts use it unless they specifically provide a subkey of their own. Enclose names that contain spaces in double quotes.
Help	This is the string that the Group Policy editor displays on the Explain tab and on the Extended tab of the policy's dialog box.
Value	This is the registry value to modify. Enabling the policy sets the REG_DWORD value to 0x01. Select the Not Configured option or disable the policy, and the policy editor removes the value from the registry. To specify values other than the default 0x01, use the VALUEON and VALUEOFF keywords directly following the VALUENAME keyword:
	VALUEON [NUMERIC] *Enabled* VALUEOFF [NUMERIC] *Disabled*
	When you use these keywords, the policy editor sets the registry value to *Enabled* when you enable the policy and sets the value to *Disabled* when you disable the policy. The default value type is REG_SZ, but you can change it to REG_DWORD by prefixing the value with the keyword NUMERIC. Regardless, setting the policy to Not Configured removes the value altogether.

Example

Listing 6-6   example.adm

```
CLASS MACHINE

CATEGORY "Disk Quotas"

  KEYNAME "Software\Policies\MS\DiskQuota"
  POLICY "Enable disk quotas"
```

```
      EXPLAIN "Enables and disables disk quotas management."
      VALUENAME "Enable"
      VALUEON NUMERIC 1
      VALUEOFF NUMERIC 0
   END POLICY

END CATEGORY
```

Keywords

The valid keywords within a POLICY section include the following:

- ACTIONLISTOFF
- ACTIONLISTON
- END
- KEYNAME
- PART
- VALUENAME
- VALUEOFF
- VALUEON
- HELP
- POLICY

> **Note**   Additional keywords are available for policies, but they are for developers creating policy extensions. For example, CLIENTEXT associates a client-side extension with a policy via the extension's GUID. I'm not covering these because they don't fit our purposes here.

EXPLAIN

The EXPLAIN keyword provides help text for a specific policy. In Windows 2000 and Windows XP, each policy's dialog box includes an Explain tab, which provides details about the policy settings. You also see this help text on the Extended tab of the editor's right pane in Windows XP. Each policy you create for Windows 2000 and Windows XP should contain one EXPLAIN keyword followed by a full description of the policy and its settings. Although I don't show this in my examples (trying to keep them simple), you should enclose this keyword between #if version >=3 and #endif to prevent earlier versions of the policy editor from choking on these keywords:

Listing 6-7   example.adm

```
#if version >= 3
   EXPLAIN "Enables and disables disk quotas management."
#endif
```

VALUENAME

The VALUENAME keyword identifies the registry value that the policy editor modifies when you enable or disable the policy. The syntax is VALUENAME *Name*. You saw an example of this keyword in the section "POLICY." Unless you set the VALUEON and VALUEOFF keywords, described in the next section, the policy editor creates the policy as a REG_DWORD value:

- **Enabled.**   Sets the value to 0x01
- **Disabled.**   Removes the value
- **Not Configured.**   Removes the value

VALUENAME, VALUEON, and VALUEOFF describe the value that enables and disables the policy. If you want to define additional settings that enable you to collect additional values to refine the policy, you must use the PART keyword. Settings in a PART section are in the bottom part of the policy's dialog box.

VALUEON and VALUEOFF

You can use the VALUEON and VALUEOFF keywords to write specific values based on the state of the policy. The section "POLICY" contains an example of how these keywords are used. The syntaxes are VALUEON [NUMERIC] *Enabled* and VALUEOFF [NUMERIC] *Disabled*. By default, the policy editor creates the value as a REG_SZ value; if you want it to create the value as a REG_DWORD value, prefix it with the NUMERIC keyword. For example:

```
VALUEON 0          // Created as a REG_SZ value containing "0"
VALUEOFF NUMERIC 1 // Created as a REG_DWORD value containing 0x01
```

ACTIONLIST

The ACTIONLIST keyword enables you to group settings together. Think of it as a list of values you want the policy editor to change when you change a policy. The following two variants of the ACTIONLIST keyword are the most commonly used:

- **ACTIONLISTON.**   A list of values to change when the policy is enabled
- **ACTIONLISTOFF.**   A list of values to change when the policy is disabled

Syntax

```
ACTIONLIST
  [KEYNAME Subkey]
  VALUENAME Value
  VALUE Data
END ACTIONLIST
```

Subkey	This is an optional subkey of HKLM or HKCU to use for the category. Do not include either root key in the path, though, because the preceding CLASS keyword specifies which of these root keys to use. If you specify a subkey, all subcategories, policies, and parts use it unless they specifically provide a subkey of their own. Enclose names that contain spaces in double quotes.
Value	This is the registry value to modify. Enabling the policy sets the REG_DWORD value to 0x01. Select the Not Configured option, and the policy editor removes the value from the registry. To specify values other than the default 0x00 and 0x01, use the VALUE keyword.
Data	This is the data to which you want to set the value. The default value type is REG_SZ, but you can change it to REG_DWORD by prefixing the value with the keyword NUMERIC. If you follow the keyword VALUE with the keyword DELETE (VALUE DELETE), policy editor removes the value from the registry. Regardless, setting the policy to Not Configured removes the value altogether.

Example

Listing 6-8   example.adm

```
POLICY "Sample Action List"
  EXPLAIN "This illustrates action lists"
  ACTIONLISTON
    VALUENAME Sample1 VALUE 1
    VALUENAME Sample2 VALUE 1
  END ACTIONLISTON

  ACTIONLISTOFF
    VALUENAME Sample1 VALUE 0
    VALUENAME Sample2 VALUE 0
  END ACTIONLISTOFF
END POLICY
```

PART

The PART keyword enables you to specify various options, including drop-down lists, text boxes, and check boxes, in the lower part of a policy's dialog box. Figure 6-5 shows an example of the settings that you want to collect in addition to enabling or disabling the policy. For simple policies that you only need to enable or disable, you won't need to use this keyword. In fact, only a relative handful of the policies in Windows XP use the PART keyword at all.

You begin a part with the PART keyword and end it with END PART. The syntax of the PART keyword is PART *Name Type*. *Name* is the name of the part, and *Type* is the type of part. Each policy can contain multiple PART keywords, and the policy editor displays them in the dialog box using the order that it found them in the administrative template. This section gives you the overall syntax of the PART keyword, and the sections following this one describe how to create the different types of parts.

Syntax

```
PART Name Type

  Keywords

  [KEYNAME Subkey]
  [DEFAULT Default]
  VALUENAME Name
END PART
```

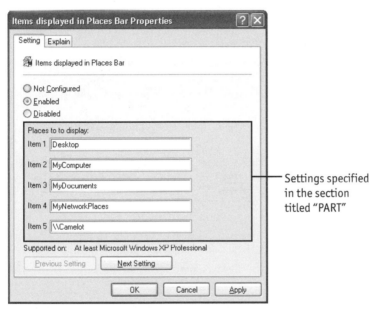

Figure 6-5 *Use the PART keyword to collect additional data that further refines the policy.*

Name	This specifies the name of the setting as you want to see it in the policy's dialog box. Enclose the name in double quotes if it contains spaces. This is the setting's prompt.
Type	This can be one of the following types:
	• **CHECKBOX.** Displays a check box. The REG_DWORD value is 0x01 if you select the check box or 0x00 if you clear it.
	• **COMBOBOX.** Displays a combo box.
	• **DROPDOWNLIST.** Displays a combo box with a drop-down list. The user can choose only one of the entries supplied.
	• **EDITTEXT.** Displays a text box that accepts alphanumeric input. The value is either REG_SZ or REG_EXPAND_SZ.
	• **LISTBOX.** Displays a list box with Add and Remove buttons. This is the only type that can be used to manage multiple values in one key.
	• **NUMERIC.** Displays a text box with an optional spin control that accepts a numeric value. The value is a REG_DWORD value.
	• **TEXT.** Displays a line of static text. It stores no data in the registry and is useful for adding help to the dialog box.
Keywords	This is information specific to each type of part. See the sections following this for more information about these keywords.
Subkey	This is an optional subkey of HKLM or HKCU to use for the category. Do not include either root key in the path, though, because the preceding CLASS keyword specifies which of these root keys to use. If you specify a subkey, all subcategories, policies, and parts use it unless they specifically provide a subkey of their own. Enclose names that contain spaces in double quotes.
Default	This is the default value for the part. When you enable the policy, the policy editor fills the control with the default value. Use a default value that's appropriate for the part's type.
Value	This is the registry value to modify. The value type and data depend entirely on the part's type.

Example

Listing 6-9   example.adm

```
POLICY "Sample Part"
  EXPLAIN "This illustrates parts"
  KEYNAME "Software\Policies"
  POLICY "Sample Policy"
    EXPLAIN "This is a sample policy including parts."
    VALUENAME "Sample"
    PART test EDITTEXT
      DEFAULT "This is the default text"
      VALUENAME Sample
    END PART
END POLICY
```

Keywords

The valid keywords within a PART section are the following:

- CHECKBOX
- COMBOBOX
- DROPDOWNLIST
- EDITTEXT
- END
- LISTBOX
- NUMERIC
- PART
- TEXT

CHECKBOX

The CHECKBOX keyword displays a check box. In the registry, it's a REG_SZ value. By default, the check box is cleared, and the settings it writes to the registry for each of its states are as follows:

- **Checked.**   Writes 1 to the REG_SZ value

- **Cleared.**   Writes 0 to the REG_SZ value

Include the keyword DEFCHECKED within the part if you want the check box selected by default. Otherwise, the check box is cleared by default.

Syntax

```
PART Name CHECKBOX
   DEFCHECKED
   VALUENAME Value
END PART
```

Name	This specifies the name of the setting as you want to see it in the policy's dialog box. Enclose the name in double quotes if it contains spaces. You see the name next to the check box.
Value	This is the registry value to modify. Enabling the policy sets the REG_SZ value to 1. Set the Not Configured option, and the policy editor removes the value from the registry. To specify values other than the default 0 and 1, use the VALUEON and VALUEOFF keywords following the VALUENAME keyword:
	VALUEON [NUMERIC] *Enabled* VALUEOFF [NUMERIC] *Disabled*
	When you use these keywords, the policy editor sets the registry value to *Enabled* when you enable the policy and sets the value to *Disabled* when you disable the policy. The default value type is REG_SZ, but you can change it to REG_DWORD by prefixing the value with the keyword NUMERIC. Regardless, setting the policy to Not Configured removes the value altogether. You can also use the ACTIONLISTON and ACTIONLISTOFF keywords to associate multiple values with a check box.

Example

Listing 6-10   example.adm

```
CLASS USER

CATEGORY "Sample Policies"
  EXPLAIN "These are sample policies that illustrate parts."

  POLICY "Sample Policy"
    SUPPORTED "At least Microsoft Windows XP Professional"

    EXPLAIN "This is a sample policy that illustrates a part."
    KEYNAME "Software\Policies"

    PART Sample1 CHECKBOX
      VALUENAME Sample1
    END PART

    PART Sample2 CHECKBOX
      DEFCHECKED
      VALUENAME Sample2
      VALUEON NUMERIC 11
      VALUEOFF NUMERIC 12
    END PART

  END POLICY

END CATEGORY
```

Keywords

The valid keywords within a CHECKBOX section include the following:

- ACTIONLISTOFF
- ACTIONLISTON
- DEFCHECKED
- END
- KEYNAME
- VALUENAME
- VALUEOFF
- VALUEON

COMBOBOX

The COMBOBOX keyword adds a combo box to the policy's dialog box. It has one additional keyword you must use, SUGGESTIONS. This creates a list of suggestions that the policy editor places in the drop-down list. Separate the items in this list with white space and enclose items containing spaces within double quotation marks. End the list with the END SUGGESTIONS.

A few keywords modify the behavior of the combo box:

- `DEFAULT.` Specifies the default value of the combo box
- `EXPANDABLETEXT.` Creates the value as a `REG_EXPAND_SZ` value
- `MAXLENGTH.` Specifies the maximum length of the value
- `NOSORT.` Prevents the policy editor from sorting the list
- `REQUIRED.` Specifies that a value is required

Syntax

```
PART Name COMBOBOX
  SUGGESTIONS
    Suggestions
  END SUGGESTIONS
  [DEFAULT Default]
  [EXPANDABLETEXT]
  [MAXLENGTH Max]
  [NOSORT]
  [REQUIRED]
  VALUENAME Value
END PART
```

Name	This specifies the name of the setting as you want to see it in the policy's dialog box. Enclose the name in double quotes if it contains spaces. You see the name next to the combo box.
Suggestions	This is a list of items to put in the drop-down list. Separate each suggestion with white space (line feeds, tabs, spaces and the like), and enclose any suggestion that includes a space in double quotes.
Default	This is the default value for the part. When you enable the policy, the policy editor fills the control with the default value. Use a default value that's appropriate for the part's type.
Max	This is the maximum length of the value's data.
Value	This is the registry value to modify. The policy editor creates this in the registry as a REG_SZ value and fills it with any text that you typed or selected in the combo box.

Example

Listing 6-11 example.adm

```
CLASS USER

CATEGORY "Sample Policies"
  EXPLAIN "These are sample policies that don't do anything but illustrate
parts."

  POLICY "Sample Policy"
```

```
SUPPORTED "At least Microsoft Windows XP Professional"

EXPLAIN "This is a sample policy that illustrates creating a part."
KEYNAME "Software\Policies"

PART Sample COMBOBOX
  SUGGESTIONS
    Sample1 Sample2 "Another Sample"
  END SUGGESTIONS
  VALUENAME Sample
END PART

END POLICY

END CATEGORY
```

Keywords

The valid keywords within a COMBOBOX section are the following:

- DEFAULT
- END
- EXPANDABLETEXT
- KEYNAME
- MAXLENGTH
- NOSORT
- REQUIRED
- SUGGESTIONS
- VALUENAME

DROPDOWNLIST

The DROPDOWNLIST keyword adds a drop-down list to the policy's dialog box. It has one additional keyword you must use, and that is ITEMLIST. This creates a list of items that the policy editor places in the drop-down list. Define each item within the ITEMLIST section using the syntax NAME *Name* VALUE *Value*. Enclose items containing spaces within double quotation marks. End the list with the END ITEMLIST.

A few keywords modify the behavior of the drop-down list:

- **DEFAULT.**   Specifies the default value of the drop-down list

- **EXPANDABLETEXT.**   Creates the value as a REG_EXPAND_SZ value

- **NOSORT.**   Prevents the policy editor from sorting the list

- **REQUIRED.**   Specifies that a value is required

Syntax

```
PART Name DROPDOWNLIST
  ITEMLIST
    NAME Item VALUE Data
  END ITEMLIST
  [DEFAULT Default]
  [EXPANDABLETEXT]
  [NOSORT]
  [REQUIRED]
  VALUENAME Value
END PART
```

Name	This specifies the name of the setting as you want to see it in the policy's dialog box. Enclose the name in double quotes if it contains spaces. You see the name next to the drop-down list.
Item	This is the name of each item in the list. This is the text that you'll see in the drop-down list. This isn't the value that the policy editor stores in the registry, though.
Data	This is the data you want the policy editor to store in the value when you select the associated item.
Default	This is the default value for the part. When you enable the policy, the policy editor fills the control with the default value. Use an item defined in ITEMLIST.
Value	This is the registry value to modify. The policy editor creates this in the registry as a REG_SZ value and fills it with the value of *Data* associated with the selected item.

Example

Listing 6-12   example.adm

```
CLASS USER

CATEGORY "Sample Policies"
  EXPLAIN "These are sample policies that illustrate parts."

  POLICY "Sample Policy"
    SUPPORTED "At least Microsoft Windows XP Professional"

    EXPLAIN "This is a sample policy that illustrates creating a part."
    KEYNAME "Software\Policies"

    PART Sample DROPDOWNLIST
      ITEMLIST
        NAME Sample1 VALUE 0
        NAME Sample2 VALUE 1
        NAME "Another Sample" VALUE 2
      END ITEMLIST
      VALUENAME Sample
    END PART
```

```
END POLICY

END CATEGORY
```

Keywords

The valid keywords within a DROPDOWNLIST section are the following:

- DEFAULT
- END
- EXPANDABLETEXT
- KEYNAME
- NOSORT
- REQUIRED
- ITEMLIST
- VALUENAME

EDITTEXT

The EDITTEXT keyword enables you to input alphanumeric text in a text box. Policy editor stores the text in a REG_SZ value. A few keywords modify the behavior of the text box:

- **DEFAULT.**   Specifies the default value of the text box

- **EXPANDABLETEXT.**   Creates the value as a REG_EXPAND_SZ value

- **MAXLENGTH.**   Specifies the maximum length of the value

- **REQUIRED.**   Specifies that a value is required

Syntax

```
PART Name EDITTEXT
  [DEFAULT Default]
  [EXPANDABLETEXT]
  [MAXLENGTH Max]
  [REQUIRED]
  VALUENAME Value
END PART
```

Name	This specifies the name of the setting as you want to see it in the policy's dialog box. Enclose the name in double quotes if it contains spaces. You see the name next to the text box.
Default	This is the default value for the part. When you enable the policy, the policy editor fills the control with the default value. Use a default value that's appropriate for the part's type.
Max	This is the maximum length of the value's data.
Value	This is the registry value to modify. The policy editor creates this in the registry as a REG_SZ value and fills it with any text that you typed.

Example

Listing 6-13   example.adm

```
CLASS USER

CATEGORY "Sample Policies"
  EXPLAIN "These are sample policies that illustrate parts."

  POLICY "Sample Policy"
    SUPPORTED "At least Microsoft Windows XP Professional"

    EXPLAIN "This is a sample policy that illustrates creating a part."
    KEYNAME "Software\Policies"

    PART Sample EDITTEXT
      VALUENAME Sample
    END PART

  END POLICY

END CATEGORY
```

Keywords

The valid keywords within an EDITTEXT section are the following:

- DEFAULT
- END
- EXPANDABLETEXT
- KEYNAME
- MAXLENGTH
- REQUIRED
- VALUENAME

LISTBOX

The LISTBOX keyword adds a list box with Add and Remove buttons to the policy's dialog box. This is the only type of part that you can use to manage multiple values in one key. You can't use the VALUENAME option with the LISTBOX part because it doesn't associate just a single value with it. Use the following options with the LISTBOX part type:

- **ADDITIVE.**   By default, the content of list boxes overrides values already set in the registry. That means that the Windows XP client-side extensions remove values before setting them. When you use this keyword, the client-side extensions do not delete existing values before adding the values set in the list box.

- **EXPLICITVALUE.**   This keyword makes you specify the value name and data. The list box shows two columns, one for the name and one for the data. You can't use this keyword with the VALUEPREFIX keyword.

- **VALUEPREFIX.**   The prefix you specify determines value names. If you specify a prefix, the policy editor adds an incremental number to it. For example, a prefix of Sample generates the value names Sample1, Sample2, and so on. The prefix can be empty ("") , causing the value names to be 1, 2, and so on.

By default, without using either the EXPLICITVALUE or VALUEPREFIX keywords, only one column appears in the list box. For each entry in the list, the policy editor creates a value using the entry's text for the value's name and data. For example, the entry Sample in the list box creates a value called Sample whose data is Sample. The default behavior is seldom the desirable result.

Syntax

```
PART Name LISTBOX
  [EXPANDABLETEXT]
  [NOSORT]
  [ADDITIVE]
  [EXPLICITVALUE | VALUEPREFIX Prefix]
END PART
```

Name	This specifies the name of the setting as you want to see it in the policy's dialog box. Enclose the name in double quotes if it contains spaces.
Prefix	This is the prefix to use for incremental names. If you specify a prefix, the policy editor adds an incremental number to it. For example, a prefix of Sample generates the value names Sample1, Sample2, and so on. The prefix can be empty (""), causing the value names to be 1, 2, and so on.

Example

Listing 6-14   example.adm

```
CLASS USER

CATEGORY "Sample Policies"
  EXPLAIN "These are sample policies that illustrate parts."

  POLICY "Sample Policy"
    SUPPORTED "At least Microsoft Windows XP Professional"

    EXPLAIN "This is a sample policy that illustrates creating a part."
    KEYNAME "Software\Policies"

    PART Sample LISTBOX
      EXPLICITVALUE
    END PART
```

```
    END POLICY

END CATEGORY
```

Keywords

The valid keywords within a LISTBOX section are the following:

- ADDITIVE
- END
- EXPANDABLETEXT
- EXPLICITVALUE
- KEYNAME
- NOSORT
- VALUEPREFIX

NUMERIC

The NUMERIC keyword enables you to input alphanumeric text using a spinner control that adjusts the number up and down. Policy editor stores the number in a REG_DWORD value, but you can change the value's type to REG_SZ using the TXTCONVERT keyword. A few other keywords modify the behavior of the text box:

- **DEFAULT.** Specifies the initial value of the text box

- **MAX.** Specifies the maximum value. The default is 9999

- **MIN.** Specifies the minimum value. The default is 0.

- **REQUIRED.** Specifies that a value is required

- **SPIN.** Specifies the increment to use for the spinner control. The default value is 1, and using 0 removes the spinner control.

- **TXTCONVERT.** Writes values as REG_SZ values rather than REG_DWORD

Syntax

```
PART Name NUMERIC
  [DEFAULT Default]
  [MAX Max]
  [MIN Min]
  [REQUIRED]
  [SPIN]
  [TXTCONVERT]
  VALUENAME Value
END PART
```

Name	This specifies the name of the setting as you want to see it in the policy's dialog box. Enclose the name in double quotes if it contains spaces. You see the name next to the text box.
Default	This is the default value for the part. When you enable the policy, the policy editor fills the control with the default value. Use a default value that's appropriate for the part's type.
Max	This is the maximum value. The default is 9999.
Min	This is the minimum value. The default is 0.
Value	This is the registry value to modify. The policy editor creates this in the registry as a REG_DWORD value, setting it to the value that you specify in the dialog box. To change the value's type to REG_SZ, use the TXTCONVERT keyword.

Example

Listing 6-15   example.adm

```
CLASS USER

CATEGORY "Sample Policies"
  EXPLAIN "These are sample policies that illustrate parts."

  POLICY "Sample Policy"
    SUPPORTED "At least Microsoft Windows XP Professional"

    EXPLAIN "This is a sample policy that illustrates creating a part."
    KEYNAME "Software\Policies"

    PART Sample NUMERIC
      DEFAULT 11
      MIN 10
      MAX 20
      VALUENAME Sample
    END PART

  END POLICY

END CATEGORY
```

Keywords

The valid keywords within a NUMERIC section are the following:

- DEFAULT
- END
- KEYNAME
- MAX
- MIN

- REQUIRED
- SPIN
- TXTCONVERT
- VALUENAME

TEXT

The TEXT keyword adds static text to the bottom part of the policy's dialog box.

Syntax

```
PART Text TEXT
END PART
```

Text	This is the text you want to add to the dialog box.

Example

Listing 6-16   example.adm

```
CLASS USER

CATEGORY "Sample Policies"
  EXPLAIN "These are sample policies that illustrate parts."

  POLICY "Sample Policy"
    SUPPORTED "At least Microsoft Windows XP Professional"

    EXPLAIN "This is a sample policy that illustrates creating a part."
    KEYNAME "Software\Policies"

    PART "This is sample text added to the dialog box." TEXT
    END PART

  END POLICY

END CATEGORY
```

Deploying Registry-Based Policy

To use an administrative template, whether you created it or an application such as Office XP provides it, you must load it in the Administrative Templates extension. You load template files into each GPO in which you want to use them. Because we're talking about the local GPO in this chapter, you only have to load template files once. If you use a template with Active Directory, you'd have to load it in each GPO in which you want to use it, though.

Here's how to load a template in the local GPO:

1. Right-click Administrative Templates, under Computer Configuration or User Configuration, and then click Add/Remove Templates.

2. In the Add/Remove Templates dialog box, click Add.

3. In the Policy Templates dialog box, type the path and file name of the administrative template you want to load in to the local GPO.

Windows XP Group Policy Improvements

Windows XP includes improved policy management, enabling IT professionals to fine tune, manage, or simply turn off features they don't want users to access. IT professionals can deploy any of the policy settings in Windows XP from Active Directory, too, without fear of wrecking their Windows 2000 configurations. Here's a brief list of the improvements you find in Windows XP:

- Windows XP supports all 421 Windows 2000 policies.

- Windows XP adds 212 new policy settings, and Windows 2000 ignores them.

- The Group Policy editor uses Web view to display useful information about policies that IT professionals use to assess and verify settings.

- The Group Policy editor includes integrated help that makes learning and tracking down policies easier.

- Windows XP doesn't wait for the network to fully initialize before presenting the desktop, using cached credentials in the meantime, and allowing users to get to work faster. It applies policies in the background when the network is ready.

These improvements are big advantages. However, you'll be happy to know that the big picture doesn't change much. You use roughly the same tools in the same ways to configure and manage user settings. If you're already familiar with Windows 2000 Group Policy, you're equally familiar with Windows XP Group Policy.

Windows 2000 Server-Based Networks

The Windows XP policy templates are fully compatible with Windows 2000 Server and its version of Active Directory. Microsoft Windows .NET Server includes the Windows XP administrative templates by default. You have to load them in each GPO in which you want to use them, though, and the steps for doing that are the same as you learned in the previous sections.

You can avoid having to load the Windows XP administrative templates in each GPO by copying them to %SYSTEMROOT%\Inf on the server. Just copy all the files with the *.adm* extension from %SYSTEMROOT%\Inf on a computer running Windows XP to the same folder on the server. The server operating system automatically updates each GPO when you open it for editing. If you're uncomfortable with replacing your Windows 2000 administrative templates, you should continue loading the Windows XP templates in GPOs where you want to use them. I've replaced my Windows 2000 administrative templates with Windows XP administrative templates, however, and haven't felt any pain.

Consider these best practices when using Windows XP administrative templates in Windows 2000 Server:

- In a mixed environment, use Windows XP template files to administer your GPOs. Windows 2000 ignores Windows XP–specific settings.

- Apply the same policy settings to both Windows XP and Windows 2000 to give roaming users a consistent experience.

- Test interoperability of the various settings before deployment.

- Configure policy settings only on client machines using GPOs. Do not try to create these registry values by other methods.

Windows NT-Based and Other Networks

Like Group Policy, System Policy configures and manages settings for groups of computers and groups of users. I assume you're familiar with System Policy Editor if you're facing this issue. Table 6-2 describes the differences between the two technologies. The policy file that System Policy Editor creates, Ntconfig.pol normally, contains the registry settings for all the users, groups, and computers that use those settings. To deploy this file on a network, put it in the NETLOGON share of the domain controller. Unlike Group Policy, separate policy files aren't necessary.

Table 6-2   Group Policy Compared to System Policy

	Group Policy	**System Policy**
Tool	Group Policy editor	System Policy Editor
Number of settings	620 registry-based settings	72 registry-based settings
Applied to	Users and computers in a specific Active Directory container, such as sites, domains, and organizational units	Users and computers in a domain
Security	Secure	Not secure
Extensions	Microsoft Management Console and administrative templates	Administrative templates
Persistence	Does not make permanent changes to the registry	Makes permanent changes to the registry that you must manually remove
Usage	• Implementing registry-based policy settings • Configuring security settings • Applying logon, logoff, startup, and shutdown scripts • Deploying and maintaining software • Optimizing and maintaining Internet Explorer	Implementing registry-based policy settings

Windows XP behaves differently depending on what kind of server authenticates the user and computer accounts. If a Windows 2000–based server authenticates the account, Windows XP looks for Group Policy, not System Policy. If a Windows NT-based server authenticates the account, Windows XP looks for System Policy. (It uses the file Ntconfig.pol in the NETLOGON share.) You can use this to your advantage when you haven't deployed Active Directory but you still want to configure policies.

To configure System Policies, use System Policy Editor. You load the Windows XP policy templates in System Policy Editor before using them. Using System Policy, you can configure and deliver all the registry-based policies that these templates define. Note that Windows XP doesn't provide System Policy Editor but Windows 2000 Server does. Also, you will find System Policy Editor in the Office XP Resource Kit, which you learn about in Chapter 14, "Deploying Office XP Settings." You create the Ntconfig.pol file and drop it in the NETLOGON share. If Windows XP authenticates the account using that Windows NT-based server, it downloads and parses the policies from the Ntconfig.pol file it finds in the NETLOGON share.

If you're not using Active Directory or a Windows NT domain, you can still configure System Policy. You configure Windows XP to look for the Ntconfig.pol file in any share by specifying a path to the policy file. You must make this change on each individual computer, however, which makes it a labor-intensive process unless you configure it on your disk images. Set the UpdateMode REG_DWORD value to 0x02, which changes Windows XP from automatic (0x01) to manual mode (0x02). (Set this value to 0x00 to turn off system policy.) Then set the REG_SZ value NetworkPath to the UNC path and name of the policy file you want to use. These values are in the key HKLM\SYSTEM\CurrentControlSet\Control\Update. You might have to create them.

Customizing Windows XP

The key reason that power users want to create administrative templates is to customize settings that have no user interface. By creating an administrative template, you give those settings a user interface, preventing human error. The following listing is a sample administrative template that does just that. It defines a handful of custom settings that Tweak UI (see Chapter 5, "Mapping Tweak UI") contains. Figure 6-6 on page 180 shows what this administrative template looks like in the Group Policy editor.

Listing 6-17   Tweakui.adm

```
CLASS USER

CATEGORY "Tweak UI Settings"
  EXPLAIN "These are settings from Tweak UI."

  CATEGORY "Mouse"
    EXPLAIN "Settings that customize the mouse."

    POLICY "Menu Show Delay"
      EXPLAIN "Delay before Windows XP opens a menu when you point at it."
      KEYNAME "Control Panel\Desktop"
      PART "Menu Delay (milliseconds)" NUMERIC
```

```
        MIN 0
        MAX 65534
        DEFAULT 400
        TXTCONVERT
        VALUENAME MenuShowDelay
      END PART
    END POLICY

    POLICY "Drag Height and Width"
      EXPLAIN "Number of pixels the mouse moves before Windows XP thinks you're
dragging it."
      KEYNAME "Control Panel\Desktop"
      PART "Height" NUMERIC
        MIN 0
        MAX 16
        TXTCONVERT
        VALUENAME DragHeight
      END PART
      PART "Width" NUMERIC
        MIN 0
        MAX 16
        TXTCONVERT
        VALUENAME DragWidth
      END PART
    END POLICY

  END CATEGORY

  CATEGORY "Taskbar"
    EXPLAIN "Settings that customize the taskbar."

    POLICY "Balloon Tips"
      EXPLAIN "Enable or disable balloon tips."
      KEYNAME Software\Microsoft\Windows\CurrentVersion\Explorer\Advanced
      VALUENAME EnableBalloonTips
      VALUEOFF NUMERIC 0
      VALUEON NUMERIC 1
    END POLICY

    POLICY "Taskbar Grouping"
      EXPLAIN "Control how buttons group on the taskbar."
      KEYNAME Software\Microsoft\Windows\CurrentVersion\Explorer\Advanced

      PART Grouping DROPDOWNLIST
        ITEMLIST
          NAME "Group least used applications first" VALUE 0
          NAME "Group applications with the mouse windows first" VALUE 1
          NAME "Group applications with at least 2 windows" VALUE 2
          NAME "Group applications with at least 3 windows" VALUE 3
```

```
        NAME "Group applications with at least 4 windows" VALUE 4
        NAME "Group applications with at least 5 windows" VALUE 5
        NAME "Group applications with at least 6 windows" VALUE 6
        NAME "Group applications with at least 7 windows" VALUE 7
      END ITEMLIST
      NOSORT
      VALUENAME TaskbarGroupSize
    END PART

  END POLICY

 END CATEGORY

END CATEGORY
```

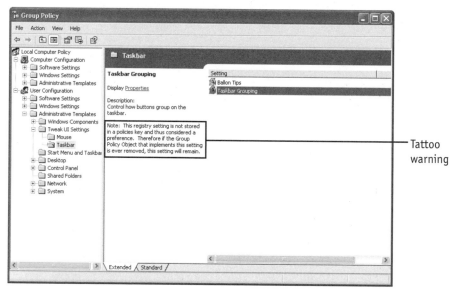

Figure 6-6 *Notice the warning that says the setting will tattoo the registry.*

This administrative template does not contain proper policies. The settings aren't in an official policy branch in the registry, so Windows XP can't manage them. That means if you remove the policy, the setting remains. The change is permanent. By default, the Group Policy editor does not display unmanaged settings because they tattoo the registry—a negative side effect you don't normally want to happen. In this case, I'm consciously choosing to do this to provide a user interface for user preferences that don't normally have a user interface. In Group Policy editor, unmanaged settings have red icons rather than the normal blue icons. To display these settings, you must show unmanaged settings in Group Policy editor:

1. Right-click Administrative Templates under Computer Configuration or User Configuration, point to View, and click Filtering.

2. In the Filtering dialog box, clear the Only Show Policy Settings That Can Be Fully Managed check box.

Using the Group Policy Tools

The Group Policy tools in Windows XP contain a lot of improvements. The sections following this one describe each of these tools and how to use them. Some of these enhancements deserve special mention, though. First is Group Policy Update Tool (Gpupdate.exe). Group Policy refreshes policies every 90 minutes by default. In Windows 2000, if you change a policy and want to see the results immediately, you had to use the commands `secedit /refreshpolicy user_policy` and `secedit /refreshpolicy machine_policy`. Gpupdate.exe replaces both of these commands in one easy to use command. You don't need to use this tool when updating the local GPO, though, because changes to the local GPO are instant.

Second is Resultant Set of Policy (RSoP). Windows XP includes new tools for seeing which policies the operating system is applying to the current user and computer and the location where they originated. One of the toughest parts of administering Group Policy on a large network is tracking down behaviors that result from combinations of GPOs that you didn't intend or didn't know were occurring. These tools help you track down these behaviors much faster than you could with Windows 2000 because they give you a snapshot of how the operating system is applying them and where they originated.

Gpresult

Group Policy Result Tool displays the effective policies and RSoP for the current user and computer. This section describes its command-line options.

Syntax

```
gpresult [/s Computer [/u Domain\User /p Password]] [/user TargetUserName] [/
scope {user|computer}] [/v] [/z]
```

/s *Computer*	This specifies the name or IP address of a remote computer (don't use back-slashes). It defaults to the local computer.
/u *Domain\User*	This runs the command with the account permissions of the user specified by *User* or *Domain\User*. The default is the permissions of the current console user.
/p *Password*	This specifies the password of the user account that the /u option specifies.
/user *TargetUserName*	This specifies the user name of the user for whom you want to display RSoP.
/scope {user|computer}	This displays either user or computer results. Valid values for the /scope option are user or computer. If you omit the /scope option, Gpresult.exe displays both user and computer settings.
/v	This specifies that the output display verbose policy information.

(continued)

/z	This specifies that the output display all available information about Group Policy. Because this option produces more information than the /v option, redirect output to a text file when you use this parameter: `gpresult /z >policy.txt`.
/?	This displays help.

Examples

```
gpresult /user jerry /scope computer
gpresult /s camelot /u honeycutt\administrator /p password /user jerry
gpresult /s camelot /u honeycutt\administrator /p password /user jerry /z
>policy.txt
```

Gpupdate

Group Policy Update Tool (Gpupdate.exe) refreshes local and network policy settings, including registry-based settings. As I mentioned, this command replaces the obsolete command `secedit /refreshpolicy`.

Syntax

```
gpupdate [/target:{computer|user}] [/force] [/wait:value] [/logoff] [/boot]
```

/target:{computer|user}	This processes only the computer settings or the current user settings. By default, both the computer and user settings are processed.
/force	This ignores all processing optimizations and reapplies all settings.
/wait:value	This is the number of seconds that policy processing waits to finish. The default is 600 seconds. 0 means don't wait, and -1 means wait forever.
/logoff	This logs the user off after the refresh has completed. This is required for those Group Policy client-side extensions that do not process on a background refresh cycle but that do process when the user logs on, such as user Software Installation and Folder Redirection. This option has no effect if there are no extensions called that require the user to log off.
/boot	This restarts the computer after the refresh is finished. This is required for those Group Policy client-side extensions that do not process on a background refresh cycle but that do process when the computer starts up, such as computer Software Installation. This option has no effect if there are no extensions called that require the computer to be restarted.
/?	This displays help.

Examples

```
gpupdate
gpupdate /target:computer
gpupdate /force /wait:100
gpupdate /boot
```

Simulating Folder Redirection

IT professionals often ask me about Folder Redirection. Specifically, they want to know how to simulate this policy when they haven't yet deployed Active Directory. Active Directory is a requirement for this policy, after all.

Not so fast! Although you can't achieve automatic folder redirection without Active Directory, you can simulate it. Configure the key User Shell Folders to redirect My Documents and other folders to a network location. This key is in HKCU\Software\Microsoft\Windows \CurrentVersion\Explorer and contains one value for each of the special folders that Windows XP supports. They are REG_EXPAND_SZ values, so you can use environment variables, such as %USERNAME% and %HOMESHARE%, in the path. This means that even on a Windows NT–based network, you can use redirected folders.

I suggest you script this customization so you can apply it uniformly. Chapter 4, "Hacking the Registry," describes the key User Shell Folders in great detail, and it also contains a sample script that automatically redirects folders.

Help and Support Center

Although of limited use for IT professionals because you can't use it remotely, users can run Help and Support Center's Resultant Set of Policy Report on their own computers to check policy settings. This tool provides a user-friendly, printable report of most policies in effect for the computer and console user. Figure 6-7 on the next page shows a sample of this report. Here's how to use this tool:

1. Click Start, and then click Help And Support Center.

2. Under Pick A Task, click Use Tools To View Your Computer Information And Diagnose Problems.

3. Click Advanced System Information, and then click View Group Policy Settings Applied.

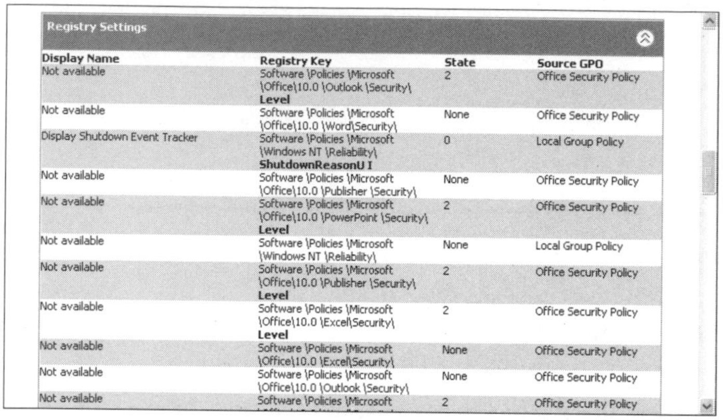

Registry Settings

Display Name	Registry Key	State	Source GPO
Not available	Software \Policies \Microsoft \Office\10.0 \Outlook \Security\ **Level**	2	Office Security Policy
Not available	Software \Policies \Microsoft \Office\10.0 \Word\Security\	None	Office Security Policy
Display Shutdown Event Tracker	Software \Policies \Microsoft \Windows NT \Reliability\ **ShutdownReasonU I**	0	Local Group Policy
Not available	Software \Policies \Microsoft \Office\10.0 \Publisher \Security\	None	Office Security Policy
Not available	Software \Policies \Microsoft \Office\10.0 \PowerPoint \Security\ **Level**	2	Office Security Policy
Not available	Software \Policies \Microsoft \Windows NT \Reliability\	None	Local Group Policy
Not available	Software \Policies \Microsoft \Office\10.0 \Publisher \Security\ **Level**	2	Office Security Policy
Not available	Software \Policies \Microsoft \Office\10.0 \Excel\Security\ **Level**	2	Office Security Policy
Not available	Software \Policies \Microsoft \Office\10.0 \Excel\Security\	None	Office Security Policy
Not available	Software \Policies \Microsoft \Office\10.0 \Outlook \Security\	None	Office Security Policy
Not available	Software \Policies \Microsoft	2	Office Security Policy

Figure 6-7 *Help and Support Center's RSoP report contains the same type of information as Gpresult.exe, but it's more readable and more suitable for printing.*

Resultant Set of Policy

Although Help and Support Center's RSoP report isn't suitable for use by IT professionals, the RSoP snap-in is suitable because you can use it to view RSoP data for remote computers. You use this tool to predict how policies work for a specific user or computer, as well as for entire groups of users and computers. Sometimes, GPOs applied at different levels in Active Directory conflict with each other. Tracking down these conflicting settings is difficult without a tool like this snap-in.

The RSoP snap-in checks Software Installation for applications associated with the user or computer. It reports all other policy settings, too, including registry-based policies, redirected folders, Internet Explorer maintenance, security settings, and scripts. You've already seen two tools that report RSoP data: Gpresult.exe and Help and Support Center. The RSoP snap-in is almost as easy to use (your account must be in the computer's local Administrators group to use this tool):

1. Click Start, Run, and type **mmc**.
2. Click File, Add/Remove Snap-In; and then click Add.
3. In the Available Standalone Snap-Ins dialog box, select Resultant Set Of Policy, and then click Add.
4. Click Next in Resultant Set of Policy Wizard; and click Next again.
5. On the Computer Selection page, click Another Computer, type the name of the computer you want to inspect, and then click Next.
6. On the User Selection page, select the user for which you want to display RSoP data, and then click Next.
7. Click Next, and then click Finish to close the wizard.

Figure 6-8 shows the results. In this example, you see the password policies applied to the computer. For each setting, you see the GPO that's the source for it.

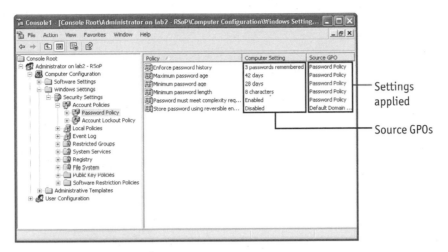

Figure 6-8 *The RSoP snap-in is the best tool for figuring out the source of policy settings when multiple GPOs apply to a computer.*

Finding More Resources

This chapter focused on local registry-based policies. This is a registry book after all. If you're interested in learning more about Group Policy, Microsoft's Web site contains a plethora of good information. You don't even need to buy a book to learn more about it. Here's a list of resources that I found valuable when I was first learning about Group Policy:

- *http://www.microsoft.com/windows2000/techinfo/howitworks/management /grouppolwp.asp*   This is the Windows 2000 Group Policy white paper, and it's the best starting point for understanding how to create GPOs and apply them to containers in Active Directory. This paper is long but a worthy read.

- *http://www.microsoft.com/Windows2000/techinfo/howitworks/management /rbppaper.asp*   This is the Implementing Registry-Based Group Policy white paper. The bulk of this paper is about creating administrative templates for Windows XP. It's the paper I used most when writing this chapter because it describes the syntaxes for each of the keywords you can use in administrative templates.

- *http://www.microsoft.com/WINDOWSXP/pro/techinfo/administration/policy /default.asp*   This is the Managing Windows XP in a Windows 2000 Server Environment white paper. It's a bit long, and all it really says is that Windows 2000 ignores Windows XP policies, and you can copy the Windows XP administrative templates to %SYSTEMROOT%\Inf on a Windows 2000–based server to use those templates for both Windows 2000 and Windows XP. Still, it's an interesting read because it goes into detail about the Group Policy improvements that Windows XP provides. Of note, this Web page includes a spreadsheet that lists all the policies. You can use it as a start for your own specification, recording which policies you're going to deploy.

Managing Registry Security

Security is not the most interesting registry-related topic, nor is it the most popular. I don't use a lot of pages talking about it because, well, there's just not much to tell you. You can change a key's access control list (ACL). You can audit keys. You can also take ownership of keys. You can't do any of these things with individual values, though. Power users generally won't care much about registry security, but IT professionals often have no choice.

Just because you can edit keys' ACLs doesn't mean you should, however. Messing with your registry's security is not a good idea unless you have a specific reason to do so. At best, you will make a change that's irrelevant, but at worst, you can prevent Microsoft Windows XP from working properly. So why am I including security in this book at all? There are cases in which IT professionals must change the registry's default permissions to deploy software. That is a totally different story than tinkering with your registry's security out of curiosity. For example, you might have an application that users can run only when they log on to the operating system as a member of the Administrators group. Ouch. In a corporate environment, you don't want to dump all your users in this group. The solution is to deploy Windows XP with custom permissions so users can run those programs as a member of the Power Users or Users group. This is the most common scenario, and it's the primary focus of this chapter.

You have two methods of deploying custom permissions. First you can do it manually. For the sake of completeness, I show you how to change a key's permissions in Registry Editor (Regedit). You can also build a security template, complete with custom registry permissions, and then apply that template to a computer manually. You wouldn't run around from desktop to desktop applying the template, though; you'd apply that template to your disk images before deployment. The second method is by using Group Policy. You create a Group Policy object (GPO) and then import a security template into it to create a security policy for your network. Windows XP automatically applies the custom permissions in your template to the computer and user if that GPO is in the Resultant Set of Policy (RSoP). I don't talk about Group Policy a whole lot in this book, but Chapter 6, "Using Registry-Based Policy," points out a lot of good, free resources for learning more about it.

Note   If you're interested in learning about the new security features in Windows XP, see the white paper "What's New in Security for Windows XP Professional and Windows XP Home Edition." You find this paper on Microsoft's Web site at *http://www.microsoft.com/technet /treeview/default.asp?url=/TechNet/prodtechnol/winxppro/evaluate/xpsec.asp*

Setting Keys' Permissions

Registry security is similar to file system security except that you can set only keys' permissions, not values' permissions. Other than that, the dialog boxes look similar; the permissions are similar, and so on. If you don't understand basic security concepts, take a moment and review them in Help and Support Center before tinkering with permissions. I don't include the basic concepts in this chapter because I assume that you're an IT professional and already have this information under your belt.

If you have full control of or own a registry key, you can edit its permissions for users and groups in its ACL:

1. In Regedit, click the key with the ACL you want to edit.

2. On the Edit menu, click Permissions (see Figure 7-1).

3. In the Group Or User Names list, click the user or group for whom you want to edit permissions, and then select the check box in the Allow or Deny column to allow or deny the following permissions:

   - **Full Control.**   Grants the user or group permission to open, edit, and take ownership of the key. It literally gives full control of it.

   - **Read.**   Grants the user or group permission to read the key's contents but not save changes made to it. Read this as *read-only*.

   - **Special Permissions.**   Grants the user or group a special combination of permissions. To grant special permissions, click Advanced. You learn more about this permission setting in the section titled "Assigning Special Permissions," later in this chapter.

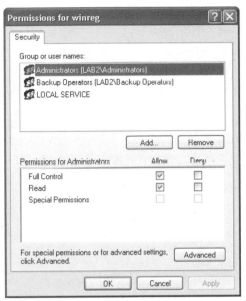

Figure 7-1 *This dialog box is almost identical to the dialog box for file system security.*

Sometimes the check boxes in the Permissions For *Name* area are shaded. You can't change them. The reason is that the key inherits that permission from the parent key. You can prevent a key from inheriting permissions, and you learn how to do that later in this chapter in "Assigning Special Permissions."

Tip OK, you had your fun. You tinkered with your registry's security and satisfied your curiosity; but now what? You can easily restore the original permissions by applying the Setup Security template. You learn how to apply this template in the section "Modifying a Computer's Configuration," later in this chapter.

Adding Users to ACLs

You can add users or groups to a key's existing ACL:

1. In Regedit, click the key with the ACL you want to edit.

2. On the Edit menu, click Permissions, and then click Add.

3. In the Select Users, Computers, Or Groups dialog box, click Locations, and then click the computer, domain, or organizational unit in which you want to look for the user or group you want to add to the key's ACL.

4. In the Enter The Object Names To Select box, type the name of the user or group you want to add to the key's ACL, and then click OK.

5. In the Permissions For *Name* list, configure the permissions you want to give the user or group by selecting the Allow or Deny check box.

The only real-world scenario I can think of for adding users to a key's ACL is allowing a group to access a computer's registry over the network, which you learn how to do in "Restricting Remote Registry Access," later in this chapter. Otherwise, adding a user or group to a key's ACL is sometimes useful as a quick fix when an application can't access the settings it needs when users run it. Generally speaking, adding users or groups to a key's ACL does little harm, but if you're not careful, you can open holes in the security of Windows XP so wide that users and hackers can walk through them. And if the edit you're making affects more than one computer or user, consider deploying it as a security template. (See "Deploying Security Templates," later in this chapter.)

Tip   In step 4, you type all or part of the user or group name you want to add to the key's ACL. If you don't have a clue what the name is, you can search for it. First, if possible, narrow your search by choosing a location as I described in step 3. Then click Advanced, and click Find Now. Click the name of the user or group you want to add, and click OK. You can further narrow the results by clicking Object Types, and then clearing the Built-In Security Principals check box.

Removing Users from ACLs

Here's how to remove a user or group from a key's ACL:

1. In Regedit, click the key with the ACL you want to edit.

2. On the Edit menu, click Permissions.

3. Click the user or group you want to remove, and click Remove.

Caution   Be wary of removing groups from keys' ACLs. Generally, the ACLs you see in Windows XP after installing it (Setup Security) are the bare minimum required for users to start and use the operating system. If you remove the Users or Power Users group from a key, users in those groups can't read the key's values, and this is likely going to mangle the operating system or an application. If you dare remove the Administrators group from a key, you might not be able to manage the computer at all. Removing individual users from a key's ACL isn't necessarily a bad thing, however. Windows XP doesn't assign permissions to individual users, so those permissions got there by devious means. You should never remove users from their profile hives' ACLs, though. Doing so prevents them from accessing their own settings, of which they should have full control.

Assigning Special Permissions

Special permissions give you more granular control of a key's ACL than the basic Full Control and Read permissions. You can allow or deny users the ability to create subkeys, set values, read values, and so on. You can get very detailed. Here's how:

1. In Regedit, click the key with the ACL you want to edit.

2. On the Edit menu, click Permissions.

3. In the Group Or User Names list, click the user or group for whom you want to edit permissions. Add the user or group if necessary. Then click Advanced.

4. Double-click the user or group to whom you want to give special permissions. You see the Permission Entry For *Name* dialog box shown in Figure 7-2.

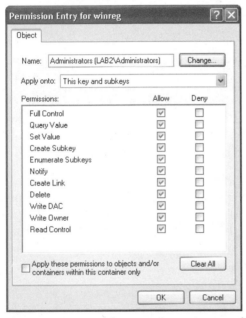

Figure 7-2   *Special permissions give you finer control of a user or group's permissions to use a key, but assigning special permissions is generally unnecessary.*

5. In the Apply Onto drop-down list, click one of the following:

- **This Key Only.**   Applies the permissions to the selected key only.

- **This Key And Subkeys.**   Applies the permissions to the selected key and all its subkeys. In other words, it applies them to the entire branch.

- **Subkeys Only.**   Applies the permissions to all the key's subkeys but not to the key itself.

6. In the Permissions list, select the Allow or Deny check box for each permission you want to allow or deny:

- **Full Control.** All the following permissions.
- **Query Value.** Read a value from the key.
- **Set Value.** Set a value in the key.
- **Create Subkey.** Create subkeys in the key.
- **Enumerate Subkeys.** Identify the key's subkeys.
- **Notify.** Receive notification events from the key.
- **Create Link.** Create symbolic links in the key.
- **Delete.** Delete the key or its values.
- **Write DAC.** Write the key's discretionary access control list.
- **Write Owner.** Change the key's owner.
- **Read Control.** Read the key's discretionary access control list.

A word about inheritance is necessary here. With inheritance enabled, subkeys inherit the permissions of their parent keys. In other words, if a key gives a group full control, all the key's subkeys also give that group full control. In fact, when you view the subkeys' ACLs, the Allow check box next to Full Control is shaded for that group because you can't change inherited permissions. There are a few things you can do to configure inheritance. First you can prevent a subkey from inheriting its parent key's permissions: In the Advanced Security Settings For *Key* dialog box, clear the Inherit From Parent The Permission Entries That Apply To Child Objects check box. Second you can replace the ACLs of a key's subkeys, effectively resetting an entire branch to match a key's ACL. Select the Replace Permission Entries On All Child Objects With Entries Shown Here That Apply To Child Objects check box.

Mapping Default Permissions

Understanding the registry's default permissions is useful if you're an IT professional deploying software. Knowing whether members of the Users group can change a particular setting helps you test applications prior to deployment and determine if the application works with default permissions. If you determine that an application does work properly with the default permissions, it's good to go. If you determine that an application doesn't work properly with the default permissions, you must either fix the program or change the offending key's permissions. The easiest way to do that, of course, is using security templates.

First you must understand the three fundamental groups in Windows XP: Users, Power Users, and Administrators. Through these groups, Windows XP provides different levels of access depending on each group's needs:

- **Users.**   This group has the highest security because the default permissions given to it don't allow its members to change operating system data or other users' settings. Generally, users in this group can't change per-computer operating system and application settings. They can usually include programs certified for Windows XP that administrators deploy to their computers. Last, this group gives its members full control over everything in their user profile, including their profile hives (HKCU). What frequently keeps IT professionals from assigning users to this group is that members can't usually run legacy applications. Rather than assign users to another group, deal with this problem by applying a compatible security template, which you learn how to do in the section titled "Deploying Security Templates," later in this chapter.

- **Power Users.**   This group provides backward compatibility for running programs that aren't certified for Windows XP. The default permissions give this group the ability to change many per-computer operating system and program settings. Generally, if you have legacy applications that users can't run as members of the Users group and you're not going to use security templates, adding those users to the Power Users group allows the applications to run. This group doesn't have enough permission to install most applications, though; members can't change operating system files or install services. The permissions given to the Power Users group is somewhere in the middle of the Users and Administrators groups. It's similar to the Users group in Microsoft Windows NT 4.0. And no, members of this group can't add themselves to the Administrators group.

- **Administrators.**   This group provides full control of the entire computer. Its members can change all operating system and application files. They can change all settings in the registry. Also, they can take ownership of keys and change a key's ACL. IT professionals are often tempted to add users to this group to avoid having trouble deploying applications that are otherwise difficult to install or run. Don't. Because users in this group can install anything they like or change any setting they like, viruses are free to do their damage and users are free to subject their configurations to the inevitable bout of human error. To secure your enterprise's desktops and reduce downtime, reserve this group for actual administrators. If you're a power user, don't add your account to this group for the same reasons. Instead, when you need to perform an administrative task, use a secondary logon to start a program as Administrator: Hold down the Shift key while you right-click the program's shortcut, click Run As, and then type the account name and password that you want to use to run the program.

Table 7-1 on the next page describes the registry's default permissions after installing Windows XP from scratch. Keep in mind that the resulting permissions are different if you upgrade from an earlier version of Windows to Windows XP. I got these permissions from the security template that you use to restore Windows XP to *out of box* security. I've focused on the Users and Power Users groups because these are the primary issue. In most of these cases, the Administrators group has full control, as do the Creator Owner and System built-in accounts. In most cases—but not all—each key's permissions replace all subkeys' permissions. This is through the magic of inheritance, which you learned about in the last section.

When you see the word *Special* in the Power Users column, it means the group has special permissions on that key (and subkeys in most cases), and that permission is usually the ability to modify values. The Power Users group doesn't ever get the Full Control, Create Link, Change Permissions, or Take Ownership permission for any key in the registry, though. The interesting thing about this table is that Windows XP gives the Users group Read permission and the Power Users group special permissions for all of HKLM\SOFTWARE. The remaining entries in the table are exceptions to this rule that limit access to specific keys in HKLM\SOFTWARE.

Table 7-1   Default Permissions in the Registry

Branch	Users	Power users
hklm\software	Read	Special
hklm\software\classes	Read	Special
hklm\software\classes\.hlp	Read	Read
hklm\software\classes\helpfile	Read	Read
hklm\software\microsoft\ads\providers\ldap\extensions	Read	Read
hklm\software\microsoft\ads\providers\nds	Read	Read
hklm\software\microsoft\ads\providers\nwcompat	Read	Read
hklm\software\microsoft\ads\providers\winnt	Read	Read
hklm\software\microsoft\command processor	Read	Read
hklm\software\microsoft\cryptography	Read	Read
hklm\software\microsoft\cryptography\calais	None	None
hklm\software\microsoft\driver signing	Read	Read
hklm\software\microsoft\enterprisecertificates	Read	Read
hklm\software\microsoft\msdtc	None	None
hklm\software\microsoft\netdde	None	None
hklm\software\microsoft\non-driver signing	Read	Read
hklm\software\microsoft\ole	Read	Read
hklm\software\microsoft\protected storage system provider	None	None
hklm\software\microsoft\rpc	Read	Read
hklm\software\microsoft\secure	Read	Read
hklm\software\microsoft\systemcertificates	Read	Read
hklm\software\microsoft\upnp device host	Read	None
hklm\software\microsoft\windows nt\currentversion\accessibility	Read	Read

Branch	Users	Power users
hklm\software\microsoft\windows nt\currentversion\aedebug	Read	Read
hklm\software\microsoft\windows nt\currentversion\asr\commands	Read	Read
hklm\software\microsoft\windows nt\currentversion\classes	Read	Read
hklm\software\microsoft\windows nt\currentversion\drivers32	Read	Read
hklm\software\microsoft\windows nt\currentversion\efs	Read	Read
hklm\software\microsoft\windows nt\currentversion\font drivers	Read	Read
hklm\software\microsoft\windows nt\currentversion\fontmapper	Read	Read
hklm\software\microsoft\windows nt\currentversion \image file execution options	Read	Read
hklm\software\microsoft\windows nt\currentversion\inifilemapping	Read	Read
hklm\software\microsoft\windows nt\currentversion\perflib	None	None
hklm\software\microsoft\windows nt\currentversion\perflib\009	None	None
hklm\software\microsoft\windows nt\currentversion\profilelist	Read	Read
hklm\software\microsoft\windows nt\currentversion\secedit	Read	Read
hklm\software\microsoft\windows nt\currentversion\setup \recoveryconsole	Read	Read
hklm\software\microsoft\windows nt\currentversion\svchost	Read	Read
hklm\software\microsoft\windows nt\currentversion\terminal server\install\software\microsoft\windows\currentversion\runonce	Read	Read
hklm\software\microsoft\windows nt\currentversion\time zones	Read	Read
hklm\software\microsoft\windows nt\currentversion\windows	Read	Read
hklm\software\microsoft\windows nt\currentversion\winlogon	Read	Read
hklm\software\microsoft\windows\currentversion\explorer \user shell folders	Read	Read
hklm\software\microsoft\windows\currentversion\group policy	None	None
hklm\software\microsoft\windows\currentversion\installer	None	None
hklm\software\microsoft\windows\currentversion\policies	None	None
hklm\software\microsoft\windows\currentversion\reliability	Read	Read
hklm\software\microsoft\windows\currentversion\runonce	Read	Read
hklm\software\microsoft\windows\currentversion\runonceex	Read	Read
hklm\software\microsoft\windows\currentversion\telephony	Read	Special
hklm\software\policies	Read	Read
hklm\system	Read	Read
hklm\system\clone	None	None

Table 7-1   Default Permissions in the Registry *(continued)*

Branch	Users	Power users
hklm\system\controlset001	None	None
hklm\system\controlset001\services\dhcp\configurations	Read	Read
hklm\system\controlset001\services\dhcp\parameters	Read	Read
hklm\system\controlset001\services\dhcp\parameters\options	Read	Read
hklm\system\controlset001\services\dnscache\parameters	Read	Read
hklm\system\controlset001\services\mrxdav\encrypteddirectories	None	None
hklm\system\controlset001\services\netbt\parameters	Read	Read
hklm\system\controlset001\services\netbt\parameters\interfaces	Read	Read
hklm\system\controlset001\services\tcpip\linkage	Read	Read
hklm\system\controlset001\services\tcpip\parameters	Read	Read
hklm\system\controlset001\services\tcpip\parameters\adapters	Read	Read
hklm\system\controlset001\services\tcpip\parameters\interfaces	Read	Read
hklm\system\controlset002	None	None
hklm\system\controlset003	None	None
hklm\system\controlset004	None	None
hklm\system\controlset005	None	None
hklm\system\controlset006	None	None
hklm\system\controlset007	None	None
hklm\system\controlset008	None	None
hklm\system\controlset009	None	None
hklm\system\controlset010	None	None
hklm\system\currentcontrolset\control\class	None	None
hklm\system\currentcontrolset\control\keyboard layout	Read	Read
hklm\system\currentcontrolset\control\keyboard layouts	Read	Read
hklm\system\currentcontrolset\control\network	Read	Read
hklm\system\currentcontrolset\control\securepipeservers\winreg	None	None
hklm\system\currentcontrolset\control\session manager\executive	None	Special
hklm\system\currentcontrolset\control\timezoneinformation	None	Special
hklm\system\currentcontrolset\control\wmi\security	None	None
hklm\system\currentcontrolset\enum	None	None
hklm\system\currentcontrolset\hardware profiles	None	None
hklm\system\currentcontrolset\services\appmgmt\security	None	None
hklm\system\currentcontrolset\services\clipsrv\security	None	None

Branch	Users	Power users
hklm\system\currentcontrolset\services\cryptsvc\security	None	None
hklm\system\currentcontrolset\services\dnscache	Read	Read
hklm\system\currentcontrolset\services\ersvc\security	None	None
hklm\system\currentcontrolset\services\eventlog\security	None	None
hklm\system\currentcontrolset\services\irenum\security	None	None
hklm\system\currentcontrolset\services\netbt	Read	Read
hklm\system\currentcontrolset\services\netdde\security	None	None
hklm\system\currentcontrolset\services\netddedsdm\security	None	None
hklm\system\currentcontrolset\services\remoteaccess	Read	Read
hklm\system\currentcontrolset\services\rpcss\security	None	None
hklm\system\currentcontrolset\services\samss\security	None	None
hklm\system\currentcontrolset\services\scarddrv\security	None	None
hklm\system\currentcontrolset\services\scardsvr\security	None	None
hklm\system\currentcontrolset\services\stisvc\security	None	None
hklm\system\currentcontrolset\services\sysmonlog\log queries	None	None
hklm\system\currentcontrolset\services\tapisrv\security	None	None
hklm\system\currentcontrolset\services\tcpip	Read	Read
hklm\system\currentcontrolset\services\w32time\security	None	None
hklm\system\currentcontrolset\services\wmi\security	None	None
hku\.default	Read	Read
hku\.default\software\microsoft\netdde	None	None
hku\.default\software\microsoft\protected storage system provider	None	None
hku\.default\software\microsoft\systemcertificates\root \protectedroots	None	None

Figuring out which keys an application uses is part science but mostly art. Sometimes I simply open the program's binary file in a text editor and look for strings that look like keys. Most often, I use a tool such as Winternals Registry Monitor, which you learn how to use in Chapter 8, "Finding Registry Settings," to monitor registry activity while I run the program I'm putting through its paces. Then I record the different keys that the program references and check to see whether the Users or Power Users groups have the required permissions for those keys. Last, well-behaved applications report errors when they can't read or write a value in the registry. I wouldn't count on this behavior, however, because ill-behaved programs just bounce along happily even after encountering a registry error.

Taking Ownership of Keys

By default, Windows XP assigns ownership to the HKLM and HKCU as follows:

- Administrators own each subkey in HKLM.

- Users own each subkey in their profile hives, HKCU.

If you have full control of a key (and administrators usually do), you can take ownership of it if you're not already the owner:

1. In Regedit, click the key for which you want to take ownership.

2. On the Edit menu, click Permissions; then click Advanced.

3. On the Owner tab, click the new owner.

Auditing Registry Access

Auditing registry access is a great way to track down registry settings, and it's one of the methods that I discuss in Chapter 8, "Finding Registry Settings." It's also a reasonable way to monitor access to sensitive settings. The problem with auditing the registry is that you must either get very specific about which key you're auditing or pay a severe performance penalty by auditing too much of the registry. It's a fine line between getting the information you need and grinding the computer to a halt.

Auditing a key is a three-step process. First you must enable Audit Policy. You can do that on the network using Group Policy, but that seems silly considering the scope of the performance impact. If you're using auditing as a troubleshooting tool or to track down a setting, turn on Audit Policy locally. Click Start, Control Panel, Performance And Maintenance, Administrative Tools, and Local Security Policy. In the left pane, under Local Policies, click Audit Policy. In the right pane, double-click Audit Object Access, and then select the Success and Failure check boxes. After you've enabled Audit Policy, use Regedit to audit individual keys:

1. In Regedit, click the key you want to audit.

2. On the Edit menu, click Permission; then click Advanced.

3. On the Auditing tab, shown in Figure 7-3, click Add.

4. In the Select Users, Computers, Or Groups dialog box, click Locations, and then click the computer, domain, or organizational unit in which you want to look for the user or group you want to audit.

5. In the Enter The Object Names To Select box, type the name of the user or group you want to add to the key's audit list, and then click OK.

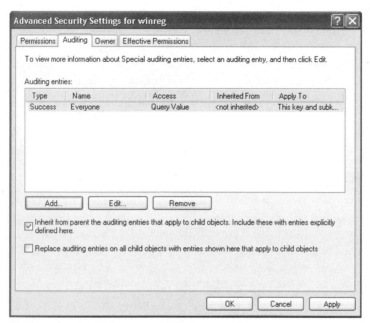

Figure 7-3   *Audit keys sparingly because doing so can significantly impact performance.*

6. In the Auditing Entry For *Name* dialog box, in the Access list, select both the Successful and Failed check boxes next to the activities for which you want to audit successful and failed attempts. These correspond to the permissions you learned about in the section tilted "Setting Keys' Permissions," earlier in this chapter:

- Full Control
- Query Value
- Set Value
- Create Subkey
- Enumerate Subkeys
- Notify
- Create Link
- Delete
- Write DAC
- Write Owner
- Read Control

After enabling Audit Policy and auditing specific keys, check the results using Event Viewer. To open Event Viewer, click Start, Control Panel, Performance And Maintenance, Administrative Tools, and Event Viewer. In Event Viewer's left pane, click Security. You see each hit in the right pane, and the most recent hits are at the top of the list. Double-click any entry to see more details. The Event Properties dialog box tells you what type of access Windows XP detected, the object type, and the process that accessed the key or value. Chapter 8, "Finding Registry Settings," shows you how to use this information to figure out where Windows XP or a program stores certain settings in the registry.

Preventing Local Registry Access

Whenever I bring up registry security, the inevitable question is always how to prevent users from accessing the registry. You can't. Remember that the registry contains settings that the user must be able to read for Windows XP to work properly. Users also must have full control of their profile hives for the operating system and applications to save their preferences. You can't prevent access—nor do you want to prevent it. The best you should hope for is limiting users' ability to edit the registry using Regedit or other registry editors.

The most elegant way to prevent access to Regedit is by enabling the Prevent access to registry editing tools policy. When users start Regedit, all they see is an error message that says, *Registry editing has been disabled by your administrator.* The problem with this policy is that not all registry editors honor this policy. Nothing prevents a determined user from downloading a shareware registry editor, of which there are plenty, and using it. That's the type of user you either want to fire or hire for your IT department. Another possibility is using Software Restriction Policies, which you can learn more about in Help and Support Center. Even this doesn't prevent users from running shareware registry editors unless you completely restrict them to a short list of acceptable applications.

Restricting Remote Registry Access

Securing local access to the Windows XP registry is one thing; securing remote access is another. Windows XP gives members of the local Administrators and Backup Operators groups remote access to the registry. Because the Domain Admins group is a member of each computer's local Administrators group, all domain administrators can connect the registry of any computer that's joined to the domain. So far so good, and Windows XP limits remote access to the registry more than earlier versions of Windows.

There might be limited scenarios in which you want to open remote access to computers' registries. For example, in Active Directory, you might create an administrators group for each organizational unit and want to give it the ability to edit computers' registries if they belong to the organizational unit. To enable that group to remotely edit a computer's registry, add that group to the ACL of the key HKLM\SYSTEM\CurrentcontrolSet\Control \SecurePipeServers\winreg. The problem you're going to run into is that although adding a group to winreg allows remote access, each key's ACL still determines which keys the group can change. So to allow a remote user or group to change a setting on the computer, add that user or group to the local Users, Power Users, or Administrators group.

Caution Don't go nuts and open each computer's registry to security threats by willy-nilly adding groups to the winreg key's ACL. Doing so creates a hole large enough for many Trojan viruses to get their hooks into Windows XP and invites predators to hack away at your infrastructure. The best practice is to leave well enough alone, and limit remote registry access to domain administrators.

Deploying Security Templates

You use security templates to create a security policy for your computer or network. Rather than using the techniques you learned about in this chapter to hunt-and-peck security on a computer, security templates give you a single place to configure a range of security settings and then deploy those settings to numerous computers. It's a little used, often misunderstood tool that organizes many of the available security settings in one place to make managing security a far easier job. It saddens me when administrators tell me their security woes and yet they've never heard of security templates, which would deal with most of their problems admirably. Security templates are an IT professional's best friend. Sold yet? I hope so.

You use a variety of tools to create and apply templates. First you use security templates to create and edit templates. Then you use either Security Configuration And Analysis or Group Policy to apply templates. This section walks you through the process of using these tools, starting with creating the Microsoft Management Console (MMC) that you'll use to edit templates, and ending with deploying templates on a network.

First here's an explanation of the different security settings in a template. The following list shows the different categories of settings you see in a security template. Following each category is a description of the settings you can define within it.

- **Account Policies.**   Password Policy, Account Lockout Policy, and Kerberos Policy
- **Local Policies.**   Audit Policy, User Rights Assignment, and Security Options
- **Event Log.**   Application, System, and Security Event Log settings
- **Restricted Groups.**   Membership of security-sensitive groups
- **System Services.**   Startup and permissions for system services
- **Registry.**   Permissions for registry keys (the topic of this section)
- **File System.**   Permissions for files and folders

Security templates are nothing more than text files that have the *.inf* extension. You can copy them, edit them, and so on. The file looks much like an INI file. You can create your own security templates from scratch, which I don't recommend because it's too much work with so much risk, or you can customize one of the predefined templates that come with

Windows XP. Customizing a predefined template is definitely the way to go because most of the work is already done for you. Note that because only the Administrators group has permissions to change the default security template folder, %SYSTEMROOT%\Security \Templates, only administrators can edit and apply security templates.

Creating a Security Management Console

To make your job easier, create an MMC console that includes all the tools you'll need for editing, analyzing, and applying security templates:

1. Click Start, Run; then type **mmc**, and click OK.

2. On the File menu, click Add/Remove Snap-in.

3. In the Add/Remove Snap-in dialog box, click Add.

4. Click Security Templates, and click Add.

5. Click Security Configuration And Analysis, and click Add.

After creating your console, save it to a file for quick access. On the File menu, click Save. I like to call the file *Templates.msc*. MMC saves your file in your Administrative Tools folder. To open it again quickly, click Start, All Programs, Administrative Tools, and then Templates (or what ever you called it). Figure 7-4 shows the console that I created as described in this section.

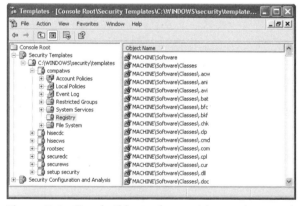

Figure 7-4   *You build templates with security templates, and you analyze and apply templates using Security Configuration And Analysis.*

Choosing a Predefined Security Template

Windows XP comes with a small gaggle of predefined security templates. You almost never need to create a new template because you can usually just customize one of the predefined templates and save it to a different file. They provide starting points for applying security policies in different scenarios, whether those scenarios include one, one hundred, or thousands of computers. The following predefined security policies are in %SYSTEMROOT% \Security\Templates by default:

- **Default security (Setup security.inf).**   This template contains the default security settings that the setup program applies when you install Windows XP. It includes file system and registry permissions, too. If you need information about the operating system's default permissions, you'll find that information here. You can use this template to restore a computer to the original Windows XP security settings, which you'd do by applying it with Security Configuration And Analysis, but don't deploy it using Group Policy.

- **Compatible (Compatws.inf).**   This template contains security settings that relax restrictions on the Users group enough to allow legacy applications to run. This is preferable to moving users from the Users group to the Power Users or, oh my, the Administrators groups. Specifically, this template changes the file system and registry permissions granted to the Users group so that they're consistent with legacy and other applications that aren't certified for Windows XP. This template also assumes that the administrator doesn't want users in the Power Users group, so it moves users from Power Users to the Users group. This template applies to workstations only, and you shouldn't apply it to servers.

- **Secure (Secure*.inf).**   These templates tighten security settings that are least likely to affect application compatibility. Securedc.inf is for domain controllers, and Securews.inf is for workstations. It applies strong password, lockout, and audit settings, for example. It also limits the user of LAN Manager and NTLM authentication protocols by configuring Windows XP to send only NTLM version 2 responses and configuring servers to refuse LAN Manager responses. Last, this template restricts anonymous users by preventing them from enumerating account names, enumerating shares, and translating SIDs (see Chapter 1, "Learning the Basics"). Test this template carefully before deploying it.

- **Highly Secure (hisec*.inf).**   These templates are supersets of the previous templates, and they apply even more restrictions. Hisecdc.inf is for domain controllers, and Hisecws.inf is for workstations. For example, this template sets the levels of encryption and signing that Windows XP requires for authentication and for data moving over secure channels. It requires strong encrypting and signing. Last, it removes all members of the Power Users groups and makes sure that only the Domain Admins group and the local Administrator are members of the local Administrators group. Test these templates to ensure compatibility with your infrastructure and applications because only certified applications are likely to run after applying it.

- **System root security (Rootsec.inf).**   This template defines root permissions for the Windows XP file system. It contains no registry permissions. It does apply permissions for the root of %SYSTEMDRIVE%. You can apply this template to a computer to restore these permissions to the root of the system drive or to apply the same permissions to additional volumes.

- **No Terminal Server user SID (Notssid.inf).**   This template removes unnecessary Terminal Server SIDs from the file system and registry when running Terminal Server in application compatibility mode. If possible, run Terminal Server in full security mode instead, a mode in which the Terminal Server SID isn't used at all.

Most of these security templates are incremental. They modify the default or existing security settings if those settings are already configured on the computer. Other than the Setup Security template, they don't configure the default security settings before changing the computer's security configuration. Also, you can't use security templates to secure Windows XP when you use the FAT file system.

You can view these templates in your new MMC console. In the console's left pane, double-click a security template to open it. By default, the templates are under C:\Windows \Security\Templates in Security Templates. You can add a new path, however. Right-click Security Templates, and then click New Template Search Path. You'll see both paths in Security Templates. If you want to remove a path from Security Templates, right-click it, and then click Delete.

Building a Custom Security Template

The hard way to create a custom security template is to start from scratch:

1. In Security Templates, right-click the folder in which you want to create the new template, and then click New Template.

2. In Template Name, type the name of the new template in Description, type a brief but useful description of your new template, and click OK.

3. In the left pane, double-click the new security template to open it. Select a security area, such as Registry, in the left pane, and configure that area's security settings in the right pane.

That's the hard way, and definitely not the way I recommend. First it's too labor-intensive. Second it's error-prone. The best way to create a security template is to start with one of the predefined templates, save it to a new file, and then edit it—carefully. Most of the times I've done this, I started with the Compatws.inf template file and customized it as necessary to give a legacy application enough room to work. Here's how:

1. In Security Templates, double-click C:\Windows\Security\Templates.

2. Right-click the predefined template you want to customize, click Save As, type a new file name for the security template, and click Save.

3. In the left pane, double-click the new security template to open it. Select a security area, such as Registry, in the left pane, and configure that area's security settings in the right pane.

Because this is a registry book, I'll give you a little more detail about configuring registry security in a template. In the left pane of Security Templates, double-click your template, and then click Registry. You'll see a list of registry keys in the right pane. To add a key to the list, right-click Registry, and then click Add Key. Because the list already covers all of HKLM, add exceptions to the settings that the template defines for HKLM\SOFTWARE and HKLM \SYSTEM. To edit a key's settings, double-click it, and then select one of the following options:

- **Configure This Key Then.** After selecting this option, select one of the following:

  - **Propagate Inheritable Permissions To All Subkeys.** The key's subkey inherits the key's security settings, assuming that the subkeys' security settings don't block inheritance. In case of a conflict, the subkey's explicit permissions override the permissions they inherit from the parent key.

  - **Replace Existing Permissions On All Subkeys With Inheritable Permissions.** The key's permissions override all its subkey's permissions. In other words, each subkey's permissions will be identical to the parent key's permissions. If you select this option and apply the template, the change is permanent unless you change it by applying a different template to the registry.

- **Do Not Allow Permissions On This Key To Be Replaced.** Select this option if you don't want to configure the key or its subkey's permissions.

To edit the actual permissions that you want the template to apply to the key, click Edit Security. You do this in the same Security For *Name* dialog box that you saw earlier in this chapter. You can add and remove groups. You can allow or deny permissions for different users and groups to perform various tasks. You can audit users' and groups' access to the key. You can also change ownership of the key. When you apply the template to a computer or deploy the template through Group Policy, the key receives the permissions you define here.

Analyzing a Computer's Configuration

With your custom template in hand, you can use it to analyze a computer's security configuration. Security Configuration And Analysis enables you to compare the current state of the computer's security configuration to the settings defined in the template. You can use this tool to make immediate changes to the computer's configuration, such as when troubleshooting a problem. You can also use it to track and ensure a certain level of security as part of your enterprise risk management program, detecting flaws in security as they occur over time.

Here's how to analyze a computer's security using Security Configuration And Analysis:

1. Right-click Security Configuration And Analysis, which you added to your console in the section titled "Creating a Security Management Console," earlier in this chapter, and then click Open Database.

2. In the Open Database dialog box, do one of the following:

   - To create a new analysis database, type the name of your new database in File Name, and click Open (you don't have a database initially). Then in the Import Template dialog box, click a template and click Open.

   - To open an existing analysis database, type the name of an existing database in File Name, and click Open.

3. Right-click Security Configuration And Analysis, click Analyze Computer Now, and then accept the default log file path or specify a new one.

Security Configuration And Analysis compares the computer's current security against the analysis database. If you import multiple templates into the database, which you can do by right-clicking Security Configuration And Analysis and then clicking Import Template, the tool merges the templates together to create one template. If it detects a conflict, the last template you loaded has precedence (last in, first out). After Security Configuration And Analysis analyzes the computer, it displays results that you can browse. The organization of these results is the same as in security templates. The difference is that Security Configuration And Analysis displays indicators that show whether a current setting matches or is inconsistent with a setting defined in the template:

- **Red X.**   The setting is in the analysis database and on the computer, but the two versions don't match. The trick is to drill down through settings that have a red X next to them until you isolate the specific problem.

- **Green Check Mark.**   The setting is in the analysis database and on the computer, and the two match.

- **Question Mark.**   The setting is not in the analysis database and was not analyzed. This might also mean that the user who ran Security Configuration And Analysis didn't have permissions necessary to do so.

- **Exclamation Point.**   The setting is in the analysis database but not on the computer. A registry key might exist in the database but not on the computer.

- **No Indicator.**   The setting is not in the database or on the computer.

What do you do with any discrepancies you find between the analysis database and the computer's settings? First you can update the database by double-clicking the troublesome setting and clicking Edit Security (see Figure 7-5). This updates the database but not the template, however. Also, it doesn't change the computer's settings. To do that, see the next section. You can also import a more appropriate template for that computer or an updated template into the database and then analyze it again. To avoid problems that result from merging templates, consider creating a new database if you use a new or updated template.

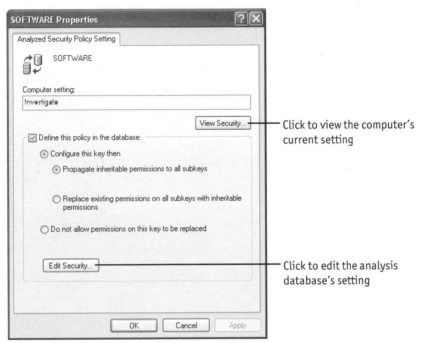

Figure 7-5   *You can view and edit settings in this dialog box.*

Modifying a Computer's Configuration

After you've created a security template and verified it by analyzing computers using Security Configuration And Analysis, you're ready to apply it to the computer:

1. Right-click Security Configuration And Analysis, and then click Open Database.

2. In the Open Database dialog box, do one of the following:

   - To create a new database, type the name of your new database in File Name, and click Open. Then in the Import Template dialog box, click a template, and click Open.

   - To open an existing database, type the name of an existing database in File Name, and click Open. If you modified a database without updating the template on which it's based, make sure you open the existing database.

3. Right-click Security Configuration And Analysis, click Configure Computer Now, and then accept the default log file path or specify a new one.

Deploying Security Templates on the Network

In "Modifying a Computer's Configuration," you learned how to apply a security template to a computer manually. This is fine for one-off scenarios, but it's not the way to deploy security templates to multiple computers on the network. To deploy templates on a network, use Group Policy: Create a new GPO, and then edit it. In the Group Policy editor, right-click Security Settings, and then click Import Policy. Click the template you want to apply, and then click Open.

It's so simple, but I don't want to make light of this. Deploying security templates on your network requires careful planning. You must first identify the templates that your network requires. Then you must identify which organizational units get which security templates. For example, if the sales department uses a legacy application that requires the Users group to have full control of certain registry keys, document and test the security template, and then import the template into a GPO that you assign to the sales department's organizational unit. Ideally, you'll account for security templates early in the deployment planning process. What really ends up happening, unless they planned carefully, is that IT professionals use security templates as a big fire hose to put out fires created by lack of foresight and planning.

Finding Registry Settings

This chapter shows you how to relate a setting in the user interface to a value in the registry. Power users can use this information to find their own registry hacks. IT professionals get the long end of this stick, though; they can use the information to locate settings in the registry for a variety of purposes. For example, after they've found settings, they can build administrative templates for them and deploy the settings on their network. They can write scripts that automatically apply the settings they found. They can even use this information to help build and deploy better default user profiles.

Three basic techniques are available for tracking down settings. The first, and often most effective, is comparing two snapshots of the registry. Take one snapshot before changing a setting and the second after you've made a change. The second method is monitoring the registry to detect changes that a program makes. Monitoring is often difficult because of the way Microsoft Windows XP and programs thrash the registry. Nonetheless, with a good tool and the tips you read here, it is an occasionally useful method. The last is auditing, which is the most difficult to use effectively and causes performance degradation. Because the first method is often most effective, that's where I start.

Comparing REG Files

Comparing two REG files is often the easiest way to discover where in the registry Windows XP stores a setting. Create these REG files before and after changing a setting that is in the user interface and that you know is somewhere in the registry. This is how I found the location of the settings that Tweak UI includes and that I documented in Chapter 5, "Mapping Tweak UI." First I exported HKCU to a REG file. I changed a setting in Tweak UI and exported the same branch to a second REG file. Then I compared the two files to figure out which value changed when I changed the setting in Tweak UI. You can use this method to trace just about any setting that has a user interface to its location in the registry.

The only disadvantage to comparing two registry files is that the process requires a file-comparison tool. Windows XP comes with such a tool, though, which I'll tell you about later in this section. The advantages of this method are many. First it's quick and easy. Second its results are dead-on accurate. If you don't let a lot of time pass between each snapshot, the differences between the two should include only those settings you changed. Also, REG files are easy to read, so you won't have any problems deciphering the results.

Now for some details. Recall that Registry Editor (Regedit) can export all or part of the registry to text files that have the *.reg* extension (REG files). A REG file looks similar to an INI file. It contains one or more sections; the name of each section is the path of a registry key. Each section contains the key's values. The format of each value is *name=value*. If the value is a string containing spaces, *value* must be quoted. Each key's default value looks like @=*value*. Chapter 9, "Scripting Registry Changes," describes REG files in all their glory, including how to interpret the different types of values in them. To export the registry to a REG file, click the key that you want to export. Then on the File menu, click Export. In the Export Registry File dialog box, click Win9x/NT4 Registration Files (*.reg) to export to a version 4 ANSI REG file. Remember from Chapter 2, "Using the Registry Editor," that Regedit supports REG files in two different file formats: ANSI and Unicode. Many file-comparison tools work only with the first, thus you must create version 4 ANSI REG files for them. The tools I talk about in this chapter support Unicode text files, though. If you're not familiar with ANSI and Unicode character encoding, see Chapter 1, "Learning the Basics."

The sections following this one describe tools you can use to compare two REG files. My personal favorite is WinDiff, which comes with Windows XP. I like this tool so much because of its simple user interface and, more importantly, the speed at which it compares very large text files. Another choice is probably already installed on your computer: Microsoft Word 2002. It's slower than WinDiff, but you're probably already familiar with how to use this word processor. In any case, the overall process is the same:

1. Export the registry to a REG file. Name the file something like Before.reg. If you have a general idea where the setting is in the registry, export that branch; otherwise, export the entire registry, including HKCU and HKLM.

2. Change a setting in the user interface or perform some other action that you're trying to trace to the registry. For example, if you want to see where a program stores its settings during installation, install the program.

3. Export the registry to a second REG file. Name it After.reg. Make sure you export the same branch using the same file format as you did in step 1. If you don't duplicate the process exactly, the files won't match, and finding the difference will be difficult.

4. Compare Before.reg and After.reg using your favorite file-comparison utility. The differences between the two files are your changes. The file-comparison tool points out only the values that changed, because only the values under each section heading change, but if you look a little higher in the file, you'll see the key that contains the values.

All-in-One Solutions

LastBit Software produces a program called RegSnap that performs the process I described in this section. You don't have to create any REG files or compare two REG files with a file-comparison tool. RegSnap does the whole bit for you, making it a cool program to have around if you do this sort of thing on a regular basis. You can download the shareware version of RegSnap from *http://www.webdon.com*. Give it a try; if you like it, it's very inexpensive. It comes in a standard edition and a professional edition. The professional edition enables you to work with remote registries; otherwise, the standard edition is sufficient to locate a setting in the registry. The only problem I have with RegSnap is that its user interface is very clunky.

That leads me to RegView, from Vincent Chiu. This program is available at *http://home.xnet.com/~vchiu/regview.shtml*. I like this program because it has a cleaner user interface. You can use it to edit and search the registry and to compare different versions of it. RegView doesn't have a setup program, but it really doesn't need one. Figure 8-1 shows the result in RegView of comparing a snapshot to the current registry. RegView's output is a little easier to read than RegSnap's output, but RegView is quite a bit slower at producing it.

Figure 8-1   *RegView is an enhanced registry editor.*

If turn-around time is important to you, use RegSnap. If you're after an enhanced registry editor that can do a search-and-replace as well as compare snapshots of the registry, you should consider RegView. Both shareware programs are inexpensive, but if you don't want to shell out the money, stick with the methods you learn in this chapter.

There are a few ways to make this process more efficient. Comparing two large REG files can take a while—even using WinDiff. If you're pretty certain you know the general vicinity of a setting in the registry, export just that branch. For example, if you know a setting is a per-user setting, export just HKCU. If you suspect it's somewhere in HKLM\SOFTWARE\Microsoft, search just that branch. You can always resort to exporting the entire registry if your hunch isn't right. Another way to streamline the process is to ignore differences that are irrelevant. Some settings change whether or not you doing anything. For example, Plug and Play values change frequently, as does the configuration of some services. The easiest way to eliminate the confusion that these inherent changes cause is to exclude HKLM\SYSTEM in your REG files. Also, the less time that elapses between snapshots, the less noise you'll have in your comparison results.

Using WinDiff

WinDiff is the ultimate tool for comparing two versions of a text file. Its roots are as a developer tool for comparing different versions of source files to see changes before checking them into version control. It was also useful as a debugging tool to figure out which changes in a source file might have introduced a problem. WinDiff was originally available in the Windows Software Development Kit (SDK). Microsoft included it in the last several Windows resource kits. It comes with Windows XP as part of the Windows XP Support Tools. Install the tools from \Support\Tools on your Windows XP CD. Type **windiff** in the Run dialog box to start it.

After starting WinDiff, here's how to compare two REG files with it:

1. On the File menu, click Compare Files.

2. Type the path and name of the first file, and click Open.

3. Type the path and name of the second file, and click Open.

4. On the View menu, click Expand, or double-click the files in the list.

After comparing the two files, you see results similar to Figure 8-2. WinDiff combines both files and highlights the differences in red and yellow. Differences are relative to the second file, which is why I had you open the second file after the first one. Deleted lines, present in the first file but not in the second, are red. Inserted lines, absent in the first file but present in the second, are yellow. White lines are the same in both files. You also see arrows that indicate whether a line is deleted or inserted. A left arrow (<!) indicates a line deleted from the second file, and a right arrow(!>) indicates a line inserted into the second file. WinDiff represents changed lines as deletions followed by insertions, as shown in Figure 8-2. Because WinDiff compares files line by line instead of character by character, you have to judge for yourself whether a deleted line followed by an inserted line represents a changed line of text. Press F8 to move to the next block of differences that WinDiff found; press F7 to move to the previous block of differences.

Figure 8-2   *The two columns you see on the left side of the window represent the two files that you're comparing. These columns are a roadmap of the files' differences.*

Using Word 2002

On the odd chance that WinDiff isn't available to you (for example, if you're not free to install the support tools on a customer's computer), you can use the comparison features of Word to compare REG files. You might also prefer using Word if you're already familiar with the word processor and don't want to install or learn how to use WinDiff. The only drawback is that using Word to compare REG files is often a slow and tedious process because it's not designed for this purpose.

When using Word to compare REG files, open the second REG file first, and compare it to the first REG file. This order ensures that Word indicates insertions and deletions properly. Here's how to compare two REG files using Word:

1. On the File menu, click Open, type the path and name of the first REG file in the File Name box, and click Open.

2. If the File Conversion dialog box appears, select the encoding method that makes the text in the Preview area readable, and then click OK.

   You can choose between Windows (Default), MS-DOS, and Other Encoding. Windows (Default) corresponds to ANSI, which is what version 4 REG files use. If the file is a version 5 REG file, select the Other Encoding option, and then click Unicode in the list.

3. On the Tools menu, click Compare And Merge Documents, type the path and name of the second REG file, and then click Merge.

4. If the File Conversion dialog box appears, select the encoding method that makes the text in the Preview area readable.

Word displays the results as shown in Figure 8-3. To see the next change, click the Next button on the Reviewing toolbar. To see the previous change, click the Previous button. Word displays the results differently depending on the view:

- **Normal view.** To switch to the normal view, click Normal on the View menu. This is the view shown in Figure 8-3. By default, insertions are underlined. Deletions are crossed out.

- **Print Layout view.** To switch to Print Layout view, click Print Layout on the View menu. In this view, you see bubbles in the right column that describe the differences between the two files. This view is often the easiest to read.

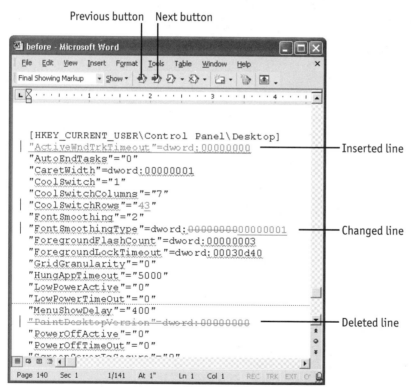

Figure 8-3 *Word is effective at comparing large REG files, but much slower than WinDiff.*

Tip   When comparing two REG files in Word, make sure that you disable grammar and spelling checking. Word isn't likely to find many correctly spelled words in a REG file, so it burns up a lot of resources checking them. To disable both features, on the Tools menu, click Options. In the Options dialog box, click the Spelling & Grammar tab, and clear the Check Spelling As You Type and Check Grammar As You Type check boxes.

Comparing with Reg.exe

The Windows XP Support Tools, which include WinDiff, as you've already learned, install Console Registry Tool for Windows (Reg.exe). This program can compare two branches of the registry and has a useful feature that helps you track down settings in the registry. Copy the branch you think contains the value to the temporary key (this is your first snapshot), change the setting you're tracking, and then compare the current key to the temporary key. Using Reg.exe this way has the advantage of being quite straightforward. It has the disadvantage of relying on a command line rather than a graphical user interface, and if you don't remove the temporary keys from the registry, you can end up with an oversized registry that contains a bunch of data you don't need.

Chapter 9, "Scripting Registry Changes," describes all the command-line options available in Reg.exe. For now, here are the steps necessary to locate a setting in the registry:

1. At the MS-DOS command prompt, type **reg copy** *source destination* **/s /f**, where *source* is the key you want to copy to the temporary key *destination*.

   Make sure the destination doesn't exist first; otherwise, you'll end up with a lot of differences when you compare the two keys. Also, if the name of either key contains spaces, enclose the entire key in quotation marks. Don't use the full names of root keys; use HKCU and HKLM instead.

2. Make changes to the setting.

3. At the MS-DOS command prompt, type **reg compare** *key temp* **/s**, where *key* is the current key and *temp* is the temporary key.

The following listing is a sample of the output that Reg.exe generates. Reg.exe indicates lines that are missing from the current key with a right arrow (>) and indicates lines that were added or changed in the current key with a left arrow (<). In other words, you see > next to deleted values and < next to new or changed values.

```
< Value:  HKEY_CURRENT_USER\control panel\desktop ActiveWndTrkTimeout REG_DWORD  0x0
> Value:  HKEY_CURRENT_USER\backup ActiveWndTrkTimeout REG_DWORD  0x400
< Value:  HKEY_CURRENT_USER\control panel\desktop DragFullWindows REG_SZ  1
> Value:  HKEY_CURRENT_USER\backup DragFullWindows REG_SZ  0
< Value:  HKEY_CURRENT_USER\control panel\desktop DragHeight REG_SZ  4
< Value:  HKEY_CURRENT_USER\control panel\desktop DragWidth REG_SZ  4
```

```
Result Compared:  Different

The operation completed successfully
```

After you're done with the temporary key, make sure that you delete it; otherwise, you're going to fill up the registry with junk, and you won't be able to use the same temporary key for future comparisons. To quickly remove the temporary key, at the MS-DOS command prompt, type **reg delete** *key* **/f**, where *key* is the name of the temporary key. The command-line option **/f** prevents Reg.exe from prompting you to confirm that you want to remove the key.

Tip   An alternative method is to save a branch as a hive file, and load the hive file into HKU. Then change a setting in the user interface, and compare the original branch to the hive file you loaded in HKU. Don't forget to unload the hive file when you are finished. This has the advantage of not cluttering the registry with temporary keys. Chapter 9, "Scripting Registry Changes," shows you the Reg.exe commands that enable you to save, load, and unload hive files.

Auditing the Registry

As I mentioned, comparing snapshots of the registry is just one method of finding a setting; monitoring is another. The first method of monitoring the registry I'm going to show you is built into Windows XP: auditing. Use auditing only if you don't have other monitoring tools available to you, however, because its disadvantages far outweigh its advantages for the purpose of tracing settings. The first drawback is that auditing the registry for changes requires that you know in advance the general vicinity where a setting is located because auditing the entire registry isn't practical. Second, deciphering the results of an audit is rather cumbersome. It relies on viewing security events in Event Viewer, and the output isn't friendly.

Auditing the registry for changes is a three-step process. First you must enable Audit Policy. You do this by editing Local Security Policy. After that, you audit branches in the registry where you think the setting is located. You can't just audit the entire registry because doing so would bring even the fastest computer running Windows XP to a grinding halt. On average, the operating system and the applications access the registry thousands of times during a session, so recording the details of every one of these hits just isn't practical. Last, after changing the setting or performing the action you're tracking, look in Event Viewer to see which values changed. The following sections describe each step.

Setting Audit Policy

The first step in auditing the registry is to enable Audit Policy:

1. Click Start, Control Panel, Performance And Maintenance, Administrative Tools, and Local Security Policy.

2. In the left pane, under Local Policy, click Audit Policy.

3. In the right pane, double-click Audit Object Access, and then select both the Success and Failure check boxes.

Auditing Registry Keys

After enabling Audit Policy, audit the specific keys in which you think you're going to find the setting:

1. In Regedit, click the key you want to audit.

2. On the Edit menu, point to Permission, and then click Advanced.

3. On the Auditing tab of the Advanced Security Settings dialog box, shown in Figure 8-4, click Add.

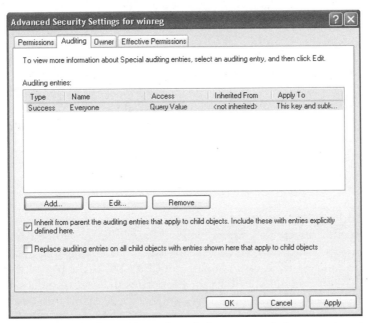

Figure 8-4 *Auditing the registry helps you track down settings in the registry.*

4. In the Select Users, Computers, Or Groups dialog box, click Locations. Then click the computer, domain, or organizational unit in which you want to look for the user or group you want to audit.

5. In the Enter The Object Names To Select box, type the name of the user or group you want to add to the key's audit list, and then click OK.

6. In the Access list, select the Successful and Failed check boxes next to the activities you want to audit. The following list of permissions corresponds to the permissions you learned about in Chapter 7, "Managing Registry Security."

- Full Control
- Query Value
- Set Value
- Create Subkey
- Enumerate Subkeys
- Notify
- Create Link
- Delete
- Write DAC
- Write Owner
- Read Control

Tip   Audit carefully to avoid too much of a performance penalty. For example, if you're trying to find the location where an application saves a setting, audit for Set Value, change the value in the user interface, and then check your results.

Analyzing the Results

The final step after enabling Audit Policy and auditing specific keys is checking the results using Event Viewer. To open Event Viewer, click Start, Control Panel, Performance And Maintenance, Administrative Tools, and Event Viewer. In Event Viewer's left pane, click Security. You see each hit in the right pane, and the most recent hits are at the top of the list. Double-click any entry to see more details. The Event Properties dialog box tells you what type of access Windows XP detected, the object type, and the process that accessed the key or value.

Monitoring the Registry

Monitoring the registry for changes is different than comparing snapshots in that you're watching registry access as it happens. Thus, you can change a setting in the user interface and then look at the monitor to see what value Windows XP wrote to the registry. I tend to monitor the registry instead of compare snapshots when I'm looking for a large number of settings. When doing this, it's helpful to keep the noise down to a minimum. I'll show you how to reduce the noise in the section "Filtering for Better Results," later in this chapter.

My favorite monitoring tool is Regmon from Winternals. You can download a freeware version of this tool from *http://www.sysinternals.com*. Regmon Enterprise Edition is available at *http://www.winternals.com* and is inexpensive. The difference between the two is that the enterprise edition enables you to monitor a remote registry, which makes the process a little easier if you can work on one computer and see the results on a different computer. Although the freeware version of Regmon contains all the enterprise edition's other features, I purchased and use Regmon Enterprise Edition for the convenience of remote monitoring.

Download either version of Regmon. The freeware version doesn't have a setup program, so you just run it from the directory in which you unzip it. Regmon Enterprise Edition comes with a setup program that adds a shortcut for Regmon to the Start menu. The following sections show you how to use this hot product.

Using Winternals Regmon

Figure 8-5 shows the freeware version of Regmon. Every time Windows XP or programs access the registry, Regmon adds a row to the window. The first two columns are a line number and time. The next column displays the name of the process that accessed the registry, which is usually the program's file name. Next you see the type of access, followed by the path and result. The last column gives you additional information, such as the contents of a value. The most interesting information here is the type of access, the path of the key, and the Other column. Any time a column is too narrow to display the entire contents of a row, you can point to the data, and Regmon displays its full contents in a balloon. Nifty.

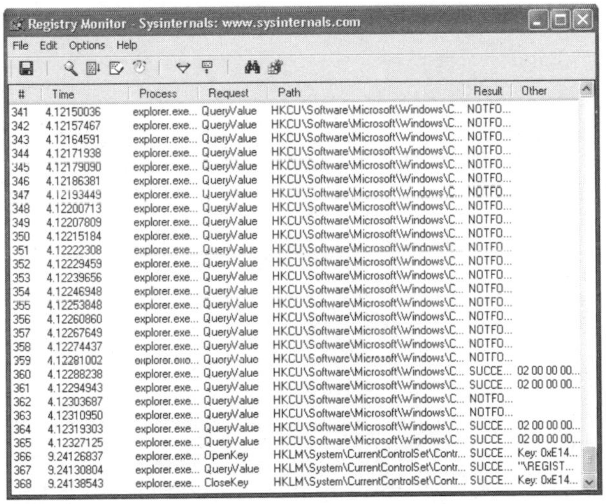

Figure 8-5 *Regmon's window quickly fills up with uninteresting information. This is Regmon's window seconds after starting it.*

Two columns, *Request* and *Other,* need more attention. Request tells you what Windows XP or a program was trying to do. The requests you see in the Request column are different registry application programming interface (API) functions and are shown in Table 8-1. The most interesting type of request is SetValue, of course. The Other column contains a variety of information, depending on the type of request. Again, see Table 8-1. For example, if the request is QueryValue, the Other column contains the data in the value. If the request is OpenKey, the Other column contains the key's handle.

Table 8-1   Regmon Request Types and Data

Request type	Data in the Other column
CloseKey	Handle of closed key
CreateKey	Handle of new key
CreateKeyEx	Handle of new key
DeleteKey	None
DeleteValue	None
DeleteValueKey	None
EnumerateKey	Name of next subkey
EnumKeyEx	Name of next subkey
EnumerateValue	None
FlushKey	None
OpenKey	Handle of open key
OpenKeyEx	Handle of open key
QueryKey	Name of key
QueryValue	Value's data
QueryValueEx	Value's data
SetValue	Data stored in value
SetValueEx	Data stored in value

Filtering for Better Results

If you start Regmon and change some settings in the Windows XP user interface, you won't have a lot of luck sifting through Regmon's output to find the setting. For example, opening Windows Explorer accesses the registry about 5,000 times. Clicking Options on Windows Explorer's Tools menu accesses the registry a few hundred times. Sorting through all that output isn't practical. Your experience improves dramatically if you learn how to use filtering.

The first thing you can do, particularly if you're interested in finding the value in which Windows XP stores a setting, is filter out everything but write requests. On Regmon's Edit menu, click Filter/Highlight. Then clear all the check boxes except Log Successes and Log

Writes. Regmon will report only successful writes to the registry. This alone significantly reduces the amount of output you see. Get more specific, though, and Regmon will all but hand you the setting for which you're looking. The asterisk (*) in the Include box is a wildcard that matches everything; this is the default filter.

To get more specific, limit Regmon to certain processes. For example, if you're searching for a setting in Windows Explorer, look only for registry access by the process *explorer.exe*. If you're searching for settings in Tweak UI, look only for registry access by the process *Tweakui.exe*. On Regmon's Edit menu, click Filter/Highlight. In the Include box, type the name of the process you want Regmon to display in the window. Include multiple processes separated by a semicolon. The easiest way to figure out the name of a process is to look in Windows Task Manager. Press Ctrl+Shift+Esc, and then look on the Processes tab. If in doubt, you can also look in Regmon's output for the process name, which is how I usually find it. You might see the process Rundll32.exe. This is a special program that executes APIs in Dynamic Link Libraries (DLL). Because you might have many different instances of this process running at any time, filtering this process is more difficult.

My last tip for how you can limit the output of Regmon is to filter for specific keys. If you have general knowledge of where Windows XP stores a setting in the registry, filter the output to display only lines that contain that key. For example, if you know that a setting is somewhere in HKLM\SOFTWARE\Microsoft, filter Regmon's output so it shows only SetValue requests on that key. You'll see very little output in Regmon's window when you change that value in the user interface, and one of the lines is likely to be the value for which you're searching.

Tip   You can combine subkeys and process names in your filter. Separate each with a semicolon. Regmon compares your criteria to all the columns you see in the window, so you can filter multiple columns at one time. You can filter results by process, request type, and key at the same time, for instance.

Registry in Deployment

There are two ways to deploy Windows XP and other applications: throw them out there and see what sticks, or carefully plan and design configurations. I prefer the second option, and that's the point of this part. You learn how the registry fits into the deployment of Windows XP.

This part begins with building and deploying user profiles. Then you learn about the registry settings for Windows Installer and how to remove errant Windows Installer–based settings from the registry. Three chapters in this part are about how to deploy settings with Windows XP and Office XP. And the last chapter in this part describes how to fix a variety of IT problems that have solutions in the registry. This part of the book is primarily for IT professionals.

Scripting Registry Changes

Think of what life would be like for an IT professional without any sort of automation. To change settings, you'd have to get up from your desk, take the 10-minute elevator ride to the 12th floor, and find the user's computer in the maze of cubicles. And at the end of *this* maze, you don't get cheese; you get a user who's angry that you're interrupting his or her game of Spider. Life is better when you don't have to deal face-to-face with real users (wink).

Scripting is a more efficient way to deploy and change settings. Notice that I didn't use the word *manage*, which better applies to policies than scripting. If you need to manage settings, see Chapter 6, "Using Registry-Based Policy." Scripting is useful on many levels. You can write a script that changes some group of settings and then test it in the lab before deploying. And if you need to update the script, you can easily regression-test it to see how your changes affect the results. Simply put, I like scripting registry changes because scripts are repeatable without the potential for human error each time I use them to change settings. You can also deploy scripts without visiting desktops. You can use your software management infrastructure or some dodgier methodology if you don't have an infrastructure to deploy scripts without having to interrupt users' work.

This chapter describes five of my favorite scripting methods. The first is INF files. I like the simplicity of INF files and the fact that there's no registry setting they can't edit, so I describe them first. The second is REG files, which are easy to make by exporting settings from Registry Editor (Regedit). I also describe how to use Console Registry Tool for Windows (Reg.exe) to edit the registry from the MS-DOS command prompt, which is a terrific tool for changing settings from batch files. Also, I describe how to write scripts that change settings. Microsoft Windows XP comes with Windows Script Host, and this chapter shows you how to write scripts using the JScript and VBScript languages. Finally, I describe how to build a Windows Installer package file to deploy settings. This technique is great because you can deploy those settings through Active Directory and Group Policy. Because I cover so many different techniques, the first section, "Choosing a Technique," helps you choose the scripting method that's best for you.

Choosing a Technique

Table 9-1 lays out the substantial differences—as I see them—between the scripting methods covered in this chapter. Each column represents one of the five scripting methods that I describe in this chapter. For example, the Batch column describes using Reg.exe in a batch file. The MSI column describes Windows Installer package files that include registry settings. First the similarities: All five methods enable you to change values as well as add keys or values. Also, Windows XP supports all five methods without installing third-party tools or any resource kits.

Table 9-1   Comparison of Scripting Methods

Features	INF	REG	Batch	Script	MSI
Difficulty	Medium	Low	Medium	High	Medium
OS access	Basic	None	Full	Full	Basic
Built-in support	Yes	Yes	Yes	Yes	Yes
Change values	Yes	Yes	Yes	Yes	Yes
Add keys/values	Yes	Yes	Yes	Yes	Yes
Delete keys/values	Yes	Keys only	Yes	Yes	Yes
Querying values	No	No	Yes	Yes	No
Support for value types	High	Medium	Medium	Low	Medium
Bitwise support	Yes	No	No	Yes	No

Nine times out of ten, my preference is to write an INF file. You'll notice that most of the scripts in this book are INF files. I chose this method because I'm familiar with INF files, they're easy to create, and they're easy to read. I use scripts only when I have to query values from the registry. INF files' strong suit is that they offer the flexibility to do anything I want in the registry without requiring me to put on a programmer hat for the weekend. Choose whatever methods best suit you, but give more weight to INF files and scripts. You won't end up using just one of these techniques, though. In fact, you'll find that you'll use a combination of these methods, depending on the scenario. After you start using the script methods I describe in this chapter, you'll master them in no time.

Now I'll describe the differences. As the table shows, using REG files is the easiest method, scripts and Windows Installer package files are the most difficult, and the rest fall somewhere in between. No matter which method you choose, they all become rather easy after you learn how to use them. Access to the operating system is important only if you're trying to do more than just edit the registry. For example, if you want to read values from the registry and then dump them to a text file, you're going to need access to the operating system. The most important difference is that only INF files and scripts provide high support for the many different types of values you can store in the registry. The remaining methods support the basic value types, though, and that's often all you need. If you need to edit more esoteric types, though, you're better off writing an INF file or a script. Likewise, INF files and scripts are the only two methods you can use to set and clear bits in values. For example, the bits in the value UserPreferencesMask indicate different user interface settings, and you enable or disable them by setting or clearing the corresponding bit. If this is your requirement, you're left with INF files or scripts as your method of choice.

Installing INF Files

Setup Information files have the *.inf* extension; I call them INF files. The Windows XP setup API (Application Programming Interface) uses INF files to script installations. Most people associate INF files with device-driver installation, but applications often use them, too. Most actions that you associate with installing device drivers and applications are available through INF files. You can copy, remove, and rename files. You can add, change, and delete registry values. You can install and start services. You can install most anything using INF files. For example, you can use them to customize registry settings—obviously. You can also create INF files that users can uninstall using Add Or Remove Programs.

INF files look similar to INI and REG files. They're text files that contain sections that look like [*Section*]. Each section contains items, sometimes called properties, that look like *Name=Value*. Windows XP happens to come with the perfect INF-file editor: Notepad. When you create a new INF file using Notepad, make sure that you enclose the file name in quotation marks or choose All Files in the Save As Type list in the Save As dialog box. That way, your file will have the *.inf* extension instead of the *.txt* extension. Installing an INF file is straightforward: Right-click the INF file, and then click Install. To deploy an INF file and prevent users from having to install it manually, use the following command, replacing *Filename* with the name of your INF file. (This is the command line that Windows XP associates with the *.inf* file extension in the registry.)

```
rundll32.exe setupapi,InstallHinfSection DefaultInstall 132 Filename.inf
```

Listing 9-1 shows a simple INF file. The first section, [Version], is required. The name of the second section is arbitrary but usually [DefaultInstall] so that users can right-click the file to install it. The linkage to this section is through the command line you saw just before this paragraph. The command is rundll32.exe, which executes the API in Setupapi.dll called InstallHinfSection. The next item on the command line, DefaultInstall, is the name of the section to install. The 132 you see before the file name tells the setup API to prompt the user before rebooting the computer, if necessary. The last item on the command line is the name of the INF file to install. Like I mentioned, because this is the command that Windows XP associates with the *.inf* file extension, you should usually name this section [DefaultInstall]. Within this section you see two directives, AddReg and DelReg. The directive AddReg=Add.Settings adds the settings contained in the section [Add.Settings].

The directive `DelReg=Del.Settings` deletes the settings listed in the section `[Del.Settings]`. The names of these sections are arbitrary; you should adopt names that make sense to you and stick with them so you don't confuse yourself down the road.

Listing 9-1   Example.inf

```
[Version]
Signature=$CHICAGO$

[DefaultInstall]
AddReg=Add.Settings
DelReg=Del.Settings

[Add.Settings]
HKCR,regfile\shell,,0,"edit"

[Del.Settings]
HKCU,Software\Microsoft\Windows\CurrentVersion\Applets\Regedit
```

Now you've had my two-dollar tour of an INF file. The sections that follow describe how to write the different parts of an INF file. I'm focusing on using INF files to edit the registry, but you can do much more with them. The ultimate resource for writing INF files is *http://msdn.microsoft.com/library/en-us/install/hh/install/inf-format_7soi.asp* on Microsoft's Web site. This is the INF File Sections and Directives section of the Windows Driver Development Kit (DDK). Don't let the fact that this information is in the DDK scare you; it's really straightforward and useful for much more than installing device drivers.

Starting with a Template

I never start INF files from scratch. I can't be bothered to remember the format of the sections and directives, so I use a template. I'm lazy enough (or efficient enough) that I add the template you see in Listing 9-2 to the Templates folder in my user profile so that I can right-click in a folder, and then click New, Setup Information File. The easiest way is to first create the file Setup Information File.inf with the contents of Listing 9-2. Then use Tweak UI, which you learn about in Chapter 5, "Mapping Tweak UI," to add the template. It's a real timesaver.

The reason this template makes creating INF files so easy is because I've added comments to it. Comments begin with the semicolon (;) and add descriptive information to the file. In this case, for each section, I described the format of the different directives. In the `[Reg.Settings]` section, for example, you see the syntax for adding values to the registry. In the `[Bits.Set]` section, you see the format for setting individual bits in a number. I often write INF files that users can uninstall using Add Or Remove Programs; the template in Listing 9-2 shows you how to do that. If you don't want users to uninstall the file and its settings, remove the `[DefaultUninstall]`, `[Reg.Uninstall]`, `[Inf.Copy]`, `[DestinationDirs]`, `[SourceDisksNames]`, and `[SourceDisksFiles]` sections and any linkages to those sections. In this template, all-capitalized words are placeholders that I replace when I create an INF file. For example, I replace `FILENAME` with the INF file's actual name.

Listing 9-2   Setup Information File.inf

```
[Version]
Signature=$CHICAGO$

[DefaultInstall]
BitReg=Bits.Set
AddReg=Reg.Settings
AddReg=Reg.Uninstall
CopyFiles=Inf.Copy

[DefaultUninstall]
BitReg=Bits.Clear
DelReg=Reg.Settings
DelReg=Reg.Uninstall
DelFiles=Inf.Copy

[Reg.Settings]

; ROOT,SUBKEY[,NAME[,FLAG[,DATA]]]
;
; FLAG:
;
;  0x00000 - REG_SZ
;  0x00001 - REG_BINARY
;  0x10000 - REG_MULTI_SZ
;  0x20000 - REG_EXPAND_SZ
;  0x10001 - REG_DWORD
;  0x20001 - REG_NONE

[Bits.Set]

; ROOT,SUBKEY,NAME,FLAG,MASK,BYTE
;
; FLAG:
;
;  0x00000 - Clear bits in mask
;  0x00001 - Set bits in mask

[Bits.Clear]

; ROOT,SUBKEY,NAME,FLAG,MASK,BYTE
;
; FLAG:
;
;  0x00000 - Clear bits in mask
;  0x00001 - Set bits in mask

[Reg.Uninstall]
```

```
HKCU,Software\Microsoft\Windows\CurrentVersion\Uninstall\%NAME%
HKCU,Software\Microsoft\Windows\CurrentVersion\Uninstall\%NAME%,DisplayName\
,,"%NAME%"
HKCU,Software\Microsoft\Windows\CurrentVersion\Uninstall\%NAME%,UninstallString\
,,"Rundll32.exe setupapi.dll,InstallHinfSection DefaultUninstall 132"\
" %53%\Application Data\Custom\FILENAME"

; ROOT:
;
;   HKCU
;   HKLM

[Inf.Copy]
FILENAME

[DestinationDirs]
Inf.Copy=53,Application Data\Custom

; DIRID:
;
;   10 - %SystemRoot%
;   11 - %SystemRoot%\System32
;   17 - %SystemRoot%\Inf
;   53 - %UserProfile%
;   54 - %SystemDrive%
;   -1 - Absolute path

[SourceDisksNames]
55=%DISKNAME%

[SourceDisksFiles]
FILENAME=55

[Strings]
NAME     = "Jerry's NAME"
DISKNAME = "Setup Files"
```

The first two lines in Listing 9-2 are the only ones required. The [Version] section and the Signature property identify the file as a valid INF file. You must include these two lines at the top of all your INF files. Incidentally, *Chicago* was Microsoft's code name for Microsoft Windows 95, and so version=$CHICAGO$ identifies the file as a Windows 95 INF file. These days, $CHICAGO$ indicates an INF file that's compatible with all versions of Windows. Use $Windows 95$ if you want to indicate that your INF file is compatible with 16-bit versions of Windows only. Use $Windows NT$ to indicate that your INF file is compatible with 32-bit versions of Windows only. Generally, I leave Signature set to $CHICAGO$.

Linking Sections Together

After the [Version] section is usually the [DefaultInstall] section. As I said earlier, the name of this section is arbitrary, but you should use [DefaultInstall] if you want users to be able to install your INF file by right-clicking it. The command associated with the *.inf* file extension references this section by name. This is the section that links together your INF file. You fill it with directives that tell the Setup API which sections in the INF file to process and what to do with them.

You saw this section in Listing 9-2. Each line in this section is a directive. The Setup API supports a number of different directives, but the ones we care about in this book are AddReg, DelReg, and BitReg. In the listing, you see a line that says AddReg=Reg.Settings. This adds the settings listed in the [Reg.Settings] section. The line BitReg=Bits.Set sets the bit masks listed in the section [Bits.Set]. As well, you can list more than one section for each directive. You can duplicate a directive on multiple lines, for example, or you can assign multiple sections to it: AddReg=*Section1*,*Section2*,*SectionN*. For an example, see Listing 9-3.

Listing 9-3   Example.inf

```
[Version]
Signature=$CHICAGO$

[DefaultInstall]
AddReg=Reg.Settings1,Reg.Settings2,Reg.Settings3
AddReg=Reg.Settings4
AddReg=Reg.Settings5
DelReg=Reg.Settings6

[Reg.Settings1]
; Registry settings to add or change

[Reg.Settings2]
; Registry settings to add or change

[Reg.Settings3]
; Registry settings to add or change

[Reg.Settings4]
; Registry settings to add or change

[Reg.Settings5]
; Registry settings to add or change

[Reg.Settings6]
; Registry keys and values to remove
```

Note   The order of the AddReg and DelReg directives doesn't matter. The Setup API processes all DelReg directives first, followed by the AddReg sections.

Adding Keys and Values

As you just saw, the AddReg directive in [DefaultInstall] indicates the names of sections that contain settings you want to add to the registry. These are [*add-registry-section*] sections. You can add new keys, set default values, create new values, or modify existing values using an [*add-registry-section*] section. And each section can contain multiple entries. Each [*add-registry-section*] name must be unique in the INF file.

Syntax

```
[add-registry-section]
rootkey, [subkey], [value], [flags], [data]
```

rootkey	This is the root key containing the key or value you're modifying. Use the abbreviations HKCR, HKCU, HKLM, or HKU.
subkey	This is the subkey to create or the subkey in which to add or change a value. This is optional. If missing, all operations are on the root key.
value	This is the name of the value to create or modify if it exists. This value is optional. If *value* is omitted and the *flags* and *data* parameters are given, operations are on the key's default value. If *value*, *flags*, and *data* are omitted, you're adding a subkey.
flags	• **0x00000000.** *Value* is REG_SZ. This is the default if you omit *flags*. • **0x00000001.** *Value* is REG_BINARY. • **0x00010000.** *Value* is REG_MULTI_SZ. • **0x00020000.** *Value* is REG_EXPAND_SZ. • **0x00010001.** *Value* is REG_DWORD. • **0x00020001.** *Value* is REG_NONE. • **0x00000002.** Don't overwrite existing keys and values. Combine this flag with others by ORing them together. • **0x00000004.** Delete *subkey* from the registry, or delete *value* from *subkey*. Combine this flag with others by ORing them together. • **0x00000008.** Append *data* to *value*. This flag is valid only if *value* is REG_MULTI_SZ. The string *data* is not appended if it already exists. Combine this flag with 0x00010000 by ORing them together. • **0x00000010.** Create *subkey*, but ignore *value* and *data* if specified. Combine this flag with others by ORing them together. • **0x00000020.** Set *value* only if it already exists. Combine this flag with others by ORing them together. • **0x00001000.** Make the specified change in the 64-bit registry. If not specified, the change is made to the native registry. Combine this flag with others by ORing them together. • **0x00004000.** Make the specified change in the 32-bit registry. If not specified, the change is made to the native registry. Combine this flag with others by ORing them together.
data	This is the data to write to *value*. If the value doesn't exist, the Setup API creates it; if the value exists, the API overwrites it; if the value is REG_MULTI_SZ and you set the 0x00010008 flag, the API adds the value to the existing string list. If you omit *data*, the Setup API creates the value without setting it. See the following example to learn how to format each type of value.

Example

```
[Version]
Signature=$CHICAGO$

[DefaultInstall]
AddReg=Reg.Settings

[Reg.Settings]
; Sets the default value of HKCU\Software\Sample
HKCU,Software\Sample,,,"Default"

; Creates a REG_SZ value called Sample
HKCU,Software\Sample,String,0x00000,"String"

; Creates a REG_BINARY value called Binary
HKCU,Software\Sample,Binary,0x00001,00,01,30,05

; Creates a REG_MULTI_SZ value called Multisz
HKCU,Software\Sample,Multisz,0x10000,"String list"

; Creates a REG_DWORD value called Dword
HKCU,Software\Sample,Dword,0x10001,0x01010102

; Creates a REG_SZ value called Hello
HKLM,SOFTWARE\Sample,Hello,,"World"

; Creates a REG_DWORD value and sets it to 0x0000
HKLM,SOFTWARE\Sample,Nothing,0x10001
```

Deleting Keys and Values

The [DefaultInstall] section's DelReg directive specifies sections containing registry keys and values to delete. These are [*del-registry-section*] sections. They are much simpler than the [*add-registry-section*] sections but have similar rules: Each section can contain multiple entries, and the name of each section must be unique.

Syntax

```
[del-registry-section]
rootkey, [subkey], [value], [flags], [data]
```

rootkey	This is the root key containing the key or value you're deleting. Use the abbreviations HKCR, HKCU, HKLM, or HKU.
subkey	This is the subkey to delete or subkey from which to delete a value. This is optional. If missing, all operations are on the root key.
value	This is the name of the value to delete. This value is optional. If *value* is omitted, you're deleting *subkey*.
flags	• **0x00002000.** Delete the entire subkey.
	• **0x00004000.** Make the specified change in the 32-bit registry. If not specified, the change is made to the native registry. Combine this flag with others by ORing them together.
	• **0x00018002.** If *value* is REG_MULTI_SZ, remove all strings matching the string indicated by *data*.
data	This is used only when *flags* is 0x00018002. This specifies the string to remove from a REG_MULTI_SZ value.

Example

```
[Version]
Signature=$CHICAGO$

[DefaultInstall]
DelReg=Reg.Settings

[Reg.Settings]
; Removes the key HKCU\Software\Sample
HKCU,Software\Sample

; Removes the value Hello from HKCU\Software\Sample
HKCU,Software\Sample,Hello

; Removes the string "World" from the REG_MULTI_SZ value Hello
HKCU,Software\Sample,Hello,0x00018002,"World"
```

Setting and Clearing Bits

The BitReg directive is similar to the AddReg directive. You add it to the [DefaultInstall] section to indicate the names of sections that contain bits you want to set and clear. These are [*bit-registry-section*] sections. Use the BitReg directive when you want to work with bit masks in the registry. For example, if you want to enable certain user-interface features in the value UserPreferencesMask, use this directive. Like the other directives you learned about, each section can contain multiple entries, and the name of each section must be unique.

In the following description of the syntax, notice the differences between the [*bit-registry-section*] and [*add-registry-section*] sections. The parameter *value* is not optional. Also, the parameters *mask* and *byte* replace the value *data*. The parameter *mask* is 8 bits long and indicates which bit you want to enable or disable. The parameter *byte* indicates which byte in the binary value you want to modify. This indicates bytes left to right starting from 0. This is straightforward when working with REG_BINARY values but less so when working with REG_DWORD values. As discussed in Chapter 1, "Learning the Basics," Windows XP stores REG_DWORD values in the registry in reverse-byte order (little-endian architecture). To be sure, test your INF files carefully to make sure you're masking the bits you think you're masking. Figure 9-1 shows the relationship between *value*, *mask*, and *byte*. The value to which I'm applying the mask is a REG_DWORD value stored in the registry in reverse-byte notation: 0x0180C000. Set the mask in byte 0, and the result is 0x0180C080. Clear the mask in byte 1, and the result is 0x0140C080.

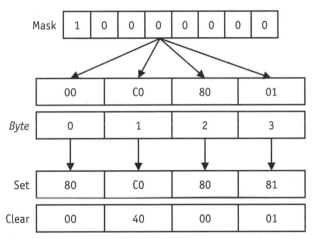

Figure 9-1 *The parameter byte indicates to which of a number's bytes you want to apply mask.*

Syntax

```
[bit-registry-section]
rootkey, [subkey], value, [flags], mask, byte
```

rootkey	This is the root key containing the value you're modifying. Use the abbreviations HKCR, HKCU, HKLM, or HKU.
subkey	This is the subkey in which to change a value. This is optional. If missing, all operations are on the root key.
value	This is the name of the value to modify. This value is *not* optional and should be a REG_DWORD or REG_BINARY value.
flags	• **0x00000000.** Clear the bits specified by *mask*. • **0x00000001.** Set the bits specified by *mask*. • **0x00040000.** Make the specified change in the 32-bit registry. If not specified, the change is made to the native registry. Combine this flag with others by ORing them together.
mask	This is the byte-sized mask specifying the bits to set or clear in the specified byte of *value*. Specify this value in hexadecimal notation. Bits that are 1 will be set or cleared, depending on *flags*, and bits that are 0 will be ignored.
byte	This specifies the byte in *value* to which you want to apply *mask*. The left-most byte is 0, the next is 1, and so on. Keep in mind that Windows XP stores REG_DWORD values in reverse-byte order when specifying which byte on which to apply *mask*. Thus, in REG_DWORD values, the right-most byte is stored first in memory.

Example

```
[Version]
Signature=$CHICAGO$

[DefaultInstall]
BitReg=Bit.Settings

[Bit.Settings]
; Changes 50,00,10,00 to 31,00,10,00
HKCU,Software\Sample,Mask,0x0001,0x01,0

; Changes 50,00,F0,00 to 30,00,70,00
HKU,Software\Sample,Mask,0x0000,0x80,2
```

Using Strings in INF Files

You can make your INF files far easier to read if you use the [Strings] section. Each line in this section is a string in the format *name="string"*. Then you can use that string elsewhere in the INF file by referencing it as *%name%*. This makes INF files easier to read in numerous ways (see Listing 9-4, which is also a good example of using the BitReg directive):

• The [Strings] section collects strings at the bottom of your INF file so that you can see them in one place.

- The [Strings] section enables you to type a string one time and then use that string in numerous places. The string is consistent throughout your INF file.
- The [Strings] section makes translating INF files easier because localizable strings are at the bottom of the file.

Listing 9-4   Strings.inf

```
[Version]
Signature=$CHICAGO$

[DefaultInstall]
BitReg=Bits.Set
AddReg=Add.Settings
DelReg=Del.Settings

[Add.Settings]
HKCU,%HK_DESKTOP%,ActiveWndTrkTimeout,0x10001,1000
HKLM,%HK_SETUP%,RegisteredOwner,,%OWNER%

[Del.Settings]
HKCU,%HK_EXPLORER%\MenuOrder
HKCU,%HK_EXPLORER%\RunMRU
HKCU,%HK_EXPLORER%\RecentDocs
HKCU,%HK_EXPLORER%\ComDlg32\LastVisitedMRU
HKCU,%HK_SEARCH%\ACMru
HKCU,%HK_INTERNET%\TypedURLs

[Bits.Set]
HKCU,%HK_DESKTOP%,UserPreferencesMask,1,0x01,0
HKCU,%HK_DESKTOP%,UserPreferencesMask,1,0x40,0

[Strings]
HK_DESKTOP="Control Panel\Desktop"
HK_EXPLORER="Software\Microsoft\Windows\CurrentVersion\Explorer"
HK_SEARCH="Software\Microsoft\Search Assistant"
HK_INTERNET="Software\Microsoft\Internet Explorer"
HK_SETUP="SOFTWARE\Microsoft\Windows NT\CurrentVersion"
OWNER="Fuzzy Wuzzy Was a Bear"
```

Note   Here's the truth-in-advertising bit: I seldom use strings because I don't often localize INF files. I use strings only when doing so really does make the INF file easier to read. In particular, when a line becomes so long that it wraps, I use a string to shorten it. Alternatively, you can use the line-continuation character, a backslash (\), to split lines. I also use strings for values that change frequently, particularly in template INF files. Strings make using templates easier.

Setting Values with REG Files

You learned how to create REG files using Regedit in Chapter 2, "Using the Registry Editor." REG files are the classic method for adding and changing values in the registry, but as I said in the section "Choosing a Technique," they're not as powerful as the other methods you learn about in this chapter. Their big weakness is that you can't remove values using a REG file; you can only add or modify values, or remove keys.

After you've created a REG file, which has the *.reg* file extension, you import it into the registry by double-clicking the file. This is great if you want users to import the file themselves, but you need the following command if you want to import a REG file using your software management infrastructure or some method such as providing a link to it on the intranet: regedit /s *filename*.reg. Replace *filename*.reg with the path and name of your REG file. The /s command-line option imports the file into the registry without prompting the user, which is what you want to do most of the time. To edit a REG file, right-click it, and then click Edit. Don't accidentally double-click a REG file thinking that you're going to open it in Notepad because double-clicking a REG file imports it into the registry.

Remember that Regedit supports two different file formats for REG files. Version 4 REG files are ANSI. ANSI character encoding uses one byte to represent each character. Also, Regedit writes REG_EXPAND_SZ and REG_MULTI_SZ strings to REG files using ANSI character encoding, so each character is a single byte. Unicode character encoding uses two bytes for each character, and when you create a Unicode REG file, Regedit writes REG_EXPAND_SZ and REG_MULTI_SZ strings to the file using the two-byte Unicode encoding scheme. Chapter 1, "Learning the Basics," tells you more about the differences between the two encoding standards. Chapter 2, "Using Registry Editor," describes the differences between the two different types of REG files. What you need to know is that choosing to create a version 4 REG file means that the file and the values in the file use ANSI; likewise, creating a version 5 REG file means that the file and the values in the file use Unicode. I tend to use version 4, ANSI REG files, except when I know the registry data contains localized text that requires Unicode to represent it. If in doubt, always create version 5, Unicode files.

Listing 9-5 shows a sample REG file. The first line in this file is the header, which identifies the file's version. The header Windows Registry Editor Version 5.00 indicates a version 5, Unicode REG file. The header REGEDIT4 indicates a version 4, ANSI REG file. A blank line usually follows the header, but the file works fine without it. Notice how similar the remainder of this file looks to INF and INI files. Each section contains the fully qualified name of a key. They use the full names of root keys, not the abbreviations. Listing 9-5 is importing settings into three keys: HKCU\Control Panel\Desktop, HKCU\Control Panel \Desktop\WindowMetrics, and HKCU\Control Panel\Mouse. The lines below each section are values that Regedit will add to that key when Regedit imports the file in to the registry. The format is *"name"*=*value*. The value named @ represents the key's default value. Some of the values in Listing 9-5 contain dword and hex, whereas others are enclosed in quotation marks. Values enclosed in quotation marks are strings. Values in the form dword:*value* are REG_DWORD values. Values in the form hex:*values* are REG_BINARY values. This gets more complicated when you add subtypes, such as hex(*type*):*value*, and I'll talk about those a bit later.

Listing 9-5   Example.reg

```
Windows Registry Editor Version 5.00

[HKEY_CURRENT_USER\Control Panel\Desktop]
"ActiveWndTrkTimeout"=dword:00000000
"ForegroundFlashCount"=dword:00000003
"ForegroundLockTimeout"=dword:00030d40
"MenuShowDelay"="400"
"PaintDesktopVersion"=dword:00000000
"UserPreferencesMask"=hex:9e,3e,07,80

[HKEY_CURRENT_USER\Control Panel\Desktop\WindowMetrics]
"Shell Icon BPP"="16"
"Shell Icon Size"="32"
"MinAnimate"="1"

[HKEY_CURRENT_USER\Control Panel\Mouse]
@="Rodent"
"ActiveWindowTracking"=dword:00000000
"DoubleClickHeight"="4"
"DoubleClickSpeed"="500"
"DoubleClickWidth"="4"
"MouseSensitivity"="10"
"MouseSpeed"="1"
"MouseThreshold1"="6"
"MouseThreshold2"="10"
"SnapToDefaultButton"="0"
"SwapMouseButtons"="0"
```

Exporting Settings to REG Files

The easiest way to create a REG file is by using Regedit to export keys to REG files. Follow these steps to export branches of the registry to files:

1. Click the key at the top of the branch you want to export.

2. On the File menu, click Export.

    The Export Registry File dialog box appears, shown in Figure 9-2 on the next page.

3. In the File Name box, enter a name for the file you're creating.

4. Select the option for the export range you want:

    - To back up the entire registry, select the All option.

    - To back up the selected branch, select the Selected Branch option.

5. In the Save As Type list, click the type of file you want to create: Registration (*.reg) or Win9x/NT4 Registration (*.reg).

6. Click Save.

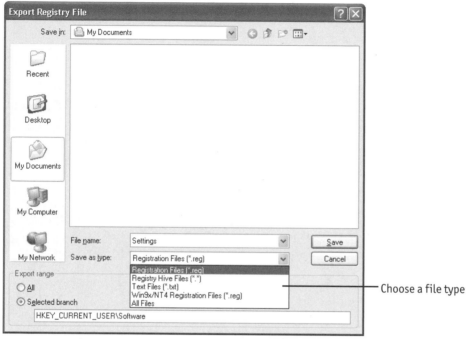

Figure 9-2   *The only two types of files that create REG files are Registration Files (*.reg) and Win9x/NT4 Registration Files (*.reg).*

The REG file you create contains all the subkeys and values under the key you exported. The likelihood that you want all the key's subkeys and values isn't very high, so you should open the file in Notepad by right-clicking it and clicking Edit; then remove any keys and values that you don't want to keep in the file. You can also change any of the values in the REG file. For example, you can export a key from your own computer, just to get you started, and then edit it to suit your requirements, removing keys, changing values, and so on.

Caution   If you're creating a REG file for versions of Windows that don't support version 5, Unicode REG files, use version 4, ANSI REG files. Microsoft Windows 95, Windows 98, and Windows Me do not support Unicode REG files, and any attempt to import Unicode REG files into their registries could yield results that you don't like.

Creating REG Files Manually

Creating REG files by hand is an error-prone process that I don't recommend. Nonetheless, many of you are likely to do it anyway, so I'm going to show you how. First decide whether you're going to create an ANSI or Unicode REG file, and then follow these instructions to create it:

1. Create a new file in Notepad.

2. At the top of the file, add one of the following, followed by a blank line:

   - Add REGEDIT4 at the top of the file to create a version 4 REG file.

   - Add Windows Registry Editor Version 5.00 at the top of the file to create a version 5 REG file.

3. For each key into which you want to import values, add a section to the file in the format [*key*], where *key* is the fully qualified name of the key. Don't use the root-key abbreviations; use their full names: HKEY_CURRENT_USER.

4. For each value that you want to import into the registry, add the value in the format "name"=value to the key's section. Use @ for a key's default value. See Table 9-2 for information about how to format the different types of values in a REG file. You can continue an entry from one line to the next using the line-continuation character, a backslash (\).

5. Click File, Save As, type the name of the file in File Name, including the extension *.reg* (enclose the file name in quotation marks so that Notepad doesn't use the *.txt* extension), do one of the following, and then click Save:

   - In the Encoding list, choose ANSI to create a version 4 REG file.

   - In the Encoding list, choose Unicode to create a version 5 REG file.

Table 9-2   Value Formats in REG files

Type	Version 4	Version 5
REG_SZ	"String"	"String"
REG_DWORD	dword:00007734	dword:00007734
REG_BINARY	hex:00,00,01,03	hex:00,00,01,03
REG_EXPAND_SZ	hex(2):25,53,59,53,54,45,4d,52, 4f,4f,54,25,00	hex(2):25,00,53,00,59,00,53,00, 54,00,45,00,4d,00,52,00,4f,00, 4f,00,54,00,25,00,00,00
REG_MULTI_SZ	hex(7):48,65,6c,6c,6f,20,57,6f, 72,6c,64,00,4a,65,72,72,79,20, 77,61,73,20,68,65,72,65,00,00	hex(7):48,00,65,00,6c,00,6c,00, 6f,00,20,00,57,00,6f,00,72,00, 6c,00,64,00,00,00,4a,00,65,00, 72,00,72,00,79,00,20,00,77,00, 61,00,73,00,20,00,68,00,65,00, 72,00,65,00,00,00,00,00

Encoding Special Characters

Within REG files, certain characters have special meaning. Quotation marks begin and end strings. The backslash character is a line-continuation character. So how do you include these characters in your values? You use *escaping*, which is an ages-old method for prefixing special characters with a backslash. For example, the string \n represents a newline character and the string \" represents a quotation mark. Table 9-3 describes the special characters you can use and shows you examples.

Table 9-3   Special Characters in REG Files

Escape	Expanded	Example
\\	\	`C:\\Documents and Settings\\Jerry`
\"	"	`A \"quoted\" string`
\n	*newline*	`This is on \n two lines`
\r	*return*	`This is on \r two lines`

Deleting Keys Using a REG File

You can't use a REG file to remove individual values, but you can certainly use one to delete entire keys. This is an undocumented feature of REG files: Just prefix a key's name with
a minus (–) sign: [-*key*]. Here's a brief example that removes the key HKCU\Software \Honeycutt when you import the REG file in to the registry:

```
Windows Registry Editor Version 5.00

[-HKEY_CURRENT_USER\Software\Honeycutt]
```

Rather than manually create a REG file to remove keys, I prefer to export a key to a REG file and then edit it. After exporting the key to a REG file, remove all the values and keys that you don't want to delete. Then add the minus sign to the names of the keys that you want to delete. Then you can remove those keys quickly and easily by double-clicking the REG file or using the command regedit /s *filename*.reg.

Editing from the Command Prompt

Windows XP comes with Console Registry Tool for Windows (Reg.exe). This tool is nothing short of marvelous. You use it to edit the registry from the MS-DOS command prompt. You can do with Reg.exe just about anything you can do with Regedit, and more. The best part of Reg.exe is that you can use it to write simple scripts in the form of batch files that change the registry. And unlike in earlier versions of Windows, you don't have to install Reg.exe. It's installed by default and combines the numerous registry tools that came with the resource kits for earlier versions of Windows.

This tool is so cool I can just start with an example. Listing 9-6 is a simple batch file that installs Microsoft Office XP the first time the batch file runs (think logon script). After installing Office XP, the batch file calls Reg.exe to add the REG_DWORD value Flag to HKCU \Software\Example. The batch file checks for this value's presence each time the file runs and skips the installation if it exists. Thus, the batch file installs the application only one time. This is a method you can use to deploy software through users' logon scripts. Instead of checking for a value that you add, as Listing 9-6 does, you can check for a value that the application stores in the registry. For example, the second line in the batch file could just as easily been Reg QUERY HKCU\Software\Microsoft\Office\10.0 >nul, which checks to see if Office XP is installed for the user.

Listing 9-6   Login.bat

```
@Echo Off

Reg QUERY HKCU\Software\Example /v Flag >nul

goto %ERRORLEVEL%

:1

    Echo Installing software the first time this runs
    \\Camelot\Office\Setup.exe /settings setup.ini

    Reg ADD HKCU\Software\Example /v Flag /t REG_DWORD /d "1"
    goto CONTINUE

:0

    Echo Software is already installed, skipping this section

:CONTINUE

Set HKMS=HKCU\Software\Microsoft
Set HKCV=HKCU\Software\Microsoft\Windows\CurrentVersion

REM Clear the history lists

Reg DELETE %HKCV%\Explorer\MenuOrder /f
Reg DELETE %HKCV%\Explorer\RunMRU /f
Reg DELETE %HKCV%\Explorer\RecentDocs /f
Reg DELETE %HKCV%\Explorer\ComDlg32\LastVisitedMRU /f
Reg DELETE "%HKMS%\Search Assistant\ACMru" /f
Reg DELETE "%HKMS%\Internet Explorer\TypedURLs" /f
```

The syntax of the Reg.exe command line is straightforward: `reg` *command options*. *Command* is one of the many commands that Reg.exe supports, including ADD, QUERY, and DELETE. *Options* is the options that the command requires. Options usually include the name of a key, and sometimes a value's name and data. If any key or value name contains spaces, you must enclose the name in quotation marks. It gets more complicated for each of the different commands you can use with it, however, and I cover each of those in the sections following this one. If you're without this book and need a quick refresh, just type **reg /?** at the MS-DOS command prompt to see a list of commands that Regexe supports.

Adding Keys and Values

Use the ADD command to add keys and values to the registry.

Syntax

```
REG ADD [\\computer\]key [/v value | /ve] [/t type] [/s separator] [/d data]
[/f]
```

\\computer	If omitted, Reg.exe connects to the local computer; otherwise, Reg.exe connects to the remote computer.
key	This is the key's path, beginning with the root key. Use the root-key abbreviations HKCR, HKCU, HKLM, and HKU. Only HKLM and HKU are available when connecting to remote computers.
/v value	This will add or change *value*.
/ve	This will change the key's default value.
/t type	This is the value's type: REG_BINARY, REG_DWORD, REG_DWORD_LITTLE_ENDIAN, REG_DWORD_BIG_ENDIAN, REG_EXPAND_SZ, REG_MULTI_SZ, or REG_SZ. The default is REG_SZ.
/s separator	This specifies the character used to separate strings when creating REG_MULTI_SZ values. the default is \0, or null.
/d data	This is the data to assign to new or existing values.
/f	This forces Reg.exe to overwrite existing values with prompting.

Example

```
REG ADD \\JERRY1\HKLM\Software\Honeycutt
REG ADD HKLM\Software\Honeycutt /v Data /t REG_BINARY /d CCFEF0BC
REG ADD HKLM\Software\Honeycutt /v List /t REG_MULTI_SZ /d Hello\0World
REG ADD HKLM\Software\Honeycutt /v Path /t REG_EXPAND_SZ /d %%SYSTEMROOT%%
```

Note The percent sign (%) has a special purpose on the MS-DOS command prompt and within batch files. You enclose environment variables in percent signs to expand them in place. Thus, to use them on the Reg.exe command line, and elsewhere for that matter, you must use double percent signs (%%). In the previous example, if you had used single percent signs, the command prompt would have expanded the environment variable before running the command. Using double percent signs prevents the command prompt from expanding the environment variable.

Querying Values

The QUERY command works three ways. First it can display the data in a specific value. Second it can display all of a key's values. Third it can list all the subkeys and values in a key by adding the /s command-line option. How it works depends on the options you use.

Syntax

```
REG QUERY [\\computer\]key [/v value | /ve] [/s]
```

\\computer	If omitted, Reg.exe connects to the local computer; otherwise, Reg.exe connects to the remote computer.
key	This is the key's path, beginning with the root key. Use the root-key abbreviations HKCR, HKCU, HKLM, and HKU. Only HKLM and HKU are available when connecting to remote computers.
/v value	This will query value in key. If you omit /v, Reg.exe queries all values in the key.
/ve	This will query the key's default value.
/s	This will query all the key's subkeys and values.

Example

```
REG QUERY HKLM\SOFTWARE\Microsoft\Windows\CurrentVersion /s
REG QUERY HKLM\SOFTWARE\Microsoft\Windows NT\CurrentVersion /v CurrentVersion
```

Note Reg.exe sets ERRORLEVEL to 0 if the command succeeds and 1 if it doesn't. Thus, you can test ERRORLEVEL in a batch file to determine if a value exists or not. You saw an example of this in Listing 9-6. Although you can use the If statement to test ERRORLEVEL, I prefer creating labels in my batch file, one for each level, as shown in Listing 9-6 earlier in this chapter. Then I can just write statements that look like Goto %ERRORLEVEL% or Goto QUERY%ERRORLEVEL%, which branches to the label QUERY1 if ERRORLEVEL is 1.

Deleting Keys and Values

Use the DELETE command to remove keys and values from the registry.

Syntax

```
REG DELETE [\\computer\]key [/v value | /ve | /va] [/f]
```

\\computer	If omitted, Reg.exe connects to the local computer; otherwise, Reg.exe connects to the remote computer.
key	This is the key's path, beginning with the root key. Use the root-key abbreviations HKCR, HKCU, HKLM, and HKU. Only HKLM and HKU are available when connecting to remote computers.
/v value	This will delete value from key.
/ve	This will delete the key's default value.
/va	This will delete all values from key.
/f	This will force Reg.exe to delete values with prompting.

Example

```
REG DELETE \\JERRY1\HKLM\Software\Honeycutt
REG DELETE HKLM\Software\Honeycutt /v Data /f
REG DELETE HKLM\Software\Honeycutt /va
```

Comparing Keys and Values

Use the COMPARE command to compare two registry keys. Those keys can be on the same computer or different computers, making this a useful troubleshooting tool.

The /on command-line option seems odd at first. Why would you compare keys or values and not show the differences? Reg.exe sets ERRORLEVEL depending on the comparison's result, and you can use that in your batch files to execute different code depending on whether the two are the same or different—without displaying any results. Here's the meaning of ERRORLEVEL:

- **0.**   The command was successful and the keys or values are identical.

- **1.**   The command failed.

- **2.**   The command was successful and the keys or values are different.

```
REG COMPARE [\\computer1\]key1 [\\computer2\]key2 [/v value | /ve]
[/oa|/od|/os|/on] [/s]
```

\\computer1	If omitted, Reg.exe connects to the local computer; otherwise, Reg.exe connects to the remote computer.
\\computer2	If omitted, Reg.exe connects to the local computer; otherwise, Reg.exe connects to the remote computer.

key1	This is the key's path, beginning with the root key. Use the root-key abbreviations HKCR, HKCU, HKLM, and HKU. Only HKLM and HKU are available when connecting to remote computers.
key2	This is the key's path, beginning with the root key. Use the root-key abbreviations HKCR, HKCU, HKLM, and HKU. Only HKLM and HKU are available when connecting to remote computers.
/v *value*	This compares *value*.
/ve	This compares the key's default value.
/oa	This shows all differences and matches.
/od	This shows only differences.
/os	This shows only matches.
/on	This shows nothing.
/s	This compares all the key's subkeys and values.

Example

```
REG COMPARE HKCR\txtfile HKR\docfile /ve
REG COMPARE \\JERRY1\HKCR \\JERRY2\HKCR /od /s
REG COMPARE HKCU\Software \\JERRY2\HKCU\Software /s
```

Copying Keys and Values

The COPY command copies a subkey to another key. This command is useful to back up subkeys, as you learned in Chapter 3, "Backing Up the Registry."

```
REG COPY [\\computer1\]key1 [\\computer2\]key2 [/s] [/f]
```

computer1	If omitted, Reg.exe connects to the local computer; otherwise, Reg.exe connects to the remote computer.
computer2	If omitted, Reg.exe connects to the local computer; otherwise, Reg.exe connects to the remote computer.
key1	This is the key's path, beginning with the root key. Use the root-key abbreviations HKCR, HKCU, HKLM, and HKU. Only HKLM and HKU are available when connecting to remote computers.
key2	The key's path, beginning with the root key. Use the root-key abbreviations HKCR, HKCU, HKLM, and HKU. Only HKLM and HKU are available when connecting to remote computers.
/s	This copies all the key's subkeys and values.
/f	This forces Reg.exe to copy with prompting.

Example

```
REG COPY HKCU\Software\Microsoft\Office HKCU\Backup\Office /s
REG COPY HKCR\regfile HKCU\Backup\regfile /s /f
```

Exporting Keys to REG Files

Use the EXPORT command to export all or part of the registry to REG files. This command has a few limitations, though. First it works only with the local computer. You can't create a REG file from a remote computer's registry. Second it creates only version 5, Unicode REG files. There's no option available to create ANSI REG files. The EXPORT command is the same as clicking File, Export in Regedit.

```
REG EXPORT key filename
```

key	This is the key's path, beginning with the root key. Use the root-key abbreviations HKCR, HKCU, HKLM, and HKU. This is the key you want to export to a REG file.
filename	This is the path and name of the REG file to create.

Example

```
REG EXPORT "HKCU\Control Panel" Preferences.reg
```

Importing REG Files

Use the IMPORT command to import a REG file in to the registry. This command does the same thing as running regedit /s filename. It imports a REG file silently. This command can handle both version 4 and version 5 REG files, but it works only on the local computer.

```
REG IMPORT filename
```

filename	This is the path and name of the REG file to import.

Example

```
REG IMPORT Settings.reg
```

Saving Keys to Hive Files

The SAVE command saves a key as a hive file. This command is similar to clicking File, Export in Regedit, and then changing the file type to Registry Hive Files (*.*). It's a convenient method for backing up the registry before making substantial changes. Chapter 3, "Backing Up the Registry," describes this technique. This command works only on the local computer.

```
REG SAVE key filename
```

key	This is the key's path, beginning with the root key. Use the root-key abbreviations HKCR, HKCU, HKLM, and HKU. This is the key you want to save as a hive file.
filename	This is the path and name of the hive file to create.

Example

```
REG SAVE HKU Backup.dat
```

Restoring Hive Files to Keys

The RESTORE command overwrites a key and all of its contents with the contents of a hive file. This is similar to importing a hive file in Regedit. The difference between this command and loading a hive file is that this command overwrites any existing key, whereas loading a hive file creates a new temporary key to contain the hive file's contents. Use this command to restore a backup hive file. This command works only on the local computer.

```
REG RESTORE key filename
```

key	This is the key's path, beginning with the root key. Use the root-key abbreviations HKCR, HKCU, HKLM, and HKU. This is the key you want to overwrite with the contents of the hive file.
filename	This is the path and name of the hive file to restore.

Example

```
REG RESTORE HKCU Backup.dat
```

Loading Hive Files

The LOAD command loads a hive file into a temporary key. You reference the hive file's keys and values through the temporary key you specify on the command line. This command is similar to loading hive files in Regedit. This command works only on the local computer.

```
REG LOAD key filename
```

key	This is the key's path, beginning with the root key. Use the root-key abbreviations HKCR, HKCU, HKLM, and HKU. This is the new temporary key into which you want to load the hive file.
filename	This is the path and name of the hive file to load.

Example

```
REG LOAD HKU\Temporary Settings.dat
```

Unloading Hive Files

The UNLOAD command removes a hive file that you've loaded using the LOAD command. It simply unhooks the hive file from the registry. You must remember to unload a hive file that you've loaded before trying to copy or do anything else with the hive file because Windows XP locks the file while it's in use.

```
REG UNLOAD key
```

key	This is the key's path, beginning with the root key. Use the root-key abbreviations HKCR, HKCU, HKLM, and HKU. This is the name of the key containing the hive file you want to unload.

Example

```
REG UNLOAD HKU\Temporary
```

Scripting Using Windows Script Host

Scripts give IT professionals the ultimate ability to control and automate Windows XP. These aren't batch files; they're full-fledged administrative programs that are surprisingly easy to create considering the wealth of power they enable. You can write a script that inventories a computer and writes the result to a file on the network, for example. You can automate an application to perform redundant steps automatically. The sky is the limit, really, but I'm here to tell you how to use scripts to edit the registry, so I'm confining myself a bit.

The scripting technology in Windows XP is Windows Script Host. The current version is 5.6 and is technologically leaps and bounds over what Microsoft Windows 2000 provided. Windows Script Host is called a *host* because it's not aware of a script's language. Microsoft calls this *language agnostic*. Windows Script Host uses different scripting engines to parse the different languages in which you might write a script. Windows XP provides two scripting engines: VBScript and JScript. If you've ever used the C or C++ languages, you'll be more comfortable writing scripts using JScript. If you've ever used Visual Basic in any of its incarnations, you're going to be more comfortable using VBScript to write scripts.

The problem with focusing this chapter on how to use scripts to edit the registry is that doing so assumes that you're already familiar with Windows Script Host. If that's not true, I suggest that you find a good book about scripts. If you don't want a book about it, see *http://www.microsoft.com/scripting*. This is Microsoft's Scripting Web site, and it contains everything you need to know about writing scripts for Windows XP, including accessing Windows Management Instrumentation (WMI) through scripts. After you've mastered the languages, which aren't difficult, you'll appreciate this Web site's reference content. The content describes the object model and how to use it—the hardest part of writing scripts for Windows XP.

Creating Script Files

Script files can have two file extensions, and the script's file extension indicates which language the file contains. Use the *.js* extension for files that contain JScript. Use the *.vbs* extension for files that contain VBScript. Regardless, script files are nothing more than text files that contain the language's keywords, so you can use your favorite text editor, Notepad, to create them. When you save a script file, make sure you enclose the file's name in quotation marks or choose All Files from the Save As Type list so Notepad doesn't add the *.txt* extension to the file.

Without going into detail about the object model, you access the registry through the Shell object. This object contains the methods you call to add, remove, and update values in the registry. You'll add one of the following statements to every script in which you want to access the registry. The first line shows you how to create the Shell object using VBScript, and the second shows you how to do it using JScript. Just to show you how easy it is to create a script, open Notepad, and type Listing 9-7. The JScript language is case sensitive, so type Listing 9-7 carefully. VBScript has the benefit of not being case sensitive. Save the file using the *.js* extension, and then double click the file to run it. You'll see a message from me. Because double-clicking the script file runs it, you must right-click the file and then click Edit to edit the file.

```
set WshShell = WScript.CreateObject( "WScript.Shell")
var WshShell = WScript.CreateObject( "WScript.Shell");
```

Listing 9-7   Example.js

```
var WshShell = WScript.CreateObject( "WScript.Shell");

WshShell.Popup( "Hello from Jerry Honeycutt" );
```

Why write scripts when INF files are easier?

I usually write INF files to edit the registry. If I'm not using INF files, I write batch files and use Reg.exe. I like the simplicity of these methods. There are times when writing a script is the only suitable method, however.

Writing a script is necessary in a number of cases. The first is when you must have a user interface. If you want to display settings to or collect settings from users, scripting is the best choice. Also, scripting is the only method that provides rather full access to Windows XP. For example, you can use a script to inventory the computer and dump the information to a text file on the network. You can use a script to configure users' computers using logic, if-this-then-that, which isn't possible with the other methods. So if you're doing anything more complicated than just adding, changing, or removing values, you're going to end up writing scripts. I've seen some fairly complicated scripts. For example, one fellow I worked with wrote a script that searched the registry for services that Sysprep disabled, and then permanently removed them from the registry. This is a great example of scripting.

Combined with WMI, scripting is nothing short of amazing. The script on the next page shows you how to use VBScript and WMI to inventory a computer's configuration. It displays the amount of physical memory installed on the computer, the name of the computer, the BIOS version, the type of processor, and more. This script and many more like it are available on Microsoft's Script Center, which is a large library of scripts that you can download, modify, and use. All these scripts are at *http://www.microsoft.com/technet/scriptcenter*.

```
strComputer = "."
Set objWMIService = GetObject("winmgmts:" _
    & "{impersonationLevel=impersonate}!\\" & strComputer & "\root\cimv2")
Set colSettings = objWMIService.ExecQuery _
    ("Select * from Win32_OperatingSystem")
For Each objOperatingSystem in colSettings
    Wscript.Echo "OS Name: " & objOperatingSystem.Name
    Wscript.Echo "Version: " & objOperatingSystem.Version
    Wscript.Echo "Service Pack: " & _
        objOperatingSystem.ServicePackMajorVersion _
            & "." & objOperatingSystem.ServicePackMinorVersion
    Wscript.Echo "OS Manufacturer: " & objOperatingSystem.Manufacturer
    Wscript.Echo "Windows Directory: " & _
        objOperatingSystem.WindowsDirectory
    Wscript.Echo "Locale: " & objOperatingSystem.Locale
    Wscript.Echo "Available Physical Memory: " & _
        objOperatingSystem.FreePhysicalMemory
    Wscript.Echo "Total Virtual Memory: " & _
        objOperatingSystem.TotalVirtualMemorySize
    Wscript.Echo "Available Virtual Memory: " & _
        objOperatingSystem.FreeVirtualMemory
    Wscript.Echo "OS Name: " & objOperatingSystem.SizeStoredInPagingFiles
Next
Set colSettings = objWMIService.ExecQuery _
    ("Select * from Win32_ComputerSystem")
For Each objComputer in colSettings
    Wscript.Echo "System Name: " & objComputer.Name
    Wscript.Echo "System Manufacturer: " & objComputer.Manufacturer
    Wscript.Echo "System Model: " & objComputer.Model
    Wscript.Echo "Time Zone: " & objComputer.CurrentTimeZone
    Wscript.Echo "Total Physical Memory: " & _
        objComputer.TotalPhysicalMemory
Next
Set colSettings = objWMIService.ExecQuery _
    ("Select * from Win32_Processor")
For Each objProcessor in colSettings
    Wscript.Echo "System Type: " & objProcessor.Architecture
    Wscript.Echo "Processor: " & objProcessor.Description
Next
Set colSettings = objWMIService.ExecQuery _
    ("Select * from Win32_BIOS")
For Each objBIOS in colSettings
    Wscript.Echo "BIOS Version: " & objBIOS.Version
Next
```

Running Script Files

Windows XP provides two scripting hosts. The Windows-based version runs scripts when you double-click a script file. The script engine is Wscript.exe. You can also use the command-line version, which is handy when the script outputs data similar to how most command-line programs do. The example given in the sidebar "Why write scripts when INF files are easier?" in Listing 9-7 is one script that's better from the command-line. The command-line scripting engine is Cscript.exe:

```
cscript script [//B|//I] [//D] [//E:engine] [//H:cscript|//H:wscript] [//
Job:name] [//Logo|//Nologo] [//S] [//T:time] [//X] [//?]
```

//B	This specifies batch mode, which does not display alerts, scripting errors, or input prompts.
//I	This specifies interactive mode, which displays alerts, scripting errors, and input prompts. This is the default and the opposite of //B.
//D	This turns on the debugger.
//E:engine	Specifies the scripting language that is used to run the script.
//H:cscript | //H:wscript	This registers either Cscript.exe or Wscript.exe as the default script host for running scripts. If neither is specified, the default is Wscript.exe.
//Job:name	This runs the job identified by name in a .wsf script file.
//Logo	This specifies that the Windows Script Host banner is displayed in the console window before the script runs. This is the default and the opposite of //Nologo.
//Nologo	This specifies that the Windows Script Host banner is not displayed before the script runs.
//S	This saves the current command-line options for the current user.
//T:time	This specifies the maximum time the script can run (in seconds). You can specify up to 32,767 seconds. The default is no time limit.
//X	This starts the script in the debugger.
//?	This displays available command parameters and provides help for using them. (This is the same as typing **Cscript.exe** with no parameters and no script.)

You can specify some of the same options when using the Windows-based scripting host. Right-click the script file, and then click Properties. You'll see the dialog box shown in Figure 9-3 on the next page. You can set the amount of time that the script is allowed to run and whether or not the host displays a log. The result is a file with the *.wsh* extension that contains these settings. It looks like your average INI file. You then execute the script by double-clicking the WSH file.

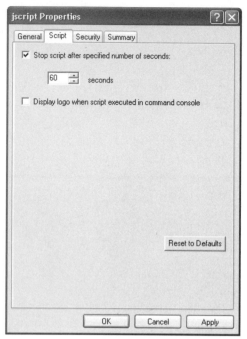

Figure 9-3   *You create a WSH file, which contains a script file's settings, by right-clicking the script, clicking Properties, and then clicking the Script tab.*

Formatting Key and Value Names

Before I show you how to edit the registry with a script, there's one more detail: how to format the names of keys and values in a script. Unlike other scripting methods I've described in this chapter, the Windows Script Host object model doesn't have separate parameters for the key and value name. Thus, you distinguish key names and value names by how you format them. The rule is simple: If a string ends with a backslash, it's a key name; if a string doesn't end with a backslash, it's a value name. Also, the JScript language reserves the backslash character (\) as the escape character: \n is a newline character and \t is a tab, for example. That means that you must escape the backslashes in your keys. Thus, any time you have a backslash in a key, you must use two backslashes (\\). To keep these clear, see Table 9-4.

Table 9-4   Key and Value Formatting

Object	VBScript	JScript
Value	`"HKLM\Subkey\Value"`	`"HKLM\\Subkey\\Value"`
Key	`"HKLM\Subkey\"`	`"HKLM\\Subkey\\"`

Adding and Updating Values

The Shell object's RegWrite method adds keys and values or changes existing values. If you want to change a key's default value, set *strName* to the name of the key, including the trailing backslash, and then assign a value to it.

Tip One of the RegWrite method's biggest weaknesses is that it writes only four bytes of REG_BINARY values. It can't handle larger binary values. If you want to change longer binary values or change types of values that this method doesn't support, use the Shell object's Run method to import a REG file. For example, you can put your settings in a REG file called Settings.reg. Then import that REG file using the statement WshShell.Run("Settings.reg").

---

object.RegWrite(*strName*, *anyValue* [,*strType*])

object	This is the Shell object.
strName	This is the string indicating the name of the key or value. You can add keys. You can add or change values. strName must be a fully-qualified path to a key or value and begin with one of the root keys: HKCR, HKCU, HKLM, or HKU.
anyValue	This is the data to assign to new or existing values. Use the format appropriate for the value's type.
strType	This is the type of value to create: REG_SZ, REG_EXPAND_SZ, REG_DWORD, or REG_BINARY. The RegWrite method doesn't support the REG_MULTI_SZ value type. Also, this method writes only four byte REG_BINARY values.

Example (VBScript)

```
Set WshShell = WScript.CreateObject( "WScript.Shell" )

WshShell.RegWrite "HKCU\Software\Sample\", 1, "REG_BINARY"
WshShell.RegWrite "HKCU\Software\Sample\Howdy", "World!", "REG_SZ"
```

Example (JScript)

```
var WshShell = WScript.CreateObject( "WScript.Shell" );

WshShell.RegWrite( "HKCU\\Software\\Sample\\", 1, "REG_BINARY" );
WshShell.RegWrite( "HKCU\\Software\\Sample\\Howdy", "World!", "REG_SZ");
```

Removing Keys and Values

The Shell object's RegDelete method removes keys and values from the registry. Be careful, however, because removing an entire branch is easy; there's no confirmation. To remove a key, end *strName* with a backslash; otherwise, you're removing a value.

```
object.RegDelete( strName )
```

object	This is the shell object.
strName	This is the string indicating the name of the key or value to delete. strName must be a fully qualified path to a key or value and begin with one of the root keys: HKCR, HKCU, HKLM, or HKU.

Example (VBScript)

```
Set WshShell = WScript.CreateObject( "WScript.Shell" )

WshShell.RegDelete "HKCU\Software\Honeycutt\Howdy"
WshShell.RegDelete "HKCU\Software\Honeycutt\"
```

Example (JScript)

```
var WshShell = WScript.CreateObject( "WScript.Shell" );

WshShell.RegDelete ( "HKCU\\Software\\Honeycutt\\Howdy" );
WshShell.RegDelete ( "HKCU\\Software\\Honeycutt\\" );
```

Querying Registry Values

The Shell object's RegRead method returns a value's data. To read a key's default value, end *strName* with a backslash; otherwise, you're reading a value.

```
object.RegRead( strName )
```

object	This is the shell object.
strName	This is the string indicating the name of the value to read. strName must be a fully qualified path to a key or value and begin with one of the root keys: HKCR, HKCU, HKLM, or HKU.

Example (VBScript)

```
Dim WshShell, dwFlag, strValue
Set WshShell = WScript.CreateObject( "WScript.Shell" )

dwFlag = WshShell.RegRead( "HKCU\Software\Honeycutt\" )
strValue = WshShell.RegRead( "HKCU\Software\Honeycutt\Howdy" )
```

Example (JScript)

```
var WshShell = WScript.CreateObject( "WScript.Shell" );

var dwFlag = WshShell.RegRead( "HKCU\\Software\\Honeycutt\\" );
var strValue = WshShell.RegRead( "HKCU\\Software\\Honeycutt\\Howdy" );
```

Creating Windows Installer Packages

The last method of deploying registry settings I discuss in this chapter is creating Windows Installer package files. You've undoubtedly encountered package files by now. Microsoft Office 2000 and Office XP both ship as package files, which are databases of files and settings that Windows Installer installs on the computer. Creating a package file for a large application is an intense process, but creating package files that contain registry settings is straightforward.

To create a package file, you need an editor. One of the most popular package editors is VERITAS WinINSTALL, and you can learn more about this enterprise-class tool at *www.veritas.com*. If you don't want to fork over the cash necessary to purchase a full version of WinINSTALL, you can get a free version if you still have your Microsoft Windows 2000 Professional CD lying around. Look in the Valueadd\3rdparty\Mgmt\Winstle folder. This is an older limited edition version of WinINSTALL. It's clunky and short on features when compared to recent versions of WinINSTALL, but it's suitable for creating package files to deploy registry settings. Install the program by double-clicking Swiadmle.msi. This installs WinINSTALL on the Start menu: Click Start, All Programs, VERITAS Software, VERITAS Software Console to run it.

Package files contain features, and features contain components. To deploy registry settings in a package file, you must create all of the above. Follow these steps to create a new package file and add registry settings to it:

1. In the left pane of Veritas Software Console, right-click Windows Installer Package Editor, and then click New. In the Filename box, type the path and name of the package file, and click OK.

2. In the left pane, right-click the package file you created, and then click Add Feature. In the Name box in the right pane, type a new name for the feature.

   This is likely to be the only feature that you add to the package file, because all you're doing is deploying registry settings. You can create multiple features, though, and each feature can contain different registry settings. That way, users can install or not install individual features.

3. In the left pane, right-click the feature you created in step 2, and then click Add Component.

   The package editor automatically gives the component a GUID. Components typically contain all the files and settings required to implement a program unit, so applications often have multiple components. When using a package file to deploy settings, creating multiple components doesn't make a lot of sense.

4. In the left pane, select the component you added, and click Registry.

5. In the right pane, right-click the root key that you want to edit, and click New Key. Continue creating subkeys by right-clicking a key and clicking New Key until you've created the full path of the key that you want to edit.

6. In the right pane, click the key in which you want to add or change a value, and then click New Value. In the Value Name box, type the name of the value. In the Data Type list, select the value's type; click OK. In the *Type* Editor dialog box, type the value's data, and then click OK.

7. Click File, Save to save your package file.

After you've created a package file, you can deploy it just like any other package file. For example, users can simply double-click the package file to install it. If the package file contains settings that users don't have permission to change, you can deploy it through Active Directory and Group Policy, which installs package files with elevated privileges. You can also execute the command that installs a package file, which is `msiexec.exe" /i filename.msi`.

Deploying User Profiles

Microsoft Windows XP stores user settings separate from computer settings. The computer's settings affect every user who logs on to Windows XP. Computer settings include hardware configuration, network configuration, and so on. Typically, only the administrators group can change computer settings, but some settings are within reach of the Power Users group. On the other hand, a user profile contains settings for a specific user. Users customize the operating system to their liking, and their settings don't affect other users. Users have full control of their own profiles, which contain more than just settings. They also contain files and folders specific to each user.

Deploying and managing user profiles are two of the most significant issues facing IT professionals. Properly deploying and managing user profiles can save companies money. That's because most of the behaviors that users experience in Windows XP have settings in user profiles, and IT professionals can deploy user profiles that contain defaults for these settings, starting users off on the right foot. For example, they can populate the Favorites folder with links to the intranet so users don't have to find those links for themselves. They can add printer connections to a default user profile so users can print right away without having to figure out how to add a printer. Importantly, most of the useful policies that manage operating system and application settings are in user profiles. IT professionals manage the settings in user profiles by applying policies to them.

Mastering user profiles isn't just for IT professionals; power users, particularly those who use multiple accounts on their computers or who work on a home network, can create user profiles to simplify their experience. They can customize a default user profile. Then whenever they reinstall Windows XP or create a new account, they start with familiar settings and don't have to spend an hour customizing the operating system to suit their tastes. User profiles aren't so complicated that power users shouldn't use them to their full advantage.

I've written this chapter primarily for the IT professional; power users need master only portions of it. First you learn about the contents of a user profile. Then you learn how to use roaming user profiles on a business network. The most compelling part of this chapter shows you how to build and deploy default user profiles. In that part, I show you two techniques for building default user profiles. The first is traditional but rather dirty. I prefer the second method, which is a more surgical (and tidy) method of building default user profiles. I wrap up this chapter with a discussion of the User State Migration Tool, which can help overcome the difficulties involved with migrating users' settings from earlier versions of Windows.

Exploring User Profiles

Windows XP loads users' profiles when they log on to the computer and unloads their profiles when they log off. A user profile contains a registry hive with per-user settings and folders, which contain documents and data files. The following section, "Profile Hives," describes the registry hive that the operating system loads. The section "Profile Folders" describes the folders in a user profile.

Before delving into the contents of user profiles, knowing their location on the file system is useful. The default location is different than it was in Microsoft Windows NT 4.0 or other operating systems of that era. Remember that Windows NT 4.0 stored user profiles in %SYSTEMROOT%\Profiles, but this location made it difficult to secure the operating system files while allowing access to users' data. Microsoft Windows 2000 and Windows XP store user profiles in a different location, which enables you to pull user data out from under an operating system folder: %SYSTEMDRIVE%\Documents and Settings, C:\Documents and Settings on most computers. This is the case only with a clean installation of Windows XP, however.

If you upgrade from a version of Windows earlier than Windows 2000, the profiles remain where they were in the previous operating system. For example, if you upgrade from Windows NT 4.0 to Windows XP, the profiles remain in %SYSTEMROOT%\Profiles. The location of user profiles after upgrading from Windows 2000 to Windows XP depends on whether you installed Windows 2000 cleanly or upgraded from an earlier version of Windows. In other words, the setup program never moves user profiles during an upgrade. Table 10-1 summarizes where you'll find profile folders, scenario by scenario.

Windows XP creates and stores a list of user profiles. Table 10-1 shows the locations of user profiles depending on the scenario. The key HKLM\SOFTWARE\Microsoft\Windows NT \CurrentVersion\ProfileList corresponds to the list you see in the User Profiles dialog box. To open the User Profiles dialog box, click Start, Control Panel, Performance And Maintenance, and System. In the System Properties dialog box, on the Advanced tab, click Settings in the User Profiles area. Each subkey is a user profile, and the subkey's name is the

SID of the account that owns the profile. Each profile in `ProfileList` contains the `REG_SZ` value `ProfileImagePath` that points to a user profile folder in %SYSTEMROOT% \Documents and Settings. Figure 10-1 illustrates the relationship between the `ProfileList` key and the user profile folders. This relationship is the reason you shouldn't just remove a user profile from the file system. Instead, use the User Profiles dialog box to remove user profiles, which cleans the user profile out of the `ProfileList` key as well as off the file system.

Table 10-1   Location of User Profiles

Scenario	Location
Clean installation	%SYSTEMDRIVE%\Documents and Settings
Upgrade from Windows 2000	%SYSTEMDRIVE%\Documents and Settings
Upgrade from Windows NT 4.0	%SYSTEMROOT%\Profiles
Upgrade from Windows 98	%SYSTEMDRIVE%\Documents and Settings

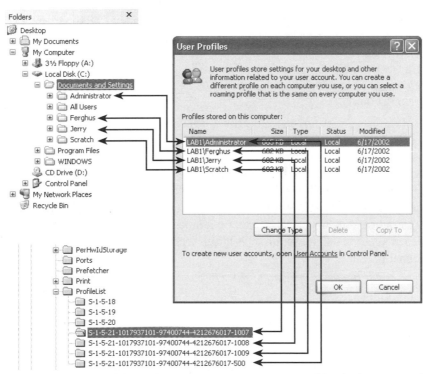

Figure 10-1   *The subkeys of* `ProfileList` *contain a wealth of information about the user profiles that Windows XP has created, including their paths on the file system.*

Note   In enterprises that use Windows NT 4.0, IT professionals sometimes move profiles to %SYSTEMROOT%\Profiles when deploying Windows XP because managing the profiles is often easier if they are in the same location regardless of the platform. Windows XP answer files offer a setting that enables you to do that. The setting is `ProfilesDir`, and it's in the `[GuiUnattended]` section. Set `ProfilesDir` to the path of the folder in which you want to store profiles. You should begin the path with either %SYSTEMROOT% or %SYSTEMDRIVE%; otherwise, the setup program ignores it.

Advantages of User Profiles

The primary goal of user profiles is to keep each user's settings and data distinct from that of other users as well as from the computer's settings. This has several advantages for enterprise environments and makes Windows XP more convenient to use at home, too. User profiles enable *stateless* computing. A company can configure Windows XP to store key user settings and data separately from the computer. This makes backing up and replacing computers much easier because users' data is tucked safely away on the network and maintained separately from the computer's configuration. The first time users log on to a replacement computer, the operating system copies their settings from the network. They get back to work more quickly.

User profiles also allow users' settings to follow them from computer to computer. They don't have to reconfigure settings at each computer. When they log on to a network that supports roaming user profiles, the operating system downloads their settings from the network. When they log off of the computer, the operating system copies users' settings back to the network. Roaming user profiles makes sharing computers more feasible because each user has his or her personalized configuration. Roaming user profiles are a must-have in environments such as call centers, where users aren't guaranteed to sit down at the same computer twice. You learn about roaming user profiles in the section "Using Roaming User Profiles," later in this chapter.

Profile Hives

The first half of a user profile is the profile hive: Ntuser.dat. You learn about the second half in "Profile Folders." This file is in the root of users' profile folders. Chapter 1, "Learning the Basics," and Chapter 2, "Using the Registry Editor," describe hive files and how to work with them. Users' operating system and application settings are stored in profile hives. For example, you find all the per-user settings for Windows Explorer and persistent network connections in profile hives. Profile hives also contain per-user taskbar, printer, and Control Panel settings. Accessories that come with Windows XP store per-user settings in the profile hive.

When Windows XP loads a user profile, the operating system loads the hive file Ntuser.dat into the subkey HKU\SID, where SID is the user's SID. (See Chapter 1, "Learning the Basics," for more information about SIDs.) Then Windows XP links the root key HKCU to HKU\SID. Figure 10-2 shows this relationship. Windows XP and most applications reference users' settings through HKCU, not HKU\SID, because HKCU resolves which subkey of HKU contains the console user's settings. HKU contains a second hive file, HKU\SID_Classes, which contains per-user file associations and class registrations. You learn about this in Appendix A, "File Associations."

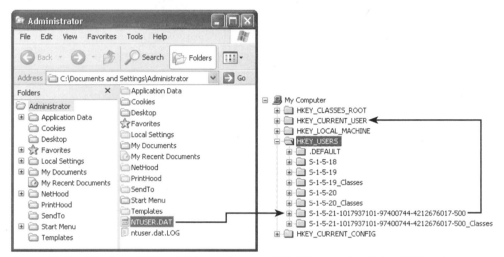

Figure 10-2   *Windows XP loads Ntuser.dat into HKU\SID and then links HKCU to it.*

The list of profile hives is in the key ProfileList, which you learned about in the previous section. It contains one subkey for each user profile. The subkey's name is the name of the hive in HKU or the account's SID. The REG_SZ value ProfileImagePath is the path of the profile hive file Ntuser.dat for that user profile. ProfileList does not contain a value for the SID_Classes hives, however. HKLM\SYSTEM\CurrentControlSet\Control\hivelist contains one REG_SZ value for each hive in HKLM and HKU that the operating system is currently using. The difference between the values ProfileList and hivelist is that ProfileList contains a list of all user profiles that Windows XP knows about, loaded or not, and hivelist contains a list of all currently loaded hive files.

Tip   You can load and edit profile hives in Registry Editor (Regedit) without logging on to the computer using the account that owns that user profile. This is one of the techniques you use later in this chapter to build default user profiles.

Profile Folders

The folders in a user profile contain per-user application files. For example, Office XP installs templates and custom dictionaries in the user profile. Internet Explorer stores its cookies and shortcuts in the user profile. The most interesting folder in a user profile is the Application Data folder. Figure 10-3 shows a user profile in Windows Explorer. Some of the folders are hidden; show the hidden files in Windows Explorer if you want to see all the following folders for yourself:

- **Application Data.**   This folder contains application files, such as mail files, shortcuts, templates, and so on. Each application's vendor chooses what files to store here. You can redirect this folder to a network location using Group Policy.

- **Cookies.**   This folder contains Internet Explorer cookies.

- **Desktop.**   This folder contains files, folders, and shortcuts on the desktop. Users see the contents of this folder on the Windows XP desktop. You can redirect this folder to a network location using Group Policy.

- **Favorites.**   This folder contains Internet Explorer favorite shortcuts. Users see the contents of this folder on Internet Explorer's Favorites menu. Group Policy doesn't support redirecting this folder, but you can redirect it manually as shown in Chapter 15, "Working Around IT Problems."

- **Local Settings.**   This folder contains application files that do not roam with the profile. The files you find in this folder are either per-computer or too large to copy to the network. This folder contains four interesting subfolders:

  - **Application Data.**   This subfolder contains computer-specific application data.

  - **History.**   This subfolder contains Internet Explorer history.

  - **Temp.**   This subfolder contains per-user temporary files.

  - **Temporary Internet Files.**   This subfolder contains Internet Explorer offline files.

- **My Documents.**   This folder contains the default location for users' documents. Applications should save users' documents to this folder by default, and this is the location to which the common dialog boxes open by default. This folder also contains the My Pictures folder, which is the default location for users' pictures, and optionally the My Music folder, which is the default location for users' music files. You can redirect this folder to a network location using Group Policy.

- **NetHood.**   This folder contains shortcuts to objects on the network. Users can browse the folders to which these shortcuts are linked in the My Network Places folder.

- **PrintHood.**   This folder contains shortcuts to printer objects. Users see the contents of this folder in the Printers folder.

- **Recent.**   This folder contains shortcuts to the most recently used documents. Users see these shortcuts on the My Recent Documents menu, which is on the Start menu.

- **SendTo.**   This folder contains shortcuts to drives, folders, and applications that are copy targets. Users see the contents of this folder when they right-click an object and then click Send To.

- **Start Menu.**   This folder contains shortcuts to program items. Users see the contents of this folder on the Start menu and on the Start menu's All Programs menu. IT professionals can redirect this folder to a network location using Group Policy.

- **Templates.**   This folder contains template files. Users see the contents of this folder when they right-click in a folder and then click New.

Figure 10-3   *The user profile folders you see in this figure are the default folders in a clean installation of Windows XP.*

`HKCU\Software\Microsoft\Windows\CurrentVersion\Explorer\User Shell Folders` is the key where Windows XP stores the location of each folder that's part of a user profile. Each value in this key represents a folder as shown in Table 10-2. These are REG_EXPAND_SZ values, so you can use environment variables in them. Use %USERPROFILE% to direct the folder somewhere inside users' profile folders and %USERNAME% to include users' names, particularly when you want to redirect a profile folder to a network location. Redirect users' Favorites folders to the network by setting Favorites to *Server**Share*\%USERNAME% \Favorites, where *Server**Share* is the server and share containing the folders, for example. Windows XP does not use the similar key Shell Folder.

Table 10-2   User Profile Folders

Name	Default path
AppData	%USERPROFILE%\Application Data
Cache	%USERPROFILE%\Local Settings\Temporary Internet Files
Cookies	%USERPROFILE%\Cookies
Desktop	%USERPROFILE%\Desktop
Favorites	%USERPROFILE%\Favorites
History	%USERPROFILE%\Local Settings\History
Local AppData	%USERPROFILE%\Local Settings\Application Data
Local Settings	%USERPROFILE%\Local Settings

Table 10-2   User Profile Folders *(continued)*

Name	Default path
My Pictures	%USERPROFILE%\My Documents\My Pictures
NetHood	%USERPROFILE%\NetHood
Personal	%USERPROFILE%\My Documents
PrintHood	%USERPROFILE%\PrintHood
Programs	%USERPROFILE%\Start Menu\Programs
Recent	%USERPROFILE%\Recent
SendTo	%USERPROFILE%\SendTo
Start Menu	%USERPROFILE%\Start Menu
Startup	%USERPROFILE%\Start Menu\Programs\Startup
Templates	%USERPROFILE%\Templates

Special Profiles

The profile folders you saw in Figure 10-1 contain more than the standard user profiles that Windows XP creates when users log on to the operating system. The figure shows four special user profiles about which any IT professional should learn:

- **All Users.**   This profile folder contains settings that apply to all users who log on to the computer. This profile folder contains a profile hive, Ntuser.dat, which the operating system doesn't load. Also, this profile folder contains the shared documents and music folders; shared Start menu shortcuts, and so on. The key User Shell Folders in HKLM\SOFTWARE\Microsoft\Windows\CurrentVersion\Explorer contains the linkages to the subfolders in the All Users profile folder.

- **Default User.**   This profile folder contains the default user profile that Windows XP copies when it creates new user profiles. It contains most of the files and folders that you learned about in the previous section. Customizing this folder is a good way to start each user who logs on to the computer with the same settings. Windows XP first checks for a Default User folder on the NETLOGON share of the server and uses the local Default User folder only if the network copy isn't available. Customizing this folder is a good way to deploy settings that you don't want to manage. You learn how to customize it in the section "Deploying Default User Profiles," later in this chapter.

- **LocalService.**   This profile folder is for the built-in LocalService account, which Service Control Manager uses to host services that don't need to run in the LocalSystem account. This is a normal user profile with limited data. You don't see it in the User Profiles dialog box, and the LocalService folder is super-hidden.

- **NetworkService.**   This profile folder is for the built-in NetworkService account, which the Service Control Manager uses to host network services that don't need to run in the LocalSystem account. This is a normal user profile. You don't see it in the User Profiles dialog box, and the NetworkService folder is super-hidden.

In the previous list, the first two profile folders are far more interesting than the last two. IT professionals often customize the All Users profile folder on disk images. The customization, such as a shortcut on the Start menu, affects all users who log on to the computer. IT professionals more frequently customize the \Default User folder, though. Doing so is a great way to create custom settings that you don't want to manage. In other words, it's one method for deploying common user preferences while still allowing users to change those preferences if necessary. As you'll learn throughout this chapter, customizing the Default User folder on a disk image isn't necessarily the most efficient means to deploy default user settings. Instead, create a customized Default User folder on the server's NETLOGON share. See the section "Deploying Default User Profiles," later in this chapter.

Tip   Many programs install themselves for use by a single user when you really want all users who share the computer to use them. You can tell when a program is installed per-user because its shortcut is in the profile folder belonging to the account you used to install it. If the program re-creates missing settings as it starts, you can change the program from per-user to per-computer by simply moving its shortcut from the user profile folder in which it installed the shortcut to the All Users profile folder. This works the other way, too. You can move a shortcut from the All Users profile folder to a specific user's profile folder so that only a single user sees the shortcut.

Improvements to User Profiles

In Windows 2000, poorly written applications and services that keep registry keys open during logoff prevent Windows 2000 from unloading the user's registry hive. When this occurs, changes that a user made to his or her profile are not saved to the server. This has three symptoms:

- The user experience is affected because changes are not saved when users log on to another computer.

- Because *locked* profiles never get unloaded, they end up using a lot of memory on a terminal server that has many users logging on to it.

- If a profile is marked for deletion at logoff (to clean up the machine or for temporary profiles), profiles do not get deleted.

The three symptoms are solved as follows:

- In Windows XP, when a user logs off and the profile is locked, the operating system polls the profile for 60 seconds before giving up. Windows XP then saves the user's profile hive and roams the profile correctly.

- When the application or service closes the registry key and unlocks the profile, Windows XP unloads the users profile hive, freeing memory used by the profile.

- If a profile is marked for deletion, when the reference count drops to zero, Windows XP unloads and deletes it. In the event that the application never releases the registry key, Windows XP deletes all profiles marked for deletion at the next machine boot.

Getting User Profiles

How users get their profiles depends on the type of profile you've configured their accounts to use:

- **Local user profile.**   This profile is created the first time users log on to their computers. Local user profiles are stored on the local hard disk. Changes that users make to their profiles don't follow them from computer to computer.

- **Roaming user profile.**   This profile is available to users from any computer on the network, and changes that users make to their profiles follow them from computer to computer.

- **Mandatory user profile.**   This profile is similar to roaming user profiles. Administrators assign mandatory user profiles to users, and Windows XP throws away users' changes when they log off of the operating system. In other words, users start with the same settings every time they log on to the operating system. Microsoft provides mandatory user profiles to provide compatibility with Windows NT 4.0, but you should consider using Group Policy instead.

The following sections describe how Windows XP creates a profile when users log on to the operating system. The section "Using Roaming User Profiles" describes how to create and manage roaming user profiles. Also, the section "Managing Roaming User Profiles" shows you how to prevent Windows XP from merging the local copy of a profile with the server copy using Group Policy.

Local Profiles

Here's an overview of how Windows XP creates and uses a local user profile for users the first time they log on to their computers:

1. The user logs on to Windows XP.

2. Windows XP checks the list of user profiles in the key `ProfileList` to determine if a local profile exists for the user. If an entry exists, the operating system uses it; otherwise, the operating system does one of the following:

   - If the computer is a domain member, Windows XP checks the NETLOGON share on the domain controller for a default user profile in a subfolder called Default User. If it exists, the operating system copies NETLOGON\Default User to %SYSTEMDRIVE%\Documents and Settings*Username*, where *Username* is the name of the user's account.

   - If the computer is not a domain member or if Windows XP doesn't find a default user profile on the NETLOGON share, it uses the local default user profile. It copies %SYSTEMDRIVE\Documents and Settings\Default User to %SYSTEMDRIVE%\Documents and Settings*Username*.

3. Windows XP loads the profile hive Ntuser.dat into HKU and links the root key HKCU to it.

When the user logs off of Windows XP, the operating system saves any changes to the profile in the user profile folder. It doesn't copy the profile folder to the network. It also unloads the profile hive from the registry.

Roaming Profiles

Here's an overview of how Windows XP creates and uses a roaming user profile for users the first time they log on to their computers:

1. The user logs on to Windows XP.

2. Windows XP checks the list of user profiles in the key ProfileList to determine if a local profile exists for the user. If an entry exists, the operating system merges the network copy of the profile into the local profile folder; otherwise, the operating system does one of the following:

   - Windows XP checks the NETLOGON share on the domain controller for the Default User folder. If it exists, the operating system copies the Default User folder to %SYSTEMDRIVE%\Documents and Settings*Username*, where *Username* is the name of the user's account.

   - If Windows XP doesn't find a default user profile on the NETLOGON share, it copies %SYSTEMDRIVE\Documents and Settings\Default User to %SYSTEMDRIVE%\Documents and Settings*Username*.

3. Windows XP loads the profile hive Ntuser.dat into HKU and links the root key HKCU to it.

When users log off of Windows XP, the operating system saves their changes to the local profile folders and then unloads the profile hives from HKU. Afterward, the operating system copies their profile folders to the network location specified by the administrator. If the profile folder already exists on the network, the operating system merges the local copy into the network copy. For more information, see "Understanding the New Merge," later in this chapter.

Note   There are two differences between roaming and mandatory user profiles. First you create the mandatory profile and copy it to the user's profile folder instead of allowing Windows XP to create it when the user logs on to the computer. Second you rename the Ntuser.dat to Ntuser.man. Windows XP uses the *.man* file extension to make the profile mandatory. Windows XP doesn't merge mandatory user profiles to the network when the user logs off of the computer.

Using Roaming User Profiles

You configure roaming user profiles on the server, so the user must be a member of and log on to the domain to use a roaming user profile. Both Microsoft Windows NT Server 4.0 and Microsoft Windows 2000 Server support roaming user profiles, as does Microsoft Windows .NET Server. The following instructions show you how to configure roaming user profiles in Active Directory on Windows 2000 Server:

1. Create a folder on the server where you want to store user profiles. This is the top-level folder that will contain individual user profile folders.

2. Share the folder, giving all users full control. (I sometimes reduce users' permissions to read and execute in this folder, and then give them full control of their individual profile folders.

3. In Active Directory Users and Computer, double-click the account that you want to configure to use a roaming user profile.

4. On the Profile tab of the *Name* Properties dialog box, shown in Figure 10-4, type the path where you want to store the user's profile in the Profile Path box. The path is *Server\Share\Username*, where *Server* is the name of the server, *Share* is the share you created in step 1, and *Username* is the name of the account. Optionally, use %USERNAME% for *Username*, and Active Directory substitutes the current account's name for it.

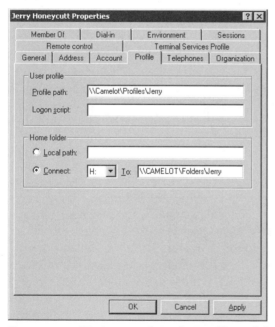

Figure 10-4   *Typing a path in the Profile Path box is all it takes to enable roaming user profiles.*

If you want to configure a lot of accounts to use roaming user profiles, doing the job by hand is a monumental task. Instead, use a third-party tool or write an Active Directory Scripting Interface (ADSI) script to do the job. You access ADSI through Windows Script Host using VBScript or JScript. This subject is beyond the scope of this book, but you can find more information about it on Microsoft's Web site: *http://www.microsoft.com.*

Folder Redirection is a great complement to user profiles, particularly the roaming variety. It enables an IT professional to redirect the location of some profile folders to the network. There's nothing magical about Folder Redirection. Group Policy simply changes the folder's location in the User Shell Folders key so that applications automatically look for the folder on the network. From users' perspectives, redirected folders are similar to roaming user profiles because their documents follow them from computer to computer. Unlike roaming user profiles, however, redirected folders always remain in the same place. You can use redirected folders with or without roaming user profiles. If you use them with roaming user profiles, you can reduce the amount of data that Windows XP transfers when users log on to and off of the operating system. Furthermore, redirected folders are often useful even when you don't intend to use roaming user profiles; you can allow users' documents to follow them without the complexity and sometimes difficulty of using roaming user profiles. You learn about roaming user profiles in the earlier section "Getting User Profiles."

Table 10-3   Roaming and Redirecting Folders

Folder	Can roam?	Can redirect?
Application Data	Yes	Yes
Cookies	Yes	No
Desktop	Yes	Yes
Favorites	Yes	No
Local Settings	No	No
My Documents	Yes	Yes
My Recent Documents	Yes	No
NetHood	Yes	No
PrintHood	Yes	No
SendTo	Yes	No
Start Menu	Yes	Yes
Templates	Yes	No

Best Practices for Roaming User Profiles

The following are best practices for roaming user profiles:

- Redirect the My Documents folder outside of roaming user profiles. Doing so decreases logon time. Folder Redirection is the best way to do this, but you can redirect the My Documents folder manually, as Chapter 15, "Working Around IT Problems," describes.

- Don't use Encrypted File System (EFS) on files in a roaming user profile. EFS is not compatible with roaming user profiles. Encrypting a roaming user profile prevents the user profile from roaming.

- Don't make disk quotas for roaming user profiles too restrictive. If they're too low, roaming user profile synchronization might fail. The server debits the user's quota for temporary files that Windows XP creates during the synchronization process, so ensure that enough disk space is available on the server. Also, make sure enough disk space is available on the workstation to create temporary duplicate copies of the profile.

- Don't make folders in roaming user profiles available offline. If you use Offline Folders with roaming user profile folders, synchronization problems occur because both Offline Folders and roaming user profiles try to synchronize at the same time. However, you can use Offline Folders with folders you redirect, such as My Documents.

- Use Group Policy loopback policy processing in moderation if you're also using roaming user profiles. Loopback processing enables you to apply different per-user Group Policy settings to users based on the computer they're using.

- When redirecting the My Documents folder outside of a roaming user profile, set the home folder to the redirected My Documents folder for compatibility with applications that aren't compatible with folder redirection.

- Disable fast network logon using Group Policy if you're using roaming user profiles. This prevents conflicts that occur when user profiles change from local to roaming. For more information, see "Understanding Fast Network Logon," later in this chapter.

Managing Roaming User Profiles

Group Policy provides a number of policies that you can use to manage how Windows XP handles user profiles. You can configure these policies in a local Group Policy Object (GPO) or in a network GPO. Chapter 6, "Using Registry-Based Policy," gives more information. For now, here's a description of policies for user profiles:

- **Connect home directory to root of the share.** This policy restores the definitions of the %HOMESHARE% and %HOMEPATH% environment variables to those used in Windows NT 4.0 and earlier.

- **Limit profile size.** This policy sets the maximum size of each roaming user profile and determines the system's response when a roaming user profile reaches the maximum size. If user profiles become excessively large, consider redirecting the My Documents folder to a location outside of the profile.

- **Exclude directories in a roaming profile.** This policy enables you to add to the list of folders excluded from the user's roaming profile.

- **Delete cached copies of roaming profiles.** This policy determines whether the system saves a copy of a user's roaming profile on the local computer's hard disk when the user logs off.

- **Do not detect slow network connections.** This policy disables the slow link detection feature.

- **Slow network connection timeout for user profiles.** This policy defines a slow connection for roaming user profiles.

- **Wait for remote user profile.** This policy directs the system to wait for the remote copy of the roaming user profile to load, even when loading is slow. Also, the system waits for the remote copy when the user is notified about a slow connection but does not respond in the time allowed.

- **Prompt user when slow link is detected.** This policy notifies users when their roaming profile is slow to load. Users can then decide whether to use a local copy or to wait for the roaming user profile.

- **Timeout for dialog boxes.** This policy determines how long the system waits for a user response before it uses a default value.

- **Log users off when roaming profile fails.** This policy logs a user off automatically when the system cannot load the user's roaming user profile.

- **Maximum retries to unload and update user profile.** This policy determines how many times the system will try to unload and update the profile hive. When the number of trials specified by this setting is exhausted, the system stops trying. As a result, the user profile might not be current, and local and roaming user profiles might not match.

- **Add the Administrators security group to roaming user profiles.** This policy adds the Administrator security group to the roaming user profile share. The default behavior prevents administrators from managing individual profile folders without taking ownership of them.

- **Prevent Roaming Profile changes from propagating to the server.** This policy determines if the changes a user makes to his or her roaming profile are merged with the server copy of their profile. This is a policy-based method for implementing mandatory user profiles.

- **Only allow local user profiles.** This policy determines if roaming user profiles are available on a particular computer. By default, when roaming-profile users log on to a computer, their roaming profile is copied to the local computer. If they have already logged on to this computer in the past, the roaming profile is merged with the local profile. Similarly, when the users logs off this computer, the local copy of their profile, including any changes they have made, is merged with the server copy of their profile.

The first three policies in this list are per-user and the remaining are per-computer policies; Figure 10-5 shows them in Group Policy editor. All of them are administrative policies in System\User Profiles under User Configuration and Computer Configuration.

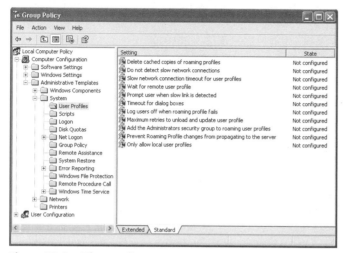

Figure 10-5   *These policies give you management control of how Windows XP uses profiles.*

Understanding Fast Network Logon

Windows XP doesn't wait for the network to start before displaying the Logon To Windows dialog box. This substantially improves start time over Windows 2000. Users who've previously logged on to the computer get to their desktops faster because the operating system uses cached credentials and loads Group Policy in the background after the network becomes available. Although fast network logon improves perceived performance, it has effects you should understand. The most important thing to take away from this section is that Windows XP doesn't use fast network logon if you use roaming user profiles.

Because background refresh is the default behavior, users might have to log on to Windows XP up to three times for Group Policy extensions like Software Installation and Folder Redirection to take effect. Windows XP must process these types of extensions in the background without any users logged on to it. Also, because advanced Folder Redirection is based on group membership, users must log on to Windows XP three times: once to update the cached user object and group membership, a second time to detect the change in group membership and require a foreground policy application, and a third time to apply folder redirection policy in the foreground. The operating system might require users to log on two times to update the properties of other Group Policy objects.

Another thing to keep in mind is the effect that fast network logon has on Windows XP when users' profiles change from local to roaming. When the operating system uses fast network logon, it always uses the locally cached copy of the profile. By the time the operating system detects that the user has a roaming user profile, it's already loaded the local profile hive and changed its timestamp. The result is that if users log on to multiple computers, the operating system can replace newer profile hives with older ones. To handle this scenario, Windows XP treats the change from local to roaming as a special case. First the operating system checks the following conditions:

- Is the user changing from a local to a roaming profile?
- Is a copy of the user profile on the server?

If both these conditions are true, Windows XP merges the contents of the local user profile with the server copy, without the profile hive Ntuser.dat. Then the operating system copies the server copy of the profile to the local copy, regardless of the profile hives' time stamps. After the user's profile becomes a roaming profile, Windows XP always waits for the network so it can download the user profile. In other words, fast network logon and roaming user profiles don't work together.

Note   Considering the changes that Windows XP makes to roaming user profiles, if you remove the roaming profile path from a user in Active Directory, you should remove the profile folder from the server. If you reconfigure the user to use roaming user profiles and you use the same path, the user will receive the older, server copy of the user profile.

Understanding the New Merge

Many IT professionals are shy about using roaming user profiles because they have experience with the merge algorithm that Windows NT 4.0 uses. That algorithm assumes that there is a single, master copy of the user profile. When the user logs on to the computer, the operating system assumes that the master profile is on the local computer, and when the user logs off of the computer, it assumes that the master profile is on the server. It mirrors the entire profile from the local computer to the server and visa versa, completely replacing the profile at the target location. This works perfectly well when people use a single computer, but it creates havoc when they use multiple computers.

The merge algorithm in Windows XP is more advanced; it merges user profiles at the file level. In other words, it's a real merge, not a wipe-and-load. The merged profile then becomes a superset of the files in the local and server copies of the user profile, and when a file exists in both copies, the operating system uses the most recent version of the file. New files don't turn up missing, and updated files are not replaced—both of which are symptoms that occur with the merge algorithm in Windows NT 4.0. In the case of the Windows NT 4.0 merge, if a profile changes on two computers, only the last one copied to the network persists.

Behind the new and improved merge algorithm is the timestamp that Windows XP saves in the ProfileList key. When a user logs on to the computer, the operating system saves the current time in ProfileList. When the user logs off of the computer, the operating system uses the timestamp to determine which files have been added or removed from the server's copy of the user profile. For example, if a file called Example.doc is in the server copy of the user profile but not in the local copy, the timestamp helps Windows XP determine whether the file was added to the server copy or removed from the local copy. If the timestamp of the file is later than the timestamp of the local user profile, the file was added to the server copy. The result is that Windows XP doesn't touch the file when it merges the local profile into the server copy. If the timestamp of the file is earlier than the timestamp of the local user profile, the file was removed from the local user profile. The result is that Windows XP removes the file from the server copy of the profile when the operating system merges the local copy into it. With Windows XP, if a profile changes on two computers, both of them are merged file by file into the server copy.

> **Note** There is another issue that keeps many IT professionals from using roaming user profiles. Roaming user profiles are terrific when configurations are similar from desktop to desktop. When users log on to different computers with different sets of applications, screen sizes, power management requirements, and so on, roaming user profiles are cumbersome and users' experiences aren't very good. Roaming user profiles are great in scenarios such as call centers and other environments in which configurations are standardized, but they are not very useful when configurations are not standardized in the organization.

Deploying Default User Profiles

Deploying default user profiles is one of the easiest ways to deploy settings to new users. You can't use default user profiles to deploy settings to existing users, though, because they already have user profiles. These aren't settings that you want to manage. They're defaults that you want to establish for users while allowing users to change them when necessary. Essentially, deploying default user profiles is like modifying the default settings in Windows XP. If you want to define a setting that users *can't* change, use policies. Chapter 6, "Using Registry-Based Policies," contains more information about managing settings.

To deploy a default user profile, follow these steps:

1. Create a template account.

   You can use a local or a domain account, but the user profile is generally cleaner if you use a local account on a computer that's not joined to a domain. (Because I include network shortcuts in my profiles, I usually use a domain account to create default user profiles.) Also, use a name for the template account that you're sure is unique in the registry and is shorter than eight characters. You'll learn why using a unique name is important a bit later.

2. Log on to the computer using the template account, and customize its settings. The section "Customizing User Settings," later in this chapter, describes settings that I frequent.

3. Clean up the user profile to remove artifacts that you don't want to deploy. The section "Cleaning the User Profile," later in this chapter, describes how to clean the profile.

4. Copy the template account's user profile folder to a new location and name it Default User.

   Don't replace %SYSTEMDRIVE%\Documents and Settings\Default User, however, because you might need to repeat the process a few times to get it right and you'll want the original default user profile handy. In the section "Creating the Default User Folder," later in this chapter, I describe an alternative method for building the Default User folder, which I think is more precise and yields a cleaner default user profile.

5. Deploy the default user profile.

   You can put the Default User folder in %SYSTEMDRIVE%\Documents and Settings on disk images and then deploy them, or you can put the Default User folder on the NETLOGON share of the server. I prefer the second method because it separates settings from the disk images, which allows me to update settings much more easily.

Alternatives to Default User Profiles

An alternative to customizing a bunch of settings in default user profiles is scripting. Create a script that configures Windows XP user settings per your company's requirements. This assumes that you have a specification, or at the very least, a list of settings that you want to customize for users. Then edit the Ntuser.dat hive file in the disk image's Default User folder, adding the command that executes the script to the key HKCU\Software\Microsoft \Windows\CurrentVersion\RunOnce. The Ntuser.dat hive file in the Default User folder doesn't contain the RunOnce key by default, so you must add it. Then add a REG_SZ value to this key—the name is arbitrary—and put the command line you want to execute in it. Each time Windows XP creates a new user profile, it executes the script to customize the user's settings.

Also, you can add a script that customizes the current user profile to HKLM\Software \Microsoft\Windows\CurrentVersion\Run. Windows XP runs this script every time a user logs on to the computer. If you want only to configure settings the first time the user logs on to the computer, add code to the script that checks for a value in HKCU and runs only if that value doesn't exist. Then end the script with code that creates the missing value so that the script doesn't run the next time the user logs on to the computer. Chapter 9, "Scripting Registry Changes," shows you how to write scripts using Windows Scripting Host, and these are ideal for this scenario.

Customizing User Settings

Log on to the template account you created in step 1 of the previous section and customize the account's settings. When customizing settings for a default use profile, less is more. Preferably, you'll work from a list of settings that you've vetted with other members of the deployment planning team. The following list will give you an idea of the settings I frequently target with default user profiles:

- Taskbar
- Quick Launch toolbar
- Start menu
- Windows Explorer
- Internet Explorer
- My Network Places
- Search Assistants
- Tweak UI
- Control Panel, in particular:
  - Display
  - Folder Options
  - Mouse
  - Power Options
  - Printers and Faxes
  - Sounds and Audio Devices
  - Taskbar and Start Menu

You want to customize per-user settings because those are the only settings that are in the user profile. How do you know that a setting is per-user when you're customizing a user profile? You don't necessarily. That's why you must test the settings in your list ahead of time. Sitting down to construct a default user profile isn't the time to begin wondering whether a particular setting is per-user or per-computer. The easiest way to figure this out is to log on to a new account and customize the settings in your list. Then copy that user profile to a clean installation of Windows XP and see which settings made it. The settings that didn't make it are per-computer settings, and you'll want to scratch them off of your list. There are a small number of settings that are per-user but still don't work well in default user profiles, and there's generally little you can do about it except hack the profile to make them work. The most prominent example is desktop wallpaper. Including wallpaper in a default user profile requires you to include the wallpaper graphic file inside the profile folder and then hack the profile hive to point to the new location.

You might also want to include settings for applications you're deploying, whether you include them on your disk images or deploy them using other methods. First a caveat: Don't include settings for Windows Installer–based applications in a default user profile. Windows Installer provides superior methods for deploying settings. That means you shouldn't deploy settings for Office XP using default user profiles. Instead, use tools such as Custom Installation Wizard and Office Profile Wizard. Both tools come with the Office XP Resource Kit, and Chapter 14, "Deploying Office XP Settings," describes how to use them. Install other types of applications and customize their settings to your requirements just as you would customize Windows XP settings.

This last part is optional but I recommend it: Remove artifacts from the user profile that you don't want to deploy. Artifacts include history lists and the like. I have a preset route that I use to clean up a user profile. First I clear the Start menu and Internet Explorer's history lists. To do this:

- Click Start, Control Panel, Appearance And Themes, and Taskbar And Start Menu. On the Start Menu tab, click Customize. On the Customize Start Menu dialog box's Advanced tab, click the Clear List button.

- Click Start, Control Panel, Network And Internet Connections, and Internet Options. In the Internet Options dialog box, click Clear History to remove Internet Explorer's history lists.

You don't need to worry about removing temporary Internet files because these are in the profile's Local Settings folder and Windows XP doesn't copy them with the profile. If you opened Internet Explorer to customize it, however, you might clear out the cookies and AutoComplete lists. In the Internet Options dialog box, on the General tab, click Delete Cookies, and then on the Content tab, click AutoComplete followed by Clear Forms and Clear Passwords.

After you're finished customizing and cleaning the account's settings, log off of Windows XP. My last word of advice is to tread lightly; don't open dialog boxes and programs you don't intend to customize. Doing so keeps their settings out of the default user profile. For example, if you don't intend to customize Windows Media Player, don't open the program.

Cleaning User Profiles

You cleaned the user profile a wee bit in the previous section, but only to remove some artifacts from the profile hive. The next major step is to open the profile hive in Regedit and scour it for settings that you don't want to deploy or that you must change before deploying.

The most significant example is paths. User profiles contain references to the profile folder: %SYSTEMDRIVE%\Documents and Settings*Name*. If you deploy the user profile to countless users, they'll all have different profile folders. When they try accessing the profile folder *Name*, Windows XP and programs will fail because the user doesn't have access to that folder. A more concrete example will make this clear. Assume you created a user profile using a template account called DefUser and deployed that profile to a user named Jerry. The user Jerry has access to %SYSTEMDRIVE%\Documents and Settings\Jerry, but the folder %SYSTEMDRIVE%\Documents and Settings\DefUser doesn't even exist. When the user Jerry runs a program that uses a setting containing the path to the DefUser user profile folder, the program causes an error. To correct this situation, follow these steps:

1. Log on to the computer containing the template user profile as Administrator.

2. In Regedit, load the Ntuser.dat hive file from the template user profile folder. (See Chapter 2, "Using the Registry Editor" to learn about using hive files.)

3. Search the hive file for references to the template user profile folder. If the name of the folder is longer than eight characters, search for the long and short versions of the folder's name.

4. Remove values that contain the path of the template user profile folder.

5. Unload the hive file and restart the computer.

   Restarting the computer is often necessary because Windows XP locks the file and you can't copy it. Restarting the computer is the quickest way to force it to let go of the file.

When you remove values that contain the path of the template user profile folder in step 4, you're assuming that Windows XP and other programs re-create missing settings. This isn't always true. Some of my favorite applications fail to re-create missing settings. You'll learn which do and which don't through trial and error. You can handle the problem easily, though. Rather than removing the value permanently, replace a REG_SZ value with a REG_EXPAND_SZ value of the same name. Then set the value to the original path, substituting %USERPROFILE% for the portion that is the user profile folder. For example, if you see a REG_SZ value called Templates that contains C:\Documents and Settings\Jerry\Templates, remove the value; then add the value Templates back as a REG_EXPAND_SZ value and set it to %USERPROFILE%\Templates. Test these changes in your lab to make sure they work properly.

In the previous section, you cleared some of the history lists using the Windows XP user interface. Take this opportunity to further cover your tracks by removing the keys listed in Table 10-4. These correspond to most of the history lists that Windows XP keeps, including the Search Assistant and common dialog boxes.

Table 10-4 History Lists to Remove

History list	Key
Internet Explorer's address bar	`HKCU\Software\Microsoft\Internet Explorer\TypedURLs`
Run dialog box	`HKCU\Software\Microsoft\Windows\CurrentVersion\Explorer\RunMRU`
Documents menu	`HKCU\Software\Microsoft\Windows\CurrentVersion\Explorer\RecentDocs`
Common dialog boxes	`HKCU\Software\Microsoft\Windows\CurrentVersion\Explorer\ComDlg32` `\LastVisitedMRU`
Search Assistant	`HKCU\Software\Microsoft\Search Assistant\ACMru`

Creating Default User Folders

The template user profile is ready to go. All you have to do now is copy it. To open the User Profiles dialog box, click Start, Control Panel, Performance And Maintenance, and then System. On the Advanced tab, click Settings in the User Profiles area. In the User Profiles dialog box, click the template user profile and then click Copy To. In the Copy Profile To box, shown in Figure 10-6, type the path to which you want to copy the profile. To keep things simple, I usually copy the profile folder to C:\Default User. Just make sure that the folder doesn't already exist. Also, give the Everyone group permission to use the profile, which is appropriate for a default user profile: Click Change, type **Everyone**, and then click OK. The default user profile is ready to deploy, and you learn how to do that in the next section.

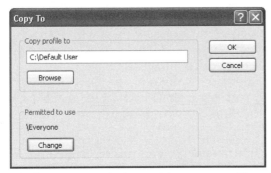

Figure 10-6 *Copy the template user profile using this dialog box; don't copy the folder using Windows Explorer because doing so copies artifacts that you don't want in the profile.*

The method I just described is common for creating a default user profile from a template user profile. I don't like it because user profiles expand greatly in size and complexity after Windows XP loads and uses them. A default user profile created using the method I just described contains more files and folders than necessary. To use the more surgical method that I prefer, follow these steps:

1. Copy %SYSTEMDRIVE%\Documents and Settings\Default User to another location, such as C:\Default User. You want to keep the original Default User folder around, just in case you have to start over again.

2. Copy the Ntuser.dat hive file from the template user profile to your copy of the Default User folder, C:\Default User.

3. Copy other files from the template user profile folder to your copy of the Default User folder, C:\Default User. I tend to copy files from the following folders, assuming they contain files I want to deploy:

   - \Application Data\Microsoft\Internet Explorer\Quick Launch
   - \Desktop
   - \Favorites
   - \NetHood
   - \PrintHood
   - \SendTo
   - \Templates

Deploying Default User Folders

After completing the steps in the last section, you have a default user profile that's ready to deploy. You have two choices. If you're deploying Windows XP using disk-imaging techniques, you can include the default user profile on the disk image. Replace %SYSTEMDRIVE%\Documents and Settings\Default User with your own Default User folder. After replacing the Default User folder with your own, clone and deploy the disk image. When new users log on to the computer, they'll receive your default user profile and thus your settings.

I don't like customizing the local Default User folder as my sole means of deploying default settings, though. I prefer to separate settings from configurations. What if I need to update a setting down the line? I don't want to update the Default User folder on each computer in the organization.

The alternative is to copy the customized Default User folder to the NETLOGON share of the server. As you learned earlier in the chapter, Windows XP looks first for the network version of the Default User folder and then the local version. The first time users log on to a computer, Windows XP gets my default user profile from the network. Of course, the benefit is that I can always update it later. The primary problem with this method is that if users log on to their computers locally, they still get the local default user profile. That's the reason that I prefer doing both at the same time. I replace the Default User folder on disk images and also copy the same folder to the NETLOGON share of the server.

Note   An alternative to copying a default user profile to the NETLOGON share is keeping a user profile handy on the network and then copying it to users' network profile folders when you create new accounts. For example, stash away a default user profile somewhere on your server. Assuming that you're using roaming user profiles, copy the default user profile into new accounts' profile folders. The first time those users log on to Windows XP, the operating system downloads their roaming user profile, which you've already preconfigured. This is useful in one-off scenarios when you want users to have a profile other than the default. It's also useful in a heterogeneous environment, which often requires different user profiles for different versions of Windows.

Coexisting with Earlier Versions of Windows

Coexistence is an issue that affects roaming user profiles only. If you're not using roaming user profiles on your network, coexistence isn't an issue because you won't be deploying user profiles to different versions of Windows. In general, though, roaming user profiles are compatible between Windows 2000 and Windows XP. Here are a few precautions you can take to minimize problems:

- Try to make sure that users with roaming user profiles are logging on to the same version of Windows on each computer. That means you should choose your rollout units so that you're picking up all the computers that users can access.

- At the very least, make sure the same application versions are on each computer and that you've installed applications to the same path on each computer.

- If you're using roaming user profiles with Windows 2000 and Windows XP, make sure your %SYSTEMDRIVE% and %SYSTEMROOT% are the same. Also, make sure that profiles are stored in the same path. If you're using roaming user profiles with Windows NT 4.0 and Windows XP, you should move the location of user profiles that Windows XP uses by setting the ProfilesDir property in the [GuiUnattended] section of your answer file.

There's nothing in the documentation that says user profiles don't roam between Windows NT and Windows XP. However, I suspect that this scenario isn't workable. First Windows XP converts Windows NT-based profiles. Second having knowledge of both versions of the registry, I suspect that subtle differences between the two are likely to cause configuration problems in the long run. If anybody suggests that you can use roaming user profiles with any combination other than Windows 2000 and Windows XP, I'd ask for more information and test these scenarios carefully in a lab.

Migrating User Settings to Windows XP

Default user profiles give settings to new users, but what do you do about users who already have user profiles? You can let Windows XP migrate the user profile. Throw disk imaging into the mix and you have a whole different bag of problems. One of the drawbacks of using disk imaging to deploy the operating system is that users lose their documents and settings. This doesn't have to be a barrier to deployment, though. A variety of third-party utilities are available to migrate users' settings. Also, Microsoft provides two tools, one for the user and one for the IT professional.

All these tools work roughly the same way. First you siphon users' documents and settings off of their computers and store them on the network. You install a new disk image to their computers, and then you re-apply their settings. Users get to keep their documents and settings. Here are the tools that Microsoft provides:

- **Files And Settings Transfer Wizard.**   This tool is designed for the user. This wizard is also useful in enterprise environments when employees want to migrate their own documents and settings without the IT department's help.

- **User State Migration Tool (USMT).**   This tool is designed for IT professionals performing large-scale deployments of Windows XP Professional in an enterprise. USMT provides the same functionality as File And Settings Transfer Wizard, but on a larger scale. USMT gives IT professionals precise control over the documents and settings that it migrates.

Files And Settings Transfer Wizard

Files And Settings Transfer Wizard is a fast and easy way for you to copy all your documents and settings from your previous configuration to Windows XP. To start it, click Start, All Programs, Accessories, System Tools, Files And Settings Transfer Wizard. It migrates settings in four major groups:

- **Action.**   This group includes settings such as the key repeat rate, whether double-clicking a folder opens it in a new window or the same window, and whether you need to double-click or single-click an object to open it.

- **Internet.**   This group includes settings that enable you to connect to the Internet and control how Internet Explorer works. They include settings such as your home page URL, favorites, Internet shortcuts, cookies, security settings, dial-up connections, and so on.

- **Mail.**   This group includes settings for connecting to your mail server, your signature file, views, mail rules, local mail, and contacts. The wizard supports only Outlook and Outlook Express.

- **Application.**   This group includes application settings such as Microsoft Office. The wizard migrates only application settings, not the applications. You must reinstall each after upgrading to Windows XP.

Files And Settings Transfer Wizard also migrates your documents. It does so by type (*.doc), folder (C:\Documents and Settings\Administrator\My Documents), or name (C:\Documents and Settings\Administrator\My Documents\Jerry.doc). The wizard is preconfigured to copy the most common types of files and the most useful folders. It also gives you the option to change the folders, file types, and files lists.

User State Migration Tool

User State Migration Tool (USMT) is similar to Files And Settings Transfer Wizard but it adds the ability for you to fully customize exactly what it migrates. USMT is designed for IT professionals only; individual users do not need to use USMT. The tool is designed for large-scale migrations, and it requires a domain controller on which to store settings during migration.

USMT consists of two programs, ScanState.exe and LoadState.exe, and four migration rule information files: Migapp.inf, Migsys.inf, Miguser.inf, and Sysfiles.inf. ScanState.exe collects users' documents and settings based on the information contained in Migapp.inf, Migsys.inf, Miguser.inf and Sysfiles.inf. LoadState.exe deposits this user state data on a computer running a clean installation of Windows XP. Both of these tools are on the Windows XP CD in the \Valueadd\Msft\Usmt folder. The shared set of INF files drive USMT. IT professionals can modify these files to customize the documents and settings that the tool migrates. In fact, during any real deployment project, you'll most likely have to modify the INF files to handle your unique requirements.

Note   The whitepaper "Step-by-Step Guide to Migrating Files and Settings" is a good guide for learning how to use USMT. This whitepaper is on the Web at *www.microsoft.com /windowsxp/pro/techinfo/deployment/filesettings/default.asp*.

Mapping Windows Installer

Windows Installer is a component of Microsoft Windows XP that simplifies application deployment, management, and removal. It manages installation by applying the setup rules that a package file contains. These rules define which files to install and the configuration of the application. After installing Windows Installer–based applications, you can change, repair, or remove them with a high degree of reliability—much greater than with applications that use legacy setup programs. In Windows XP, Windows Installer is an operating system service.

Windows Installer is a big subject. Component management, customization with transforms, deployment through Active Directory, and resiliency are some of the topics in the vast list of things you should learn about Windows Installer before deploying applications based on the technology. This is a book about the registry, however, so I must focus on how Windows Installer interacts with the registry. With that said, you don't necessarily need to run out and buy a book to learn how to deploy Windows Installer–based applications. Microsoft posted incredibly useful documentation on the company's Web site. The whitepaper that I'd suggest you start with is "Windows Installer: Benefits and Implementation for System Administrators" at *www.microsoft.com/windows2000/techinfo/administration /management/wininstaller.asp*. Also, the Office XP Resource Kit, *www.microsoft.com/office/ork*, is the ultimate resource for learning how to deploy big Windows Installer–based applications like Microsoft Office XP. From this point forward, I'm assuming that you're familiar with Windows Installer and want to know more about how it interacts with the registry.

In this chapter, I describe Windows Installer registry settings. First I describe how to repair a Windows Installer–based application's user and computer settings. One of the really cool things about Windows Installer is that it heads off helpdesk calls by repairing applications automatically when it detects a problem (missing or corrupt files, for example) and enabling users to repair an application's user and computer settings manually. This chapter also describes the policies IT professionals use to manage Windows Installer and the applications that use it. Some policies are more useful than others, so I'll describe the ones that offer solutions to common deployment problems. Last, I wrap up by describing the tools you can use to remove an application's Windows Installer settings from the registry. These tools are sometimes essential because when an application's Windows Installer settings become corrupt, you can't remove the application using Add Or Remove Programs and you can't reinstall or repair it.

Repairing Registry Settings

One of the most common things you'll find yourself doing with a Windows Installer–based application's registry settings is repairing them. The most common scenario is when a user's settings are so out of whack that the only choice is to restore them to their original values. This goes for computer settings, too. After the helpdesk call has exceeded a reasonable amount of time, the technician can put a quick end to the call by repairing the application. The most straightforward ways to repair a Windows Installer–based application are in the user interface:

- On the application's Help menu, click Detect And Repair.

- In Add Or Remove Programs, select the application you want to repair, click Change, and then follow the directions you see on the screen.

Some applications don't provide a user interface for repairing them, so you must use the command line. The syntax of the command you use to repair an application follows this paragraph. The variable *package* is the path and name of the package file from which you installed the application. To repair user settings, type **msiexec /fu** *package*. To repair computer settings, type **msiexec /fm** *package*. The command **msiexec /fmu** *package* gets them both at the same time. These commands work rather well, which you can witness for yourself. Install Office XP. Remove its settings from the registry, which are in HKCU \Software\Microsoft\Office, and then repair user settings. Windows Installer rebuilds the missing settings.

```
msiexec /f[p|o|e|d|c|a|u|m|v|s] package
```

p	Reinstall missing files but don't check version
o	Reinstall missing files or files that are from an earlier version
e	Reinstall missing files or files that are from the same or earlier version
d	Reinstall missing files or files that aren't from the same version
c	Reinstall missing files or files that are corrupt. This option repairs only files that have a checksum in the package file.
a	Reinstall all files regardless of their versions or checksums
u	Rewrite the essential registry values described in the package file. This includes values in the per-user branches HKU and HKCU.
m	Rewrite essential registry values described in the package file. This includes values in the per-computer branches HKLM and HKCR.
s	Reinstall all shortcuts and overwrite existing icons.
v	Recache the source package locally.

Note   Repairing an application using Windows Installer is a bit extreme considering that you have System Restore at your disposal. Chapter 3, "Backing Up the Registry," describes how to use this awesome feature to protect configurations. If users' settings get out of whack, going back to an earlier restore point will likely fix the problem. IT professionals can easily script this operation, too, which enables the helpdesk to automatically go back to the most recent restore point.

Managing Windows Installer with Policies

Windows Installer provides a number of policies for managing how it installs applications and interacts with users. Some policies are more important and more useful than others; I'll get to that in just a bit. First here's the lineup (the parentheses contain the policies' registry values):

- User Configuration\Administrative Templates\Windows Components \Windows Installer (HKCU\Software\Policies\Microsoft\Windows\Installer)

  - **Always install with elevated privileges (AlwaysInstallElevated).**   Directs Windows Installer to use system permissions when it installs any program on the system. You must also set the per-computer version of this policy for it to work.

- **Search order (SearchOrder).** Specifies the order in which Windows Installer searches for installation files. In other words, you can specify the order in which it looks at network, local media, and Web locations for installation files.

- **Prohibit rollback (DisableRollback).** Prohibits Windows Installer from generating and saving the files it needs to reverse an interrupted or unsuccessful installation. This is useful when you know that the disks won't have enough space to hold the rollback files. However, it's dangerous because Windows Installer won't be able to restore the computer if the installation fails.

- **Prevent removable media source for any install (DisableMedia).** Prevents users from installing programs from removable media. Using this policy is a nifty way to prevent users from installing applications themselves, circumventing IT policies. This controls only Windows Installer–based applications, though.

- Computer Configuration\Administrative Templates\Windows Components \Windows Installer (HKLM\Software\Policies\Microsoft\Windows\Installer)

  - **Disable Windows Installer (DisableMSI).** Disables or restricts the use of Windows Installer. Use this policy to limit Windows Installer to managed applications. Your choices are to allow users to install Windows Installer–based applications, never allow them, or allow them to install only managed applications.

  - **Always install with elevated privileges (AlwaysInstallElevated).** Directs Windows Installer to use system permissions when it installs any program on the system. You must also set the per-user version of this policy for it to work.

  - **Prohibit rollback (DisableRollback).** Prohibits Windows Installer from generating and saving the files it needs to reverse an interrupted or unsuccessful installation. This is useful when you know that the user's hard disk doesn't have enough space to hold the rollback files. However, it's dangerous because Windows Installer won't be able to restore the computer if the installation fails.

  - **Remove browse dialog box for new source (DisableBrowse).** Prevents users from searching for installation files when they add features or components to an installed program. By default, if Windows Installer can't find the application's source files, it displays a dialog box allowing users to browse for the files.

  - **Prohibit patching (DisablePatch).** Prevents users from using Windows Installer to install patches. Prevent users from patching their applications to protect them from malicious code.

  - **Disable IE security prompt for Windows Installer scripts (SafeForScripting).** Allows Web-based programs to install software on the computer without notifying the user.

  - **Enable user control over installs (EnableUserControl).** Permits users to change installation options that typically are available only to system administrators. Use this policy only in environments that don't lock down and carefully control configurations because it bypasses some of the security features built into Windows Installer.

- **Enable user to browse for source while elevated (AllowLockdownBrowse).**
  Allows users to search for installation files during privileged installations.
  By default, Windows Installer doesn't allow users to browse for installation
  source files when it's running with elevated privileges.

- **Enable user to use media source while elevated (AllowLockdownMedia).**
  Allows users to install programs from removable media, such as floppy disks
  and CD-ROMs, during privileged installations. By default, Windows Installer
  doesn't allow users to install applications from local media when it's running
  with elevated privileges.

- **Enable user to patch elevated products (AllowLockdownPatch).** Allows
  users to upgrade programs during privileged installations. By default, Windows
  Installer doesn't allow users to patch applications when the installation program
  is running with elevated privileges.

- **Allow admin to install from Terminal Services session (EnableAdminTSRemote).**
  Allows Terminal Services administrators to install and configure programs
  remotely. Windows Installer allows administrators to install applications only
  when they are console users. This policy allows them to install applications using
  Terminal Services.

- **Cache transforms in secure location on workstation (TransformsSecure).**
  Saves copies of transform files in a secure location on the local computer. Windows
  Installer stores transforms in users' profile folders so that transforms follow
  users from computer to computer. Users can change the transforms, however.
  This policy causes Windows Installer to store transforms in a secure location,
  preventing users from changing them, but the transforms don't follow users.

- **Logging (Logging).** Specifies the types of events that Windows Installer
  records in its transaction log for each installation. The log, Msi.log, appears
  in the Temp directory of the system volume.

- **Prohibit user installs (DisableUserInstalls).** Allows IT professionals
  to prevent user installs. This policy has three choices. Allow per-user installations,
  which is the default, and Windows Installer favors per-user installations over
  per-computer. Hide per-user installations, and Windows Installer favors per-
  computer installations over per user. Prohibit user installations, and Windows
  Installer prevents applications from installing per user. The last option is desirable
  to ensure a standard configuration that's available to all users on all computers.

- **Turn off creation of System Restore checkpoints
  (LimitSystemRestoreCheckpointing).** Prevents Windows Install from
  creating System Restore check points. System Restore enables users, in the
  event of a problem, to restore their computers to a previous state without losing
  personal data files. By default, the Windows Installer automatically creates
  a System Restore checkpoint each time an application is installed so that users
  can restore their computer to the state it was in before installing the application.

Of all the policies I just described, the most useful are AlwaysInstallElevated, which loosens up security enough to allow restricted users to install applications, TransformsSecure, which stores transforms to prevent tampering, and the other policies that you can use to significantly restrict Windows Installer. Both ends of the spectrum are available to you.

Installing with Elevated Privileges

The policy InstallAlwaysElevated installs Windows Installer–based applications with elevated privileges. Microsoft documentation often calls this a *privileged installation*. This policy is one way to enable users to install applications that they couldn't otherwise install because they're in restricted groups or you've locked down the desktops in your enterprise. A better way is to deploy those applications through Active Directory or by using something like SMS (Microsoft Systems Management Server). If neither product is available to you, consider using this policy, but keep in mind that the consequences of doing so can be severe.

These consequences are due to the fact that users can take advantage of this policy to gain full control of their computers. Potentially, users could permanently change their privileges and circumvent your ability to manage their accounts and computers. In addition, this policy opens the door to viruses disguised as Windows Installer package files. For these reasons, this isn't a setting that I recommend in any but the most dire situations in which there's no method available other than tossing users in the local Administrators group.

For this policy to be effective, you must enable both the per-computer and per-user versions of it at the same time. In other words, enable it in Computer Configuration as well as User Configuration.

Tip   Deploying applications to locked-down desktops is a common and sticky scenario. Using the AlwaysInstallElevated policy isn't the best solution, either. Other than the typical fare, such as Active Directory and SMS, elegant solutions do exist for this problem. Chapter 7, "Managing Registry Security," describes many of them, including using Security Templates and Security Configuration And Analysis to open up security just enough to allow legacy programs to run in Windows XP. Chapter 15, "Working Around IT Problems," shows you a few techniques for launching setup programs with elevated privileges.

Caching Transforms in Secure Location

Transforms are essentially answer files for Windows Installer–based applications. Chapter 14, "Deploying Office XP Settings," describes transforms, but chances are good that you already know all about them. Transforms, which you build using the Office XP Resource Kit's Custom Installation Wizard, customize the way an application installs.

When you install an application using a transform, Windows Installer stores the transform with a *.mst* extension in the Application Data folder of the user profile. Windows Installer needs this file to reinstall, remove, or repair the application. Keeping it in the user profile ensures that the file is always available. For example, if users have roaming user profiles, the transform follows them from computer to computer. This is not secure, however. When you set the TransformsSecure policy, Windows Installer saves transforms in %SYSTEMROOT%, instead, where users don't have permissions to change files. But because Windows Installer requires access to the transform used to install an application, the user must use the same computer on which he or she installed the application or have access to the original installation source to install, remove, or repair the software. The idea behind this policy is to secure transforms in enterprises when IT professionals can't risk users' maliciously changing the files.

Locking Down Windows Installer

Table 11-1 describes the policies that provide the most security for Windows Installer–based applications and Windows XP in general. The first part of the table contains per-user policies and the second part contains per-computer policies. In the Setting column, *Not Configured* means that you don't define the policy. *Enabled* speaks for itself.

Table 11-1   Secure Windows Installer Settings

Policy	Setting
User Configuration	
Always install with elevated privileges	Not Configured
Prevent removable media source for any install	Enabled
Computer Configuration	
Always install with elevated privileges	Not Configured
Enable user to browse for source while elevated	Not Configured
Enable user to use media source while elevated	Not Configured
Enable user to patch elevated products	Not Configured
Remove browse dialog box for new source	Enabled
Disable Windows Installer	Enabled for non-managed apps only
Prohibit patching	Enabled
Enable user control over installs	Not Configured
Disable IE security prompt for Windows Installer scripts	Not Configured
Cache transforms in secure location on workstation	Enabled

You can configure these policies directly in the registry. I gave you the key and value names earlier in this chapter. To enable a policy, add it to the appropriate key as a REG_DWORD value and set it to 0x01. To disable the policy, set it to 0x00. Delete the value to remove the policy. These policies are typical of enterprise-style deployments, however, so I wouldn't configure them in the registry, which is totally unmanaged. Instead, configure them using Group Policy locally or on the network so you can manage them properly.

Removing Windows Installer Data

If you thought manually removing legacy applications was difficult, try removing a Windows Installer–based application manually. More than once I've broken Windows Installer–based applications so badly that I couldn't remove them, repair them, or reinstall them. In these cases, I had to manually remove the application's Windows Installer data from the registry or reinstall Windows XP. Tools are available that automate this process, and you learn about them in this chapter. Removing Windows Installer data without these tools is akin to replacing transistors on your computer's mainboard—it's not really possible.

Before I introduce the tools, I'm going to point you to the location in the registry where Windows Installer stores data about the applications it installs. Don't modify these settings using Registry Editor (Regedit) because doing so will likely inflict pain on you. Straightening out the relationships between all the different bits of data that Windows Installer stores in the registry is difficult. This is just good information to have available:

* HKCU\Software\Microsoft\Installer.   This branch contains per-user Windows Installer data for applications that you install per user.

* HKLM\SOFTWARE\Microsoft\Windows\CurrentVersion\Installer.   This branch contains Windows Installer data for per-computer applications and managed applications.

* HKLM\SOFTWARE\Microsoft\Windows\CurrentVersion\Uninstall.   This branch contains removal information for Windows Installer–based programs.

* HKCR\Installer.   This branch contains information similar to the Installer key under HKLM.

The tools you learn about in the next two sections come with Windows XP Support Tools. You install the tools from \Support\Tools on your Windows XP CD.

Msizap.exe

Msizap is a tool that removes most of the data that Windows Installer maintains for an application. It doesn't remove the application's files or settings from the hard disk however; you have to clean those up yourself. You can focus this utility on a single application or you can make sweeping changes to the Windows Installer data. I've had good luck using Msizap to remove a single application's Windows Installer data from the registry, but I don't trust it to make huge changes, such as allowing it to remove all the Windows Installer folders and registry keys.

The following examples show the different forms of the Msizap program's command line. The first two forms are the most useful. In the first case, you specify the product code, which is the product's unique GUID. You're not likely to know the product code off the top of your head, so you're going to want to use the second form. In the second form, you specify the path and name of the package file. Then Msizap will look up the product code for you. An example is in order. Assuming that you've installed Microsoft Office XP and can't remove it using Add Or Remove Programs, you'd type **msizap T!** *path\proplus.msi* in the Run dialog box. *Path* is the path containing the package file Proplus.msi. After Msizap finishes removing the application's Windows Installer data from the registry, you'll still have plenty of cleaning to do. You'll want to get rid of the application's files and other settings that it might have stored in the registry. For example, you'll still see the application's shortcut on the Start menu, but when you click it, you'll see an error message telling you that the application isn't installed. Chapter 3, "Backing Up the Registry," describes how to manually remove a program after you've got it to this step.

```
msizap T[A!] productcode
msizap T[A!] packagefile
msizap *[A!] ALLPRODUCTS
msizap PSA?!
```

*	Remove all Windows Installer folders and registry keys, adjusting shared DLL counts and stopping the service
T	Remove all Windows Installer information for a product
P	Remove the in-progress key
S	Remove rollback information
A	Give administrators full control to targeted folders and keys instead of removing them
W	Apply changes for all users instead of just the current user
G	Remove cached Windows Installer files that are orphaned
!	Automatically respond *Yes* to all prompts
?	Display help

Tip   I'm not comfortable with manually removing a program's files and registry settings after using Msizap. Most large applications store settings in the registry beyond the typical HKU\Software*Vendor**Product**Version* keys. For example, they register components in HKCR, and you might not get rid of them all. My solution seems odd, but it works well. Zapping a program's Windows Installer data from the registry should enable me to reinstall it. So I reinstall the application and then use Add Or Remove Programs to remove it. Windows Installer is likely to do a much cleaner job of removing the application than I am.

Msicuu.exe

Windows Installer Clean Up (Msicuu.exe in the Windows XP Support Tools) puts a graphical user interface on Msizap.exe. If you're sitting at the computer, use this tool instead of using Msizap at the command prompt. It's less error-prone:

1. In the Run dialog box, type **Msicuu**, and click OK.

2. In the Windows Installer Clean Up dialog box, shown in Figure 11-1, click the application for which you want to remove Windows Installer data from the registry, and then click Remove.

3. Confirm that you want to remove the application's Windows Installer data from the registry by clicking OK.

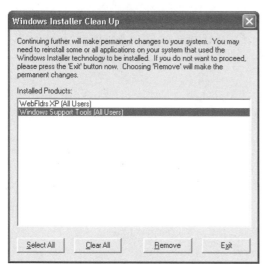

Figure 11-1   *Windows Installer Clean Up is a friendly interface for Msizap.*

Inventorying Applications

One of the more common requests I receive regarding Windows Installer–based applications is about inventorying the applications and features installed on users' computers. If you have a software management infrastructure already in place, you should use the tools that it provides. Otherwise, Microsoft's TechNet Script Center (*www.microsoft.com/technet /scriptcenter*), which contains an awesome collection of useful scripts, has a few scripts that suit the purpose very well.

Listing 11-1 is a script that inventories the software installed on a computer. Listing 11-2 is a script that inventories the features for all software installed on a computer. These inventory only Windows Installer–based applications though. Using Notepad, type each script and save it as a text file with the *.vbs* extension. To run each script, double-click the file.

> ## Updating Source Lists
>
> After inventorying Windows Installer–based applications, the next most common request I receive is about updating an application's source list. When you deploy a Windows Installer-based application, you specify a list of alternative locations from which Windows Installer can install files. This supports multiple installation locations from a single set of configuration files. If you deployed an application with an incorrect source list or moved your administration installations, you must update the source lists on each client computer.
>
> With earlier versions of Windows Installer, updating source lists was a difficult task. You had to deploy a registry hack. With the current versions, you can use Custom Maintenance Wizard to deploy an updated source list. This is a far more elegant solution than deploying a registry hack. Chapter 14, "Deploying Office XP Settings," tells you more about using Custom Maintenance Wizard.

Listing 11-1   Inventory.vbs

```
Set objFSO = CreateObject("Scripting.FileSystemObject")
Set objTextFile = objFSO.CreateTextFile("c:\scripts\software.tsv", True)
strComputer = "."
Set objWMIService = GetObject("winmgmts:" _
    & "{impersonationLevel=impersonate}!\\" & strComputer & "\root\cimv2")
Set colSoftware = objWMIService.ExecQuery _
    ("Select * from Win32_Product")
objTextFile.WriteLine "Caption" & vbtab & _
    "Description" & vbtab & "Identifying Number" & vbtab & _
    "Install Date" & vbtab & "Install Location" & vbtab & _
    "Install State" & vbtab & "Name" & vbtab & _
    "Package Cache" & vbtab & "SKU Number" & vbtab & "Vendor" & vbtab _
        & "Version"
For Each objSoftware in colSoftware
    objTextFile.WriteLine objSoftware.Caption & vbtab & _
    objSoftware.Description & vbtab & _
    objSoftware.IdentifyingNumber & vbtab & _
    objSoftware.InstallDate2 & vbtab & _
    objSoftware.InstallLocation & vbtab & _
    objSoftware.InstallState & vbtab & _
    objSoftware.Name & vbtab & _
    objSoftware.PackageCache & vbtab & _
    objSoftware.SKUNumber & vbtab & _
    objSoftware.Vendor & vbtab & _
    objSoftware.Version
Next
objTextFile.Close
```

Listing 11-2   Software.vbs

```
strComputer = "."
Set objWMIService = GetObject("winmgmts:" _
    & "{impersonationLevel=impersonate}!\\" & strComputer & "\root\cimv2")
Set colFeatures = objWMIService.ExecQuery _
    ("Select * from Win32_SoftwareFeature")
For each objFeature in colfeatures
    Wscript.Echo "Accesses: " & objFeature.Accesses
    Wscript.Echo "Attributes: " & objFeature.Attributes
    Wscript.Echo "Caption: " & objFeature.Caption
    Wscript.Echo "Description: " & objFeature.Description
    Wscript.Echo "Identifying Number: " & objFeature.IdentifyingNumber
    Wscript.Echo "Install Date: " & objFeature.InstallDate
    Wscript.Echo "Install State: " & objFeature.InstallState
    Wscript.Echo "LastUse: " & objFeature.LastUse
    Wscript.Echo "Name: " & objFeature.Name
    Wscript.Echo "ProductName: " & objFeature.ProductName
    Wscript.Echo "Vendor: " & objFeature.Vendor
    Wscript.Echo "Version: " & objFeature.Version
Next
```

Deploying with Answer Files

Users installing Microsoft Windows XP on their own computers don't often worry about automating the setup program. Instead, they drop the CD in the drive, the setup programs starts, and they answer the setup program's prompts. That won't work in a business because most business users don't know the answers to all the setup program's questions. Automating the setup program prevents users from having to fumble with the installation. Furthermore, as an IT professional, you want to ensure that users have a positive experience so that they say good things about you.

You should still consider automating Windows XP installation even if you are a power user. It makes installing Windows XP more convenient, and options are available to you through answer files that just aren't available through the setup program's user interface.

Microsoft provides several tools that help you to deploy automated and customized Windows XP installations. Each tool has purposes, strengths, and weakness that are different from the other tools in various deployment scenarios. Examples of deployment tools include Sysprep for disk imaging and Remote Installation Service, both of which come with the Microsoft Windows 2000 Server and Microsoft Windows .NET Server family of products. Every deployment method and tool has unattended answer files, which you use to automate the setup program so that it runs with little or no user interaction. The operating system's setup program uses the information contained in the answer files rather than prompting users for it.

Answer files are text files that look like INI files. Answer files have many sections, and each section contains settings. Because this book is about Windows XP's registry and user settings rather than desktop deployment, I only introduce you to answer files.

After you learn the basics, I'll describe two answer file features that specifically enable you to deploy user settings as part of the Windows XP setup process. If you're interested in learning more about deploying Windows XP, see the Microsoft Windows XP Corporate Deployment Tools User's Guide. You find it in Deploy.chm, which is in the Deploy.cab cabinet file in the Support\Tools folder of your Windows XP CD. You start this chapter by learning how to add files to Windows XP distribution files (the i386 folder).

Creating Distribution Folders

To add files to Windows XP's distribution folder, you start by making a copy of the CD's i386 folder on your hard disk because you can't modify the CD. You don't need the rest of the files or folders on the CD—just the i386 folder. In a corporate deployment, you'll eventually replicate the customized i386 folder on distribution servers and then deploy the command that installs Windows XP from them. If you're a power user, you'll likely burn a custom CD that contains your files. You add files to the distribution folder by creating the structure shown in Figure 12-1.

Figure 12-1   *In addition to creating this folder structure, you must set* OEMPreinstall=Yes *in your Windows XP answer file.*

Here's a description of each folder shown in Figure 12-1:

- **i386 folder.**   This is the i386 folder from the Windows XP CD, including all of its subfolders and files.

- **OEM.**   This is the OEM distribution folder that contains additional files you want to deploy and are required to install Windows XP. If you use the OemFilesPath setting in the [Unattended] section of the answer file, you can create the OEM folder outside the i386 folder. I often create multiple OEM folders (one for each different configuration) and deploy each along with a single i386 folder. To do that, I create an answer file for each configuration that points to a unique OEM folder. You must include OemPreinstall=Yes in the [Unattended] section of the answer file if you are using the OEM folder to add files to the system or if you are using Cmdlines.txt to run other programs during installation.

- **Cmdlines.txt.**   This file contains the commands that the setup program runs during installation. The file format is similar to an INI file. You create this file in the OEM folder, adding each command in the [Commands] section. For more information about using Cmdlines.txt, particularly to deploy user settings with Windows XP, see "Cmdlines.txt," later in this chapter.

- **$$Rename.txt.** This is an optional file that setup uses during installations you start from MS-DOS to convert short file names to long file names. You can create a $$Rename.txt file for each folder containing short file names you want to rename, or you can use one $$Rename.txt file for an entire folder tree. I often use this file when deploying third-party device drivers that use long file names.

- **OEM\Textmode.** This folder contains hardware-dependent files that Setup Loader and the text-mode setup program install on the target computer during text-mode setup. These files include OEM HALs (hardware abstraction layers), mass storage device drivers, and the Txtsetup.oem file, which describes how to load and install these components. List these files in the [OEMBootFiles] section of your answer file. This folder isn't as necessary as it was when hardware configurations varied more wildly.

- **OEM\$$.** This is the folder into which you add files and subfolders that you want the setup program to copy to the target computer's %SYSTEMROOT% folder. This is how to customize Windows XP Professional system folders. To add a file called Sample.dll to %SYSTEMROOT%\System32, add it to OEM\$$\System32. The setup program creates subfolders that don't exist on the target computer. Therefore, you can create a new subfolder in %SYSTEMROOT% called Drivers to deploy third-party device drivers with Windows XP. OemPnPDriversPath must indicate the location of the third-party device drivers on the target computer; in this case, OemPnPDriversPath=%SYSTEMROOT%\Drivers.

- **OEM\$1.** This folder enables you to add files and folders to %SYSTEMDRIVE% on the target computer. It works in a similar way as OEM\$$, except that you use OEM\$1 to add files to the root of the drive on which you're installing Windows XP. A typical example is creating a folder on %SYSTEMDRIVE% called OEM\$1\Sysprep, which automatically adds the Sysprep folder and files necessary to prepare the target computer's drive for duplication. (See Chapter 13, "Cloning Disks with Sysprep," for more information about disk imaging.)

Tip You can use Setup Manager to create the i386 distribution folder for Sysprep, Remote Installation Service, or an unattended installation using an answer file. Setup Manager is in Deploy.cab, which is located in \Support\Tools on the Windows XP CD. Open Deploy.cab in Windows Explorer, and extract its contents to a folder on your hard disk. I prefer to create the distribution folder manually because many options aren't available through Setup Manager's user interface.

Customizing Default Settings

Windows XP doesn't invent its settings out of thin air. It uses four INF files in the i386 distribution folder to create the registry's hive files when you install the operating system. These INF files use the same syntax I described in Chapter 9, "Scripting Registry Changes," and you should be able to customize them easily. Here are those four INF files:

- **Hivecls.inf.** This INF file creates the settings in `HKLM\SOFTWARE\Classes` (HKCR).

- **Hivedef.inf.** This INF file creates the settings in `HKU\.DEFAULT`. It also creates the settings for the default user profile.

- **Hivesft.inf.** This INF file creates the settings in `HKLM\SOFTWARE`.

- **Hivesys.inf.** This INF file creates the settings in `HKLM\SYSTEM`.

You can change any of the Windows XP default settings by changing the setting in the hive files listed. For example, if you want to deploy some of the per-user hacks shown in Chapter 4, "Hacking the Registry," change those values in the file Hivedef.inf. This is in lieu of creating a default user profile for Windows XP. If you want to change file associations for every computer in the organization, change them in the file Hivecls.inf.

Customizing Answer Files

As you have already learned, an answer file is a script that looks much like an INI file. The script drives the setup program, rather than the setup program prompting the user for information. Not only does an answer file automate the setup program's user interface, but it also enables you to configure Windows XP in ways that aren't possible through the user interface. I use an answer file to change the location of user profiles from %SYSTEMDRIVE% \Documents and Settings to %SYSTEMDRIVE%\Profiles, for example, because I'm a command-line junkie and do not like typing **C:\Documents and Settings** over and over again.

Unattend.txt is the traditional name for answer files, but I prefer to give answer files names that make it easy to decipher their purpose. Just make sure that you limit their names to eight characters so you can read their names when installing Windows XP using MS-DOS. Also, I don't like to use the *.txt* extension for answer files. I prefer to use *.sif*, which is the file extension for Setup Information Files, so I can easily differentiate a text file from an answer file. For example, I might have an answer file to install Windows XP on a lab computer called Labprep.sif. You might create different answer files for different departments called Sales.sif, Legal.sif, and so on. Regardless, use descriptive names that help you discern the differences between answer files because you'll grow a collection.

Listing 12-1 shows a sample answer file (most tend not to be this complicated and so well-documented with comments).

Listing 12-1 Unattend.txt

```
[Unattended]
UnattendMode = FullUnattended
TargetPath = Windows
FileSystem = LeaveAlone
OemPreinstall = Yes
OemSkipEula = Yes

[GuiUnattended]
; Set the TimeZone. For example, to set the TimeZone for the
; Pacific Northwest, use a value of "004." Be sure to use the
; numeric value that represents your own time zone. To look up
; a numeric value, see the Deploy.chm file on the Windows XP Professional CD.
; The Deploy.cab file is in the \Support\Tools folder.
TimeZone = "YourTimeZone"
OemSkipWelcome = 1
; The OemSkipRegional key allows Unattended Installation to skip
; RegionalSettings when the final location of the computer is unknown.
OemSkipRegional = 1

[UserData]
; Tip: Avoid using spaces in the ComputerName value.
ComputerName = "YourComputerName"
; To ensure a fully unattended installation, you must provide a value
; for the ProductKey key.
ProductKey = "Your product key"[LicenseFilePrintData]
; This section is used for server installs.
AutoMode = "PerServer"AutoUsers = "50"[Display]
BitsPerPel = 16
XResolution = 800
YResolution = 600
VRefresh = 60

[Components]
; This section contains keys for installing the components of
; Windows XP Professional. A value of On installs the component, and a
; value of Off prevents the component from being installed.
iis_common = On
iis_inetmgr = Off
iis_www = Off
iis_ftp = Off
iis_doc = Off
iis_smtp = On
; The Fp_extensions key installs Front Page Server Extensions.
Fp_extensions = On
; If you set the TSEnabled key to On, Terminal Services is installed on
; a current version of Windows Server.
TSEnabled = On
```

```
; If you set the TSClients key to On, the files required to create
; Terminal Services client disks are installed. If you set this key
; to On, you must also set the TSEnabled key to On.
TSClients = On
Indexsrv_system = On
Accessopt = On
Calc = On
Charmap = On
Chat = Off
Clipbook = On
Deskpaper = On
Dialer = On
Freecell = Off
Hypertrm = On
Media_clips = On
Media_utopia = On
Minesweeper = Off
Mousepoint = Off
Mplay = On
Mswordpad = On
Paint = On
Pinball = Off
Rec = On
Solitaire = Off
Templates = On
Vol = On

[TapiLocation]
CountryCode = "1"
Dialing = Pulse
; Indicates the area code for your telephone. This value must
; be a 3-digit number.
AreaCode = "Your telephone area code"
LongDistanceAccess = 9

[Networking]

[Identification]
JoinDomain = YourCorpNet
DomainAdmin = YourCorpAdmin
DomainAdminPassword = YourAdminPassword

[NetOptionalComponents]
; Section contains a list of optional network components to install.
Snmp = Off
```

```
Lpdsvc = Off
Simptcp = Off

[Branding]
; This section brands Microsoft® Internet Explorer with custom
; properties from the Unattended answer file.
BrandIEUsingUnattended = Yes

[URL]
; This section contains custom URL settings for Microsoft
; Internet Explorer. If these settings are not present, the
; default settings are used. Specifies the URL for the
; browser's default home page. For example, you might use the
; following: Home_Page = www.microsoft.com.
Home_Page = YourHomePageURL
; Specifies the URL for the default search page. For example, you might
; use the following: Search Page = www.msn.com
Search_Page = YourSearchPageURL
; Specifies a shortcut name in the link folder of Favorites.
; For example, you might use the following: Quick_Link_1_Name =
; "Microsoft Product Support Services"
Quick_Link_1_Name = "Your Quick Link Name"
; Specifies a shortcut URL in the link folder of Favorites. For example,
; you might use this: Quick_Link_1 = http://support.microsoft.com/.
Quick_Link_1 = YourQuickLinkURL

[Proxy]
; This section contains custom proxy settings for Microsoft
; Internet Explorer. If these settings are not present, the default
; settings are used. If proxysrv:80 is not accurate for your
; configuration, be sure to replace the proxy server and port number
; with your own values.
HTTP_Proxy_Server = proxysrv:80
Use_Same_Proxy = 1
```

You tell the setup program about your answer file using the /unattend command-line option. You can shorten this to /u (we all know that technology professionals and enthusiasts have a limited number of keystrokes in their lifetime). You also must use the setup program's /source command-line option to tell it where to find the Windows XP source files. You can shorten it to /s. The setup program's command line has many other options that control how it works. For more information about them, see Deploy.chm in Deploy.cab in the Support \Tools folder of the Windows XP CD. The following sample commands run the setup program from \\camelot\wxppro:

```
net use w: \\camelot\wxppro
w:\i386\winnt /s:w:\i386 /u:w:\winnt.sif
```

Setup Manager

You can use Setup Manager to create answer files for unattended Windows XP installations, automated installations using Sysprep, or automated installations using Remote Installation Service. Setup Manager is on the Windows XP CD in the Deploy.cab file of the Support\Tools folder. Setup Manager is a wizard that helps you create and modify answer files by prompting for the information required to create answer files. Setup Manager can create new answer files, import existing answer files, and create new answer files based on a computer's current configuration. The last option is useful when you want to configure network settings in an answer file and you don't understand all the settings available or you don't want to risk errors, which are likely considering how complex these sections are sometimes.

To install and run Setup Manager, double-click Deploy.cab in the Windows XP CD's Support\Tools folder, and then copy the cabinet file's contents to a folder on your disk and double-click Setupmgr.exe to run Setup Manager, as shown in Figure 12-2. The result of the wizard is an answer file. Table 12-1 describes Setup Manager's different pages, in the order you see them.

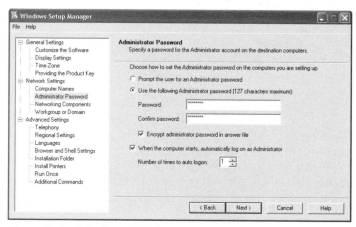

Figure 12-2   *Windows XP's Setup Manager is greatly improved over Windows 2000's version. Most of the changes are in its user interface, but encrypting the local administrator password is a new feature.*

Table 12-1   Setup Manager Pages

Page	Description
Set User Interaction	Use this page to set the level of user interaction during the setup process. Select Provide Defaults to display the configurable values supplied in the answer file, or select Fully Automated to create a setup process that requires no user interaction.
Customize the Software	Use this page to specify an organization and user name.

Page	Description
Display Settings	Use this page to configure the display color depth, screen resolution, and refresh frequency display settings. I prefer to allow Windows XP to automatically adjust these settings to the best available, and you should generally avoid setting a refresh frequency if you're not 100 percent sure that all the monitors in use by your organization can support that frequency. Generally, 70 is a safe bet, and LCD monitors perform best with 60.
Time Zone	Use this page to set the time zone.
Providing the Product Key	Use this page to specify a product key, which is required for a fully automated installation.
Computer Names	Use this page to tell Setup Manager to generate a Uniqueness Database File (UDF) that the setup program will use to give each computer a unique name. If you import names from a text file, Setup Manager converts them into a UDF file. You can also set an option to generate unique computer names.
Administrator Password	Use this page to tell Setup Manager to encrypt the local administrator password in the answer file so that users can't gain unauthorized access to the local administrator account. You can also configure the answer file to prompt users for the local administrator password during installation. If the Administrator Password box is blank, you can use the AutoLogon feature to automatically log on to the client computer as an administrator. For more information about using the AutoLogon feature with [GuiRunOnce] to deploy user settings with Windows XP, see "[GuiRunOnce]," later in this chapter.
Networking Components	Use this page to configure any network setting in Setup Manager that you can configure on the desktop. The interface for setting network settings in Setup Manager is the same as you see in Windows XP.
Workgroup or Domain	Use this page to join computers to a domain or workgroup. You can also automatically create accounts in the domain.
Telephony	Use this page to set telephony properties, such as area codes and dialing rules.
Regional Settings	Use this page to set regional options, such as date, time, and currency formats.
Languages	Use this page to add support for other language groups.
Browser and Shell Settings	Use this page to configure Internet connections, including proxy server settings. If you need to customize the browser, you can use Setup Manager to access the Internet Explorer Administration Kit (IEAK), available from *http://www.microsoft.com*, and the Office XP Resource Kit toolbox at *http://www.microsoft.com/office/ork*.
Installation Folder	Use this page to specify the default Windows folder, generate a unique folder during setup, or install Windows XP in a custom folder. For example, if you plan to keep Microsoft Windows 2000 in parts of your company or are upgrading to Windows XP from Windows 2000, you can move Windows XP from the Windows folder to the Winnt folder so that you have a consistent folder structure throughout the organization.
Install Printers	Use this page to install printers as part of the installation process.
Run Once	Use this page to add commands that run automatically the first time a user logs on to the computer. Setup Manager adds these commands to the answer file's [GuiRunOnce] section. For example, you can fire off Microsoft Office XP's setup program from here. For more information about using this feature to deploy user settings, see "GuiRunOnce," later in this chapter.
Additional Commands	Use this page to add commands that run at the end of the setup process and before users log on to the system, such as starting a setup program or adding user settings. For more information, see "Cmdlines.txt," later in this chapter.

Notepad and Other Text Editors

Even with all of Setup Manager's features, I prefer to create answer files manually. Now, before you think I'm silly and just making work for myself, let me add that I have a library of answer-file templates that I call on when required. After you've created your first answer file and you've got it just right, you can reuse it over and over again because little changes from job to job. I've got another surprise for you that I'm holding onto until you get to the end of this section.

You can use a text editor, Notepad for example, to create answer files. They look just like INI files; both have sections and their sections contain settings. You don't have to use all the sections or values available in the answer file if you don't need them. In fact, a typical answer file for a computer that you're joining to a Microsoft-based network is only about 20 lines long. If you add errors to an answer file, the setup program reports the line number containing the syntax error.

The answer file in Listing 12-2 is one that I use frequently. Notice that I've commented out the AdminPassword and FullName values by preceding them with a semicolon (;), so the setup program prompts the user for both values. You must provide your own product key for this sample (wink). Also notice that I don't use the [Display] section in this answer file, but Windows XP automatically optimizes the display settings when the user logs on to the computer. Last, I've commented out the DomainAdmin and DomainAdminPassword values in this answer file so the setup program will prompt the user for the credentials necessary to join the domain. I do this to avoid putting my domain administrator's credentials in an answer file. This isn't a problem, though, because I delegate ownership of each computer object to users so they can use their own account to join their own computers to the domain.

Listing 12-2   Unattend.txt

```
[Unattended]
    FileSystem=ConvertNTFS
    OemPreinstall=Yes
    OemSkipEula=Yes
    TargetPath=\Windows
    UnattendMode=ReadOnly

[GuiUnattended]
;   AdminPassword=
    OEMSkipRegional=1
    OEMSkipWelcome=1
    ProfilesDir=%SYSTEMDRIVE%\Profiles
    TimeZone=020

[UserData]
    ComputerName=*
;   FullName=
    OrgName="Jerry Honeycutt"
    ProductID="Your Product ID"
```

```
[TapiLocation]
    AreaCode=972
    CountryCode=1
    Dialing=Tone

[Identification]
;    DomainAdmin=
;    DomainAdminPassword=
    JoinDomain=HONEYCUTT

[Networking]
    InstallDefaultComponents=Yes

;end
```

This answer file is just one example. I built this answer file to do a clean installation of Windows XP from MS-DOS. I also have answer files that upgrade Windows 2000 to Windows XP. I have answer files that build disk images for deployment. I have still other answer files for deploying Windows XP through Remote Installation Services, building lab computers, installing Windows XP on mobile computers, installing Windows XP on Novell networks, and so on.

Jerry's Answer File Editor

Here's the surprise I promised. I don't use Notepad to edit answer files. I use Microsoft Word 2002. Here's why:

- Word includes built-in version control, enabling me to manage the different versions of an answer file over time. I can refer back to an earlier version of an answer file to see what I've changed.

- Word includes revision tracking, which enables me to see the changes I've made to the current version of my answer file. This is a great feature for documenting answer files as well as sending answer files out for review.

- Word enables reviewers to comment on answer files without actually changing them. This is another great feature for sending answer files out for review.

- Word enables me to build custom dictionaries. I build custom dictionaries that include answer file section and value names, which ensures that I don't add errors to answer files with something as silly as a typo.

I'm willing to bet that these four features are enough to convince you to start using Word to edit answer files. Doing so will make you many times more productive as an IT professional. The process requires one bit of explanation, though. I edit and review answer files as document files (DOC files). Only when I'm ready to build a distribution share do I export the answer file from Word to a text file. Enjoy!

Adding Settings to Unattend.txt

Now you know how to build answer files and how to use them. It's time to get to the heart of the matter, which is how to deploy user settings with your answer file. To deploy settings with Windows XP, you need a mechanism for running a program during the setup process. Windows XP's setup program provides two different mechanisms, but first, think of all the different ways to add settings to the registry (and this is only a partial list):

- **REG files.** For more information about creating REG files, see Chapter 2, "Using the Registry Editor," and Chapter 9, "Scripting Registry Changes." You import a REG file using the command `regedit` *filename*`.reg /s`.

- **INF files.** For more information about building and installing INF files, see Chapter 9, "Scripting Registry Changes." You install an INF file by running the command `rundll32.exe setupapi,InstallHinfSection DefaultInstall 132` *filename*`.inf`.

- **Scripts.** For more information about writing scripts for Windows Scripting Host, see Chapter 9, "Scripting Registry Changes." You run a script using the command `wscript` *filename.ext*, where *ext* is either `vbs` or `js`.

- **OPS files.** For more information about creating and installing OPS files, see Chapter 14, "Deploying Office XP Settings." You import an OPS file into the user's profile using the command `proflwiz /r` *filename*`.ops /q`.

- **Console Registry Tool for Windows (Reg).** For more information about using Reg to edit the registry, see Chapter 2, "Using the Registry Editor," and Chapter 9, "Scripting Registry Changes." Reg has a robust command-line interface that enables you to edit the registry using batch files.

- **Windows Installer package files (MSI files).** For more information about package files, see Chapter 11, "Mapping Windows Installer." To learn how to build MSI files that install registry settings, see Chapter 9, "Scripting Registry Changes."

Now that I've reminded you of the many tools and commands that I describe in this book for installing registry settings, see the following two sections, "[GuiRunOnce]" and "Cmdlines.txt," to learn how to deploy those commands with Windows XP.

[GuiRunOnce]

The [GuiRunOnce] section contains a list of commands that run the first time a user logs on to the computer after the Windows XP setup program runs. Enclose each command in quotation marks. The commands in the [GuiRunOnce] section run in the context of the console user, so you must ensure that the user has the privileges necessary to run each command. You can use this feature to install a REG file when a user logs on to the computer. For example, add the following lines to your answer file to import Settings.reg into the registry the first time a user logs on to the computer:

```
[GuiRunOnce]
"regedit %SYSTEMROOT%\Settings.reg /s"
```

You must provide any programs and data files that you want to use, though, and you do that by deploying them through the OEM distribution folders that you learned about in "Creating Distribution Folders," earlier in this chapter. In the previous example of a [GuiRunOnce] section, I'd put Settings.reg in i386\$OEM$\$$ to make sure that the setup program copied it to %SYSTEMROOT% on the target computer. Also, you want to make sure that a program you run from [GuiRunOnce] has a command-line option to run quietly; you don't want to display a user interface while installing registry settings. All the commands I listed in the section "Adding Settings to Unattend.txt" include the command-line option to run without displaying a user interface.

Another method of deploying settings is running Profile Wizard from the Office XP Resource Kit. Add the following lines to your answer file. You must also make sure that the Windows XP setup program copies Proflwiz.exe and Settings.ops to the target computer. In this case, I put both files in i386\$OEM$\$$:

```
[GuiRunOnce]
"%SYSTEMROOT%\Proflwiz.exe /r %SYSTEMROOT%\Settings.ops /q"
```

Here are three things you should consider when using [GuiRunOnce]:

- From [GuiRunOnce]you can't run programs that force Windows XP to restart. That's because Windows XP loses any entries remaining in [GuiRunOnce] when it restarts, and those command will not run. If you can't prevent the program from restarting the computer, try repackaging it as a Windows Installer package file or add it as the last command in [GuiRunOnce]. This isn't an issue for any of the commands I've given you that add registry settings.

- Any program that relies on Windows Explorer will not work properly because Windows Explorer is not running when the commands in the [GuiRunOnce] section are. Again, you can consider repackaging these applications.

- If you're trying to install Windows Installer package files from [GuiRunOnce], you must use the /wait command-line option to ensure that two packages don't try to install at the same time. Otherwise, both packages fail. This is an issue only when installing Windows Installer packages using Setup.exe, however, because Setup.exe launches Windows Installer and then returns, allowing the next package to begin installing immediately. If you install Windows Installer packages using Msiexec (the Windows Installer command-line interface) instead, this problem isn't an issue.

Tip   The commands in the [GuiRunOnce] section run asynchronously, which means that they could potentially all run at the same time. If you'd rather run commands synchronously—one at a time—create a batch file that runs the program using the Start command's /wait command-line option. The syntax is Start /wait *program*, where *program* is the path and name of the program file. The /wait command-line option prevents the Start program from returning control to the batch file until *program* finishes. Then run this batch file from [GuiRunOnce].

Cmdlines.txt

The file Cmdlines.txt contains commands that the GUI-mode portion of the setup program runs when installing optional components, including applications the setup program must install immediately after installing Windows XP. The commands in Cmdlines.txt run as a system service, so they run with elevated privileges. You put Cmdlines.txt in the OEM subfolder of the Windows XP distribution folder. You put the same kinds of commands in Cmdlines.txt that you'd put in [GuiRunOnce]. You also have to use the OEM folder to copy data files, such as REG files, INF files, and scripts, to the target computer.

The format of Cmdlines.txt is simple. It has a single section called [Commands], followed by zero or more commands. Enclosing each command in quotation marks is a good idea if the command contains spaces. Here's a sample that imports a REG file called Settings.reg and installs an INF file called Config.inf, assuming that I added both files to OEM\$$ in the distribution folder:

```
[Commands]
"regedit.exe %SYSTEMROOT%\Settings.reg /s"
"rundll32.exe setupapi,InstallHinfSection DefaultInstall 132"\
" %SYSTEMROOT%\Config.inf"
```

Using Cmdlines.txt is different than [GuiRunOnce] in some important aspects, though:

- You must create the OEM distribution folders, and you must set OEMPreinstall=Yes in your answer file.

- When the setup program runs the command in Cmdlines.txt, no user is logged on to Windows XP, and for that matter, no network connection is guaranteed. As a result, Windows XP stores settings in the default user hive file so all users receive the same settings.

- You can't install Windows Installer packages using Cmdlines.txt.

Logging On Automatically After Installation

If you're using the [GuiRunOnce] section to deploy settings or run programs after installing Windows XP, you'll want to automatically log on to the operating system immediately after installation is finished. On top of that, you'll likely want to log on as local Administrator to install applications that require elevated privileges or change settings in HKLM that restricted users can't change. For that, use the AutoLogon setting in the [GuiUnattended] section of your answer file. Set AutoLogon=Yes. This sets the value AutoAdminLogon in the key HKLM\Software \Microsoft\Windows\CurrentVersion\WinLogon, which you learn about in Chapter 15, "Working Around IT Problems."

You must also set AutoLogonCount in the [GuiUnattended] section. This setting specifies the number of times you want to automatically log on to Windows XP as local Administrator. This sets the value AutoLogonCount in the key HKLM\Software\Microsoft\Windows \CurrentVersion\WinLogon. Normally, you'd log on to Windows XP only one time by setting AutoLogonCount=1. However, you can log on to the operating system as many times as necessary, such as when a setup programs restarts the computer in the middle of the installation process. The following lines show you the settings necessary to use this feature:

```
[GuiUnattended]
AutoLogon=Yes
AutoLogonCount=1

[GuiRunOnce]
"regedit %SYSTEMROOT%\Settings.reg /s"
```

When you set a password using the AdminPassword setting in the [GuiUnattended] section, Windows XP uses that password to log the local Administrator on to it. However, if you encrypt the password and set EncryptedAdminPassword=Yes, Windows XP disables this feature. It's a trade off between security and deployment convenience. Don't panic, though; when Windows XP finishes installing, it removes the password from any local copies of the answer file, such as %SYSTEMROOT%\System32\$winnt$.sif.

Cloning Disks with Sysprep

Disk imaging entails taking a snapshot of a computer's configuration, which includes Microsoft Windows XP and applications such as those in Microsoft Office XP, and then deploying that snapshot to other computers in the organization. It's essentially like installing Windows XP on a computer's hard disk and then copying that hard disk to other computers. Use disk imaging to deploy clean Windows XP installations in large organizations when hundreds of computers require the same configuration. Disk imaging is more effective when organizations have standard hardware configurations, but with a tweak here and there, it is a method that can be used in companies that tend to purchase the computer *du jour*.

Even though I say that disk imaging is for large organizations, I use it in my small 10-PC shop. It's more convenient and much quicker to install Windows XP from a disk image than by running the setup program from scratch. This is a major productivity boost for me because I install Windows XP a dozen times a week.

Disk imaging has two personalities: good and bad (no ugly). First the good: Disk imaging is the fastest way to deploy Windows XP. Rather than installing the operating system from the CD, which can take up to 45 minutes, a disk image installs in less than 10 minutes. And with multicasting technologies, you can deploy disk images to many computers at the same time. Possibly the biggest benefit of disk imaging is that you can include third-party applications and custom settings to standardize desktop computers throughout the enterprise, and you do all that without requiring user interaction. Now for the bad: You can't use disk imaging to upgrade from an earlier version of Windows because you're replacing the hard disk's contents. That means users' documents, settings, and applications are lost unless you use the User State Migration Tool that's on the Windows XP CD.

Also, disk imaging requires somewhat compatible sample and target hardware configurations, although you can mitigate this issue a bit using the techniques you learn in this chapter. An additional concern is that multicasting can bring a network to its knees, so you must manage the rollout so that it doesn't affect the productivity of users. The last problem is that deploying disk images to remote computers is difficult—but it's not impossible if you can fit the images on CDs.

The benefits of disk imaging far outweigh the potential problems, particularly in large enterprises. Disk imaging got better with Windows XP than it was with Microsoft Windows 2000; new Windows XP disk-imaging tools significantly reduce the number of disk images that you maintain now. Microsoft's Web site is full of case studies of companies that have reduced their image count by 60 percent. One company reduced its image count from 50 with Windows 2000 to one with Windows XP. That's impressive! This chapter shows you how to reap those benefits for yourself. After I introduce you to disk imaging, I'll focus on how the registry fits in to the disk imaging process.

Cloning Windows XP

The best way to understand disk imaging is to walk through the entire process; you'll learn more about this process later in this chapter, though (see Figure 13-1 as you're working through these steps):

1. Install Windows XP on the sample computer.

   Install the operating system from a fully customized distribution folder, as you learned in Chapter 12, "Deploying with Answer Files." Doing so ensures that you can regression test your disk images after fixing problems. Do not join the computer to a domain; just join a workgroup.

2. Log on to the computer as Administrator, and do any of the following:

   - Install and customize each application you want to include in the disk image. For example, install Office XP. As a rule, don't customize per-user settings on a disk image; save those for a network-based default user profile (see Chapter 10, "Deploying User Profiles").

   - Install any third-party device drivers that are not included in Drivers.cab, the file in which Microsoft distributes the Windows XP device drivers, and that you didn't add to your distribution folders.

3. Customize the %SYSTEMDRIVE%\Sysprep folder.

   Copy Sysprep.exe and Setupcl.exe to this folder. Also, copy the Sysprep.inf file, which you build ahead of time. Sysprep.inf automates Mini-Setup Wizard, a stripped-down version of the full setup program that runs when users start a computer to which you've deployed the disk image. I'll tell you where to get these files in the next section.

4. Run Sysprep.exe, select the Mini-Setup check box, and then click Reseal.

If the computer is ACPI-compliant, Sysprep automatically shuts down the PC; otherwise, turn off the computer when you see a message that says it's safe to shut down the computer.

5. Clone the disk to an image file.

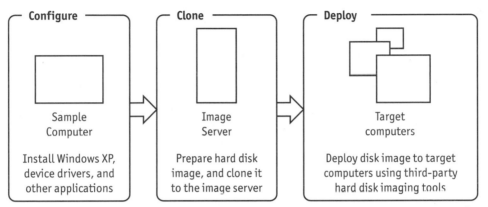

Figure 13-1 *Using disk imaging, you deploy the contents of a sample computer's hard disk to many other computers' hard disks. It's an effective way to deploy many desktops.*

After you deploy the disk image to users' computers and they turn them on, Mini-Setup Wizard starts. First the wizard detects the computers' Plug and Play devices. Then the wizard prompts users to accept the license agreement, type their name and organization, join a domain or workgroup, specify regional options, configure TAPI, and choose the networking protocols and services to install. The wizard can skip some or all of these settings if you configure them in Sysprep.inf. Last, Mini-Setup Wizard removes %SYSTEMDRIVE% \Sysprep and restarts the computer. The whole process takes less than five minutes.

Before we move on to actual techniques, I'm going to introduce you to the tools necessary for doing the job. You'll find everything you need for preparing disk images on Windows XP's CD. The following sections describe these tools, their limitations, and a list of third-party disk imaging suites to evaluate. (Third-party tools are necessary to duplicate disk images after you prepare them.)

Windows XP Tools

Disk imaging has two phases: preparing the disk image and cloning the disk image. All the tools you need for preparing a disk image are on the Windows XP CD in the Deploy.cab file. This file is in the Support\Tools folder; extract its contents by opening the file in Windows Explorer. The disk imaging tools in Deploy.cab include:

- **Sysprep.exe.**   Prepares the disk for duplication by configuring Windows XP so that Setupcl.exe runs the next time it starts.

- **Setupcl.exe.**   Regenerates the computer's security identifier (SID) because every computer on the network must have a unique SID. It also starts Mini-Setup Wizard to configure Windows XP on the computer.

- **Sysprep.inf.**   Automates Mini-Setup Wizard by providing settings for users.

The tools are a given, but I'm jazzed about the documentation in the file Deploy.cab—it's a huge improvement over the deployment documentation for Windows 2000. First Ref.chm describes how to build answer files and includes a reference that describes all the settings you can use. Second Deploy.chm describes how to use the disk imaging tools in Deploy.cab. It also contains a complete reference for all the settings you can use in answer files. This is the resource from which you're going to learn the most about disk imaging.

Sysprep Limitations

Due to the nature of disk imaging—copying a hard disk's image to other computers—Sysprep has a few requirements (call them limitations if you like):

- The sample and target computers must have the identical hardware abstraction layers (HALs). For example, a disk image created on a computer using a single processor HAL is not compatible with one that uses a multiprocessor HAL.

- The sample and target computers must have compatible BIOS types. For example, a disk image created on a computer with an ACPI BIOS is not compatible with a computer that has an APM BIOS. A disk image created using an APM BIOS is often compatible with a computer that has an ACPI BIOS, though.

- The target computer's hard disk must be the same size or larger than the sample computer's hard disk. If the target computer's hard disk is larger, you can set ExtendOEMPartition in Sysprep.inf to extend the disk image to the end of the disk. The Sysprep.inf sample on the facing page shows an example of using this setting to extend a partition.

- Sysprep only prepares the disk image; it doesn't clone the disk. Thus, to deploy the disk image, you'll have to use a third-party disk imaging product. The sidebar "Third-Party Disk Imaging Suites," on the facing page, gives you choices to evaluate. My preference is Symantec Ghost, but there are many good products.

Windows XP's documentation also says that the mass-storage controllers (IDE, SCSI, and the like) must be identical on the sample and target computers. This isn't so if you tell Sysprep in advance about the mass-storage controllers you're anticipating. For more information, see the section titled, "Reducing Image Count," later in this chapter. I've had good luck building images using one mass-storage controller and deploying to computers with completely different mass-storage controllers.

The sample and target computers' remaining devices do not have to be the same. That includes Plug and Play devices, such as modems, sound cards, network cards, video adapters, and so on. If you anticipate devices for which Windows XP doesn't include native support (the device doesn't have a driver in Drivers.cab), you should include those device drivers in your image so that Mini-Setup Wizard can detect and install them during installation. This usually includes devices that come to market after Windows XP. Chapter 12, "Deploying with Answer Files," describes how to deploy third-party device drivers with Windows XP.

Tip   Often, device drivers that you download from a vendor's Web site aren't suitable for deployment. They install from package files, so you can't easily extract the device driver files and then figure out which files are necessary and which aren't. You can almost always get the latest device drivers from Windows Update, though, and these device drivers are in a suitable format for deployment through an answer file and on a disk image. The trick is to use the Windows Update Catalog. In Internet Explorer, click Tools, Windows Update. In the Web page's left pane, click Personalize Windows Update. In the right pane, select Display The Link To The Windows Update Catalog under See Also, and click Save Settings. Now you'll see the Windows Update Catalog link in left pane of the Windows Update Web site, and you can search for and download device drivers that are packaged and ready for deployment.

Third-Party Disk Imaging Suites

Sysprep only prepares disks for duplication; it doesn't clone them. Thus, you're going to need a third-party tool to deploy disk images. A small selection of the tools with which I'm familiar includes the following:

- **Symantec Ghost.**   *http://www.symantec.com*
- **Altiris eXpress 5.**   *http://www.altiris.com*
- **Phoenix ImageCast.**   *http://www.it-infusion.com*
- **PowerQuest DeployCenter.**   *http://www.powerquest.com*

Symantec Ghost is at the top of the list because it's the tool that I know best and the one I use most often. It's a robust disk imaging tool that does much more than just clone disk images. For example, you can deploy a disk image to a remote computer without ever getting up from your desk. You can use it to manage configurations, too, not just disk images. When I talk to administrators around the world, this is the tool that 90 percent of them use, whereas the other tools tend to have a small but loyal following. Regardless, the disk imaging process is roughly the same with all these tools, and most of them are high quality.

Building a Disk Image

You got the overview earlier in this chapter. Now it's time for some detail.

The first step is to configure a sample computer, and you start the ball rolling by installing Windows XP. Don't just drop the Windows XP CD in the drive and install the operating system manually, however. If you find an error in your disk image, you're likely to repeat it or introduce different errors because you're using a manual process. (Picture playing Whack-a-Mole.) Instead, install Windows XP from a fully customized distribution folder. Chapter 12, "Deploying with Answer Files," describes how to customize the distribution folders so that Windows XP installs without any user interaction. Just make sure that your answer file joins a workgroup and not a domain because Sysprep will remove the computer from the domain anyway and you don't want the extra junk in the registry.

Next install the applications you want to include in your disk image. Include only applications that you want to install on every computer to which you deploy the disk image. For example, include Office XP and your antivirus software, but don't include line of business applications that only one department uses if you want to use that disk image for other departments. I don't like to install applications manually for the same reasons that I don't like to install Windows XP manually: regression testing. Instead, install Windows Installer-based applications from fully customized administrative installations. Install other applications using any quiet mode switches they provide or consider repackaging them as Windows Installer packages, which you can install without interaction. After you automate each application's installation, you can easily install each from your Windows XP answer file.

Tip   Whether it's superstition or has some basis in fact, I usually build custom computers for the express purpose of building disk images. I use the most generic hardware I can find and I leave out any unnecessary devices (sound cards, and so on). My thinking, and what I want to pass on to you, is that by using generic hardware, I have a better chance of producing a disk image that works on many different configurations. The goal, of course, is to manage fewer disk images.

Customizing Mini-Setup

Sysprep.inf automates Mini-Setup Wizard. In other words, the wizard avoids prompting users for settings that you provide in Sysprep.inf. If your goal is a 100-percent automated installation, you'll want to create a robust Sysprep.inf. Completely automating Mini-Setup Wizard can be difficult in three cases, though:

- **User name.**   You can provide a user name, such as *Valued Microsoft Employee* in Sysprep.inf, or you can allow the wizard to prompt users for their names.

- **Computer name.** This is the toughest of all to automate. You can accept the random computer names that Mini-Setup Wizard generates when you set ComputerName=* in Sysprep.inf, or you can allow the wizard to prompt users for a computer name. This is one of the reasons that many organizations send technicians to desktops to install Windows XP. Alternatively, you can accept the random computer name and then change the name after installation using scripts. The TechNet Script Center provides Windows Script Host scripts for renaming computers and joining them to domains, and you can run these scripts from Sysprep.inf. See Chapter 12, "Deploying with Answer Files," to learn how to run programs after Windows XP finishes installation. The Script Center is at *www.microsoft.com/technet/ /scriptcenter/default.asp.*

- **Joining a domain.** To automatically join a domain, you must provide domain administrator credentials in your answer file. But, grrrr, they are plain text. (Documentation that says you can encrypt the domain Administrator password is inaccurate.) One solution is to create a domain account with just enough rights and permissions to join computers to the domain and then use those credentials in the answer file. Otherwise, you can delegate ownership of computers to users so that they can join their own computers to the domain. You can also use the scripts from the TechNet Script Center to automatically join computers to domains after Windows XP finishes installing.

The remaining settings in a typical Sysprep.inf file will be easy to understand because you already learned about answer files in Chapter 12, "Deploying with Answer Files." The ultimate reference is Ref.chm in Deploy.cab, however. Microsoft's documentation is full of sample answer files, but Listing 13-1 on the next page shows you one that I typically use. A few notes about this listing:

- ExtendOemPartition causes Mini-Setup Wizard to extend the partition to the end of the disk, which is necessary if the target computer's hard disk is bigger than that of the sample computer.

- InstallFilesPath tells Mini-Setup Wizard where to find additional installation files, including the OEM folder, which contains a Cmdlines.txt file (more on that later).

- OemPnPDriversPath tells Mini-Setup Wizard where to find third-party device drivers that I've included in the disk image (helps reduce image count).

- ComputerName and Username are missing from this Sysprep.inf file, so Mini-Setup Wizard prompts users for both values.

- DomainAdmin and DomainAdminPassword are absent from this Sysprep.inf file, so Mini-Setup Wizard prompts users for the credentials necessary to join the computer to the domain.

- [Sysprep] and [SysprepMassStorage] help to reduce the number of disk images you must maintain. I discuss both these sections in "Reducing Image Count," later in this chapter.

Listing 13-1   Sysprep.inf

```
[Unattended]
    ExtendOemPartition=1
    InstallFilesPath=\Sysprep\i386
    OemPnPDriversPath=\Windows\Drivers
    OemPreinstall=Yes
    OemSkipEula=Yes

[GuiUnattended]
    OemSkipRegional=1
    OemSkipWelcome=1
    TimeZone=020

[UserData]
    OrgName="Jerry Honeycutt"
    ProductID=#####-#####-#####-#####-#####

[TapiLocation]
    AreaCode=972
    CountryCode=1
    Dialing=Tone

[Identification]
    JoinDomain=HONEYCUTT

[Networking]
    InstallDefaultComponents=Yes

[Sysprep]
    BuildMassStorageSection=Yes

[SysprepMassStorage]

;end
```

The easiest way to build your own Sysprep.inf file is to use a template and then edit it in Notepad. You can use the previous listing with very little modification. If you prefer, you can use Setup Manager. Chapter 12, "Deploying with Answer Files," introduced Setup Manager to you. There are a few more settings available to you in Setup Manager that this listing doesn't show, such as installing printers; thus, you might build a Sysprep.inf file using Setup Manager and then use that as your template for future jobs.

> **Note** Chapter 12, "Deploying with Answer Files," describes how to deploy settings in an answer file. It shows how to use REG files, INF files, and so on from an answer file. You can use those same methods in the Sysprep.inf file, too. Just like in any normal answer file, you can run a command in the [GuiRunOnce] section or run a command from the Cmdlines.txt file that edits the registry. Because Chapter 12 covers these topics thoroughly, I won't duplicate them here.

Preparing for Duplication

You're almost done; now you must prepare the sample computer's hard disk for duplication. On the surface, this is the easy part but, as I sometimes do, I'm going to throw a curveball. To prepare for duplication, create %SYSTEMDRIVE%\Sysprep and copy Sysprep.exe, Setupcl.exe, and the Sysprep.inf file you created to it.

That's it—now for the curveball: Fully automated disk image production is the ideal. It enables regression testing. If you can swing it (and you can with a good bit of work), you'll want to modify your Windows XP answer file so that it runs Sysprep after it installs all the applications. Here's how:

1. Create a Sysprep folder in the Windows XP distribution folder under OEM\$1 so that the setup program creates %SYSTEMDRIVE%\Sysprep for you during installation. This prevents you from having to interact with the disk image at all.

2. Add the following to the answer file you're using to build the disk image. This installs each application. The placeholders *setup1* and *setup2* are the commands necessary to install the applications you want to include on the disk image. If you prefer, you can run a batch file from the [GuiRunOnce] section, and install all the applications from that batch file. Running each setup program with no user interaction is preferable. This script quietly runs Sysprep configured to use Mini-Setup Wizard, which prepares the disk for duplication:

```
[GuiRunOnce]
"setup1"
"setup2"
"%SYSTEMDRIVE%\Sysprep\Sysprep.exe -mini -quiet -reseal -forceshutdown"
```

3. Add the following to the answer file you're using to build the disk image. This automatically logs the local Administrator on to Windows XP to run the programs in [GuiRunOnce] (set AutoLogonCount to the number of times you need to log on to Windows XP to complete the installation process in [GuiRunOnce]):

```
[GuiUnattended]
    AutoLogon=Yes
    AutoLogonCount=1
```

4. In the answer file you're using to install Windows XP on the sample computer, leave the local Administrator password null: AdminPassword=*. Doing so ensures that you can change the local Administrator password in Sysprep.inf.

Cloning the Disk Image

The last step is to run Sysprep and clone the disk to an image file. If you're fully automating disk image production, this occurs automatically. Otherwise, run Sysprep manually. The following steps describe how to run Sysprep so that it prepares the disk for duplication and configures it to automate Mini-Setup Wizard:

1. Run %SYSTEMDRIVE%\Sysprep.exe.

   You see the Sysprep window shown in Figure 13-2.

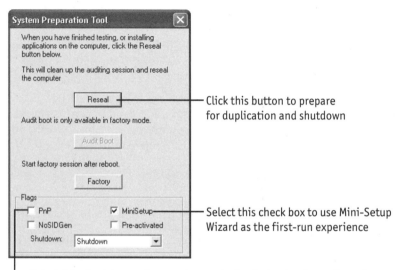

Click this button to prepare for duplication and shutdown

Select this check box to use Mini-Setup Wizard as the first-run experience

Select this check box to detect a legacy device during hardware detection

Figure 13-2   *Earlier versions of Sysprep had no user interface, so this look and feel is truly new.*

2. Select the MiniSetup check box.

   This causes Sysprep to use Mini-Setup Wizard as the first-run experience instead of Windows Welcome, which is the default. Mini-Setup Wizard is the first-run experience that you customize with Sysprep.inf.

3. Optionally, select the PnP check box.

   Do this only if you want Mini-Setup Wizard to detect legacy devices during hardware detection, which adds about 10 minutes to the installation process.

4. Click Reseal to prepare the disk for duplication, and shut down the computer.

   I'm not a fan of graphical user interfaces when there is a perfectly good command I can type at the MS-DOS command prompt. As a result, I almost always use Sysprep's command-line options instead:

```
sysprep {[-clean] | [-activated] [-audit] [-factory] [-forceshutdown] [-mini]
[-noreboot] [-nosidgen] [-pnp] [-quiet] [-reboot] [-reseal]}
```

-activated	Does not reset the grace period for Windows Product Activation. Use this option only if you have activated Windows XP in Factory mode. The product key you use to activate Windows XP must match the product key located on the COA sticker attached to that particular computer.
-audit	Reboots the computer into Factory mode without generating new SIDs or processing any items in the [OEMRunOnce] section of Winbom.ini. Use this command-line option only if the computer is already in Factory mode.
-clean	Clears the critical devices database used by the [SysprepMassStorage] section in Sysprep.inf. You learn about this setting in the section titled, "Reducing Image Count," later in this chapter.
-factory	Restarts in a network-enabled state without displaying Windows Welcome or Mini-Setup Wizard. This option is useful for updating drivers, running Plug and Play enumeration, installing applications, testing, configuring the computer with customer data, and making other configuration changes in your factory environment. For companies that use disk imaging, Factory mode can reduce the number of images required. When you have finished your desired set of tasks in Factory mode, run Sysprep with the -reseal option selected to prepare the computer for end-user delivery.
-forceshutdown	Shuts down the computer after Sysprep is complete. Use this option with a computer that has ACPI BIOS and that does not shut down properly with Sysprep's default behavior.
-mini	Configures Windows XP Professional to use Mini-Setup Wizard rather than Windows Welcome. This option has no effect on Windows XP Home Edition, in which the first-run experience is always Windows Welcome.
-noreboot	Modifies registry keys (SID, OemDuplicatorString, and so on) without the system rebooting or preparing for duplication. This option is used mainly for testing, specifically to see if the registry is modified properly. This option is not recommended because making changes to a computer after Sysprep has run can invalidate the preparation done by Sysprep. Do not use this option in a production environment.
-nosidgen	Runs Sysprep without generating new SIDs. You must use this option if you are not duplicating the computer on which you are running Sysprep or if you are pre-installing domain controllers.
-pnp	Runs the full Plug and Play device enumeration and installation during Mini-Setup Wizard. This command-line option has no effect if the first-run experience is Windows Welcome. Use -pnp only when you need to detect and install legacy, non-Plug and Play devices. Do not use sysprep -pnp on computer systems that use only Plug and Play devices. If you do, you will increase the time required for the first-run experience without providing any additional benefit to the user.
-quiet	Runs Sysprep without displaying onscreen confirmation messages. This is useful if you are automating Sysprep. Select this option if you plan to run Sysprep immediately following installation, for example.
-reboot	Forces the computer to automatically reboot and then start Windows Welcome, Mini-Setup Wizard, or Factory mode. This is useful when you want to audit the system and verify that the first-run experience is operating correctly.
-reseal	Clears the Event Viewer logs and prepares the computer for delivery to the customer. Windows Welcome or Mini-Setup Wizard is set to start at the next boot. If you run the command sysprep -factory, you must seal the installation as the last step in your pre-installation process, either by running the command sysprep -reseal or by clicking Reseal in the Sysprep window.

After you've prepared the disk for duplication, use your third-party disk imaging product to clone the disk to an image file. For example, with Symantec Ghost, the product I know and love, you run the Ghost Multicast client on the sample computer to transfer the disk image to the Ghost Multicast server on another computer. This is the simplistic way to clone a disk image, though. The product gets more complicated when you configure disk images so that you can deploy them remotely. In the case of Symantec Ghost, you use the Ghost Enterprise Console to manage and deploy images. For more information, see your vendor's documentation.

Tip   Sysprep doesn't always shut down the computer properly. Sometimes it just reboots the computer. If Mini-Setup Wizard starts, however, you can't use the image. To prevent a surprise reboot, stick a blank floppy disk in drive A before running Sysprep so if the computer does restart, the computer will boot from the floppy disk and Mini-Setup Wizard won't run.

Reducing Image Count

I'm getting to the meat in this section: how to reduce the number of images that you manage, and how the registry fits into that process. To reduce image count, you have to make sure that Windows XP starts on each hardware configuration because Windows XP must start before Mini-Setup Wizard can. Without additional effort on your part, this isn't always possible. Windows XP only knows about the devices installed on the sample computer, and if the target computer has different boot hardware (mass-storage controllers and system devices), it won't start.

The secret is to tell Windows XP about the other boot hardware you expect it to encounter when you deploy the operating system. I'll show you the hard way first, which is to manually customize the Sysprep.inf file's [SysprepMassStorage] section, and then I'll show you the easy way, which is to allow Sysprep to build this section for you automatically. The manual method is what you used for Windows 2000, and you must use it with Windows XP if the operating system doesn't include native support for all the boot hardware in your organization. In either case, customizing [SysprepMassStorage] allows for the following combinations:

- **IDE to IDE.**   The sample computer uses a different IDE controller than the target computers.

- **IDE to SCSI.**   The sample computer uses an IDE controller, and the target computers use SCSI controllers.

- **SCSI to SCSI.**   The sample computer uses a different SCSI controller than the target computers.

- **SCSI to IDE.**   The sample computer uses a SCSI controller, and the target computers use IDE controllers.

Note   When deploying disk images to computers that use SCSI controllers, the target computers' hard disks must support the extended INT13 BIOS functions. They must be able to start using a Boot.ini file that uses the `multi()` syntax in lieu of the `scsi()` or `signature()` syntax. To ensure the use of the `multi()` syntax, add `AddBiosToBoot` to your answer file.

Filling SysprepMassStorage Manually

To fill the [`SysprepMassStorage`] section, you need to dig up the Plug and Play ID for each boot device on the target computers. There's a few ways to get this ID. One is to look for it in the INF files that come with Windows XP. Search %SYSTEMROOT%\Inf for the name of the device, look in the INF file that you find, and record the device's ID as well as the name of the INF file in which you found it. For example, if I'm deploying a disk image to computers that have the Intel 82801BA Bus Master IDE Controller, I'd look in Mshdc.inf to get its Plug and Play ID, which is `PCI\VEN_8086&DEV_244A`. All your hits will be in Machine.inf, Scsi.inf, Pnpscsi.inf, and Mshdc.inf.

After you've identified boot devices, add them to your Sysprep.inf file in the [`SysprepMassStorage`] section. The following listing shows the format. *PNPID* is the device's Plug and Play ID, and *INF* is the path and file name of the INF file that contains the Plug and Play ID of the device.

```
[SysprepMassStorage]
PNPID = INF
```

Here's an excerpt from a Sysprep.inf file that I used recently:

```
[SysprepMassStorage]
Primary_IDE_Channel=%SYSTEMROOT%\Inf\Mshdc.inf
Secondary_IDE_Channel=%SYSTEMROOT%\Inf\Mshdc.inf
PCI\VEN_8086&DEV_1222=%SYSTEMROOT%\Inf\Mshdc.inf
PCI\VEN_8086&DEV_1230=%SYSTEMROOT%\Inf\Mshdc.inf
PCI\VEN_8086&DEV_7010=%SYSTEMROOT%\Inf\Mshdc.inf
PCI\VEN_8086&DEV_7111=%SYSTEMROOT%\Inf\Mshdc.inf
PCI\VEN_8086&DEV_2411=%SYSTEMROOT%\Inf\Mshdc.inf
PCI\VEN_8086&DEV_2421=%SYSTEMROOT%\Inf\Mshdc.inf
PCI\VEN_8086&DEV_2441=%SYSTEMROOT%\Inf\Mshdc.inf
PCI\VEN_8086&DEV_244A=%SYSTEMROOT%\Inf\Mshdc.inf
```

If Windows XP doesn't provide native support for a boot device, you use a different format. First copy the device driver's files to a folder on the disk image. The easiest way is to add them to the Windows XP distribution folder OEM\$$\Drivers so that the setup program automatically copies them to %SYSTEMROOT%\Drivers on the sample computer. Then add lines to the [`SysprepMassStorage`] section that look like the following listing. *PNPID* is the Plug and Play ID of the device. *INF* is the path and file name of the INF file that contains the Plug and Play ID, such as %SYSTEMROOT%\Drivers*Filename*.inf. *DIR* is the name of the directory on the floppy disk that contains the device driver. *DESC* is a description of the disk as specified in the Txtsetup.oem file, and *TAG* is the disk tag as specified in the Txtsetup.oem file. The last three items are optional.

```
PNPID = INF[, DIR[, DESC[, TAG]]]
```

Filling SysprepMassStorage Automatically

New for Windows XP is the ability to automatically build the Sysprep.inf file's `[SysprepMassStorage]` section. By adding the lines that you see in the following listing to your Sysprep.inf file, Sysprep extracts all the Plug and Play IDs from Machine.inf, Scsi.inf, Pnpscsi.inf, and Mshdc.inf and adds the appropriate entries. Make sure that you leave the `[SysprepMassStorage]` section empty, and double-check your spelling of `BuildMassStorageSection`. (I've spent hours troubleshooting a file in which I misspelled the name of this setting.)

```
[Sysprep]
    BuildMassStorageSection=Yes

[SysprepMassStorage]
```

Note When you build the `[SysprepMassStorage]` section automatically, Sysprep takes much longer to run. Rather than shutting down the computer after a few seconds, which is Sysprep's typical behavior, Sysprep grinds away for about 15 minutes while it builds this section. Be patient as long as you see hard disk activity and a spinning hourglass. Reducing image count is worth the wait.

Cleaning Up After Sysprep

You're not finished yet. Sysprep adds the devices in the `[SysprepMassStorage]` section to Windows XP's critical device's database. This database is in the registry at `HKLM\SYSTEM \CurrentControlSet\Control\CriticalDeviceDatabase`. Each subkey corresponds to a device you added to `[SysprepMassStorage]` and contains a link to the actual device driver in the registry. Windows XP tries to start each device in the database every time it boots. The problem is that this increases boot time significantly—something you don't want to inflict on users.

Don't I always have a solution? On each target computer, run `sysprep.exe -clean -quiet`. This command disables all the devices that Windows XP didn't find when it started. The next time the operating system starts, it doesn't try to start device drivers for those devices that it didn't find. The trick is when to run this command. You don't do it when you build the image. Instead, you run the command during Mini-Setup Wizard. Add the command to the Cmdlines.txt file that you create in %SYSTEMDRIVE%\Sysprep \i386\OEM. The file looks like this (make sure that `InstallFilesPath` points to the folder containing the OEM folder, which is usually %SYSTEMDRIVE%\Sysprep\i386, and you set OemPreinstall=Yes):

```
[Commands]
"%SYSTEMDRIVE%\Sysprep\Sysprep.exe -clean -quiet"
```

Mapping Sysprep Settings

When you run Sysprep, it modifies hundreds if not thousands of registry settings to prepare the computer's hard disk for duplication. Table 13-1 on the next page describes the settings that relate directly to Sysprep. These are settings that prepare Mini-Setup Wizard to run the next time Windows XP starts. I tracked these down by comparing snapshots of the registry before and after running Sysprep. I divided this table into sections, with each key in a different section.

Sysprep changes other settings that I don't describe in Table 13-1. The settings that it changes depend on the computer's configuration. For example, it disables Remote Desktop and Remote Assistance. It configures System Restore to create an initial system checkpoint the next time Windows XP starts. It also resets the computer's digital ID and resets the Windows Product Activation timer. Last, if you're using [SysprepMassStorage], Sysprep fills the critical devices database and configures the device drivers for each device. The changes that Sysprep makes to the registry are numerous, but the following list summarizes some of the most significant that I found while sniffing out the changes that it makes:

- Sysprep resets the event system. These settings are in HKLM\SOFTWARE\Microsoft \EventSystem.

- Sysprep removes certificate templates and certificates from the keys HKLM\SOFTWARE \Microsoft\Cryptography and HKLM\SOFTWARE\Microsoft\EnterpriseCertificates.

- Sysprep resets the configuration of Group Policy in the key HKLM\SOFTWARE\Microsoft \Windows\CurrentVersion\Group Policy.

- Sysprep removes the computer from the domain, if it's a domain member, by deleting the appropriate values from the keys HKLM\SOFTWARE\Microsoft\Windows NT \CurrentVersion\Winlogon, HKLM\SOFTWARE\Microsoft\Windows NT\CurrentVersion \Winlogon\DomainCache, and elsewhere.

- Sysprep removes policies from the key HKLM\SOFTWARE\Policies.

- Sysprep removes networking components from the keys HKLM\SYSTEM \CurrentControlSet\Control, HKLM\SYSTEM\CurrentControlSet\Enum, and HKLM\SYSTEM\CurrentControlSet\Services.

- Sysprep resets the application compatibility data in HKLM\SYSTEM\CurrentControlSet \Control\Session Manager\AppCompatibility.

- Sysprep resets power management settings in the key HKLM\SYSTEM\ControlSet001 \Control\Session Manager\Power.

- Sysprep configures the Netlogon service to load on demand instead of automatically in HKLM\SYSTEM\CurrentControlSet\Services\Netlogon.

- Sysprep adds the devices specified in [SysprepMassStorage] to the critical devices database. This database is in the key HKLM\SYSTEM\CurrentControlSet\Control \CriticalDeviceDatabase.

- Sysprep installs and configures device drivers for the devices listed in the [SysprepMassStorage] section. It configures these device drivers in the key HKLM\SYSTEM\CurrentControlSet\Services.

Table 13-1   Sysprep Registry Settings

Value	Type	Description
HKLM\SOFTWARE\Microsoft\Sysprep		
SidsGenerated	REG_DWORD	Sysprep sets this value to 0x01, indicating that it removed the computer's SID and Setupcl.exe will regenerate it.
CriticalDevicesInstalled	REG_DWORD	Sysprep sets this value to 0x01, indicating that it created the critical devices database.
HKLM\SOFTWARE\Microsoft\Windows\CurrentVersion\Setup		
SourcePath	REG_DWORD	Sysprep sets this to the value of InstallFilesPath in Sysprep.inf, which indicates to the setup program where to find installation files.
HKLM\SOFTWARE\Microsoft\Windows\CurrentVersion\Setup\OOBE		
RunWelcomeProcess	REG_DWORD	Sysprep sets this value to 0x00, which disables the Windows Welcome out-of-box experience.
HKLM\SYSTEM\CurrentControlSet\Control\Lsa\Kerberos\SidCache		
MachineSid	REG_BINARY	Sysprep deletes this value to remove the computer's SID.
HKLM\SYSTEM\CurrentControlSet\Control\Session Manager		
SetupExecute	REG_MULTI_SZ	Setup adds Setupcl.exe to this value. This runs Setupcl.exe when Windows XP restarts so that Setupcl.exe can regenerate the computer's SID and run Mini-Setup Wizard.
HKLM\SYSTEM\Setup		
BootDiskSig	REG_DWORD	Sysprep stores the signature of the boot disk in this value.
CloneTag	REG_MULTI_SZ	Sysprep stores the date and time that you ran the prepared disk in this value.
Cmdline	REG_SZ	Sysprep stores the setup command line setup -newsetup -mini in this value. This is the command that runs Mini-Setup Wizard.
MiniSetupInProgress	REG_DWORD	Sysprep sets this value to 0x01, indicating that Mini-Setup Wizard is in the process of running.
SetupType	REG_DWORD	Sysprep sets this value to 0x01.
SystemSetupInProgress	REG_DWORD	Sysprep Sets this value to 0x01.

Keeping Perspective

In this chapter, I've given you enough information to start testing Sysprep in your lab straightaway. Sysprep is even a great tool for those power users who install Windows XP over and over again. But I haven't told you enough about Sysprep for you to build an image and start blasting it at an enterprise's desktops.

There's much more to Sysprep than just writing a few answer files and running Sysprep.exe. Considerations include everything from defining preferred configurations to licensing to whether you've configured your routers for multicast. Disk imaging is a part of an overall deployment plan, which includes hardware and software inventories, migration plans, configuration plans, and much more. Microsoft has several resources available to help you plan large-scale deployments using disk imaging techniques. To learn more about these important resources, contact your Microsoft account manager, who'd be happy to tell you about them. The ultimate resource for online deployment information is the Desktop Deployment Resource Center at *www.microsoft.com /windowsxp/officexp/deploy/default.asp.*

Microsoft Office XP User Settings

Microsoft Office XP is extremely flexible and highly customizable. Users can customize Office XP through its settings, custom templates, tools, and much more. For example, an accounting department can create custom templates for expense reports, and IT professionals can create custom dictionaries that contain computer terminology and product names. Users can customize everything from how their toolbars look to the file formats for saving documents. Almost all these settings are in the registry.

IT professionals can customize user settings and distribute standard Office XP configurations to all users. First install Office XP on a sample computer, and then customize the toolbars, settings, templates, dictionaries, and any other options for each program. Run Profile Wizard to create a profile settings file (OPS file) that contains all these settings. If you add the OPS file to a transform (MST file), your customized settings are included when you install Office XP on client computers. Custom Installation Wizard is the tool you use to build MST files. It enables you to customize settings directly in the MST file without an OPS file. You can also use it to set user options and edit registry entries.

Profile Wizard and Custom Installation Wizard are part of the Office XP Resource Kit, which you can find in the ORK folder on any Office XP Enterprise Edition CD. You can also download it from *http://www.microsoft.com/office/ork*. Because the resource kit's tools are covered comprehensively in the resource kit book, I won't go into detail about them. Instead, I'll focus on how to use these tools to deploy user settings, which are essentially registry settings. And if you're interested in learning about specific Office XP settings, including Office XP policies, and where you find them in the registry, see Part IV, "Appendices."

> **Tip**   Most of the tools in the Office XP Resource Kit are useful for more than just deploying Office XP. For example, you can deploy settings for any program using Profile Wizard, and you can customize other Microsoft Windows Installer–based applications with Custom Installation Wizard. For that matter, you can use Profile Wizard to customize Windows XP if you're prone to frequent reinstallation.

Profile Wizard

Profile Wizard saves and restores Office XP user settings, which are in the Office XP portion of users' profiles (see Chapter 10, "Deploying User Profiles"). When you run Profile Wizard to save a user profile, you create an OPS file that you can use later to restore those settings. The Office XP Resource Kit installs Profile Wizard on the Start menu. Click Start, All Programs, Microsoft Office Tools, Microsoft Office XP Resource Kit Tools, and then click Profile Wizard. The program file Proflwiz.exe is in C:\Program Files\ORKTools \ORK10\Tools.

By default, Profile Wizard uses the file OPW10adm.ini to decide which settings and files to include in an OPS file. This file is essentially a big list of settings and files. This file also indicates which settings and files will be purposely excluded from an OPS file. The default OPW10adm.ini file is for Office XP; it nabs most Office XP settings from the registry and takes files from the user profile folder. It excludes settings that shouldn't be deployed, like user names, lists of recently used files, and so on. You can use Profile Wizard with the default OPW10adm.ini file to capture and apply Office XP settings or you can customize it to capture and deploy any settings, including settings for applications other than Office XP.

The sections following this one describe how to capture settings, apply settings, and customize settings with Profile Wizard. The following list describes Profile Wizard's command-line options:

```
proflwiz.exe [/a] [/u] [/q] [/e] [/p] [/f] [/i filename.ini] /s filename.ops |
/r filename.ops
```

/a	Starts the wizard in administrator mode (Profile Wizard). Uses the OPW10adm.ini file by default. This is the default setting if neither /a nor /u is on the command line.
/u	Starts the wizard in user mode (Save My Settings Wizard). Proflwiz.exe uses the OPW10usr.ini file if /u is present on the command line. OPW10usr.ini is available only with Office XP and not the Office XP Resource Kit.
/q	Runs the wizard in quiet mode. Runs the wizard quietly and displays no progress indicators or error messages. Use this option with either the /s or /r option but not the /p or /e option. You do not need to specify a mode of operation (/a or /u) when using the quiet mode option.
/e	Displays error messages. Displays only error messages and no progress indicators while the wizard is running. Use this option with either the /s or /r option but not with the /q option.
/p	Displays progress indicators. Displays only progress indicators and no error messages while the wizard is running. Use this option with either the /s or /r option, but not with the /q option.

/f	Displays a completion message at the end of the restore or save process. Use this option with either the /s or /r option but not with the /q option. The options /e, /p, and /f are additive. Including /e and /f in the command line displays only error messages and finish messages.
/i *filename*.ini	Specifies the INI file to use. Instructs Profile Wizard not to use the default INI file (OPW10adm.ini or OPW10usr.ini). Instead, it uses the INI file *filename*.ini to determine which settings and files to store in the OPS file.
/s *filename*.ops	Saves user configuration settings from the current computer to the OPS file *filename*.ops. The wizard displays progress indicators and error messages while it is running.
/r *filename*.ops	Restores the application settings from the specified OPS file *filename*.ops to the computer. The wizard displays progress indicators and error messages while it is running.

Note   Save My Settings Wizard in Office XP is based on Profile Wizard. It uses an INI file that saves and restores users' settings. That INI file is OPW10usr.ini. The OPS file that it creates includes personal settings and information, though, which makes it inappropriate for deployment to other users.

Customizing the Wizard

You do not need to edit Profile Wizard's INI file to include or exclude entire Office XP applications in your OPS file. On the wizard's Save Or Restore Settings page, select the check boxes next to the applications for which you want to save settings. If a setting in Office XP (or another program) that you want to capture isn't in OPW10adm.ini, you must customize OPW10adm.ini or build a new INI file to capture it in an OPS file.

Edit OPW10adm.ini in Notepad or another text editor, and then add or delete references to settings and files that you want to include or exclude. You can also run Profile Wizard from the command line with no loss in functionality. Every option available in the wizard has a corresponding command-line switch. Listing 14-1 on page 337 shows the default OPW10adm.ini file. You'll notice that it contains thorough instructions on how to customize the file. If you're capturing settings for Office XP, start with this file. If you're capturing user settings for Windows XP or another application, consider starting a new INI file using OPW10adm.ini as a reference. Make sure that your new INI file contains the [Header] section shown in listing 14-1; otherwise, Profile Wizard won't let you save the settings defined in your INI file to an OPS file. Here's an overview of what each section contains:

- **[IncludeFolderTrees].**   List the folder trees you want to include in the OPS file. Profile Wizard captures all the subfolders and files in each tree. All entries in this section must begin with one of the following tokens, which represent a subfolder in the user's profile folder: <AppData>, <Desktop>, <Favorites>, <NetHood>, <Personal>, <PrintHood>, <ProgramsMenu>, <RecentFiles>, <SendTo>, <StartMenu>, <StartupMenu>, <UserProfile>.

- **[IncludeIndividualFolders].**   List individual folders you want to include in the OPS file; the format is the same as [IncludeFolderTrees].

- **[IncludeIndividualFiles].**   List individual files you want to include in the OPS file. The format is the same as [IncludeFolderTrees].

- **[ExcludeFiles].**   List files you don't want to include in the OPS file. The format is the same as [IncludeFolderTrees] except that you can use wildcards to specify all files of a certain type.

- **[FolderTreesToRemoveToResetToDefaults].**   List the folder trees you want Profile Wizard to remove prior to restoring the settings in the OPS file. This essentially resets the application. The format is the same as [IncludeFolderTrees].

- **[IndividualFilesToRemoveToResetToDefaults].**   List individual files you want Profile Wizard to remove prior to restoring the settings in the OPS file. The format is the same as [IncludeFolderTrees].

- **[ExcludeFilesToRemoveToResetToDefaults].**   List the individual files you *don't* want Profile Wizard to remove, regardless of where they exist in the profile folder. This enables you to keep certain files within folders that you're removing through [FolderTreesToRemoveToResetToDefaults]. You can use wildcards only as the first character of the file name, and you cannot specify a path: *.doc.

- **[IncludeRegistryTrees].**   List the registry branches you want to include in the OPS file. Profile Wizard captures all the subkeys and values in each branch. Include one branch per line.

- **[IncludeIndividualRegistryKeys].**   List individual registry keys you want to include in the OPS file.

- **[IncludeIndividualRegistryValues].**   List individual registry values you want to include in the OPS files. For the default value, use a trailing backslash: HKCU \Software\. Otherwise, include the value name in each line: HKCU\Software\Value.

- **[ExcludeRegistryTrees].**   List the registry branches you want to exclude from the OPS file.

- **[ExcludeIndividualRegistryKeys].**   List the individual registry keys you want to exclude from the OPS file.

- **[ExcludeIndividualRegistryValues].**   List the individual values you want to exclude from the OPS file. The format is the same as [IncludeIndividualRegistryValues].

- **[RegistryTreesToRemoveToResetToDefaults].**   List the registry branches you want Profile Wizard to remove prior to applying the OPS file.

- **[IndividualRegistryValuesToRemoveToResetToDefaults].**   List individual values you want Profile Wizard to remove prior to applying the OPS file. The format is the same as [IncludeIndividualRegistryValues].

- **[RegistryTreesToExcludeToResetToDefaults].** List the individual registry branches you *don't* want Profile Wizard to remove when applying an OPS file. You cannot use this section if you're embedding the OPS file in a MST file. This overrides [RegistryTreesToRemoveToResetToDefaults].

- **[RegistryKeysToExcludeToResetToDefaults].** List the individual registry keys you *don't* want Profile Wizard to remove when applying the OPS file. You cannot use this section if you're embedding the OPS file in a MST file. This overrides [RegistryTreesToRemoveToResetToDefaults].

- **[RegistryValuesToExcludeToResetToDefaults].** List the individual values you *don't* want Profile Wizard to remove when applying the OPS file. You cannot use this section if you're embedding the OPS file in a MST file. This overrides [RegistryTreesToRemoveToResetToDefaults].

Listing 14-1 OPW10adm.ini

```
# Microsoft Office Save My Settings/Profile Wizard INI file

# Edit this file to change which files and registry keys are included into
# the OPS file, and/or to change what gets deleted when using the
# 'Reset to defaults before restoring settings' option.

# Syntax is documented in each section.
# All include and exclude strings are case insensitive.
# Comments are denoted with # at the beginning of the line.

# At the end of a line is a '#' followed by one or more of the following
# possible terminal symbols:
# word, xl, access, ppt, ol, pub, fp, designer, common, all
# Terminal symbols indicate which applications the line of settings belongs to.
#   "all"      indicates settings to be saved for any application.
#   "common"   indicates settings that are common among all applications.


[Header]
Version  = 10.0
Product  = Microsoft Office 10.0


# *********************** File/Folder Sections ***********************

[IncludeFolderTrees]
# List folder trees to be included into the OPS file.
# Syntax is one folder per line; no trailing backslash.
# Includes all subfolders in specified tree.
# Wildcards are not supported.
```

```
# Entries must begin with one of the following Folder tokens:
#    <AppData>, <Desktop>, <Favorites>, <NetHood>, <Personal>,
#    <PrintHood>, <ProgramsMenu>, <RecentFiles>, <SendTo>,
#    <StartMenu>, <StartupMenu>, <UserProfile>.
# Subfolder tokens of format <SubFolder_$$$$> can be embedded in lines
#    and are replaced at SAVE time by the registry data found in the $$$$
#    value of HKCU\Software\Microsoft\Office\10.0\Common\General.
<AppData>\Microsoft\<SubFolder_AddIns>              # xl word
<AppData>\Microsoft\ClipGallery                     # ppt
<AppData>\Microsoft\Excel                           # xl
<AppData>\Microsoft\FrontPage                       # fp
<AppData>\Microsoft\Graph                           # all
<AppData>\Microsoft\Office                          # common
<AppData>\Microsoft\Outlook                         # ol
<AppData>\Microsoft\PowerPoint                      # ppt
<AppData>\Microsoft\<SubFolder_Proof>               # common all
<AppData>\Microsoft\<SubFolder_Queries>             # xl access
<AppData>\Microsoft\<SubFolder_Signatures>          # ol
<AppData>\Microsoft\<SubFolder_Stationery>          # ol
<AppData>\Microsoft\<SubFolder_Templates>           # word ppt xl
<AppData>\Microsoft\<SubFolder_Themes>              # ppt
<AppData>\Microsoft\Word                            # word
# Use the following two lines for Outlook 98:
#    <AppData>\Microsoft\Shared\<SubFolder_Signatures>    # ol
#    <AppData>\Microsoft\Shared\<SubFolder_Stationery>    # ol
# Use the following line for Web Server Locations:
#    <NetHood>                                       # fp


[IncludeIndividualFolders]
# List individual folders to be included into the OPS file.
# Syntax same as [IncludeFolderTrees] but does not include subfolders.
# Wildcards are not supported.



[IncludeIndividualFiles]
# List individual files to be included into the OPS file.
# Syntax is one path\filename per line.
# Entries must begin with one of the Folder tokens listed under
#    [IncludeFolderTrees].
# Wildcards are not supported.
#
# Example for including Normal.dot:
#    <AppData>\Microsoft\<SubFolder_Templates>\Normal.dot   # word


[ExcludeFiles]
# List files to not include into the OPS file.
# Syntax is one filename or path\filename per line.
```

```
# Folder-token (e.g. <AppData>) is optional.
# Path relative to folder-token is optional.
# Wildcards are supported in the filename.
# Wildcards are not supported in the path.
#
# Examples for excluding Normal.dot:
#   Normal.dot
#   Normal.*
#   Norm??.dot
#   <AppData>\Microsoft\<SubFolder_Templates>\Normal.dot
*.OST
*.PAB
*.PST
*.TMP
*.RWZ
*.NICK
EXTEND.DAT
OutlPrnt
<AppData>\Microsoft\Outlook\*.FAV
<AppData>\Microsoft\Word\*.ASD
<AppData>\Microsoft\Word\*.WBK


[FolderTreesToRemoveToResetToDefaults]
# List folder trees to be deleted prior to restoring data from OPS file.
# Syntax is same as [IncludeFolderTrees].
# Wildcards are not supported.
# Every file in the folder and all subfolders will be deleted.
# Use this section with caution; it might delete more than you intend.
# Terminal Symbols are ignored and treated as "all".
<AppData>\Microsoft\Office\Shortcut Bar
<AppData>\Microsoft\FrontPage


[IndividualFilesToRemoveToResetToDefaults]
# List files to be deleted prior to restoring data from OPS file.
# Syntax is one path\filename per line.
# Specify all subfolders explicitly.
# Entries must begin with one of the Folder tokens listed under
#   [IncludeFolderTrees].
# Wildcards are supported in the filename.
# Wildcards are not supported in the path.
# Terminal Symbols are ignored and treated as "all".
<AppData>\Microsoft\<SubFolder_AddIns>\*.*
<AppData>\Microsoft\ClipGallery\*.*
<AppData>\Microsoft\Excel\*.*
<AppData>\Microsoft\Excel\<SubFolder_Xlstart>\*.*
<AppData>\Microsoft\Graph\*.*
<AppData>\Microsoft\Office\*.*
```

```
<AppData>\Microsoft\Office\<SubFolder_Actors>\*.*
#    <AppData>\Microsoft\Office\<SubFolder_RecentFiles>\*.*
<AppData>\Microsoft\PowerPoint\*.*
<AppData>\Microsoft\<SubFolder_Proof>\*.*
<AppData>\Microsoft\<SubFolder_Queries>\*.*
<AppData>\Microsoft\<SubFolder_Signatures>\*.*
<AppData>\Microsoft\<SubFolder_Stationery>\*.*
<AppData>\Microsoft\<SubFolder_Templates>\*.*
<AppData>\Microsoft\<SubFolder_Themes>\*.*
<AppData>\Microsoft\Word\*.*
<AppData>\Microsoft\Word\<SubFolder_Startup>\*.*


[ExcludeFilesToRemoveToResetToDefaults]
# List of files NOT to be removed regardless of where they live when
#   resetting to defaults prior to restoring data from OPS file.
#
# Syntax is one filename per line; no preceeding path.
# Wildcards "*" and "?" are supported as the first character only.
# The following are allowed:*.DIC
#NORMAL.DOC
#?FOO.FIL
#*FILE.FOO
#*.DIC
# Terminal Symbols are ignored and treated as "all".
# Your files must not be preceeded by a path.
*.PST
*.DIC
*.OST


# **************************** Registry Sections ****************************

[SubstituteEnvironmentVariables]
# List environment variables to substitute in registry values
#   that take the data type REG_EXPAND_SZ.
# Syntax is one environment variable per line.
# Wildcards are not supported.
%USERPROFILE%
%USERNAME%


[IncludeRegistryTrees]
# List registry trees to include.
# All values and subkeys within the specified tree are included.
# Syntax is one key per line.
# Wildcards are not supported.
HKCU\Software\Microsoft\Office\10.0\Access                      # access
HKCU\Software\Microsoft\Office\10.0\Common                      # common
```

```
HKCU\Software\Microsoft\Office\10.0\Excel                          # xl
HKCU\Software\Microsoft\Office\10.0\Graph                          # all
HKCU\Software\Microsoft\Office\10.0\NetFolder                      # common
HKCU\Software\Microsoft\Office\10.0\Osa                            # common
HKCU\Software\Microsoft\Office\10.0\Outlook                        # ol
HKCU\Software\Microsoft\Office\10.0\PowerPoint                     # ppt
HKCU\Software\Microsoft\Office\10.0\Shortcut Bar                   # common
HKCU\Software\Microsoft\Office\10.0\Web Server                     # fp
HKCU\Software\Microsoft\Office\10.0\Word                           # word
HKCU\Software\Microsoft\Office\10.0\Publisher                      # pub
HKCU\Software\Microsoft\Office\10.0\ClipGallery                    # common
HKCU\Software\Microsoft\Office\Access                              # access
HKCU\Software\Microsoft\Office\Common                              # common
HKCU\Software\Microsoft\Office\Excel                               # xl
HKCU\Software\Microsoft\Office\Outlook                             # ol
HKCU\Software\Microsoft\Office\PowerPoint                          # ppt
HKCU\Software\Microsoft\Office\Word                                # word
HKCU\Software\Microsoft\FrontPage                                  # fp
HKCU\Software\Microsoft\Shared Tools\Font Mapping                  # all
HKCU\Software\Microsoft\Shared Tools\Proofing Tools               # all
HKCU\Software\Microsoft\Shared Tools\Outlook\Journaling            # ol
HKCU\Software\Microsoft\VBA\Office                                 # all
HKCU\ControlPanel\International\NumShape                           # common
HKCU\ControlPanel\International\Calendars\TwoDigitYearMax          # common
HKCU\AppEvents\Schemes\Apps\Office97                               # ol


[IncludeIndividualRegistryKeys]
# List individual registry keys to include.
# Syntax is same as [IncludeRegistryTrees] but includes only values
#   in the specified key, not subkeys.
# Wildcards are not supported.
HKCU\Software\Microsoft\Exchange\Client\Options                   # ol
HKCU\Software\Microsoft\Office\10.0\Common\LanguageResources      # common
HKCU\Software\Microsoft\VBA\Trusted                               # common


[IncludeIndividualRegistryValues]
# List individual registry values to include.
# Same as [IncludeIndividualRegistryKeys] but includes only specific named
#   value, not subkeys.
# Syntax is key\valuename.
# Wildcards are not supported.
# Name can be blank to denote the default value (use a trailing backslash).


[ExcludeRegistryTrees]
# List registry trees to exclude.
# All values and subkeys within the specified tree are excluded.
```

```
# Syntax is one key per line.
# Wildcards are not supported.
HKCU\Software\Microsoft\Office\10.0\Common\Migration                    # all


[ExcludeIndividualRegistryKeys]
# List individual registry keys to exclude.
# Syntax is same as [ExcludeRegistryTrees] but excludes only values
#   in the specified key, not subkeys.
# Wildcards are not supported.
HKCU\Software\Microsoft\Office\10.0\PowerPoint\Tips                 # all
HKCU\Software\Microsoft\Office\10.0\Common\UserInfo                 # all
HKCU\Software\Microsoft\Office\10.0\Excel\Recent Files             # all
HKCU\Software\Microsoft\Office\10.0\PowerPoint\Recent File List    # all
HKCU\Software\Microsoft\Office\Outlook\OMI Account Manager\Accounts   # all
HKCU\Software\Microsoft\FrontPage\Explorer\FrontPage Explorer\Recent File List
# all
HKCU\Software\Microsoft\FrontPage\Explorer\FrontPage Explorer\Recent Page List
# all
HKCU\Software\Microsoft\FrontPage\Explorer\FrontPage Explorer\Recent Web List
# all
HKCU\Software\Microsoft\Office\10.0\PhotoDraw\Recent File List # all


[ExcludeIndividualRegistryValues]
# List individual registry values to exclude.
# Same as [ExcludeIndividualRegistryKeys] but excludes only specific named
#   value, not subkeys.
# Syntax is key\valuename.
# Wildcards are not supported.
# Name can be blank to denote the default value (use a trailing backslash).
HKCU\Software\Microsoft\Office\10.0\Access\MRU1
HKCU\Software\Microsoft\Office\10.0\Access\MRUFlags1
HKCU\Software\Microsoft\Office\10.0\Access\MRU2
HKCU\Software\Microsoft\Office\10.0\Access\MRUFlags2
HKCU\Software\Microsoft\Office\10.0\Access\MRU3
HKCU\Software\Microsoft\Office\10.0\Access\MRUFlags3
HKCU\Software\Microsoft\Office\10.0\Access\MRU4
HKCU\Software\Microsoft\Office\10.0\Access\MRUFlags4
HKCU\Software\Microsoft\Office\10.0\Access\MRU5
HKCU\Software\Microsoft\Office\10.0\Access\MRUFlags5
HKCU\Software\Microsoft\Office\10.0\Access\MRU6
HKCU\Software\Microsoft\Office\10.0\Access\MRUFlags6
HKCU\Software\Microsoft\Office\10.0\Access\MRU7
HKCU\Software\Microsoft\Office\10.0\Access\MRUFlags7
HKCU\Software\Microsoft\Office\10.0\Access\MRU8
HKCU\Software\Microsoft\Office\10.0\Access\MRUFlags8
HKCU\Software\Microsoft\Office\10.0\Access\MRU9
HKCU\Software\Microsoft\Office\10.0\Access\MRUFlags9
```

```
HKCU\Software\Microsoft\Office\10.0\Access\Settings\Prefs Migrated
HKCU\Software\Microsoft\Office\10.0\Access\UserData
HKCU\Software\Microsoft\Office\10.0\Common\General\FirstRun
HKCU\Software\Microsoft\Office\10.0\Common\UserData
HKCU\Software\Microsoft\Office\10.0\Excel\Options\FirstRun
HKCU\Software\Microsoft\Office\10.0\Excel\Options\TipShown
HKCU\Software\Microsoft\Office\10.0\Excel\UserData
HKCU\Software\Microsoft\Office\10.0\Outlook\Setup\First-Run
HKCU\Software\Microsoft\Office\10.0\Outlook\Setup\MailSupport
HKCU\Software\Microsoft\Office\10.0\Outlook\UserData
HKCU\Software\Microsoft\office\10.0\Outlook\Journal\Item log File
HKCU\Software\Microsoft\office\10.0\Outlook\Journal\Outlook Item Log File
HKCU\Software\Microsoft\Office\10.0\PowerPoint\First Run\FirstRun
HKCU\Software\Microsoft\Office\10.0\PowerPoint\UserData
HKCU\Software\Microsoft\Office\10.0\Word\Options\FirstRun
HKCU\Software\Microsoft\Office\10.0\Word\Options\ReplyMessageComment
HKCU\Software\Microsoft\Office\10.0\Word\UserData
HKCU\Software\Microsoft\Office\10.0\Outlook\Preferences\AnnotationText
HKCU\Software\Microsoft\Office\10.0\Shortcut Bar\LocalPath
HKCU\Software\Microsoft\office\10.0\Word\Options\PROGRAMDIR
HKCU\Software\Microsoft\Office\Common\Assistant\AsstFile
HKCU\Software\Microsoft\Office\Common\Assistant\CurrAsstFile


[RegistryTreesToRemoveToResetToDefaults]
# List registry trees to be removed prior to writing custom values.
# All values and subkeys within the specified tree will be removed.
# Wildcards are not supported.
# Terminal Symbols are ignored and treated as "all".
HKCU\Software\Microsoft\Office\10.0
HKCU\Software\Microsoft\Office\Access
HKCU\Software\Microsoft\Office\Common
HKCU\Software\Microsoft\Office\Excel
HKCU\Software\Microsoft\Office\Outlook
HKCU\Software\Microsoft\Office\PowerPoint
HKCU\Software\Microsoft\Office\Word
HKCU\Software\Microsoft\FrontPage
HKCU\Software\Microsoft\Shared Tools\Proofing Tools
HKCU\Software\Microsoft\VBA\Office
#   HKCU\Software\Microsoft\Windows NT\CurrentVersion\Windows Messaging
#   Subsystem\Profiles
HKCU\Software\Microsoft\VBA\Trusted


[IndividualRegistryValuesToRemoveToResetToDefaults]
# List individual registry values to be removed prior to writing custom values.
# Syntax is key\valuename.
# Wildcards are not supported.
# Valuename can be blank to denote the default value (use a trailing backslash).
```

```
# Terminal Symbols are ignored and treated as "all".


[RegistryTreesToExcludeToResetToDefaults]
# List individual registry trees that will not be removed when resetting to
# defaults.
# All values and subkeys within the specified tree will be ignored.
# Wildcards are not supported.
# Terminal symbols are ignored and treated as "all".
# This section cannot be used if the OPS file is used for custom setup in a
# transform.


[RegistryKeysToExcludeToResetToDefaults]
# List individual registry keys that will not be removed when resetting to
# defaults.
# All values within the specified tree will be ignored.
# Wildcards are not supported.
# Terminal symbols are ignored and treated as "all".
# This section cannot be used if the OPS file is used for custom setup in a
# transform.


[RegistryValuesToExcludeToResetToDefaults]
# List individual registry values that will not be removed when resetting to
# defaults.
# Wildcards are not supported.
# Only excludes only specific values, not subkeys.
# Terminal symbols are ignored and treated as "all".
# Syntax is key\valuename.
# Name can be blank to denote the default value (use a trailing backslash).
# This section cannot be used if the OPS file is used for custom setup in a
# transform.
```

Capturing Settings

Before creating an OPS file, you must start each Office XP program on a sample computer and set all the options you want to capture in the file. The most interesting settings are on each program's Tools menu. To customize toolbars and menus, click Customize on the Tools menu. To configure user settings, click Options on the Tools menu. After you've customized each program, run Profile Wizard to save the settings to an OPS file. If you're creating an OPS file based on an INI file you created for a different application, customize that application, instead.

There are two ways to capture the settings defined in your INI file. You can run Profile Wizard from the Start menu. This is interactive and sometimes a bit confusing if you're using this tool for an application other than Office XP. You can also run Profile Wizard from the MS-DOS command prompt:

```
proflwiz /i filename.ini /s filename.ops /q
```

Replace *filename.ini* with the name of the INI file that you customized. If you're using the default OPW10adm.ini file, you don't need to specify an INI file (just make sure it's in the same folder as Proflwiz.exe). Replace *filename.ops* with the name of the OPS file in which you want to store settings form the current profile. The following steps describe how to save settings to an OPS file:

1. Run Profile Wizard, and then click Next.

2. On the Save Or Restore Settings page, shown in Figure 14-1, select the Save The Settings From This Machine option. Then, in the Settings File box, type the name and path for the OPS file.

3. Select the check boxes next to each Office XP program you want to include in your OPS file. Clear the check boxes next to each program you want to exclude. If you're using an OPS file that you've customized for another program, skip this step.

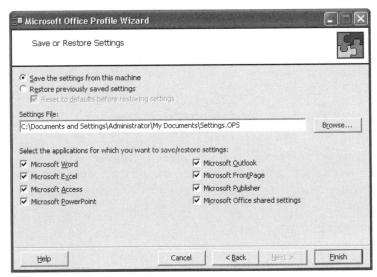

Figure 14-1   *Profile Wizard enables you to exclude settings for some Office XP programs and include settings for others. Clear the check boxes next to the settings you want to exclude.*

Deploying Settings

The primary purpose of OPS files is to deploy settings with Office XP. However, they're more useful than that. You can also use them to restore a program's default configuration, as a help desk tool to deploy settings to users' desktops, and as a convenient way to configure a computer after installing a fresh copy of Windows XP and applications.

Just as there are many ways to use OPS files, there are also different ways to deploy them. The most common method is to embed them in MST files that you create with Custom

Installation Wizard. You learn about this in the next section. If you want to apply settings outside the setup program in Office XP, you must run Profile Wizard separately, though. This is much more flexible than including OPS files in MST files, because it enables you to deploy different settings to different groups of users. To restore the settings from an OPS file to the user's profile, run the following command while logged on to Windows XP as that user:

```
proflwiz /r filename.ops /q
```

Replace `filename.ops` with the name of the OPS file that you want to restore to the user's profile. Profile Wizard must be available for users to run, so copy Proflwiz.exe from C:\Program Files\ORKTools\ORK10\Tools to a share that's available to all users, perhaps the Office XP administrative installation.

Custom Installation Wizard

Custom Installation Wizard is the tool you use to customize Office XP. You can use it to configure everything from the Office XP installation folder to the security settings. It's the one tool you'll always use when deploying Office XP. The result of running Custom Installation Wizard is a transform (MST file). You associate this MST file with the Office XP package file using the TRANSFORMS=`filename.mst` property or a the MST1 setting in the Office XP Setup.ini file.

Order of Precedence

Most of the Office XP settings are in the registry. If you define conflicting values for the same setting, Office XP has rules that determine which setting it uses. Most often, the later in the process you apply a setting, the more precedence it has. Office XP applies settings in the following order:

- Settings in an OPS file included in the transform.
- Settings on the Change Office User Settings, Specify Office Security Settings, and Outlook: Custom Default Settings pages of Custom Installation Wizard.
- Registry values specified in the transform.
- Settings applied by running Profile Wizard during installation.
- Settings that migrate from a previous version of Office XP.
- Settings applied by using Profile Wizard or Custom Maintenance Wizard after installing Office XP. This precedence assumes that users have already started each Office XP application and any migrated settings have already been applied.
- Settings managed through policies.

Four of Custom Installation Wizard's pages enable you to deploy settings with your MST file. You learn more about each page in the following sections "Add/Remove Registry Entries," "Customize Default Application Settings," "Change Office User Settings," and "Add Installations and Run Programs."

Add/Remove Registry Entries

Because most Office XP settings are in the registry, you can customize them by adding and changing registry values within MST files. The setup program applies your settings when users install Office XP. You can apply settings once per user by adding settings to HKCU, or you can apply settings once per computer by adding settings to HKLM. You can also add values to the registry that customize settings that aren't accessible through the Office XP user interface and that Profile Wizard doesn't capture in OPS files. For example, you can include settings for other programs. Here's how to add registry values to a transform:

1. On the Add Registry Entries page, shown in Figure 14-2, click Add.

2. In the Root box, select the portion of the registry you want to modify.

3. In the Data type box, select a data type for the new entry.

4. In the remaining boxes, type the full path for the registry value you want to add, enter the value name and data, and click OK.

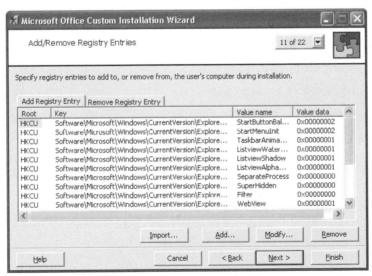

Figure 14-2 *Custom Installation Wizard is the primary tool you use to customize Office XP.*

Typing values on the Add Registry Entries page of Custom Installation Wizard is an error-prone and tedious process. It's better to export the settings to a REG file and then import that REG file into your MST file. For more information about creating REG files, see Chapter 2, "Using the Registry Editor," and Chapter 9, "Scripting Registry Changes." Of course, this assumes that the values you want to add to the transform already exist in your computer's registry. If the values aren't already present, you can add them with the benefit of Registry Editor's user interface, and then export them to a REG file. To import a registry file to a transform:

1. On Custom Installation Wizard's Add Registry Entries page, click Import.

2. In the File Name box, type the path and file name of the REG file, and then click Open.

   Custom Installation Wizard adds the values from the REG file to the list on the Add Registry Entries page. If the wizard encounters an entry in the REG file that is a duplicate and each version contains different value data, the wizard prompts you to select the entry you want to keep. To remove any values you don't want to keep, click the value, and then click Remove.

After Windows Installer finishes installing Office XP, it copies the values you added to the Add/Remove Registry Entries screen to users' computers. Options that you set by adding or modifying registry values override duplicate values that you set on other pages of Custom Installation Wizard, including the following:

- Settings in an OPS file added to a transform

- Settings on the Change Office User Settings page

- Options on the Outlook: Customize Default Settings page

- Settings on the Specify Office Security Settings page

Customize Default Application Settings

Adding an OPS file to an MST file is an easy way to deploy a bunch of settings throughout the organization. You learned how to create an OPS file earlier in this chapter. Now you need to learn how to embed that OPS file in your MST file. The big *gotcha* here is that any settings in your OPS file have lower precedence than settings you define elsewhere in your MST file. That means settings in the Change Office User Settings page overwrite settings in your OPS file, for example, as do settings defined on the Add Registry Entries page.

You embed OPS file in your MST file on Custom Installation Wizard's Customize Default Application Settings page. Select the Get Values From An Existing Settings Profile check box, and type the file name and path of the OPS file. Custom Installation Wizard creates a transform that contains your OPS file and any other customizations you have made.

> **Note**   Adding an OPS file to the MST file increases the size of the transform and requires you to re-create the MST file any time you change the OPS file. You can store the OPS file on the network and run Profile Wizard with your OPS file during the Office XP installation, instead. See "Add Installations and Run Programs," later in this chapter, for more information.

If an earlier version of Office is installed on a user's computer, Windows Installer migrates the previous version's settings to Office XP the first time the user starts an Office XP program. Users' migrated settings overwrite duplicate settings in an OPS file or MST file. On the Customize Default Application Settings page of Custom Installation Wizard, shown in Figure 14-3, you can change this behavior. If you are not including an OPS file in the MST file, the wizard selects the Migrate User Settings check box by default. When users install Office XP with your transform, Setup migrates settings from an earlier version of Office. If you add an OPS file to the transform, the wizard clears the Migrate User Settings check box and uses the values in your OPS file instead.

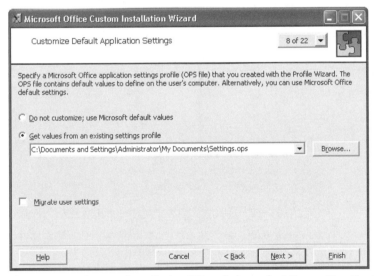

Figure 14-3   *Custom Installation Wizard clears the Migrate User Settings check box if you include an OPS file in your MST file.*

If you add an OPS file to an MST file and select the Migrate User Settings check box, the settings from your OPS file are applied during the initial installation. The first time a user runs one of the Office XP programs, Windows Installer migrates settings from an earlier version of Office and overwrites any corresponding settings previously applied.

Change Office User Settings

You can set most of the options you capture with Profile Wizard on Custom Installation Wizard's Change Office User Settings page. That includes any REG_DWORD and REG_SZ value but not REG_BINARY values. This is useful for customizing a small number of settings or changing a default configuration without rebuilding an OPS file that's already in the MST file.

To configure settings on the Change Office User Settings page, shown in Figure 14-4, click a category in the left pane. In the right pane, double-click the settings you want to configure and include in your MST file.

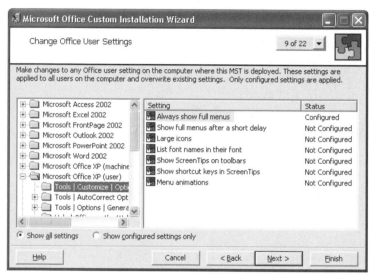

Figure 14-4 *Custom Installation Wizard's Change Office User Settings page is very similar to System Policy Editor with the Office XP policy templates (ADM files) loaded.*

When users install Office XP using your transform, the settings you configure on the Change Office User Settings page apply to every user on that computer. However, Windows Installer applies only the settings that differ from existing default settings. Settings you configure on this page of the wizard override the same settings in the OPS file you've included in the transform.

Tip The Change Office User Settings page uses templates for the settings it displays, just as Group Policy and system policies use templates. These templates are in C:\Program Files \ORKTools\ORK10\Tools and have the OPA file extension.

Add Installations and Run Programs

Custom Installation Wizard enables you to run programs during the Office XP installation. You can run Profile Wizard (Proflwiz.exe) to distribute custom settings at the end of the Office XP installation, for example. You cannot use Custom Installation Wizard's Add Installations And Run Programs page to install other Windows Installer packages, however. If Windows Installer starts installing a second package before it's finished installing the first, the entire process fails. Here's how to add Profile Wizard to the Add Installations And Run Programs page:

1. On the Add Installations And Run Programs page, click Add.

2. In the Target box, type the path and file name of Profile Wizard, typically **C:\Program Files\ORKTools\ORK10\Tools\Proflwiz.exe**.

3. In the Arguments box, add command-line options to apply the OPS file to the user's computer, usually **/r** *filename.ops* **/q**.

4. Do either of the following, as shown in Figure 14-5:

   • Click Run This Program Once Per Machine to apply your settings the first time a user logs on.

   • Click Run This Program Once Per User to apply your default settings to every user on that computer. This option requires an active network connection to the network the first time a user logs on to the computer.

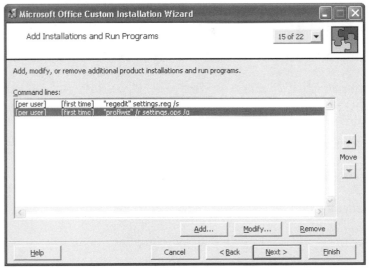

Figure 14-5   *You can also add programs to your installation by customizing the Office XP Setup.ini file.*

Custom Maintenance Wizard

You get one shot at applying an MST file to Office XP, and that's during installation. If you want to change settings after installing Office XP, you can use Custom Maintenance Wizard to modify almost everything that you can configure in Custom Installation Wizard, including user settings, security levels, Outlook profile settings, and so on. Custom Maintenance Wizard is one of the bigger improvements in the Office XP Resource Kit over the Office 2000 version.

The resource kit installs Custom Maintenance Wizard on the Start menu. Click Start, All Programs, Microsoft Office Tools, Microsoft Office XP Resource Kit Tools, and then click Custom Maintenance Wizard. The program file Maintwiz.exe is in C:\Program Files \ORKTools\ORK10\Tools. The result of running the wizard is a CMW file that contains your configuration changes. For users to apply the CMW files that the wizard creates, you must copy Maintwiz.exe and the CMW files to the Office XP administrative share, which gives Custom Maintenance Wizard elevated privileges by proxy. Alternatively, you can use the policy `Allow CMW files at any location to be applied`.

The user interfaces of both wizards are almost identical, so I won't use much space describing how to use Custom Maintenance Wizard here. You specify new settings using Custom Maintenance Wizard's Change Office User Settings page, for instance. You can't use Custom Maintenance Wizard to deploy a new OPS file, however, so you have to run Profile Wizard separately (think logon script, and so on). Chapter 15, "Working Around IT Problems," has recommendations for pushing command-lines to users' computers.

Group and System Policy

Everything I've presented to this point helps you deploy user settings for Office XP and sometimes other programs. If you want to manage settings, however, you must use Group Policy or system policies. Group Policy is a feature of Windows 2000 and Active Directory. System policies is a legacy policy-based management technology that's still available if you've not yet deployed Active Directory.

Chapter 6, "Using Registry-Based Policies," describes policies in detail. Part IV, "Appendices," describes many of the policies in Office XP and tells you where to find them in the registry. The Office XP Resource Kit provides policy templates (ADM files) that you can use with either Group Policy or system policies. It installs several ADM files in %SYSTEMROOT%\Inf, such as OFFICE10.ADM, which contains policy settings that are common to all Office XP programs.

When to Use What

Scenario	Method	Tool
Distribute a standard default Office XP configuration	Add an OPS file to a transform	Profile Wizard and Custom Installation Wizard (Customize Default Application Settings page)
Configure a few options or override the OSP file's settings without rebuilding it	Add user settings to a transform	Custom Installation Wizard (Change Office User Settings page)
Set default security levels and customize trusted sources list	Specify security settings in a transform	Custom Installation Wizard (Specify Office Security Settings page)
Set migration and e-mail options for Outlook	Specify Outlook settings in a transform	Custom Installation Wizard (Outlook: Custom Default Settings page)
Specify settings that are not captured in an OPS file	Add registry values to a transform	Custom Installation Wizard (Add/Remove Registry Entries page)
Distribute a default Office XP configuration but store one or more OPS files separately from the MST file	Run Profile Wizard during Setup	Profile Wizard and Custom Installation Wizard (Add Installations and Run Programs page)
Preserve users' custom settings from a previous version instead of specifying new default settings	Enable Setup to migrate ettings from a previous version of Office	Default behavior
Set unique options for Office XP Multilingual User Interface Packs or other chained packages	Specify settings in the transform applied to the chained package	Custom Installation Wizard and Setup INI Customization Wizard
Distribute a default Office XP configuration that overrides individual users' settings	Run Profile Wizard as a stand-alone tool after installing Office XP	Profile Wizard
Modify user settings after installing Office XP	Distribute a CMW file after installing Office XP	Custom Maintenance Wizard
Prevent users from modifying settings	Set policies	System Policy Editor or Windows 2000 Group Policy

Working Around IT Problems

IT professionals often have to struggle with getting configurations just right before *and* after deployment. They try to play by the rules, but they sometimes must bend them to get things to work well in their environments. Bending the rules often means using the registry to achieve a goal that's not usually possible. Chapter 4, "Hacking the Registry," showed good examples of bending the rules. If you want to use Folder Redirection without Active Directory, for example, you have to hack the registry. This chapter follows that example with many more.

I could fill an entire book (I'd sure like to try) with the dirty tricks that IT professionals use to get things to work the way they want. I've focused this chapter on the topics that I'm asked about most frequently, though. For example, I don't know many professionals who aren't frustrated with the Microsoft Outlook Express icons that keep popping up on users' desktops. This chapter shows you how to rid your business of them. I also know that many professionals want to permanently remove some components from Microsoft Windows XP, and of course, this chapter shows you how to do that as well. Last, this chapter shows you how to run processes with elevated privileges, something you must do if you want to distribute applications without the benefit of a software management infrastructure, and how to customize the logon process.

Controlling Just-in-Time Setup

Every IT professional I've spoken with, particularly desktop-deployment types, have the same problem: They want to know how to prevent Windows XP from creating icons for Outlook Express on the Quick Launch toolbar and Start menu when users log on to the computer the first time. More specifically, Windows XP creates these icons when it creates user profiles for new users. These icons aren't in the default user profile, which you learned about in Chapter 10, "Deploying User Profiles," so you can't just remove them from it to avoid creating them.

At this point, you might be asking why you can't just remove those components from Windows XP. Well, the operating system doesn't provide a user interface for doing that. In the section "Removing Components," later in this chapter, I show you how to limit which components the setup program installs, though. Still, other components are required for the operating system to work properly. For example, Windows XP requires Internet Explorer. If you're deploying Microsoft Outlook 2002, you must install Outlook Express, because Outlook 2002 depends on many of the components in Outlook Express. The best you can do is not advertise these programs so users don't get sidetracked while using their computers.

Windows XP actually creates these icons as part of its *just-in-time* setup process for user profiles. The operating system creates a user profile for a new user, and then runs this just-in-time setup process to finish configuring it. Another way to think of the process is that the setup program defers configuring per-user settings until Windows XP creates user profiles, when decisions about those settings are better made. This just-in-time setup process is what you need to control to prevent the pesky Outlook Express icons from showing up on the desktop.

The key `HKLM\SOFTWARE\Microsoft\Active Setup\Installed Components` drives the just-in-time setup process. Each subkey is a component. For example, the subkey `{2179C5D3-EBFF-11CF-B6FD-00AA00B4E220}` is for NetShow. Within each subkey, you might see the `REG_EXPAND_SZ` value `StubPath`. If this value exists, Windows XP executes the command it contains when the operating system creates a new user profile. If you don't see this value or the value is empty, it does nothing. So to keep Windows XP from running a component's just-in-time setup process, remove the value `StubPath` from that component's subkey in `Installed Components`. The next several sections describe how to use this hack to control different components. You should include changes to `Installed Components` on disk images. Chapter 13, "Cloning Disks with Sysprep," describes how to deploy settings on your disk images.

Note Why care if Outlook Express has an icon on the Quick Launch toolbar? It's distracting and keeps users from their work. Specifically, your enterprise isn't likely to use Outlook Express as its mail client; you probably deployed a full-featured client like Outlook 2002 or similar. If you advertise Outlook Express on the desktop, users are going to have two mail clients. If that doesn't confuse them and cause problems, it'll certainly tease them into playing with Outlook Express. This goes for many of the other programs that come with Windows XP, including Windows Media Player, NetMeeting, and so on.

Outlook Express

When Windows XP creates a new user profile, it executes the command in the `REG_EXPAND_SZ` value `HKLM\SOFTWARE\Microsoft\Active Setup\Installed Components\{44BBA840-CC51-11CF-AAFA-00AA00B6015C}\StubPath` to create the Outlook Express icon in the Start menu and on the Quick Launch toolbar. This command is `"%ProgramFiles%\Outlook Express\setup50.exe" /APP:OE /CALLER:WINNT /user /install`. To prevent this command from running, remove the `StubPath` value or, alternatively, change its name to `HideStubPath`, as shown in Figure 15-1.

Name	Type	Data
(Default)	REG_SZ	Microsoft Outlook Express 6
CloneUser	REG_DWORD	0x00000001 (1)
ComponentID	REG_SZ	MailNews
HideStubPath	REG_EXPAND_SZ	"%ProgramFiles%\Outlook Express\setup50.exe" /APP:OE /C...
IsInstalled	REG_DWORD	0x00000001 (1)
Locale	REG_SZ	EN
Version	REG_SZ	6,0,2600,0000

Figure 15-1 *Prevent Windows XP from creating Outlook Express shortcuts by hiding* `StubPath`.

This customization is common on disk images, so I'm providing you with a script to do it. Save the script shown in Listing 15-1 to a text file with the *.inf* extension. Right-click it, and then click Install. Keep this script handy as a disk-image customization tool.

Listing 15-1 Outlook.inf

```
[Version]
Signature=$CHICAGO$

[DefaultInstall]
DelReg=Reg.Settings

[Reg.Settings]
HKLM,SOFTWARE\Microsoft\Active Setup\Installed Components\{44BBA840-\
CC51-11CF-AAFA-00AA00B6015C},StubPath
```

> **Tip** An alternative to hiding the Outlook Express icon is making Outlook Express a news-reader client only. Add the option /outnews to the target of each icon (put this command-line option outside of the quotation marks). When users choose the shortcut, Outlook Express opens with all its news-client features working, but its mail-client features don't work. This is useful in scenarios when you must provide newsgroup access to users, like developers, who usually require access to Microsoft and developer newsgroups. To easily deploy this customized Outlook Express shortcut, add it to the default user profile. Alternatively, because this hack usually accompanies an Outlook 2002 deployment, you can add this shortcut to your Microsoft Office XP transform.

Windows Media Player

Windows Media Player has two subkeys in HKLM\SOFTWARE\Microsoft\Active Setup \Installed Components:

- {22d6f312-b0f6-11d0-94ab-0080c74c7e95} is for version 6.4 and the value StubPath is rundll32.exe advpack.dll,LaunchINFSection C:\WINDOWS\INF \mplayer2.inf,PerUserStub.NT.

- {6BF52A52-394A-11d3-B153-00C04F79FAA6} is for version 8 and the value StubPath is rundll32.exe advpack.dll,LaunchINFSection C:\WINDOWS \INF\wmp.inf,PerUserStub.

These values are responsible for the numerous Windows Media Player shortcuts. Remove both StubPath values to prevent Windows XP from adding the Windows Media Player shortcut to the Quick Launch toolbar. Also, if you want to keep the Windows Media Player shortcut off the top of the Start menu, remove it from the default user profile (see Chapter 10, "Deploying User Profiles"). You also find Windows Media Player shortcuts in the All Users profile folder in %SYSTEMDRIVE%\Documents and Settings\All Users\Start Menu \Programs\Accessories\Entertainment. Ideally, remove the shortcut from your network-based Default User profile, and then remove the shortcut from the All Users profile folder on your disk images.

Desktop Themes

Preventing Windows XP from configuring desktop themes when it creates a user profile is an easy way to revert to the classic user interface (see Figure 15-2). Remove or hide the REG_EXPAND_SZ value StubPath from the key HKLM\SOFTWARE\Microsoft\Active Setup \Installed Components\{2C7339CF-2B09-4501-B3F3-F3508C9228ED}. The command that this value contains is %SystemRoot%\system32\regsvr32.exe /s /n /i:/UserInstall %SystemRoot%\system32\themeui.dll.

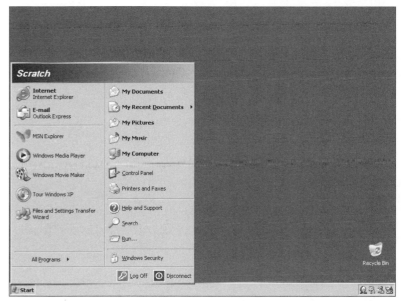

Figure 15-2 *Removing the value StubPath from the subkey {2C7339CF-2B09-4501-B3F3-F3508C9228ED} prevents Windows XP from configuring the new user interface.*

Other Shortcuts

The key `HKLM\SOFTWARE\Microsoft\Active Setup\Installed Components` contains other components with `StubPath` values that I haven't mentioned yet. You can prevent Windows XP from configuring any of the components when the operating system creates a user profile by removing or hiding the `StubPath` value in the corresponding subkey. Table 15-1 lists all the components I've already described plus the ones that I haven't.

Table 15-1 Components in Installed Components

Component	Subkey	StubPath
Address Book 6	{7790769C-0471-11d2-AF11-00C04FA35D02}	"%ProgramFiles%\Outlook Express\setup50.exe" /APP:WAB /CALLER:WINNT /user /install
Internet Explorer 6	{89820200-FCBD-11cf-8B85-00AA005B4383}	%SystemRoot%\system32\ie4uinit.exe
Internet Explorer Access	{ACC563BC-4266-43f0-B6ED-9D38C4202C7E}	rundll32 iesetup.dll,IEAccessUserInst
Microsoft Outlook Express 6	{44BBA840-CC51-11CF-AAFA-00AA00B6015C}	"%ProgramFiles%\Outlook Express\setup50.exe" /APP:OE /CALLER:WINNT /user /install

Table 15-1   Components in Installed Components *(continued)*

Component	Subkey	StubPath
Microsoft Windows Media Player 6.4	{22d6f312-b0f6-11d0-94ab-0080c74c7e95}	rundll32.exe advpack.dll,LaunchINFSection C:\WINDOWS\INF \mplayer2.inf,PerUserStub.NT
Microsoft Windows Media Player 8	{6BF52A52-394A-11d3-B153-00C04F79FAA6}	rundll32.exe advpack.dll,LaunchINFSection C:\WINDOWS\INF \wmp.inf,PerUserStub
NetMeeting 3.01	{44BBA842-CC51-11CF-AAFA-00AA00B6015B}	rundll32.exe advpack.dll,LaunchINFSection C:\WINDOWS\INF \msnetmtg.inf,NetMtg.Install.PerUser.NT
Theme Component	{2C7339CF-2B09-4501-B3F3-F3508C9228ED}	%SystemRoot%\system32\regsvr32.exe /s /n /i: /UserInstall %SystemRoot%\system32 \themeui.dll
Windows Desktop Update	{89820200-ECBD-11cf-8B85-00AA005B4340}	regsvr32.exe /s /n /i:U shell32.dll
Windows Messenger 4.0	{5945c046-1e7d-11d1-bc44-00c04fd912be}	rundll32.exe advpack.dll,LaunchINFSection C:\WINDOWS\INF \msmsgs.inf,BLC.Install.PerUser

Keep in mind that even if you prevent Windows XP from configuring every component I show in the table, you might still have unwanted icons. These icons come from the Default User and All User profile folders. Remove the shortcuts that you don't want from any default user profile you've deployed. Remove the shortcuts you don't want from the All Users folder on your disk images.

Caution   Be wary of preventing Windows XP from configuring the Windows Desktop Update. This component is necessary to provide resiliency for Windows Installer–based applications. For example, when a user opens the shortcut of a Windows Installer–based application, the Windows Desktop Update passes it on to Windows Installer so that Windows Installer can check and repair the application if necessary. If you prevent the operating system from configuring the Windows Desktop Update, you remove Windows Installer from the process. Even though this prevents Windows Installer from repairing broken shortcuts, it doesn't prevent Windows Installer from repairing components within an application.

Removing Components

Whereas the previous section showed you how to prevent Windows XP from configuring components when it creates a user profile, this section shows you how to prevent Windows XP from installing certain components altogether. Be careful when you prevent the operating system from installing components, though, because doing so could cripple some features and applications. For example, Office XP requires Internet Explorer, Outlook Express, and NetMeeting for a lot of its features, particularly its collaboration features. The moral is to test your configurations in a lab before deploying them to unsuspecting users.

The Windows XP setup program doesn't provide a user interface for removing components during installation. You can use an answer file to remove components, however; Chapter 12, "Deploying with Answer Files," shows you what the [Components] section looks like in an answer file, and I summarize that information in this chapter. The operating system does allow users to add or remove components using Windows Components Wizard, though: click Start, Control Panel, Add Or Remove Programs, Add/Remove Windows Components. Still, the wizard and answer files do not allow you to remove and disable some of the features that enterprises would rather not install. There's no option to remove Movie Maker, for example, nor is there an option to remove Windows Messenger.

This section shows you some alternative ways to get rid of components, if possible, or to hide them. The most common requests that I get are to get rid of Tour Windows XP, Movie Maker, Outlook Express, and Files And Settings Transfer Wizard. Strangely, I'm not often asked about removing the games, but you can do that easily enough through your Windows XP answer file.

Answer File [Components] Section

Chapter 12, "Deploying with Answer Files," describes how to build an answer file. If you're an IT professional deploying Windows XP, you're probably already familiar with answer files. The [Components] section of answer files enables you to prevent the operating system from installing certain components. Listing 15-2 on the next page shows what this section looks like, and the listing contains all the components that Windows XP answer files support (I omitted server-specific components). The names of each component are self-explanatory. To install a component, set it to On. To prevent its installation, set it to Off. In the listing, I've set each component to its default installation value.

Microsoft doesn't document a way to prevent the setup program from installing Windows Messenger—a common request. I've added the component msmsgs to Listing 15-2, however, which prevents the setup program from installing it. The file Sysoc.inf, which you learn about in the next section, hides this component in Windows Components Wizard. You can edit that file to show Windows Messenger in the wizard, but doing so relies on users to remove Windows Messenger. Instead, you can add the component to the [Components] section of your answer file to prevent the setup program from installing it.

Listing 15-2   Unattend.txt

```
[Components]
accessopt=On; Accessibility wizard
calc=On; Calculator
charmap=On; Character Map
chat=Off; Chat
deskpaper=On; Desktop backgrounds
dialer=On; Phone Dialer
fax=Off; Fax
fp_extensions=Off; FrontPage server extensions
fp_vdir_deploy=Off; Visual InterDev RAD Remote Deployment Support
freecell=On; Freecell
hearts=On; Hearts
hypertrm=On; HyperTerminal
IEAccess=On; Visible entry points to Internet Explorer
iis_common=Off; Internet Information Services (IIS) common
iis_ftp=Off; FTP service
iis_htmla=Off; HTML-based administration for IIS
iis_inetmgr=Off; MMC-based administration for IIS
iis_pwmgr=Off; Personal Web Manager
iis_smtp=Off; SMTP service for IIS
iis_smtp_docs=Off; SMTP service documentation
iis_www=Off; WWW service for IIS
iis_www_vdir_printers=Off; Web printing components for IIS
iisdbg=Off; Microsoft Script Debugger
indexsrv_system=Off; Indexing Service
media_clips=On; Sample sound clips
media_utopia=Off; Utopia Sound Scheme
minesweeper=On; Minesweeper
mousepoint=On; Mouse pointers
mplay=On; Windows Media Player
msmq_ADIntegrated=Off; Integrates Message Queuing (MSMQ) with AD
msmq_Core=Off; MSMQ core files
msmq_HTTPSupport=Off; MSMQ support for HTTP
msmq_LocalStorage=Off; MSMQ support for local storage
msmq_MQDSService=Off; MSMQ support for down-level clients
msmq_RoutingSupport=Off; MSMQ support for efficient routing
msmq_TriggersService=Off; MSMQ support for Component Object Model
msmsgs=On; Windows Messenger
msnexplr=On; MSN Explorer
mswordpad=On; WordPad
Netcis=Off; COM Internet Services
netoc=On; Optional networking components
objectpkg=On; Object Packager
paint=On; Paint
pinball=On; Pinball
rec=On; Sound Recorder
solitaire=On; Solitaire
```

```
spider=On; Spider
templates=On; Document templates
Vol=On; Volume Control
zonegames=On; Gaming Zone Internet games
```

This is a great technique for preventing the operating system from installing things such as the games, but it doesn't prevent the installation of components such as Movie Maker, because the [Components] section doesn't include settings for those components. You can use it to prevent the installation of Windows Media Player and Windows Messenger, though, which strikes two components off of my checklist.

Extending Windows Components Wizard

Just because you don't see a component in Windows Components Wizard doesn't mean that Windows XP isn't prepared to remove it. The file Sysoc.inf controls which components appear in the wizard. This file is in %SYSTEMROOT%\Inf, and Listing 15-3 shows its default contents. You must display super-hidden files to see the Inf folder: In Windows Explorer, click Tools, Folder Options. On the View tab, select the Show Hidden Files And Folders check box.

The important section in this file is [Components]. Each line in this section is either a specific component or a category of components. If you see the word hide, Windows XP doesn't display the component or category in Windows Components Wizard. To allow users to remove the component, or the components in the category, remove the word hide. For example, to allow users to remove Windows Messenger, change the line msmsgs=msgrocm.dll,OcEntry,msmsgs.inf,hide,7 to msmsgs=msgrocm.dll,OcEntry,msmsgs.inf,,7.

Listing 15-3   Sysoc.inf

```
[Version]
Signature = "$Windows NT$"
DriverVer=07/01/2001,5.1.2600.0

[Components]
NtComponents=ntoc.dll,NtOcSetupProc,,4
WBEM=ocgen.dll,OcEntry,wbemoc.inf,hide,7
Display=desk.cpl,DisplayOcSetupProc,,7
Fax=fxsocm.dll,FaxOcmSetupProc,fxsocm.inf,,7
NetOC=netoc.dll,NetOcSetupProc,netoc.inf,,7
iis=iis.dll,OcEntry,iis.inf,,7
com=comsetup.dll,OcEntry,comnt5.inf,hide,7
dtc=msdtcstp.dll,OcEntry,dtcnt5.inf,hide,7
IndexSrv_System = setupqry.dll,IndexSrv,setupqry.inf,,7
TerminalServer=TsOc.dll, HydraOc, TsOc.inf,hide,2
msmq=msmqocm.dll,MsmqOcm,msmqocm.inf,,6
ims=imsinsnt.dll,OcEntry,ims.inf,,7
```

```
fp_extensions=fp40ext.dll,FrontPage4Extensions,fp40ext.inf,,7
AutoUpdate=ocgen.dll,OcEntry,au.inf,hide,7
msmsgs=msgrocm.dll,OcEntry,msmsgs.inf,hide,7
RootAutoUpdate=ocgen.dll,OcEntry,rootau.inf,,7
IEAccess=ocgen.dll,OcEntry,ieaccess.inf,,7


Games=ocgen.dll,OcEntry,games.inf,,7
AccessUtil=ocgen.dll,OcEntry,accessor.inf,,7
CommApps=ocgen.dll,OcEntry,communic.inf,HIDE,7
MultiM=ocgen.dll,OcEntry,multimed.inf,HIDE,7
AccessOpt=ocgen.dll,OcEntry,optional.inf,HIDE,7
Pinball=ocgen.dll,OcEntry,pinball.inf,HIDE,7
MSWordPad=ocgen.dll,OcEntry,wordpad.inf,HIDE,7
ZoneGames=zoneoc.dll,ZoneSetupProc,igames.inf,,7

[Global]
WindowTitle=%WindowTitle%
WindowTitle.StandAlone="*"

[Components]
msnexplr=ocmsn.dll,OcEntry,msnmsn.inf,,7

[Strings]
WindowTitle="Windows Professional Setup"
WindowTitle_Standalone="Windows Components Wizard"
```

Removing Components After Installation

The first option I gave you enables you to prevent the Windows XP setup program from installing components during installation. The second option enables you to expose additional components in Windows Components Wizard. This last option is for scenarios in which you want to remove a component without exposing it in Windows Components Wizard. This is also useful when you want to script the removal so that you don't have to visit the desktop.

The first step is to find the component's INF file in %SYSTEMROOT%\Inf. Remember that this is a super-hidden folder, and I gave you instructions for showing it earlier in this chapter. The easiest way to find the component's INF file is to use Search Assistant. Look for all files with the *.inf* extension that contain the name of the component. For example, to find the INF file for Windows Messenger, search for all files with the *.inf* extension in %SYSTEMROOT%\Inf that contain *Windows Messenger*. You should come up with the file Msmsgs.inf as shown in Figure 15-3. Then look in the file for a section with the words *remove* or *uninstall* in it. In this case, the section is called [BLC.Remove]. Then execute the following command, whether in a script or in the Run dialog box, where *Filename.inf* is the name of the INF file and *Section* is the name of the uninstall section:

```
rundll32 advpack.dll,LaunchINFSection %systemroot%\Inf\Filename.inf,Section
```

Thus, to remove Windows Messenger, run the command:

```
rundll32 advpack.dll,LaunchINFSection %systemroot%\Inf\Msmsgs.inf,BLC.Remove.
```

Alas, many components don't have uninstall sections in their INF files, and that leaves you looking for other ways to remove them. You can use this method for many device drivers, programs, and components that do provide INF files, though.

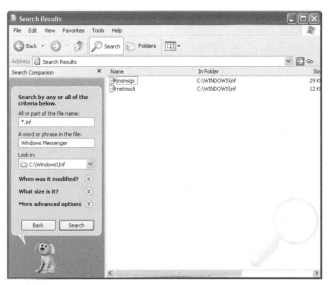

Figure 15-3   *Search the %SYSTEMROOT%\Inf folder for all files with the .inf extension that contain the name of the component you want to remove.*

Hiding Non-Removable Components

None of the methods I've shown will help you get rid of some components, including Tour Windows XP, Movie Maker, Outlook Express, and Files And Settings Transfer Wizard, which is what started me on this rampage in the first place. To prevent users from accessing these applications, you're going to have to get creative. Tour Windows XP is easy to hide, if not get rid of altogether. Create a new subkey in HKLM\Software\Microsoft\Windows\CurrentVersion\Applets\Tour called Tour. Then create the REG_DWORD value RunCount and set it to 0x00. Do this on your disk images so that users aren't accosted by Tour Windows XP the first time they log on to the operating system; they can run the tour from the Start menu.

The remaining bits aren't as easy. You can't just remove the program files because Windows File Protection immediately restores them. You could disable Windows File Protection, but I don't recommend doing so because it protects users' configurations from accidents and misbehaved applications that like to replace files they have no business replacing. Instead, on your disk images, hide the shortcuts, and use Software Restriction Policies to prevent users from running the programs by opening the program files:

1. Prevent Windows XP from creating new shortcuts by removing the appropriate `StubPath` values from `HKLM\SOFTWARE\Microsoft\Active Setup\Installed Compo-nents`. See the section "Controlling Just-in-Time Setup," earlier in this chapter, for more information.

2. Hide existing shortcuts to the program (do this on your disk images):

   - Search %SYSTEMDRIVE%\Documents and Settings\All Users for shortcuts to the program, and remove them.

   - Search %SYSTEMDRIVE%\Documents and Settings\Default User for shortcuts to the program, and remove them.

   - Search the Default User folder in *Server*\NETLOGON\Default User share for the program's shortcuts, and remove them.

3. Create a new Group Policy object (GPO) in Active Directory or locally on your disk images that prevents users from running the program.

That last step requires more explanation. Chapter 6, "Using Registry-Based Policy," contains more information about Group Policy, but I'll get you started. The following instructions assume that you're defining Software Restriction Policies in the local GPO, but the steps transfer to network-based Group Policy:

1. In Group Policy Editor's left pane, click Software Restriction Policies.

   To start Group Policy Editor, type **gpedit.msc** in the Run dialog box. Software Restriction Policies is under `Computer Configuration\Windows Settings \Security Settings`.

2. Right-click Software Restriction Policies, and then click Create New Policies.

3. Under Software Restrictions Policies, right-click Additional Rules, and then click New Hash Rule.

4. Click Browse, and select the file that you want to prevent users from executing. For example to prevent users from running Files And Settings Migration Wizard, select %SYSTEMROOT%\system32\usmt\migwiz.exe.

After you select the file that you want to prevent users from running, Group Policy Editor creates a hash for the file. Figure 15-4 shows an example that prevents users from running Files And Settings Transfer Wizard. Users won't be able to run any program that matches that hash value. That way, users can't trick the system by copying the file to a different location (clever). After you save the policy, you must log off of Windows XP for the change to take affect. When users try to run the program, they see an error message that says, *Windows cannot open this program because it has been prevented by a software restriction policy.* So between hiding the advertisements and preventing the program file from executing, you can prevent programs such as Movie Maker and Files And Settings Transfer Wizard from distracting users.

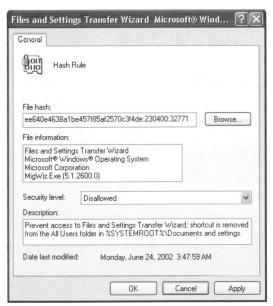

Figure 15-4 *Without a Files And Settings Transfer Wizard shortcut on the Start menu, users will not usually try to run the wizard. Those who do will see an error message.*

Removing Policy Tattoos

Tattoos are a significant problem with System Policy, which versions of Windows before Windows 2000 supported. Tattooing means that policies make permanent changes to the registry. The administrator must explicitly remove those policies. For example, if you create a policy file, which has the *.pol* extension, and Windows applies its settings to the registry, when you remove the policy file, the settings remain. To remove those policies, you must remove the settings from the registry or edit the policy file to remove the settings.

Tattoos become more problematic when you upgrade to Windows XP from an earlier version of Windows. It's also a problem when you deploy Windows XP on a network that doesn't have Active Directory but uses System Policy, and then deploy Active Directory down the line. The upgrade process doesn't remove System Policy settings from the registry during an upgrade, so those settings remain. The shotgun approach is to remove the following keys from each computer's registry and each user's profile hive before upgrading to Windows XP; the surgical approach is to remove individual policies, but that's too tedious:

* `HKLM\SOFTWARE\Policies`

* `HKLM\SOFTWARE\Microsoft\Windows\CurrentVersion\Policies`

* `HKCU\Software\Policies`

* `HKCU\Software\Microsoft\Windows\CurrentVersion\Policies`

How you remove these keys during the upgrade is the question. This isn't an issue for disk images because the problem occurs only during an upgrade. If technicians are visiting desktops during the upgrade, and I hope they aren't doing that, they can remove these keys manually. Otherwise, run the Windows XP setup program from a batch file or script. Then you can precede the command that starts the setup program with the commands that remove these keys. Listing 15-4 is an example of an INF file that removes them. To run this INF file from a batch file, save it in a file called Tattos.inf; then add the command `%SystemRoot%` `\System32\rundll32.exe setupapi,InstallHinfSection DefaultInstall 132 Tattoos.inf` to the batch file that starts the Windows XP installation. You can also script this edit using Windows Script Host, which Chapter 9, "Scripting Registry Changes," describes how to do.

Listing 15-4   Tattoos.inf

```
[Version]
Signature=$CHICAGO$

[DefaultInstall]
DelReg=Reg.Settings

[Reg.Settings]
HKLM,SOFTWARE\Policies
HKLM,SOFTWARE\Microsoft\Windows\CurrentVersion\Policies
```

There a few major issues with this script, however. The first is that the user must be an administrator to remove the policy branches from the registry. You can use the techniques described in the next section, "Elevating Processes' Privileges," to take care of this issue or rely on your software management infrastructure. The second issue is that it removes only the per-computer policies. It doesn't remove policies from users' profile hives. You won't be able to use a script like this from a logon script or allow the user to run it because they don't have the privileges required to remove the policy branches from the registry. This is true unless you've dumped all users in to the local Administrators group, which I hope you haven't done. The only reasonable solution is to load each user's profile hive in Registry Editor (Regedit), and then remove the two policy branches from it. You can more or less automate this process by writing a script that connects to a remote computer, loads each profile hive file that exists in `HKLM\SOFTWARE\Microsoft\Windows NT\CurrentVersion` `\ProfileList`, removes the policy branches, and then unloads the hive file.

Elevating Processes' Privileges

Privileges are a nasty little paradox. On one hand, you don't want to add users to the local Administrators group. Restricting users is a best practice that prevents human error, senseless distractions, opportunistic viruses, and so on. On the other hand, deploying software to restricted users is difficult. They don't have the privileges necessary to install most applications, such as Office XP. Chapter 7, "Managing Registry Security," shows you a variety of features that you can use to reach a happy medium between unbridled access and totally locked-down desktops. What I want to show you in this chapter is how to run processes elevated so you can perform many of the tasks I've described in locked-down environments.

The sections following this one go from elegant to dodgy. Group Policy, specifically the InstallAlwaysElevated policy, is one way to allow restricted users to install Windows Installer–based applications. You can also use the Secondary Logon feature or Scheduled Tasks. The section "AutoLogon," later in this chapter, describes a method that SMS uses, and I tend to like this solution. The last two methods I describe in this section are very dodgy and can be used against you if you're not careful.

Group Policy

The policy InstallAlwaysElevated installs Windows Installer–based applications with elevated privileges. This policy is one way to allow users to install Windows Installer–based applications that they couldn't otherwise install because their accounts are in restricted groups or you've locked down the desktops.

Keep in mind the consequences of using this policy. Users can take advantage of this policy to gain full control of their computers. Potentially, users can even permanently change their privileges and circumvent your ability to manage their accounts and computers. Not only that, this policy opens the door to viruses disguised as Windows Installer package files. For these reasons, this isn't a setting that I recommend in any but the most necessary scenarios when there's no other method available other than to toss users in the local Administrators group.

For this policy to be effective, you must enable both the per-computer and per-user versions of it at the same time. In other words, enable it in Computer Configuration as well as User Configuration. If you're going to use this policy, I recommend that you enable it for each rollout unit prior to deploying software to it. Deploy your package, and then immediately remove the policy for that unit. You can at least limit your exposure to the perils that this policy creates.

Note If you have Active Directory and Group Policy, you shouldn't consider using the `InstallAlwaysElevated` policy. The only reason you'd use this policy is in lieu of a software management infrastructure. If you have Active Directory and Group Policy, however, you have at your disposal an elegant solution for small and medium businesses: Software Installation And Maintenance. This feature enables you to deploy software through GPOs. The best part is that you can deploy Windows Installer–based software to restricted users and locked-down desktops because applications you deploy through Group Policy install with elevated privileges. The paper "Understanding Software Installation" is an excellent walkthrough for the subject. The URL is *http://www.microsoft.com/technet/prodtechnol/winxppro/proddocs/sag_ADEconcepts_01.asp*.

Secondary Logon

Secondary Logon, also called *Run As*, enables users to run programs in the context of accounts other than their own. For example, if I'm logged on to the computer using the account Jerry, which is in the Power Users group, but I need to run a program as an administrator, I hold down the Shift key, right-click the program's shortcut icon, click Run As, and then type the Administrator account's name and password. The program runs under the Administrator account. Because Secondary Logon relies on users knowing the credentials (which they won't know), it's not a really useful tool for software deployment. I include it here to answer the inevitable question about whether you can use it for that purpose.

You can use Secondary Logon from the command prompt, too. The following shows you the syntax for this command:

```
RUNAS [ [/noprofile | /profile] [/env] [/netonly] ] /user:Username Program
RUNAS [ [/noprofile | /profile] [/env] [/netonly] ] /smartcard [/user:Username]
Program
```

`/noprofile`	Specifies that Runas should not load the user profile. Programs load faster but often don't work properly.
`/profile`	Specifies that Runas should load the user profile.
`/env`	Uses the current environment instead of the user's.
`/netonly`	Specifies that the credentials are for remote access only.
`/savecred`	Uses the credentials previously saved by the user.
`/smartcard`	Specifies that the credentials are provided by a smartcard.
`/user` *Username*	Specifies the account name to use. This should be in the form of *user@domain* or *domain\user*.
Program	Specifies the command to execute.

Scheduled Tasks

One thing I like about Scheduled Tasks is that you have remote access to the Scheduled Tasks folder on each computer. Also, you can include an account name and password in each task. You're not relying on users to provide the credentials necessary to run a job, such as installing software. For this reason, Scheduled Tasks beats Secondary Logon. In My Network Places, find the computer on which you want to add a task. Open the computer's Scheduled Tasks folder, right-click the folder, point to New, click Scheduled Task, and then rename the task. Configure the task as follows (shown in Figure 15-5).

- In the Task tab's Run box, type the command you want to execute. Remember to keep the command's path relative to the computer on which you're running it.

- In the Task tab's Run As box, type the account in which you want to run the task, and then click Set Password to set the matching password. As shown in Figure 15-5, type the account in the form *domain\username*.

- On the Schedule tab, configure the task's schedule. In the scenarios that I've described (deploying software and settings), you'd want to schedule the task to run once.

- On the Settings tab, configure Windows XP to remove the task from the Scheduled Tasks folder after it runs. No reason to leave behind artifacts.

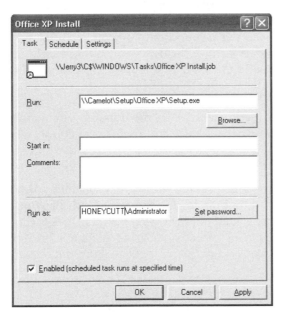

Figure 15-5 *Scheduled Tasks is a useful way to run programs on remote computers with elevated privileges, particularly in one-off scenarios.*

Note   Be careful not to schedule tasks that require user interaction. Users won't see the task running unless they look in Windows Task Manager and view tasks for all users. For example, if you schedule a task to run on a computer as the local administrator and the user Jerry is the current console user, Jerry won't be able to interact with the task. If the task requires user interaction, it'll hang. Many programs, particularly setup programs, have command-line options that run them quietly. Install Office XP with no user interaction, for example, using the /qn command-line option. Also, use this method to install software or run programs that don't interact with the current console user's profile because this method will affect only the profile of the user you typed in the Run As box. In other words, install applications that support per-computer installations or run programs that interact with HKLM.

AutoLogon

This is my favorite method when I don't have a software management infrastructure available for deploying software: I use AutoLogon. This is the same capability that you can configure in answer files, as described in Chapter 12, "Deploying with Answer Files," but you can use it after deployment. Table 15-2 describes the settings you need to configure for AutoLogon. To enable this feature, you must set the REG_SZ value AutoAdminLogon to 1. Then you set the REG_SZ value DefaultUserName to the account that you want to use, and the REG_SZ value DefaultPassword to the account's password. If the user name doesn't include the domain, set the REG_SZ value DefaultDomainName to the name of the domain authenticating the account. Just remember that you must add the account to one of the local groups in order to log on to Windows XP using that account. The domain administrator is already a member of the local Administrators group, but I don't recommend using the domain administrator account with this technique. Instead, you can use the local Administrator account, which is always available. The last value you set is the REG_DWORD value AutoLogonCount. Set this value to the number of times you want to automatically log on to Windows XP.

Here's how it works. If the AutoAdminLogon value is 1 and the AutoLogonCount value is not 0, Windows XP automatically logs on to the computer using the credentials provided in the values DefaultUserName, DefaultDomainName, and DefaultPassword. The operating system then decrements the value in AutoLogonCount. When AutoLogonCount reaches zero, Windows XP removes the values AutoLogonCount and DefaultPassword from the registry and no longer logs the user on to it automatically.

The last step is to put the command you want to run in HKLM\SOFTWARE\Microsoft\Windows\CurrentVersion\RunOnce. Because you're putting this command in the RunOnce key, Windows XP runs this command one time and then removes the value from the registry. Each value in RunOnce is a command. The name of each REG_SZ value doesn't matter, but you store the command line you want to execute in it.

Table 15-2 Configuring Autologon

Setting	Name	Type	Data
HKLM\SOFTWARE\Microsoft\Windows NT\CurrentVersion\Winlogon			
Enable Autologon	AutoAdminLogon	REG_SZ	0 | 1
User name	DefaultUserName	REG_SZ	*Name*
User domain	DefaultDomainName	REG_SZ	*Domain*
User password	DefaultPassword	REG_SZ	*Password*
Number of times to log on to Windows XP	AutoLogonCount	REG_DWORD	*N*
HKLM\SOFTWARE\Microsoft\Windows\CurrentVersion\RunOnce			
Program to run	*Name*	REG_SZ	*Command*

An example will tie everything together for you. I want to deploy an application to a computer but the users in my organization are restricted and can't install it. I'd configure the values described in Table 15-2 so that when the current user logs off or when Windows XP restarts, the operating system automatically logs the domain Administrator on to the computer. I know that the application reboots the computer one time during the installation process, so I have to set AutoLogonCount to 2. The first time Windows XP logs the user on to it starts the setup program, and the second continues the setup program. The script shown in Listing 15-5 shows a way to automatically configure Windows XP for this scenario.

Listing 15-5 Install.inf

```
[Version]
Signature=$CHICAGO$

[DefaultInstall]
AddReg=Reg.Settings

[Reg.Settings]
HKLM,SOFTWARE\Microsoft\Windows NT\CurrentVersion\Winlogon,AutoAdminLogon,0,"1"
HKLM,SOFTWARE\Microsoft\Windows NT\CurrentVersion\Winlogon,DefaultUserName,0\
,"Administrator"
HKLM,SOFTWARE\Microsoft\Windows NT\CurrentVersion\Winlogon,DefaultDomainName,0\
,"HONEYCUTT"
HKLM,SOFTWARE\Microsoft\Windows NT\CurrentVersion\Winlogon,DefaultPassword,0\
,"PASSWORD"
HKLM,SOFTWARE\Microsoft\Windows NT\CurrentVersion\Winlogon,AutoLogonCount\
,0x10001,0x02
HKLM,SOFTWARE\Microsoft\Windows\CurrentVersion\RunOnce,Setup,0\
,"\\Server\Share\Setup.exe"
```

The last thing that you should know about this technique is that after Windows XP automatically logs the user on to it and the task completes, you're going to want to log the account off of the computer. Otherwise, you leave Windows XP vulnerable because anybody wandering by the computer has access to the account you used. The Windows XP Support

Tools, which you install from the Windows XP CD in the Support\Tools folder, contain a utility called Shutdown. After installing the application, run the command `shutdown -l` to log the user off of Windows XP. To restart the computer, run `shutdown -r`. To chain the application's setup program to the Shutdown command, use a batch file and the Start command with the `/wait` command-line option, which enables you to run programs synchronously, one after the other. To see the command-line options for the Shutdown command, type **shutdown /?** at the command prompt. Type **start /?** to see the options for the Start command.

Severing File Associations

There are two scenarios in which severing the default file associations is useful to IT professionals. The first is when you're concerned about users accidentally running scripts that they receive as mail attachments. If you don't have a virus filter on your mail server and you're not using a mail client like Outlook 2002, which blocks dangerous attachments, you can break the associations between the script files' extensions and the program class that opens them. Appendix A, "File Associations," describes how Windows XP associates file extensions with program classes. In the first scenario, you'd break the file association between the *.vbs* and *.js* file extensions and Windows Script Host. To do that, clear the default values of `HKCR\.vbs` and `HKCR\.js`. This isn't foolproof, however, because you can't break other dangerous file associations without affecting users' ability to use the operating system.

The second common scenario is when deploying Office XP in coexistence scenarios. For example, if you need to keep Microsoft Access 97 in the field until after you migrate those databases to Microsoft Access 2002, you might consider blocking the installation of Access 2002 until later. However, some businesses deploy Access 2002 so that it coexists with Access 97. Technically, this scenario works, but you have to tend to your license agreement. The problem with this scenario is that the default file association for the *.mdb* extension will be with Access 2002, which isn't usually appropriate. Instead, you'll want to restore the association with Access 97. Better yet, to prevent confusion, don't associate the *.mdb* file extension with any program class. To do this, clear the default value of `HKCR\.mdb`, and then teach users to use one of the following methods to ensure that they're opening each database in the appropriate version of Access:

- Open either version of Access first, and then open the database through the File menu.
- Create a shortcut for each database file that opens the file in the right version of Access.

Note   In the second scenario, you'll want to prevent Access 2002 users from accidentally converting down-level databases to the Access 2002 file format. You accomplish this by using the policies that come with the Office XP Resource Kit. The kit installs these policy templates in %SYSTEMROOT%\Inf, and you must load them into a GPO to use them. Be sure to enable the policy `Do Not Prompt To Convert Older Databases`, which prevents accidental database conversions.

Deploying Office XP Trusted Sources

If you're deploying Windows XP, odds are good that you're deploying Office XP. And if you're deploying Office XP, odds are good that you're concerned about security. Rightfully so, too. The security best practices that Microsoft prescribes will protect your business from most macro viruses. Those best practices are first to set the security level to high for all Office XP programs, which means that users can run only signed macros from trusted sources, and then to lock the list of trusted sources so users can't add to it. But how are users going to work if they can't run unsigned macros and they can't add sources to the list of trusted sources?

When a user opens a document that contains signed code, enables those macros, and then adds the source to the list of trusted sources, HKCU\Software\Microsoft\VBA\Trusted is where Office XP stores those certificates. To enable user to add sources to the list of trusted sources, distribute the list of trusted sources along with Office XP. The deployment tools don't provide a user interface for doing this, so here's my solution:

1. Create a document that contains code, and then sign the code using a certificate you want to deploy. Repeat this for each certificate.

2. Install Office XP on a lab computer and set the security levels to high.

3. Open each document containing a certificate you want to deploy. Enable the document's macros, and then add the source to the list of trusted sources. Figure 15-6 shows you an example.

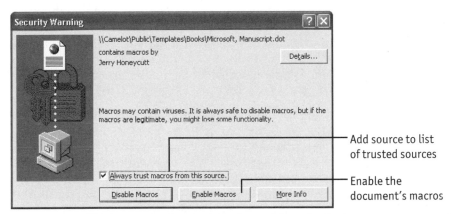

Figure 15-6 *High security in combination with code signing protects your business from viruses.*

4. Export the key HKCU\Software\Microsoft\VBA\Trusted to a REG file, and include this REG file in your deployment. Chapter 14, "Deploying Office XP Settings," describes how to deploy registry settings with Office XP.

Enabling Remote Desktop Remotely

Remote Desktop is one of my all-time favorite Windows XP features. I've raved about it numerous times throughout this book because it enables me to use several computers from the comfort of a single screen and keyboard. In an enterprise environment, Remote Desktop enables users to connect to their desktop computers from any other computer in the organization. It also enables administrators to manage computers remotely and even install software on remote computers.

My main problem with Remote Desktop is that Windows XP doesn't enable it by default. As a result, you must enable it on your disk image or enable it using the System Properties dialog box. Click Start, Control Panel, Performance And Maintenance, and System. On the Remote tab, select the Allow Users To Connect Remotely To This Computer check box.

I've got a better solution. Use Regedit to edit the remote computer's registry. Change the REG_DWORD value fDenyTSConnections in the key HKLM\SYSTEM\CurrentControlSet\Control \Terminal Server to 0x00. Setting this value to 0x01 disables Remote Desktop. After you change this value, you'll be able to log on to the computer using Remote Desktop. The account you use to edit this setting must belong to the remote computer's local Administrators group.

Customizing the Windows XP Logon

I'll wrap this chapter up by showing you how to customize the logon process in Windows XP. The first thing I want to show you is how to customize the screen saver that Windows XP uses when it's displaying the Log On To Windows dialog box. There's no user interface for configuring this screen saver. However, you can change it in the key HKU\.DEFAULT \Control Panel\Desktop. Set the value of SCRNSAVE.EXE to the name of the screen saver file you want to use. The default value is Logon.scr, which is the logon screen saver. If you want to use the Starfield screen saver instead, set SCRNSAVE.EXE to Ssstars.scr.

The second customization is a bit more serious. Companies often want to display an acceptable usage policy when users log on to their computers. You can do that by setting the REG_SZ value LegalNoticeCaption to the caption you want to display in the window's title bar, and the REG_SZ value LegalNoticeText to the text you want to display in the window. Both values are in the key HKLM\SOFTWARE\Microsoft\Windows NT\CurrentVersion \Winlogon. For example, you can set LegalNoticeCaption to Corporate Policy and LegalNoticeText to Corporate policy prohibits the use of this computer for actual work.

Appendices

The appendices in this part describe how Windows XP organizes the registry. They also describe some of the more interesting settings in the registry. They don't describe every key and every setting, but they give you the information you'll need to find your way. Both power users and IT professionals can use this information as a roadmap to help them navigate the thousands of settings that the registry contains.

File Associations

The bulk of the registry's content is in HKCR, which is where Microsoft Windows XP stores file associations and class registrations. These settings associate different types of files with the programs that can open, edit, and print them. They also register different program classes so that Windows XP can create objects using them.

A large number of the customizations I make on a regular basis are simple ones in HKCR. For example, I like to add commands to the file association for folders so I can open an MS-DOS command prompt with the selected folder set as the current working directory. I've also added commands to the My Computer object so I can quickly access Registry Editor (Regedit) and Tweak UI. If you master the contents of HKCR, the opportunities for tweaking Windows XP so it looks and feels the way you want are boundless.

The root key HKCR is many times more complex than it was back in the days of Microsoft Windows 95, when I wrote my first registry book. I'm not even going to attempt to describe all the different values you find in HKCR. Instead, I'm going to describe the most useful subkeys and values so you can customize Windows XP using the same techniques that I use.

Merge Algorithm

Recall from Chapter 1, "Learning the Basics," that HKCR was a link to the key HKLM\SOFTWARE\Classes before Microsoft Windows 2000, but it is more complicated now. Windows XP merges HKLM\SOFTWARE\Classes and HKCU\Software\Classes. The data in HKLM is default file associations and class registrations, whereas the data in HKCU is per-user file associations and class registrations. HKCU\Software\Classes is really a link to HKU\SID_Classes, which Windows XP loads when it loads the profile hive in HKU\SID. If the same value appears in both branches, the value in HKCU\Software\Classes has higher precedence and wins over the value in HKLM\SOFTWARE\Classes.

Chapter 1 described the benefits of this merge algorithm, but in short, it enables users to install applications and use file associations that don't affect other users. Thus, two users who share a computer can use two different programs to edit the same types of files.

When you create a new key in the root of HKCR, Windows XP actually creates it in HKLM \SOFTWARE\Classes. Windows XP doesn't provide a user interface other than Registry Editor to add class registrations to HKCU\Software\Classes because the intention is to allow programs to register per-user program classes. When you edit an existing program class, however, the change is reflected in HKLM or HKCU, depending on where the program class already exists. If the program class exists in both places, Windows XP updates only the version in HKCU.

File Extension Keys

Files containing particular types of data usually have the same file extension. For example, Microsoft Word 2002 documents have the *.doc* file extension. Although three-character extensions are the norm, extensions can be longer. Files with the same extension are members of a *file class*. File classes define behaviors common to all files that share that file name extension. By customizing file associations, you can specify which application opens a file, add commands to the shortcut menu, or even specify a custom icon that Windows Explorer will use for that type of file.

File associations have two parts. The first is a file extension key, HKCR\.*ext*. When Windows XP needs information about a file type, it looks up this key. The default value of the file extension key contains the name of the program class associated with it, which is the second part. Program classes are in HKCR*progid*, where *progid* is the program ID of the application. The default value of *progid* contains the friendly name of the application. For example, the file extension key HKCR\.txt has a default value of txtfile. Look in HKCR\txtfile to find the program class associated with it, and you'll find the description Text File. Figure A-1 illustrates this relationship with the *.ani* file extension.

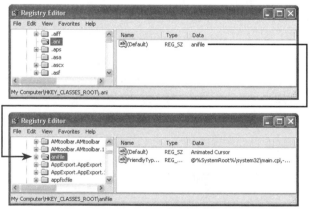

Figure A-1   *The default values of file extension keys associate these keys with program classes.*

File extension keys can have a variety of subkeys and values. The following list describes the most common:

- **PerceivedType.** This REG_SZ value indicates the file's perceived type. Windows XP is the only version of Windows that uses this key. See "PerceivedType" below, for more information.

- **Content Type.** This REG_SZ value indicates the MIME type.

- **OpenWithProgids.** This subkey contains a list of alternate program classes associated with the file extension. Windows XP displays these programs in the Other Programs area in the Open With dialog box.

- **OpenWithList.** This subkey contains one or more keys bearing the names of the applications to appear in the Recommended Programs area in the Open With dialog box. See "OpenWithList," later in this appendix, for more information.

- **ShellNew.** This subkey defines a template from which Windows XP creates a new file when users choose this file type on the New menu. See "ShellNew," later in this appendix, for more information.

OpenWithList

Sometimes users want to open files with applications that aren't associated with the file class. For example, a user might want to open a document in WordPad instead of Microsoft Word 2002. In other cases, users might want to open files that have no file associations. The Open With dialog box allows both scenarios.

The applications you see in the Open With dialog box are registered in HKCR\Applications. This key contains one subkey for each application, and the subkey bears the name of the program's executable file. You can prevent Windows XP from displaying an application in the Open With dialog box by adding the REG_SZ value NoOpenWith to HKCR\Applications \program.exe.

PerceivedType

Perceived types are similar to file types, except perceived types refer to broad categories of file format types, rather than to specific types of files. Think of them as super types. Perceived types include images, text files, audio files, and compressed files. In Windows XP, you can associate a perceived type with each file type. For example, the file extensions *.bmp*, *.png*, *.jpg*, and *.gif* are perceived as image files. Windows XP defines several perceived file types. In the file extension key, you set the REG_SZ value PerceivedType to one of the following:

- Image
- Text
- Audio
- Video
- Compressed
- System

ShellNew

When users right-click in a folder and click New, they see a list of template files that they can create in the folder. You can extend the New menu with additional file templates. First make sure that HKCR contains a file extension key for the type of file you're creating. Then create the ShellNew subkey under the file extension key. For example, to define a template for files with the *.inf* extension, create the key HKCR\.inf\ShellNew. Then in ShellNew, create one of the following values:

- **Command.**   Executes an application. This is a REG_SZ value command to execute. For example, you use a command to launch a wizard.

- **Data.**   Creates a file containing specified data. This is a REG_BINARY value that contains the file's data. Windows XP ignores this value if either NullFile or FileName exists.

- **FileName.**   Creates a file that is a copy of a specified file. This is a REG_SZ value that contains the path and name of the file to copy. If the file is in the user profile's Templates folder, you can leave off the path.

- **NullFile.**   Creates an empty file. This is a REG_SZ value that contains no data. If the value NullFile exists, Windows XP ignores Data and FileName.

Program Class Keys

Program classes define a program and the behaviors associated with it. Program classes are in HKCR*progid*, where progid is a program identifier. For example, HKCR\txtfile is a program class. Windows XP associates file extension keys with program classes through the file extension keys' default values. The default value of the program class contains the class's friendly name. The proper format of a program ID is *application.component.version*. For example, Word.Document.6 is a proper program ID. This format isn't always used, though, not even by Windows XP.

Program classes contain the following values and subkeys:

- **AlwaysShowExt.**   This empty REG_SZ value indicates that Windows Explorer should always show the file extension, even if the user has hidden it.

- **CurVer.**   The default value of this subkey contains the program ID of the most current version.

- **DefaultIcon.**   The default value of this subkey is the default icon that Windows XP displays for files associated with this program class. This value can be either a REG_SZ or a REG_EXPAND_SZ string, but it must use the format *file,index*, where *file* is the path and name of the file containing the icon, and *index* is the index of the icon in the file. Optionally, if you know the exact resource ID, you can use the format *file,-resource*. See "DefaultIcon," on the facing page, for more information.

- **FriendlyTypeName.**   This REG_SZ value is the friendly name for the program class. You see this value in Windows Explorer. In Windows XP, this value supercedes the program class's default value, which earlier versions of Windows still use and Windows XP maintains for backwards compatibility. Still, the default value of the program class and this value should remain the same for consistency. Windows XP commonly specifies a resource instead of a string in this value. The format is *@file,index* or *@file,-resource.*

- **EditFlags.** This is a REG_DWORD value that controls how Windows XP handles file classes linked to this program class. You can also use the EditFlags value to control users' ability to modify certain aspects of these file classes. See "EditFlags," later in this appendix, for more information.

- **InfoTip.** This REG_SZ value contains a brief message that Windows XP displays for this program class when users position the mouse pointer at a file or folder linked to it. This value can be a string or a resource as described for the FriendlyTypeName value.

- **IsShortcut.** This empty REG_SZ values indicates that the file is a shortcut. Windows Explorer displays the shortcut overlay on top of the file's icon.

- **NeverShowExt.** This empty REG_SZ value indicates that Windows Explorer should never show the file extension, even if the user has configured Windows Explorer to show file extensions for known types.

- **Shell.** This subkey contains commands (called *verbs*) defined for the program class. For example, the txtfile program class defines the commands for opening and printing text files. See "Shell," later in this appendix, for more information. This is the heart of most customizations you'll do in HKCR.

Special Program Classes

The program classes Directory, Drive, and Folder are specialized program classes that are useful to customize. The organization of these program classes is just like any other. They contain Shell subkeys that you can customize to add, change, and remove the commands you see on their shortcut menus. The trick is knowing which program classes apply to which types of objects:

- **Directory.** This program class applies to any normal folder that you can view in Windows Explorer.

- **Drive.** This program class applies only to drives that you see in My Computer.

- **Folder.** This program class applies to all system folders, drives, and other folders that you can view in Windows Explorer.

The program class Folder is the most inclusive. It includes all folders and all special system folders, such as Control Panel, My Computer, and so on. As such, this is typically the program class that you want to customize unless you need to restrict your customization to specifically drives or non-system folders.

DefaultIcon

Windows XP provides default icons for every type of object you see in Windows Explorer. That includes files, drives, and so on. You can customize these icons as described in

Chapter 4, "Hacking the Registry." Each file class's DefaultIcon value contains the path and name of the file containing the icon. You can assign an icon file, which has the *.ico* extension to this value, or you can assign an icon from program files using the formats *file,index* or *file,-resource. Index* is an incremental index number of a resource, and *resource* is a specific resource ID. Doing this requires that you know either the relative location of an icon in a file or the icon's exact resource ID. To find this value, you can use a third-party resource editor, many of which are shareware tools you can download from your favorite shareware Web site.

EditFlags

The REG_DWORD value EditFlags gives you some control of a program class's behavior. You can also use it to limit the ways in which users can change a program class. Each bit in this value represents a different setting, and Table A-1 describes the bit mask of each. See Chapter 1, "Learning the Basics," to refresh your memory on how to use bit masks.

Table A-1   Bits in EditFlags

Bit mask	Description
0x00000001	Excludes the file class.
0x00000002	Shows file classes, such as folders, that aren't associated with a file extension.
0x00000004	Denotes that the file class has a file extension.
0x00000008	Prevents users from editing the registry entries associated with this file class. They can't add new entries or change existing entries.
0x00000010	Prevents users from deleting the registry entries associated with this file class.
0x00000020	Prevents users from adding new verbs to the file class.
0x00000040	Prevents users from changing verbs.
0x00000080	Prevents users from deleting verbs.
0x00000100	Prevents users from changing the description of the file class.
0x00000200	Prevents users from changing the icon assigned to the file class.
0x00000400	Prevents users from changing the default verb.
0x00000800	Prevents users from changing the commands associated with verbs.
0x00001000	Prevents users from modifying or deleting verbs.
0x00002000	Prevents users from changing or deleting DDE-related values.
0x00008000	Prevents users from changing the content type associate with this file class.
0x00010000	Allows users to safely use the file class's open verb for downloaded files.
0x00020000	Disables the Never Ask Me check box.
0x00040000	Denotes that the file class's file name extension is always shown, even if the user hides known file extensions in the Folder Options dialog box.
0x00100000	Denotes that members of this file class are not added to the Recent Documents folder.

Shell

File classes contain verbs, which are commands that Windows XP executes to complete certain actions. Verbs are related to the shortcut menus that you see when you right-click a file. Each item on the shortcut menu is a verb. A program class's verbs are in HKCR \progid\Shell, which contains one subkey for each verb. For example, HKCR\txtfile\Shell contains the subkeys open and print, which are the Open and Print verbs. The default value of the Shell key indicates the name of the default verb. For example, if the default value of Shell is edit, this indicates that the subkey edit is the default verb. If the default value of Shell is empty, Windows XP uses the verb open. If that verb is missing, it uses the first verb as the default. Figure A-2 shows an example that relates the Shell key to shortcut menus.

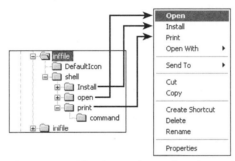

Figure A-2 *This figure shows the relationship of a program class's verbs to the shortcut menu.*

Canonical verbs are built in to the operating system. Examples of canonical verbs are Open, Edit, and Print. One thing that makes canonical verbs special is that Windows XP automatically translates them to different languages as necessary. The following list shows typical canonical verbs, some of which are special verbs that users don't see on menus:

- **Edit.** This is usually the same as Open, but enables the user to edit the file's contents.

- **Explore.** This opens the selected folder in Windows Explorer.

- **Find.** This opens Search Assistant with the selected folder as the default search location.

- **Open.** This is typically the default verb, which opens a file in the associated application.

- **Open As.** This opens the Open With dialog box.

- **Play.** This indicates that the contents of the file will be opened and played, rather than just opening the file and waiting for the user to play it.

- **Print.** This causes the application to print the file's contents and exit. Applications should display as little user interface as possible.

- **PrintTo.** This is a special verb that supports drag-and-drop to printers. Users don't see this verb on shortcut menus.

- **Preview.**   This enables users to preview files without opening or editing them. An example is previewing images, rather than opening to edit them.

- **Properties.**   This opens the *Name* Properties dialog box.

- **RunAs.**   This is a special verb that enables users to open a file or run an application in the context of a different user. They can see this verb on shortcut menus by holding down the Shift key while right-clicking the file.

You can add supplemental verbs to any program class. For example, you can add the verb Edit in WordPad to the txtfile program class to have the option of editing text files in WordPad without changing the default verbs. To add verbs to a program class, create a new subkey for it in the Shell key. The new subkey is HKCR*progid*\Shell*verb*. Then set the default value of *verb* to the text you want to see on the shortcut menu. You can make any character in the description a hotkey by prefixing it with an ampersand (&). For example, Open in &WordPad makes the letter *W* a hotkey for that verb. Add the subkey command to *verb*, and set its default value to the command you want to execute when you choose that verb. Figure A-3 shows an example.

Figure A-3   *Add supplemental verbs to a program class by creating new subkeys in* Shell.

The default value of command needs a bit more explanation. First if the path and name of the program file contain spaces, you should enclose the command in quotation marks. Second you use %1 as a placeholder for the file name that you right-clicked. For example, assume the command is Notepad "%1". If you right-click C:\Sample\Text.txt, the command is *Notepad "C:\Sample\Text.txt."* Note that you should always enclose %1 in quotation marks so that the command works with long file names.

You see extended verbs only when you press the Shift key while right-clicking a file. Creating extended verbs is a handy way to remove clutter from shortcut menus. For example, you can add extended verbs that you don't use often to shortcut menus, hiding them behind the Shift key. To make a verb an extended verb, add the empty REG_SZ value extended to the verb's subkey, Shell*verb*.

Specialized Keys

When Windows XP queries a file association, it checks the following keys in the order shown; that is, locations further down the list have a higher order of precedence than locations higher in the list:

- HKCR*progid.*   This is the program class associated with the file extension key through the file extension key's default value.

- HKCR\SystemFileAssociations.   This key defines perceived file types, and associates commands with each. See "SystemFileAssociations," later in this appendix, for more information.

- HKCR*.   This is the base class for files of all types. You see the commands in this key on the shortcut menus of all files.

- HKCR\AllFileSystemObjects.   This key defines commands for all files and folders. By default, this key just adds the Send To item on shortcut menus.

The sections following this one describe some of the keys in the previous list as well as others that are useful for customizing Windows XP. Notably, the section "SystemFileAssociations" describes how to customize the commands you see on files perceived as a certain type. The section "Applications" describes how to customize the Open With dialog box and more.

Applications

To display an application in the Open With dialog box, that application must register in HKCR \Applications. Each subkey in Applications bears the name of the program file. For example, Notepad is in HKCR\Applications\Notepad.exe. You must also add the OpenWithList key to the file extension key, as described earlier in this appendix. You find combinations of the following values and subkeys in the program's subkeys:

- NoOpenWith.   This empty REG_SZ value indicates that Windows XP should not add the program to the Open With list.

- FriendlyAppName.   This REG_SZ value contains the application's friendly name. This value can contain a string, but it more likely contains a value in the format *@file,-resource*, where *file* is the name of the program file containing the string resource identified by *resource*.

- SupportedTypes.   This subkey contains a list of file extensions, including the leading period, which indicates which type of files the program can open. For example, HKCR \Applications\mplayer2.exe\SupportedTypes contains the empty REG_SZ values .asf and .mp3, indicating that the program can open files that have these file extensions. This list filters the Open With list.

SystemFileAssociations

The key HKCR\SystemFileAssociations is a cool way to customize the shortcut menus of files by their perceived purposes. For example, you can customize the verbs you see for all files you perceive as text files or all files you perceive as image files.

HKCR\SystemFileAssociations contains subkeys for the different perceived types you can set in the value PerceivedType. You learned about this value in "PerceivedType," earlier in this appendix. Thus, setting PerceivedType in a file extension key associates that file name extension with the commands in this key. For example, if you set the value PerceivedType in HKCR \.inf to text, you'll see the commands in HKCR\SystemFileAssociations\text on the shortcut menu of any file that has the *.inf* extension. Perceived types in SystemFileAssociations include audio, image, system, text, and video. You can add additional perceived types to SystemFileAssociations, though. The organization of HKCR\SystemFileAssociations\type is the same as program classes, which you learned about in the section "Program Class Keys," earlier in this appendix.

Unknown

When users try opening files that have an extension not registered in HKCR, Windows XP looks in HKCR\Unknown. By default, the only verb in Unknown\Shell is Open As. Windows XP displays the Open With dialog box for unknown types of files.

COM Class Keys

The key HKCR\CLSID contains COM class registrations. HKCR\CLSID*clsid* is an individual class registration, where *clsid* is the class's class ID, which is a GUID. See Chapter 1, "Learning the Basics," to learn more about GUIDs. The default value of each class registration contains the class's name, but it's not all that friendly. There's not a lot to customize in HKCR\CLSID. Programs register these classes when you install them so they can create objects from these classes.

Class registrations sometimes contain the same subkeys as program classes in HKCR. For example, class registrations support the DefaultIcon and InfoTip values. They also contain many more subkeys and values that program classes don't support. Listing them here is senseless because they are in the programmer's domain and not useful for a power user or IT professional customizing Windows XP. However, knowing the class ID of certain COM classes is useful when customizing other parts of the registry. For example, adding some classes to the desktop's namespace enables you to customize the objects you see on it. You can use this same information to hide icons that you see in My Network Places. Chapter 4, "Hacking the Registry," describes how to show and hide desktop icons using these class IDs. Thus, Table A-2 lists the most interesting COM classes that are in HKCR\CLSID.

Table A-2   Special Classes in HKCR\CLSID

Object	Class identifier
Shell folders	
ActiveX Cache	{88C6C381-2E85-11D0-94DE-444553540000}
Computer Search Results	{1F4DE370-D627-11D1-BA4F-00A0C91EEDBA}
History	{FF393560-C2A7-11CF-BFF4-444553540000}
Internet Explorer	{871C5380-42A0-1069-A2EA-08002B30309D}
My Computer	{20D04FE0-3AEA-1069-A2D8-08002B30309D}
My Documents	{450D8FBA-AD25-11D0-98A8-0800361B1103}
My Network Places	{208D2C60-3AEA-1069-A2D7-08002B30309D}
Offline Files	{AFDB1F70-2A4C-11D2-9039-00C04F8EEB3E}
Programs	{7BE9D83C-A729-4D97-B5A7-1B7313C39E0A}
Recycle Bin	{645FF040-5081-101B-9F08-00AA002F954E}
Search Results	{E17D4FC0-5564-11D1-83F2-00A0C90DC849}
Shared Documents	{59031A47-3F72-44A7-89C5-5595FE6B30EE}
Start Menu	{48E7CAAB-B918-4E58-A94D-505519C795DC}
Temporary Internet Files	{7BD29E00-76C1-11CF-9DD0-00A0C9034933}
Web	{BDEADF00-C265-11D0-BCED-00A0C90AB50F}
Control Panel folders	
Administrative Tools	{D20EA4E1-3957-11D2-A40B-0C5020524153}
Fonts	{D20EA4E1-3957-11D2-A40B-0C5020524152}
Network Connections	{7007ACC7-3202-11D1-AAD2-00805FC1270E}
Printers And Faxes	{2227A280-3AEA-1069-A2DE-08002B30309D}
Scanners And Cameras	{E211B736-43FD-11D1-9EFB-0000F8757FCD}
Scheduled Tasks	{D6277990-4C6A-11CF-8D87-00AA0060F5BF}
Control Panel icons	
Folder Options	{6DFD7C5C-2451-11D3-A299-00C04F8EF6AF}
Taskbar And Start Menu	{0DF44EAA-FF21-4412-828E-260A8728E7F1}
User Accounts	{7A9D77BD-5403-11D2-8785-2E0420524153}
Other	
Add Network Places	{D4480A50-BA28-11D1-8E75-00C04FA31A86}
Briefcase	{85BBD920-42A0-1069-A2E4-08002B30309D}
E-mail	{2559A1F5-21D7-11D4-BDAF-00C04F60B9F0}
Help And Support	{2559A1F1-21D7-11D4-BDAF-00C04F60B9F0}
Internet	{2559A1F4-21D7-11D4-BDAF-00C04F60B9F0}
Network Setup Wizard	{2728520D-1EC8-4C68-A551-316B684C4EA7}
Run	{2559A1F3-21D7-11D4-BDAF-00C04F60B9F0}
Search	{2559A1F0-21D7-11D4-BDAF-00C04F60B9F0}
Windows Security	{2559A1F2-21D7-11D4-BDAF-00C04F60B9F0}

Per-User Settings

Chapter 4, "Hacking the Registry," and Chapter 15, "Working Around IT Problems," described numerous useful registry settings. This appendix continues by describing the most interesting settings in the Microsoft Windows XP registry.

The settings in this appendix are per user; they're in HKCU. The root key HKLM contains similar settings, but the settings in HKCU are more interesting because these are often useful for deployment and customization. Also, many of my favorite IT hacks are in HKCU rather than HKLM because they affect per-user behaviors instead of the overall computer configuration. I'm not able to describe every setting in HKCU, incidentally. Even if I could figure out every setting, documenting them all would require hundreds of pages. Instead, I'm focusing on the most interesting and useful settings in the registry with a dab of just-plain-cool settings thrown into the mix.

The resources that I used to discover these settings vary. Many times I just know what a setting does from experience. Other times, I used Microsoft's Developer Network, Knowledge Base, or resource kits. If I get really desperate to figure out a setting, I'll install the Windows Software Development Kit and then search for the setting in the header files, which yields surprisingly good results.

The headings in this appendix follow the organization of HKCU to make finding information easier. Thus, you'll see top-level headings for HKCU\Control Panel, and so on. This appendix doesn't describe the relationship of HKCU to HKU and the profile hives that the operating system loads, though. For more information about this relationship, see Chapter 1, "Learning the Basics."

AppEvents

Windows XP associates sounds with certain events. The most notable are the sounds you hear when you log on to or off of the operating system. You assign sounds to different events, including minimizing windows, opening menus, and so on, in the Sounds And Audio Devices dialog box shown in Figure B-1. To open this dialog box, click Start; Control Panel; Sounds, Speech, And Audio Devices; Sounds And Audio Devices. Figure B-1 shows which subkeys of AppEvents provide this dialog box's values. Many applications also associate sounds with certain events. For example, you can download and install sounds for use with Microsoft Office XP. These sounds provide great feedback that I've missed when they're not available. If you don't like the sound that a particular event produces, you can change the sound file associated with it. For example, you can create your own recording that says, "You've got spam!" and associate that sound file with Windows Messenger's New Mail event.

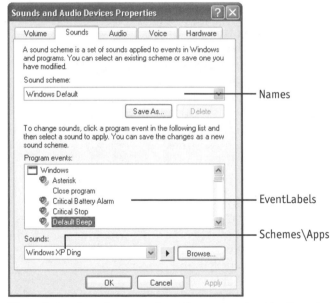

Figure B-1   *Associate sounds with events using the Sounds And Audio Devices Properties dialog box.*

These events and the sounds associated with them are in HKCU\AppEvents. There are two subkeys in AppEvents. The first is EventLabels, which contains one subkey for each event, and the subkey's default value is the name of the event as you see it in Control Panel. The second is Schemes. This is the more interesting subkey because it actually associates sound files with each event. You can customize AppEvents, but doing so isn't worth the extra effort. Configuring sounds is far easier through Control Panel. My suggestion is that you configure your sounds the way you like them, and then export AppEvents to a REG file that you can use to configure sounds down the line. Just make sure the sound files are available if you're using the REG file on a different computer. Most times, you'll find all these sound files in %SYSTEMROOT%\media.

Console

The key HKCU\Console contains the default configuration for the MS-DOS command prompt (console subsystem). This is the environment that hosts all character-mode applications. To change console settings, click the System icon (top-left corner of the window), and then click Properties. After changing the properties, Windows XP prompts you to change the default settings or save the settings for console windows that have the same title:

- If you change the default settings, the operating system stores those settings in HKCU\Console.

- If you save the settings for console windows with the same title, the operating system creates the subkey HKCU\Console*Title*, where *Title* is the window's title, and stores the custom settings in it (see Figure B-2).

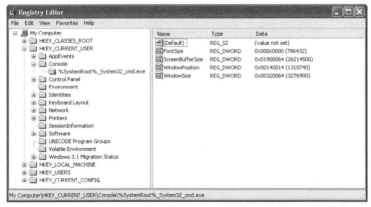

Figure B-2   *Each subkey in* Console *is the title of a customized console window. You typically see this key only after starting a command prompt from the Run dialog box.*

Like AppEvents, there's seldom a good reason to customize these settings directly. It's not really a cool hack, and a user interface is available for all these settings. What is cool is that after you've configured your console windows just the way you want them, you can export Console to a REG file. Then the next time you install Windows XP, import the REG file to restore your console settings. You'll never configure a command prompt again.

Control Panel

The key HKCU\Control Panel has a wealth of customization possibilities. This is the key where Windows XP stores most of the settings you configure in Control Panel. The most interesting subkeys are Desktop and Mouse. The following list gives you an overview of what's in most of the subkeys, and I describe the Desktop and Mouse subkeys in more detail in the sections following this one:

- **Accessibility.**   This subkey stores accessibility settings you set using the Accessibility Options dialog box. To open this dialog box, click Start, Control Panel, Accessibility Options. The values' names are self-explanatory, and you can easily map them to the user interface.

- **Appearance.**   This subkey contains values for each scheme you see on the Appearance tab of the Display Properties dialog box. To open this dialog box, click Start, Control Panel, Appearance And Themes, Display. Customizing themes in the registry is too cumbersome to do reliably, so stick with the user interface.

- **Colors.**   This subkey defines the color of each element in the Windows XP user interface. ActiveBorder defines the color of each active window's border, for instance. Each value is a REG_SZ value that contains three decimal numbers that correspond to the RGB color notation.

- **Current.**   Windows XP does not use this subkey.

- **Cursors.**   This subkey contains values that associate the name of a mouse pointer with a file containing the mouse pointer. The file has the *.cur* extension, or if the pointer is animated, the *.ani* extension. The value's name is the name of the pointer. This key's default value contains the name of the current pointer scheme. You don't see values in this key unless you've customized your pointers in the Mouse Pointers dialog box. To open the Mouse Pointers dialog box, click Start, Control Panel, Printers And Other Hardware, Mouse.

- **Custom Colors.**   This subkey defines the custom colors in the color palette. The values in the Custom Colors subkey are named ColorA through ColorP, and all have a default value of 0xFFFFFF.

- **Desktop.**   See "Desktop," on the facing page.

- **don't load.**   This subkey indicates which Control Panel files to load. Windows XP consults the values in don't load to decide whether to display the file in Control Panel. The operating system looks for a value whose name is the same as the file. If the REG_SZ value is Yes, the operating system displays the file's icon in Control Panel; otherwise, it doesn't display the icon.

- **International.**   This subkey contains a value called Locale that contains the ID of the user's locale. See Intl.inf in %SYSTEMROOT%\Inf for a list of the locale IDs available. Configure this setting in the Regional And Language Options dialog box. To see this dialog box, click Start; Control Panel; Date, Time, Language, And

Regional Options; Regional And Language Options. You see many other values in this subkey, which define settings such as the currency symbol, date format, list separator, and so on.

- **Keyboard.**   This subkey stores options configured in the Keyboard Properties dialog box. To display the Keyboard Properties dialog box, click Start, Control Panel, Printers And Other Hardware, Keyboard. The most interesting value in this subkey is the REG_SZ value InitialKeyboardIndicators. If the value is 0, Windows XP turns NUMLOCK off when it starts. If the value is 2, the operating system turns on NUMLOCK. The operating system stores the current state of NUMLOCK in this value when users log off of or restart the computer.

- **Mouse.**   See "Mouse," later in this appendix.

- **PowerCfg.**   This subkey defines the schemes that you see in the Power Options dialog box. To open the Power Options dialog box, click Start, Control Panel, Performance And Maintenance, Power Options. The REG_SZ value CurrentPowerPolicy indicates the current power scheme. You find that scheme in PowerCfg\PowerPolicies.

- **Screen Saver.Name.**   These subkeys contain settings unique to each screen saver. *Name* is the name of the screensaver.

- **Sound.**   This subkey contains the REG_SZ value Beep, which indicates whether Windows XP beeps on errors. The operating system beeps on errors if this value is Yes.

Desktop

The values in HKCU\Control Panel\Desktop control many aspects of the Windows XP user interface. A good number of them don't have a user interface for configuring them, however, so there's a lot of potential in this subkey for customizing the operating system. The following list describes these values:

- **ActiveWndTrkTimeout.**   This REG_DWORD value indicates the time in milliseconds that the mouse pointer must remain over a window before Windows XP actives the window. The default value is 0.

- **AutoEndTasks.**   This REG_SZ value determines whether the operating system ends tasks automatically when users log off of or shut down Windows XP. If the value is 0, the operating system doesn't end processes automatically; instead, it waits until the timeout in HungAppTimeout expires and then displays the End Task dialog box. If the value is 1, the operating system automatically ends processes.

- **CaretWidth.**   This REG_DWORD value specifies the width of the blinking caret. The default value is 1. This value is not in the registry by default.

- **CoolSwitch.**   Windows XP doesn't use this value.

- **CoolSwitchColumns.**   This REG_SZ value determines how many columns of icons you see in Task Switcher (Alt+Tab). The default value is 7.

- **CoolSwitchRows.**   This REG_SZ value determines how many rows of icons you see in Task Switcher (Alt+Tab). The default value is 3.

- **CursorBlinkRate.**   This REG_SZ value determines the amount of time in milliseconds that elapses between each blink of the selection cursor. The default value is 530, which is a little more than a half a second.

- **DragFullWindows.**   This REG_SZ value determines whether users see windows' contents when they drag them. The default value is 1, which means users see full window contents when dragging. Set this value to 0 to see window outlines only.

- **DragHeight.**   This REG_SZ value indicates the height of the rectangle that determines the start of a drag operation. The default value is 4.

- **DragWidth.**   This REG_SZ value indicates the width of the rectangle that determines the start of a drag operation. The default value is 4.

- **FontSmoothing.**   This REG_SZ value determines whether Windows XP smoothes the edges of large fonts using anti-aliasing techniques. The default value is 0, which disables font smoothing. To enable font smoothing, set it to 2.

- **ForegroundFlashcount.**   This REG_DWORD value indicates the number of times that a taskbar button flashes to get the user's attention. The default value is 3. If the timeout value in ForegroundLockTimeout expires without user input, Windows XP automatically brings the window to the foreground.

- **ForegroundLockTimeout.**   This REG_DWORD value specifies the time in milliseconds that must elapse since the last user input before Windows XP allows windows to come to the foreground. The default value is 200000 (200 seconds).

- **GridGranularity.**   Windows XP doesn't use this value.

- **HungAppTimeout.**   This REG_SZ value controls how long Windows XP waits for processes to end in response to users' clicking the End Task button in Task Manager. If the timeout expires, Windows XP displays the End Task dialog box, which tells the user that the process did not response to the request. The default value is 5000, or five seconds.

- **LowPowerActive.**   This REG_SZ value indicates the status of the low-power alarm. If this value is 0, no alarm activates when batter power is low. This is the default value. If this value is 1, an alarm activates when battery power is low. This value affects only computers that use Advanced Power Management (APM).

- **LowPowerTimeOut.**   This REG_SZ value determines if a lower-power timeout is set. If this value is 0, the timeout is not set. This is the default value. If this value is 1, the timeout is set. This value affects only computers that use Advanced Power Management (APM).

- **MenuShowDelay.**   This REG_SZ value determines the time in milliseconds that elapses between when the user points to a menu and when Windows XP displays it. The default value is 400, which is almost half a second.

- **PaintDesktopVersion.** This REG_DWORD value determines whether Windows XP displays its version and build number on the desktop. The default value is 0, which doesn't display the version. Set this value to 1 to display the version of Windows XP on the desktop.

- **Pattern.** This REG_SZ value defines a two-color, 8-pixel-by-8-pixel bitmap used for the background. The default value is an empty string. To define a bitmap, set this value to *B1 B2 B3 B4 B5 B6 B7 B8*. *BN* is an 8-bit binary number that represents a row of 8 pixels. Bits that are 0 show the background color, whereas bits that are 1 show the foreground color.

- **ScreenSaveActive.** This REG_SZ value determines whether the user has selected a screen saver. The default value is 1, indicating that a screen saver is active. Set this value to 0 to indicate that a screen saver is not active.

- **ScreenSaverIsSecure.** This REG_SZ value has a default value of 0. This value indicates whether or not the screen saver is password-protected. The value 1 indicates the screen saver is password-protected; 0 indicates that it's not protected.

- **ScreenSaveTimeOut.** This REG_SZ value specifies the time in seconds that the computer must remain idle before the screen saver starts. The default is 600, which is 10 minutes.

- **SCRNSAVE.EXE.** This REG_SZ value has no default value. This value specifies the path and name of the screen saver executable file. If the screen saver file is in %SYSTEMROOT%\System32, no path is necessary.

- **TileWallpaper.** This REG_SZ value indicates how to format wallpaper on the screen. If the value is 0, Windows XP centers the wallpaper. This is the default value. If the value is 1, Windows XP tiles the wallpaper.

- **WaitToKillAppTimeout.** This REG_SZ value indicates the time in milliseconds that Windows XP waits for processes to end after users log off of or shut down Windows XP. If the timeout expires and processes are still running, Windows XP displays the End Task dialog box, unless you've set the value AutoEndTasks to end processes automatically. The default value is 20000, which is 20 seconds.

- **Wallpaper.** This REG_SZ value is the path and file name of the image to use for wallpaper. The default value is an empty string. You don't need to include the path if the file is in %SYSTEMROOT% or %SYSTEMROOT%\System32. If you want to include wallpaper in a default user profile, copy the image file to the user profile folder and then specify the full path in this value.

- **WallpaperStyle.** This REG_SZ value determines how to display the wallpaper on the desktop. The default value is 0, which centers the bitmap on the desktop. Set this value to 2 to stretch the wallpaper.

- **WheelScrollLines.** This REG_SZ value specifies the number of lines to scroll for each one-notch rotation of the mouse wheel when users don't use modifier keys such as Ctrl or Alt. The default value is 3. To turn off wheel scrolling, set this value to 0.

I left the value UserPreferencesMask out of the list because this value represents some of the most interesting and most useful ways to customize Windows XP. It's also more complicated than other values in the list because it's a bit mask that contains a large number of settings in one value. Lately, Microsoft has stayed away from using large bit masks like this one, favoring REG_DWORD values that you set to 0x00 to disable a feature and 0x01 to enable a feature. This value is a holdover from earlier versions of Windows, however. It's a 4-byte REG_BINARY value that might as well be a REG_DWORD value. The default value is 0x80003E9E, which will make more sense after you know what the different bits in this value represent.

Table B-1 describes each bit. Because this is a REG_BINARY value, count the bits from left to right, beginning with 0. If this were a REG_DWORD value, you'd count the bits from right to left instead. The table indicates each setting's bit number, describes the feature that it controls, and shows the bit mask. For any feature you see in the table, setting the bit to 0 disables the feature and setting it to 1 enables the feature. If you'd like to see an example of writing a script that changes settings in UserPreferencesMask, see Chapter 4, "Hacking the Registry." Chapter 4 contains a script that updates this value to cause Windows XP to raise windows to the foreground when you point at them. For more information about doing bitwise math, see Chapter 1, "Learning the Basics."

Table B-1   Bits in UserPreferencesMask

Bit	Bit mask	Default	Description
0	0x00000001	0	Active window tracking. Windows get focus when the user positions the mouse pointer over them.
1	0x00000002	1	Menu animation. This depends on the value of bit 9.
2	0x00000004	1	Combo box animation. The combo boxes slide open.
3	0x00000008	1	List box smooth scrolling. The list boxes scroll smoothly.
4	0x00000010	1	Gradient captions. The title bars display a gradient.
5	0x00000020	0	Keyboard cues. Menu hotkeys are underlined only when accessed from the keyboard.
6	0x00000040	0	Active window tracking Z order. Windows that gain focus through active window tracking are brought to the foreground.
7	0x00000080	1	Mouse hot tracking.
8	0x00000100	0	Reserved for future use.
9	0x00000200	1	Menu fade animation. Menus fade when closed; otherwise, menus use slide animation.
10	0x00000400	1	Selection fade animation. Lists fade after users make a section.
11	0x00000800	1	Tooltip animation. This depends on bit 12.
12	0x00001000	1	Tooltip fade animation. Tooltips fade when they close. When the bit is set to 0, tooltips use slide animation.
13	0x00002000	1	Cursor shadow. This requires more than 256 colors.
31	0x80000000	1	All user-interface effects. This enables combo box animation, cursor shadow, gradient captions, hot tracking, list box smooth scrolling, menu animation, menu hotkey underlining, selection fade, and tooltip animation.

Desktop\Window Metrics

The key HKCU\Control Panel\Desktop\Windows Metrics contains settings that govern the dimensions of the elements you see on the screen. Some of these settings represent dimensions in pixels whereas others are actually coordinates. The following list describes the settings in Window Metrics, which you define by clicking Advanced on the Display Properties dialog box's Appearance tab, as shown in Figure B-3.

Figure B-3 *After you've configured the settings in this dialog box, consider exporting them to a REG file so you can use the same settings on other computers.*

- **BorderWidth.** This REG_SZ value determines the width of the borders for all windows that users can't resize. The default is -15, which is 15 twips. (The minus sign indicates a twip, which is 1/1440th of an inch.) Valid values are 0 to -750.

- **CaptionFont.** This REG_BINARY value contains the name of the font to use in window captions. The default is Trebuchet MS.

- **CaptionHeight.** This REG_SZ value specifies the height of caption buttons. This value is measured in twips, and the default value is -375.

- **CaptionWidth.** This REG_SZ value specifies the width of caption buttons. This value is measured in twips, and the default value is -270.

- **IconFont.** This REG_BINARY value contains the name of the font used to display icon text. The default value is Tahoma.

- **IconSpacing.** This REG_SZ value specifies the width of the grid cell used to display the large view of an icon. This value is measured in twips and the default is -1125.

- **IconTitleWrap.** This REG_SZ value determines whether icon text wraps or truncates when it's too long to fit on one line. The default value is 1, which causes icon text to wrap; 0 causes icon text to truncate.

- **IconVerticalSpacing.** This REG_SZ value specifies the vertical space between icons. This value is measured in twips, and the default is -1125.

- **MenuFont.** This REG_BINARY value specifies the font to use in menu bars. The default value is Tahoma.

- **MenuHeight.** This REG_SZ value specifies the height of menu bars. This value is measured in twips, and the default is -285.

- **MenuWidth.** This REG_SZ value specifies the width of buttons on menu bars. This value is measured in twips, and the default is -270.

- **MessageFont.** This REG_BINARY value contains the name of the font to use in message boxes. The default value is Tahoma.

- **MinAnimate.** This REG_SZ value determines whether Windows XP uses animation for minimizing and restoring windows. The default value is 1, which uses animation. Set this value to 0 to prevent window animation.

- **ScrollHeight.** This REG_SZ value specifies the height of horizontal scroll bars. The default value, measured in twips, is -255.

- **ScrollWidth.** This REG_SZ value specifies the width of vertical scroll bars. The default value, measured in twips, is -255.

- **Shell Icon BPP.** This REG_SZ value determines the color depth of icons on the desktop. The default value is 4, but valid values include 4 (16 colors), 8 (256 colors), 16 (65,536 colors), 24 (16,777,216 colors), and 32 (16,777,216 colors).

- **Shell Icon Size.** This REG_SZ value specifies the size in pixels of icons that Windows Explorer displays. The default value is 32. Valid values range from 16 to 48 pixels.

- **SmCaptionFont.** This REG_BINARY value specifies the font to use for small captions. The default value is Tahoma.

- **SmCaptionHeight.** This REG_SZ value specifies the height of small captions. This value is measured in twips, and the default is -255.

- **SmCaptionWidth.** This REG_SZ value specifies the width of small captions. This value is measured in twips, and the default is -255.

- **StatusFont.** This REG_BINARY value specifies the font to use in status bars. The default value is Tahoma.

Mouse

The values in HKCU\Control Panel\Mouse configure the mouse. The following list describes these values, including their types and default values:

- **DoubleClickHeight.** This REG_SZ value specifies the height of the rectangle that Windows XP uses to detect double-clicks. If two clicks are within the rectangle and within the time specified by the value DoubleClickSpeed, the clicks are combined into a double-click. The default value is 4.

- **DoubleClickSpeed.** This REG_SZ value specifies the amount of time that can elapse between two mouse clicks for Windows XP to consider them a double-click. If the amount of time between clicks is greater than this timeout, the operating system considers them separate clicks. The default value is 500, which is half a second, and the valid range is 100 to 900.

- **DoubleClickWidth.** This REG_SZ value specifies the width of the rectangle that Windows XP uses to detect double-clicks. If two clicks are within the rectangle and within the time specified by the value DoubleClickSpeed, the clicks are combined into a double-click. The default value is 4.

- **MouseSpeed.** This REG_SZ value determines how fast the pointer moves in response to mouse movements. Valid values are 0, 1, and 2. The default value is 1. When this value is 0, Windows XP doesn't accelerate the mouse. When this value is 1, Windows XP doubles the mouse speed when it exceeds the value in MouseThreshold1. When this value is 2, Windows XP doubles the mouse speed when it exceeds the value in MouseThreshold1, and quadruples the mouse speed when it exceeds the value in MouseThreshold2.

- **MouseThreadhold1.** This REG_SZ value, measured in pixels, specifies the mouse speed that triggers mouse acceleration. The default value is 6.

- **MouseThreshold2.** This REG_SZ value, measured in pixels, specifies the mouse speed that triggers quadruple mouse acceleration. The default is 10.

- **MouseTrails.** This REG_SZ value specifies whether mouse trails is enabled or disabled. Setting this value to 0 disables mouse trails; setting it to 1 enables them.

- **SnapToDefaultButton.** This REG_SZ value determines whether the mouse snaps to the default button when you open a dialog box. The default value is 0, which turns off this feature. To enable this feature, set it to 1.

- **SwapMouseButtons.** This REG_SZ value determines whether Windows XP swaps the left and right mouse buttons. The default value is 0, which disables this feature. To swap the mouse buttons, set this value to 1.

Environment

The key HKCU\Environment defines per-user environment variables. Normally, all you see in this key are two values: TEMP and TMP. Both are REG_EXPAND_SZ values. You can add environment variables to Environment, however, and then use those from within batch files, REG_EXPAND_SZ values, and so on. Of course, you can also rely on the user interface to add environment variables. Click Start, Control Panel, Performance And Maintenance, System, and then click Environment Variables on the System Properties dialog box's Advanced tab. Per-user environment variables are at the top of the dialog box, and per-computer environment variables are at the bottom.

Keyboard Layout

The key HKCU\Keyboard Layout defines the keyboard layouts that you configure using the Regional And Language Options dialog box. In essence, a keyboard layout maps the physical keys on your keyboard to the characters they generate. Keyboard layouts enable you to write German text using a U.S. English keyboard, for example. This key sometimes contains a single REG_DWORD value, Attributes, which determines which key to use for Caps Lock. If this value is 0, Windows XP uses the Caps Lock key. If this value is 0x10000, the operating system uses the Shift key. You sometimes see three subkeys in HKCU\Keyboard Layout:

- **Preload.** This subkey contains the ID of each keyboard layout the user chooses through the Regional And Language Options dialog box. Windows XP uses this data to restore the keyboard layout when the user logs back on. The first value is 1, the second is 2, and so on. The value 1 is the default keyboard layout.

- **Substitutes.** This subkey stores the IDs of alternate keyboard layouts. Windows XP checks this subkey when loading a keyboard layout, and if it finds a substitute, it uses that instead of the default layout. This key is usually empty until the user chooses substitute keyboard layouts.

- **Toggle.** This subkey specifies the key sequences that toggle between input locales. It contains the REG_SZ value Hotkey, which can have one of four values. The value 1 specifies that Left Alt+Shift switches locales. The value 2 specifies Ctrl+Shift, 3 disables the key sequence altogether, and 4 specifies the accent grave key when the default locale is Thai.

Network

The key HKCU\Network contains data about the user's mapped network drives. Each subkey represents a mapped drive that Windows XP restores the next time the user logs on to the computer. The name of the subkey is HKCU\Network*Drive*, where *drive* is the drive letter mapped to the network path. The following values are in each mapped drive's subkey:

- **ConnectionType.**   This REG_DWORD value specifies how to connect the drive to the local computer. A value of 1 means drive redirection and 2 means print redirection. The default value is 1.

- **ProviderName.**   This REG_SZ value specifies the connection's network provider. The default value is Microsoft Windows Network.

- **ProviderType.**   This REG_DWORD value identifies the provider that makes the network connection. The value for the Microsoft LanMan provider is 0x20000. Other network providers use different values.

- **RemotePath.**   This REG_SZ value contains the network connection's UNC path using the notation *Computer**Share*.

- **UserName.**   This REG_SZ value contains the user's name, including the domain. It identifies the user who made the network connection, and Windows XP uses it to fill the Connect As box in the Map Network Drive dialog box.

Printers

The key HKCU\Printers defines the user's printer connections. The following list describes the three subkeys you find in this key:

- **Connections.**   This subkey contains one subkey for each printer connection The name of the key defines the printer connection: ,,*Server*,*Printer*. Also, values in this subkey define the print provider and server.

- **DevModePerUser.**   This subkey contains per-user printer settings.

- **Settings.**   This subkey contains settings for Add Printer Wizard, including the users' preferences from the last time they used the wizard to add a printer.

SessionInformation

The itty-bitty key HKCU\SessionInformation contains a single value. The REG_DWORD value ProgramCount indicates how many programs are running in the foreground. Each time you open a program on the desktop, Windows XP increments this value. Each time you close a foreground program, Windows XP decrements this value.

Software

The key HKCU\Software contains per-user program settings. Windows XP stores much of its own configuration in this key, too. Microsoft standardized this key's organization, which makes finding settings easier because you generally know where in the registry to look for a program's settings. Applications store their settings in HKCU\Software*Vendor**Program* *Version*\. *Vendor* is the name of the program's publisher, *Program* is the name of the program, and *Version* is the program's version number. Often, *Version* is simply CurrentVersion. Figure B-4 shows an example of a program that stores its settings in this key.

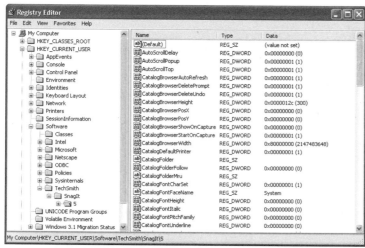

Figure B-4 *TechSmith SnagIt stores its settings in HKCU\Software\TechSmith\SnagIt\5.*

By far, the most interesting subkey is Microsoft because it contains most of the Windows XP per-user settings. This subkey is discussed in detail in "Software\Microsoft\Windows \CurrentVersion," later in this appendix. Other interesting subkeys are Classes and Policies, which I describe in the following sections.

Classes

The key HKCU\Software\Classes contains per-user file associations and class registrations. It's really a link to HKU*SID*_Classes, which you learned about in Chapter 1, "Learning the Basics." File associations in HKCU have precedence over file associations in HKLM. Per-user file associations began with Microsoft Windows 2000, and they enable users to install applications without affecting the file associations of other users who share the same computer. They also enable users' file associations to follow them when roaming user profiles are enabled. The contents of this key are the same as HKCR, so see Appendix A, "File Associations," for more information.

Microsoft\Command Processor

The MS-DOS command prompt supports file and folder name completion, as well as a few other features. You can configure these features using Tweak UI, as described in Chapter 5, "Mapping Tweak UI," or you can hack them directly in the registry. These are settings that I apply to just about every computer I use, so I keep them handy in a script. The following list describes the settings in the subkey Command Processor, which configure the MS-DOS command prompt:

- **AutoRun.**   This REG_SZ value, which has no default, contains a list of commands that run automatically when you start the MS-DOS command prompt.

- **CompletionChar.**   This REG_DWORD value specifies the ASCII character code of the key to use for file name completion. You can set this value to 0x00, 0x01 through 0x1F, 0x20, or 0x40. The Tab key is 0x09 and is the default.

- **DefaultColor.**   This REG_DWORD value specifies the default background and foreground color for the MS-DOS command prompt. The first hexadecimal digit specifies the background color, and the second digit specifies the foreground color. Valid values range from 0x00 to 0xFE; the default is 0. The digits correspond to the colors shown in Table B-2.

Table B-2   Values for DefaultColor

Value	Color
0	Black
1	Blue
2	Green
3	Aqua
4	Red
5	Purple
6	Yellow
7	White
8	Gray
9	Light Blue
A	Light Green
B	Light Aqua
C	Light Red
D	Light Purple
E	Light Yellow
F	Bright White

- **DelayedExpansion.** This REG_DWORD value specifies whether the command prompt delays environment variable expansion. If the value is 0x01, the command prompt interprets the exclamation point (!) as an environment variable that expands only when used. The default is 0x00.

- **EnableExtensions.** This REG_DWORD value determines whether command-processor extensions are enabled or not. Setting this value to 0x00 disables extensions. You need to disable extensions only when they interfere with a script language with which they aren't compatible. The default value is 0x01.

- **PathCompletionChar.** This REG_DWORD value specifies the ASCII character code of the key to use for path completion. Set this value to 0x00, 0x01 through 0x1F, 0x20, or 0x40. The Tab key is 0x09. You can use the same key that you use for file name completion, which expands both.

Microsoft\Internet Connection Wizard

The key HKCU\Software\Microsoft\Internet Connection Wizard contains a single value that indicates whether users have run the wizard. Unlike earlier versions of Windows, the wizard doesn't run automatically when users first open Internet Explorer, so this value is only interesting for inventorying. If the REG_BINARY value Completed is 0x0000, the user has not run the wizard. If the value is 0x0001, the user has run the wizard.

Microsoft\Internet Explorer

The key HKCU\Software\Microsoft\Internet Explorer contains per-user settings for Internet Explorer. Many of the subkeys in Internet Explorer are difficult to understand or uninteresting. There are settings in this key that are very useful to customize, however:

- **Help_Menu_URLs.** This subkey is used to redirect Internet Explorer's online support feature to an intranet location, instead of Microsoft's Web site. To do that, add the REG_SZ value Online_Support to this subkey, and then set its value to the URL of your Internet Explorer support page. After customizing this setting, when users click Help, Online Support, Internet Explorer opens your support page. As far as I can discover, this is the only choice that you can redirect.

- **IntelliForms.** This subkey contains the REG_DWORD value AskUser that indicates whether Internet Explorer should ask users whether they want to use the Auto-Complete feature. You can set this value to 0x00 to prevent the prompt, but in a business environment where you're more likely to disable this feature, you should disable it using Group Policy.

- **Main.** This subkey contains many settings for Internet Explorer. For example, you can configure whether Internet Explorer shows its status bar and toolbar.

- **Settings.**   This subkey contains five values that specify the colors used in Internet Explorer: Anchor Color, Anchor Color Visited, Background Color, Text Color, and Use Anchor Color Hover. Each is a REG_SZ value in the format R,G,B, where you specify each color component, red, green, and blue, using decimal numbers 0 through 255.

- **Toolbar.**   This subkey contains information about the Internet Explorer toolbars. The REG_DWORD value Locked indicates whether the toolbars are locked. The REG_SZ value LinksFolderName contains the name of the annoying Links folder, which you can rename if you like so that it better matches the contents of your Favorites folder. You can also create the REG_SZ value BackBitmap to customize the bitmap that you see on the toolbar.

- **TypedURLs.**   This subkey contains a list of the URLs that users type in the address bar. You can quickly clear this history list by removing this subkey.

The subkey Internet Explorer contains two other subkeys that enable some pretty cool customizations. The first subkey is MenuExt. This subkey enables you to extend Internet Explorer's menus with your own scripts. The second subkey is SearchURL, which makes searching the Internet a snap. You add custom search URLs to this subkey, and then search the Internet by typing one of their names in the address bar. It's a real timesaver and one of my all-time favorite customizations, which I also describe in Chapter 4, "Hacking the Registry."

Microsoft\Internet Explorer\MenuExt

Right-click a Web page, and Internet Explorer displays a shortcut menu. You can customize this shortcut menu by adding commands to it that you link to scripts in an HTML file. For example, you can add a command to the shortcut menu that opens the current Web page in a new window or highlights the selected text on it.

Internet Explorer looks for extensions in HKCU\Software\Microsoft\Internet Explorer \MenuExt. Add this key if it doesn't exist, and then add a subkey for each command that you want to add. Then set that subkey's default value to the path and name of the HTML file containing the script that carries out the command. For example, to add the command Magnify to the shortcut menu that runs the script in the HTML file C:\Windows\Web \Magnify.htm, add the subkey Magnify and set its default value to C:\Windows\Web \Magnify.htm. When you choose this command on Internet Explorer's shortcut menu, it executes the script that the file contains. Then you need to create Magnify.htm. Listing B-1 on the next page is Magnify.htm. external.menuArguments is a property that contains the window object in which you executed the command. Because you have access to the window object, you can do almost anything in that window, such as reformatting its contents, and so on.

Listing B-1   Magnify.htm

```
<HTML>
<SCRIPT LANGUAGE="JavaScript" defer>
var objWin = external.menuArguments;
var objDoc = objWin.document;
var objSel = objDoc.selection;
var objRange = objSel.createRange();
objRange.execCommand( "FontSize", 0, "+2" );
</SCRIPT>
</HTML>
```

You can choose the shortcut menus to which Internet Explorer adds your command. In the subkey you created for the extension, add the REG_DWORD value Contexts, and apply the bit masks shown in Table B-3 to it. For example, to limit the previous example so that Internet Explorer displays it only for text selections, add the REG_DWORD value Contexts to Magnify, and set it to 0x10.

Table B-3   Internet Explorer Menu Extensions

Bit mask	Menu
0x01	Default
0x02	Image
0x04	Control
0x08	Table
0x10	Text Selection
0x11	Anchor
0x12	Unknown

Microsoft\Internet Explorer\SearchURL

Search URLs are a convenient way to use different Internet search engines. For example, you might have a search URL called *shop* that searches eBay. As shown in Figure B-5, Type **shop casino chip** (yes, I collect them) in the address bar to automatically search eBay for all items that contain the words *casino* and *chip*.

Figure B-5   *Customizing the key* SearchURL *is the ultimate shortcut for searching the Internet.*

`HKCU\Software\Microsoft\Internet Explorer\SearchURL` is where you create search URLs. If you don't see this subkey, create it. Then add a subkey for each search prefix you want to use. To use the example I just gave you, create the subkey `shop`. Set the default value of the prefix's subkey to the URL of the search engine. Use `%s` as a placeholder for the search string. Internet Explorer replaces the `%s` with any text you type to the right of the prefix. In my example, set it to `http://search.ebay.com/search/search.dll?MfcISAPICommand=GetResult&ht=1&SortProperty=MetaEndSort&query=%s`.

Add the `REG_SZ` values shown in Table B-4 to the prefix key you created. These values describe what to substitute for special characters in your search string, including a space, percent sign (%), ampersand (&), and plus sign (ı). These characters have special meaning when submitting forms to Web sites, so you must substitute a plus sign for a space, for example, or %26 for an ampersand. Thus, the browser translates the string *casino & chip* to *casino+%26+chip*.

Finding the URL to use is easy. Open the search engine that you want to add to Internet Explorer's search URLs, and then search for something. When the browser displays the results, copy the URL from the address bar to the default value of the search URL you're creating, replacing your search word with a `%s`. For example, after searching eBay for *sample*, the resulting URL is *http://search.ebay.com/search/search.dll?MfcISAPICommand=GetResult&ht=1&SortProperty=MetaEndSort&query=sample*. Replace *sample* with `%s` to get `http://search.ebay.com/search/search.dll?MfcISAPICommand=GetResult&ht=1&SortProperty=MetaEndSort&query=%s`.

Table B-4 Values in SearchURLs

Name	Data
`<space>`	+
%	%25
&	%26
+	%2B

Microsoft\MessengerService

The key `HKCU\Software\Microsoft\MessengerService` contains the settings for Windows Messenger:

- **`AlwaysOnTop`.** This `REG_BINARY` value is `0x01` when you've configured Windows Messenger to appear on top of other windows; otherwise, it's `0x00`.

- **`DSBkgndMode`.** The first time users close Windows Messenger, this `REG_BINARY` value displays a prompt that tells them it's running in the background. Setting this `REG_BINARY` value to `0x01` disables that prompt.

- **FirstTimeUser.**   This REG_BINARY value is 0x01 for first-time users, and it's 0x00 for old-timers. That's the best explanation I've got.

- **FtReceiveFolder.**   This REG_BINARY value contains the folder into which Windows Messenger downloads files it receives. The default value is the My Received Files folder in the user's My Documents folder.

- **PassportBallon.**   This REG_BINARY value indicates the number of times that Windows Messenger has displayed its prompt to sign up for a Passport. To prevent it from prompting to create a Passport, set this value to 0x0a. (Remember to reverse the bits because this is a REG_BINARY value.)

- **PassportWizard.**   This REG_BINARY value indicates whether the user has run .NET Passport Wizard. If this value is 0x01, the user has run the wizard.

- **Server.**   This REG_SZ value specifies the server to which Windows Messenger connects. messenger.hotmail.com;64.4.13.143:1863 is the default value.

- **StatusBar.**   This REG_BINARY value indicates whether to display the status bar. If this value is 0x01, you see the status bar.

- **TabsShowHide.**   This REG_BINARY value indicates which tabs to show or hide.

- **Toolbar.**   This REG_BINARY value is 0x01 if Windows Messenger displays its toolbar; otherwise, it's 0x00.

- **WindowMax.**   This REG_BINARY value is 0x01 when the Windows Messenger window is maximized; otherwise, it's 0x00.

- **WindowRect.**   This REG_BINARY value indicates the coordinates of the normal Windows Messenger window.

Microsoft\Office

This is where Office XP stores its per-user settings. In reality, most IT professionals will use the tools outlined in Chapter 14, "Deploying Office XP Settings," instead of customizing these settings for deployment. However, a brief tour of these settings is useful, and a handful of settings are important enough to explain a bit more about them here.

First I'll describe what's in HKCU\Software\Microsoft\Office. At the top of this key, you'll see one subkey for each version of Office that's installed on the computer. For example, you'll see the subkeys 10.0 and 9.0. Version 10.0 is Office XP. Note that installing Office XP creates the keys 8.0, 9.0, and 10.0, even though you don't have Office 2000 or an earlier version of Office on the computer. You'll also see a subkey for the different programs in Office at the top of Office. Although user settings are in HKCU\Software\Microsoft\Office*version*, information about add-ins is in HKCU\Software\Microsoft\Office*program*, and all Office applications share this information.

The subkey 10.0 contains the majority of the Office XP settings, whereas the remaining subkeys contain only a handful of settings. For example, in the key 10.0, you see subkeys for each application, Excel, FrontPage, Outlook, Word, and so on. You also see the subkey Common, which contains settings that are common to all the programs in Office XP. Some of these settings are important to know about for two reasons. First the more you understand about them, the more successful you'll be at customizing Office XP. Second you can deploy some Office XP settings only as registry values in Custom Installation Wizard. Simply put, the only way to customize a REG_BINARY value in Custom Installation Wizard is by using the Add/Remove Registry Entries screen. You can't customize these settings on the Change Office User Settings screen. Here's a description of these and other important settings:

- **First-run settings.**   The first time a user starts one of the Office XP programs, Office XP goes through its first-run process to configure the computer for the user. It prompts the user for his or her name and initials, for example, and it customizes settings in HKCU\Software\Microsoft\Office. A handful of values prevent the first-run process from starting a second time. These values are in HKCU\Software\Microsoft\Office\10.0. The value UserData in the subkey Common is 0x01 after the first-run process. You'll find this value in each program's subkey, too. A second, related setting is FirstRun. This value indicates whether the first-run process is complete or not. You find this value in different subkeys of HKCU\Software\Microsoft\Office*version*:

  - HKCU\Software\Microsoft\Office\10.0\Common\General

  - HKCU\Software\Microsoft\Office\10.0\Excel\Options

  - HKCU\Software\Microsoft\Office\10.0\Outlook\Setup

  - HKCU\Software\Microsoft\Office\10.0\PowerPoint\First Run

  - HKCU\Software\Microsoft\Office\10.0\Word\Options

- **Toolbar settings.**   Office XP stores most programs' toolbar settings in REG_BINARY values. This means that you can't customize them using the Change Office User Settings screen in Custom Installation Wizard. You can capture those toolbar settings using Profile Wizard, as described in Chapter 14, but what if you don't want to deploy an OPS file? The solution is to customize the toolbars and then export HKCU\Software \Microsoft\Office\10.0\Common\Toolbars to a REG file. Import that REG file into your transform using the Add/Remove Registry Entries screen of Custom Installation Wizard. Office XP maintains a number of other REG_BINARY values that you can deploy the same way. If you don't find a setting in the Change Office User Settings screen, track down the setting using the techniques you learn about in Chapter 8, "Finding Registry Settings." The setting is likely a REG_BINARY value.

Microsoft\Search Assistant

The key HKCU\Software\Microsoft\Search Assistant contains the configuration for the Windows Explorer and Internet Explorer Search Assistant. The REG_SZ value Actor contains the file name of the character that the assistant uses. The REG_DWORD value UseAdvanced-SearchAlways is 0x01 if you've configured the assistant to always display its advanced search features. You don't see the REG_DWORD value SocialUI unless you've turned off the animated character. If this value is 0x01, you'll see the animated character. If this value is 0x00, you won't. Most folks don't like the new search interface, and they can restore it to a user interface more similar to the one in Windows 2000 by setting SocialUI to 0x00 and UseAdvancedSearchAlways to 0x01. I admit that I like the little dog, so I usually leave SocialUI set to 0x01 but use the advanced search features.

Search Assistant's history list is in the subkey ACMru. This subkey contains a variety of subkeys, depending on the types of things for which you've searched. For example, if you search for files and folders, you'll see the subkey 5603, and that subkey contains a list of the different search strings. If you search the Internet using Search Assistant, you'll see the subkey 5001. You can remove each subkey individually to clear a specific type of query's history list, or you can remove the key ACMru to clear all of Search Assistant's history lists. Table B-5 contains a list of the subkeys that I've found in ACMru.

Table B-5   History Lists in Search Assistant

Subkey	Description
5001	Internet
5603	Files and folders
5604	Pictures, music, and video
5647	Printers, computers, and people

Microsoft\VBA\Trusted

The key HKCU\Software\Microsoft\VBA\Trusted is an important subkey if you're deploying Office XP. This is where Office XP stores its list of trusted sources. When users open a document that contains signed code, enable those macros, and then add the source to the list of trusted sources, Office XP stores those certificates in this key. The reason this key is important is that most businesses should lock the list of trusted sources so that users can't add to it, and then set the security level to high. This prevents users from accidentally running malicious code.

The problem with this scenario is that users can't run legitimate macros that they require to do their jobs. The solution is to distribute the list of trusted sources along with Office XP, but the deployment tools don't provide a user interface for doing this. So here's my solution:

1. Create a document that contains code and then sign the code using a certificate you want to deploy. Repeat this for each certificate.

2. Install Office XP on a lab computer and set the security levels to high.

3. Open each document containing a certificate you want to deploy. Enable the document's macros and then add the source to the list of trusted sources. Figure B-6 shows you an example.

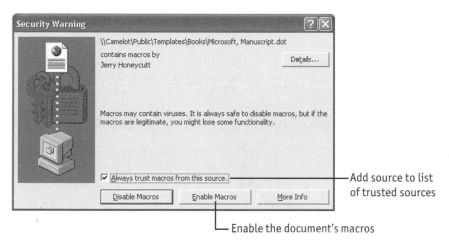

Add source to list of trusted sources

Enable the document's macros

Figure B-6   *High security in combination with code signing protects your business from viruses.*

4. Export the key HKCU\Software\Microsoft\VBA\Trusted to a REG file, and include this REG file in your deployment. Chapter 14, "Microsoft Office XP Settings," describes how to deploy registry settings with Office XP.

Policies

Windows XP stores policies in the key HKCU\Software\Policies, the preferred branch for registry-based policies. These are per-user policies, so they are in the HKCU branch of the registry. Restricted users don't have permission to change the Policies subkey, which prevents them from circumventing policies by editing the registry. Windows XP supports hundreds of policies that enable IT professionals to control users' experiences, lock down the desktop, and so on. Chapter 6, "Using Registry-Based Policy," shows you how to customize policies by building custom administrative templates. Appendix D, "Group Policy," lists all the policies that Windows XP creates in this key.

Very often, using policies is the best and most interesting way to customize Windows XP. For example, many of the customizations you learn about in Chapter 4, "Hacking the Registry," rely on policy settings in the registry to change behaviors. Some of the most interesting policies you learn about in Chapter 4 change how the Start menu and taskbar look and feel. Still other policies enable you to obliterate annoying behavior. Ever wanted to prevent Windows Messenger from running? You can set a policy in this subkey that does that.

Although editing the registry directly is one way to customize these policies, there are better ways. The first way is to use Group Policy Editor to edit the local Group Policy Object (GPO). This provides a user interface for the policies, limiting your settings to valid choices. Chapter 6 describes how to create a local GPO. In short, type **gpedit.msc** in the Run dialog box, and then edit the policies under Computer Configuration and User Configuration in Administrative Templates. The second way is to write scripts that change policies. I use scripts when I want to repeat the same setting many times, such as when I'm configuring my user profile on multiple computers or when I reinstall Windows XP on computers repeatedly. Chapter 9, "Scripting Registry Changes," shows you how to write scripts to edit the registry. Personally, my favorite method is writing INF files.

Software\Microsoft\Windows\CurrentVersion

This branch of HKCU is one of the most interesting because this is where you find most of the Windows XP per-user settings. The following list describes some of the more interesting subkeys, and the sections following this one go into more detail:

- **Applets.**   This subkey contains subkeys for many of the different programs that come with Windows XP. For example, it contains the subkeys Regedit, SysTray, Tour, and Volume Control. If you don't want to see the tour when you create a new user profile, set the REG_DWORD value RunCount in the subkey Tour to 0x00, for example.

- **Internet Settings.**   This subkey contains Internet Explorer settings. A large number of these settings are security settings, such as security zones.

- **NetCache.**   This subkey contains settings for the Windows XP Offline Files feature. It contains the subkey AssignedOfflineFolders, which is a list of the offline folders assigned to that user through Group Policy.

- **Policies.**   This subkey is the per-user policy branch that Windows XP inherits from earlier versions of Windows. You learn about policies in Chapter 6, "Using Registry-Based Policy." Appendix D, "Group Policies," lists the policies that are available in this key, which are some of the best customizations for Windows XP.

- **Run.**   This subkey contains programs that run after the user logs on to the computer. The name of each REG_SZ value is arbitrary. The value's data contains the command to execute after the user logs on to the computer.

- **RunOnce.**   This subkey contains programs that run after the user logs on to the computer. The name of each REG_SZ value is arbitrary, and the value's data contains the command to execute after the user logs on to the computer. The difference between this key and Run is that Windows XP removes commands from this key after they've run, so they only run one time.

HKCU\Software\Microsoft\Windows\CurrentVersion\Explorer is one of the most interesting branches in the registry. For that reason, the remaining sections in this appendix discuss this branch, beginning with the Advanced subkey.

Explorer\Advanced

`HKCU\Software\Microsoft\Windows\CurrentVersion\Explorer\Advanced` contains settings for Windows Explorer and the Start menu. You configure these settings in two places. The first is the Folder Options dialog box. The second is the Taskbar And Start Menu Properties dialog box. Table B-6 describes these settings.

Table B-6   Start Menu Settings

Name	Data
Folder Options dialog box	
ClassicViewState	0x00—Use the classic folder view 0x01—Don't use the classic folder view
SeparateProcess	0x00—Don't run folders in separate processes 0x01—Launch folders in separate processes
DisableThumbnailCache	0x00—Cache thumbnails 0x01—Do not cache thumbnails
FolderContentsInfoTip	0x00—Do not display file sizes in folder tips 0x01—Display file sizes in folder tips
FriendlyTree	0x00—Don't display simple folder tree 0x01—Display simple folder tree in Folders list
Hidden	0x01—Don't show hidden files and folders 0x02—Show hidden files and folders
HideFileExt	0x00—Show known file extensions 0x01—Don't show known file extensions
NoNetCrawling	0x00—Don't search for network folders, printers 0x01—Search for network folders, printers
PersistBrowsers	0x00—Don't restore previous folders 0x01—Restore previous folders at logon
ShowCompColor	0x00—Don't display compressed files in color 0x01—Display compressed files in color
ShowInfoTip	0x00—Don't display tips for folders, desktop items 0x01—Display tips for folders, desktop items
ShowSuperHidden	0x00—Don't show protected operating system files 0x01—Show protected operating system files
WebViewBarricade	0x00—Don't display contents of system folders 0x01—Display contents of system folders
Customize Classic Start Menu dialog box	
StartMenuAdminTools	NO—Hide Administrative Tools YES—Display Administrative Tools
CascadeControlPanel	NO—Display Control Panel as link YES—Display Control Panel as menu
CascadeMyDocuments	NO—Display My Documents as link YES—Display My Documents as menu
CascadeMyPictures	NO—Display My Pictures as link YES—Display My Pictures as menu

Table B-6   Start Menu Settings *(continued)*

Name	Data
CascadePrinters	NO—Display Printers as link YES—Display Printers as menu
IntelliMenus	0x00—Don't use personalized menus 0x01—Use personalized menus
CascadeNetworkConnections	NO—Display Network Connections as link YES—Display Network Connections as menu
Start_LargeMFUIcons	0x00—Show small icons on Start menu 0x01—Show large icons on Start menu
StartMenuChange	0x00—Disable dragging and dropping 0x01—Enable dragging and dropping
StartMenuFavorites	0x00—Hide Favorites 0x01—Display Favorites
StartMenuLogoff	0x00—Hide Log Off 0x01—Display Log Off
StartMenuRun	0x00—Hide Run command 0x01—Display Run command
StartMenuScrollPrograms	NO—Don't scroll Programs menu YES—Scroll Programs menu
Customize Start Menu dialog box	
Start_ShowControlPanel	0x00—Hide Control Panel 0x01—Show Control Panel as link 0x02—Show Control Panel as menu
Start_EnableDragDrop	0x00—Disable dragging and dropping 0x01—Enable dragging and dropping
StartMenuFavorites	0x00—Hide Favorites menu 0x01—Show the Favorites menu
Start_ShowMyComputer	0x00—Hide My Computer 0x01—Show My Computer as link 0x02—Show My Computer as menu
Start_ShowMyDocs	0x00—Hide My Documents 0x01—Show My Documents as link 0x02—Show My Documents as menu
Start_ShowMyMusic	0x00—Hide My Music 0x01—Show My Music as link 0x02—Show My Music as menu
Start_ShowMyPics	0x00—Hide My Pictures 0x01—Show My Pictures as link 0x02—Show My Pictures as menu
Start_ShowNetConn	0x00—Hide Network Connections 0x01—Show Network Connections as link 0x02—Show Network Connections as menu
Start_AdminToolsTemp	0x00—Hide Administrative Tools 0x01—Show on All Programs menu 0x02—Show on All Programs menu and Start menu
Start_ShowHelp	0x00—Hide Help and Support 0x01—Show Help and Support

Name	Data
Start_ShowNetPlaces	0x00—Hide My Network Places 0x01—Show My Network Places
Start_ShowOEMLink	0x00—Hide Manufacturer Link 0x01—Show Manufacturer Link
Start_ShowPrinters	0x00—Hide Printers and Faxes 0x01—Show Printers and Faxes
Start_ShowRun	0x00—Hide Run command 0x01—Show Run command
Start_ShowSearch	0x00—Hide Search command 0x01—Show Search command
Start_ScrollPrograms	0x00—Don't scroll Programs menu 0x01—Scroll Programs menu

Windows XP defines templates, similar to the policy templates that define how to collect and store policies, for these settings. You find these templates in the following places:

- HKEY_LOCAL MACHINE\SOFTWARE\Microsoft\Windows\CurrentVersion\Explorer\StartMenu \StartMenu contains templates for the settings in the Advanced Start Menu Options area of the Customize Classic Start Menu dialog box. To open this dialog box, click Start, Control Panel, Appearance And Themes, and Taskbar And Start Menu. Then on the Start Menu tab, select the Classic Start Menu option, and click Customize.

- HKEY_LOCAL_MACHINE\SOFTWARE\Microsoft\Windows\CurrentVersion\Explorer\StartMenu \StartPanel contains templates for the settings on the Advanced tab of the Customize Start Menu dialog box. To open this dialog box, click Start, Control Panel, Appearance And Themes, and Taskbar And Start Menu. Then on the Start Menu tab, select the Start Menu option, and click Customize.

- HKLM\SOFTWARE\Microsoft\Windows\CurrentVersion\Explorer\Advanced\Folder contains templates for the settings in the Folder Options dialog box, most of which are on the View tab. To open this dialog box, click Start, Control Panel, Appearance And Themes, and Folder Options.

Explorer\AutoComplete

The subkey AutoComplete contains a single value that controls the AutoComplete feature in Windows Explorer. If the REG_SZ value AutoComplete is Yes, Windows Explorer uses AutoComplete; otherwise, it doesn't.

Explorer\ComDlg32

The subkey ComDlg32 contains two subkeys. Both are history lists. To clear the history list that the common dialog boxes use, delete both subkeys. The first is LastVisitedMRU, which contains a list of folders that you've opened.

The second is OpenSaveMRU, which is a little more complicated. Within the key OpenSaveMRU are subkeys for different types of files. For example, you see the subkey doc in OpenSaveMRU that lists all the files with the *.doc* extension that you've opened. The subkey * contains files all the files you've opened in the common dialog boxes, regardless of their extensions. Thus, the common dialog boxes can display a history list by type or display all the files in the history.

Explorer\HideDesktopIcons

In HideDesktopIcons, you see two subkeys: ClassicStartMenu and NewStartPanel. The first subkey determines which icons to hide when Windows XP is using the classic Start menu. The second determines which icons to hide when Windows XP is using the new Start menu. Add a REG_DWORD value named for the icon's class ID to either subkey to hide it in that view. Set the value to 0x01. Hide the Recycle Bin icon by creating a REG_DWORD value called {645FF040-5081-101B-9F08-00AA002F954E} in the subkey HideDesktopIcons\NewStartPanel, for example, and then set it to 0x01. Click the desktop and then press F5 to refresh. Appendix A, "File Associations," lists the class IDs you might want to hide.

Explorer\HideMyComputerIcons

The key HideMyComputerIcons enables you to hide icons in My Computer. To hide icons in My Computer, add a REG_DWORD value to HideMyComputerIcons—the name is the class ID of the icon you want to hide—and set it to 0x01. See Appendix A, "File Associations," for a list of class IDs. Refresh Windows Explorer to see your changes.

Explorer\MenuOrder

HKCU\Software\Microsoft\Windows\CurrentVersion\Explorer\MenuOrder contains the sort order of the Favorites menu and Start menu. The subkey Favorites contains the sort order of the Favorites menu. The subkey Start Menu contains the sort order of the classic Start menu, and the subkey Start Menu2 contains the sort order of the new Start menu. Deciphering the contents of these three keys is next to ridiculous, but you can remove any of them to re-sort the corresponding menu in alphabetical order. For example, to restore the All Programs menu to alphabetical order, remove the subkey Start Menu2. To restore the Favorites menu in both Windows Explorer and Internet Explorer, remove the subkey Favorites.

Explorer\RecentDocs

The subkey RecentDocs is the list of recent documents that you see on the Start menu. Within this key are subkeys for different types of files and folders. For example, you see the subkey txt that lists all the files with the *.txt* extension that you've opened. To clear your list of recent documents, remove this subkey. Along with this subkey, you must remove the documents shortcuts that Windows XP creates in your profile folder, %USERPROFILE%\Recent.

Explorer\RunMRU

The subkey RunMRU contains a list of programs that you've run using the Run dialog box. You can remove individual programs from this list or delete the RunMRU subkey to clear the list of programs.

Explorer\User Shell Folders

Special folders include the My Documents, My Pictures, and Favorites folders, among many others. Table B-7 shows the special folders that Windows XP creates after a fresh installation and their default paths. The first column contains each folder's internal name as Windows XP and other programs know it. The second column contains each folder's default path, which almost always starts with %USERPROFILE%, making these folders part of each user's profile folder. Chapter 10, "Deploying User Profiles," describes these user profile folders in depth.

Table B-7 Special Folders

Name	Default path
AppData	%USERPROFILE%\Application Data
Cache	%USERPROFILE%\Local Settings\Temporary Internet Files
Cookies	%USERPROFILE%\Cookies
Desktop	%USERPROFILE%\Desktop
Favorites	%USERPROFILE%\Favorites
History	%USERPROFILE%\Local Settings\History
Local AppData	%USERPROFILE%\Local Settings\Application Data
Local Settings	%USERPROFILE%\Local Settings
My Pictures	%USERPROFILE%\My Documents\My Pictures
NetHood	%USERPROFILE%\NetHood
Personal	%USERPROFILE%\My Documents
PrintHood	%USERPROFILE%\PrintHood

Table B-7 Special Folders *(continued)*

Name	Default path
Programs	%USERPROFILE%\Start Menu\Programs
Recent	%USERPROFILE%\Recent
SendTo	%USERPROFILE%\SendTo
Start Menu	%USERPROFILE%\Start Menu
Startup	%USERPROFILE%\Start Menu\Programs\Startup
Templates	%USERPROFILE%\Templates

HKCU\Software\Microsoft\Windows\CurrentVersion\Explorer\User Shell Folders is the key where Windows XP stores the location of per-user special folders. Each value in this key is a special folder, as shown in Table B-7. These are REG_EXPAND_SZ values, so you can use environment variables in them. Use %USERPROFILE% in a path to direct the folder somewhere inside users' profile folders or %USERNAME% in a path to include users' names. To redirect users' Favorites folders to the network, set the value Favorites, which you can look up in Table B-7, to \\Server\Share\%USERNAME%\Favorites, where \\Server\Share is the server and share containing the folders. Windows XP updates a second key, HKCU \Software\Microsoft\Windows\CurrentVersion\Explorer\Shell Folders, with the paths from User Shell Folders the next time the user logs on to the operating system, so you don't have to update it. In fact, Microsoft's documentation says Windows XP doesn't use Shell Folders.

Per-Computer Settings

In Appendix B, "Per-User Settings," you learned about many of the settings that Microsoft Windows XP creates for users in the registry. These settings are in HKCU. This appendix is about the per-computer settings in HKLM.

The branch HKLM\SOFTWARE is similar to HKCU\Software. In fact, the organization of this key is almost identical. The difference is that these settings are computer-oriented; they affect every user who logs on to the computer. However, you find some settings in both places, HKLM\SOFTWARE and HKCU\Software. This is common with Microsoft Office XP and many of the policies in Windows XP, for example. Most often, when a setting is in both places, the version in HKLM has precedence over the same setting in HKCU. Only when an administrator removes the setting from HKLM (restricted users don't usually have permission to change settings in HKLM) do users' own preferences mean anything. The only exception to this rule is the file associations in SOFTWARE\Classes in both root keys. File associations in HKCU have precedence over file associations in HKLM. This order of precedence is necessary to enable users to have custom file associations.

Other branches in HKLM are unique, though. Windows XP stores the computer's configuration in HKLM\SYSTEM. The operating system's lower-level settings are in this branch, too. Lower-level settings include the configuration of the computer's network connections, device drivers, services, and so on. Windows XP also stores local security data in HKLM. Something else unique in HKLM is that it contains more links than HKCU does. Recall that links are aliases for other subkeys, and Windows XP uses links in HKLM to support features such as hardware profiles and configuration sets. This appendix describes these links so you can better understand how different parts of the registry relate to each other.

This appendix outlines the organization of HKLM, describing its interesting and useful subkeys. But by no means do I cover this root key's entire contents. Instead, I've focused on settings that you're most likely to customize or need to understand as a power user or IT professional. Also, I don't describe the hive files or how Windows XP loads them into HKLM because Chapter 1, "Learning the Basics," already covers this.

HARDWARE

Windows XP re-creates HKLM\HARDWARE every time the operating system starts. This key contains configuration data that the operating system detects when it starts. This branch contains few values to customize because the branch's contents are volatile. Some values in it are useful for inventorying the computer's hardware, though. For example, you can read its settings to inventory the computer's processor. You find this value and similar ones in HKLM\HARDWARE\DESCRIPTION, and they're easy-to-read REG_SZ values.

The following list is an overview of the HARDWARE key's subkeys, and the sections following this one give more details about some of them:

- ACPI.   This subkey describes the computer's ACPI BIOS. The values in this subkey are a bit cryptic.

- DESCRIPTION.   This is the most interesting subkey in HARDWARE. It describes the computer's BIOS, processors, and buses. See "DESCRIPTION," on the facing page.

- DEVICEMAP.   This subkey maps the devices that the hardware recognizer detects to their device drivers in the SYSTEM branch of HKLM.

- RESOURCEMAP.   This subkey maps the computer's resources to the devices that use them. Like the ACPI subkey, this subkey is difficult to understand. Resources that the RESOURCEMAP subkey maps include bus number, DMA channels, interrupt vectors, memory ranges, and I/O ports.

Tip   You can use System Information to see the computer's hardware configuration and how Windows XP has been spending its resources. To use this feature, in the Run dialog box, type **msinfo32**. The data that System Information displays is comprehensive. Especially helpful is that you can use it to look at remote computers' configurations. And it sure beats scrounging around the registry for the same information.

DESCRIPTION

Each time Windows XP boots, its hardware recognizer collects information about the computer's hardware and stores it in HKLM\HARDWARE\DESCRIPTION\System. In this branch, you find three subkeys:

- **CentralProcessor.** This subkey contains one subkey for each CPU that the hardware recognizer finds on the computer. CentralProcessor\0 is the subkey for the first processor, CentralProcessor\1 is the second, and so on. Each subkey contains values that describe the processor. For example, the value ~MHz describes the approximate speed of the processor.

- **FloatingPointProcessor.** This subkey contains one subkey for each FPU that that hardware recognizer finds on the computer. The organization is similar to that of CentralProcessor. Because Pentium-compatible processors contain onboard FPUs, this subkey usually corresponds to CentralProcessor.

- **MultifunctionAdapter.** This subkey contains one subkey for each bus that the hardware recognizer detects. The subkeys are 0, 1, and so on. Each subkey contains the REG_SZ value Identifier, which is a description of the bus: PCI and ISA. Below each bus's subkey are subkeys that describe the devices attached to the bus. This key describes only essential devices; it's not all-inclusive.

DEVICEMAP

The DEVICEMAP subkey is another interesting subkey of HKLM\HARDWARE. It maps the devices that the hardware recognizer detects to the services that drive them. Different device classes have different subkeys in DEVICEMAP. For example, this subkey typically contains the subkeys KeyboardClass and PointerClass. You don't find subkeys for every device in the computer, though. It contains subkeys only for those devices that Windows XP requires to start the computer. Thus, you don't find subkeys for sound cards and the like.

These subkeys contain one or more values. The values' names are the devices' names. The values' data points to the subkeys that define the services associated with those devices. For example, the subkey DEVICEMAP\KeyboardClass contains the value \Device\KeyboardClass0, and its value is \REGISTRY\MACHINE\SYSTEM\ControlSet001\Services\Kbdclass. This indicates that the service driving the keyboard is in the registry, in HKLM, and in the branch SYSTEM \ControlSet001\Services\Kbdclass.

SAM

The key HKLM\SAM\SAM is a link to HKLM\SECURITY\SAM. You learn about the SECURITY subkey in the next section. This key is where the Security Account Manager (SAM) creates the local computer's security database. Examining the contents of this key is interesting, but you can't customize it. You're better off managing local security using the User Accounts dialog box.

Windows XP protects the SAM key by preventing access to it. The key's access control list (ACL) doesn't even allow the Administrators group to read its contents, much less members of the Users or Power Users groups. You can give yourself Read permission to view the key, however, if you're a member of the Administrators group, because this group owns the SAM key. If you want to tour this key, do it on a lab computer. Don't tamper with the SAM key on a production computer. To give yourself Read permission, select HKLM\SAM\SAM; click Edit, Permissions; select the Administrators group; and then select the Read check box in the Allow column. If you don't have a lab computer available, just look at Figure C-1, which shows the contents of this key.

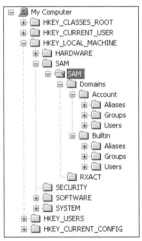

Figure C-1   *You can't normally see the contents of the SAM key, but this figure shows what you do see if you give the Administrators group permission to read it.*

The key HKLM\SAM\SAM\Domains contains two subkeys. The first subkey, Account, describes local computer accounts, user accounts, and groups. The second subkey, Builtin, describes built-in accounts and groups. You manage these subkeys using the User Accounts dialog box. Both subkeys contain the same three subkeys: Aliases, Groups, and Users. These subkeys define the computer's local accounts and membership in the computer's local groups.

SECURITY

The key HKLM\SECURITY contains Windows XP security data. You normally can't see the contents of this key, but you can give the Administrators group permission to read it so that you can examine it. The section "SAM," on the facing page, shows you how to do that. The SECURITY key contains the subkey SAM. It also contains the subkey Policies. This subkey defines local, non–registry-based policies for the computer. The key Policies\Accounts has one subkey for each SID in the local security database. Each SID contains four subkeys:

- **ActSysAc.**   This subkey defines the SID's operating system access allowed.

- **Privilgs.**   This subkey defines the SID's privileges.

- **SecDesc.**   This subkey contains the SID's security descriptor.

- **Sid.**   This subkey defines the groups to which the SID belongs.

SOFTWARE

The key HKLM\SOFTWARE is second in interest only to HKCU\Software. It contains per-computer software settings, including many Windows XP settings. Because Windows XP and most applications store settings as per-user settings, this branch is a bit slimmer than HKCU\Software, but it still contains numerous settings that are useful for customization. The types of settings you find in HKLM\SOFTWARE are typically those that an administrator defines. Because HKLM\SOFTWARE contains per-computer settings, any changes you make here affect all users who log on to the computer. Also, restricted users don't have permission to change settings in HKLM.

The key HKLM\SOTWARE is organized similarly to the way HKCU\Software is organized. Applications store settings in HKLM\SOFTWARE*Vendor**Program**Version*\. *Vendor* is the name of the program's publisher, *Program* is the name of the program, and *Version* is the program's version number. Often, *Version* is CurrentVersion. This branch also contains a handful of subkeys that don't follow this organization. For example, HKLM\SOFTWARE\Policies contains per-computer policies. The sections following this one describe the most interesting and useful parts of HKLM\SOFTWARF.

Classes

The key HKLM\CLASSES contains per-computer file associations. This key contains the vast majority of file associations, as opposed to HKCU\Classes, which contains per-user file associations. Windows XP merges both subkeys to form HKCR. Appendix A, "File Associations," describes HKCR in detail.

Clients

The key HKLM\SOFTWARE\Clients defines the client programs that Internet Explorer associates with different Internet services. You configure these clients on the Programs tab of the Internet Options dialog box, shown in Figure C-2. For example, you can choose the mail client that Internet Explorer uses when you click a mailto link, or you can choose the news client to use when you click a news link. These choices also determine the programs that Internet Explorer launches when you choose one of the tools on the Tools menu.

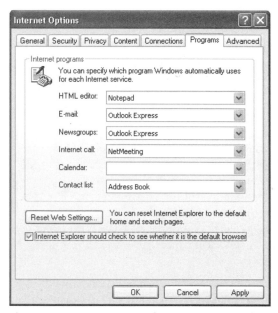

Figure C-2   *You associate client programs with Internet services by using the Programs tab.*

The Clients key contains six subkeys by default: Contacts, Internet Call, Mail, Media, News, and StartMenuInternet. The default value of each subkey specifies the name of the application that is the default tool for that category. For example, if the default value of HKLM\SOFTWARE\Clients\Mail is Outlook Express, then Outlook Express is the default mail client that Internet Explorer starts when you click a mailto link.

Drill down a bit further and you find one subkey for each client program. For example, Clients\Mail contains the Hotmail, MSN Explorer, and Outlook Express subkeys. The organization of these subkeys is almost the same as the organization of the subkeys in HKCR. Typically, you find the subkeys Protocols and shell under each client program's subkey. The subkey Protocols defines the protocols associated with the application. For example, the key HKLM\SOFTWARE\Clients\Mail\Outlook Express\Protocols describes the command to run when users click a mailto link on a Web page. The subkey shell defines the command to run when users choose an option on Internet Explorer's Tools menu. The subkey HKLM \SOFTWARE\Clients\Mail\Outlook Express\shell describes the command to run when users click Tools, Mail And News, Read Mail in Internet Explorer.

Microsoft\Active Setup

A variety of Windows XP components, notably Internet Explorer components, still use Active Setup. The key HKLM\SOFTWARE\Microsoft\Active Setup contains these components' registrations. The subkey FeatureComponentID is sometimes useful for mapping a GUID to a component. Look for the GUID in this subkey; then look at the REG_SZ value to determine the component's name.

The key HKLM\SOFTWARE\Microsoft\Active Setup\Installed Components is each component's registration. Each subkey is a component. For example, the subkey {2179C5D3-EBFF-11CF-B6FD-00AA00B4E220} is for NetShow. Within each subkey, you see several values, some more interesting than others. First the REG_BINARY value IsInstalled indicates whether the component is installed or not. The value is 0x0001 if the component is installed; if not, the value is 0x0000. The REG_SZ value Version contains the component's version.

The most interesting value is the REG_EXPAND_SZ value StubPath. If this value exists, Windows XP executes the command it contains after the operating system creates a new user profile. If you don't see this value, nothing happens. To keep Windows XP from running the command, remove the value StubPath from that components subkey in Installed Components.

Microsoft\Command Processor

The MS-DOS command prompt supports file and folder name completion, as well as a few other features. You can configure these features using Tweak UI, as described in Chapter 5, "Mapping Tweak UI," or you can hack them directly in the registry. This key is similar to HKCU\Software\Microsoft\Command Processor. The difference is that this key applies to all users, whereas the key in HKCU applies only to the current console user. The following list describes the settings in the subkey Command Processor, which configure the MS-DOS command prompt:

- **AutoRun.**   This REG_SZ value, which has no default, contains a list of commands that run automatically when you start the MS-DOS command prompt.

- **CompletionChar.**   This is a REG_DWORD value. It specifies the ASCII character code of the key to use for file name completion. You can set this value to 0x00, 0x01 through 0x1F, 0x20, or 0x40. The Tab key is 0x09 and is the default.

- **DefaultColor.**   This REG_DWORD value defaults to 0. Valid values range from 0x00 to 0xFE. It specifies the default background and foreground color of the MS-DOS command prompt. The first hexadecimal digit specifies the background color, and the second digit specifies the foreground color. The digits correspond to the colors shown in Table C-1 on the next page.

- **DelayedExpansion.**   This is a REG_DWORD value with a default of 0x00. It specifies whether the command prompt delays environment variable expansion. If the value is 0x01, the command prompt interprets the exclamation point (!) as an environment variable that expands only when used.

- **EnableExtensions.**   This REG_DWORD value has a default value of 0x01. It determines whether command-processor extensions are enabled or not. Setting this value to 0x00 disables extensions. You need to disable extensions only when they interfere with a script language with which they aren't compatible.

- **PathCompletionChar.**   This is a REG_DWORD value that specifies the ASCII character code of the key to use for path completion. Set this value to 0x00, 0x01 through 0x1F, 0x20, or 0x40. The Tab key is 0x09. You can use the same key that you use for file name completion, which expands both.

Table C-1   Values for DefaultColor

Value	Color
0	Black
1	Blue
2	Green
3	Aqua
4	Red
5	Purple
6	Yellow
7	White
8	Gray
9	Light Blue
A	Light Green
B	Light Aqua
C	Light Red
D	Light Purple
E	Light Yellow
F	Bright White

Microsoft\Driver Signing

The key HKLM\SOFTWARE\Microsoft\Driver Signing contains values that configure the Windows XP driver-signing feature. Microsoft digitally signs driver files so Windows XP can verify that Microsoft tested the driver file and that the file hasn't changed since Microsoft tested it. This key's only value, Policy, controls how Windows XP handles driver files that aren't signed. Here are the possible values:

- **0x00.**   Windows XP installs unsigned device drivers (Ignore).

- **0x01.**   Windows XP warns the user that the device driver is unsigned and enables the user to choose whether or not to install it (Warn).

- **0x02.**   Windows XP does not install unsigned device drivers (Block).

This setting comes from the Driver Signing Options dialog box, shown in Figure C-3. It applies to all users, unless you clear the Make This Action The System Default check box. The figure shows the values associated with each option.

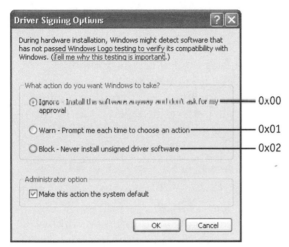

Figure C-3   *In an enterprise environment, blocking unsigned device drivers is the safest option.*

Microsoft\InternetExplorer

The key HKLM\SOFTWARE\Microsoft\Internet Explorer contains Internet Explorer settings that apply to every user who logs on to the computer. For example, the subkey AboutURLs contains the URLs of Web pages that Internet Explorer displays in special scenarios. The subkey AdvancedOptions defines templates for the options on the Internet Options dialog box's Advanced tab.

Microsoft\Sysprep

You won't see HKLM\SOFTWARE\Microsoft\Sysprep on your computer unless you installed Windows XP from a disk image that you prepared with Sysprep. Chapter 13, "Cloning Disks with Sysprep," describes how to use this tool. The values in this subkey are useful for understanding what Sysprep has done:

- **CriticalDevicesInstalled.**   This value is 0x01 if Sysprep installed the critical devices. See Chapter 13 for more information.

- **SidsGenerated.**   This value is 0x01 if Sysprep regenerated the computer's SID.

Microsoft\Windows NT\CurrentVersion

The key `HKLM\SOFTWARE\Microsoft\Windows NT\CurrentVersion` contains useful subkeys for learning more about Windows XP but not customizing it. The values in this subkey describe the current version of Windows XP, the registered owner, and the path in which you installed the operating system. For IT professionals, the three most useful subkeys are in the following list:

- `HotFix.`   This key contains one subkey for each hotfix installed on the computer. The value `Installed` is `0x01` if the hotfix is installed; it's `0x00` otherwise. The `HotFix` key fills up quickly when you use Windows Update or Automatic Update to download and install hotfixes. IT professionals can inventory the hotfixes installed on different computers by writing scripts that extract the contents of this key and dump them to text files on the network.

- `ProfileList.`   This key contains one subkey for each user profile you see in the User Profiles dialog box.

- `Winlogon.`   This key contains values that define the logon process, as well as the last user who logged on to the computer. There are two interesting customizations in this key, both of which you learn in Chapter 15, "Working Around IT Problems." The first is that you can display a legal notice when users log on to the operating system. The second is that you can use this key to automatically log on to the computer using a specific account. You can do that a specific number of times. For example, you can configure this key to automatically log on as Administrator, install an application, and then log off of the operating system. See Chapter 15 for more information about this useful IT trick.

Policies

Windows XP stores per-computer policies in the key `HKLM\SOFTWARE\Policies`, the preferred branch for registry-based policies. Restricted users don't have permission to change the `Policies` subkey, which prevents them from circumventing policies by editing the registry. Windows XP supports hundreds of policies that enable IT professionals to control the computer's configuration. Chapter 6, "Using Registry-Based Policy," shows you how to customize policies by building custom administrative templates. Appendix D, "Group Policy," lists all of the policies that Windows XP creates in this key.

Very often, using policies is the best and most interesting way to customize Windows XP. For example, many of the customizations you learn about in Chapter 4, "Hacking the Registry," rely on policy settings in the registry to change behaviors. Some policies enable you to change behavior that annoys you. In this regard, the per-user policies in `HKCU\Software \Policies` offer more customization possibilities that the policies that you find in `HKLM \SOFTWARE\Policies`.

Although editing the registry directly is certainly one way to customize policies, there are better ways. The first is to use Group Policy Editor to edit the local Group Policy Object (GPO). This provides a user interface for the policies, limiting your settings to valid choices. Chapter 6 describes how to edit the local GPO. In short, type **gpedit.msc** in the Run dialog box, and then edit the policies under Computer Configuration and User Configuration in Administrative Templates. The second way is to write scripts that change policies. I use scripts when I need to repeat the same setting many times, such as when I'm configuring multiple computers or when I reinstall Windows XP on computers often. Chapter 9, "Scripting Registry Changes," shows you how to write scripts to edit the registry.

SOFTWARE\Microsoft\Windows\CurrentVersion

The key `HKLM\SOFTWARE\Microsoft\Windows\CurrentVersion`, and all its subkeys, contains some of the most interesting settings in `HKLM`. First, this key has a number of `REG_SZ` and `REG_EXPAND_SZ` values that are interesting:

- `CommonFilesDir`. This value contains the path of Windows XP common files. The default location is `C:\Program Files\Common Files`.

- `DevicePath`. This value defines the locations where Windows XP finds device-driver INF files. `%SystemRoot%\inf;%SystemDrive%\Windows\Drivers` is the default for this value.

- `MediaPath`. This value defines the default location for media files. The default value is `C:\WINDOWS\Media`.

- `MediaPathUnexpanded`. This value is the same as `MediaPath`, except that it's a `REG_EXPAND_SZ` value that includes environment variables.

- `PF_AccessoriesName`. This value defines the name of the Accessories group on the Program Files menu. The default value is `Accessories`.

- `ProductId`. This value contains the Windows XP product ID. This is not the product key that you typed when you registered Windows XP.

- `ProgramFilesDir`. This value contains the location of profile files. The default value is `C:\Program Files`.

- `ProgramFilesPath`. This value is the same as `ProgramFilesDir`, except that it uses environment variables. The default value is `%ProgramFiles%`.

- `SM_AccessoriesName`. This value contains the name of the Accessories group on the Start menu. The default value is `Accessories`.

- `SM_GamesName`. This value contains the name of the Games group on the Start menu. The default value is `Games`.

- `WallPaperDir`. This value contains the default location for Windows XP wallpaper. The default value is `%SystemRoot%\Web\Wallpaper`.

App Paths

The subkey `App Paths` specifies the paths of specific program files. It enables you to run a program from the Run dialog box or the MS-DOS command prompt without specifying its path. For example, you can type Wordpad.exe in the Run dialog box, and Windows XP looks up the program's path in the `App Paths` key.

The default value for `App Paths\`*filename*, where filename is the program file's name including the *.exe* file extension, contains the command that executes the program. For example, the default value of `App Paths\Wordpad.exe` contains `%ProgramFiles%\Windows NT \Accessories\WORDPAD.EXE`. You can add other programs to the `App Paths` subkey so that you can run them without typing their paths. The value `Path` is optional and it specifies the working path for the program, which is the path where the program finds additional program files. This path is usually to the folder containing the program file.

Applets

The `Applets` subkey contains per-computer settings for Windows XP accessories. By default, you find a single subkey, `DeluxeCD`, but other accessories store per-computer settings here after you run them. The more interesting accessory settings are in `HKCU\Software\Microsoft \Windows\CurrentVersion\Applets`, though.

Explorer

The key `Explorer` contains Windows Explorer settings. These are per-computer settings, and they're not as interesting to customize as the same subkey in `HKCU`. The subkey `Advanced` defines the settings you see in the Folder Options dialog box. There's not a lot to customize here because they're templates, but it's interesting to see how Windows Explorer defines and collects these settings.

Explorer\AutoplayHandlers

`HKLM\SOFTWARE\Microsoft\Windows\CurrentVersion\Explorer\AutoplayHandlers \EventHandlers` is the key where you find associations between different types of media and the applications that handle them. When Windows XP detects that you've inserted a CD, DVD, or removable disk, it automatically runs the program that it associates with the type of content on that disk. In Table C-2, look up the type of content you want to customize. Then open the subkey shown in the Subkey column for `EventHandlers`. In that subkey, add any of the following handlers as an empty `REG_SZ` value:

- `MSCDBurningOnArrival`
- `MSGenericVolumeArrival`

- `MSOpenFolder`
- `MSPlayCDAudioOnArrival`
- `MSPlayDVDMovieOnArrival`
- `MSPlayMediaOnArrival`
- `MSPlayMusicFilesOnArrival`
- `MSPlayVideoFilesOnArrival`
- `MSPrintPicturesOnArrival`
- `MSPromptEachTime`
- `MSPromptEachTimeNoContent`
- `MSShowPicturesOnArrival`
- `MSTakeNoAction`
- `MSVideoCameraArrival`
- `MSWiaEventHandler`

Table C-2   Values in AutoplayHandlers

Media	Subkey
Generic	`GenericVolumeArrival`
Blank CDR	`HandleCDBurningOnArrival`
Mixed content	`MixedContentOnArrival`
CD audio	`PlayCDAudioOnArrival`
DVD	`PlayDVDMovieOnArrival`
Music files	`PlayMusicFilesOnArrival`
Video files	`PlayVideoFilesOnArrival`
Digital images	`ShowPicturesOnArrival`
Video camera	`VideoCameraArrival`

Explorer\Desktop\NameSpace

The subkey `Desktop\Namespace` defines the objects you see on the Windows XP desktop. It contains one subkey for each object, and the name is the class ID of the object's class registration in HKCR. Appendix A, "File Associations," contains more information about HKCR. Don't remove subkeys to hide desktop icons, though. The best way is to use `HideDesktopIcons`, which you learn about later in this appendix.

Explorer\FindExtensions

The subkey FindExtensions defines the different extensions that you can use to search. The subkey Static contains three subkeys: ShellSearch, WabFind, and WebSearch. The subkey ShellSearch defines the extensions that enable you to search for files, computers, and printers. The subkey WabFind defines the extensions that enable you to search address books. Last, the subkey WebSearch defines the extensions that enable you to search the Internet.

Explorer\HideDesktopIcons

The subkey HideDesktopIcons specifies which icons to show or hide on the desktop. You see two subkeys below the key HideDesktopIcons. The first is ClassicStartMenu. It affects the classic Start menu. This subkey contains REG_DWORD values. The names of these values are the GUID of the object's class registration. The value is either 0x01, which indicates that Windows XP should hide the icon, or 0x00, which indicates that Windows XP shouldn't hide the icon. The subkey NewStartPanel affects the new Start menu. Its organization is similar to the subkey ClassicStartMenu.

Explorer\HideMyComputerIcons

The subkey HideMyComputerIcons specifies which icons to show or hide in the My Computer folder. This subkey contains REG_DWORD values. The names of these values are the GUID of the object's class registration. The value is either 0x01, which indicates that Windows XP should hide the icon, or 0x00, which indicates that Windows XP shouldn't hide the icon.

Explorer\MyComputer

The MyComputer subkey specifies the path and file name of the special tools you see when you right-click a drive in My Computer and then click Properties. The following subkeys define these paths:

- BackupPath.   The default value of this subkey contains the command to run when users right-click a drive in My Computer, click Properties, and then click Backup Now on the Tools tab.

- CleanupPath.   The default value of this subkey contains the command to run when users right-click a drive in My Computer, click Properties, and then click Disk Cleanup on the General tab.

- DefragPath.   The default value of this subkey contains the command to run when users right-click a drive in My Computer, click Properties, and then click Defragment Now on the Tools tab.

The subkey MyComputer\NameSpace also serves a similar purpose to the subkey Desktop \NameSpace. It defines the objects you see in My Computer. By default, this subkey doesn't contain any GUIDs. You can add subkeys to this subkey named for the object's GUID to add objects to My Computer, though.

Explorer\NetworkNeighborhood\NameSpace

The subkey `NetworkNeighborhood\Namespace` defines the objects you see in the My Network Places folder. It contains one subkey for each object, and the name is the class ID of the object's class registration in `HKCR`. By default, you see icons for Network Setup Wizard and Add Network Place.

Explorer\RemoteComputer\NameSpace

The subkey `RemoteComputer\NameSpace` defines the objects you see when you browse remote computers in the My Network Places folder. It contains one subkey for each object, and the name is the class ID of the object's class registration in `HKCR`. You see icons for the Printers and Scheduled Tasks folders on remote computers. If browsing remote computers is a slow process, you can remove the subkeys in the `RemoteComputer\NameSpace` key. This prevents Windows XP from looking up the remote printers and scheduled tasks on remote computers and could speed up browsing a bit.

Explorer\StartMenu

The subkey `StartMenu` defines templates for the settings you see in the Taskbar And Start Menu Properties dialog box. Because these are templates, they aren't often useful to customize. Their usefulness to you as a power user or IT professional is in sorting out where Windows XP stores settings and each setting's values in the registry.

Explorer\User Shell Folders

Windows XP maintains a set of shared folders in the All Users profile folder, which is in %SYSTEMROOT%\Documents and Settings. The operating system specifies the paths of these folders in `User Shell folders` under `HKLM`. Table C-3 on the next page describes each value you find in `User Shell Folders` and the default path. The first column is the folder's internal name, and the second is the default path. You can redirect these folders to different locations by changing the path in `User Shell Folders`.

The values in Table C-3 are `REG_EXPAND_SZ` values, so you can use environment variables in them. Use %ALLUSERSPROFILE% in a path to direct the folder somewhere inside the All Users profile folder. To redirect the Common Favorites folder to the network, set the value `Common Favorites`, to *Server**Share*. The next time the operating system starts, Windows XP updates a second key, `HKLM\SOFTWARE\Microsoft\Windows\CurrentVersion\Explorer\Shell Folders`, with the paths from `User Shell Folders`. Windows XP doesn't actually use the values in `Shell Folders`.

Table C-3   Special Folders

Name	Default path
Common AppData	%ALLUSERSPROFILE%\Application Data
Common Desktop	%ALLUSERSPROFILE%\Desktop
Common Documents	%ALLUSERSPROFILE%\Documents
Common Favorites	%ALLUSERSPROFILE%\Favorites
Common Programs	%ALLUSERSPROFILE%\Start Menu\Programs
Common Start Menu	%ALLUSERSPROFILE%\Start Menu
Common Startup	%ALLUSERSPROFILE%\Start Menu\Programs\Startup
Common Templates	%ALLUSERSPROFILE%\Templates

Explorer\VisualEffects

The subkey VisualEffects contains templates for the settings you see in the Performance Options dialog box. They aren't useful for customizing Windows XP, but they are handy to map specific settings to their corresponding registry settings.

Policies

The key HKLM\SOFTWARE\Microsoft\Windows\CurrentVersion\Policies is the policy branch that Windows XP inherits from earlier versions of Windows. Windows XP still stores many policies in this branch, although the new, preferred policy branch is HKLM\SOFTWARE\Policies. Often, the settings you find in this key are leftovers from old-style policy files that have tattooed the registry.

Run

Windows XP runs the commands in the subkey Run for every user who logs on to the computer. The name of each value in this subkey is arbitrary. The operating system runs the command in each REG_SZ value, though. So if you don't want to use the Start Up group in the Program Files menu to run programs when you log on to the computer, you can add the command to the Run subkey. Although this subkey affects all users, the commands in HKCU\Software\Microsoft\Windows\CurrentVersion\Run are per-user commands. Chapter 15, "Working Around IT Problems," describes a useful workaround using this subkey.

RunOnce

The RunOnce subkey is similar to the Run subkey. The difference is that Windows XP removes commands from the RunOnce subkey after running them. Thus, commands in the RunOnce subkey execute only one time.

Uninstall

The Uninstall key describes how to remove applications using the Add Or Remove Programs dialog box. Each subkey, Uninstall*Name*, describes how to remove the program. For example, the Add Or Remove Programs dialog box uses the REG_SZ value DisplayName to display the program's name in the list, and the REG_SZ value UninstallString contains the command that it uses to uninstall the program.

Some programs store more information in the Uninstall key. For example, in Uninstall \SnagIt5, TechSmith SnagIt stores the location in which you installed the program so it can find the program files to remove. Some programs store the location of any shortcuts they create in Uninstall*Name* so they can remove those when you remove the program.

SYSTEM

The subkeys in HKLM\SYSTEM are ControlSet*N*, where *N* is a number beginning with 001. These are control sets, and they describe the computer's configuration. Of all the configuration data stored in the registry, this is by far the most important. Windows XP maintains at least two control sets to make sure that the operating system can always start. If the first fails, you can start with the second by choosing Last Known Good Configuration from the boot options menu.

The subkey CurrentControlSet is a link to the current control set ControlSet*N*. Windows XP identifies the current control set using the key HKLM\SYSTEM\Select. The REG_DWORD value Current contains the number of the current control set. The REG_DWORD value LastKnownGood contains the number of the last control set that worked properly. This is the control set that Windows XP loads when users choose Last Known Good Configuration.

All the control sets have a similar organization and similar contents. The sections following this one describe the contents of CurrentControlSet, which is a link to one of the numbered control sets.

CurrentControlSet\Control

The subkey CurrentControlSet\Control contains values that control how Windows XP starts. It defines the components to load and their configurations. The following list describes many of the interesting subkeys of Control:

- **BackupRestore.** This subkey contains subkeys that specify the files and registry keys the Windows XP won't back up or restore. You learn about this subkey in Chapter 3, "Backing Up the Registry."

- **Class.** This subkey stores configuration data for classes of hardware devices.

- **CrashControl.** This subkey contains values that specify what happens when Windows XP locks, fails, or terminates abnormally.

- `CriticalDeviceDatabase.` This subkey contains the critical device database, which you learn about in Chapter 13, "Cloning Disks with Sysprep." It contains configuration data for new devices that Windows XP must install and start before the components that the operating system normally installs are started.

- `FileSystem.` This subkey contains file system configurations.

- `GraphicsDriver.` This subkey contains DirectX and graphics drivers settings.

- `GroupOrderList.` This subkey contains the order in which Windows XP loads services in a service group when the operating system starts.

- `hivelist.` This subkey defines the locations of hive files that are loaded in the registry. You learned about this subkey in Chapter 1, "Learning the Basics."

- `IDConfigDB.` This subkey contains settings that identify the current hardware configuration for Windows XP.

- `Lsa.` This subkey contains configuration data for the Local Security Authority (LSA).

- `Network.` This subkey contains network settings.

- `NetworkProvider.` This subkey contains network provider settings.

- `Print.` This subkey contains printer settings that apply to all users.

- `PriorityControl.` This subkey specifies the relative priority of foreground applications to background applications.

- `SafeBoot.` This subkey contains data about the computer's safe-mode settings. See Chapter 3, "Backing Up the Registry," to learn about boot options.

- `SecurePipeServers.` This subkey contains the `winreg` subkey, which controls remote access to the registry. See Chapter 7, "Managing Registry Security," to learn how to use this subkey to secure remote access to the registry.

- `ServiceGroupOrder.` This subkey contains a list of all service groups in the order in which Windows XP loaded them.

- `ServiceProvider.` This subkey contains data about the installed service providers.

- `SessionManager.` This subkey contains Session Manager data.

- `Update.` This subkey contains configuration data for System Policy. Chapter 6, "Using Registry-Based Policy," describes how to use this subkey.

- `VirtualDeviceDrivers.` This subkey contains data for virtual device drivers.

- `Windows.` This subkey contains data for the Win32 subsystem.

- `WOW.` This subkey contains settings that control MS-DOS-based applications and applications created for 16-bit versions of Windows.

CurrentControlSet\Enum

The subkey CurrentControlSet\Enum is a database of all the computer's devices that Windows XP recognized. This database stores configuration data for hardware devices separately from the device drivers they use. This database is an important part of Plug and Play in Windows XP.

Tip The most common reason to hack CurrentControlSet\Enum is to remove devices that don't appear in Device Manager. Windows XP provides a better, safer alternative. In Device Manager, click View, Show Hidden Devices; then remove the devices you want to remove from the Enum subkey.

CurrentControlSet\Hardware Profiles

The subkey CurrentControlSet\Hardware Profiles stores hardware profiles, which are usually created for laptop computers that have configurations for their docked and undocked states. A hardware profile contains changes to the original hardware profile configured in HKLM \SOFTWARE and HKLM\SYSTEM keys. Windows XP doesn't change the original value, so it can change hardware profiles easily. You use the Hardware Profiles dialog box to create and choose hardware profiles. Also, Windows XP automatically creates hardware profiles when it finds scenarios that require them.

Each hardware profile is in the subkey Hardware Profiles\N, where N is an incremental number beginning with 0000. These subkeys look like stripped-down versions of HKLM \SOFTWARE and HKLM\SYSTEM keys. They contain only those values that the hardware profile changes, though. In other words, when Windows XP uses a hardware profile, the settings in the profile override the settings in SOFTWARE and SYSTEM. They represent a powerful way to customize the operating system for different scenarios, which is particularly important to laptop users.

The subkey HKLM\SYSTEM\CurrentControlSet\Hardware Profiles\Current is a link to the current hardware profile. HKCC is also a link to the current hardware profile (which explains why you don't find a separate section for HKCC in this appendix). Changing a value in any of these three locations changes the same value in the remaining two locations.

Windows XP maintains information about all its hardware profiles in the key HKLM\SYSTEM \CurrentControlSet\Control\IDConfigDB. This key contains the REG_DWORD value CurrentConfig, which indicates the number of the current hardware profile. The subkey Hardware Profiles in IDConfigDB defines each hardware profile in further detail. For example, each subkey in Hardware Profiles defines the friendly name of the hardware profile.

CurrentControlSet\Services

The subkey `CurrentControlSet\Services` defines services, such as device drivers, file system drivers, and Win32 services. The settings differ for each service. Each subkey in the `Services` key has the name of the service that uses it. This is frequently the name of the file from which Windows XP loads the service. Some of the subkeys in `Services` represent devices and services that are actually installed and running on the computer. Others aren't installed or aren't enabled. While different services might have unique values and subkeys, they all have the following values and subkeys in common:

- `DependOnGroup.` This `REG_MULTI_SZ` value specifies the service groups that Windows XP must load before loading this service. This value ensures that all of a service's prerequisites are met.

- `DependOnService.` This `REG_MULTI_SZ` value specifies the services that Windows XP must load before loading this service. This value ensures that all of a service's prerequisites are met.

- `Enum.` You see this subkey in services that store values for device drivers and other services that control devices. It stores information about the hardware associated with this service.

- `ErrorControl.` This `REG_DWORD` value specifies how to continue if the device driver fails to load or initialize properly. The following values are possible:

  - `0x00` (Ignore)   Ignore the error and continue starting Windows XP.

  - `0x01` (Normal)   Display a warning and continue starting Windows XP.

  - `0x02` (Severe)   Restart using the last known good configuration, and if that fails, continue starting Windows XP.

  - `0x03` (Critical)   Restart using the last known good configuration, and if that fails, do not continue starting Windows XP.

- `Group.` This `REG_DWORD` value specifies the service group to which the service belongs. If this value doesn't exist, the service doesn't belong to a group, and the service loads after all service groups load.

- `ImagePath.` This `REG_EXPAND_SZ` value specifies the path and name of the service's executable file. Network adapters don't use this value.

- `Linkage.` This subkey contains data for binding network components. They associate network services with protocols and devices that support them.

- `NetworkProvider.` This subkey contains the name of the device, the provider, and the provider order for a network service.

- `ObjectName.` This `REG_SZ` value specifies the name of a driver object that the I/O Manager uses to load the device driver. This value exists in services that are kernel-mode or file system drivers.

- `Parameters.` This subkey contain entries specific to each service.

- **Performance.**   This subkey contains data for the service's performance counter.
- **Security.**   This subkey contains information about a driver's or service's permissions.
- **Start.**   This REG_DWORD value specifies how Windows XP loads or starts the service. The following values are possible:
  - 0x00 (Boot)   The kernel loader loads the driver when Windows XP boots.
  - 0x01 (System)   The I/O Subsystem loads the driver during kernel initialization.
  - 0x02 (Automatic)   The Session Control Manager starts the service automatically.
  - 0x03 (Manual)   The service must be started manually.
  - 0x04 (Disabled)   The service is never started.
- **Tag.**   This REG_DWORD value specifies the services tag number, which is a unique number within the service group.
- **Type.**   This REG_DWORD value indicates the service's type. The following values are possible:
  - 0x01   Kernel-mode device drivers
  - 0x02   File system drivers
  - 0x04   Arguments for an adapter
  - 0x08   File system driver services
  - 0x10   Win32 programs that run their own processes
  - 0x20   Win32 programs that share processes
  - 0x110   Win32 programs that run in processes by themselves
  - 0x120   Win32 programs that share processs and interact with users

Group Policies

Microsoft Windows XP provides six administrative templates. This appendix cross-references each policy in these templates with its registry setting. Each section in this appendix contains a table that lists the template's settings. Each table has three columns. The first is the location of the policy in Group Policy editor. The second is the name of the policy. The third column is the policy's registry value. Use this appendix along with the descriptions you see in Group Policy editor to identify where in the registry Windows XP stores each policy.

Conf.adm

Table 19-1   Policies in Conf.adm

Location	Name	Key
Computer Configuration\Administrative Templates \Windows Components\NetMeeting	Disable remote Desktop Sharing	HKLM\Software\Policies\Microsoft \Conferencing\NoRDS
User Configuration\Administrative Templates \Windows Components\NetMeeting \Application Sharing	Disable application Sharing	HKCU\Software\Policies\Microsoft \Conferencing\NoAppSharing
User Configuration\Administrative Templates \Windows Components\NetMeeting \Application Sharing	Prevent Sharing	HKCU\Software\Policies\Microsoft \Conferencing\NoSharing
User Configuration\Administrative Templates \Windows Components\NetMeeting \Application Sharing	Prevent Desktop Sharing	HKCU\Software\Policies\Microsoft \Conferencing\NoSharingDesktop
User Configuration\Administrative Templates \Windows Components\NetMeeting \Application Sharing	Prevent Sharing Command Prompts	HKCU\Software\Policies\Microsoft \Conferencing\NoSharingDosWindows
User Configuration\Administrative Templates \Windows Components\NetMeeting \Application Sharing	Prevent Sharing Explorer windows	HKCU\Software\Policies\Microsoft \Conferencing\NoSharingExplorer
User Configuration\Administrative Templates \Windows Components\NetMeeting \Application Sharing	Prevent Control	HKCU\Software\Policies\Microsoft \Conferencing\NoAllowControl
User Configuration\Administrative Templates \Windows Components\NetMeeting \Application Sharing	Prevent Application Sharing in true color	HKCU\Software\Policies\Microsoft \Conferencing\NoTrueColorSharing
User Configuration\Administrative Templates \Windows Components\NetMeeting\Audio & Video	Limit the bandwidth of Audio and Video	HKCU\Software\Policies\Microsoft \Conferencing\MaximumBandwidth
User Configuration\Administrative Templates \Windows Components\NetMeeting\Audio & Video	Disable Audio	HKCU\Software\Policies\Microsoft \Conferencing\NoAudio
User Configuration\Administrative Templates \Windows Components\NetMeeting\Audio & Video	Disable full duplex Audio	HKCU\Software\Policies\Microsoft \Conferencing\NoFullDuplex
User Configuration\Administrative Templates \Windows Components\NetMeeting\Audio & Video	Prevent changing DirectSound Audio setting	HKCU\Software\Policies\Microsoft \Conferencing\NoChangeDirectSound
User Configuration\Administrative Templates \Windows Components\NetMeeting\Audio & Video	Prevent sending Video	HKCU\Software\Policies\Microsoft \Conferencing\NoSendingVideo
User Configuration\Administrative Templates \Windows Components\NetMeeting\Audio & Video	Prevent receiving Video	HKCU\Software\Policies\Microsoft \Conferencing\NoReceivingVideo
User Configuration\Administrative Templates \Windows Components\NetMeeting\Options Page	Hide the General page	HKCU\Software\Policies\Microsoft \Conferencing\NoGeneralPage
User Configuration\Administrative Templates \Windows Components\NetMeeting\Options Page	Disable the Advanced Calling button	HKCU\Software\Policies\Microsoft \Conferencing\NoAdvancedCalling
User Configuration\Administrative Templates \Windows Components\NetMeeting\Options Page	Hide the Security page	HKCU\Software\Policies\Microsoft \Conferencing\NoSecurityPage
User Configuration\Administrative Templates \Windows Components\NetMeeting\Options Page	Hide the Audio page	HKCU\Software\Policies\Microsoft \Conferencing\NoAudioPage

Location	Name	Key
User Configuration\Administrative Templates \Windows Components\NetMeeting\Options Page	Hide the Video page	HKCU\Software\Policies\Microsoft \Conferencing\NoVideoPage
User Configuration\Administrative Templates \Windows Components\NetMeeting	Enable Automatic Configuration	HKCU\Software\Policies\Microsoft \Conferencing\ConfigFile
User Configuration\Administrative Templates \Windows Components\NetMeeting	Disable Directory services	HKCU\Software\Policies\Microsoft \Conferencing\NoDirectoryServices
User Configuration\Administrative Templates \Windows Components\NetMeeting	Prevent adding Directory servers	HKCU\Software\Policies\Microsoft \Conferencing\NoAddingDirectoryServers
User Configuration\Administrative Templates \Windows Components\NetMeeting	Prevent viewing Web directory	HKCU\Software\Policies\Microsoft \Conferencing\NoWebDirectory
User Configuration\Administrative Templates \Windows Components\NetMeeting	Set the intranet support Web page	HKCU\Software\Policies\Microsoft \Conferencing\IntranetSupportURL
User Configuration\Administrative Templates \Windows Components\NetMeeting	Set Call Security options	HKCU\Software\Policies\Microsoft \Conferencing\CallSecurity
User Configuration\Administrative Templates \Windows Components\NetMeeting	Prevent changing Call placement method	HKCU\Software\Policies\Microsoft \Conferencing\NoChangingCallMode
User Configuration\Administrative Templates \Windows Components\NetMeeting	Prevent automatic acceptance of Calls	HKCU\Software\Policies\Microsoft \Conferencing\NoAutoAcceptCalls
User Configuration\Administrative Templates \Windows Components\NetMeeting	Prevent sending files	HKCU\Software\Policies\Microsoft \Conferencing\NoSendingFiles
User Configuration\Administrative Templates \Windows Components\NetMeeting	Prevent receiving files	HKCU\Software\Policies\Microsoft \Conferencing\NoReceivingFiles
User Configuration\Administrative Templates \Windows Components\NetMeeting	Limit the size of sent files	HKCU\Software\Policies\Microsoft \Conferencing\MaxFileSendSize
User Configuration\Administrative Templates \Windows Components\NetMeeting	Disable Chat	HKCU\Software\Policies\Microsoft \Conferencing\NoChat
User Configuration\Administrative Templates \Windows Components\NetMeeting	Disable NetMeeting 2.x Whiteboard	HKCU\Software\Policies\Microsoft \Conferencing\NoOldWhiteBoard
User Configuration\Administrative Templates \Windows Components\NetMeeting	Disable Whiteboard	HKCU\Software\Policies\Microsoft \Conferencing\NoNewWhiteBoard

Inetcorp.adm

Table 19-2   Policies in Inetcorp.adm

Location	Name	Key
Computer Configuration\Administrative Templates \Code Download	Code Download	HKLM\Software\Microsoft\Windows \CurrentVersion\Internet Settings \CodeBaseSearchPath
Computer Configuration\Administrative Templates \Related Sites and Errors	Related Sites	HKLM\SOFTWARE\Microsoft \Internet Explorer\Extensions \{c95fe080-8f5d-11d2-a20b- 00aa003c157a}
Computer Configuration\Administrative Templates \Temporary Internet Files (Machine)	Temporary Internet Files (Machine)	HKLM\Software\Microsoft\Windows \CurrentVersion\Internet Settings \5.0\Cache\Content\CacheLimit

Table 19-2   Policies in Inetcorp.adm   *(continued)*

Location	Name	Key
Computer Configuration\Administrative Templates \Temporary Internet Files (Machine)	User Profiles	`HKLM\Software\Microsoft\Windows` `\CurrentVersion\Internet Settings` `\5.0\Cache\Content\PerUserItem`
User Configuration\Administrative Templates \Temporary Internet Files (User)	Temporary Internet Files (User)	`HKCU\Software\Microsoft\Windows` `\CurrentVersion\Internet Settings` `\SyncMode5`
User Configuration\Administrative Templates \Temporary Internet Files (User)	Temporary Internet Files (User)	`HKCU\Software\Microsoft\Windows` `\CurrentVersion\Internet Settings` `\5.0\Cache\Content\CacheLimit`

Inetres.adm

Table 19-3   Policies in Inetres.adm

Location	Name	Key
Computer Configuration\Administrative Templates \Windows Components\Internet Explorer	Security Zones: Use only machine settings	`HKLM\Software\Policies\Microsoft\Windows` `\CurrentVersion\Internet Settings` `\Security_HKLM_only`
Computer Configuration\Administrative Templates \Windows Components\Internet Explorer	Security Zones: Do not allow users to change policies	`HKLM\Software\Policies\Microsoft\Windows` `\CurrentVersion\Internet Settings` `\Security_options_edit`
Computer Configuration\Administrative Templates \Windows Components\Internet Explorer	Security Zones: Do not allow users to add/delete sites	`HKLM\Software\Policies\Microsoft\Windows` `\CurrentVersion\Internet Settings` `\Security_zones_map_edit`
Computer Configuration\Administrative Templates \Windows Components\Internet Explorer	Make proxy settings per-machine (rather than per-user)	`HKLM\Software\Policies\Microsoft\Windows` `\CurrentVersion\Internet Settings` `\ProxySettingsPerUser`
Computer Configuration\Administrative Templates \Windows Components\Internet Explorer	Disable Automatic Install of Internet Explorer components	`HKLM\Software\Policies\Microsoft` `\Internet Explorer\Infodelivery` `\Restrictions\NoJITSetup`
Computer Configuration\Administrative Templates \Windows Components\Internet Explorer	Disable Periodic Check for Internet Explorer software updates	`HKLM\Software\Policies\Microsoft` `\Internet Explorer\Infodelivery` `\Restrictions\NoUpdateCheck`
Computer Configuration\Administrative Templates \Windows Components\Internet Explorer	Disable software update shell notifications on program launch	`HKLM\Software\Microsoft\Windows` `\CurrentVersion\Policies\Explorer` `\NoMSAppLogo5ChannelNotify`
Computer Configuration\Administrative Templates \Windows Components\Internet Explorer	Disable showing the splash screen	`HKLM\Software\Policies\Microsoft` `\Internet Explorer\Infodelivery` `\Restrictions\NoSplash`
User Configuration\Administrative Templates \Windows Components\Internet Explorer	Search: Disable Search Customization	`HKCU\Software\Policies\Microsoft` `\Internet Explorer\Infodelivery` `\Restrictions\NoSearchCustomization`
User Configuration\Administrative Templates \Windows Components\Internet Explorer	Search: Disable Find Files via F3 within the browser	`HKCU\Software\Policies\Microsoft` `\Internet Explorer\Restrictions` `\NoFindFiles`
User Configuration\Administrative Templates \Windows Components\Internet Explorer	Disable external branding of Internet Explorer	`HKCU\Software\Policies\Microsoft` `\Internet Explorer\Restrictions` `\NoExternalBranding`

Location	Name	Key
User Configuration\Administrative Templates\Windows Components\Internet Explorer	Disable importing and exporting of favorites	HKCU\Software\Policies\Microsoft\Internet Explorer\DisableImportExportFavorites
User Configuration\Administrative Templates\Windows Components\Internet Explorer\Internet Control Panel	Disable the General page	HKCU\Software\Policies\Microsoft\Internet Explorer\Control Panel\GeneralTab
User Configuration\Administrative Templates\Windows Components\Internet Explorer\Internet Control Panel	Disable the Security page	HKCU\Software\Policies\Microsoft\Internet Explorer\Control Panel\SecurityTab
User Configuration\Administrative Templates\Windows Components\Internet Explorer\Internet Control Panel	Disable the Content page	HKCU\Software\Policies\Microsoft\Internet Explorer\Control Panel\ContentTab
User Configuration\Administrative Templates\Windows Components\Internet Explorer\Internet Control Panel	Disable the Connections page	HKCU\Software\Policies\Microsoft\Internet Explorer\Control Panel\ConnectionsTab
User Configuration\Administrative Templates\Windows Components\Internet Explorer\Internet Control Panel	Disable the Programs page	HKCU\Software\Policies\Microsoft\Internet Explorer\Control Panel\ProgramsTab
User Configuration\Administrative Templates\Windows Components\Internet Explorer\Internet Control Panel	Disable the Advanced page	HKCU\Software\Policies\Microsoft\Internet Explorer\Control Panel\AdvancedTab
User Configuration\Administrative Templates\Windows Components\Internet Explorer	Disable changing Advanced page settings	HKCU\Software\Policies\Microsoft\Internet Explorer\Control Panel\Advanced
User Configuration\Administrative Templates\Windows Components\Internet Explorer	Disable changing home page settings	HKCU\Software\Policies\Microsoft\Internet Explorer\Control Panel\HomePage
User Configuration\Administrative Templates\Windows Components\Internet Explorer	Use Automatic Detection for dial-up connections	HKCU\Software\Policies\Microsoft\Windows\CurrentVersion\Internet Settings\DialupAutodetect
User Configuration\Administrative Templates\Windows Components\Internet Explorer	Disable caching of Auto-Proxy scripts	HKCU\Software\Policies\Microsoft\Windows\CurrentVersion\Internet Settings\EnableAutoProxyResultCache
User Configuration\Administrative Templates\Windows Components\Internet Explorer	Display error message on proxy script download failure	HKCU\Software\Policies\Microsoft\Windows\CurrentVersion\Internet Settings\DisplayScriptDownloadFailureUI
User Configuration\Administrative Templates\Windows Components\Internet Explorer	Disable changing Temporary Internet files settings	HKCU\Software\Policies\Microsoft\Windows\CurrentVersion\Internet Settings\Cache
User Configuration\Administrative Templates\Windows Components\Internet Explorer	Disable changing history settings	HKCU\Software\Policies\Microsoft\Windows\CurrentVersion\Internet Settings\History
User Configuration\Administrative Templates\Windows Components\Internet Explorer	Disable changing color settings	HKCU\Software\Policies\Microsoft\Windows\CurrentVersion\Internet Settings\Colors
User Configuration\Administrative Templates\Windows Components\Internet Explorer	Disable changing link color settings	HKCU\Software\Policies\Microsoft\Windows\CurrentVersion\Internet Settings\links
User Configuration\Administrative Templates\Windows Components\Internet Explorer	Disable changing font settings	HKCU\Software\Policies\Microsoft\Windows\CurrentVersion\Internet Settings\Fonts
User Configuration\Administrative Templates\Windows Components\Internet Explorer	Disable changing language settings	HKCU\Software\Policies\Microsoft\Windows\CurrentVersion\Internet Settings\Languages

Table 19-3   Policies in Inetres.adm   *(continued)*

Location	Name	Key
User Configuration\Administrative Templates \Windows Components\Internet Explorer	Disable changing accessibility settings	HKCU\Software\Policies\Microsoft\Windows \CurrentVersion\Internet Settings \Accessibility
User Configuration\Administrative Templates \Windows Components\Internet Explorer	Disable Internet Connection wizard	HKCU\Software\Policies\Microsoft\Windows \CurrentVersion\Internet Settings \Connwiz Admin Lock
User Configuration\Administrative Templates \Windows Components\Internet Explorer	Disable changing connection settings	HKCU\Software\Policies\Microsoft\Windows \CurrentVersion\Internet Settings \Connection Settings
User Configuration\Administrative Templates \Windows Components\Internet Explorer	Disable changing proxy settings	HKCU\Software\Policies\Microsoft\Windows \CurrentVersion\Internet Settings\Proxy
User Configuration\Administrative Templates \Windows Components\Internet Explorer	Disable changing Automatic Configuration settings	HKCU\Software\Policies\Microsoft\Windows \CurrentVersion\Internet Settings \Autoconfig
User Configuration\Administrative Templates \Windows Components\Internet Explorer	Disable changing ratings settings	HKCU\Software\Policies\Microsoft\Windows \CurrentVersion\Internet Settings \Ratings
User Configuration\Administrative Templates \Windows Components\Internet Explorer	Disable changing certificate settings	HKCU\Software\Policies\Microsoft\Windows \CurrentVersion\Internet Settings \Certificates
User Configuration\Administrative Templates \Windows Components\Internet Explorer	Disable changing Profile Assistant settings	HKCU\Software\Policies\Microsoft\Windows \CurrentVersion\Internet Settings \Profiles
User Configuration\Administrative Templates \Windows Components\Internet Explorer	Disable AutoComplete for forms	HKCU\Software\Policies\Microsoft\Windows \CurrentVersion\Internet Settings \FormSuggest
User Configuration\Administrative Templates \Windows Components\Internet Explorer	Do not allow AutoComplete to save passwords	HKCU\Software\Policies\Microsoft\Windows \CurrentVersion\Internet Settings \FormSuggest Passwords
User Configuration\Administrative Templates \Windows Components\Internet Explorer	Disable changing Messaging settings	HKCU\Software\Policies\Microsoft\Windows \CurrentVersion\Internet Settings \Messaging
User Configuration\Administrative Templates \Windows Components\Internet Explorer	Disable changing Calendar and Contact settings	HKCU\Software\Policies\Microsoft\Windows \CurrentVersion\Internet Settings \CalendarContact
User Configuration\Administrative Templates \Windows Components\Internet Explorer	Disable the Reset Web Settings feature	HKCU\Software\Policies\Microsoft\Windows \CurrentVersion\Internet Settings \ResetWebSettings
User Configuration\Administrative Templates \Windows Components\Internet Explorer	Disable changing default browser check	HKCU\Software\Policies\Microsoft\Windows \CurrentVersion\Internet Settings \Check_If_Default
User Configuration\Administrative Templates \Windows Components\Internet Explorer	Identity Manager: Prevent users from using Identities	HKCU\Software\Policies\Microsoft\Windows \CurrentVersion\Identities\Locked Down
User Configuration\Administrative Templates \Windows Components\Internet Explorer	Configure Outlook Express	HKCU\Software\Microsoft\Outlook Express \BlockExeAttachments
User Configuration\Administrative Templates \Windows Components\Internet Explorer	Configure Media Explorer Bar	HKCU\Software\Microsoft \Internet Explorer\media\Autoplay
User Configuration\Administrative Templates \Windows Components\Internet Explorer \Offline Pages	Disable adding channels	HKCU\Software\Policies\Microsoft \Internet Explorer\Infodelivery \Restrictions\NoAddingChannels

Location	Name	Key
User Configuration\Administrative Templates \Windows Components\Internet Explorer \Offline Pages	Disable removing channels	HKCU\Software\Policies\Microsoft \Internet Explorer\Infodelivery \Restrictions\NoRemovingChannels
User Configuration\Administrative Templates \Windows Components\Internet Explorer \Offline Pages	Disable adding schedules for offline pages	HKCU\Software\Policies\Microsoft \Internet Explorer\Infodelivery \Restrictions\NoAddingSubscriptions
User Configuration\Administrative Templates \Windows Components\Internet Explorer \Offline Pages	Disable editing schedules for offline pages	HKCU\Software\Policies\Microsoft \Internet Explorer\Infodelivery \Restrictions\NoEditingSubscriptions
User Configuration\Administrative Templates \Windows Components\Internet Explorer \Offline Pages	Disable removing schedules for offline pages	HKCU\Software\Policies\Microsoft \Internet Explorer\Infodelivery \Restrictions\NoRemovingSubscriptions
User Configuration\Administrative Templates \Windows Components\Internet Explorer \Offline Pages	Disable offline page hit logging	HKCU\Software\Policies\Microsoft \Internet Explorer\Infodelivery \Restrictions\NoChannelLogging
User Configuration\Administrative Templates \Windows Components\Internet Explorer \Offline Pages	Disable all scheduled offline pages	HKCU\Software\Policies\Microsoft \Internet Explorer\Infodelivery \Restrictions\NoScheduledUpdates
User Configuration\Administrative Templates \Windows Components\Internet Explorer \Offline Pages	Disable channel user interface completely	HKCU\Software\Policies\Microsoft \Internet Explorer\Infodelivery \Restrictions\NoChannelUI
User Configuration\Administrative Templates \Windows Components\Internet Explorer \Offline Pages	Disable down-loading of site subscription content	HKCU\Software\Policies\Microsoft \Internet Explorer\Infodelivery \Restrictions\NoSubscriptionContent
User Configuration\Administrative Templates \Windows Components\Internet Explorer \Offline Pages	Disable editing and creating of schedule groups	HKCU\Software\Policies\Microsoft \Internet Explorer\Infodelivery \Restrictions\NoEditingScheduleGroups
User Configuration\Administrative Templates \Windows Components\Internet Explorer \Offline Pages	Subscription Limits	HKCU\Software\Policies\Microsoft \Internet Explorer\Infodelivery \Restrictions\MaxWebcrawlLevels
User Configuration\Administrative Templates \Windows Components\Internet Explorer \Browser menus	File menu: Disable Save As menu option	HKCU\Software\Policies\Microsoft \Internet Explorer\Restrictions \NoBrowserSaveAs
User Configuration\Administrative Templates \Windows Components\Internet Explorer \Browser menus	File menu: Disable New menu option	HKCU\Software\Policies\Microsoft \Internet Explorer\Restrictions \NoFileNew
User Configuration\Administrative Templates \Windows Components\Internet Explorer \Browser menus	File menu: Disable Open menu option	HKCU\Software\Policies\Microsoft \Internet Explorer\Restrictions \NoFileOpen
User Configuration\Administrative Templates \Windows Components\Internet Explorer \Browser menus	File menu: Disable Save As Web Page Complete	HKCU\Software\Policies \Microsoft\Internet Explorer \Infodelivery\Restrictions \NoBrowserSaveWebComplete
User Configuration\Administrative Templates \Windows Components\Internet Explorer \Browser menus	File menu: Disable closing the browser and Explorer windows	HKCU\Software\Policies\Microsoft \Internet Explorer\Infodelivery \Restrictions\NoBrowserClose
User Configuration\Administrative Templates \Windows Components\Internet Explorer \Browser menus	View menu: Disable Source menu option	HKCU\Software\Policies\Microsoft \Internet Explorer\Infodelivery \Restrictions\NoViewSource

Table 19-3 Policies in Inetres.adm *(continued)*

Location	Name	Key
User Configuration\Administrative Templates \Windows Components\Internet Explorer \Browser menus	View menu: Disable Full Screen menu option	`HKCU\Software\Policies\Microsoft` `\Internet Explorer\Infodelivery` `\Restrictions\NoTheaterMode`
User Configuration\Administrative Templates \Windows Components\Internet Explorer \Browser menus	Hide Favorites menu	`HKCU\Software\Policies\Microsoft` `\Internet Explorer\Infodelivery` `\Restrictions\NoFavorites`
User Configuration\Administrative Templates \Windows Components\Internet Explorer \Browser menus	Tools menu: Disable Internet Options menu option	`HKCU\Software\Policies\Microsoft` `\Internet Explorer\Infodelivery` `\Restrictions\NoBrowserOptions`
User Configuration\Administrative Templates \Windows Components\Internet Explorer \Browser menus	Help menu: Remove 'Tip of the Day' menu option	`HKCU\Software\Policies\Microsoft` `\Internet Explorer\Restrictions` `\NoHelpItemTipOfTheDay`
User Configuration\Administrative Templates \Windows Components\Internet Explorer \Browser menus	Help menu: Remove 'For Netscape Users' menu option	`HKCU\Software\Policies\Microsoft` `\Internet Explorer\Restrictions` `\NoHelpItemNetscapeHelp`
User Configuration\Administrative Templates \Windows Components\Internet Explorer \Browser menus	Help menu: Remove 'Send Feedback' menu option	`HKCU\Software\Policies\Microsoft` `\Internet Explorer\Restrictions` `\NoHelpItemSendFeedback`
User Configuration\Administrative Templates \Windows Components\Internet Explorer \Browser menus	Disable Context menu	`HKCU\Software\Policies\Microsoft` `\Internet Explorer\Restrictions` `\NoBrowserContextMenu`
User Configuration\Administrative Templates \Windows Components\Internet Explorer \Browser menus	Disable Open in New Window menu option	`HKCU\Software\Policies\Microsoft` `\Internet Explorer\Restrictions` `\NoOpeninNewWnd`
User Configuration\Administrative Templates \Windows Components\Internet Explorer \Browser menus	Disable Save this program to disk option	`HKCU\Software\Policies\Microsoft` `\Internet Explorer\Restrictions` `\NoSelectDownloadDir`
User Configuration\Administrative Templates \Windows Components\Internet Explorer \Toolbars	Disable customizing browser toolbar buttons	`HKCU\Software\Microsoft\Windows` `\CurrentVersion\Policies` `\Explorer\NoToolbarCustomize`
User Configuration\Administrative Templates \Windows Components\Internet Explorer \Toolbars	Disable customizing browser toolbars	`HKCU\Software\Microsoft\Windows` `\CurrentVersion\Policies` `\Explorer\NoBandCustomize`
User Configuration\Administrative Templates \Windows Components\Internet Explorer \Toolbars	Configure Toolbar Buttons	`HKCU\Software\Microsoft\Windows` `\CurrentVersion\Policies` `\Explorer\Btn_Encoding`
User Configuration\Administrative Templates \Windows Components\Internet Explorer \Persistence Behavior	File size limits for Local Machine zone	`HKCU\Software\Policies\Microsoft` `\Internet Explorer\Persistence` `\0\DocumentLimit`
User Configuration\Administrative Templates \Windows Components\Internet Explorer \Persistence Behavior	File size limits for Intranet zone	`HKCU\Software\Policies\Microsoft` `\Internet Explorer\Persistence` `\1\DocumentLimit`
User Configuration\Administrative Templates \Windows Components\Internet Explorer \Persistence Behavior	File size limits for Trusted Sites zone	`HKCU\Software\Policies\Microsoft` `\Internet Explorer\Persistence` `\2\DocumentLimit`
User Configuration\Administrative Templates \Windows Components\Internet Explorer \Persistence Behavior	File size limits for Internet zone	`HKCU\Software\Policies\Microsoft` `\Internet Explorer\Persistence` `\3\DocumentLimit`

Location	Name	Key
User Configuration\Administrative Templates \Windows Components\Internet Explorer \Persistence Behavior	File size limits for Restricted Sites zone	HKCU\Software\Policies\Microsoft \Internet Explorer\Persistence \4\DocumentLimit
User Configuration\Administrative Templates \Windows Components\Internet Explorer \Administrator Approved Controls		HKCU\Software\Policies\Microsoft \Windows\CurrentVersion \Internet Settings\AllowedControls \{22D6F312-B0F6-11D0-94AB-0080C74C7E95}
User Configuration\Administrative Templates \Windows Components\Internet Explorer \Administrator Approved Controls		HKCU\Software\Policies\Microsoft \Windows\CurrentVersion \Internet Settings\AllowedControls \{F5131C24-E56D-11CF-B78A-444553540000}
User Configuration\Administrative Templates \Windows Components\Internet Explorer \Administrator Approved Controls		HKCU\Software\Policies\Microsoft \Windows\CurrentVersion \Internet Settings\AllowedControls \{D45FD31B-5C6E-11D1-9EC1-00C04FD7081F}
User Configuration\Administrative Templates \Windows Components\Internet Explorer \Administrator Approved Controls		HKCU\Software\Policies\Microsoft \Windows\CurrentVersion \Internet Settings\AllowedControls \{D6526FE0-E651-11CF-99CB-00C04FD64497}
User Configuration\Administrative Templates \Windows Components\Internet Explorer \Administrator Approved Controls	Microsoft Survey Control	HKCU\Software\Policies\Microsoft \Windows\CurrentVersion \Internet Settings\AllowedControls \{BD1F006E-174F-11D2-95C0-00C04F9A8CFA}
User Configuration\Administrative Templates \Windows Components\Internet Explorer \Administrator Approved Controls	Shockwave Flash	HKCU\Software\Policies\Microsoft \Windows\CurrentVersion \Internet Settings\AllowedControls \{D27CDB6E-AE6D-11CF-96B8-444553540000}
User Configuration\Administrative Templates \Windows Components\Internet Explorer \Administrator Approved Controls	NetShow File Transfer Control	HKCU\Software\Policies\Microsoft \Windows\CurrentVersion \Internet Settings\AllowedControls \{26F24A93-1DA2-11D0-A334-00AA004A5FC5}
User Configuration\Administrative Templates \Windows Components\Internet Explorer \Administrator Approved Controls	DHTML EditCon-trol	HKCU\Software\Policies\Microsoft \Windows\CurrentVersion \Internet Settings\AllowedControls \{2D360201-FFF5-11D1-8D03-00A0C959BC0A}
User Configuration\Administrative Templates \Windows Components\Internet Explorer \Administrator Approved Controls	Microsoft Script-let Component	HKCU\Software\Policies\Microsoft \Windows\CurrentVersion \Internet Settings\AllowedControls \{AE24FDAE-03C6-11D1-8B76-0080C744F389}
User Configuration\Administrative Templates \Windows Components\Internet Explorer \Administrator Approved Controls		HKCU\Software\Policies\Microsoft \Windows\CurrentVersion \Internet Settings\AllowedControls \{DED22F57-FEE2-11D0-953B-00C04FD9152D}
User Configuration\Administrative Templates \Windows Components\Internet Explorer \Administrator Approved Controls		HKCU\Software\Policies\Microsoft \Windows\CurrentVersion \Internet Settings\AllowedControls \{52ADE293-85E8-11D2-BB22-00104B0EA281}
User Configuration\Administrative Templates \Windows Components\Internet Explorer \Administrator Approved Controls		HKCU\Software\Policies\Microsoft \Windows\CurrentVersion \Internet Settings\AllowedControls \{2FF18E10-DE11-11D1-8161-00A0C90DD90C}

Inetset.adm

Table 19-4   Policies in Inetset.adm

Location	Name	Key
Computer Configuration \Administrative Templates \Component Updates	Periodic check for updates to Internet Explorer and Internet Tools	HKLM\Software\Microsoft\Internet Explorer\Main \Update_Check_Interval
Computer Configuration \Administrative Templates \Component Updates	Help Menu > About Internet Explorer	HKLM\Software\Microsoft\Windows\CurrentVersion \IEAKUpdateUrl
User Configuration\Administrative Templates \Advanced settings	Connection	HKCU\Software\Microsoft\Windows\CurrentVersion \Internet Settings\EnableAutodial
User Configuration\Administrative Templates \Advanced settings	Browsing	HKCU\SOFTWARE\Microsoft\Ftp \Error Dlg Displayed On Every Error
User Configuration\Administrative Templates \Advanced settings	Multimedia	HKCU\SOFTWARE\Microsoft\Internet Explorer \Show image placeholders
User Configuration\Administrative Templates \Advanced settings	Security	HKCU\SOFTWARE\Microsoft\Windows\CurrentVersion \Internet Settings\WarnonZoneCrossing
User Configuration\Administrative Templates \Advanced settings	Microsoft VM	HKCU\Software\Microsoft\Java VM\EnableJIT
User Configuration\Administrative Templates \Advanced settings	Printing	HKCU\Software\Microsoft\Java VM \Print_Background
User Configuration\Administrative Templates \Advanced settings	Searching	HKCU\Software\Microsoft\Internet Explorer \SearchURL\AutoSearch
User Configuration\Administrative Templates \Advanced settings	HTTP 1.1 settings	HKCU\SOFTWARE\Microsoft\Windows\CurrentVersion \Internet Settings\ProxyHttp1.1
User Configuration\Administrative Templates \Advanced settings	Signup Settings	HKCU\Software\Microsoft\IEAK\NoAutomaticSignup
User Configuration\Administrative Templates \Advanced settings	Internet Connection Wizard Settings	HKCU\Software\Microsoft \Internet Connection Wizard\Completed
User Configuration\Administrative Templates \AutoComplete	AutoComplete Settings	HKCU\SOFTWARE\Microsoft\Windows\CurrentVersion \Explorer\AutoComplete\FormSuggest PW Ask
User Configuration\Administrative Templates \Display settings	Text Size	HKCU\Software\Microsoft\Internet Explorer \International\Scripts\Default_IEFontSize
User Configuration\Administrative Templates \Display settings	General Colors	HKCU\Software\Microsoft\Internet Explorer \Main\Use_DlgBox_Colors
User Configuration\Administrative Templates \Display settings	Link colors	HKCU\Software\Microsoft\Internet Explorer \Main\Anchor Color Hover
User Configuration\Administrative Templates \URL Encoding	URL Encoding	HKCU\Software\Microsoft\Windows\CurrentVersion \Internet Settings\UrlEncoding

System.adm

Table 19-5 Policies in System.adm

Location	Name	Key
Computer Configuration\Administrative Templates \Network	Background Intelligent Transfer Service (BITS) inactive job timeout	HKLM\Software\Policies\Microsoft \Windows\BITS\JobInactivityTimeout
Computer Configuration\Administrative Templates \Network	Sets how often a DFS Client discovers DC's	HKLM\Software\Policies\Microsoft\System \DFSClient\DfsDcNameDelay
Computer Configuration\Administrative Templates \Network\DNS Client	Primary DNS Suffix	HKLM\Software\Policies\Microsoft\System \DNSClient\NV PrimaryDnsSuffix
Computer Configuration\Administrative Templates \Network\DNS Client	Dynamic Update	HKLM\Software\Policies\Microsoft \Windows NT\DNSClient \RegistrationEnabled
Computer Configuration\Administrative Templates \Network\DNS Client	DNS Suffix Search List	HKLM\Software\Policies\Microsoft \Windows NT\DNSClient\SearchList
Computer Configuration\Administrative Templates \Network\DNS Client	Primary DNS Suffix Devolution	HKLM\Software\Policies\Microsoft \Windows NT\DNSClient \UseDomainNameDevolution
Computer Configuration\Administrative Templates \Network\DNS Client	Register PTR Records	HKLM\Software\Policies\Microsoft \Windows NT\DNSClient \RegisterReverseLookup
Computer Configuration\Administrative Templates \Network\DNS Client	Registration Refresh Interval	HKLM\Software\Policies\Microsoft \Windows NT\DNSClient \RegistrationRefreshInterval
Computer Configuration\Administrative Templates \Network\DNS Client	Replace Addresses In Conflicts	HKLM\Software\Policies\Microsoft \Windows NT\DNSClient \RegistrationOverwritesInConflict
Computer Configuration\Administrative Templates \Network\DNS Client	DNS Servers	HKLM\Software\Policies\Microsoft \Windows NT\DNSClient\NameServer
Computer Configuration\Administrative Templates \Network\DNS Client	Connection-Specific DNS Suffix	HKLM\Software\Policies\Microsoft \Windows NT\DNSClient \AdapterDomainName
Computer Configuration\Administrative Templates \Network\DNS Client	Register DNS records with connection-specific DNS suffix	HKLM\Software\Policies\Microsoft \Windows NT\DNSClient \RegisterAdapterName
Computer Configuration\Administrative Templates \Network\DNS Client	TTL Set in the A and PTR records	HKLM\Software\Policies\Microsoft \Windows NT\DNSClient\RegistrationTtl
Computer Configuration\Administrative Templates \Network\DNS Client	Update Security Level	HKLM\Software\Policies\Microsoft \Windows NT\DNSClient \UpdateSecurityLevel
Computer Configuration\Administrative Templates \Network\DNS Client	Update Top Level Domain Zones	HKLM\Software\Policies\Microsoft \Windows NT\DNSClient \UpdateTopLevelDomainZones
Computer Configuration\Administrative Templates \Network\Network Connections	Prohibit use of Internet Connection Sharing on your DNS domain network	HKLM\Software\Policies\Microsoft \Windows\Network Connections \NC_ShowSharedAccessUI
Computer Configuration\Administrative Templates \Network\Network Connections	Prohibit use of Internet Connection Firewall on your DNS domain network	HKLM\Software\Policies\Microsoft \Windows\Network Connections \NC_PersonalFirewallConfig

Table 19-5   Policies in System.adm   *(continued)*

Location	Name	Key
Computer Configuration\Administrative Templates \Network\Network Connections	Prohibit installation and configuration of Network Bridge on your DNS domain network	HKLM\Software\Policies\Microsoft \Windows\Network Connections \NC_AllowNetBridge_NLA
Computer Configuration\Administrative Templates \Network\Network Connections	IEEE 802.1x Certificate Authority for Machine Authentication	HKLM\Software\Policies\Microsoft \Windows\Network Connections\8021X \8021XCARootHash
Computer Configuration\Administrative Templates \Network\Offline Files	Allow or Disallow use of the Offline Files feature	HKLM\Software\Policies\Microsoft \Windows\NetCache\Enabled
Computer Configuration\Administrative Templates \Network\Offline Files	Prohibit user configuration of Offline Files	HKLM\Software\Policies\Microsoft \Windows\NetCache\NoConfigCache
Computer Configuration\Administrative Templates \Network\Offline Files	Synchronize all offline files when logging on	HKLM\Software\Policies\Microsoft \Windows\NetCache\SyncAtLogon
Computer Configuration\Administrative Templates \Network\Offline Files	Synchronize all offline files before logging off	HKLM\Software\Policies\Microsoft \Windows\NetCache\SyncAtLogoff
Computer Configuration\Administrative Templates \Network\Offline Files	Synchronize offline files before suspend	HKLM\Software\Policies\Microsoft \Windows\NetCache\SyncAtSuspend
Computer Configuration\Administrative Templates \Network\Offline Files	Default cache size	HKLM\Software\Policies\Microsoft \Windows\NetCache\DefCacheSize
Computer Configuration\Administrative Templates \Network\Offline Files	Action on server disconnect	HKLM\Software\Policies\Microsoft \Windows\NetCache\GoOfflineAction
Computer Configuration\Administrative Templates \Network\Offline Files	Non-default server disconnect actions	HKLM\Software\Policies\Microsoft\Windows \NetCache\CustomGoOfflineActions\
Computer Configuration\Administrative Templates \Network\Offline Files	Remove 'Make Available Offline'	HKLM\Software\Policies\Microsoft\Windows \NetCache\NoMakeAvailableOffline
Computer Configuration\Administrative Templates \Network\Offline Files	Prevent use of Offline Files folder	HKLM\Software\Policies\Microsoft\Windows \NetCache\NoCacheViewer
Computer Configuration\Administrative Templates \Network\Offline Files	Files not cached	HKLM\Software\Policies\Microsoft\Windows \NetCache\ExcludeExtensions
Computer Configuration\Administrative Templates \Network\Offline Files	Administratively assigned offline files	HKLM\Software\Policies\Microsoft\Windows \NetCache\AssignedOfflineFolders\
Computer Configuration\Administrative Templates \Network\Offline Files	Turn off reminder balloons	HKLM\Software\Policies\Microsoft\Windows \NetCache\NoReminders
Computer Configuration\Administrative Templates \Network\Offline Files	Reminder balloon frequency	HKLM\Software\Policies\Microsoft\Windows \NetCache\ReminderFreqMinutes
Computer Configuration\Administrative Templates \Network\Offline Files	Initial reminder balloon lifetime	HKLM\Software\Policies\Microsoft\Windows \NetCache\InitialBalloonTimeoutSeconds
Computer Configuration\Administrative Templates \Network\Offline Files	Reminder balloon lifetime	HKLM\Software\Policies\Microsoft\Windows \NetCache\ReminderBalloonTimeoutSeconds
Computer Configuration\Administrative Templates \Network\Offline Files	At logoff, delete local copy of user's offline files	HKLM\Software\Policies\Microsoft\Windows \NetCache\PurgeOnlyAutoCacheAtLogoff

Location	Name	Key
Computer Configuration\Administrative Templates \Network\Offline Files	Event logging level	HKLM\Software\Policies\Microsoft\Windows \NetCache\EventLoggingLevel
Computer Configuration\Administrative Templates \Network\Offline Files	Subfolders always available offline	HKLM\Software\Policies\Microsoft\Windows \NetCache\AlwaysPinSubFolders
Computer Configuration\Administrative Templates \Network\Offline Files	Encrypt the Offline Files cache	HKLM\Software\Policies\Microsoft\Windows \NetCache\EncryptCache
Computer Configuration\Administrative Templates \Network\Offline Files	Prohibit 'Make Available Offline' for these file and folders	HKLM\Software\Policies\Microsoft\Windows \NetCache\NoMakeAvailableOfflineList\
Computer Configuration\Administrative Templates \Network\Offline Files	Configure Slow link speed	HKLM\Software\Policies\Microsoft\Windows \NetCache\SlowLinkSpeed
Computer Configuration\Administrative Templates \Network\QoS Packet Scheduler	Limit reservable bandwidth	HKLM\Software\Policies\Microsoft\Windows \Psched\NonBestEffortLimit
Computer Configuration\Administrative Templates \Network\QoS Packet Scheduler	Limit outstanding packets	HKLM\Software\Policies\Microsoft\Windows \Psched\MaxOutstandingSends
Computer Configuration\Administrative Templates \Network\QoS Packet Scheduler	Set timer resolution	HKLM\Software\Policies\Microsoft\Windows \Psched\TimerResolution
Computer Configuration\Administrative Templates \Network\QoS Packet Scheduler \DSCP value of conforming packets	Best effort service type	HKLM\Software\Policies\Microsoft\Windows \Psched\DiffservByteMappingConforming \ServiceTypeBestEffort
Computer Configuration\Administrative Templates \Network\QoS Packet Scheduler \DSCP value of conforming packets	Controlled load service type	HKLM\Software\Policies\Microsoft\Windows \Psched\DiffservByteMappingConforming \ServiceTypeControlledLoad
Computer Configuration\Administrative Templates \Network\QoS Packet Scheduler \DSCP value of conforming packets	Guaranteed service type	HKLM\Software\Policies\Microsoft\Windows \Psched\DiffservByteMappingConforming \ServiceTypeGuaranteed
Computer Configuration\Administrative Templates \Network\QoS Packet Scheduler \DSCP value of conforming packets	Network control service type	HKLM\Software\Policies\Microsoft\Windows \Psched\DiffservByteMappingConforming \ServiceTypeNetworkControl
Computer Configuration\Administrative Templates \Network\QoS Packet Scheduler \DSCP value of conforming packets	Qualitative service type	HKLM\Software\Policies\Microsoft\Windows \Psched\DiffservByteMappingConforming \ServiceTypeQualitative
Computer Configuration\Administrative Templates \Network\QoS Packet Scheduler \DSCP value of non-conforming packets	Best effort service type	HKLM\Software\Policies\Microsoft\Windows \Psched\DiffservByteMappingNonConforming \ServiceTypeBestEffort
Computer Configuration\Administrative Templates \QoS Packet Scheduler \DSCP value of non-conforming packets	Controlled load service type	HKLM\ Software\Policies \Microsoft\Windows\Psched \DiffservByteMappingNonConforming \ServiceTypeControlledLoad
Computer Configuration\Administrative Templates \Network\QoS Packet Scheduler \DSCP value of non-conforming packets	Guaranteed service type	HKLM\ Software\Policies \Microsoft\Windows\Psched \DiffservByteMappingNonConforming \ServiceTypeGuaranteed
Computer Configuration\Administrative Templates \Network\QoS Packet Scheduler \DSCP value of non-conforming packets	Network control service type	HKLM\Software\Policies\Microsoft\Windows \Psched\DiffservByteMappingNonConforming \ServiceTypeNetworkControl
Computer Configuration\Administrative Templates \Network\QoS Packet Scheduler \DSCP value of non-conforming packets	Qualitative service type	HKLM\Software\Policies\Microsoft\Windows \Psched\DiffservByteMappingNonConforming \ServiceTypeQualitative

Table 19-5 Policies in System.adm *(continued)*

Location	Name	Key
Computer Configuration\Administrative Templates \Network\QoS Packet Scheduler \Layer-2 priority value	Non-conforming packets	HKLM\Software\Policies\Microsoft\Windows \Psched\UserPriorityMapping \ServiceTypeNonConforming
Computer Configuration\Administrative Templates \Network\QoS Packet Scheduler \Layer-2 priority value	Best effort service type	HKLM\Software\Policies\Microsoft\Windows \Psched\UserPriorityMapping \ServiceTypeBestEffort
Computer Configuration\Administrative Templates \Network\QoS Packet Scheduler \Layer-2 priority value	Controlled load service type	HKLM\Software\Policies\Microsoft\Windows \Psched\UserPriorityMapping \ServiceTypeControlledLoad
Computer Configuration\Administrative Templates \Network\QoS Packet Scheduler \Layer-2 priority value	Guaranteed service type	HKLM\Software\Policies\Microsoft\Windows \Psched\UserPriorityMapping \ServiceTypeGuaranteed
Computer Configuration\Administrative Templates \Network\QoS Packet Scheduler \Layer-2 priority value	Network control service type	HKLM\Software\Policies\Microsoft\Windows \Psched\UserPriorityMapping \ServiceTypeNetworkControl
Computer Configuration\Administrative Templates \Network\QoS Packet Scheduler \Layer-2 priority value	Qualitative service type	HKLM\Software\Policies\Microsoft\Windows \Psched\UserPriorityMapping \ServiceTypeQualitative
Computer Configuration\Administrative Templates \Network\SNMP	Communities	HKLM\Software\Policies\SNMP\Parameters \ValidCommunities\
Computer Configuration\Administrative Templates \Network\SNMP	Permitted Managers	HKLM\Software\Policies\SNMP\Parameters \PermittedManagers\
Computer Configuration\Administrative Templates \Network\SNMP	Traps for Public community	HKLM\Software\Policies\SNMP\Parameters \TrapDestinations\
Computer Configuration\Administrative Templates \Printers	Allow printers to be published	HKLM\Software\Policies\Microsoft \Windows NT\Printers\PublishPrinters
Computer Configuration\Administrative Templates \Printers	Allow pruning of published printers	HKLM\Software\Policies\Microsoft \Windows NT\Printers\Immortal
Computer Configuration\Administrative Templates \Printers	Automatically publish new printers in Active Directory	HKLM\Software\Policies\Microsoft \Windows NT\Printers\Wizard \Auto Publishing
Computer Configuration\Administrative Templates \Printers	Check published state	HKLM\Software\Policies\Microsoft \Windows NT\Printers \VerifyPublishedState
Computer Configuration\Administrative Templates \Printers	Computer location	HKLM\Software\Policies\Microsoft \Windows NT\Printers\PhysicalLocation
Computer Configuration\Administrative Templates \Printers	Custom support URL in the Printers folder's left pane	HKLM\Software\Policies\Microsoft \Windows NT\Printers\SupportLink
Computer Configuration\Administrative Templates \Printers	Directory pruning interval	HKLM\Software\Policies\Microsoft \Windows NT\Printers\PruningInterval
Computer Configuration\Administrative Templates \Printers	Directory pruning priority	HKLM\Software\Policies\Microsoft \Windows NT\Printers\PruningPriority
Computer Configuration\Administrative Templates \Printers	Directory pruning retry	HKLM\Software\Policies\Microsoft \Windows NT\Printers\PruningRetries
Computer Configuration\Administrative Templates \Printers	Disallow installation of printers using kernel-mode drivers	HKLM\Software\Policies\Microsoft \Windows NT\Printers \KMPrintersAreBlocked

Location	Name	Key
Computer Configuration\Administrative Templates \Printers	Log directory pruning retry events	HKLM\Software\Policies\Microsoft \Windows NT\Printers\PruningRetryLog
Computer Configuration\Administrative Templates \Printers	Pre-populate printer search location text	HKLM\Software\Policies\Microsoft \Windows NT\Printers \PhysicalLocationSupport
Computer Configuration\Administrative Templates \Printers	Printer browsing	HKLM\Software\Policies\Microsoft \Windows NT\Printers\ServerThread
Computer Configuration\Administrative Templates \Printers	Prune printers that are not automati- cally republished	HKLM\Software\Policies\Microsoft \Windows NT\Printers\PruneDownlevel
Computer Configuration\Administrative Templates \Printers	Web-based printing	HKLM\Software\Policies\Microsoft \Windows NT\Printers\DisableWebPrinting
Computer Configuration\Administrative Templates \System	Display Shutdown Event Tracker	HKLM\Software\Policies\Microsoft \Windows NT\Reliability\ShutdownReasonUI
Computer Configuration\Administrative Templates \System	Specify Windows installation file location	HKLM\Software\Policies\Microsoft \Windows NT\Setup\SourcePath
Computer Configuration\Administrative Templates \System	Specify Windows Service Pack installa- tion file location	HKLM\Software\Policies\Microsoft \Windows NT\Setup\ServicePackSourcePath
Computer Configuration\Administrative Templates \System	Remove Boot/ Shutdown/Logon/ Logoff status messages	HKLM\Software\Microsoft\Windows \CurrentVersion\Policies\System \DisableStatusMessages
Computer Configuration\Administrative Templates \System	Verbose vs normal status messages	HKLM\Software\Microsoft\Windows \CurrentVersion\Policies\System \VerboseStatus
Computer Configuration\Administrative Templates \System	Restrict these programs from being launched from Help	HKLM\Software\Policies\Microsoft\Windows \System\DisableInHelp
Computer Configuration\Administrative Templates \System	Turn off Autoplay	HKLM\Software\Microsoft\Windows \CurrentVersion\Policies\Explorer \NoDriveTypeAutoRun
Computer Configuration\Administrative Templates \System	Do not automatically encrypt files moved to encrypted folders	HKLM\Software\Microsoft\Windows \CurrentVersion\Policies\Explorer \NoEncryptOnMove
Computer Configuration\Administrative Templates \System	Download missing COM components	HKLM\Software\Policies\Microsoft\Windows \App Management\COMClassStore
Computer Configuration\Administrative Templates \System\Disk Quotas	Enable disk quotas	HKLM\Software\Policies\Microsoft \Windows NT\DiskQuota\Enable
Computer Configuration\Administrative Templates \System\Disk Quotas	Enforce disk quota limit	HKLM\Software\Policies\Microsoft \Windows NT\DiskQuota\Enforce
Computer Configuration\Administrative Templates \System\Disk Quotas	Default quota limit and warning level	HKLM\Software\Policies\Microsoft \Windows NT\DiskQuota\ThresholdUnits
Computer Configuration\Administrative Templates \System\Disk Quotas	Log event when quota limit exceeded	HKLM\Software\Policies\Microsoft \Windows NT\DiskQuota\LogEventOverLimit
Computer Configuration\Administrative Templates \System\Disk Quotas	Log event when quota warning level exceeded	HKLM\Software\Policies\Microsoft \Windows NT\DiskQuota \LogEventOverThreshold

Table 19-5   Policies in System.adm   *(continued)*

Location	Name	Key
Computer Configuration\Administrative Templates \System\Disk Quotas	Apply policy to removable media	HKLM\Software\Policies\Microsoft \Windows_NT\DiskQuota \ApplyToRemovableMedia
Computer Configuration\Administrative Templates \System\Error Reporting	Display Error Notification	HKLM\Software\Policies\Microsoft \PCHealth\ErrorReporting\DW \DWAllowHeadless
Computer Configuration\Administrative Templates \System\Error Reporting	Report Errors	HKLM\Software\Policies\Microsoft \PCHealth\ErrorReporting\DW \DWReporteeName
Computer Configuration\Administrative Templates \System\Error Reporting \Advanced Error Reporting settings	Default application reporting settings	HKLM\Software\Policies\Microsoft \PCHealth\ErrorReporting \IncludeWindowsApps
Computer Configuration\Administrative Templates \System\Error Reporting \Advanced Error Reporting settings	List of applications to always report errors for	HKLM\Software\Policies\Microsoft \PCHealth\ErrorReporting\InclusionList\
Computer Configuration\Administrative Templates \System\Error Reporting \Advanced Error Reporting settings	List of applications to never report errors for	HKLM\Software\Policies\Microsoft \PCHealth\ErrorReporting\ExclusionList\
Computer Configuration\Administrative Templates \System\Error Reporting \Advanced Error Reporting settings	Report operating system errors	HKLM\Software\Policies\Microsoft \PCHealth\ErrorReporting \IncludeKernelFaults
Computer Configuration\Administrative Templates \System\Error Reporting \Advanced Error Reporting settings	Report unplanned shutdown events	HKLM\Software\Policies\Microsoft \PCHealth\ErrorReporting \IncludeShutdownErrs
Computer Configuration\Administrative Templates \System\Group Policy	Turn off background refresh of Group Policy	HKLM\Software\Microsoft\Windows \CurrentVersion\Policies\System \DisableBkGndGroupPolicy
Computer Configuration\Administrative Templates \System\Group Policy	Group Policy refresh interval for computers	HKLM\Software\Policies\Microsoft \Windows\System \GroupPolicyRefreshTimeOffset
Computer Configuration\Administrative Templates \System\Group Policy	Group Policy refresh interval for domain controllers	HKLM\Software\Policies\Microsoft \Windows\System \GroupPolicyRefreshTimeOffsetDC
Computer Configuration\Administrative Templates \System\Group Policy	User Group Policy loopback processing mode	HKLM\Software\Policies\Microsoft \Windows\System\UserPolicyMode
Computer Configuration\Administrative Templates \System\Group Policy	Group Policy slow link detection	HKLM\Software\Policies\Microsoft \Windows\System \GroupPolicyMinTransferRate
Computer Configuration\Administrative Templates \System\Group Policy	Turn off Resultant Set of Policy logging	HKLM\Software\Policies\Microsoft \Windows\System\RSoPLogging
Computer Configuration\Administrative Templates \System\Group Policy	Remove users ability to invoke machine policy refresh	HKLM\Software\Policies\Microsoft \Windows\System\DenyUsersFromMachGP
Computer Configuration\Administrative Templates \System\Group Policy	Disallow Interactive Users from genera-ting Resultant Set of Policy data	HKLM\Software\Policies\Microsoft \Windows\System \DenyRsopToInteractiveUser
Computer Configuration\Administrative Templates \System\Group Policy	Registry policy processing	HKLM\Software\Policies\Microsoft \Windows\Group_Policy \{35378EAC-683F-11D2-A89A-00C04FBBCFA2} \NoGPOListChanges

Location	Name	Key
Computer Configuration\Administrative Templates \System\Group Policy	Internet Explorer Maintenance policy processing	HKLM\Software\Policies \Microsoft\Windows\Group Policy \{A2E30F80-D7DE-11d2-BBDE-00C04F86AE3B} \NoGPOListChanges
Computer Configuration\Administrative Templates \System\Group Policy	Software Installation policy processing	HKLM\Software\Policies \Microsoft\Windows\Group Policy \{c6dc5466-785a-11d2-84d0-00c04fb169f7} \NoGPOListChanges
Computer Configuration\Administrative Templates \System\Group Policy	Folder Redirection policy processing	HKLM\Software\Policies \Microsoft\Windows\Group Policy \{25537BAC-77A8-11D2-9B6C-0000F8080861} \NoGPOListChanges
Computer Configuration\Administrative Templates \System\Group Policy	Scripts policy processing	HKLM\Software\Policies \Microsoft\Windows\Group Policy \{42B5FAAE-6536-11d2-AE5A-0000F87571E3} \NoGPOListChanges
Computer Configuration \Administrative Templates\System \Group Policy	Security policy processing	HKLM\Software\Policies \Microsoft\Windows\Group Policy \{827D319E-6EAC-11D2-A4EA-00C04F79F83A} \NoGPOListChanges
Computer Configuration\Administrative Templates \System\Group Policy	IP Security policy processing	HKLM\Software\Policies \Microsoft\Windows\Group Policy \{e437bc1c-aa7d-11d2-a382-00c04f991e27} \NoGPOListChanges
Computer Configuration\Administrative Templates \System\Group Policy	EFS recovery policy processing	HKLM\Software\Policies \Microsoft\Windows\Group Policy \{B1BE8D72-6EAC-11D2-A4EA-00C04F79F83A} \NoGPOListChanges
Computer Configuration\Administrative Templates \System\Group Policy	Disk Quota policy processing	HKLM\Software\Policies \Microsoft\Windows\Group Policy \{3610eda5-77ef-11d2-8dc5-00c04fa31a66} \NoGPOListChanges
Computer Configuration\Administrative Templates \System\Logon	Don't display the Getting Started welcome screen at logon	HKLM\Software\Microsoft\Windows \CurrentVersion\Policies\Explorer \NoWelcomeScreen
Computer Configuration\Administrative Templates \System\Logon	Always use classic logon	HKLM\Software\Microsoft\Windows \CurrentVersion\Policies\System \LogonType
Computer Configuration\Administrative Templates \System\Logon	Run these programs at user logon	HKLM\Software\Microsoft\Windows \CurrentVersion\Policies\Explorer\Run\
Computer Configuration\Administrative Templates \System\Logon	Do not process the run once list	HKLM\Software\Microsoft\Windows \CurrentVersion\Policies\Explorer \DisableLocalMachineRunOnce
Computer Configuration\Administrative Templates \System\Logon	Do not process the legacy run list	HKLM\Software\Microsoft\Windows \CurrentVersion\Policies\Explorer \DisableLocalMachineRun
Computer Configuration\Administrative Templates \System\Logon	Always wait for the network at computer startup and logon	HKLM\Software\Policies\Microsoft \Windows NT\CurrentVersion\Winlogon \SyncForegroundPolicy
Computer Configuration\Administrative Templates \System\Net Logon	Expected dial-up delay on logon	HKLM\Software\Policies\Microsoft \Netlogon\Parameters\ExpectedDialupDelay
Computer Configuration\Administrative Templates \System\Net Logon	Site Name	HKLM\Software\Policies\Microsoft \Netlogon\Parameters\SiteName
Computer Configuration\Administrative Templates \System\Net Logon	Negative DC Discovery Cache Setting	HKLM\Software\Policies\Microsoft \Netlogon\Parameters\NegativeCachePeriod

Table 19-5   Policies in System.adm   *(continued)*

Location	Name	Key
Computer Configuration\Administrative Templates \System\Net Logon	Initial DC Discovery Retry Setting for Background Callers	HKLM\Software\Policies\Microsoft \Netlogon\Parameters \BackgroundRetryInitialPeriod
Computer Configuration\Administrative Templates \System\Net Logon	Maximum DC Discovery Retry Interval Setting for Background Callers	HKLM\Software\Policies\Microsoft \Netlogon\Parameters \BackgroundRetryMaximumPeriod
Computer Configuration\Administrative Templates \System\Net Logon	Final DC Discovery Retry Setting for Background Callers	HKLM\Software\Policies\Microsoft \Netlogon\Parameters \BackgroundRetryQuitTime
Computer Configuration\Administrative Templates \System\Net Logon	Positive Periodic DC Cache Refresh for Background Callers	HKLM\Software\Policies\Microsoft \Netlogon\Parameters \BackgroundSuccessfulRefreshPeriod
Computer Configuration\Administrative Templates \System\Net Logon	Positive Periodic DC Cache Refresh for Non-Background Callers	HKLM\Software\Policies\Microsoft \Netlogon\Parameters \NonBackgroundSuccessfulRefreshPeriod
Computer Configuration\Administrative Templates \System\Net Logon	Scavenge Interval	HKLM\Software\Policies\Microsoft \Netlogon\Parameters\ScavengeInterval
Computer Configuration\Administrative Templates \System\Net Logon	Contact PDC on logon failure	HKLM\Software\Policies\Microsoft \Netlogon\Parameters\AvoidPdcOnWan
Computer Configuration\Administrative Templates \System\Net Logon\DC Locator DNS Records	Dynamic Registra- tion of the DC Locator DNS Records	HKLM\Software\Policies\Microsoft \Netlogon\Parameters\UseDynamicDns
Computer Configuration\Administrative Templates \System\Net Logon\DC Locator DNS Records	DC Locator or DNS records not regis- tered by the DCs	HKLM\Software\Policies\Microsoft \Netlogon\Parameters \DnsAvoidRegisterRecords
Computer Configuration\Administrative Templates \System\Net Logon\DC Locator DNS Records	Refresh Interval of the DC Locator DNS Records	HKLM\Software\Policies\Microsoft \Netlogon\Parameters \DnsRefreshInterval
Computer Configuration\Administrative Templates \System\Net Logon\DC Locator DNS Records	Weight Set in the DC Locator DNS SRV Records	HKLM\Software\Policies\Microsoft \Netlogon\Parameters\LdapSrvWeight
Computer Configuration\Administrative Templates \System\Net Logon\DC Locator DNS Records	Priority Set in the DC Locator DNS SRV Records	HKLM\Software\Policies\Microsoft \Netlogon\Parameters\LdapSrvPriority
Computer Configuration\Administrative Templates \System\Net Logon\DC Locator DNS Records	TTL Set in the DC Locator DNS Records	HKLM\Software\Policies\Microsoft \Netlogon\Parameters\DnsTtl
Computer Configuration\Administrative Templates \System\Net Logon\DC Locator DNS Records	Automated Site Coverage by the DC Locator DNS SRV Records	HKLM\Software\Policies\Microsoft \Netlogon\Parameters\AutoSiteCoverage
Computer Configuration\Administrative Templates \System\Net Logon\DC Locator DNS Records	Sites Covered by the DC Locator DNS SRV Records	HKLM\Software\Policies\Microsoft \Netlogon\Parameters\SiteCoverage
Computer Configuration\Administrative Templates \System\Net Logon\DC Locator DNS Records	Sites Covered by the GC Locator DNS SRV Records	HKLM\Software\Policies\Microsoft \Netlogon\Parameters\GcSiteCoverage
Computer Configuration\Administrative Templates \System\Net Logon\DC Locator DNS Records	Sites Covered by the Application Directory Partition Locator DNS SRV Records	HKLM\Software\Policies\Microsoft \Netlogon\Parameters \NdncSiteCoverage

Location	Name	Key
Computer Configuration\Administrative Templates \System\Net Logon\DC Locator DNS Records	Location of the DCs hosting a domain with single label DNS name	HKLM\Software\Policies\Microsoft \Netlogon\Parameters \AllowSingleLabelDnsDomain
Computer Configuration\Administrative Templates \System\Remote Assistance	Solicited Remote Assistance	HKLM\Software\policies\Microsoft \Windows NT\Terminal Services \MaxTicketExpiryUnits
Computer Configuration\Administrative Templates \System\Remote Assistance	Offer Remote Assistance	HKLM\Software\policies\Microsoft \Windows NT\Terminal Services \RAUnsolicit \fAllowUnsolicitedFullControl
Computer Configuration\Administrative Templates \System\Remote Procedure Call	RPC Troubleshooting State Information	HKLM\Software\Policies\Microsoft \Windows NT\Rpc\StateInformation
Computer Configuration\Administrative Templates \System\Remote Procedure Call	Propagation of extended error information	HKLM\Software\Policies\Microsoft \Windows NT\Rpc\ExtErrorInfoExceptions
Computer Configuration\Administrative Templates \System\Scripts	Run logon scripts synchronously	HKLM\Software\Microsoft\Windows \CurrentVersion\Policies\System \RunLogonScriptSync
Computer Configuration\Administrative Templates \System\Scripts	Run startup scripts asynchronously	HKLM\Software\Microsoft\Windows \CurrentVersion\Policies\System \RunStartupScriptSync
Computer Configuration\Administrative Templates \System\Scripts	Run startup scripts visible	HKLM\Software\Microsoft\Windows \CurrentVersion\Policies\System \HideStartupScripts
Computer Configuration\Administrative Templates \System\Scripts	Run shutdown scripts visible	HKLM\Software\Microsoft\Windows \CurrentVersion\Policies\System \HideShutdownScripts
Computer Configuration\Administrative Templates \System\Scripts	Maximum wait time for Group Policy scripts	HKLM\Software\Microsoft\Windows \CurrentVersion\Policies\System \MaxGPOScriptWait
Computer Configuration\Administrative Templates \System\System Restore	Turn off System Restore	HKLM\Software\Policies\Microsoft \Windows NT\SystemRestore\DisableSR
Computer Configuration\Administrative Templates \System\System Restore	Turn off Configuration	HKLM\Software\Policies\Microsoft \Windows NT\SystemRestore\DisableConfig
Computer Configuration\Administrative Templates \System\User Profiles	Delete cached copies of roaming profiles	HKLM\Software\Policies\Microsoft\Windows \System\DeleteRoamingCache
Computer Configuration\Administrative Templates \System\User Profiles	Do not detect slow network connections	HKLM\Software\Policies\Microsoft\Windows \System\SlowLinkDetectEnabled
Computer Configuration\Administrative Templates \System\User Profiles	Slow network connection timeout for user profiles	HKLM\Software\Policies\Microsoft\Windows \System\SlowLinkTimeOut
Computer Configuration\Administrative Templates \System\User Profiles	Wait for remote user profile	HKLM\Software\Policies\Microsoft\Windows \System\SlowLinkProfileDefault
Computer Configuration\Administrative Templates \System\User Profiles	Prompt user when slow link is detected	HKLM\Software\Policies\Microsoft\Windows \System\SlowLinkUIEnabled
Computer Configuration\Administrative Templates \System\User Profiles	Timeout for dialog boxes	HKLM\Software\Policies\Microsoft\Windows \System\ProfileDlgTimeOut
Computer Configuration\Administrative Templates \System\User Profiles	Log users off when roaming profile fails	HKLM\Software\Policies\Microsoft \Windows\System\ProfileErrorAction
Computer Configuration\Administrative Templates \System\User Profiles	Maximum retries to unload and update user profile	HKLM\Software\Policies\Microsoft\Windows \System\ProfileUnloadTimeout

Table 19-5   Policies in System.adm   *(continued)*

Location	Name	Key
Computer Configuration\Administrative Templates\System\User Profiles	Add the Administrators security group to roaming user profiles	HKLM\Software\Policies\Microsoft\Windows\System\AddAdminGroupToRUP
Computer Configuration\Administrative Templates\System\User Profiles	Prevent Roaming Profile changes from propagating to the server	HKLM\Software\Policies\Microsoft\Windows\System\ReadOnlyProfile
Computer Configuration\Administrative Templates\System\User Profiles	Only allow local user profiles	HKLM\Software\Policies\Microsoft\Windows\System\LocalProfile
Computer Configuration\Administrative Templates\System\Windows File Protection	Set Windows File Protection scanning	HKLM\Software\Policies\Microsoft\Windows NT\Windows File Protection\SfcScan
Computer Configuration\Administrative Templates\System\Windows File Protection	Hide the file scan progress window	HKLM\Software\Policies\Microsoft\Windows NT\Windows File Protection\SfcShowProgress
Computer Configuration\Administrative Templates\System\Windows File Protection	Limit Windows File Protection cache size	HKLM\Software\Policies\Microsoft\Windows NT\Windows File Protection\SfcQuota
Computer Configuration\Administrative Templates\System\Windows File Protection	Specify Windows File Protection cache location	HKLM\Software\Policies\Microsoft\Windows NT\Windows File Protection\SFCDllCacheDir
Computer Configuration\Administrative Templates\System\Windows Time Service	Global Configuration Settings	HKLM\Software\Policies\Microsoft\W32Time\Config\MinPollInterval
Computer Configuration\Administrative Templates\System\Windows Time Service\Time Providers	Enable Windows NTP Client	HKLM\Software\Policies\Microsoft\W32time\TimeProviders\NtpClient\Enabled
Computer Configuration\Administrative Templates\System\Windows Time Service\Time Providers	Configure Windows NTP Client	HKLM\Software\Policies\Microsoft\W32time\Parameters\EventLogFlags
Computer Configuration\Administrative Templates\System\Windows Time Service\Time Providers	Enable Windows NTP Server	HKLM\Software\Policies\Microsoft\W32Time\TimeProviders\NtpServer\Enabled
Computer Configuration\Administrative Templates\Windows Components\Task Scheduler	Hide Property Pages	HKLM\Software\Policies\Microsoft\Windows\Task Scheduler5.0\Property Pages
Computer Configuration\Administrative Templates\Windows Components\Task Scheduler	Prevent Task Run or End	HKLM\Software\Policies\Microsoft\Windows\Task Scheduler5.0\Execution
Computer Configuration\Administrative Templates\Windows Components\Task Scheduler	Prohibit Drag-and-Drop	HKLM\Software\Policies\Microsoft\Windows\Task Scheduler5.0\DragAndDrop
Computer Configuration\Administrative Templates\Windows Components\Task Scheduler	Prohibit New Task Creation	HKLM\Software\Policies\Microsoft\Windows\Task Scheduler5.0\Task Creation
Computer Configuration\Administrative Templates\Windows Components\Task Scheduler	Prohibit Task Deletion	HKLM\Software\Policies\Microsoft\Windows\Task Scheduler5.0\Task Deletion
Computer Configuration\Administrative Templates\Windows Components\Task Scheduler	Remove Advanced Menu	HKLM\Software\Policies\Microsoft\Windows\Task Scheduler5.0\Disable Advanced
Computer Configuration\Administrative Templates\Windows Components\Task Scheduler	Prohibit Browse	HKLM\Software\Policies\Microsoft\Windows\Task Scheduler5.0\Allow Browse
Computer Configuration\Administrative Templates\Windows Components\Terminal Services	Keep-Alive Messages	HKLM\SOFTWARE\Policies\Microsoft\Windows NT\Terminal Services\KeepAliveInterval
Computer Configuration\Administrative Templates\Windows Components\Terminal Services	Limit users to one remote session	HKLM\SOFTWARE\Policies\Microsoft\Windows NT\Terminal Services\fSingleSessionPerUser

Location	Name	Key
Computer Configuration\Administrative Templates \Windows Components\Terminal Services	Enforce Removal of Remote Desktop Wallpaper	HKLM\SOFTWARE\Policies\Microsoft \Windows NT\Terminal Services \fNoRemoteDesktopWallpaper
Computer Configuration\Administrative Templates \Windows Components\Terminal Services \Client/Server data redirection	Do not allow clip-board redirection	HKLM\SOFTWARE\Policies\Microsoft \Windows NT\Terminal Services \fDisableClip
Computer Configuration\Administrative Templates \Windows Components\Terminal Services \Client/Server data redirection	Do not allow smart card device redirection	HKLM\SOFTWARE\Policies\Microsoft \Windows NT\Terminal Services \fEnableSmartCard
Computer Configuration\Administrative Templates \Windows Components\Terminal Services \Client/Server data redirection	Allow audio redirection	HKLM\SOFTWARE\Policies\Microsoft \Windows NT\Terminal Services \fDisableCam
Computer Configuration\Administrative Templates \Windows Components\Terminal Services \Client/Server data redirection	Do not allow COM port redirection	HKLM\SOFTWARE\Policies\Microsoft \Windows NT\Terminal Services \fDisableCcm
Computer Configuration\Administrative Templates \Windows Components\Terminal Services \Client/Server data redirection	Do not allow client printer redirection	HKLM\SOFTWARE\Policies\Microsoft \Windows NT\Terminal Services \fDisableCpm
Computer Configuration\Administrative Templates \Windows Components\Terminal Services \Client/Server data redirection	Do not allow LPT port redirection	HKLM\SOFTWARE\Policies\Microsoft \Windows NT\Terminal Services \fDisableLPT
Computer Configuration\Administrative Templates \Windows Components\Terminal Services \Client/Server data redirection	Do not allow drive redirection	HKLM\SOFTWARE\Policies\Microsoft \Windows NT\Terminal Services \fDisableCdm
Computer Configuration\Administrative Templates \Windows Components\Terminal Services \Client/Server data redirection	Do not set default cli-ent printer to be default printer in a session	HKLM\SOFTWARE\Policies\Microsoft \Windows NT\Terminal Services \fForceClientLptDef
Computer Configuration\Administrative Templates \Windows Components\Terminal Services \Encryption and Security	Always prompt client for password upon connection	HKLM\SOFTWARE\Policies\Microsoft \Windows NT\Terminal Services \fPromptForPassword
Computer Configuration\Administrative Templates \Windows Components\Terminal Services \Encryption and Security	Set client connection encryption level	HKLM\SOFTWARE\Policies\Microsoft \Windows NT\Terminal Services \MinEncryptionLevel
Computer Configuration\Administrative Templates \Windows Components\Terminal Services	Limit number of connections	HKLM\SOFTWARE\Policies\Microsoft \Windows NT\Terminal Services \MaxInstanceCount
Computer Configuration\Administrative Templates \Windows Components\Terminal Services	Limit maximum color depth	HKLM\SOFTWARE\Policies\Microsoft \Windows NT\Terminal Services ColorDepth
Computer Configuration\Administrative Templates \Windows Components\Terminal Services	Do not allow new client connections	HKLM\ SOFTWARE\Policies\Microsoft \Windows NT\Terminal Services \fDenyTSConnections VALUE NUMERIC 0
Computer Configuration\Administrative Templates \Windows Components\Terminal Services	Do not allow local administrators to customize permissions	HKLM\SOFTWARE\Policies\Microsoft \Windows NT\Terminal Services \fWritableTSCCPermTab
Computer Configuration\Administrative Templates \Windows Components\Terminal Services	Remove Windows Security item from Start menu	HKLM\Software\Microsoft\Windows \CurrentVersion\Policies\Explorer \NoNTSecurity
Computer Configuration\Administrative Templates \Windows Components\Terminal Services	Remove Disconnect item from Shut Down dialog	HKLM\Software\Microsoft\Windows \CurrentVersion\Policies\Explorer \NoDisconnect

Table 19-5   Policies in System.adm   *(continued)*

Location	Name	Key
Computer Configuration\Administrative Templates \Windows Components\Terminal Services \Licensing	Prevent License Upgrade	HKLM\Software\Policies\Microsoft \Windows NT\Terminal Services \fPreventLicenseUpgrade
Computer Configuration\Administrative Templates \Windows Components\Terminal Services \Temporary folders	Do not use temp folders per session	HKLM\Software\Policies\Microsoft \Windows NT\Terminal Services \PerSessionTempDir
Computer Configuration\Administrative Templates \Windows Components\Terminal Services \Temporary folders	Do not delete temp folder upon exit	HKLM\Software\Policies\Microsoft \Windows NT\Terminal Services \DeleteTempDirsOnExit
Computer Configuration\Administrative Templates \Windows Components\Terminal Services \Session Directory	Session Directory Active	HKLM\SOFTWARE\Policies\Microsoft \Windows NT\Terminal Services \SessionDirectoryActive
Computer Configuration\Administrative Templates \Windows Components\Terminal Services \Session Directory	Session Directory Server	HKLM\SOFTWARE\Policies\Microsoft \Windows NT\Terminal Services \SessionDirectoryLocation
Computer Configuration\Administrative Templates \Windows Components\Terminal Services \Session Directory	Session Directory Cluster Name	HKLM\SOFTWARE\Policies\Microsoft \Windows NT\Terminal Services \SessionDirectoryClusterName
Computer Configuration\Administrative Templates \Windows Components\Terminal Services \Sessions	Set time limit for disconnected sessions	HKLM\SOFTWARE\Policies\Microsoft \Windows NT\Terminal Services \MaxDisconnectionTime
Computer Configuration\Administrative Templates \Windows Components\Terminal Services \Sessions	Set time limit for active sessions	HKLM\SOFTWARE\Policies\Microsoft \Windows NT\Terminal Services \MaxConnectionTime
Computer Configuration\Administrative Templates \Windows Components\Terminal Services \Sessions	Set time limit for idle sessions	HKLM\SOFTWARE\Policies\Microsoft \Windows NT\Terminal Services \MaxIdleTime REQUIRED
Computer Configuration\Administrative Templates \Windows Components\Terminal Services \Sessions	Allow reconnection from original client only	HKLM\SOFTWARE\Policies\Microsoft \Windows NT\Terminal Services \fReconnectSame
Computer Configuration\Administrative Templates \Windows Components\Terminal Services \Sessions	Terminate session when time limits are reached	HKLM\SOFTWARE\Policies\Microsoft \Windows NT\Terminal Services \fResetBroken
Computer Configuration\Administrative Templates \Windows Components\Terminal Services	Set path for TS Roaming Profiles	HKLM\SOFTWARE\Policies\Microsoft \Windows NT\Terminal Services \WFProfilePath
Computer Configuration\Administrative Templates \Windows Components\Terminal Services	TS User Home Directory	HKLM\SOFTWARE\Policies\Microsoft \Windows NT\Terminal Services \WFHomeDirDrive
Computer Configuration\Administrative Templates \Windows Components\Terminal Services	Remote control settings	HKLM\SOFTWARE\Policies\Microsoft \Windows NT\Terminal Services\Shadow
Computer Configuration\Administrative Templates \Windows Components\Terminal Services	Start a program on connection	HKLM\SOFTWARE\Policies\Microsoft \Windows NT\Terminal Services \WorkDirectory
Computer Configuration\Administrative Templates \Windows Components\Windows Installer	Disable Windows Installer	HKLM\Software\Policies\Microsoft \Windows\Installer\DisableMSI
Computer Configuration\Administrative Templates \Windows Components\Windows Installer	Always install with elevated privileges	HKLM\Software\olicies\Microsoft\Windows \Installer\AlwaysInstallElevated
Computer Configuration\Administrative Templates \Windows Components\Windows Installer	Prohibit rollback	HKLM\Software\Policies\Microsoft\Windows \Installer\DisableRollback

Location	Name	Key
Computer Configuration\Administrative Templates \Windows Components\Windows Installer	Remove browse dialog box for new source	HKLM\Software\Policies\Microsoft\Windows \Installer\DisableBrowse
Computer Configuration\Administrative Templates \Windows Components\Windows Installer	Prohibit patching	HKLM\Software\Policies\Microsoft\Windows \Installer\DisablePatch
Computer Configuration\Administrative Templates \Windows Components\Windows Installer	Disable IE security prompt for Windows Installer scripts	HKLM\Software\Policies\Microsoft\Windows \Installer\SafeForScripting
Computer Configuration\Administrative Templates \Windows Components\Windows Installer	Enable user control over installs	HKLM\Software\Policies\Microsoft\Windows \Installer\EnableUserControl
Computer Configuration\Administrative Templates \Windows Components\Windows Installer	Enable user to browse for source while elevated	HKLM\Software\Policies\Microsoft\Windows \Installer\AllowLockdownBrowse
Computer Configuration\Administrative Templates \Windows Components\Windows Installer	Enable user to use media source while elevated	HKLM\Software\Policies\Microsoft\Windows \Installer\AllowLockdownMedia
Computer Configuration\Administrative Templates \Windows Components\Windows Installer	Enable user to patch elevated products	HKLM\Software\Policies\Microsoft\Windows \Installer\AllowLockdownPatch
Computer Configuration\Administrative Templates \Windows Components\Windows Installer	Allow admin to install from Terminal Services session	HKLM\Software\Policies\Microsoft\Windows \Installer\EnableAdminTSRemote
Computer Configuration\Administrative Templates \Windows Components\Windows Installer	Cache transforms in secure location on workstation	HKLM\Software\Policies\Microsoft\Windows \Installer\TransformsSecure
Computer Configuration\Administrative Templates \Windows Components\Windows Installer	Logging	HKLM\Software\Policies\Microsoft\Windows \Installer\Logging
Computer Configuration\Administrative Templates \Windows Components\Windows Installer	Prohibit User Installs	HKLM\Software\Policies\Microsoft\Windows \Installer\DisableUserInstalls
Computer Configuration\Administrative Templates \Windows Components\Windows Installer	Turn off creation of System Restore Checkpoints	HKLM\Software\Policies \Microsoft\Windows\Installer \LimitSystemRestoreCheckpointing
Computer Configuration\Administrative Templates \Windows Components\Windows Messenger	Do not allow Windows Messenger to be run	HKLM\Software\Policies\Microsoft \Messenger\Client\PreventRun
Computer Configuration\Administrative Templates \Windows Components\Windows Messenger	Do not automatically start Windows Messenger initially	HKLM\Software\Policies\Microsoft \Messenger\Client\PreventAutoRun
User Configuration\Administrative Templates \Control Panel	Prohibit access to the Control Panel	HKCU\Software\Microsoft\Windows \CurrentVersion\Policies\Explorer \NoControlPanel
User Configuration\Administrative Templates \Control Panel	Hide specified Control Panel applets	HKCU\Software\Microsoft\Windows \CurrentVersion\Policies\Explorer \DisallowCpl\DisallowCpl
User Configuration\Administrative Templates \Control Panel	Show only specified Control Panel applets	HKCU\Software\Microsoft\Windows \CurrentVersion\Policies\Explorer \RestrictCpl\RestrictCpl
User Configuration\Administrative Templates \Control Panel	Force classic Control Panel Style	HKCU\Software\Microsoft\Windows \CurrentVersion\Policies\Explorer \RestrictCpl\ForceClassicControlPanel

Table 19-5   Policies in System.adm   *(continued)*

Location	Name	Key
User Configuration\Administrative Templates \Control Panel\Add/Remove Programs	Remove Add/Remove Programs Programs	HKCU\Software\Microsoft\Windows \CurrentVersion\Policies\Uninstall \NoAddRemovePrograms
User Configuration\Administrative Templates \Control Panel\Add/Remove Programs	Hide Change or Remove Programs page	HKCU\Software\Microsoft\Windows \CurrentVersion\Policies\Uninstall \NoRemovePage
User Configuration\Administrative Templates \Control Panel\Add/Remove Programs	Hide Add New Programs page	HKCU\Software\Microsoft\Windows \CurrentVersion\Policies\Uninstall \NoAddPage
User Configuration\Administrative Templates \Control Panel\Add/Remove Programs	Hide Add/Remove Windows Components page	HKCU\Software\Microsoft\Windows \CurrentVersion\Policies\Uninstall \NoWindowsSetupPage
User Configuration\Administrative Templates \Control Panel\Add/Remove Programs	Hide the Add a program from CD-ROM or floppy disk option	HKCU\Software\Microsoft\Windows \CurrentVersion\Policies\Uninstall \NoAddFromCDorFloppy
User Configuration\Administrative Templates \Control Panel\Add/Remove Programs	Hide the Add programs from Microsoft option	HKCU\Software\Microsoft\Windows \CurrentVersion\Policies\Uninstall \NoAddFromInternet
User Configuration\Administrative Templates \Control Panel\Add/Remove Programs	Hide the Add programs from your network option	HKCU\Software\Microsoft\Windows \CurrentVersion\Policies\Uninstall \NoAddFromNetwork
User Configuration\Administrative Templates \Control Panel\Add/Remove Programs	Go directly to Components Wizard	HKCU\Software\Microsoft\Windows \CurrentVersion\Policies\Uninstall \NoServices
User Configuration\Administrative Templates \Control Panel\Add/Remove Programs	Remove Support Information	HKCU\Software\Microsoft\Windows \CurrentVersion\Policies\Uninstall \NoSupportInfo
User Configuration\Administrative Templates \Control Panel\Add/Remove Programs	Specify default category for Add New Programs	HKCU\Software\Microsoft\Windows \CurrentVersion\Policies\Uninstall \DefaultCategory
User Configuration\Administrative Templates \Control Panel\Display	Remove Display in Control Panel	HKCU\Software\Microsoft\Windows \CurrentVersion\Policies\System \NoDispCPL
User Configuration\Administrative Templates \Control Panel\Display	Hide Desktop tab	HKCU\Software\Microsoft\Windows \CurrentVersion\Policies\System \NoDispBackgroundPage
User Configuration\Administrative Templates \Control Panel\Display	Prevent changing wallpaper	HKCU\Software\Microsoft\Windows \CurrentVersion\Policies\ActiveDesktop \NoChangingWallPaper
User Configuration\Administrative Templates \Control Panel\Display	Hide Appearance and Themes tab	HKCU\Software\Microsoft\Windows \CurrentVersion\Policies\ActiveDesktop \NoDispAppearancePage
User Configuration\Administrative Templates \Control Panel\Display	Hide Settings tab	HKCU\Software\Microsoft\Windows \CurrentVersion\Policies\ActiveDesktop \NoDispSettingsPage
User Configuration\Administrative Templates \Control Panel\Display	Hide Screen Saver tab	HKCU\Software\Microsoft\Windows \CurrentVersion\Policies\ActiveDesktop \NoDispScrSavPage
User Configuration\Administrative Templates \Control Panel\Display	Screen Saver	HKCU\Software\Policies\Microsoft\Windows \Control Panel\Desktop\ScreenSaveActive
User Configuration\Administrative Templates \Control Panel\Display	Screen Saver executable name	HKCU\Software\Policies\Microsoft\Windows \Control Panel\Desktop\SCRNSAVE.EXE
User Configuration\Administrative Templates \Control Panel\Display	Password protect the screen saver	HKCU\Software\Policies\Microsoft\Windows \Control Panel\Desktop \ScreenSaverIsSecure

Location	Name	Key
User Configuration\Administrative Templates\Control Panel\Display	Screen Saver timeout	HKCU\Software\Policies\Microsoft\Windows\Control Panel\Desktop\ScreenSaveTimeOut
User Configuration\Administrative Templates\Control Panel\Display\Desktop Themes	Remove Theme option	HKCU\Software\Microsoft\Windows\CurrentVersion\Policies\Explorer\NoThemesTab
User Configuration\Administrative Templates\Control Panel\Display\Desktop Themes	Prevent selection of windows and buttons styles	HKCU\Software\Microsoft\Windows\CurrentVersion\Policies\System\NoVisualStyleChoice
User Configuration\Administrative Templates\Control Panel\Display\Desktop Themes	Prohibit selection of font size	HKCU\Software\Microsoft\Windows\CurrentVersion\Policies\System\NoSizeChoice
User Configuration\Administrative Templates\Control Panel\Display\Desktop Themes	Prohibit Theme color selection	HKCU\Software\Microsoft\Windows\CurrentVersion\Policies\System\NoColorChoice
User Configuration\Administrative Templates\Control Panel\Display\Desktop Themes	Load a specific visual style file or force Windows Classic	HKCU\Software\Microsoft\Windows\CurrentVersion\Policies\System\SetVisualStyle
User Configuration\Administrative Templates\Control Panel\Printers	Browse a common web site to find printers	HKCU\Software\Policies\Microsoft\Windows NT\Printers\Wizard\Printers Page URL
User Configuration\Administrative Templates\Control Panel\Printers	Browse the network to find printers	HKCU\Software\Policies\Microsoft\Windows NT\Printers\Wizard\Downlevel Browse
User Configuration\Administrative Templates\Control Panel\Printers	Default Active Directory path when searching for printers	HKCU\Software\Policies\Microsoft\Windows NT\Printers\Wizard\Default Search Scope
User Configuration\Administrative Templates\Control Panel\Printers	Prevent addition of printers	HKCU\ Software\Policies\Microsoft\Windows NT\Printers\Wizard\NoAddPrinter
User Configuration\Administrative Templates\Control Panel\Printers	Prevent deletion of printers	HKCU\ Software\Policies\Microsoft\Windows NT\Printers\Wizard\NoDeletePrinter
User Configuration\Administrative Templates\Control Panel\Regional and Language Options	Restrict selection of Windows menus and dialogs language	HKCU\Software\Policies\Microsoft\Control Panel\Desktop\MultiUILanguageID
User Configuration\Administrative Templates\Desktop	Hide and disable all items on the desktop	HKCU\Software\Microsoft\Windows\CurrentVersion\Policies\Explorer\NoDesktop
User Configuration\Administrative Templates\Desktop	Remove My Documents icon on the desktop	HKCU\Software\Microsoft\Windows\CurrentVersion\Policies\NonEnum\{450D8FBA-AD25-11D0-98A8-0800361B1103}
User Configuration\Administrative Templates\Desktop	Remove My Computer icon on the desktop	HKCU\Software\Microsoft\Windows\CurrentVersion\Policies\NonEnum\{20D04FE0-3AEA-1069-A2D8-08002B30309D}
User Configuration\Administrative Templates\Desktop	Remove Recycle Bin icon from desktop	HKCU\Software\Microsoft\Windows\CurrentVersion\Policies\NonEnum\{645FF040-5081-101B-9F08-00AA002F954E}
User Configuration\Administrative Templates\Desktop	Remove Properties from the My Documents shortcut menu	HKCU\Software\Microsoft\Windows\CurrentVersion\Policies\Explorer\NoPropertiesMyDocuments
User Configuration\Administrative Templates\Desktop	Remove Properties from the My Computer shortcut menu	HKCU\Software\Microsoft\Windows\CurrentVersion\Policies\Explorer\NoPropertiesMyComputer

Table 19-5   Policies in System.adm   *(continued)*

Location	Name	Key
User Configuration\Administrative Templates \Desktop	Remove Properties from the Recycle Bin shortcut menu	HKCU\Software\Microsoft\Windows \CurrentVersion\Policies\Explorer \NoPropertiesRecycleBin
User Configuration\Administrative Templates \Desktop	Hide My Network Places icon on desktop	HKCU\Software\Microsoft\Windows \CurrentVersion\Policies\Explorer \NoNetHood
User Configuration\Administrative Templates \Desktop	Hide Internet Explorer icon on desktop	HKCU\Software\Microsoft\Windows \CurrentVersion\Policies\Explorer \NoInternetIcon
User Configuration\Administrative Templates \Desktop	Do not add shares of recently opened documents to My Network Places	HKCU\Software\Microsoft\Windows \CurrentVersion\Policies\Explorer \NoRecentDocsNetHood
User Configuration\Administrative Templates \Desktop	Prohibit user from changing My Documents path	HKCU\Software\Microsoft\Windows \CurrentVersion\Policies\Explorer \DisablePersonalDirChange
User Configuration\Administrative Templates \Desktop	Prevent adding, dragging, dropping and closing the Taskbar's toolbars	HKCU\Software\Microsoft\Windows \CurrentVersion\Policies\Explorer \NoCloseDragDropBands
User Configuration\Administrative Templates \Desktop	Prohibit adjusting desktop toolbars	HKCU\Software\Microsoft\Windows \CurrentVersion\Policies\Explorer \NoMovingBands
User Configuration\Administrative Templates \Desktop	Don't save settings at exit	HKCU\Software\Microsoft\Windows \CurrentVersion\Policies\Explorer \NoSaveSettings
User Configuration\Administrative Templates \Desktop	Remove the Desktop Cleanup Wizard	HKCU\Software\Microsoft\Windows \CurrentVersion\Policies\Explorer \NoDesktopCleanupWizard
User Configuration\Administrative Templates \Desktop\Active Desktop	Enable Active Desktop	HKCU\Software\Microsoft\Windows \CurrentVersion\Policies\Explorer \ForceActiveDesktopOn
User Configuration\Administrative Templates \Desktop\Active Desktop	Disable Active Desktop	HKCU\Software\Microsoft\Windows \CurrentVersion\Policies \Explorer\NoActiveDesktop
User Configuration\Administrative Templates \Desktop\Active Desktop	Disable all items	HKCU\Software\Microsoft\Windows \CurrentVersion\Policies\ActiveDesktop \NoComponents
User Configuration\Administrative Templates \Desktop\Active Desktop	Prohibit changes	HKCU\Software\Microsoft\Windows \CurrentVersion\Policies \Explorer\NoActiveDesktopChanges
User Configuration\Administrative Templates \Desktop\Active Desktop	Prohibit adding items	HKCU\Software\Microsoft\Windows \CurrentVersion\Policies\ActiveDesktop \NoAddingComponents
User Configuration\Administrative Templates \Desktop\Active Desktop	Prohibit deleting items	HKCU\Software\Microsoft\Windows \CurrentVersion\Policies\ActiveDesktop \NoDeletingComponents
User Configuration\Administrative Templates \Desktop\Active Desktop	Prohibit editing items	HKCU\Software\Microsoft\Windows \CurrentVersion\Policies\ActiveDesktop \NoEditingComponents
User Configuration\Administrative Templates \Desktop\Active Desktop	Prohibit closing items	HKCU\Software\Microsoft\Windows \CurrentVersion\Policies\ActiveDesktop \NoClosingComponents
User Configuration\Administrative Templates \Desktop\Active Desktop	Add/Delete items	HKCU\Software\Microsoft\Windows \CurrentVersion\Policies\ActiveDesktop \AdminComponent\Delete

Location	Name	Key
User Configuration\Administrative Templates \Desktop\Active Desktop	Active Desktop Wallpaper	`HKCU\Software\Microsoft\Windows` `\CurrentVersion\Policies\System` `\WallpaperStyle`
User Configuration\Administrative Templates \Desktop\Active Desktop	Allow only bitmapped wallpaper	`HKCU\Software\Microsoft\Windows` `\CurrentVersion\Policies\ActiveDesktop` `\NoHTMLWallPaper`
User Configuration\Administrative Templates \Desktop\Active Directory	Maximum size of Active Directory searches	`HKCU\Software\Policies\Microsoft` `\Windows\Directory UI\QueryLimit`
User Configuration\Administrative Templates \Desktop\Active Directory	Enable filter in Find dialog box	`HKCU\Software\Policies\Microsoft\Windows` `\Directory UI\EnableFilter`
User Configuration\Administrative Templates \Desktop\Active Directory	Hide Active Directory folder	`HKCU\Software\Policies\Microsoft\Windows` `\Directory UI\HideDirectoryFolder`
User Configuration\Administrative Templates \Network\Network Connections	Ability to rename LAN connections or remote access con-nections available to all users	`HKCU\Software\Policies\Microsoft\Windows` `\Network Connections\NC_RenameConnection`
User Configuration\Administrative Templates \Network\Network Connections	Prohibit access to properties of components of a LAN connection	`HKCU\Software\Policies\Microsoft\Windows` `\Network Connections` `\NC_LanChangeProperties`
User Configuration\Administrative Templates \Network\Network Connections	Prohibit access to properties of compo-nents of a remote access connection	`HKCU\Software\Policies\Microsoft\Windows` `\Network Connections` `\NC_RasChangeProperties`
User Configuration\Administrative Templates \Network\Network Connections	Prohibit TCP/IP advanced configuration	`HKCU\Software\Policies\Microsoft\Windows` `\Network Connections` `\NC_AllowAdvancedTCPIPConfig`
User Configuration\Administrative Templates \Network\Network Connections	Prohibit access to the Advanced Settings item on the Advanced menu	`HKCU\Software\Policies\Microsoft\Windows` `\Network Connections\NC_AdvancedSettings`
User Configuration\Administrative Templates \Network\Network Connections	Prohibit adding and removing components for a LAN or remote access connection	`HKCU\Software\Policies\Microsoft\Windows` `\Network Connections` `\NC_AddRemoveComponents`
User Configuration\Administrative Templates \Network\Network Connections	Prohibit access to properties of a LAN connection	`HKCU\Software\Policies\Microsoft\Windows` `\Network Connections\NC_LanProperties`
User Configuration\Administrative Templates \Network\Network Connections	Prohibit Enabling/ Disabling compo-nents of a LAN con-nection	`HKCU\Software\Policies\Microsoft\Windows` `\Network Connections\NC_ChangeBindState`
User Configuration\Administrative Templates \Network\Network Connections	Ability to change properties of an all user remote access connection	`HKCU\Software\Policies\Microsoft\Windows` `\Network Connections` `\NC_RasAllUserProperties`
User Configuration\Administrative Templates \Network\Network Connections	Prohibit changing properties of a private remote access connection	`HKCU\Software\Policies\Microsoft\Windows` `\Network Connections\NC_RasMyProperties`

Table 19-5   Policies in System.adm   *(continued)*

Location	Name	Key
User Configuration\Administrative Templates \Network\Network Connections	Prohibit deletion of remote access connections	`HKCU\Software\Policies\Microsoft\Windows \Network Connections\NC_DeleteConnection`
User Configuration\Administrative Templates \Network\Network Connections	Ability to delete all user remote access connections	`HKCU\Software\Policies\Microsoft\Windows \Network Connections \NC_DeleteAllUserConnection`
User Configuration\Administrative Templates \Network\Network Connections	Prohibit connecting and disconnecting a remote access connection	`HKCU\Software\Policies\Microsoft\Windows \Network Connections\NC_RasConnect`
User Configuration\Administrative Templates \Network\Network Connections	Ability to Enable/ Disable a LAN connection	`HKCU\Software\Policies\Microsoft\Windows \Network Connections\NC_LanConnect`
User Configuration\Administrative Templates \Network\Network Connections	Prohibit access to the New Connection Wizard	`HKCU\Software\Policies\Microsoft\Windows \Network Connections \NC_NewConnectionWizard`
User Configuration\Administrative Templates \Network\Network Connections	Ability to rename LAN connections	`HKCU\Software\Policies\Microsoft\Windows \Network Connections \NC_RenameLanConnection`
User Configuration\Administrative Templates \Network\Network Connections	Ability to rename all user remote access connections	`HKCU\Software\Policies\Microsoft\Windows \Network Connections \NC_RenameAllUserRasConnection`
User Configuration\Administrative Templates \Network\Network Connections	Prohibit renaming private remote access connections	`HKCU\Software\Policies\Microsoft\Windows \Network Connections \NC_RenameMyRasConnection`
User Configuration\Administrative Templates \Network\Network Connections	Prohibit access to the Dial-up Preferences item on the Advanced menu	`HKCU\Software\Policies\Microsoft\Windows \Network Connections\NC_DialupPrefs`
User Configuration\Administrative Templates \Network\Network Connections	Prohibit viewing of status for an active connection	`HKCU\Software\Policies\Microsoft\Windows \Network Connections\NC_Statistics`
User Configuration\Administrative Templates \Network\Network Connections	Enable Windows 2000 Network Connections settings for Administrators	`HKCU\Software\Policies\Microsoft\Windows \Network Connections \NC_EnableAdminProhibits`
User Configuration\Administrative Templates \Network\Offline Files	Prohibit user config- uration of Offline Files	`HKCU\Software\Policies\Microsoft\Windows \NetCache\NoConfigCache`
User Configuration\Administrative Templates \Network\Offline Files	Synchronize all offline files when logging on	`HKCU\Software\Policies\Microsoft\Windows \NetCache\SyncAtLogon`
User Configuration\Administrative Templates \Network\Offline Files	Synchronize all offline files before logging off	`HKCU\Software\Policies\Microsoft\Windows \NetCache\SyncAtLogoff`
User Configuration\Administrative Templates \Network\Offline Files	Synchronize offline files before suspend	`HKCU\Software\Policies\Microsoft\Windows \NetCache\SyncAtSuspend`
User Configuration\Administrative Templates \Network\Offline Files	Action on server disconnect	`HKCU\Software\Policies\Microsoft\Windows \NetCache\GoOfflineAction`
User Configuration\Administrative Templates \Network\Offline Files	Non-default server disconnect actions	`HKCU\Software\Policies\Microsoft\Windows \NetCache\CustomGoOfflineActions\`

Location	Name	Key
User Configuration\Administrative Templates \Network\Offline Files	Remove 'Make Available Offline'	HKCU\Software\Policies\Microsoft \Windows\NetCache\NoMakeAvailableOffline
User Configuration\Administrative Templates \Network\Offline Files	Prevent use of Offline Files folder	HKCU\Software\Policies\Microsoft \Windows\NetCache\NoCacheViewer
User Configuration\Administrative Templates \Network\Offline Files	Administratively assigned offline files	HKCU\Software\Policies\Microsoft \Windows\NetCache \AssignedOfflineFolders\
User Configuration\Administrative Templates \Network\Offline Files	Turn off reminder balloons	HKCU\Software\Policies\Microsoft \Windows\NetCache\NoReminders
User Configuration\Administrative Templates \Network\Offline Files	Reminder balloon frequency	HKCU\Software\Policies\Microsoft \Windows\NetCache\ReminderFreqMinutes
User Configuration\Administrative Templates \Network\Offline Files	Initial reminder balloon lifetime	HKCU\Software\Policies\Microsoft \Windows\NetCache \InitialBalloonTimeoutSeconds
User Configuration\Administrative Templates \Network\Offline Files	Reminder balloon lifetime	HKCU\Software\Policies\Microsoft \Windows\NetCache \ReminderBalloonTimeoutSeconds
User Configuration\Administrative Templates \Network\Offline Files	Event logging level	HKCU\Software\Policies\Microsoft\Windows \NetCache\EventLoggingLevel
User Configuration\Administrative Templates \Network\Offline Files	Prohibit 'Make Available Offline' for these file and folders	HKCU\Software\Policies\Microsoft\Windows \NetCache\NoMakeAvailableOfflineList\
User Configuration\Administrative Templates \Network\Offline Files	Do not automatically make redirected folders available offline	HKCU\Software\Policies\Microsoft\Windows \NetCache\DisableFRAdminPin
User Configuration\Administrative Templates \Shared Folders	Allow shared folders to be published	HKCU\Software\Policies\Microsoft \Windows NT\SharedFolders \PublishSharedFolders
User Configuration\Administrative Templates \Shared Folders	Allow DFS roots to be published	HKCU\Software\Policies \Microsoft\Windows NT\SharedFolders \PublishDfsRoots
User Configuration\Administrative Templates \Start Menu and Taskbar	Remove user's folders from the Start Menu	HKCU\Software\Microsoft\Windows \CurrentVersion\Policies\Explorer \NoStartMenuSubFolders
User Configuration\Administrative Templates \Start Menu and Taskbar	Remove links and access to Windows Update	HKCU\Software\Microsoft\Windows \CurrentVersion\Policies\Explorer \NoWindowsUpdate
User Configuration\Administrative Templates \Start Menu and Taskbar	Remove common program groups from Start Menu	HKCU\Software\Microsoft\Windows \CurrentVersion\Policies\Explorer \NoCommonGroups
User Configuration\Administrative Templates \Start Menu and Taskbar	Remove My Documents icon from Start Menu	HKCU\Software\Microsoft\Windows \CurrentVersion\Policies\Explorer \NoSMMyDocs
User Configuration\Administrative Templates \Start Menu and Taskbar	Remove Documents menu from Start Menu	HKCU\Software\Microsoft\Windows \CurrentVersion\Policies\Explorer \NoRecentDocsMenu
User Configuration\Administrative Templates \Start Menu and Taskbar	Remove programs on Settings menu	HKCU\Software\Microsoft\Windows \CurrentVersion\Policies\Explorer \NoSetFolders
User Configuration\Administrative Templates \Start Menu and Taskbar	Remove Network Connections from Start Menu	HKCU\Software\Microsoft\Windows \CurrentVersion\Policies\Explorer \NoNetworkConnections

Table 19-5   Policies in System.adm   *(continued)*

Location	Name	Key
User Configuration\Administrative Templates \Start Menu and Taskbar	Remove Favorites menu from Start Menu	HKCU\Software\Microsoft\Windows \CurrentVersion\Policies\Explorer \NoFavoritesMenu
User Configuration\Administrative Templates \Start Menu and Taskbar	Remove Search menu from Start Menu	HKCU\Software\Microsoft\Windows \CurrentVersion\Policies\Explorer\NoFind
User Configuration\Administrative Templates \Start Menu and Taskbar	Remove Help menu from Start Menu	HKCU\Software\Microsoft\Windows \CurrentVersion\Policies\Explorer \NoSMHelp
User Configuration\Administrative Templates \Start Menu and Taskbar	Remove Run menu from Start Menu	HKCU\Software\Microsoft\Windows \CurrentVersion\Policies\Explorer\NoRun
User Configuration\Administrative Templates \Start Menu and Taskbar	Remove My Pictures icon from Start Menu	HKCU\Software\Microsoft\Windows \CurrentVersion\Policies\Explorer \NoSMMyPictures
User Configuration\Administrative Templates \Start Menu and Taskbar	Remove My Music icon from Start Menu	HKCU\Software\Microsoft\Windows \CurrentVersion\Policies\Explorer \NoStartMenuMyMusic
User Configuration\Administrative Templates \Start Menu and Taskbar	Remove My Network Places icon from Start Menu	HKCU\Software\Microsoft\Windows \CurrentVersion\Policies\Explorer \NoStartMenuNetworkPlaces
User Configuration\Administrative Templates \Start Menu and Taskbar	Add Logoff to the Start Menu	HKCU\Software\Microsoft\Windows \CurrentVersion\Policies\Explorer \ForceStartMenuLogOff
User Configuration\Administrative Templates \Start Menu and Taskbar	Remove Logoff on the Start Menu	HKCU\Software\Microsoft\Windows \CurrentVersion\Policies\Explorer \StartMenuLogOff
User Configuration\Administrative Templates \Start Menu and Taskbar	Remove and prevent access to the Shut Down command	HKCU\Software\Microsoft\Windows \CurrentVersion\Policies \Explorer\NoClose
User Configuration\Administrative Templates \Start Menu and Taskbar	Remove Drag-and-drop context menus on the Start Menu	HKCU\Software\Microsoft\Windows \CurrentVersion\Policies\Explorer \NoChangeStartMenu
User Configuration\Administrative Templates \Start Menu and Taskbar	Prevent changes to Taskbar and Start Menu Settings	HKCU\Software\Microsoft\Windows \CurrentVersion\Policies\Explorer \NoSetTaskbar
User Configuration\Administrative Templates \Start Menu and Taskbar	Remove access to the context menus for the taskbar	HKCU\Software\Microsoft\Windows \CurrentVersion\Policies\Explorer \NoTrayContextMenu
User Configuration\Administrative Templates \Start Menu and Taskbar	Do not keep history of recently opened documents	HKCU\Software\Microsoft\Windows \CurrentVersion\Policies\Explorer \NoRecentDocsHistory
User Configuration\Administrative Templates \Start Menu and Taskbar	Clear history of recently opened documents on exit	HKCU\Software\Microsoft\Windows \CurrentVersion\Policies\Explorer \ClearRecentDocsOnExit
User Configuration\Administrative Templates \Start Menu and Taskbar	Turn off personalized menus	HKCU\Software\Microsoft\Windows \CurrentVersion\Policies\Explorer \Intellimenus
User Configuration\Administrative Templates \Start Menu and Taskbar	Turn off user tracking	HKCU\Software\Microsoft\Windows \CurrentVersion\Policies\Explorer \NoInstrumentation
User Configuration\Administrative Templates \Start Menu and Taskbar	Add Run in Separate Memory Space check box to Run dialog box	HKCU\Software\Microsoft\Windows \CurrentVersion\Policies\Explorer \MemCheckBoxInRunDlg

Location	Name	Key
User Configuration\Administrative Templates \Start Menu and Taskbar	Do not use the search-based method when resolving shell shortcuts	HKCU\Software\Microsoft\Windows \CurrentVersion\Policies\Explorer \NoResolveSearch
User Configuration\Administrative Templates \Start Menu and Taskbar	Do not use the tracking-based method when resolving shell shortcuts	HKCU\Software\Microsoft\Windows \CurrentVersion\Policies\Explorer \NoResolveTrack
User Configuration\Administrative Templates \Start Menu and Taskbar	Gray unavailable Windows Installer programs Start Menu shortcuts	HKCU\Software\Microsoft\Windows \CurrentVersion\Policies\Explorer \GreyMSIAds
User Configuration\Administrative Templates \Start Menu and Taskbar	Prevent grouping of taskbar items	HKCU\Software\Microsoft\Windows \CurrentVersion\Policies\Explorer \NoTaskGrouping
User Configuration\Administrative Templates \Start Menu and Taskbar	Turn off notification area cleanup	HKCU\Software\Microsoft\Windows \CurrentVersion\Policies\Explorer \NoAutoTrayNotify
User Configuration\Administrative Templates \Start Menu and Taskbar	Lock the Taskbar	HKCU\Software\Microsoft\Windows \CurrentVersion\Policies\Explorer \LockTaskbar
User Configuration\Administrative Templates \Start Menu and Taskbar	Force classic Start Menu	HKCU\Software\Microsoft\Windows \CurrentVersion\Policies\Explorer \NoSimpleStartMenu
User Configuration\Administrative Templates \Start Menu and Taskbar	Remove Balloon Tips on Start Menu items	HKCU\Software\Microsoft\Windows \CurrentVersion\Policies\Explorer \NoSMBalloonTip
User Configuration\Administrative Templates \Start Menu and Taskbar	Remove pinned programs list from the Start Menu	HKCU\Software\Microsoft\Windows \CurrentVersion\Policies\Explorer \NoStartMenuPinnedList
User Configuration\Administrative Templates \Start Menu and Taskbar	Remove frequent programs list from the Start Menu	HKCU\Software\Microsoft\Windows \CurrentVersion\Policies\Explorer \NoStartMenuMFUprogramsList
User Configuration\Administrative Templates \Start Menu and Taskbar	Remove All Programs list from the Start menu	HKCU\Software\Microsoft\Windows \CurrentVersion\Policies\Explorer \NoStartMenuMorePrograms
User Configuration\Administrative Templates \Start Menu and Taskbar	Remove and disable the Turn Off Computer button	HKCU\Software\Microsoft\Windows \CurrentVersion\Policies\Explorer \NoClose
User Configuration\Administrative Templates \Start Menu and Taskbar	Remove the Undock PC button from the Start Menu	HKCU\Software\Microsoft\Windows \CurrentVersion\Policies\Explorer \NoStartMenuEjectPC
User Configuration\Administrative Templates \Start Menu and Taskbar	Remove user name from Start Menu	HKCU\Software\Microsoft\Windows \CurrentVersion\Policies\Explorer \NoUserNameInStartMenu
User Configuration\Administrative Templates \Start Menu and Taskbar	Remove Clock from the system notification area	HKCU\Software\Microsoft\Windows \CurrentVersion\Policies\Explorer \HideClock
User Configuration\Administrative Templates \Start Menu and Taskbar	Hide the notification area	HKCU\Software\Microsoft\Windows \CurrentVersion\Policies\Explorer \NoTrayItemsDisplay
User Configuration\Administrative Templates \Start Menu and Taskbar	Do not display any custom toolbars in the taskbar	HKCU\Software\Microsoft\Windows \CurrentVersion\Policies\Explorer \NoToolbarsOnTaskbar

Table 19-5　Policies in System.adm　*(continued)*

Location	Name	Key
User Configuration\Administrative Templates \System	Don't display the Getting Started welcome screen at logon	`HKCU\Software\Microsoft\Windows \CurrentVersion\Policies\Explorer \NoWelcomeScreen`
User Configuration\Administrative Templates \System	Century interpretation for Year 2000	`HKCU\Software\Policies\Microsoft \Control Panel\International\Calendars \TwoDigitYearMax\1`
User Configuration\Administrative Templates \System	Configure driver search locations	`HKCU\Software\Policies\Microsoft \Windows\DriverSearching \DontSearchWindowsUpdate`
User Configuration\Administrative Templates \System	Code signing for device drivers	`HKCU\Software\Policies\Microsoft \Windows NT\Driver Signing \BehaviorOnFailedVerify`
User Configuration\Administrative Templates \System	Custom user interface	`HKCU\Software\Microsoft\Windows \CurrentVersion\Policies\System\Shell`
User Configuration\Administrative Templates \System	Prevent access to the command prompt	`HKCU\Software\Policies\Microsoft \Windows\System\DisableCMD`
User Configuration\Administrative Templates \System	Prevent access to registry editing tools	`HKCU\Software\Microsoft\Windows \CurrentVersion\Policies\System \DisableRegistryTools`
User Configuration\Administrative Templates \System	Run only allowed Windows applications	`HKCU\Software\Microsoft\Windows \CurrentVersion\Policies\Explorer \RestrictRun\RestrictRun`
User Configuration\Administrative Templates \System	Don't run specified Windows applications	`HKCU\Software\Microsoft\Windows \CurrentVersion\Policies\Explorer \DisallowRun\DisallowRun`
User Configuration\Administrative Templates \System	Turn off Autoplay	`HKCU\Software\Microsoft\Windows \CurrentVersion\Policies\Explorer \NoDriveTypeAutoRun`
User Configuration\Administrative Templates \System	Restrict these programs from being launched from Help	`HKCU\Software\Policies\Microsoft\Windows \System\DisableInHelp`
User Configuration\Administrative Templates \System	Download missing COM components	`HKCU\Software\Policies\Microsoft\Windows \App Management\COMClassStore`
User Configuration\Administrative Templates \System	Windows Automatic Updates	`HKCU\Software\Microsoft\Windows \CurrentVersion\Policies\Explorer \NoAutoUpdate`
User Configuration\Administrative Templates \System\Ctrl+Alt+Del Options	Remove Task Manager	`HKCU\Software\Microsoft\Windows \CurrentVersion\Policies\System \DisableTaskMgr`
User Configuration\Administrative Templates \System\Ctrl+Alt+Del Options	Remove Lock Computer	`HKCU\ Software\Microsoft\Windows \CurrentVersion\Policies\System \DisableLockWorkstation`
User Configuration\Administrative Templates \System\Ctrl+Alt+Del Options	Remove Change Password	`HKCU\Software\Microsoft\Windows \CurrentVersion\Policies\System \DisableChangePassword`
User Configuration\Administrative Templates \System\Ctrl+Alt+Del Options	Remove Logoff	`HKCU\Software\Microsoft\Windows \CurrentVersion\Policies\Explorer \NoLogoff`
User Configuration\Administrative Templates \System\Group Policy	Group Policy refresh interval for users	`HKCU\Software\Policies\Microsoft\Windows \System\GroupPolicyRefreshTimeOffset`
User Configuration\Administrative Templates \System\Group Policy	Group Policy slow link detection	`HKCU\Software\Policies\Microsoft\Windows \System\GroupPolicyMinTransferRate`

Location	Name	Key
User Configuration\Administrative Templates \System\Group Policy	Group Policy domain controller selection	HKCU\Software\Policies\Microsoft\Windows \Group Policy Editor\DCOption
User Configuration\Administrative Templates \System\Group Policy	Create new Group Policy object links disabled by default	HKCU\Software\Policies\Microsoft\Windows \Group Policy Editor\NewGPOLinksDisabled
User Configuration\Administrative Templates \System\Group Policy	Default name for new Group Policy objects	HKCU\Software\Policies\Microsoft\Windows \Group Policy Editor\GPODisplayName
User Configuration\Administrative Templates \System\Group Policy	Enforce Show Policies Only	HKCU\Software\Policies\Microsoft\Windows \Group Policy Editor\ShowPoliciesOnly
User Configuration\Administrative Templates \System\Group Policy	Turn off automatic update of ADM files	HKCU\Software\Policies\Microsoft\Windows \Group Policy Editor \DisableAutoADMUpdate
User Configuration\Administrative Templates \System\Group Policy	Disallow Interactive Users from generating Resultant Set of Policy data	HKCU\Software\Policies\Microsoft\Windows \System\DenyRsopToInteractiveUser
User Configuration\Administrative Templates \System\Logon	Run these programs at user logon	HKCU\Software\Microsoft\Windows \CurrentVersion\Policies\Explorer\Run\
User Configuration\Administrative Templates \System\Logon	Do not process the run once list	HKCU\Software\Microsoft\Windows \CurrentVersion\Policies\Explorer \DisableLocalUserRunOnce
User Configuration\Administrative Templates \System\Logon	Do not process the legacy run list	HKCU\Software\Microsoft\Windows \CurrentVersion\Policies\Explorer \DisableLocalUserRun
User Configuration\Administrative Templates \System\Power Management	Prompt for password on resume from hibernate/suspend	HKCU\Software\Policies\Microsoft\Windows \System\Power\PromptPasswordOnResume
User Configuration\Administrative Templates \System\Scripts	Run logon scripts synchronously	HKCU\Software\Microsoft\Windows \CurrentVersion\Policies\System \RunLogonScriptSync
User Configuration\Administrative Templates \System\Scripts	Run legacy logon scripts hidden	HKCU\Software\Microsoft\Windows \CurrentVersion\Policies\System \HideLegacyLogonScripts
User Configuration\Administrative Templates \System\Scripts	Run logon scripts visible	HKCU\Software\Microsoft\Windows \CurrentVersion\Policies\System \HideLogonScripts
User Configuration\Administrative Templates \System\Scripts	Run logoff scripts visible	HKCU\Software\Microsoft\Windows \CurrentVersion\Policies\System \HideLogoffScripts
User Configuration\Administrative Templates \System\User Profiles	Connect home directory to root of the share	HKCU\Software\Microsoft\Windows \CurrentVersion\Policies\System \ConnectHomeDirToRoot
User Configuration\Administrative Templates\ System\User Profiles	Limit profile size	HKCU\Software\Microsoft\Windows \CurrentVersion\Policies\System \WarnUserTimeout
User Configuration\Administrative Templates \System\User Profiles	Exclude directories in roaming profile	HKCU\Software\Policies\Microsoft\Windows \System\ExcludeProfileDirs
User Configuration\Administrative Templates \Windows Components \Microsoft Management Console	Restrict the user from entering author mode	HKCU\Software\Policies\Microsoft\MMC \RestrictAuthorMode
User Configuration\Administrative Templates \Windows Components \Microsoft Management Console	Restrict users to the explicitly permitted list of snap-ins	HKCU\Software\Policies\Microsoft\MMC \RestrictToPermittedSnapins

Table 19-5 Policies in System.adm *(continued)*

Location	Name	Key
User Configuration\Administrative Templates \Windows Components \Microsoft Management Console \Restricted/Permitted snap-ins	Active Directory Users and Computers	HKCU\Software\Policies\Microsoft\MMC \{E355E538-1C2E-11D0-8C37-00C04FD8FE93} \Restrict_Run
User Configuration\Administrative Templates \Windows Components \Microsoft Management Console \Restricted/Permitted snap-ins	Active Directory Domains and Trusts	HKCU\Software\Policies\Microsoft\MMC \{EBC53A38-A23F-11D0-B09B-00C04FD8DCA6} \Restrict_Run
User Configuration\Administrative Templates \Windows Components \Microsoft Management Console \Restricted/Permitted snap-ins	Active Directory Sites and Services	HKCU\Software\Policies\Microsoft\MMC \{D967F824-9968-11D0-B936-00C04FD8D5B0} \Restrict_Run
User Configuration\Administrative Templates \Windows Components \Microsoft Management Console \Restricted/Permitted snap-ins	ADSI Edit	HKCU\Software\Policies\Microsoft\MMC \{1C5DACFA-16BA-11D2-81D0-0000F87A7AA3} \Restrict_Run
User Configuration\Administrative Templates \Windows Components \Microsoft Management Console \Restricted/Permitted snap-ins	ActiveX Control	HKCU\Software\Policies\Microsoft\MMC \{C96401CF-0E17-11D3-885B-00C04F72C717} \Restrict_Run
User Configuration\Administrative Templates \Windows Components \Microsoft Management Console \Restricted/Permitted snap-ins	Certificates	HKCU\Software\Policies\Microsoft\MMC \{53D6AB1D-2488-11D1-A28C-00C04FB94F17} \Restrict_Run
User Configuration\Administrative Templates \Windows Components \Microsoft Management Console \Restricted/Permitted snap-ins	Component Services	HKCU\Software\Policies\Microsoft\MMC \{C9BC92DF-5B9A-11D1-8F00-00C04FC2C17B} \Restrict_Run
User Configuration\Administrative Templates \Windows Components \Microsoft Management Console \Restricted/Permitted snap-ins	Computer Management	HKCU\Software\Policies\Microsoft\MMC \{58221C67-EA27-11CF-ADCF-00AA00A80033} \Restrict_Run
User Configuration\Administrative Templates \Windows Components \Microsoft Management Console \Restricted/Permitted snap-ins	Device Manager	HKCU\Software\Policies\Microsoft\MMC \{90087284-d6d6-11d0-8353-00a0c90640bf} \Restrict_Run
User Configuration\Administrative Templates \Windows Components \Microsoft Management Console \Restricted/Permitted snap-ins	Disk Management	HKCU\Software\Policies\Microsoft\MMC \{8EAD3A12-B2C1-11d0-83AA-00A0C92C9D5D} \Restrict_Run
User Configuration\Administrative Templates \Windows Components \Microsoft Management Console \Restricted/Permitted snap-ins	Disk Defragmenter	HKCU\Software\Policies\Microsoft\MMC \{43668E21-2636-11D1-A1CE-0080C88593A5} \Restrict_Run
User Configuration\Administrative Templates \Windows Components \Microsoft Management Console \Restricted/Permitted snap-ins	Distributed File System	HKCU\Software\Policies\Microsoft\MMC \{677A2D94-28D9-11D1-A95B-008048918FB1} \Restrict_Run
User Configuration\Administrative Templates \Windows Components \Microsoft Management Console \Restricted/Permitted snap-ins	Event Viewer	HKCU\Software\Policies\Microsoft\MMC \{975797FC-4E2A-11D0-B702-00C04FD8DBF7} \Restrict_Run

Location	Name	Key
User Configuration\Administrative Templates\Windows Components\Microsoft Management Console\Restricted/Permitted snap-ins	FAX Service	HKCU\Software\Policies\Microsoft\MMC\{753EDB4D-2E1B-11D1-9064-00A0C90AB504}\Restrict_Run
User Configuration\Administrative Templates\Windows Components\Microsoft Management Console\Restricted/Permitted snap-ins	FrontPage Server Extensions	HKCU\Software\Policies\Microsoft\MMC\{FF5903A8-78D6-11D1-92F6-006097B01056}\Restrict_Run
User Configuration\Administrative Templates\Windows Components\Microsoft Management Console\Restricted/Permitted snap-ins	Indexing Service	HKCU\Software\Policies\Microsoft\MMC\{95AD72F0-44CE-11D0-AE29-00AA004B9986}\Restrict_Run
User Configuration\Administrative Templates\Windows Components\Microsoft Management Console\Restricted/Permitted snap-ins	Internet Authentication Service (IAS)	HKCU\Software\Policies\Microsoft\MMC\{8F8F8DC0-5713-11D1-9551-0060B0576642}\Restrict_Run
User Configuration\Administrative Templates\Windows Components\Microsoft Management Console\Restricted/Permitted snap-ins	Internet Information Services	HKCU\Software\Policies\Microsoft\MMC\{A841B6C2-7577-11D0-BB1F-00A0C922E79C}\Restrict_Run
User Configuration\Administrative Templates\Windows Components\Microsoft Management Console\Restricted/Permitted snap-ins	IP Security	HKCU\Software\Policies\Microsoft\MMC\{DEA8AFA0-CC85-11d0-9CE2-0080C7221EBD}\Restrict_Run
User Configuration\Administrative Templates\Windows Components\Microsoft Management Console\Restricted/Permitted snap-ins	IP Security Policy Management	HKCU\Software\Policies\Microsoft\MMC\{DEA8AFA0-CC85-11d0-9CE2-0080C7221EBD}\Restrict_Run
User Configuration\Administrative Templates\Windows Components\Microsoft Management Console\Restricted/Permitted snap-ins	IP Security Monitor	HKCU\Software\Policies\Microsoft\MMC\{57C596D0-9370-40C0-BA0D-AB491B63255D}\Restrict_Run
User Configuration\Administrative Templates\Windows Components\Microsoft Management Console\Restricted/Permitted snap-ins	Link to Web Address	HKCU\Software\Policies\Microsoft\MMC\{C96401D1-0E17-11D3-885B-00C04F72C717}\Restrict_Run
User Configuration\Administrative Templates\Windows Components\Microsoft Management Console\Restricted/Permitted snap-ins	Local Users and Groups	HKCU\Software\Policies\Microsoft\MMC\{5D6179C8-17EC-11D1-9AA9-00C04FD8FE93}\Restrict_Run
User Configuration\Administrative Templates\Windows Components\Microsoft Management Console\Restricted/Permitted snap-ins	Performance Logs and Alerts	HKCU\Software\Policies\Microsoft\MMC\{7478EF61-8C46-11d1-8D99-00A0C913CAD4}\Restrict_Run
User Configuration\Administrative Templates\Windows Components\Microsoft Management Console\Restricted/Permitted snap-ins	QoS Admission Control	HKCU\Software\Policies\Microsoft\MMC\{FD57D297-4FD9-11D1-854E-00C04FC31FD3}\Restrict_Run
User Configuration\Administrative Templates\Windows Components\Microsoft Management Console\Restricted/Permitted snap-ins	Remote Desktops	HKCU\Software\Policies\Microsoft\MMC\{3D5D035E-7721-4B83-A645-6C07A3D403B7}\Restrict_Run

Table 19-5   Policies in System.adm   *(continued)*

Location	Name	Key
User Configuration\Administrative Templates \Windows Components \Microsoft Management Console \Restricted/Permitted snap-ins	Removable Storage Management	HKCU\Software\Policies\Microsoft\MMC \{3CB6973D-3E6F-11D0-95DB-00A024D77700} \Restrict_Run
User Configuration\Administrative Templates \Windows Components \Microsoft Management Console \Restricted/Permitted snap-ins	Routing and Remote Access	HKCU\Software\Policies\Microsoft\MMC \{1AA7F839-C7F5-11D0-A376-00C04FC9DA04} \Restrict_Run
User Configuration\Administrative Templates \Windows Components \Microsoft Management Console \Restricted/Permitted snap-ins	Security Configuration and Analysis	HKCU\Software\Policies\Microsoft\MMC \{011BE22D-E453-11D1-945A-00C04FB984F9} \Restrict_Run
User Configuration\Administrative Templates \Windows Components \Microsoft Management Console \Restricted/Permitted snap-ins	Security Templates	HKCU\Software\Policies\Microsoft\MMC \{5ADF5BF6-E452-11D1-945A-00C04FB984F9} \Restrict_Run
User Configuration\Administrative Templates \Windows Components \Microsoft Management Console \Restricted/Permitted snap-ins	Services	HKCU\Software\Policies\Microsoft\MMC \{58221C66-EA27-11CF-ADCF-00AA00A80033} \Restrict_Run
User Configuration\Administrative Templates \Windows Components \Microsoft Management Console \Restricted/Permitted snap-ins	Shared Folders	HKCU\Software\Policies\Microsoft\MMC \{58221C65-EA27-11CF-ADCF-00AA00A80033} \Restrict_Run
User Configuration\Administrative Templates \Windows Components \Microsoft Management Console \Restricted/Permitted snap-ins	System Information	HKCU\Software\Policies\Microsoft\MMC \{45ac8c63-23e2-11d1-a696-00c04fd58bc3} \Restrict_Run
User Configuration\Administrative Templates \Windows Components \Microsoft Management Console \Restricted/Permitted snap-ins	Telephony	HKCU\Software\Policies\Microsoft\MMC \{E26D02A0-4C1F-11D1-9AA1-00C04FC3357A} \Restrict_Run
User Configuration\Administrative Templates \Windows Components \Microsoft Management Console \Restricted/Permitted snap-ins	Terminal Services Configuration	HKCU\Software\Policies\Microsoft\MMC \{B91B6008-32D2-11D2-9888-00A0C925F917} \Restrict_Run
User Configuration\Administrative Templates \Windows Components \Microsoft Management Console \Restricted/Permitted snap-ins	WMI Control	HKCU\Software\Policies\Microsoft\MMC \{5C659257-E236-11D2-8899-00104B2AFB46} \Restrict_Run
User Configuration\Administrative Templates \Windows Components \Microsoft Management Console\Restricted /Permitted snap-ins\Extension snap-ins	AppleTalk Routing	HKCU\Software\Policies\Microsoft\MMC \{1AA7F83C-C7F5-11D0-A376-00C04FC9DA04} \Restrict_Run
User Configuration\Administrative Templates \Windows Components \Microsoft Management Console\Restricted /Permitted snap-ins\Extension snap-ins	Certification Authority	HKCU\Software\Policies\Microsoft\MMC \{3F276EB4-70EE-11D1-8A0F-00C04FB93753} \Restrict_Run
User Configuration\Administrative Templates \Windows Components \Microsoft Management Console\Restricted /Permitted snap-ins\Extension snap-ins	Connection Sharing (NAT)	HKCU\Software\Policies\Microsoft\MMC \{C2FE450B-D6C2-11D0-A37B-00C04FC9DA04} \Restrict_Run

Location	Name	Key
User Configuration\Administrative Templates \Windows Components \Microsoft Management Console\Restricted /Permitted snap-ins\Extension snap-ins	DCOM Configuration Extension	HKCU\Software\Policies\Microsoft\MMC \{9EC88934-C774-11d1-87F4-00C04FC2C17B} \Restrict_Run
User Configuration\Administrative Templates \Windows Components \Microsoft Management Console\Restricted /Permitted snap-ins\Extension snap-ins	Device Manager	HKCU\Software\Policies\Microsoft\MMC \{74246bfc-4c96-11d0-abef-0020af6b0b7a} \Restrict_Run
User Configuration\Administrative Templates \Windows Components \Microsoft Management Console\Restricted /Permitted snap-ins\Extension snap-ins	DHCP Relay Management	HKCU\Software\Policies\Microsoft\MMC \{C2FE4502-D6C2-11D0-A37B-00C04FC9DA04} \Restrict_Run
User Configuration\Administrative Templates \Windows Components \Microsoft Management Console\Restricted /Permitted snap-ins\Extension snap-ins	Event Viewer	HKCU\Software\Policies\Microsoft\MMC \{394C052E-B830-11D0-9A86-00C04FD8DBF7} \Restrict_Run
User Configuration\Administrative Templates \Windows Components \Microsoft Management Console\Restricted /Permitted snap-ins\Extension snap-ins	Extended View (Web View)	HKCU\Software\Policies\Microsoft\MMC \{B708457E-DB61-4C55-A92F-0D4B5E9B1224} \Restrict Run
User Configuration\Administrative Templates \Windows Components \Microsoft Management Console\Restricted /Permitted snap-ins\Extension snap-ins	IAS Logging	HKCU\Software\Policies\Microsoft\MMC \{2E19B602-48EB-11d2-83CA-00104BCA42CF} \Restrict_Run
User Configuration\Administrative Templates \Windows Components \Microsoft Management Console\Restricted /Permitted snap-ins\Extension snap-ins	IGMP Routing	HKCU\Software\Policies\Microsoft\MMC \{C2FE4508-D6C2-11D0-A37B-00C04FC9DA04} \Restrict_Run
User Configuration\Administrative Templates \Windows Components \Microsoft Management Console\Restricted /Permitted snap-ins\Extension snap-ins	IP Routing	HKCU\Software\Policies\Microsoft\MMC \{C2FE4500-D6C2-11D0-A37B-00C04FC9DA04} \Restrict_Run
User Configuration\Administrative Templates \Windows Components \Microsoft Management Console\Restricted /Permitted snap-ins\Extension snap-ins	IPX RIP Routing	HKCU\Software\Policies\Microsoft\MMC \{90810502-38F1-11D1 9345 00C04FC9DA04} \Restrict_Run
User Configuration\Administrative Templates \Windows Components \Microsoft Management Console\Restricted /Permitted snap-ins\Extension snap-ins	IPX Routing	HKCU\Software\Policies\Microsoft\MMC \{90810500-38F1-11D1-9345-00C04FC9DA04} \Restrict_Run
User Configuration\Administrative Templates \Windows Components \Microsoft Management Console\Restricted /Permitted snap-ins\Extension snap-ins	IPX SAP Routing	HKCU\Software\Policies\Microsoft\MMC \{90810504-38F1-11D1-9345-00C04FC9DA04} \Restrict_Run
User Configuration\Administrative Templates \Windows Components \Microsoft Management Console\Restricted /Permitted snap-ins\Extension snap-ins	Logical and Mapped Drives	HKCU\Software\Policies\Microsoft\MMC \{6E8E0081-19CD-11D1-AD91-00AA00B8E05A} \Restrict_Run
User Configuration\Administrative Templates \Windows Components \Microsoft Management Console\Restricted /Permitted snap-ins\Extension snap-ins	OSPF Routing	HKCU\Software\Policies\Microsoft\MMC \{C2FE4506-D6C2-11D0-A37B-00C04FC9DA04} \Restrict_Run

Table 19-5   Policies in System.adm   *(continued)*

Location	Name	Key
User Configuration\Administrative Templates \Windows Components \Microsoft Management Console\Restricted /Permitted snap-ins\Extension snap-ins	Public Key Policies	HKCU\Software\Policies\Microsoft\MMC \{34AB8E82-C27E-11D1-A6C0-00C04FB94F17} \Restrict_Run
User Configuration\Administrative Templates \Windows Components \Microsoft Management Console\Restricted /Permitted snap-ins\Extension snap-ins	RAS Dialin - User Node	HKCU\Software\Policies\Microsoft\MMC \{B52C1E50-1DD2-11D1-BC43- 00C04FC31FD3}\Restrict_Run
User Configuration\Administrative Templates \Windows Components \Microsoft Management Console\Restricted /Permitted snap-ins\Extension snap-ins	Remote Access	HKCU\Software\Policies\Microsoft\MMC \{5880CD5C-8EC0-11d1-9570-0060B0576642} \Restrict_Run
User Configuration\Administrative Templates \Windows Components \Microsoft Management Console\Restricted /Permitted snap-ins\Extension snap-ins	Removable Storage	HKCU\Software\Policies\Microsoft\MMC \{243E20B0-48ED-11D2-97DA-00A024D77700} \Restrict_Run
User Configuration\Administrative Templates \Windows Components \Microsoft Management Console\Restricted /Permitted snap-ins\Extension snap-ins	RIP Routing	HKCU\Software\Policies\Microsoft\MMC \{C2FE4504-D6C2-11D0-A37B-00C04FC9DA04} \Restrict_Run
User Configuration\Administrative Templates \Windows Components \Microsoft Management Console\Restricted /Permitted snap-ins\Extension snap-ins	Routing	HKCU\Software\Policies\Microsoft\MMC \{DAB1A262-4FD7-11D1-842C-00C04FB6C218} \Restrict_Run
User Configuration\Administrative Templates \Windows Components \Microsoft Management Console\Restricted /Permitted snap-ins\Extension snap-ins	Shared Folders Ext	HKCU\Software\Policies\Microsoft\MMC \{58221C69-EA27-11CF-ADCF-00AA00A80033} \Restrict_Run
User Configuration\Administrative Templates \Windows Components \Microsoft Management Console\Restricted /Permitted snap-ins\Extension snap-ins	Send Console Message	HKCU\Software\Policies\Microsoft\MMC \{B1AFF7D0-0C49-11D1-BB12-00C04FC9A3A3} \Restrict_Run
User Configuration\Administrative Templates \Windows Components \Microsoft Management Console\Restricted /Permitted snap-ins\Extension snap-ins	Service Dependencies	HKCU\Software\Policies\Microsoft\MMC \{BD95BA60-2E26-AAD1-AD99-00AA00B8E05A} \Restrict_Run
User Configuration\Administrative Templates \Windows Components \Microsoft Management Console\Restricted /Permitted snap-ins\Extension snap-ins	SMTP Protocol	HKCU\Software\Policies\Microsoft\MMC \{03f1f940-a0f2-11d0-bb77-00aa00a1eab7} \Restrict_Run
User Configuration\Administrative Templates \Windows Components \Microsoft Management Console\Restricted /Permitted snap-ins\Extension snap-ins	SNMP	HKCU\Software\Policies\Microsoft\MMC \{7AF60DD3-4979-11D1-8A6C-00C04FC33566} \Restrict_Run
User Configuration\Administrative Templates \Windows Components \Microsoft Management Console\Restricted /Permitted snap-ins\Extension snap-ins	System Properties	HKCU\Software\Policies\Microsoft\MMC \{0F3621F1-23C6-11D1-AD97-00AA00B88E5A} \Restrict_Run
User Configuration\Administrative Templates \Windows Components \Microsoft Management Console\Restricted /Permitted snap-ins\Group Policy	Group Policy snap-in	HKCU\Software\Policies\Microsoft\MMC \{8FC0B734-A0E1-11D1-A7D3-0000F87571E3} \Restrict_Run

Location	Name	Key
User Configuration\Administrative Templates \Windows Components \Microsoft Management Console\Restricted /Permitted snap-ins\Group Policy	Group Policy tab for Active Directory Tools	HKCU\Software\Policies\Microsoft\MMC \{D70A2BEA-A63E-11D1-A7D4-0000F87571E3} \Restrict_Run
User Configuration\Administrative Templates \Windows Components \Microsoft Management Console\Restricted /Permitted snap-ins\Group Policy	Resultant Set of Policy snap-in	HKCU\Software\Policies\Microsoft\MMC \{6DC3804B-7212-458D-ADB0-9A07E2AE1FA2} \Restrict_Run
User Configuration\Administrative Templates \Windows Components \Microsoft Management Console\Restricted /Permitted snap-ins\Group Policy \Group Policy snap-in extensions	Administrative Templates (Computers)	HKCU\Software\Policies\Microsoft\MMC \{0F6B957D-509E-11D1-A7CC-0000F87571E3} \Restrict_Run
User Configuration\Administrative Templates \Windows Components \Microsoft Management Console\Restricted /Permitted snap-ins\Group Policy \Group Policy snap-in extensions	Administrative Templates (Users)	HKCU\Software\Policies\Microsoft\MMC \{0F6B957E-509E-11D1-A7CC-0000F87571E3} \Restrict_Run
User Configuration\Administrative Templates \Windows Components \Microsoft Management Console\Restricted /Permitted snap-ins\Group Policy \Group Policy snap-in extensions	Folder Redirection	HKCU\Software\Policies\Microsoft\MMC \{88E729D6-BDC1-11D1-BD2A-00C04FB9603F} \Restrict_Run
User Configuration\Administrative Templates \Windows Components \Microsoft Management Console\Restricted /Permitted snap-ins\Group Policy \Group Policy snap-in extensions	Internet Explorer Maintenance	HKCU\Software\Policies\Microsoft\MMC \{FC715823-C5FB-11D1-9EEF-00A0C90347FF} \Restrict_Run
User Configuration\Administrative Templates \Windows Components \Microsoft Management Console\Restricted /Permitted snap-ins\Group Policy \Group Policy snap-in extensions	Remote Installation Services	HKCU\Software\Policies\Microsoft\MMC \{3060E8CE-7020-11D2-842D-00C04FA372D4} \Restrict_Run
User Configuration\Administrative Templates \Windows Components \Microsoft Management Console\Restricted /Permitted snap-ins\Group Policy \Group Policy snap-in extensions	Scripts (Logon/Logoff)	HKCU\Software\Policies\Microsoft\MMC \{40B66650-4972-11D1-A7CA-0000F87571E3} \Restrict_Run
User Configuration\Administrative Templates \Windows Components \Microsoft Management Console\Restricted /Permitted snap-ins\Group Policy \Group Policy snap-in extensions	Scripts (Startup/Shutdown)	HKCU\Software\Policies\Microsoft\MMC \{40B6664F-4972-11D1-A7CA-0000F87571E3} \Restrict_Run
User Configuration\Administrative Templates \Windows Components \Microsoft Management Console\Restricted /Permitted snap-ins\Group Policy \Group Policy snap-in extensions	Security Settings	HKCU\Software\Policies\Microsoft\MMC \{803E14A0-B4FB-11D0-A0D0-00A0C90F574B} \Restrict_Run
User Configuration\Administrative Templates \Windows Components \Microsoft Management Console\Restricted /Permitted snap-ins\Group Policy \Group Policy snap-in extensions	Software Installation (Computers)	HKCU\Software\Policies\Microsoft\MMC \{942A8E4F-A261-11D1-A760-00C04FB9603F} \Restrict_Run

Table 19-5   Policies in System.adm   *(continued)*

Location	Name	Key
User Configuration\Administrative Templates \Windows Components \Microsoft Management Console\Restricted /Permitted snap-ins\Group Policy \Group Policy snap-in extensions	Software Installation (Users)	HKCU\Software\Policies\Microsoft\MMC \{BACF5C8A-A3C7-11D1-A760-00C04FB9603F} \Restrict_Run
User Configuration\Administrative Templates \Windows Components \Microsoft Management Console\Restricted /Permitted snap-ins\Group Policy \Resultant Set of Policy snap-in extensions	Administrative Templates (Computers)	HKCU\Software\Policies\Microsoft\MMC \{B6F9C8AE-EF3A-41C8-A911-37370C331DD4} \Restrict_Run
User Configuration\Administrative Templates \Windows Components \Microsoft Management Console\Restricted /Permitted snap-ins\Group Policy \Resultant Set of Policy snap-in extensions	Administrative Templates (Users)	HKCU\Software\Policies\Microsoft\MMC \{B6F9C8AF-EF3A-41C8-A911-37370C331DD4} \Restrict_Run
User Configuration\Administrative Templates \Windows Components \Microsoft Management Console\Restricted /Permitted snap-ins\Group Policy \Resultant Set of Policy snap-in extensions	Folder Redirection	HKCU\Software\Policies\Microsoft\MMC \{c40d66a0-e90c-46c6-aa3b-473e38c72bf2} \Restrict_Run
User Configuration\Administrative Templates \Windows Components \Microsoft Management Console\Restricted /Permitted snap-ins\Group Policy \Resultant Set of Policy snap-in extensions	Internet Explorer Maintenance	HKCU\Software\Policies\Microsoft\MMC \{d524927d-6c08-46bf-86af-391534d779d3} \Restrict_Run
User Configuration\Administrative Templates \Windows Components \Microsoft Management Console\Restricted /Permitted snap-ins\Group Policy \Resultant Set of Policy snap-in extensions	Scripts (Logon/Logoff)	HKCU\Software\Policies\Microsoft\MMC \{40B66661-4972-11d1-A7CA-0000F87571E3} \Restrict_Run
User Configuration\Administrative Templates \Windows Components \Microsoft Management Console\Restricted /Permitted snap-ins\Group Policy \Resultant Set of Policy snap-in extensions	Scripts (Startup/Shutdown)	HKCU\Software\Policies\Microsoft\MMC \{40B66660-4972-11d1-A7CA-0000F87571E3} \Restrict_Run
User Configuration\Administrative Templates \Windows Components \Microsoft Management Console\Restricted /Permitted snap-ins\Group Policy \Resultant Set of Policy snap-in extensions	Security Settings	HKCU\Software\Policies\Microsoft\MMC \{fe883157-cebd-4570-b7a2-e4fe06abe626} \Restrict_Run
User Configuration\Administrative Templates \Windows Components \Microsoft Management Console\Restricted /Permitted snap-ins\Group Policy \Resultant Set of Policy snap-in extensions	Software Installation (Computers)	HKCU\Software\Policies\Microsoft\MMC \{7E45546F-6D52-4D10-B702-9C2E67232E62} \Restrict_Run
User Configuration\Administrative Templates \Windows Components \Microsoft Management Console\Restricted /Permitted snap-ins\Group Policy \Resultant Set of Policy snap-in extensions	Software Installation (Users)	HKCU\Software\Policies\Microsoft\MMC \{1BC972D6-555C-4FF7-BE2C-C584021A0A6A} \Restrict_Run
User Configuration\Administrative Templates \Windows Components\Task Scheduler	Hide Property Pages	HKCU\Software\Policies\Microsoft\Windows \Task Scheduler5.0\Property Pages
User Configuration\Administrative Templates \Windows Components\Task Scheduler	Prevent Task Run or End	HKCU\Software\Policies\Microsoft\Windows \Task Scheduler5.0\Execution

Location	Name	Key
User Configuration\Administrative Templates \Windows Components\Task Scheduler	Prohibit Drag-and-Drop	HKCU\Software\Policies\Microsoft\Windows \Task Scheduler5.0\DragAndDrop
User Configuration\Administrative Templates \Windows Components\Task Scheduler	Prohibit New Task Creation	HKCU\Software\Policies\Microsoft\Windows \Task Scheduler5.0\Task Creation
User Configuration\Administrative Templates \Windows Components\Task Scheduler	Prohibit Task Deletion	HKCU\Software\Policies\Microsoft\Windows \Task Scheduler5.0\Task Deletion
User Configuration\Administrative Templates \Windows Components\Task Scheduler	Remove Advanced Menu	HKCU\Software\Policies\Microsoft\Windows \Task Scheduler5.0\Disable Advanced
User Configuration\Administrative Templates \Windows Components\Task Scheduler	Prohibit Browse	HKCU\Software\Policies\Microsoft\Windows \Task Scheduler5.0\Allow Browse
User Configuration\Administrative Templates \Windows Components\Terminal Services	Start a program on connection	HKCU\SOFTWARE\Policies\Microsoft \Windows NT\Terminal Services \fInheritInitialProgram
User Configuration\Administrative Templates \Windows Components\Terminal Services\Sessions	Set time limit for disconnected sessions	HKCU\SOFTWARE\Policies\Microsoft \Windows NT\Terminal Services \MaxDisconnectionTime
User Configuration\Administrative Templates \Windows Components\Terminal Services\Sessions	Set time limit for active sessions	HKCU\SOFTWARE\Policies\Microsoft \Windows NT\Terminal Services \MaxConnectionTime
User Configuration\Administrative Templates \Windows Components\Terminal Services\Sessions	Set time limit for idle sessions	HKCU\SOFTWARE\Policies\Microsoft \Windows NT\Terminal Services \MaxIdleTime REQUIRED
User Configuration\Administrative Templates \Windows Components\Terminal Services\Sessions	Allow reconnection from original client only	HKCU\SOFTWARE\Policies\Microsoft \Windows NT\Terminal Services \fReconnectSame
User Configuration\Administrative Templates \Windows Components\Terminal Services\Sessions	Terminate session when time limits are reached	HKCU\SOFTWARE\Policies\Microsoft \Windows NT\Terminal Services \fResetBroken
User Configuration\Administrative Templates \Windows Components\Terminal Services	Remote control settings	HKCU\SOFTWARE\Policies\Microsoft \Windows NT\Terminal Services\Shadow
User Configuration\Administrative Templates \Windows Components\Windows Explorer	Turn on Classic Shell	HKCU\Software\Microsoft\Windows \CurrentVersion\Policies\Explorer \ClassicShell
User Configuration\Administrative Templates \Windows Components\Windows Explorer	Removes the Folder Options menu item from the Tools menu	HKCU\Software\Microsoft\Windows \CurrentVersion\Policies\Explorer \NoFolderOptions
User Configuration\Administrative Templates \Windows Components\Windows Explorer	Remove File menu from Windows Explorer	HKCU\Software\Microsoft\Windows \CurrentVersion\Policies\Explorer \NoFileMenu
User Configuration\Administrative Templates \Windows Components\Windows Explorer	Remove Map Network Drive and Disconnect Network Drive	HKCU\Software\Microsoft\Windows \CurrentVersion\Policies\Explorer \NoNetConnectDisconnect
User Configuration\Administrative Templates \Windows Components\Windows Explorer	Remove Search button from Windows Explorer	HKCU\Software\Microsoft\Windows \CurrentVersion\Policies\Explorer \NoShellSearchButton
User Configuration\Administrative Templates \Windows Components\Windows Explorer	Remove Windows Explorer's default context menu	HKCU\Software\Microsoft\Windows \CurrentVersion\Policies\Explorer \NoViewContextMenu
User Configuration\Administrative Templates \Windows Components\Windows Explorer	Hides the Manage item on the Windows Explorer context menu	HKCU\Software\Microsoft\Windows \CurrentVersion\Policies\Explorer \NoManageMyComputerVerb

Table 19-5   Policies in System.adm   *(continued)*

Location	Name	Key
User Configuration\Administrative Templates \Windows Components\Windows Explorer	Allow only per user or approved shell extensions	`HKCU\Software\Microsoft\Windows \CurrentVersion\Policies\Explorer \EnforceShellExtensionSecurity`
User Configuration\Administrative Templates \Windows Components\Windows Explorer	Do not track Shell shortcuts during roaming	`HKCU\Software\Microsoft\Windows \CurrentVersion\Policies\Explorer \LinkResolveIgnoreLinkInfo`
User Configuration\Administrative Templates \Windows Components\Windows Explorer	Hide these specified drives in My Computer	`HKCU\Software\Microsoft\Windows \CurrentVersion\Policies\Explorer \NoDrives`
User Configuration\Administrative Templates \Windows Components\Windows Explorer	Prevent access to drives from My Computer	`HKCU\Software\Microsoft\Windows \CurrentVersion\Policies\Explorer \NoViewOnDrive`
User Configuration\Administrative Templates \Windows Components\Windows Explorer	Remove Hardware tab	`HKCU\Software\Microsoft\Windows \CurrentVersion\Policies\Explorer \NoHardwareTab`
User Configuration\Administrative Templates \Windows Components\Windows Explorer	Remove DFS tab	`HKCU\Software\Microsoft\Windows \CurrentVersion\Policies\Explorer \NoDFSTab`
User Configuration\Administrative Templates \Windows Components\Windows Explorer	Remove Security tab	`HKCU\Software\Microsoft\Windows \CurrentVersion\Policies\Explorer \NoSecurityTab`
User Configuration\Administrative Templates \Windows Components\Windows Explorer	Remove UI to change menu animation setting	`HKCU\Software\Microsoft\Windows \CurrentVersion\Policies\Explorer \NoChangeAnimation`
User Configuration\Administrative Templates \Windows Components\Windows Explorer	Remove UI to change keyboard navigation indicator setting	`HKCU\Software\Microsoft\Windows \CurrentVersion\Policies\Explorer \NoChangeKeyboardNavigationIndicators`
User Configuration\Administrative Templates \Windows Components\Windows Explorer	No Computers Near Me in My Network Places	`HKCU\Software\Microsoft\Windows \CurrentVersion\Policies \Explorer\NoComputersNearMe`
User Configuration\Administrative Templates \Windows Components\Windows Explorer	No Entire Network in My Network Places	`HKCU\Software\Microsoft\Windows \CurrentVersion\Policies\Network \NoEntireNetwork`
User Configuration\Administrative Templates \Windows Components\Windows Explorer	Maximum number of recent documents	`HKCU\Software\Microsoft\Windows \CurrentVersion\Policies\Network \MaxRecentDocs`
User Configuration\Administrative Templates \Windows Components\Windows Explorer	Do not request alternate credentials	`HKCU\Software\Microsoft\Windows \CurrentVersion\Policies\Network \NoRunasInstallPrompt`
User Configuration\Administrative Templates \Windows Components\Windows Explorer	Request credentials for network installations	`HKCU\Software\Microsoft\Windows \CurrentVersion\Policies\Network \PromptRunasInstallNetPath`
User Configuration\Administrative Templates \Windows Components\Windows Explorer	Remove CD Burning features	`HKCU\Software\Microsoft\Windows \CurrentVersion\Policies\Network \NoCDBurning`
User Configuration\Administrative Templates \Windows Components\Windows Explorer	Do not move deleted files to the Recycle Bin	`HKCU\Software\Microsoft\Windows \CurrentVersion\Policies\Network \NoRecycleFiles`
User Configuration\Administrative Templates \Windows Components\Windows Explorer	Display confirmation dialog when deleting files	`HKCU\Software\Microsoft\Windows \CurrentVersion\Policies\Network \ConfirmFileDelete`
User Configuration\Administrative Templates \Windows Components\Windows Explorer	Maximum allowed Recycle Bin size	`HKCU\Software\Microsoft\Windows \CurrentVersion\Policies\Network \RecycleBinSize`

Location	Name	Key
User Configuration\Administrative Templates \Windows Components\Windows Explorer	Remove Shared Documents from My Computer	HKCU\Software\Microsoft\Windows \CurrentVersion\Policies\Network \NoSharedDocuments
User Configuration\Administrative Templates \Windows Components\Windows Explorer	Turn off caching of thumbnail pictures	HKCU\Software\Microsoft\Windows \CurrentVersion\Policies\Network \NoThumbnailCache
User Configuration\Administrative Templates \Windows Components\Windows Explorer \Common Open File Dialog	Items displayed in Places Bar	HKCU\Software\Microsoft\Windows \CurrentVersion\Policies\comdlg32 \Placesbar\Place4
User Configuration\Administrative Templates \Windows Components\Windows Explorer \Common Open File Dialog	Hide the common dialog places bar	HKCU\Software\Microsoft\Windows \CurrentVersion\Policies\comdlg32 \Placesbar\NoPlacesBar
User Configuration\Administrative Templates \Windows Components\Windows Explorer \Common Open File Dialog	Hide the common dialog back button	HKCU\Software\Microsoft\Windows \CurrentVersion\Policies\comdlg32 \Placesbar\NoBackButton
User Configuration\Administrative Templates \Windows Components\Windows Explorer \Common Open File Dialog	Hide the dropdown list of recent files	HKCU\Software\Microsoft\Windows \CurrentVersion\Policies\comdlg32 \Placesbar\NoFileMru
User Configuration\Administrative Templates \Windows Components\Windows Installer	Always install with elevated privileges	HKCU\Software\Policies\Microsoft\Windows \Installer\AlwaysInstallElevated
User Configuration\Administrative Templates \Windows Components\Windows Installer	Search order	HKCU\Software\Policies\Microsoft\Windows \Installer \SearchOrder
User Configuration\Administrative Templates \Windows Components\Windows Installer	Prohibit rollback	HKCU\Software\Policies\Microsoft\Windows \Installer\DisableRollback
User Configuration\Administrative Templates \Windows Components\Windows Installer	Prevent removable media source for any install	HKCU\Software\Policies\Microsoft\Windows \Installer\DisableMedia
User Configuration\Administrative Templates \Windows Components\Windows Messenger	Do not allow Windows Messenger to be run	HKCU\Software\Policies\Microsoft \Messenger\Client\PreventRun
User Configuration\Administrative Templates \Windows Components\Windows Messenger	Do not automatically start Windows Messenger initially	HKCU\Software\Policies\Microsoft \Messenger\Client\PreventAutoRun
User Configuration\Administrative Templates \Windows Components\Windows Update	Remove access to use all Windows Update featues	HKCU\Software\Microsoft\Windows \CurrentVersion\Policies\WindowsUpdate \DisableWindowsUpdateAccess

Wmplayer.adm

Table 19-6 Policies in Wmplayer.adm

Location	Name	Key
User Configuration\Administrative Templates \Windows Components\Windows Media Player \User Interface	Set and Lock Skin	HKCU\Software\Policies\Microsoft \WindowsMediaPlayer\DefaultSkin
User Configuration\Administrative Templates \Windows Components\Windows Media Player \User Interface	Do Not Show Anchor	HKCU\Software\Policies\Microsoft \WindowsMediaPlayer\DoNotShowAnchor
User Configuration\Administrative Templates \Windows Components\Windows Media Player \Playback	Prevent Codec Download	HKCU\Software\Policies\Microsoft \WindowsMediaPlayer \PreventCodecDownload

Table 19-6   Policies in Wmplayer.adm   *(continued)*

Location	Name	Key
User Configuration\Administrative Templates\Windows Components\Windows Media Player\Networking	Hide Network Tab	HKCU\Software\Policies\Microsoft\WindowsMediaPlayer\HideNetworkTab
User Configuration\Administrative Templates\Windows Components\Windows Media Player\Networking	Streaming Media Protocols	HKCU\Software\Policies\Microsoft\WindowsMediaPlayer\Protocols\HTTP
User Configuration\Administrative Templates\Windows Components\Windows Media Player\Networking	Configure HTTP Proxy	HKCU\Software\Policies\Microsoft\WindowsMediaPlayer\Protocols\HTTP\BypassProxyLocalAddress
User Configuration\Administrative Templates\Windows Components\Windows Media Player\Networking	Configure MMS Proxy	HKCU\Software\Policies\Microsoft\WindowsMediaPlayer\Protocols\MMS\BypassProxyLocalAddress
User Configuration\Administrative Templates\Windows Components\Windows Media Player\Networking	Configure Network Buffering	HKCU\Software\Policies\Microsoft\WindowsMediaPlayer\NetworkBuffering

Index

Symbols

Numerics

A

B

Jerry Honeycutt empowers people to work and play better by helping them use popular technologies, including the Microsoft Windows product family, IP-based networking, and the Internet. He reaches out through his frequent writings and talks but prefers to get his hands dirty by helping companies deploy and manage their desktop computers.

As a best-selling author, Jerry has written over 25 books. His most recent include *Windows 2000 Professional* (New Riders, 2000), *Microsoft Windows 2000 Registry Handbook* (Macmillan, 2000), and *Introducing Microsoft Windows 2000 Professional* (Microsoft Press, 1999). He has written six other books about the registry. Most of his books are sold internationally and are available in a variety of languages.

Jerry is also a columnist for Microsoft Expert Zone, a Web site for Windows XP enthusiasts, and makes frequent contributions to a variety of content areas on Microsoft's Web site: Office XP, TechNet, and so on. He also contributes to various trade publications including Smart Business and CNET. Jerry is also a frequent speaker at assorted public events, including COMDEX, Developer Days, Microsoft Exchange Conference, and Microsoft Global Briefing, and occasionally hosts chats on Microsoft's TechNet Web site.

In addition to writing and speaking, Jerry has a long history of using his skills for more practical purposes: providing technical leadership to business. He specializes in desktop deployment and management, particularly using the Windows product family. Companies like Capital One, Travelers, IBM, Nielsen North America, IRM, Howard Systems International, and NCR have all leveraged his expertise. He continues writing, training, and consulting to serve the business community.

Jerry graduated from University of Texas at Dallas in 1992 with a Bachelor of Science in Computer Science. He also studied at Texas Tech University in Lubbock, TX. In his spare time, Jerry plays golf, dabbles with photography, and travels. He is an avid collector of rare books and casino chips. Jerry lives in the Dallas suburb of Frisco, TX.

See Jerry's Web site at *www.honeycutt.com* or send mail to *jerry@honeycutt.com*.

Get a **Free**
e-mail newsletter, updates,
special offers, links to related books,
and more when you

register on line!

Register your Microsoft Press® title on our Web site and you'll get
a FREE subscription to our e-mail newsletter, *Microsoft Press
Book Connections.* You'll find out about newly released and upcoming
books and learning tools, online events, software downloads, special
offers and coupons for Microsoft Press customers, and information
about major Microsoft® product releases. You can also read useful
additional information about all the titles we publish, such as detailed book descriptions, tables of contents and indexes, sample
chapters, links to related books and book series, author biographies,
and reviews by other customers.

Registration is easy. Just visit this Web page and fill in your information:

http://www.microsoft.com/mspress/register

Microsoft®

Proof of Purchase

Microsoft® Windows® XP Registry Guide
0-7356-1788-0

CUSTOMER NAME

Microsoft Press, PO Box 97017, Redmond, WA 98073-9830